The Iraq crisis and world order

This is a joint project of the United Nations University (UNU) and the International Peace Academy (IPA), in partnership with King Prajadhipok's Institute

UNITED NATIONS
UNIVERSITY

International
Peace Academy

The Iraq crisis and world order: Structural, institutional and normative challenges

Edited by Ramesh Thakur and Waheguru Pal Singh Sidhu

United Nations
University Press

TOKYO · NEW YORK · PARIS

United Nations University Press
United Nations University, 53-70, Jingumae 5-chome,
Shibuya-ku, Tokyo, 150-8925, Japan
Tel: +81-3-3499-2811   Fax: +81-3-3406-7345
E-mail: sales@hq.unu.edu   general enquiries: press@hq.unu.edu
http://www.unu.edu

United Nations University Office at the United Nations, New York
2 United Nations Plaza, Room DC2-2062, New York, NY 10017, USA
Tel: +1-212-963-6387   Fax: +1-212-371-9454
E-mail: unuona@ony.unu.edu

United Nations University Press is the publishing division of the United Nations University.

Cover design by Rebecca S. Neimark, Twenty-Six Letters
Cover photograph by Peter Payne

Printed in Hong Kong

ISBN 92-808-1128-2

Library of Congress Cataloging-in-Publication Data

The Iraq crisis and world order : structural, institutional and normative challenges / edited by Ramesh Thakur and Waheguru Pal Singh Sidhu.
    p.   cm.
  Includes bibliographical references and index.
  ISBN 9280811282 (pbk.)
  1. Iraq War, 2003– 2. World politics—21st century. I. Thakur, Ramesh Chandra, 1948– II. Sidhu, Waheguru Pal Singh.
  DS79.76.I7255   2006
  956.7044'31—dc22   2006019926

Contents

List of contributors ix

Part I: Framing the issues 1

1 Iraq's challenge to world order 3
   Ramesh Thakur and Waheguru Pal Singh Sidhu

2 Lines in the sand: The United Nations in Iraq, 1980–2001 16
   David M. Malone and James Cockayne

Part II: Structural and normative challenges 35

3 The unipolar concert: Unipolarity and multilateralism in the
   age of globalization 37
   Mohammed Ayoob and Matthew Zierler

4 International peace and security and state sovereignty:
   Contesting norms and norm entrepreneurs 57
   Brian L. Job

5 The world says no: The global movement against war
   in Iraq 75
   David Cortright

Part III: Perspectives from within the region 93

6 Iraq and world order: A Lebanese perspective 95
   Latif Abul-Husn

7 Iraq and world order: A Turkish perspective 114
   Ayla Göl

8 Iran's assessment of the Iraq crisis and the post-9/11
   international order 134
   Anoushiravan Ehteshami

9 The Iraq crisis and world order: An Israeli perspective 161
   Mark A. Heller

10 Egypt and the Iraq war 175
   Ibrahim A. Karawan

11 Reactions in the Muslim world to the Iraq conflict 187
   Amin Saikal

Part IV: External actor perspectives 201

12 The United States and the United Nations in light of wars on
   terrorism and Iraq 203
   Jane Boulden and Thomas G. Weiss

13 Baghdad to Baghdad: The United Kingdom's odyssey 217
   A. J. R. Groom and Sally Morphet

14 Explaining France's opposition to the war against Iraq 234
   *Jean-Marc Coicaud, with Hélène Gandois and Lysette
   Rutgers*

15 Iraq and world order: A Russian perspective 249
   Ekaterina Stepanova

16 Iraq and world order: A German perspective 265
   Harald Müller

17 Avoiding a strategic failure in the aftermath of the Iraq war:
   Partnership in peacebuilding 282
   Chiyuki Aoi and Yozo Yokota

18 Iraq and world order: A Latin American perspective 298
    Mónica Serrano and Paul Kenny

19 Iraq and world order: A Pakistani perspective 315
    Hasan-Askari Rizvi

20 Iraq and world order: A perspective on NATO's relevance 328
    Fred Tanner

21 The Iraq crisis and world order: A perspective from the
    European Union 344
    Luis Martinez

22 Quicksand? The United Nations in Iraq, 2001–2005 357
    David M. Malone and James Cockayne

Part V: International legal and doctrinal issues 379

23 The war in Iraq as illegal and illegitimate 381
    David Krieger

24 Legitimacy as an assessment of existing legal standards:
    The case of the 2003 Iraq war 397
    Charlotte Ku

25 The multinational action in Iraq and international law 413
    Ruth Wedgwood

26 Iraq and the social logic of international security 426
    Jean-Marc Coicaud

27 Justifying the Iraq war as a humanitarian intervention:
    The cure is worse than the disease 444
    Nicholas J. Wheeler and Justin Morris

28 The responsibility to protect and the war on Saddam
    Hussein 464
    Ramesh Thakur

29 Post-war relations between occupying powers and the United
    Nations 479
    Simon Chesterman

30 "Common enemies": The United States, Israel and the world
   crisis 497
      Tarak Barkawi

Part VI: Conclusion 517

31 Structural and normative challenges 519
      James Cockayne and Cyrus Samii

Index 535

Contributors

Professor **Ramesh Thakur** is Senior Vice-Rector of the United Nations University, Tokyo, Japan, and Assistant Secretary-General of the United Nations

Dr **Waheguru Pal Singh Sidhu** is a Faculty Member at the Geneva Centre for Security Policy, Switzerland, and was formerly Senior Associate at the International Peace Academy directing the Iraq Crisis and World Order project

Dr **Latif Abul-Husn** is Lecturer in the Department of Political Studies & Public Administration, American University of Beirut, Lebanon

Dr **Chiyuki Aoi** is Associate Professor in the School of International Politics, Economics and Communication, Aoyama Gakuin University, Tokyo, Japan

Dr **Mohammed Ayoob** is University Distinguished Professor of International Relations, Michigan State University, USA

Dr **Tarak Barkawi** is Lecturer at the Centre of International Studies, University of Cambridge, UK

Dr **Jane Boulden** is Canada Research Chair in International Relations and Security Studies, Department of Politics and Economics, Royal Military College of Canada, Ontario, Canada

Dr **Simon Chesterman** is Executive Director of the Institute for International Law and Justice, New York University School of Law, USA

Mr **James Cockayne** is an Associate at the International Peace Academy, New York, USA

Dr **Jean-Marc Coicaud** is Head of the United Nations University Office of the United Nations, New York, USA

Dr **David Cortright** is president of the Fourth Freedom Forum, Goshen, Indiana, USA

Professor **Anoushiravan Ehteshami** is Head of the School of Government and International Affairs and Professor of International Relations at Durham University, UK

Ms **Hélène Gandois** is a PhD candidate in international relations at St Antony's College, Oxford University, UK

Dr **Ayla Göl** is Lecturer in the Department of International Politics, University of Wales, Aberystwyth, UK

Professor **A. J. R. Groom** is Emeritus Professor of International Relations in the Department of Politics and International Relations, University of Kent, Canterbury, UK

Dr **Mark A. Heller** is Director of Research at the Jaffee Center for Strategic Studies, Tel-Aviv University, Israel

Dr **Brian L. Job** is Professor of Political Science and Director of the Centre of International Relations, University of British Columbia, Vancouver, Canada

Dr **Ibrahim A. Karawan** is Director of the Middle East Center and Professor of Political Science at the University of Utah, Salt Lake City, USA

Dr **Paul Kenny** is a former lecturer in humanities at King's College London, University of London, UK

Dr **David Krieger** is President of the Nuclear Age Peace Foundation, California, USA

Dr **Charlotte Ku** is Executive Director and Executive Vice President of the American Society of International Law, Washington, DC, USA

Dr **David M. Malone** is Assistant Deputy Minister (Global Issues), Department of Foreign Affairs, Canada

Dr **Luis Martinez** is Research Director at the Fondation National des Sciences Politiques (FNSP), Center for International Studies and Research, Paris, France

Ms **Sally Morphet** is Visiting Professor at the University of Kent, Canterbury, UK

Dr **Justin Morris** is Senior Lecturer in International Politics, Department of Politics and International Studies, and Deputy Dean of the Faculty of Arts and Social Sciences, University of Hull, UK

Dr **Harald Müller** is Director of the Peace Research Institute Frankfurt, Germany, and Professor of International Relations at the Johann Wolfgang Goethe Universität, Frankfurt am Main, Germany

Professor **Hasan-Askari Rizvi** is an independent security analyst and former Professor at Punjab University, Lahore, Pakistan

Ms **Lysette Rutgers** heads TaalParaat in Rotterdam, the Netherlands, a company that writes and edits texts in the field of politics and intellectual property law

Professor **Amin Saikal** is Director of the Centre for Arab & Islamic Studies (the Middle East & Central

Asia), Australian National University, Canberra, Australia

Mr **Cyrus Samii** was formerly Senior Program Officer at the International Peace Academy, New York, USA, and is a PhD candidate in Political Science at Columbia University, New York, USA

Dr **Mónica Serrano** is Professor of Politics at the Centro de Estudios Internacionales of El Colegio de México, Mexico, and Senior Research Associate at the Centre for International Studies, University of Oxford, UK

Dr **Ekaterina Stepanova** heads a research group on non-traditional threats at the Center for International Security, Institute of World Economy and International Relations, Moscow, Russia, and is an Associate Professor in the Department of World Politics, Moscow State University, Russia

Dr **Fred Tanner** is Acting Director of the Geneva Centre for Security Policy, Switzerland

Professor **Ruth Wedgwood** is Edward B. Burling Professor of International Law and Diplomacy at the Paul H. Nitze School of Advanced International Studies, Johns Hopkins University, Washington, DC, USA

Dr **Thomas G. Weiss** is Presidential Professor of Political Science and Director of the Ralph Bunche Institute for International Studies, The Graduate Center, City University of New York, USA

Dr **Nicholas J. Wheeler** is Professor in the Department of International Politics, University of Wales, Aberystwyth, UK

Dr **Yozo Yokota** is Special Adviser to the Rector, United Nations University, and Professor of International Law, Chuo Law School, Tokyo, Japan

Dr **Matthew Zierler** is Assistant Professor of International Relations, James Madison College, Michigan State University, USA

Part I

Framing the issues

1

Iraq's challenge to world order

Ramesh Thakur and Waheguru Pal Singh Sidhu

The United Nations (UN) is a collective instrument for organizing a volatile and dangerous world on a more predictable and orderly basis than would be possible without the existence of the international organization. It is the symbol of humanity's hopes and dreams for a more secure world. If it did not exist, the United Nations surely would have to be invented. Most people still look to the United Nations as our best hope for a shared future, especially if it could be reformed to reflect today's needs and realities. Yet, if some of its fiercest critics are to be believed, the damage the United Nations causes is such that it deserves to be de-invented.

Indeed, because of these divergent views, the basis of world order, with the United Nations at the centre of the system of global governance, has come under increasing strain in recent years. One reason for this is inflated expectations of what the United Nations could accomplish. A second is that threats to peace and security and obstacles to economic development lie increasingly within rather than between states. A third is the growing gravity of threats rooted in non-state actors, including but not limited to terrorists. A fourth is the growing salience of weapons of mass destruction that, in their reach and destructiveness, challenge the basis of the territorial state. And the fifth is the growing disparity between the power of the United States and that of all other states, and the challenge that this poses to the Westphalian fiction of sovereign states equal in status, capacity, power and legitimacy.

The Iraq war of March 2003 was a multiple assault on the foundations and rules of the existing UN-centred world order as well as the critical transatlantic relationship. Post-war Iraq confirms that it is easier to wage war without UN blessing than it is to win the peace – but victory in war is pointless without a resulting secure peace. Speaking to the General Assembly on 23 September 2003, Secretary-General Kofi Annan noted that "we have come to a fork in the road ... a moment no less decisive than 1945 itself, when the United Nations was founded".[1] In a number of key meetings during and after World War II, world leaders drew up rules to govern international behaviour and established a network of institutions, centred on the United Nations, to work together for the common good. Both the rules and the institutions – the system of global governance with the United Nations as the core – face an existential challenge. On the one hand, Annan noted, the Iraq war could set a precedent for the "proliferation of the unilateral and lawless use of force". On the other hand, he asked to what extent states might be resorting to unilateral instruments because of a loss of faith in "the adequacy and effectiveness of the rules and instruments" at their disposal. Consequently, the Iraq crisis became the primary motivation for Annan to announce the establishment of the High-level Panel on Threats, Challenges and Change.[2] Although the mandate for the Panel did not explicitly mention the need to examine the crucial relationship between the United Nations and the United States, possibly its single most important member, there is no doubt that most of the deliberations as well as the recommendations of the report were informed by the state of relations between these two key actors in the world order.[3]

Relations between the United States and the United Nations

The relationship between the United Nations and the United States is as critical as it is difficult to get right. The central challenge of global governance is a double disconnect. First, there is a disconnect between the distribution of "hard" and "soft" power in the real world, on the one hand, and the distribution of decision-making authority in the existing intergovernmental institutions, on the other. The second disconnect is between the numbers and types of actor playing ever-expanding roles in civil, political and economic affairs within and among nations and the concentration of decision-making authority in intergovernmental institutions.

In turn this has provoked a double crisis of legitimacy. With regard to the second disconnect, legitimacy is the conceptual rod that grounds the exercise of power by public authorities in the consent of the people, so the circuit is broken with the growing gulf between the will of the people and the actions of governments. As regards the first disconnect, legitimacy is the conceptual rod that connects power to authority, so the circuit is broken when power and authority diverge. The dominant power of the United States – military, economic, cultural, educational and media – is *the* characteristic of contemporary international relations. The United States has an unparalleled capacity to use its "hard" and "soft" power to push its own agenda. Without Washington's participation, the provision of global public goods is impossible. Although major powers have always been able to play more important roles than lesser powers, the US capacity at present is historically unique for the Westphalian order.

The United States is the world's indispensable power; the supreme power and the hyper-power are other synonyms that have been used in recent times to describe this phenomenon. But the United Nations is the world's indispensable institution, with unmatched legitimacy and authority, together with convening and mobilizing power. The Security Council is the core of the international law enforcement system and the chief body for building, consolidating and using the authority of the international community. For any international enforcement action to be efficient, it must be legitimate; for it to be legitimate, it must be in conformity with international law; for it to conform to international law, it must be consistent with the UN Charter. There will be times when UN-centred international diplomacy must be backed up by the credible threat of force. This can come only from the United States and its allies. In truth, the maintenance of world order since 1945 has depended more on US than UN ability and will. But the will to wage war will weaken if force is used recklessly, unwisely and prematurely. Progress towards a world of a rules-based, civilized international order requires that US force be put to the service of lawful international authority.

The United Nations is the main embodiment of the principle of multilateralism and the principal vehicle for the pursuit of multilateral goals. After World War II, Washington was the chief architect of the normative structure of world order based on the international rule of law. There was, alongside this, deep and widespread confidence in the United States as a fundamentally trustworthy, balanced and responsible custodian of world order, albeit with occasional lapses and eccentricities. In the past few years Washington has engaged in a systematic belittling, denigrating and hollowing out of a whole series of treaties with respect to nuclear weapons, landmines, international criminal prosecution, climate change and other regimes. In Iraq, the United States signalled that it would play by the rules of the world security institution that it helped create if, but only if, that institution bends to America's will. Coming after years of US exceptionalism, this united most of the rest of the world against American unilateralism.

The United Nations has the primary responsibility to maintain international peace and security, and is structured to discharge this responsibility in a multipolar world where the major powers have permanent membership of the key collective security decision-making body, namely the UN Security Council. The emergence of the United States as the sole superpower after the end of the Cold War distorted the structural balance in the UN schema. The ending of the Cold War also shifted the balance away from inter-state warfare to intra-state conflicts. The double question for the decision makers in Washington often became one of determining:

- whether US security and political interests were better served by engaging with distant and possibly inconsequential conflicts unilaterally, or through UN peace operations, or not at all; and
- whether the consequences of this choice for the United Nations' authority and capacity to keep the peace would have any rebound effects on the United States itself.

The Security Council is the proper locus for authorizing and legitimizing the creation, deployment and use of military force under international auspices. But it is singularly ill suited to take charge of the command and control of fighting forces. The United Nations' own panel on peacekeeping concluded that "the United Nations does not wage war".[4] Accordingly, the burden of responsibility for international military engagement typically falls on the United States and its allies, which, as the world's most powerful group, often can make the greatest difference. What is the optimal "mode of articulation" between the United Nations as the authoritative custodian of international peace and world order and the United States as its de facto underwriter? Many American decision makers find it difficult to understand why countries that do not contribute a "fair share" of the military burden should be given any determining role in deciding on the deployment of US military forces. In 1992, Richard Cheney, then Defense Secretary in the administration of George H. W. Bush, remarked that critics of the United States should remember that world order was maintained by the United States, not the United Nations. As William Pfaff notes, the statement reflected two dominant American views. First, given its history of isolationism, the United States did not seek such a role but accepted the responsibility (flowing from its power) thrust upon it after World War II. Second, the United States is uniquely qualified to be the sole superpower because it is a virtuous power.[5]

One of the main reasons for the US rejection of the League of Nations after World War I was fear of an automatic requirement to use military force as decided by the League. The symbolic shift of the world organization's headquarters after World War II from Geneva to New York did not lessen the innate American suspicion of overseas entanglements at others' behest. As Sarah Sewell notes, the United Nations remains a lightning rod for many US concerns about distracting entanglements of US forces overseas.[6] The US Congress was careful to enunciate that decisions by the Security Council could not encroach upon the internal constitutional distribution of war-making power in the United States.

Operation Desert Storm, launched in 1991 to expel Iraqi troops from Kuwait, generated unwarranted and unsustainable optimism about the centrality of the United Nations in the new world order, and about the degree to which the United States was prepared to place its military power at the disposal of the United Nations. This idealism was ephemeral because it was based on a unique confluence of circumstances that had produced a fortuitous conjunction of national US interests and the international interest. President George H. W. Bush left office on a cautiously optimistic note with regard to US–UN relations in the realm of international peace operations. The initial, naive enthusiasm of the succeeding Clinton administration, which assumed office committed to enlarging US involvement in expanding UN peace operations, quickly faded in the face of hard realities, notably the complexities of external intervention in civil wars. Since then it has become evident that the administration of the day must grapple with five interlinked and challenging questions concerning when and how Washington should:
1. offer political support to UN missions;
2. provide military assistance to them;
3. participate in possible combat operations through them;
4. enhance the peacekeeping credentials of the United Nations; and
5. opt for military action outside the UN framework.

The five policy dilemmas suggest that the division between unilateralism and multilateralism in American foreign policy with respect to international peace operations is a false dichotomy. The relationship is dynamic, not static; and multifaceted, not unidimensional. The United States remained essentially multilateral throughout the 1990s. Significant signs of unilateralism surfaced only in 2001, after President George W. Bush took office. But what did change over the course of the 1990s was the centrality of the United Nations in the US scheme of multilateralism. Learning from experience in a world no longer divided by the Cold War blocs yet facing messy internal conflicts, Washington progressively divided its multilateral impulse between the United Nations as the global mobilizing and legitimizing organization, the North Atlantic Treaty Organization (NATO) as the strategic enforcement arm for peace operations in Europe, and ad hoc coalitions of the willing for theatres beyond NATO's traditional area of operations. Outside Europe, Washington progressively retrenched from direct participation in UN peacekeeping, but not necessarily from all forms of involvement in them. At the end of the spectrum, if the United Nations is unable or unwilling to acquit itself of the "responsibility to protect"[7] victims of genocide, ethnic cleansing or other egregious humanitarian atrocities, Washington can forge multilateral coalitions of the willing to lead military interventions to stop the atrocities.

Multilateralism – the coordination of relations among several states in accordance with certain principles (such as sovereign equality)[8] – remains important to US foreign policy and the United States remains the pivot of multilateral action in the maintenance of international peace and security. Because the world is essentially anarchic, it is fundamentally insecure, characterized by strategic uncertainty and complexity resulting from too many actors with multiple goals and interests and variable capabilities and convictions. Collective action embedded in international institutions that mirror mainly American value preferences and interests enhances predictability, reduces uncertainty and cuts the transaction costs of international action in the pursuit of US foreign policy. "America First" nationalists are sceptical of the value of the United Nations to US foreign policy, viewing it more as a constraint. Why should US power be harnessed to the goals of others? Multilateralism implies bargaining and accommodation, and compromise is integral to such multilateral negotiation. But US power and assets are such that Washington does not need to compromise on core values and interests. Liberal institutionalists, in contrast, believe that multilateral organizations can externalize such bedrock US values as respect for the rule of law, due process and human rights. Multilateralism rests on assumptions of the indivisibility of the benefits of collective public goods such as peace (as well as international telecommunications, transportation, and so on) and diffuse reciprocity (whereby collective action arrangements confer an equivalence of benefits, not on every issue and every occasion, but in aggregate and over time).[9]

US power, wealth and politics are too deeply intertwined with the cross-currents of international affairs for disengagement to be a credible or sustainable policy posture for the world's only superpower. In their insular innocence and in-your-face exceptionalism,[10] Americans had long embraced the illusion of security behind supposedly impregnable lines of continental defence. The terrorist attacks of 11 September 2001 proved the vulnerability of the US homeland to quarrels rooted in complex conflicts in distant lands.

If isolationism is not an option in today's globally interconnected world, unilateralism – the robust use of military force to project US interests and promote American values overseas – cannot be the strategy of choice either. Like the two world wars, the "war" against global terrorism is neither one from which America can stay disengaged, nor one that it can win on its own, nor is it one that can be won without full US engagement.[11] A world in which every country retreated into unilateralism would not provide a better guarantee of US national security, now and for the foreseeable future, than do multilateral regimes.

Exceptionalism is also deeply flawed. Washington cannot construct a world in which all others have to obey universal norms and rules, whereas the United States can opt out whenever, as often, and for as long as it likes with respect to nuclear tests, landmines, international criminal prosecution, climate change and other regimes. Richard Haass, former Director of the Policy Planning Unit at the US State Department, called this "a la carte multilateralism",[12] and some others privately call it, even more insultingly, "disposable multilateralism".

In the case of non-UN operations, the United States would *prefer* to obtain the legitimating approbation of the United Nations if possible, in the form of enabling UN Security Council resolutions authorizing the operations. But the United States is most unlikely to accept a prior Security Council resolution as a *mandatory* requirement for the use of military force overseas. The problematic element in this comes from the equally compelling US interest in promoting the norm of the United Nations being the only collective legitimator of international military action. Washington thus faces an unresolved and irreconcilable dilemma between instilling the principle of multilateralism as the world order norm, and exempting itself from the same principle because of its sustaining and enduring belief in exceptionalism, in its identity as the virtuous power.

The contradiction came to a head in 2003 in relation to the Iraq war. Most non-Americans found it difficult to see how one country could enforce UN resolutions by defying the authority of the world body, denigrating it as irrelevant and belittling its role in reconstruction efforts after the war. As the year drew to a close, the future and prestige of the United Nations were under scrutiny as never before. The Iraq war proved to be doubly damaging to the United Nations. Those who went to war condemned the world organization for lacking the courage of its convictions with regard to 12 years of Security Council resolutions demanding full Iraqi compliance. Those who opposed the war condemned the United Nations for lacking the courage of its convictions as an anti-war organization by not censuring an illegal war and punishing the aggressors.

Was the war inevitable?

In September 2002 President George W. Bush famously warned the United Nations of irrelevance if the organization failed to enforce its resolutions on recalcitrant outlaws. The confusing compromises of multilateralism were cornered by the moral clarity of an administration willing to distinguish good from evil and determined to promote one and destroy the other. For Washington, the issues could hardly have been more serious. Could one of the world's most brutal regimes be permitted to remain in power until it succeeded in acquiring the world's most destructive weapons? The concurrent crisis with North Korea proved the wisdom of dealing with Saddam Hussein before he got his hands on nuclear or other equally powerful weapons – for it would have been next to impossible to defang him after he had usable weapons of mass destruction and delivery systems.[13] America's threat of war, unilaterally if necessary, galvanized the United Nations into putting teeth into the inspection machinery and produced unprecedented cooperation from the Iraqis.

However, cooperation from Baghdad would not have lasted forever. Based on all previous experience, international pressure would have slackened with the passage of time, and Saddam would have returned to his familiar game of cheat, deny, defy and retreat. His survival after full US military mobilization would have gravely dented US global credibility. In that case, the United Nations, with no independent military capability, would have lost its most potent enforcement agent (the United States) even as other would-be tyrants would have been emboldened. The resulting political backlash in the United States would have imperilled continued American membership, and the United Nations would have become the twenty-first century's League of Nations.

The contrary argument accepted UN authorization as necessary, but not sufficient, and preferred UN irrelevance to complicity. For all its moral authority, many feared that the United Nations lacks moral clarity. The record of the Security Council is not especially notable for a sense of moral compass and the courage of international convictions. There was a growing sentiment that, if the United Nations was bribed and bullied into submission and sanctioned war, the legitimacy of the United Nations itself, as the guardian of the rule of law and the protector of the weak, would have been eroded instead of being stamped on military action against Iraq. People look to the United Nations to stop war, not to wage one, especially one based on the revolutionary doctrine of pre-emption.

In the ensuing six months leading up to the war, instead of a pro forma test of UN relevance, the agenda shifted to being a litmus test of US legitimacy. In the end, the US argument failed to carry the world. Among the reasons for the strong worldwide anti-war sentiment were doubts over the justification for going to war; anxiety about the human toll, uncontrollable course and incalculable consequences of war in an already inflamed and extremely volatile region; and scepticism that the United States would stay engaged – politically, economically and militarily – for the years of reconstruction required after a war. Washington found it especially difficult to convince others of the need to go to war – against Iraq rather than against other states that posed a clearer and more present danger in their programmes of weapons of mass destruction or in their culpability with respect to links to international terrorism, and now rather than later – and did not help its cause by a continually shifting justification. The costs incurred, even before the war began, included fissures in the three great institutions of peace and order since World War II: the United Nations, NATO and the European Union.

Moreover, the war (without UN authorization), though swift and decisive, does not appear to have been as effective as the threat of war. The ousting of Saddam Hussein might eventually pave the way for a brighter future for Iraqis but the credibility and authority of the United Nations appear to have been gravely damaged, and it is not clear that the prestige of the United States has been greatly enhanced. There was grave disquiet that the United Nations was being subverted by the US agenda, and that it risked becoming to the United States what the Warsaw Pact was to the old Soviet Union: a collective mechanism for legitimizing the dominant power's hegemonism. In a worrying portent for the United Nations, significant groups in many countries voiced the heretical thought that they would not have supported a war against Iraq even if backed by the United Nations. For many of them, the United Nations subsequently largely legitimized the Iraq war through its recognition and endorsement of the aftermath of the Iraq war, in particular the occupation of the country by the coalition forces and the transfer of Iraqi sovereignty to the transitional government.

Iraq as a political earthquake

Wars are cataclysmic events. Out of the destruction of major wars emerge new fault-lines of international politics. To this extent, wars are the international, political equivalent of earthquakes, eruptions on the surface reflecting deeper underlying seismic shifts in the pattern of major power relations. The Cold War was unusual because of the longevity of the conflict and because of the peaceful manner in which it ended. The tectonic shifts ushered in by the realignment of forces after the Cold War were all the more significant, but they were hidden from view for an unusually long time because of the peaceful resolution. It took the 9/11 terrorist attacks to force the pace of change and sharpen the new post–Cold War contours of international politics. This new shape became more visible after the Iraq war.

The most pressing task in "post-war" Iraq became to stabilize the security situation, establish a transitional political authority, initiate the necessary steps for post-war reconstruction, peacebuilding and reconciliation, and embed these in durable institutions and structures sufficiently resilient to survive the withdrawal of a foreign presence in due course. The larger goal in the region was to assuage the humiliation inflicted on the collective Arab identity, deal with legitimate Palestinian grievances with the same mix of boldness and firmness shown in Iraq, impress upon the Arab world in general the need for deep political, social and economic reforms, eradicate terrorism from the region, and assure Israel's long-term security and survival.

There was also the larger question of the changing nature of threats in the modern world, the inadequacy of existing norms and laws in addressing such threats, and thus the need for new "rules of the game" to replace them. The urgent task was to devise an institutional framework that could marry prudent anticipatory self-defence to the centuries-old dream of a world in which force is put to the service of law, which protects the innocent without shielding the criminals.

This is why the Iraq war has the potential to reshape the bases of world order in fundamental, profound and long-lasting ways. For, arguably, the Bush administration seeks to replace:

- self-defence (wars of necessity) with preventive aggression (wars of choice);
- the tried, tested and successful strategy of containment with the untried, untested, potentially destabilizing yet possibly unavoidable doctrine of pre-emption;
- negative deterrence with positive compulsion;
- non-proliferation and disarmament, as represented in the Treaty on the Non-proliferation of Nuclear Weapons (NPT) package, with non-proliferation on its own;
- universal non-proliferation as per the NPT with differentiated non-proliferation, where the proliferating countries' relationship with the NPT is subordinated to their relations with the United States. US-friendly countries such as Israel are not on the list of countries of concern, whereas US-hostile countries are grouped into the "axis of evil" and US-ambivalent/neutral countries such as India become objects of watchful caution;
- a multilateral system of global governance centred on the United Nations with a unilateral system of US pre-eminence;
- leadership by consent-cum-persuasion with leadership by command and control;
- the European search for a new world order, based on the Kantian transition from barbarism to culture through liberal institutionalism, with the old world order, discarded by Europe after centuries of increasingly destructive warfare, based on force of arms; and
- the Westphalian order of sovereign and equal states with a post-Westphalian order of one pre-eminent if virtuous power.

The long list of fundamental changes suggests that we will continue to live in interesting times. It is difficult to deny that many of today's institutions and systems are indeed out of date and incapable of meeting contemporary challenges. Even if Washington was wrong with regard to the particular case of Iraq, it may still be right in respect of the general argument about the institutionalized incapacity of existing mechanisms to cope with today's changed and fast-changing threats. The evolution of institutions of international governance has lagged behind the rapid emergence of collective problems with on-border and cross-border dimensions. Any one intervention does not simply violate the sovereignty of any given target state in any one instance; it also challenges the principle of a society of states resting on a system of well-understood and habitually obeyed rules. Does the solution – or even one possible solution – to this lie in amending existing rules and institutions? If these are incapable of change, do they deserve to be abandoned? Or should they be jettisoned only when replaced by new and improved successor laws and institutions, because otherwise, in the resulting authority vacuum, anarchy rules – and this is not acceptable? If regime change is to be a legitimate goal, must we make the argument for that, agree on the criteria of legitimate statehood, and amend or replace the UN Charter accordingly? The report of the UN Secretary-General's High-level Panel on Threats, Challenges and Change is both an acknowledgement of this dilemma as well as a valiant, if partial, effort to address it.

Outline of the book

The key questions provoked by the above observations are: was the Iraq war a symptom of tectonic change or, alternatively, was it an event that might precipitate a collapse of the current world order? That is, do we need to think in terms of an impending paradigmatic shift, or will modifications to the current architecture suffice?

In the wake of Iraq, how will key countries, significant regional organizations and surviving international institutions deal with an unfamiliar post-Westphalian order of one pre-eminent if virtuous power? How will the growing divergence between legality and legitimacy, which bitterly divided not only the international community but also domestic opinion, be bridged in the course of this significant transition?

To address these issues, the volume begins with a historical chapter that examines the origins of the Iraq crisis in 1980. This chapter draws attention to two critical moments in the story: first, the Security Council's inadequate, indeed misguided, reaction to Iraq's attack on Iran in 1980;

and, second, the unilateral imposition by France, the United Kingdom and the United States of "no-fly zones" over Iraq in early 1991 and the launch of Operation Provide Comfort, a harbinger of unilateral initiatives that would sunder the unity of the Security Council's purpose and decisions on Iraq after 1998. The rest of the volume is divided into area and thematic/conceptual chapters.

Part II examines some crucial structural and normative issues in the light of the Iraq crisis: unipolarity and Westphalian sovereignty; the disconnect between threats to international peace and security and state sovereignty; and the rise of a global public opinion against the war. The six chapters in Part III offer perspectives from Iraq's immediate neighbourhood – the so-called broader Middle East – and examine the implications of the ongoing Iraq crisis for the key countries in the region and their evolving relationships with both the UN-centred world order as well as the United States. Part IV provides perspectives on the Iraq crisis from further afield. It looks at the role played by four of the permanent five members of the Security Council (the United States, the United Kingdom, France and Russia), as well as by Germany, Japan, Pakistan, Latin America, NATO, the European Union and the UN Security Council throughout the Iraq crisis and the implications of their actions in the emerging world order. Part V looks at the legal and doctrinal implications of the Iraq war, including the responsibility to protect norms; the universalization of human rights norms; the international use of force and the legality and legitimacy of the war on Iraq; and post-war relations between occupying powers and the United Nations.

Conclusion

The United States has global power, soft as well as hard; the United Nations is the fount of international authority. Progress towards international civilization requires that US power be harnessed to UN authority, so that force is put to the service of law. Through their bitter separation over Iraq, the United States and the United Nations provoked a legitimacy crisis about both US power and UN authority. The United States' certainty of moral clarity – values that it espouses and principles in defence of which it is prepared to stand up and be counted – put the US leadership on a course that seriously eroded its moral authority in the exercise of world power. The United Nations' lack of a sense of moral clarity diminished its moral authority. The United Nations is the arena for collective action, not a forum where nations that are unable to do anything individually get together to decide that nothing can be done collectively.

Notes

1. The text of the Secretary-General's address can be found at ⟨http://www.un.org/apps/sg/printsgstats.asp?nid=517⟩.
2. Ibid.
3. The report of the Panel can be found at ⟨http://www.un.org/secureworld/⟩.
4. *Report of the Panel on United Nations Peace Operations*, UN Doc. A/55/305-S/2000/809, 21 August 2000, para. 53.
5. William Pfaff, "Europe Is Unqualified for the World Role It Seeks", *International Herald Tribune*, 26–27 May 2001.
6. Sarah B. Sewell, "Multilateral Peace Operations", in Stewart Patrick and Shepard Forman, eds, *Multilateralism and US Foreign Policy: Ambivalent Engagement* (Boulder, CO: Lynne Rienner, 2002), p. 209.
7. The phrase is from *The Responsibility to Protect: Report of the International Commission on Intervention and State Sovereignty* (Ottawa: International Development Research Centre for ICISS, 2001). Ramesh Thakur served as one of the ICISS Commissioners.
8. John G. Ruggie, "Multilateralism: The Anatomy of an Institution", in John G. Ruggie, ed., *Multilateralism Matters: The Theory and Praxis of an Institutional Form* (New York: Columbia University Press, 1993), pp. 8–11.
9. Robert Keohane, "Reciprocity in International Relations", *International Organization*, Vol. 40, No. 1 (Winter 1986), pp. 1–27.
10. For the importance of the sense of exceptionalism in US foreign policy, see Samuel P. Huntington, "American Ideals versus American Institutions", in G. John Ikenberry, ed., *American Foreign Policy: Theoretical Essays* (3rd edn, New York: Longman, 1999), pp. 221–253.
11. See Ramesh Thakur and Hans van Ginkel, "An International Perspective on Global Terrorism", *United Nations Chronicle*, Vol. 38, No. 3 (September–November 2001), pp. 71–73.
12. Quoted in Thom Shanker, "Bush's Way: 'A la Carte' Approach to Treaties", *International Herald Tribune*, 1 August 2001.
13. The issue of "weapons of mass destruction" was the focus of the second workshop of this project held in Japan on 18–23 October 2004, starting at the Asia-Pacific University in Beppu and concluding at Ritsumeikan University in Kyoto. That work will be published as a companion volume to this book: *Arms Control after Iraq: Normative and Operational Challenges*, edited by Waheguru Pal Singh Sidhu and Ramesh Thakur (Tokyo: United Nations University Press, forthcoming).

2

Lines in the sand: The United Nations in Iraq, 1980–2001

David M. Malone and James Cockayne

Introduction

Since the establishment of the United Nations almost 60 years ago, some situations have remained almost permanently on the agenda of the Security Council – most obviously the Israeli–Palestinian conflict, Kashmir and Cyprus. In the past 20 years, however, it has been Iraq – even more than the splintering conflicts in the Balkans – that has provided a staple item of Security Council meeting agendas. The United Nations has been engaged with Iraq since the outbreak of its war with Iran in 1980, and has had an on-the-ground presence in Iraq since 1988, when it stepped in to monitor a ceasefire between Iran and Iraq, through to the present. The form of that presence has changed significantly, from a truce-monitoring group, to a coalition of states assembled under a Security Council mandate to repel Iraq's invasion of Kuwait, to weapons inspections, sanctions enforcement and now political brokerage, electoral assistance and state-building.

The role of the United Nations in managing the Iraq crisis of 2003 – and its aftermath – can be fully understood only in this historical context. The Iraq crisis of 2003 was the climax of a drama that has engaged the United Nations, and particularly the Security Council, for almost a quarter of a century – a little less than half of the life of the United Nations. To understand the implications of the 2003 crisis for the United Nations' role, not simply in Iraq but more broadly in maintaining world order, we must understand how this drama has shaped the role of the United

Nations. United Nations peace operations in Iraq since 1980 offer a unique window on the changing role of the United Nations in world order, particularly as envisaged and realized by the Security Council. Each new peace operation in Iraq has framed, in microcosm, a new role for the United Nations in managing threats to international peace and security and maintaining world order: from border monitor to sanctions enforcer, from peace broker to peace builder.

This chapter seeks to place the role of the United Nations in the Iraq crisis of 2003 and its aftermath in this historical context. In this chapter, we describe five phases of UN involvement in Iraq from 1980 to 2001. In the first phase, the United Nations acted as Cold War peace keeper, using its neutral position to broker peace between Iran and Iraq and then to monitor the peace it had brokered. In the second phase, the United Nations' universal legitimacy provided the basis for an international police action, led by the United States, when Iraq invaded Kuwait in 1990. As a result, UN member states adopted a more assertive stance in peace operations. This played out immediately, in a third phase, in the creation of a border-monitoring force, the United Nations Iraq–Kuwait Observation Mission (UNIKOM), modelled on earlier peacekeeping lines but grafted on to a Chapter VII mandate. This muscular peacekeeping seemed to herald, in President George H. W. Bush's words, a New World Order. The complex realities of this order – with its challenges of internal conflicts, global media coverage of human rights violations and UN paralysis on peace enforcement – became clear only in the years that followed. A fourth phase saw the United Nations adopt a more multidisciplinary approach to peacekeeping, reflected in operations such as the deployment of UN Guards to northern Iraq, and also saw increased willingness by Western powers to act outside, or at the edges of, the authority provided by UN Security Council resolutions, as was made clear by both Operation Provide Comfort in northern Iraq and the no-fly zone in southern Iraq. As a result, the United Nations was drawn in two different directions during a fifth period of evolution of peace operations in Iraq. The Security Council increasingly played the role of global regulator, setting down and enforcing detailed administrative standards to control Iraqi military capacity; at the same time, the UN system more broadly (including a number of its programmes and agencies) increasingly took on the role of proxy administration in areas not under sovereign control.

This chapter draws attention to two critical moments in the story, whose significance was overlooked at the time: first, the Security Council's inadequate, indeed misguided, reaction to Iraq's attack on Iran in 1980, which doubtless contributed to Saddam Hussein's contempt for the United Nations; and, second, the unilateral imposition by France, the United Kingdom and the United States of no-fly zones over Iraq in early

1991 and the launch of Operation Provide Comfort, a harbinger of unilateral initiatives to come that would sunder the unity of the Security Council's purpose and decisions on Iraq after 1998. More systemically, the chapter examines a drift of the Council towards regulatory and administrative approaches to conflict prevention and humanitarian mitigation – approaches it may not yet possess the capacity to discharge well. In our later chapter (Chapter 22), we continue the story from this point, and provide more extensive analysis of the implications for the future of UN peace operations of the United Nations' current engagement with Iraq.

Iran–Iraq: Cold War peacekeeping

The United Nations' initial engagement with Iraq in 1980 fitted neatly into the pattern that emerged during the Cold War of diplomatic good offices of the Secretary-General and limited military peacekeeping operations. Article 42 of the UN Charter had proposed the establishment of a body of national military forces available on the Security Council's call as the instrument of collective security. Cold War antagonisms soon frustrated the realization of that vision, while simultaneously increasing the need for an independent and impartial actor on the world stage that could ensure that conflicts did not spiral out of control and further fuel the confrontation between the capitalist and communist camps. In response, the United Nations used its neutral position and moral authority to broker consensual peace, where possible, improvising peacekeeping operations to act as buffers between warring parties. These "blue helmets" (as they came to be known) were peace keepers not peace enforcers; they were said to draw their mandate not from Chapter VII but from "Chapter VI and a half",[1] since they required an invitation or consent from the recipient state(s). They operated under UN command, mostly undertaking activities agreed upon by belligerents, such as the cantonment and separation of warring parties, border monitoring, oversight of the withdrawal of foreign troops, and monitoring of the cessation of aid to irregular or insurrectionist movements. Cold War peace operations were guided by the principle that they must not give an advantage to either side involved in the conflict, lest they lose the perceived neutrality and moral authority that were their main source of political capital.

In 1980, seeking to capitalize on the upheavals in Iran attendant on its revolution, which had brought to power the regime of Ayatollah Khomeini, Iraq – unprovoked – attacked Iran.[2] Geopolitical considerations conspired against an even-handed Security Council response. The United States was still smarting over the loss of its regional ally, the Shah of Iran, and over the US hostage crisis in Iran, which had provoked an embarrassingly botched military rescue operation. The Soviet Union had faced sharp criticism from Iran over its 1979 invasion of Afghanistan. Further, Iraq had long been a major trade and military client of the Soviet Union and of France. The United Kingdom was perhaps the most neutral of the five permanent members of the Security Council (the "P-5") vis-à-vis Saddam Hussein's totalitarian Iraq and Ayatollah Khomeini's chaotic Iran, while China would tap into a gold-mine of arms sales to both sides in the murderous war, which was to drag on until 1988. Thus, the balance of interests in the Council heavily favoured Iraq. In Resolution 479, the Council ignominiously failed to condemn Iraq's attack, alienating Iran for many years, rather calling blandly for a peaceful resolution of the dispute.[3] Saddam Hussein can only have concluded from this episode that the Council was prepared to go to great lengths to accommodate his regional ambitions, with fateful consequences for Iraq 10 years down the line.

Indeed, in an unvarnished oral history recorded in 2001, Joseph C. Wilson, US Chargé d'Affaires in Baghdad in 1990, argued that Saddam Hussein miscalculated his attack on Kuwait in two ways: he believed that the United States would not waste the lives of US youths in the sands of Arabia to defend Kuwait; and he hoped the United Nations could be used to absorb and deflect international outrage:

He had basically made the bet that if he could get the Iraq-Kuwait issue thrown into the United Nations system, then he could have 20 years in Kuwait.... He envisioned some toothless resolutions. He had already been the recipient of two resolutions on his use of chemical weapons. Nobody remembered them because they had no biting sanctions to them.[4]

The United Nations' response over the next decade provides a catalogue of the measures available to it as a peace broker in the Cold War years.[5] It began with Secretary-General Kurt Waldheim's quick offer to use his good offices to mediate the conflict, and his use of his powers under Article 99 of the UN Charter to bring a threat to the maintenance of international peace and security to the attention of the Security Council. When these early measures – including the unconvincing Security Council call for peaceful resolution – failed, Waldheim appointed a Special Representative, who was able to negotiate only very limited concessions by the warring parties.

In 1984, Secretary-General Javier Pérez de Cuéllar managed briefly to secure both parties' agreement to refrain from the deliberate military attacks on purely civilian centres of population that had been devastating both populations and were to leave long-lasting scars on both societies, perhaps most poignantly recorded in Iran's cinema production of the 1980s and 1990s. The United Nations moved to deploy two small inspection teams in the region, to investigate attacks on civilian areas and monitor this truce in the "war of the cities". As attacks on merchant shipping in the Gulf increased, Western powers (and to a degree the Soviet Union) moved to protect commercial sea-lanes, threatening escalation of the conflict.[6]

Gorbachev's rise to power in the USSR triggered an increased willingness of the P-5 to cooperate on matters of international peace and security, especially where their own interests clearly overlapped, as they did on the issue of maintaining the supply of oil from the Persian Gulf. This provided an opening for a diplomatic offensive by Pérez de Cuéllar in the first half of 1987, leading to the adoption of Resolution 598, whose cornerstone was the demand for a ceasefire to be monitored by a group dispatched by the Secretary-General.[7] Several days before the ceasefire eventually commenced on 20 August 1988 (after much further military jockeying between the parties), the United Nations Iran–Iraq Military Observer Group (UNIIMOG) deployed in the region to verify, confirm and supervise the cessation of hostilities and the withdrawal of all forces to the internationally recognized boundaries without delay.

UNIIMOG was a classic Cold War peacekeeping operation. With joint headquarters in Tehran and Baghdad, it had 400 personnel (including 350 military observers), drawn from contributing states on every continent.[8] Its Terms of Reference[9] mandated it to establish and monitor ceasefire lines, investigate ceasefire violations and restore calm, supervise troop withdrawals, build confidence and reduce tensions. The role UNIIMOG was designed to play in maintaining order in the Gulf was, like the broader role of the United Nations in maintaining world order at that time, to use the political capital of neutrality to provide a buffer between warring parties.

UNIIMOG's work proceeded relatively smoothly, even following the Iraqi invasion and occupation of Kuwait in August 1990, immediately after which Saddam Hussein essentially acceded to all of Iran's terms for a de facto disengagement.[10] By the end of September 1990, the withdrawal of forces to the internationally recognized boundaries was almost complete. UNIIMOG completed its mandate on 28 February 1991. Civilian offices were established in Tehran and Baghdad to allow the Secretary-General to fulfil the remaining political tasks under Resolution 598 (1987), but were phased out by the end of 1992.

Iraq–Kuwait: Towards peace enforcement

Iraq's invasion of Kuwait in August 1990 triggered events that transformed the United Nations' role in maintaining the peace (or world order) and both the nature and scale of the peace operations it was subsequently to deploy. Iraq's invasion of Kuwait represented more than the passage of an army across a long-disputed border in the remote sands of Araby. It also signalled the transgression of two lines in the sand: the prohibition on aggression, and the common global interest in stable oil supply and prices from the Persian Gulf.

Whether it was to protect international law or the international oil market, the United States moved immediately following the invasion to build a coalition of states to reverse Saddam Hussein's aggression. This was initially attempted through the imposition of sanctions and a naval blockade,[11] and ultimately by an expeditionary force authorized in Resolution 678 to use "all necessary means" to remove Iraqi occupiers from Kuwait.[12] The United Nations provided a framework that was both obvious and convenient for this international strategy, lending it legal authority and political legitimacy. For the first time since the UN action in Korea in the early 1950s, the United Nations was used to reverse a clear case of inter-state aggression (compounded by Saddam Hussein's decision to annex Kuwait outright a few days after the initial invasion), acting under Chapter VII of the UN Charter to enforce peace.

The shape of the crisis of 1990–1991 is well known, and does not require detailed discussion here. It is, however, worth reflecting on the central political role of the United Nations in the management of the crisis, because it indicates the expectations and assumptions carried forward by various actors into the crisis of 2003. Iraq invaded Kuwait on 2 August 1990; the Security Council acted the very same day, adopting Resolution 660, which condemned the invasion and demanded a complete withdrawal. Four days later the Security Council adopted Resolution 661, which imposed comprehensive sanctions on both Iraq and Kuwait and established the 661 Committee to implement the resolution. This swift action served as more than a show of strength: it signalled a fundamental shift in the United Nations' capacity to act, promising a new decisiveness in the post–Cold War era.

The United Nations' centrality in this new era was made clear by Russian unwillingness to support military action except under UN auspices, and by the use made by other diplomatic intervener powers, such as France and the Organization of the Islamic Conference, of the General Assembly and the Security Council to try to shape events.[13] The drama was played out *through* the United Nations.

At the same time, embedded within this script as it unfolded were a number of clues to the future direction of UN peace operations. The sanctions regime imposed by the Security Council included, almost from its inception, a humanitarian exception, which highlighted tensions between peace enforcement and humanitarian considerations that were later to dog the United Nations' involvement in Iraq. Resolution 686, adopted on 2 March 1991, provided the formal framework for a permanent ceasefire, pointing to the future complexity of UN roles. Among other provisions, it required Iraq to accept liability under international law for war damages[14] and to disarm, demands that would lead to a vast expansion in the Council's normative, regulatory and administrative functions for which it was ill prepared.

UNIKOM and muscular peacekeeping: The New World Order?

The success of peace enforcement against Saddam Hussein emboldened the Council to take a more assertive and intrusive stance even on traditional tasks such as border monitoring. This became apparent with the establishment of the United Nations Iraq–Kuwait Observer Mission (UNIKOM) by Resolution 689 of 9 April 1991. UNIKOM in many ways resembled earlier, classic peacekeeping operations such as UNIIMOG. But these traditional duties were grafted on to a Chapter VII mandate.[15] In line with that mandate, the Security Council increased UNIKOM's strength to three mechanized infantry battalions in 1993, following a series of Iraqi transgressions. This new approach to border monitoring heralded a period of muscular peacekeeping, a break from the past. It suggested, in the memorable phrase of President George H. W. Bush in an address to Congress on 6 March 1991, a "New World Order" – robust international police action enforcing clearly demarcated lines in the sand.

The watershed nature of UNIKOM was further underlined by the fact that all five permanent members of the Security Council (the P-5), for the first time ever, provided military staff to a UN peace operation. This signalled an unprecedented level of cooperation between the P-5, in keeping with the spirit of Soviet President Mikhail Gorbachev's famous *Pravda* and *Izvestia* article on 17 September 1987, which called for "wider use of ... the institution of UN military observers and UN peacekeeping forces in disengaging the troops of warring sides, observing ceasefires and armistice agreements".[16]

The P-5 cooperation underpinning UNIKOM represented the highwater mark of P-5 concord, whose residue continues to underwrite unprecedented Security Council activism in Africa – but which over time became notably absent in relation to Iraq. In the period between March 1991 and October 1993, the Council passed 185 resolutions (a rate about five times greater than that of previous decades) and launched 15 new peacekeeping and observer missions (as against 17 in the preceding 46 years).[17] Vetoes also dropped by roughly 80 per cent. P-5 cooperation largely continued throughout the 1990s, with Russian concerns over Yugoslavia and Chinese concerns over Taiwan mostly quarantined from other issues. There were, of course, exceptions, notably on Israel–Palestine, Bosnia, Kosovo and – of course – Iraq. In some ways, however, these exceptions serve to prove the importance of the new pattern of P-5 concord, which paved the way for UN peace operations around the globe.

UNIKOM operated smoothly for almost a dozen years. In March 2003, the coalition attack on Iraq made the force redundant by suppressing Saddam Hussein's continuing threat to Kuwait's security (although Iraqi irredentism in the future is at the very least plausible). On 17 March, Secretary-General Kofi Annan suspended UNIKOM's operations and withdrew the Mission, formally terminating it on 6 October 2003.

Insurgencies and humanitarian crisis: The new Iraqi disorder

Events in Iraq in the early 1990s soon put the lie to perceptions that the tasks ahead would prove easy to achieve. Internal insurgencies, humanitarian crises, black marketeering and human rights violations have all played out in Iraq since President George H. W. Bush announced the New Order's arrival. They have all influenced the United Nations' role in seeking to maintain international peace, both in Iraq and throughout the world. In the fourth phase of UN involvement in Iraq, the Kurdish and Shiite insurgencies in 1991 and the resulting humanitarian crises brought about a new multidisciplinarity in UN and other international responses.

On 15 February 1991, as the war in Iraq raged, President Bush called on the people of Iraq to "take matters into their own hands and force Saddam Hussein, the dictator, to step aside". On 26 February, Bush reiterated his intention to drive Saddam Hussein from power. But on 28 February, coalition military action was called to a temporary halt, and on 2 March the Security Council passed Resolution 686, which established the framework for peace, including the establishment of a formal ceasefire, with Saddam Hussein very much still in place.[18] On the same day, Shiite militias rose in rebellion in southern Iraq, hoping to capitalize on Saddam Hussein's momentary weakness and expecting American support. Within days, the rebellion had spread to all major Shia centres – Nasiriyeh, Basra, Najaf and Karbala – and Kurdish rebels mounted their own offensive in northern Iraq. In a betrayal still keenly resented by the Shiites, the coalition stood by as Iraq's Republican Guard swiftly quelled the rebellions, exacting terrible retribution particularly against the Shiites.

As the military tide also turned against the Kurds, Kurdish leaders

called on the West to prevent Saddam Hussein from committing genocide against their people. On 5 April, in the face of mounting pressure,
the Security Council passed Resolution 688, which condemned the Iraqi
repression, particularly of Kurds, and deemed the resulting refugee flows
a threat to international peace and security.[19] But Resolution 688 did not
condemn the repression itself as a threat to international peace and security, nor did it take steps under Chapter VII to put a stop to it. Although
Resolution 688's linking of refugee flows and threats to peace and security provided a normative template for later Council decisions in Yugoslavia, Somalia, Haiti and Kosovo, it also signalled that the Council was
not yet ready to abandon its long-held attachment to sovereignty and
non-interference in internal affairs.

What resulted prefigured subsequent impulses in Kosovo and some
other theatres of conflict in response to intensive if highly selective global
media coverage of humanitarian crises (the so-called "CNN effect"[20]):
unsatisfied with the UN response, and confronted by domestic public
opinion, Western powers acted unilaterally, fudging the legality of their
actions with creative interpretations of Security Council resolutions and
appeals to public conscience. Here, this new unilateralism took the form
of a humanitarian intervention to protect Kurdish refugees in the moun-
tainous border region with Turkey. US President Bush and UK Prime
Minister John Major argued, in a pattern that foreshadowed the arguments of their political heirs a decade later, that earlier UN resolutions
already provided them with all the authorization they needed to send
troops into northern Iraq. Ultimately, this Operation "Provide Comfort"
involved 16,000 US, UK, Dutch, French, German, Spanish, Canadian and
Turkish troops, protecting Kurds in an area of 5,500 square kilometres.

UN officials, under pressure from a variety of interested parties,
worked towards creating a more permanent, less controversial solution.
What emerged was a highly innovative stopgap, the UN Guards Contingent in Iraq (UNGCI):[21] up to 500 UN Guards, drawn from the
United Nations Security and Safety Section (UNSSS – the previously
near-invisible operational security arm of the UN Secretariat), supplemented by individuals seconded from national civilian police or militaries, were permitted into the northern governorates to protect humanitarian supply lines. The UNGCI was a creative face-saving initiative of
the type Ralph Bunche, the United Nations' first and possibly most creative peace negotiator, would have admired, which succeeded in establishing a UN bridge between an initiative of some P-5 members and the
opposition thereto of others.[22] Its deployment permitted the return of
hundreds of thousands of Kurdish refugees and the safe delivery of a
large international assistance programme carried out by the UN High
Commissioner for Refugees, other United Nations agencies and non-

governmental organizations. These programmes supported roughly 1.25 million people in northern Iraq, including 650,000 displaced persons. They served in a limited but effective way to deter offensives against the Kurds by Saddam Hussein's troops.

The situation on the ground remained tense, however. Iraqi forces moved decisively against southern marsh Shiites. In response, in August 1992 the Western powers imposed a no-fly zone in the south to match one they had declared in northern Iraq in April 1991 to protect Kurdish refugees, drawing a line in the sand to defend the ceasefire.[23] The unilaterally established no-fly zones – which the Western powers argued were, like Operation Provide Comfort, authorized by the earlier ceasefire resolutions – became the source of much tension in later years, not only between those powers and Iraq, but also between Security Council members over the correct interpretation of those earlier resolutions. This tension was heightened after France's position on enforcement within Iraq shifted in 1996 when it pulled out of enforcing the northern no-fly zones after the Western aid presence on the ground ended there. It grew far worse when France pulled out of enforcing the southern zone at the end of 1998, after the United States and the United Kingdom first proposed expanding the zone in September, then bombed Baghdad in Operation Desert Fox in December in response to Saddam's blocking of weapons inspections.

These developments in the aggregate yielded a complex security environment within Iraq that fuelled tension between UN Security Council members over acceptable enforcement of Security Council resolutions. The UN Secretariat, specifically the Secretary-General, was often caught in the middle – a hint of things to come. Similarly, the Kurdish and Shiite uprisings foreshadowed much greater UN involvement in essentially internal conflicts[24] and in complex humanitarian situations. But much of this was yet to become clear. While events in Iraq played out, Yugoslavia was just beginning to disintegrate; the international response to Somalia's crisis was a year off; and Secretary-General Boutros Boutros-Ghali had not yet issued *An Agenda for Peace*,[25] which called for the United Nations to take a stronger lead in preventive diplomacy, peacemaking, peacekeeping and peacebuilding.

Inspections plus sanctions: The United Nations as global regulator and proxy administrator

Operation Provide Comfort, the UNGCI and the no-fly zones signalled a more complex operational environment for the United Nations. Iraq never fully complied with the terms of Resolution 687, so there was never a formal peace with Saddam Hussein for the United Nations to keep. But the United Nations had become a lifeline for large tracts of Kurdish-controlled northern Iraq. Just as innovative solutions were crafted to meet the Kurdish population's needs in the immediate post-war environment, so creative approaches were designed to ensure containment of Iraqi belligerence.

These innovations ushered in the fifth phase for the United Nations in Iraq, involving a multidisciplinary effort to regulate Iraq's military capacity while also addressing some of its humanitarian needs.[26] Inspection of Iraqi weapons capabilities through the United Nations Special Commission (UNSCOM) signalled a movement by the Security Council towards the role of global regulator, and the "Oil-for-Food" and other humanitarian programmes vastly expanded the United Nations' administrative footprint.

Resolution 687, known informally as the "mother of all resolutions", required not only Iraq's withdrawal from Kuwait and reparations for the damages inflicted, but also disarmament. In seeking to implement the terms of this complex, ambitious resolution, the UN Secretariat and some UN agencies ventured into new territory. The complex regulatory machinery the United Nations established relied on two methods then thought to be complementary: first, disarming Iraq through weapons inspections and destruction; and, second, restricting Iraq's capacity to develop new military capabilities by imposing comprehensive sanctions in a determined (if imperfect) effort to control Iraqi belligerence. But these sanctions proved perverse: they inflicted terrible suffering on civilians in Iraq while allowing the targeted government to develop and control a lucrative black market. In response, ambitious humanitarian objectives were added by the Council to a mix of policy and regulatory initiatives that were already difficult to manage constructively with the available resources.

Developments affecting these programmes also generated changing perceptions of the role the United Nations could properly play in maintaining the peace. UNSCOM was established to implement the disarmament demands of Resolution 687. In retrospect, its meticulous auditing did a great deal to limit Saddam Hussein's military capacity.[27] But the climate of controversy and brinkmanship fostered by Saddam Hussein around the weapons inspectors served to undermine, in many quarters, faith in the efficacy of that regulatory approach. UNSCOM's successes usually came from the help of informers and defectors, and the Iraqis appeared to retreat only when caught cheating, stimulating the view in Washington that Hussein was hiding both weapons aspirations and materiel.[28] Over time, Washington's fears led to a ratcheting up of pressure on Hussein, eventually leading to open confrontation in late 1998 between Hussein and Richard Butler, the Australian UNSCOM head, over access to sensitive sites. At that point, France joined Russia and China in arguing that the containment approach of inspections-plus-sanctions had run its course, leaving Washington and London to act unilaterally when in Operation Desert Fox they bombed Baghdad for failing to allow UN-SCOM access to the disputed sites.[29] These changing attitudes to the success of inspections, and the nature of UNSCOM's relationship to Western intelligence agencies,[30] greatly influenced assessments of the United Nations' ability to carry through such a meticulous regulatory approach to security management, and particularly of what it had to offer to the United States.

Assessments of the success of this approach were also coloured by different conceptions of the approach's purpose. Whereas most countries saw the inspections-plus-sanctions regime as aimed at Iraqi disarmament, signs emerged that the United States and the United Kingdom aimed instead at removing Hussein from power. As early as 26 March 1997, US Secretary of State Albright stated:

We do not agree with the nations who argue that if Iraq complies with its obligations concerning weapons of mass destruction, sanctions should be lifted ... Iraq must prove its peaceful intentions ... the evidence is overwhelming that Saddam Hussein's intentions will never be peaceful.[31]

Eventually these differences amongst the P-5 brought UNSCOM to a grinding halt. Three panels formed in early 1999 to conduct a "comprehensive review" of the inspections-plus-sanctions approach could not arrive at a formula for improving the effectiveness of inspections while weakening the severity of sanctions.[32] Inspections were suspended, and sanctions stayed in place.

Remarkably, the diversionary tactics of Saddam Hussein over weapons issues succeeded in blinding many experts, including intelligence analysts, to the success of the inspections-plus-sanctions approach in containing Iraq's military potential. But, owing to political posturing and intelligence mistakes, what the weapons inspectors could not find attracted more attention than the fact that they found nothing much, contributing to a slowly accumulating sense of crisis amongst Western decision makers, much aggravated after the events of 11 September 2001.

Meanwhile, global civil society and many political actors, particularly in the West and in the developing world, focused increasing attention on the plight of Iraqi civilians under the UN sanctions regime. These were even harder to justify once inspections had reached stalemate. The Oil-for-Food (OFF) programme, established by Resolution 986 in April 1995,[33] commenced operations in December 1996 after a Memorandum of Understanding was agreed by the United Nations and the Government of Iraq in May 1996.[34] It was, as Secretary-General Annan noted, "one of the largest, most complex and most unusual tasks [the Security Council] has ever entrusted to the Secretariat – the only humanitarian programme ever to have been funded entirely from resources belonging to the nation it was designed to help".[35] Over its lifetime, the OFF handled US$46 billion worth of Iraqi oil revenues, and served as the sole source of sustenance for 60 per cent of Iraq's estimated 27 million people. But Saddam Hussein turned both the sanctions and this programme to his advantage, through the control of lucrative sanctions evasion schemes, while heavy costs were borne by the most vulnerable segments of Iraqi society.[36]

As the Security Council slowly permitted Iraqi exports to grow (if only to fund OFF), import-approval procedures consequently underwent two fundamental changes. First, in 1999, the Council introduced "fast track" procedures, which allowed the Secretary-General to approve contracts for the importation of specific goods on a "green list" without reference to the 661 Committee.[37] The green list was slowly expanded to include petroleum production spare parts and equipment, water and sanitation supplies, electricity supplies and health sector supplies, and finally housing sector supplies. Second, in 2002, the Security Council established the "Goods Review List", which reversed the presumption against importation: following the change to the Goods Review List, import contracts were presumptively approved by the Secretary-General unless they contained a listed item.[38] Member states were thus allowed to export to Iraq all items not on the list.

Both the OFF programme and the weapons inspections programmes reflect a movement towards the creation of regulatory regimes administered or supervised by agencies of the Security Council, with a complex relationship to the UN Secretariat. That regulatory approach has been used with increasing frequency by the Security Council; committees of the Security Council have recently proliferated, charged with overseeing the implementation of specific administrative standards or regimes.[39] This has important ramifications for the balance of the United Nations' activities – not least through resource-allocation – that are still not fully digested by the UN membership.

But the United Nations' ability to operate such a complex regulatory scheme should be carefully questioned. By 2004, OFF was being investigated for mismanagement and possible corruption by a dozen inquiries,[40] including investigations by the US Senate Permanent Subcommittee on Investigations, other congressional committees, a New York Justice Department attorney, and, most promisingly, an Independent Inquiry Committee, established by the Secretary-General and led for the United Nations itself by former US Federal Reserve chief Paul Volcker.[41] It now seems likely that billions of dollars were siphoned off from oil export and other import contracts into Iraqi state and private accounts, a slow-moving process of which the Security Council was at least passively aware. Seriously adverse findings by some or all of these inquiries could reverse the growth in the United Nations' regulatory and administrative ambitions in the security field.

Conclusion

The inspections-plus-sanctions experience of the United Nations in Iraq suggests an effort to attain not just a thin cessation of hostilities, but rather the more ambitious goal of a durable peace through a multidisciplinary approach. Today's peace operations have complex mandates extending far beyond the classic model represented by UNIIMOG, for example.[42] The mandates often aim to provide humanitarian assistance, civil administration, police monitoring and training, human rights monitoring, economic reconstruction and other essentially civilian functions. The role of the United Nations in Iraq throughout much of the 1990s anticipated and shaped this trend.

The diversification of tasks performed by contemporary peace operations creates significant challenges of coordination, increasingly addressed by a civilian leadership. Although the military components of these missions often remain the largest, the mission objectives are not necessarily ones to which the military can or may wish to contribute greatly. Sometimes, as in the Balkans and Afghanistan, the military components retain their own lines of command and control outside the UN structure. The United Nations' Iraq programmes in the 1990s were similar – essentially civilian activities overseen by civilian coordinators (Benon Sevan for OFF, Rolf Ekeus and Richard Butler for UNSCOM, Hans Blix for UNMOVIC, and Mohamed ElBaradei for the International Atomic Energy Agency), with military components operating outside UN command structures enforcing the sanctions regime and no-fly zones.

The Security Council has continued to look to sanctions regimes as an alternative – or an addition – to the use of force, even as blanket economic sanctions have fallen out of vogue given their humanitarian costs first in Haiti, then in Iraq, and as the ability of the targeted governments to manipulate sanctions for their own ends has slowly sunk in.[43] After Iraq, sanctions regimes have often become targeted to specific individuals and their assets.[44]

Western unilateralism in both Operation Provide Comfort and the establishment and enforcement of the no-fly zones (in which France initially participated, somewhat ironically in light of its subsequent opposition to American unilateralism) also pointed to a future trend. Through operations such as Desert Fox in 1998,[45] Western powers have increasingly resorted to enforcement action without explicit Security Council authorization.

These developments set the stage for the fateful confrontations over Iraq that took place at the United Nations in 2002–2003 and continue, in a more muted way, today. We turn to them and to their implications in Chapter 22.

Notes

James Cockayne is a graduate scholar at the Institute for International Law and Justice at New York University Law School; David M. Malone is Assistant Deputy Minister (Africa and Middle East), Department of Foreign Affairs, Canada. The chapter does not necessarily represent the views of either organization.

1. The term was given currency by Secretary-General Dag Hammarskjöld. For further discussion of the historical evolution of peacekeeping, see James Cockayne and David Malone, "The Ralph Bunche Centennial: Peace Operations Then and Now", *Global Governance*, Vol. 11, No. 3 (2005), pp. 331–350.
2. See Dilip Hiro, *The Longest War: The Iran–Iraq Military Conflict* (London: Paladin, 1990); Charles Tripp, *A History of Iraq* (2nd edn, Cambridge: Cambridge University Press, 2002), Ch. 6.
3. S/RES/479 (1980).
4. David Ignatius, "Saddam Hussein Revisited", *Washington Post*, 14 September 2004.
5. See, generally, Brian Urquhart, *A Life in Peace and War* (New York: HarperCollins, 1987).
6. These patrols at times threatened to drag Western nations into the conflict. On 3 July 1988, the USS *Vincennes*, a United States cruiser, mistakenly shot down an Iranian commercial airliner, killing all 290 passengers and crew on board. In other incidents, Iranian attacks on US naval vessels led to US retaliatory strikes on Iranian oil platforms, which have only recently been resolved through litigation before the International Court of Justice: see Oil Platforms (*Islamic Republic of Iran* v. *United States of America*), ICJ, Judgment (6 November 2003).
7. S/RES/598 (1987). The P-5 diplomacy involved in negotiating this text, much of it conducted in private in New York, was to set the pattern of P-5 initiatives, often domination, within the Council ever since. See Cameron Hume, *The United Nations, Iran and Iraq: How Peacemaking Changed* (Bloomington, IN: Indiana University Press, 1994), pp. 71–72, 90–102; and see David Malone, "The UN Security Council in the 1990s: Inconsistent, Improvisational, Indispensable," in Ramesh Thakur and Edward Newman, *New Millennium, New Perspectives* (Tokyo: United Nations University Press, 2000), pp. 21–45.
8. Argentina, Australia, Austria, Bangladesh, Canada, Denmark, Finland, Ghana, Hungary, India, Indonesia, Ireland, Italy, Kenya, Malaysia, New Zealand, Nigeria, Norway, Peru, Poland, Senegal, Sweden, Turkey, Uruguay, Yugoslavia and Zambia. New Zealand operated an air unit, and the Observer Group also included military police provided by Ireland and medical orderlies from Austria.

9. UN Doc. S/20093.
10. See the exchange of letters between Saddam Hussein and Iranian President Rafsanjani on 30 July and 8 August 1990, respectively, in UN Doc. S/21556, 17 August 1990, p. 4.
11. See Resolution 661 (6 August 1990); Resolution 665 (25 August 1990); Resolution 666 (13 September 1990); Resolution 670 (25 September 1990).
12. Resolution 678 (29 November 1990).
13. On 24 September 1990, French President François Mitterrand, speaking at the UN General Assembly, proposed a four-phase peace plan, including dealing with the Arab–Israeli problem. On 3 October, the foreign ministers of the Organization of the Islamic Conference, meeting on the margins at the United Nations, demanded Iraqi adherence to UN resolutions and expressed support for those Gulf states seeking foreign military assistance. The stance of the OIC was crucial: it signalled regional legitimacy for UN peace enforcement. On 15 January 1991, France unexpectedly took centre-stage, suggesting that the Security Council agree to an international conference on Palestine if Iraq withdrew from Kuwait. The United States and the United Kingdom strongly opposed the suggestion. The French withdrew the proposal, then blocked a British resolution making a last-minute appeal to Iraq to withdraw unconditionally from Iraq.
14. This led in Resolution 692 (1991) to the establishment of the UN Compensation Commission in Geneva, which has dealt with 2.6 million claims for death, injury, loss of or damage to property, commercial claims and claims for environmental damage. It has paid out more than US$18 billion in compensation, funded by Iraqi oil sales under the Oil-for-Food programme. See especially Andrea Gattini, "Old Rules, New Procedures on War Reparations", David Caron and Brian Morris, "The United Nations Compensation Commission: Practical Justice, Not Retribution" and Merritt B. Fox, "Imposing Liability for Losses from Aggressive War: An Economic Analysis of the UNCC", all in *European Journal of International Law*, Vol. 13, No. 1 (2002), pp. 161–182, 183–200, 201–222.
15. S/RES/687 (3 April 1991) and S/RES/689 (9 April 1991).
16. Mikhail S. Gorbachev, "Reality and the Guarantees of a Secure World", in Foreign Broadcast Information Service, *Daily Report: Soviet Union*, 17 September 1987, pp. 23–28.
17. See David Malone, "The UN Security Council in the Post-Cold War World: 1987–97", *Security Dialogue*, Vol. 28, No. 4 (December 1997), p. 394.
18. S/RES/686 (2 March 1991).
19. S/RES/688 (5 April 1991). Both Turkey and Iran had written letters to the Council characterizing Kurdish refugee flows as a threat to their security, and the Council apparently saw resemblances between that claim and the Indian characterization of Bengali refugee flows in 1971 as an act of indirect aggression.
20. The term refers to the effect that global media have on the determination of foreign policy. See Steven Livingston, *Clarifying the CNN Effect: An Examination of Media Effects According to Type of Military Intervention*, Joan Shorenstein Center, John F. Kennedy School of Government, Harvard University, Research Paper R-18, June 1997.
21. A similar arrangement was considered for Burundi in 1996, when the government lost control of parts of its territory, which required humanitarian assistance. The option was not ultimately pursued.
22. Although the Russian Federation and China objected to enforcement of the no-fly zones and Operation Provide Comfort, they did so in a low-key way, suggesting initially at least pragmatic acquiescence.
23. In the north, the United States, the United Kingdom and France proclaimed a no-fly

zone on 10 April 1991, relying specifically on Resolutions 678, 687 and 688. In the south, they relied on Resolutions 687, 688 and, later, 949 (1994).

24. In describing certain conflicts as internal or civil, we generally add the prior qualifier "essentially" because these conflicts rarely remain strictly internal for long – neighbouring countries often spilled in (as in the Democratic Republic of Congo) or the conflict spilled over (as with Colombia's turmoil spilling over into border areas of Ecuador and Peru and into the domestic politics of Venezuela).

25. *An Agenda for Peace, Preventive Diplomacy, Peacemaking and Peace-keeping*, UN Doc. A/47/277–S/24111 (17 June 1992).

26. *Multidisciplinary Peace-keeping: Lessons from Recent Experience* (New York: United Nations Department of Peacekeeping Operations, April 1999).

27. As Fareed Zakaria has noted, US weapons-tracker David Kay's assertion after the 2003 Iraq war that "we were all wrong" in expecting to find weapons of mass destruction in Iraq overlooks the accuracy of the UN inspectors' reporting; see Fareed Zakaria, "We Had Good Intel – The U.N.'s", *Newsweek*, 9 February 2004.

28. See Lawrence Freedman, "War in Iraq: Selling the Threat", *Survival*, Vol. 46, No. 2 (Summer 2004), pp. 7–50.

29. See Richard Butler, *Saddam Defiant: The Threat of Mass Destruction and the Crisis of Global Security* (London: Weidenfeld & Nicolson, 2000); and see David Malone, "Goodbye UNSCOM: A Sorry Tale in US-UN Relations", *Security Dialogue*, Vol. 30, No. 4 (December 1999), pp. 393–411.

30. Susan Wright, "The Hijacking of UNSCOM", *Bulletin of the Atomic Scientists*, Vol. 55, No. 4 (July/August 1999).

31. Madeline Albright, Remarks at Georgetown University, Washington, D.C., 26 March 1997, available at ⟨http://secretary.state.gov/www/statements/970326.html⟩.

32. See UN Doc. S/1999/356 (27 March 1999).

33. Resolution 986 (14 April 1995).

34. See *Memorandum of Understanding between the Secretariat of the United Nations and the Government of Iraq on the Implementation of Security Council Resolution 986 (1995)*, in *Letter Dated 20 May 1996 from the Secretary-General Addressed to the President of the Security Council*, UN Doc. S/1996/356* (20 May 1996).

35. UN News Centre, "On Eve of Its Expiry, Annan Hails 'Unprecedented' Iraq Oil-for-Food Programme", 20 November 2003.

36. See David Cortright and George A. Lopez, "Reforming Sanctions", in David M. Malone, ed., *The UN Security Council from the Cold War to the 21st Century* (Boulder, CO: Lynne Rienner, 2004), pp. 167–179; Peter van Walsum, "The Iraq Sanctions Committee", in ibid., pp. 181–193; David J. R. Angell, "The Angola Sanctions Committee", in ibid., pp. 195–204; David Cortright and George A. Lopez, *Sanctions and the Search for Security: Challenges to UN Action* (Boulder, CO: Lynne Rienner, 2002); see, generally, ⟨http://www.globalpolicy.org/security/sanction/theindex.htm⟩.

37. See S/RES/1284 (17 December 1999).

38. S/RES/1409 (14 May 2002).

39. See, for example, the committees established by Resolutions 1540 (2004) – weapons of mass destruction; 1533 (2004) – Democratic Republic of Congo; 1521 (2003) – Liberia; 1518 (2003) – Iraq; 1373 (2001) – Counter-Terrorism Committee; 1343 (2001) – Liberia; 1298 (2000) – Ethiopia and Eritrea; 1267 (1999) – Al Qaeda and the Taliban; 1160 (1998) – Kosovo; 1132 (1997) – Sierra Leone; 985 (1995) – Liberia; 918 (1994) – Rwanda; 864 (1993) – UNITA (National Union for the Total Independence of Angola); 751 (1992) – Somalia; 748 (1992) – Libya. The International Criminal Tribunal for the Former Yugoslavia and the International Criminal Tribunal for Rwanda can also be considered as subsidiary organs of the Security Council designed to enforce detailed ad-

ministrative standards – namely those regulating the conduct of hostilities. In addition, Council-mandated expert bodies, for example on economic factors in a variety of conflicts, have been proliferating.

40. See David M. Malone, "Goodbye UNSCOM: A Sad Tale in US-UN Relations", *Global Governance*, Vol. 30, No. 4 (December 1999), pp. 393–411, and "Iraq: No Easy Response to 'the Greatest Threat'", *American Journal of International Law*, Vol. 95 (2001), pp. 236–245.

41. See ⟨http://www.iic-offp.org/index.html⟩; see also William Safire, "Kofigate Gets Going", *New York Times*, 12 July 2004; "The Great Cash Cow", *New York Times*, 23 June 2004; "Tear Down this U.N. Stonewall", *New York Times*, 14 June 2004; "Scandal with No Friends", *New York Times*, 19 April 2004; "Follow-up to Kofigate", *New York Times*, 19 March 2004; "Scandal at the U.N.", *New York Times*, 17 March 2004.

42. See Thomas G. Weiss, David P. Forsythe and Roger A. Coate, *The United Nations in a Changing World* (2nd edn, Boulder, CO: Westview Press, 1997).

43. See, generally, David Cortright and George A. Lopez, *Sanctions and the Search for Security; Making Targeted Sanctions Effective: Guidelines for the Implementation of UN Policy Options*, Report of the Stockholm Process, 14 February 2003, available at ⟨http://www.smartsanctions.se⟩.

44. See, for example, the resolutions on UNITA (1127 (1997) and 1173 (1998)), Usama bin Laden and Al-Qaida (1267 (1999), 1333 (2000) and 1390 (2002)) and Charles Taylor (1532 (2004)).

45. This was the name given by the United States and the United Kingdom to the air bombardment carried out in the wake of Iraqi expulsions of Western UNSCOM officials in late 1998.

Part II

Structural and normative challenges

3

The unipolar concert: Unipolarity and multilateralism in the age of globalization

Mohammed Ayoob and Matthew Zierler

An article in the *New York Times* on the eve of the 2004 US presidential election began by asserting that the predominant view in Europe seemed to be that, "[n]o matter who wins the presidential election next week, the consequences for American-European relations will be bad". The author traced this conclusion to the strong feeling among Europeans that neither France nor Germany, the two linchpins of the Continent's transatlantic relationship, would be willing to come to the aid of the United States in Iraq regardless of who won the US election.[1] Analyses such as this one tend to portray the United States' relations with major European powers in one-dimensional terms. They argue that everything hinges on Iraq and ignore the dense web of interlocking security and economic interests that bind the industrialized countries of Western Europe and the United States together. As Joseph Nye has put it very aptly, "[i]n their relations with each other all advanced democracies are from Venus."[2]

The clear recognition of this commonality of interests was demonstrated by the atmosphere surrounding, and the rhetoric during, US Secretary of State Condoleezza Rice's trip to Europe in February 2005. Rice's trip was aimed above all at mending fences with the two leading European allies – France and Germany – that had differed from the US on the invasion of Iraq. The United States' relations with France had particularly soured on this issue. However, Rice made clear in her major foreign policy speech on 8 February in Paris that "history will surely judge us not by our old disagreements but by our new achievements".[3]

In this chapter we suggest that, although substantial changes to the international system have occurred since the end of the Cold War, the relationship among the industrialized, affluent and powerful countries of the global North basically has not been altered. This is because these relationships were only partly driven by the common Soviet threat. They were driven in equal, if not greater, measure by the need to protect and enhance the interests that Western industrialized states had in common vis-à-vis the majority of states in the economic, political and security spheres. It was recognized even during the Cold War era that potentially serious threats to the economic and security interests of the powerful and affluent countries of the global North could arise from other parts of the world, especially from the more recalcitrant and radical states from the global South, whose interests were likely to diverge fundamentally from states that composed the overlapping membership of the Organisation for Economic Co-operation and Development, the North Atlantic Treaty Organization (NATO) and the Group of Seven (G-7).

This conclusion was based on the assumption that there was a "structural conflict" built into the relationship between the North and the South and that this was likely to drive Southern states to "gang up" on the North and use their numbers in international organizations to push through agendas deleterious to the interests of the industrialized powers. Stephen Krasner made this argument most cogently and forcefully in 1985. He advised Western/Northern states to "disengage" as far as feasible from the countries of the global South. He considered this essential to prevent the North's undue dependence, especially in the economic sphere, on a web of intertwining relationships with potential adversaries.[4]

The Achilles' heel of Krasner's analysis was that it attributed greater cohesion to the groupings of third world states, such as the Group of 77 (G-77) and the Non-Aligned Movement, than they possessed. He also overestimated the will and capacity of third world states to challenge the major industrialized countries on issues vital to the latter. He did so because he ignored the vulnerabilities of individual post-colonial states, including the major oil producers such as Saudi Arabia, and their consequent dependence in economic and security matters on the major powers of the global North. Such dependence gravely hampered the translation of their collective rhetoric into meaningful collective action.[5] Despite these shortcomings, Krasner's diagnosis that the interests of the Northern and the Southern states diverged, and continue to diverge, significantly in the economic and political arenas was not far off the mark.

From the perspective of the rich and the powerful, events since the ending of the Cold War have added to the saliency of challenges emerging from the global South, whether in the shape of political Islam, especially in its more extreme manifestations, "rogue" states engaged in clandestine proliferation activities, or forces in the global South that resist the Northern conception of globalization, in the economic as well as the cultural spheres, because they perceive it to be deleterious to the interests of their societies. A recent report sponsored by the Council on Foreign Relations and chaired by Henry Kissinger and Lawrence Summers suggests that "[t]here is a consensus within the transatlantic community on the numerous challenges facing common interests. These include terrorism, authoritarianism, economic incompetence, environmental degradation, and the kind of misrule that exacerbates poverty, encourages discrimination, tolerates illiteracy, allows epidemics, and proliferates weapons of mass destruction."[6] This is a polite way of saying that the major threats to international order as conceived in the capitals of the global North come from the South, particularly from those forces that the major powers are not in a position to control.

We argue that there are remarkable continuities in crucial areas between the Cold War and post–Cold War epochs, especially the contradictions inherent in the political and economic relations between the global North and the global South that are a function of the position in which they find themselves in terms of stages of state-making and phases of economic development. It is no coincidence, therefore, that North–South relations are increasingly taking centre-stage in contemporary international affairs. This is demonstrated by the division of opinions visible in several important areas, including the US-led invasion of Iraq, the Israel–Palestine conflict, and humanitarian intervention, as well as major economic issues relating to tariff and non-tariff trade barriers, terms determining foreign investment, and questions of equity in relation to intellectual copyright and patents.

Neatly dividing the history of international relations into distinct phases often obscures the enduring elements of international politics. The end of the Cold War did mean the end to bipolarity and competition between the United States and the Soviet Union in the strategic arena. However, this by itself did not lead to a fundamental restructuring of international politics that would require a completely brand-new set of tools to explain and understand it. Analysts of the post–Cold War era who argued that systemic change had occurred with the end of superpower competition ignored the fact that today's key concepts, such as globalization, multilateralism and fundamentalism, have their roots in the Cold War period and indeed in earlier epochs.[7] We need to acknowledge the historical roots of such phenomena in order to explicate the current structure of international society. It is only by examining both the changes and the continuities in the international system that we can assess what has fundamentally changed and what has not in the politics and economics of international relations.

Structure and process in the international system

Understanding the structure and process of the international system provides the basic framework for the systematic study of international relations. According to Joseph Nye, "[t]he *structure* of a system refers to its distribution of power, and the *process* refers to patterns and types of interaction among its units".[8] Logically, in order to explain the process by which states interact – for example, whether they act multilaterally or unilaterally, or whether states act in response to economic or military pressures – it is necessary to know what the structure of the international system is and how it conditions states to act in a certain manner.

However, Nye's definition of structure is unduly restrictive if by the distribution of power he means only the allocation of capabilities among the major powers. Such a definition might suffice for neo-realists, and Nye cannot be counted among them, but it ignores the fact that the distribution of capabilities between the strong and the weak within the international system is as important as the distribution of power among the strong themselves. This is because the gap in the capabilities between the powerful and the weak determines in large measure the structural power that powerful states or groups of them wield in particular issue areas as well as in the international system as a whole. It is the variable that explains the *concentration* of power as opposed to its mere distribution. It is essential to understand this phenomenon of concentration in order to comprehend the nature and degree of structural dominance in international society and its long-term consequences.

The current era has certainly changed from the Cold War in the sense not only that the United States is the most powerful state in the international system but also that there is no credible challenger to its pre-eminence after the demise of the Soviet Union. Therefore, describing the current distribution of power as unipolar is, on the surface, not terribly problematic.[9] However, every new arrangement in terms of power distribution among the major powers does not lead states automatically to discard the patterns of behaviour that existed before the power shift. Furthermore, unlike earlier major changes in the distribution of power in the international system, for example in the aftermath of the two world wars in the twentieth century, the current redistribution of power did not result from a systemic conflict. The relatively peaceful transition from bipolarity to unipolarity has, therefore, not resulted in major disruptions in patterns of state behaviour, in already existing alliance relationships, or in the rules and norms governing the system. Consequently, unlike in the aftermath of the two world wars, when new power relations and the rules governing them had to be established afresh, the transition to US unipolarity did not mean that the relationships and processes that had been developed during the 50 years before that suddenly disappeared.

The continuity of behaviour is evident not only in the case of the mutual relationships among the states of the global North but also in the case of North–South relations. Indeed, the ending of the Cold War has made issues of North–South asymmetry more salient. Although the new vocabulary of post–Cold War analysis developed in US and European academia, emphasizing as it does terms such as globalization, unipolarity and multilateralism and the apparent tensions among them, may succeed in hiding these continuities both among the states of the North and between the North and the South for some time, analysts of international affairs with a keen sense of history and sociology, not to mention economics, are bound to realize that in many spheres the post–Cold War era is the linear descendant of the Cold War period.

Unipolarity, globalization and the Concert of Powers

At a superficial level, there seems to be tremendous tension today between the existence of a unipolar world that appears to privilege the dominance of the United States and the dramatic development of globalization, which promises both economic integration throughout the system and, in the form of touted changes in the norms of global society, the democratization of international relations. The terms "unipolarity" and "globalization" are often juxtaposed as if they are antithetical to each other or, at the least, in a state of great friction. However, a deeper analysis that focuses on structural power, that is the distribution of economic, military and technological capabilities throughout the system, would make clear that the two actually complement each other very well. They do so not merely in terms of unipolarity ruling the roost in military-political affairs while globalization dominates the economic arena. They complement each other because, in the final analysis, both underwrite the same set of power relations in the international system. They are instruments for advancing the interests of the dominant Concert of Powers – an overlapping group of actors that can be termed the Concert of the North Atlantic plus Japan – in all major spheres of international activity.

This club of rich and powerful states, now known as the global North, seemed to have come to the conclusion in the aftermath of World War II and decolonization that it was in the interest of its members to act in concert. The motivation for this was only in part the presumed threat from the Soviet Union. These states were motivated in equal measure by the need to protect their interests, indeed their dominance over the international system, from the economic and political claims of the newly independent states that had just emerged into statehood after decades, and in some cases centuries, of colonial subjugation. The need to do so had become particularly urgent because, with decolonization, the states of the West/North had been rendered a numerical minority in the system of states and the new entrants into the system had begun to clamour for "justice", "representation" and, in some cases, "reparation" in the form of a transfer of resources from the North to the South.[10] That such concerted action was deemed necessary by the industrialized powers was clearly demonstrated during the negotiations in the second half of the 1970s on the New International Economic Order (NIEO). These negotiations ended without agreement because the North, led by the United States, was unwilling to make the concessions necessary to make a dent in the industrialized countries' privileged position in the world economy. The stalemate on NIEO left intact the status quo that favoured the global North.[11]

The conclusion that the industrialized states must act in relative unison was reinforced by the end of the Cold War, which removed the veneer of superpower competition from the reality of a North–South contradiction, which was economic, political, military and, some would argue, civilizational and cultural as well. This understanding was reflected in the popularity in the global North of the neoliberal argument that privileged absolute gains over relative gains.[12] This argument depicted, among other things, the common interests of the affluent and the powerful states in cooperating with each other to further their economic and security goals. Although the neoliberals argued for the universal validity of their paradigm in an increasingly integrating world, it was clear that the neoliberal model was basically grounded in the realities of the global North. The ethnocentric nature of the neoliberal enterprise demonstrated by implication the difference between the states of the global North and those of the global South. The latter, as some analysts were quick to point out, continued to work under the supposedly discredited realist framework and, therefore, could not be assimilated into a neoliberal world.[13]

More importantly, the neoliberal rhetoric provided a cover for the realist foundations on which North–South relations, in the economic as well as the political-military fields, were and are based. James Richardson has pointed this out very succinctly. According to him, neoliberalism has "a striking resemblance to certain forms of realism. Both seek to reinforce the interests of the powerful by enjoining accommodation to them ... The major contrast is that realism places power at the center of its theorizing, whereas neoliberalism shows its respect for power through total silence."[14] Neoliberalism did yeoman service to the industrialized countries by promoting the status quo and making it intellectually respectable while concealing the element of raw power that underwrote this status quo. It did so by implicitly acknowledging the critical role of power while obfuscating its importance by means of the absolute gains rhetoric.

The concept of absolute gains that informs the mutual relationships of the industrialized countries in both the economic and security spheres can neither explain nor determine either the security predicament or the economic quandary faced by states in the third world. This is better explained by a realist, but not neo-realist, logic that is informed by the inequality in North–South relations, as well as by the security predicament faced by many states in the global South, which is related to their early stage of state-making and late entry into the system of states.[15] These circumstances make for greater disorder within states of the global South as well as a higher propensity for intra-state and inter-state conflict in the third world. They also explain the high degree of economic inequality within these states as well as the great chasm separating them from the industrialized countries in terms of economic development and affluence.

The chasm between the global North and the global South also helps explain the nature of the Concert and its objective of creating an international order that preserves its privileged position in the international system while containing the level of disorder within it, seen as mostly emanating from the global South. Given the congruence of interests among the industrialized states of the global North, the United States' unrivalled power does not undermine the unity of the Concert; it augments its power vis-à-vis those outside the Concert. Therefore, in the current context, unipolarity is quite compatible with the notion of a Concert of Powers, albeit one in which one of the members is far more powerful than the others and, therefore, demands and is accorded due deference. It would be apt to describe it as a "unipolar concert", a term that simultaneously depicts the unrivalled power of the Concert's leader and demonstrates the basic cohesion of its members' interests.

The use of the term "unipolarity", itself a derivative of polarity, in much of the Western discussion of contemporary international affairs serves a useful rhetorical purpose because it portrays the image that the return to the good old days of balance of power politics is not far away. By doing so, it diverts analytical attention from, and thus obscures the reality of, the real clash of interests between the strong and affluent states represented by the Concert, on the one hand, and the weak and poor states, a much more amorphous group, on the other. By emphasizing unipolarity and the tactical differences that emerge from time to time between the leading power and the pack that it leads, members of the Concert hide the fact that there is a basic agreement among them about the rules and norms of the international system and the basic premises on which international order should be organized. Unipolarity is, therefore, a convenient smokescreen by which much of the blame for excesses committed on behalf of the Concert is shifted to the leader of the pack, with the other members of the Concert portrayed as "reasonable" actors unable to control the more rapacious instincts of the unipolar power. It allows members of the Concert to play the "good cop, bad cop" routine for the consumption of those outside the Concert.

This became very clear in the case of the invasion of Iraq and, subsequently, the issue of the presumed threat of Iranian nuclear proliferation. European powers, especially France and Germany, were portrayed in both cases as trying to restrain the aggressively interventionist proclivities of the United States. In the case of Iraq, this allowed them to remain relatively unscathed in terms of the criticism heaped upon the United States in the Muslim world and indeed in much of the global South. In the case of Iran, it has provided them leverage with Tehran; it adds strength to their argument that, if Iran turns down their "reasonable" offer, the United States may decide to go it alone and Iran may have to face dire consequences for its recalcitrance.

The term "globalization", which has become synonymous with market fundamentalism, serves the same purpose of providing a veneer that hides more than it depicts. Moreover, it has the added merit of meaning many things to many people. As Graham Allison has pointed out, "[a]s currently used, globalization is too often an ill-defined pointer to a disparate array of phenomena – frequently accompanied by heavy breathing that implies that behind these phenomena, or at their root, is some yet-to-be-discovered substance".[16] The term "globalization" portrays a false image of an interdependent international economy in which, once again, absolute gains for all are bound to outweigh relative gains if the market alone is allowed to determine economic outcomes unhindered by political and governmental interference.

This strategy makes a great deal of sense from the point of view of the Concert that sits atop the international economic structure as well as the international security structure. It is rational for the powerful to portray their own relative gains vis-à-vis the rest as absolute gains for the entire international society. It also makes great sense for them to put a strong case that the status quo that protects (in fact enhances) the advantages they enjoy is best for all human kind. However, serious analysts must not take such claims at face value. Samuel Huntington has portrayed this reality very bluntly: "The West is attempting and will continue to attempt to sustain its preeminent position and defend its interests by defining those interests as the interests of the 'world community.' That phrase has become the euphemistic collective noun ... to give global legitimacy to actions reflecting the interests of the United States and other Western powers."[17]

Globalization has the potential to augment inequality both within states and between them unless it is carefully monitored and shepherded by sophisticated regulatory institutions established by the state. This is the core argument of Stiglitz's critique of market-driven globalization. He has argued convincingly that, for globalization to work effectively and spread wealth around, it must be a "managed" process in which democratic governments exercise more power than the International Monetary Fund (IMF) or global markets.[18] Even the pro-globalization guru Jagdish Bhagwati acknowledges the importance of appropriate governance to manage globalization better.[19] Unfortunately, not merely is there a dearth of democratic governments in the global South, but most postcolonial states do not possess the managerial resources effectively to operate regulatory institutions that would mitigate the more perverse effects of unfettered globalization. Consequently, in the developing world unmanaged globalization acting through the instrument of indiscriminate economic liberalization has the potential to create far more losers than winners.[20]

Regrettably, multilateral regimes, which are often portrayed as mechanisms with the capacity to curtail the more predatory outcomes of free market globalization and economic liberalization, frequently fail to do so. They fail because most such regimes, especially the IMF and the World Bank, reflect the power inequalities – embodied among other things in the weighted voting rules under which they operate – within the international system. Therefore, those who wield financial and economic power heavily influence the decisions of these regimes. They thus become a part of the problem rather than a part of the solution. In many ways, they conform to Sean Kay's definition of globalization. Kay suggests that "[g]lobalization is best understood as a technologically facilitated proliferation of the means through which power within the international system is channeled and pursued".[21] Such a nuanced understanding of globalization forces us to reconsider assumptions that globalization is a fundamental break from the power relations of the past and the harbinger of a new future.

Multilateralism and unipolarity: Artificial contradiction

Recent disagreements within the Concert and an increase in unilateral activities by the United States, principally in Iraq but also on issues such as the environment, have led many to predict the demise of the post–World War II order and the emergence of an international system predicated on different sets of relationships. Some have proclaimed that this is the "end of the West" as we have known it in international relations.[22]

This chapter does not mean to belittle these fissures, because they are in fact quite real in terms of strategy and tactics. However, we do not believe that these developments will result in a radical change in intra-Concert relations or in the use of multilateralism as we know it, for two reasons.

First, the Concert of the North Atlantic – with the United States in the lead – maintains its power in the international system by exploiting the multilateral regimes (be they in the financial, trade or security realm) it has worked so hard to create over the past 50 years. It is, therefore, unlikely that the United States or the major European powers will eviscerate a mechanism that has served them so well for so long and that has become embedded in their conception of the international system. There have always been disagreements about, and various levels of ambivalence toward, specific forms of multilateralism. Although the disagreements may seem more pronounced today, there is nothing to suggest that powerful states have given up on the fundamental features of the multilateral order over which they preside.

Second, disagreements in the Concert are often around policy choices, as opposed to the fundamental rules of the system or the basic objectives set by the Concert of Powers. Deterring and punishing "rogue" states and denying unconventional capabilities to those outside the Club were, and are, shared objectives from which no member of the Concert dissents. This was very clear in the run-up to the invasion of Iraq in 2003. A careful reading of the UN Security Council debates on Iraq from 1991 to 2003 makes it obvious that there was hardly any dissent among the club of powerful states that steps should be taken in relation to Iraq that would severely derogate from Iraq's sovereignty and eventually bring about regime change in that country. The imposition of no-fly zones and invasive inspections under UN auspices between 1991 and 2003 clearly demonstrated this unity of purpose. The differences were over the tactics that should be employed in order to achieve these ends. It was these differences that came to a head in 2003 on the eve of the invasion of Iraq by the United States and the United Kingdom. The same applies to the Concert's objectives regarding Iran. The shared objective is to deny Iran nuclear weapons capabilities and to curb its regional influence; the debate is about how best to attain these goals. The differences among leading members of the Concert are, once again, tactical rather than fundamental.

A similar situation prevails in the economic arena. Although there may be differences over details and even intra-Concert bickering about certain issues (for example, the US attempt to impose tariffs on European steel), there is a basic consensus about prying open world markets under the guise of free trade and liberal investment policies, thus making it easier for developed countries to market their high-valued-added products and to invest in profitable ventures abroad. This is accompanied by the imposition of conditionalities known as structural adjustments on third world economies that would ostensibly help to reduce their fiscal deficit. It is clear that none of this can be achieved without the use of multilateral mechanisms, such as the World Bank, the IMF, the World Trade Organization, and many others. The Concert of industrialized states, working through the G-7 in particular, harmonizes its economic policy in such a fashion that it can effectively use these multilateral forums to promote its neoliberal agenda.

Multilateralism is a difficult mechanism to operate and we do not suggest that the arrangements and initiatives that currently exist under the rubric of multilateralism will remain exactly the same. However, it is unlikely that the instrument as a whole will be jettisoned, if only because of the deep commitment many members of the Concert have made to maintain it and the way multilateral institutions have by and large served the purposes of the dominant Concert. In addition, we can also argue that multilateral institutions in the global North are being strengthened as the states from Eastern Europe try to gain acceptance in the rest of Europe by seeking membership in the European Union and NATO. The deepening and broadening of multilateral institutions in the North have had the added effect of reinforcing the divide between those in the Concert and those on the outside. In short, multilateralism has not proved to be antithetical to unipolarity. In fact, the two have worked in tandem to promote the interests of the global North in both the economic and the security spheres.

The North versus the South: Economics

The self-serving nature of Northern claims about unfettered globalization and the integration of the world economy on terms determined by the industrialized countries is obvious in the economic arena. Bringing down barriers imposed by state boundaries allows the economically powerful states to penetrate weak and vulnerable societies, especially those without adequate regulatory mechanisms and with unrepresentative regimes, many of which are dependent upon the major powers for their security. Moreover, the majority of economic interactions that make for interdependence in a "globalizing" world take place among the triad of North America, Europe and Japan. As Hirst and Thompson have pointed out, "[c]apital mobility is not producing a massive shift of investment and employment from the advanced to the developing countries. Rather foreign direct investment (FDI) is highly concentrated among the advanced industrial economies and the Third World remains marginal in both investment and trade, a small minority of newly industrializing countries apart."[23] Another analyst has concluded recently that, "[o]ver the past eight years, Americans invested twice as much in the Netherlands as in Mexico and ten times as much as in China ... Conversely, Europe provides 75 per cent of all investment in the United States."[24]

The disproportionate benefits of globalization that go to the developed states are not limited to FDI flows alone. In different forms this argument applies also to the protection of intellectual copyrights and patents as well as access to markets and cheap labour in the third world by multinational corporations headquartered in the global North. It applies too to the hundreds of billions of dollars in farm export subsidies by countries of the global North, as well as the imposition by the same countries of tariff and non-tariff barriers on the import of selected commodities, both agricultural and non-agricultural, on grounds of dumping. If everything else fails, the "primitive" social conditions under which exportable goods are produced in the countries of the global South are used as the clinching argument to disqualify them from being sold in the markets of "civilized" countries.

The skewed nature of globalization is demonstrated above all by the fact that, although much is made of the need to provide for the unfettered mobility of goods and capital globally, no voices are raised in the global North in favour of the free mobility of labour, and therefore of human beings, across the globe. Even Turkey's prospective, and not too certain, membership of the European Union has been made contingent by the European Commission on Ankara's accepting very limited migration to Europe from Turkey in contrast to unregulated movement among peoples of the existing EU member states.[25] The logic of economic globalization is supposed to apply selectively to cases that enhance the interests of the powerful against the weak, of the rich against the poor, but not vice versa. Furthermore, these rules are becoming embedded in an increasingly institutionalized and legalized multilateral order that would make it difficult to bring about radical transformations in the near future.

The North versus the South: Politics and security

In the political arena, tearing down the sovereignty barrier in the name of humanitarian intervention serves much the same purpose of preserving the dominance of the global North. Such interventions undertaken selectively to punish "rogue" states such as Iraq and Yugoslavia that are unwilling to fall in line with the wishes of the great powers send the clear message that opposing the international establishment is likely to incur heavy costs. The selectivity with which the normative injunctions of the emerging global society are applied makes this charade very clear. Interventions take place when it suits the strategic and economic interests of the "coalition of the willing and the able" (read, the North Atlantic Concert). Where it does not suit the global hegemon or the dominant Concert, the evolving norms of supposedly global society are disdainfully disregarded. The cases of Rwanda and Sudan exemplify this outlook.[26]

The selectivity demonstrated in the application of the norms of global society leads one to draw two important conclusions. First, sovereignty continues to be a cherished value as far as powerful states and their clients are concerned. Advising the weak to dispense with sovereignty and with their preoccupation with state security and relative gains is one thing; applying it to powerful states and their coalitions is quite another. As Lyons and Mastanduno have pointed out, the argument that sovereignty has been superseded as the organizing principle of international political life cannot be successfully sustained unless it is demonstrated "by reference to 'critical' cases ... The clearest set of critical cases would involve instances in which the exertion of some form of international authority significantly constrained major powers in their pursuit of their interests ... If we look at the present processes of international decision making [the veto power of the P-5 in the UN Security Council and the G-7's domination of international financial institutions], however, the prospect of finding such critical cases appears to be unlikely."[27]

Second, the rhetoric of globalization and of the global society is employed to provide a facade for the operation of a very realist paradigm by the powerful states of the global North in their relationship with the states of the global South, many of which continue to be weak and vulnerable and, therefore, incapable of ensuring their own security. Australian scholar James Richardson has captured this reality very lucidly. Analysing the post–Cold War period, he concludes: "Self interest now appears to dictate that the leading powers remain associates rather than rivals, as balance of power logic would have required, but the anarchic system structure points to their retaining a military capability to protect their favored position against the less favored."[28]

The retention of vastly superior military capability is currently achieved through what has come to be known as the Revolution in Military Affairs (RMA) or the Military Technological Revolution (MTR). RMA capacity has been summed up succinctly by Eliot Cohen in the following words: "What can be seen by high-tech sensors can be hit, what can be hit will be destroyed."[29] The concentration of such capacity in the hands of a very few states makes one thing very clear, namely that the hierarchy of military power has seldom been as rigidly stratified as it has become today as a result of RMA. The United States, the leading RMA power, sits in lonely glory at the top of the technological-military pyramid.[30] A group of major industrialized countries plus Israel is clustered probably two-thirds of the way up the pyramid. The rest form the base of the pyramid, except for a few, such as China and maybe India, that have been able to claw their way up to about a quarter of the pyramid's height. For those located at the base of the pyramidal structure or close to it, the prospects could range from the very uncomfortable to the extremely scary.

The RMA's lessons regarding the extreme disparity in military power and its political consequences have been emphasized over and over again since 1990. They were made explicit during the first Gulf war and, with increasingly greater clarity, during the bombing of Yugoslavia in 1999 and the US-led military campaign in Afghanistan in 2001–2002. They have been most dramatically driven home by the US campaign of "shock and awe" conducted against Iraq in March–April 2003. What impressed much of the global South with regard to these military ventures was not the righteousness or otherwise of the causes espoused by the dominant Concert or the unipolar power acting on its behalf. What overawed countries of the global South most was the enormous destructive power that the coalition, and especially the United States, brought to bear on its enemies from long distances, thereby making itself immune to retaliation. The precision and impunity with which the US-led Concert was able to destroy the vital military nerve centres of Iraq and Yugoslavia, which rendered them incapable of defending themselves, were perceived as technological miracles that dwarfed even the nuclear weapons revolution in terms of their actual impact on military affairs.

The use of RMA weaponry by the United States and its allies has left an indelible mark on the psyche of the third world political élites. On the one hand, it has markedly increased their feeling of insecurity. On the other, those among third world élites who continue to harbour a defiant streak or perceive their countries to be in danger of being labelled "rogue" states have been spurred to find a counterbalance that might deter RMA powers from initiating military action against them. These counterbalances are obtainable in only two forms. They can be procured either as weapons of mass destruction, however rudimentary, accompanied by delivery systems that can reach RMA troop and weapons concentrations at relatively long distances (nuclear, chemical or biological warheads plus missiles) or as "terror" tactics that render RMA weapons militarily irrelevant, thereby making them politically useless. A highly asymmetrical distribution of conventional military capabilities, a product of the military-technological revolution, has brought about equally asymmetrical responses that threaten to obliterate the distinction between conventional and unconventional warfare.

The attempt by "states of concern", including North Korea and Iran, to acquire weapons of mass destruction and missile capability, as well as terrorist attacks on soft US and other Northern targets, which seem to be on the rise as witnessed in Iraq, Afghanistan and elsewhere, should be seen at least in part as the response of certain states and non-state actors in the third world to the acquisition and use of RMA weapons by the United States and its allies and their deployment against immeasurably weaker adversaries. For those in the global South bent on defying the dominant Concert, and especially the unipolar power, weapons of mass destruction and terrorist tactics seem to be the only instruments that can act as a counterbalance of sorts against the precision guided conventional weaponry that can be unleashed by the United States and the coalition it leads. This adds to their attraction for those who are unwilling to embrace the New World Order, with its military, economic and normative corollaries, that the dominant coalition is intent on imposing on the rest of the members of the international system. Iraq has become the prime example of asymmetrical unconventional warfare, just as it had been the model of asymmetrical conventional warfare in 2003.

Conclusion

What does all this mean for the issue of unipolarity and multilateralism in a globalizing world? It means first that unipolarity, although it gives the impression of US hegemony, is, despite intra-alliance differences, a pretence for what is really a Concert of Powers, which we have dubbed the Concert of the North Atlantic. Where differences emerge within the Concert, they appear on issues of strategy and tactics not those of objectives and goals. The Concert is clearly led by the United States, which, as all leaders do, sometimes moves so far ahead of the pack that it makes the rest very uncomfortable. Manoeuvrings then start to bring it back into line. It is in this context that arguments about the value of institutions that bind the hegemon are made.[31] The Kissinger and Summers report cited earlier makes it plain that "[d]isagreements on policy, not differences over the utility of international institutions, have caused most of these [recent] clashes" in the transatlantic relationship.[32] The European insistence that the United States give more attention to multilateralism is a plea for consultation among members of the Concert, not an argument to strengthen institutions of global governance in which the less powerful would have a major voice. This is a distinction that must clearly be borne in mind by analysts engaged in debating the merits of multilateralism versus unilateralism. For those outside the Concert, multilateralism and unilateralism often appear as variations on the same theme of uninvited intervention.

The institutional constraint argument is made largely to draw the leader back in to the pack rather than make it accountable through the medium of international institutions to the entire membership of international society. Those outside the pack continue to remain marginal actors in the international arena, if not mere spectators to these manoeuvrings. Eventually compromises are reached that restore the unity of the pack without embarrassing the leader too much. This is clearly demonstrated by what has been happening in the wake of the war against Iraq both in the Security Council and outside. The fact that these manoeuvrings have not been completely successful is owing in large part to the all-pervasive insecurity in Iraq thanks to the resilience of, and resistance put up by, insurgent forces in that country. It is reasonable to assume that, without the insurgency and the accompanying insecurity in Iraq, the United States on the one hand and France and Germany on the other would have reconciled their differences much earlier and would be working together in Iraq through a number of multilateral instruments and organizations.

Therefore, when viewed from beyond the confines of the Concert, the discussion about unipolarity and globalization, as well as about unipolarity and multilateralism, that portrays the two sets of concepts as diametrically opposed appears to be an elaborate pretence. To many, they appear two sides of the same coin. This is the reason the unipolar power's near-hegemonic image does not bother the other members of the Concert too much. It is also the reason globalization is seen as a benign phenomenon from within the Concert because it does not imply any real shift in the distribution of capabilities and, therefore, of power positions within the international system.

What we have tried to do is to point out that the discussion about unipolarity versus other forms of polarity, bipolarity and multipolarity, or about the relevance or irrelevance of unipolarity to the age of globalization, is really marginal to the major problem facing international society in the contemporary era. The main impasse facing international society today is the huge disparity in power between the Concert of the North Atlantic (including Japan, and with Russia and possibly China co-opted as peripheral appendages to the Concert), on the one hand, and the rest of the members of the international system, on the other. This disparity and the cavalier use of power by the dominant Concert, and not just the United States, against selected targets have created a situation that threatens the already fragile normative consensus underpinning international society. The unilateral actions on the part of the United States, as in Iraq, threaten not so much the integrity of the Concert as the foundational norms of international society, such as sovereignty and non-intervention, which had provided the basis for that society in the first place. If this trend continues, we may end up with a hyper-realist world in which "the strong do what they can and the weak suffer what they must". This backsliding from society to anarchy, despite the solidarists' naive claims to the contrary, is a prelude to a serious breakdown of order in the international system.[33]

We see signs of this impending anarchy in unilateral military actions in defiance of international consensus and in doctrines justifying preventative, and not merely pre-emptive, war. We see it in escalating international terrorism and what appears to many as an approaching "clash of civilizations" between the "Judeo-Christian" North/West and the Muslim world. We see it also in the attraction that weapons of mass destruction (WMD) hold for the weak. The episode linked to Pakistani nuclear scientist A. Q. Khan has demonstrated that the dissemination of nuclear material and technology is no longer all that difficult to achieve. Notwithstanding the Libyan decision to renounce WMD and Iran's greater, although hesitant, cooperation with the International Atomic Energy Agency, the incentive to proliferate has increased during the past decade. North Korea's recent public admission that it possesses nuclear weapons may be an indication of things to come.[34] This may very well be because, as stated earlier, acquisition of WMD capacity appears to the weak and the vulnerable as their most effective defence against the possession of RMA weaponry by members of the powerful Concert led by the United States. Efforts to acquire WMD and the spread of international terrorism demonstrate that the imposition of order, without it being tempered by justice, creates its own backlash. This is a lesson that the capitals of the major powers forget at their own peril.

Similarly, unless globalization is tempered by a genuine concern for intra-state and inter-state justice, it is likely to become a serious source of destabilization both domestically and internationally. Resentment against globalization among those who feel left out, indeed hurt badly, by its relentless free market logic, which disregards negative social consequences, is building up in the global South. Such resentment is likely to increase as Southern polities democratize and previously disempowered segments of their populations undergo rapid political mobilization and access to political power. This is why it is important to heed the words of *Foreign Policy* in its study of globalization, which suggest that "those most interested in promoting global integration must do more to heed the concerns of those who feel marginalized by it, lest the backlash against globalization becomes a self-fulfilling prophecy".[35] The rejection by the Indian electorate in 2004 of the globalization-friendly ruling Hindu nationalist party's slogan "India Shining" can in part be directly attributed to the backlash among the rural and urban poor against the growing economic inequalities in the world's largest electoral democracy.

To conclude, we do not believe that there is any inherent contradiction either between unipolarity and multilateralism or between unipolarity and globalization. All three, as currently conceived and practised, serve the interests of what we have called the dominant, unipolar Concert. However, the danger we see is that the growing chasm between the Concert and other members of international society is increasingly becoming a major source of instability and disorder in the international system. It is time that those engaged in the practice of international relations in the global North redefined their conceptions of globalization and multilateralism to make these concepts, and the strategies that emanate from them, more inclusive and less subservient to the interests only of those who dominate the international security and economic power structures.

Notes

A previous version of this chapter appeared as "The Unipolar Concert: The North–South Divide Trumps Transatlantic Differences", *World Policy Journal*, Vol. 22, No. 1 (2005).

1. Richard Bernstein, "Many in Europe See U.S. Vote as a Lose-Lose Affair", *New York Times*, 29 October 2004.
2. Joseph S. Nye, *Soft Power: The Means to Success in World Politics* (New York: Public Affairs, 2004), p. 20. This, of course, counters Robert Kagan's argument that, "on major strategic and international questions today, Americans are from Mars and Europeans are from Venus". Robert Kagan, *Of Paradise and Power: America and Europe in the New World Order* (New York: Knopf, 2003), p. 3.
3. Stephen R. Weisman, "Rice Calls on Europe to Join in Building a Safer World", *New York Times*, 9 February 2005.
4. Stephen D. Krasner, *Structural Conflict* (Berkeley: University of California Press, 1985).
5. For an analysis that juxtaposes the collective aspirations of third world states and their individual vulnerabilities, thus elucidating the apparently schizophrenic tendencies they demonstrate, see Mohammed Ayoob, "The Third World in the System of States: Acute Schizophrenia or Growing Pains?", *International Studies Quarterly* (March 1989), pp. 67–79.
6. Henry A. Kissinger and Lawrence H. Summers (co-chairs) and Charles A. Kupchan (project director), *Renewing the Atlantic Partnership: Report of an Independent Task Force Sponsored by the Council on Foreign Relations* (New York: Council on Foreign Relations, 2004), p. 7.
7. For prominent analyses that posit that the end of the Cold War heralded fundamental systemic transformation, see Samuel Huntington, *The Clash of Civilizations and the Making of World Order* (New York: Simon & Schuster, 1996), and Francis Fukuyama, *The End of History and the Last Man* (New York: Free Press, 1992).
8. Joseph S. Nye, Jr, *Understanding International Conflicts* (5th edn, New York: Pearson, 2005), p. 37.
9. For a succinct case that the United States' current global predominance constitutes unipolarity, see Stephen G. Brooks and William C. Wohlforth, "American Primacy in Perspective", *Foreign Affairs*, Vol. 18, No. 4 (July/August 2002), pp. 20–33.
10. This is what Hedley Bull had aptly termed "the revolt against the West", which went beyond issues of politics and economics to the norms and rules governing international

society. Hedley Bull, "The Revolt against the West", in Hedley Bull and Adam Watson, *The Expansion of International Society* (Oxford: Clarendon Press, 1984), pp. 217–228.

11. Krasner, *Structural Conflict*; Robert Mortimer, *The Third World Coalition in International Politics* (2nd edn, Boulder, CO: Westview, 1986).

12. For a classic assertion of neoliberalism, see Robert Keohane, *After Hegemony* (Princeton, NJ: Princeton University Press, 1984).

13. For example, James M. Goldgeier and Michael McFaul, "A Tale of Two Worlds: Core and Periphery in the Post-Cold War Era", *International Organization*, Vol. 46, No. 2 (Spring 1992).

14. James L. Richardson, *Contending Liberalisms in World Politics: Ideology and Power* (Boulder, CO: Lynne Rienner, 2001), pp. 89–90.

15. For a theoretical exposition of this perspective, see Mohammed Ayoob, "Inequality and Theorizing in International Relations: The Case for Subaltern Realism", *International Studies Review* (Fall 2002), pp. 27–48.

16. Graham Allison, "The Impact of Globalization on National and International Security", in Joseph S. Nye and John D. Donahue, eds, *Governance in a Globalizing World* (Washington, DC: Brookings Institution Press, 2000), p. 72.

17. Samuel P. Huntington, *The Clash of Civilizations and the Remaking of World Order* (New York: Simon & Schuster, 1996), p. 184.

18. Joseph E. Stiglitz, *Globalization and Its Discontents* (New York: W. W. Norton, 2002).

19. Jagdish Bhagwati, *In Defense of Globalization* (New York: Oxford University Press, 2004).

20. Dani Rodrik, *The New Global Economy and Developing Countries: Making Openness Work* (Washington, DC: Overseas Development Council, 1999).

21. Sean Kay, "Globalization, Power, and Security", *Security Dialogue*, Vol. 35, No. 1 (2004), p. 11.

22. For example, see Charles Kupchan, *The End of the American Era* (New York: Knopf, 2002), and Robert Kagan, *Of Paradise and Power: America and Europe in the New World Order* (New York: Knopf, 2003).

23. Paul Hirst and Grahame Thompson, *Globalization in Question* (2nd edn, Cambridge: Polity, 1999), p. 2.

24. William Drozdiak, "The North Atlantic Drift", *Foreign Affairs*, Vol. 84, No. 1 (January–February 2005), p. 89.

25. Elaine Sciolino, "Turkey Advances in Its Bid to Join European Union", *New York Times*, 7 October 2004.

26. For details of this argument, see Mohammed Ayoob, "Humanitarian Intervention and State Sovereignty", *International Journal of Human Rights*, Vol. 6, No. 1 (Spring 2002), pp. 81–102.

27. Gene M. Lyons and Michael Mastanduno, "Introduction: International Intervention, State Sovereignty, and the Future of International Society", in Gene M. Lyons and Michael Mastanduno, *Beyond Westphalia? State Sovereignty and International Intervention* (Baltimore, MD: Johns Hopkins University Press, 1995), p. 17.

28. James L. Richardson, "The End of Geopolitics?", in Richard Leaver and James L. Richardson, eds, *Charting the Post-Cold War Order* (Boulder, CO: Westview, 1993), pp. 45–46.

29. Eliot A. Cohen, "A Revolution in Warfare", *Foreign Affairs*, Vol. 75, No. 2 (March–April 1996), p. 45. Also see Lawrence Freedman, "Revolutions in Military Affairs", in Gwyn Prins and Hylke Tromp, eds, *The Future of War* (Boston, MA: Kluwer Law International, 2000).

30. Joseph S. Nye, Jr and William A. Owens, "America's Information Edge", *Foreign Affairs*, Vol. 75, No. 2 (March–April 1996), pp. 20–36.

31. John Ikenberry, *After Victory* (Princeton, NJ: Princeton University Press, 2001).

32. Kissinger and Summers (co-chairs) and Kupchan (project director), *Renewing the Atlantic Partnership*, p. 20.

33. For a discussion of the notion of international society in an anarchic international system, see Hedley Bull, *The Anarchical Society* (New York: Columbia University Press, 1977), and Robert Jackson, *The Global Covenant* (New York: Oxford University Press, 2000). For a sophisticated solidarist conception of international society, see Nicholas Wheeler, *Saving Strangers* (New York: Oxford University Press, 2000).

34. James Brooke, "North Korea Says It Has Nuclear Weapons and Rejects Talks", *New York Times*, 10 February 2005.

35. A. T. Kearney, "Measuring Globalization: Who's Up, Who's Down?", *Foreign Policy* (January/February 2003), p. 72.

4

International peace and security and state sovereignty: Contesting norms and norm entrepreneurs

Brian L. Job

Introduction

This chapter provides some analytical purchase towards an understanding of the structural and normative forces that contend within the contemporary international order. Daily headlines, comment columns and titles of academic treatises trumpet these tensions, referring to US imperialism, unilateralism, pre-emption, the circumvention (indeed the irrelevance) of the United Nations, the abrogation of treaties, the utility of coalitions of the willing, the crisis of failed states, a war on terrorism, etc. Taken in sum, these present a picture of an international system unable to cope with the dramatic structural upheaval of the past decade and a half and struggling against the onslaught of a singular global power determined to remake a global order to meet its own interests.

Although much of this is hype and thus ephemeral, it is a symptomatic indication of the deeper challenges to the fundamental norms of state sovereignty, non-intervention, the legitimate use of force and multilateralism that have underpinned the international institutional order since World War II. Not surprisingly, these challenges are particularly evident concerning the United Nations – the world's core institution responsible for international peace and security – and the United States – a state that, although the world's dominant power, perceives itself simultaneously under threat and ill served by contemporary multilateral security organizations.

Within this context, this chapter reminds the reader that, although the intensity of these tensions may be remarkable, the existence of such tensions is a defining feature of international life, reflecting an ongoing, dynamic, social construction of norms and institutions by states and non-state actors.[1]

The chapter proceeds to make the following arguments. In general, reliance on the logics of structural change, hierarchy and the distribution of material capabilities is itself insufficient to explain the motivations and actions of states concerning the use of force and the use of multilateral institutions. Thus, the formation and operation of international institutions cannot be explained (away) as an "institutional bargain" dictated by the relative power distribution between leading and weaker states. Nor can structural changes in the distribution of power themselves account for dramatic transformations in international institutions or the reshaping of such institutions in the aftermath of major wars or systemic upheaval. Ideational forces, the normative precepts of key states and their actors and the "binding" influence of the norms underpinning existing institutions are key. The institutions and their operational modalities that emerge, therefore, reflect the "institutional compact" that can be sustained at any particular moment in the system. Change comes about through the evolution of actors' normative agendas, which, although prompted through structural change and dramatic events, are not determined by them.

The application of this abstract argument to the present sees the United Nations as an institution that reflects an evolving institutional compact mediating the tensions between norms of sovereignty, non-intervention and the use of force to gain peace and security. In turn, the United States is seen as a leading state actor, one acting as a "norm entrepreneur" to shape international institutions and to operate multilaterally to advance its national interest, as articulated by an élite political and bureaucratic cohort. In this regard, the United States has unilateral impulses and capacities but is more appropriately viewed as a self-interested, instrumental multilateral player. Thus, the United States, and its reactions to the events of 1989 and 2001, in particular, must be given due attention. These tensions and pressures, however, are being countered by the accumulating momentum of perceived imperatives to act on behalf of civilians caught in intra-state conflicts and to intervene in the context of "failed states" where governments have failed to protect or have preyed upon their own citizens. In this regard, certain middle power states, along with the Secretary-General of the United Nations and select individual personalities, were the key norm entrepreneurs over the course of the 1990s. The past decade thus reflects a trend (one that I regard as irreversible) towards institutional compacts that entrench norms of human security and sovereignty as entailing a responsibility to protect.

International institutions and institutional change

The formation of institutions: Two perspectives

One can compare and contrast two general approaches to explaining why, how and what types of international institution states form to manage their economic, political and security relations.[2] The first is that the major powers or dominant power in the system dictate the form and operative rules of institutions in a manner that facilitates maximization of their (its) interests, accepting "strategic restraints" as balanced against the costs of influence or coercion to gain the compliance of weaker states. In Ikenberry's words:

> In this institutional bargain, the leading state wants to reduce compliance costs and weaker states want to reduce their costs of security protection or the costs they would incur trying to protect their interests against the actions of a dominant lead state.... [T]he leading state agrees to restrain its own potential for domination and abandonment in exchange for the long-term institutionalized cooperation of subordinate states.[3]

Ikenberry's logic is essentially a rationalist one applied to actors defined according to the asymmetric distribution of capabilities, particularly as these emerge from the conclusion of a systemic war or arise from an unexpected structural shift in the distribution of power. The onus and opportunity rest with the leading state or coalition of major states to shape the parameters of the ensuing international institutional order. If a satisfactory institutional bargain is reached, institutions will persist to the extent that they continue to satisfy the competing interests of the strong and the weak, but in particular, for Ikenberry, of the strongest state.[4] Indeed, as institutions sustain their effectiveness and states perceive functional benefits to cooperation within their contexts, the institutions develop qualities of "stickiness" that promote their continued existence, despite minor disagreements among members and systemic perturbances.[5] This explains the longevity of the global economic and regional security institutions that were central during and indeed following the Cold War.

An alternative perspective regards institutions as "social constructions", i.e. as informal or formal mechanisms that emerge through the achievement of a consensus on norms of identity and of procedure among state actors. Institutions thus display a "collective identity", insofar as there is agreement among members about their common interests and the extent and purposes of their cooperative endeavour. There is a "bargain" in such an institutional model as well, namely that members perceive sufficiently common components of their individual identities to reveal a core set of norms around which to structure a cooperative framework.[6] This core may be a minimalist one, in that little more than collective recognition of other actors is involved; it could involve trade-offs, in that states balance their privileging of territorial sovereignty against their desire to protect human rights. But this "bargain" or "institutional compact", as it will be termed in this chapter, is not determined by a balancing of material capabilities and governed by rationalist calculations. Structural characteristics are relevant – some states are more important than others. However, in this constructivist approach to institutions, there is a capacity for leadership by non-major powers to the extent that they can articulate and create coalitions around common normative agendas and institutional procedures. In this context, non-state actors can play important roles in shaping ideas and advancing normative change. Central, too, is the understanding that institutions evolve as the normative agendas of their members evolve because of domestic developments and international interaction.[7]

Institutional change in the aftermath of "great events"

Major structural upheavals in the international order, particularly those arising in the aftermath of "world" wars, provide opportunities for the restructuring of international institutions. Thus, the years 1648, 1713, 1815, 1919, 1945 and 1989 all saw "great events", as Holsti calls them, that involved the leading state or states struggling to design what was hoped to be a peaceful and lasting international order.[8]

Not surprisingly, however, the alternative perspectives on international institutional formation take differing views of the underlying dynamics of institutional change. For some analysts, determination of the distribution of material capabilities is sufficient to dictate the key parameters of the emergent international order.[9] For Ikenberry, and many other contemporary analysts, the interests of a dominant state are the key – the extent of the asymmetry in the power distribution between it and the other states determines the nature of and the advantages to be accrued in constructing new, or reconstructing previous, institutional bargains. Thus, the international order after World War II came to reflect the international pre-eminence of the United States, with differing regional orderings of Europe and of Asia indicating the relative power asymmetries between the United States and the states in these respective regional contexts.

However, a reordered distribution of state capabilities is not by itself sufficient to explain the transforming of international institutions. The "big bang" theory of great events is challenged on two fronts. In the first instance, there is a growing body of evidence to suggest that "great events", which are marked by dramatic alterations in the distribution of material capabilities, are themselves preceded by – indeed motivated by – ideational shifts in the world views and priorities of leading actors. Such normative shifts are now acknowledged to have been substantially responsible for the ending of the East–West Cold War.[10]

Second, once the systemic order has been upset, there is no single answer to the question of the nature of the subsequent institutional order. A variety of institutional forms can be created within the context of any one distribution of power, even (perhaps especially) a distribution dominated by a single state. It is "ideas" that matter; i.e. it is the normative preferences of the lead or leading states in the system that heavily influence the framework of any international order. Thus, as many have observed regarding the period since the Cold War, the United States has open to it a spectrum of institutional management options. And, as already seen in the course of the past 15 years, changes in US leadership have resulted in several different and, in the present instance, quite distinctive normative priorities for the role and functioning of international institutions.

Norm entrepreneurs

In this regard, the role of "norm entrepreneurs" is critical. Established norms, especially as they become institutionalized in the functioning of formal organizations, are difficult to change. Members who support the outcomes that derive from their realization and bureaucrats whose institutional roles depend upon them can and do create strong resistance to change. "Bucking the system" is difficult: it requires resources, both ideational and material; a capacity to absorb the costs of nonconformity; and innovative and distinctive leadership.[11] In light of these constraints, one might expect the leaders and select élites of leading states to be better positioned to take on norm entrepreneurial roles; and they often do, and did after 1919, 1945 and 1989. However, the major powers, often those states benefiting the most from the status quo, do not hold a monopoly on norm entrepreneurship. This role has often been taken up by middle power states and non-state actors seeking to advance norms that challenge the established order. In such instances, success may well be dependent on the activism of powerful individual personalities.

Thus, tensions in the current institutional order can be viewed as arising from the clash between the distinctive agendas of two different norm entrepreneurs – the present leadership of the United States and the proactive leaders of the human security agenda. In turn, both are meeting the resistance of states whose interests are satisfied by sustaining Westphalian norms of state sovereignty, non-intervention, consensus decision-making and the exclusive role of the United Nations in authorizing the use of force.

The United Nations: Fundamental tensions, evolving norms

The institutional compact

The United Nations was created in the mid-twentieth century in the aftermath of the "great event" of World War II. As one of the key components of the institutional systemic framework orchestrated by the victorious powers, the United Nations bears the mark of their interests and aspirations. The United States, just emerging as the post-war leading state, had significant influence in this context but was not in a position to overrule the positions of its key Western allies.[12] The UN Charter must be viewed as a particularly complex "institutional bargain" – a bargain among the major powers themselves and a bargain between these leading states and the remaining independent states of that era. Thus, the UN architecture balances the General Assembly, an inclusive and consensual body of equals, with the Security Council, a great power management committee mandated to authorize the use of force but self-constrained by the veto power given to its permanent five members.

The "institutional compact", i.e. the core set of normative principles embodied in the United Nations, is fraught with inherent tension. The enshrining of the principles of state sovereignty, territoriality, non-intervention and the right of self-defence for all members is juxtaposed against the rights of the major powers not only to authorize the use of force but to call for, indeed compel, other states to undertake action on behalf of the United Nations. Presumably, this trade-off was acceptable to the leading states, as security providers, and to the other states, which anticipated both a more secure environment and a restraint upon adventurism by the major powers. However, the United Nations' institutional compact involved more than this sovereignty/security logic; for the Western allies, a fundamental mission was the advancement and protection of the human rights of the "peoples of the world". From its inception, the United Nations and the post-war international community as a whole wrestled with normative challenges to the absolutist interpretations of state sovereignty.

The forces of change

The dramatic increase in the membership of the international system with the decolonization of Asia and Africa brought with it sharpened tensions over the key norms of the international order. In effect, these states owed their existence to the combined impact of profound normative change (the overthrowing of historical norms underpinning colonialism), on the one hand, and the reinforcement of traditional norms (the claim to sovereign equality and inviolability), on the other. However, the "quasi-state" status of many of these new members raised increasing concerns for others, both in terms of their practical capacities to sustain productive international relations with their neighbours and in terms of the plight of their civilian populations, often exacerbated by government actions. During the Cold War, these tensions were muted through the major powers' exercise of influence on their clients and proxies. But they were by no means dispelled. As Ted Gurr and his associates have demonstrated, the rising trend of deadly intra-state violence began several decades ago. What has changed is the level of attention given to these conflicts, owing to the combined effects of Western publics' awareness through the media of the suffering of civilians, the recognition of the trans-border and trans-regional spillover effects of such conflicts, and a more congenial atmosphere within the United Nations for responding to these situations.[13]

An invigorated United Nations Security Council, enabled in particular by a US leadership committed to the advancement of a "new world order", took up the challenge of responding to these conflicts – the first few years of the 1990s witnessed the Council's authorization of more peace operations than in its previous four decades.[14] This enthusiasm quickly subsided as the practical challenges of mounting substantial multilateral missions, the intractability of communal violence, and the financial, but more centrally the human, costs of undertaking such missions were brought home to Western governments. From the mid-1990s onwards, the role of the UN Security Council increasingly became limited to legitimization, i.e. authorizing regional bodies or groups of member states to intercede in conflict situations.[15] The United States, in particular, backed away from engagement in UN missions, in light of the narrowed parameters of its international role as articulated in President Clinton's Presidential Decision Directive 25, and an accompanying preference for operating in US-led multilateral coalitions.

The redefining of security, responsibility and the use of force

Debates over the authorization and the legitimacy of the use of force came to the fore towards the end of the 1990s. In simplistic terms, these have been portrayed as pitting those who seek to maintain the primacy of state sovereignty, non-intervention and national security against those who argue for the higher priority of securing the safety and well-being of citizens. From this latter, "human security" perspective,[16] states have an overriding "responsibility to protect" their citizens. Regimes that are either incapable or unwilling to sustain order and basic freedoms should not be allowed to shelter behind state sovereignty barriers. Equally important, the international community, especially through the United Nations, is seen to have a responsibility to act on behalf of civilians under threat, intervening within state boundaries as necessary for their protection and well-being.

These debates were fuelled by the dilemmas attending a series of difficult crises, including Rwanda, Bosnia, Sudan and Kosovo, and by a virtual industry of writings in the academic, think-tank and non-governmental organization (NGO) communities, especially focused on humanitarian intervention. The basic "Westphalian" principles of state sovereignty and non-intervention are under challenge. The tensions at the heart of the institutional compact underlying the United Nations, in particular, and the international order, more generally, have not been, nor can they be, resolved.

Several key dimensions of the movement for normative transformation deserve attention. First is its rethinking of the traditional concepts of security and sovereignty, which has four essential components:

(a) The "broadening of security", i.e. the realization that achieving security involves much more than attending to perceived military threats from external enemies.[17]

(b) The advancement of "human security", based on the premise that the person, not the state, should be the primary "object" of security and that governments and international institutions should necessarily function to promote the well-being of citizens, even if doing so involves moving beyond the traditional barriers of territorial sovereignty.[18] In the words of UN Secretary-General Kofi Annan, "individual sovereignty" must at times take precedence over state sovereignty and national security.[19]

(c) The reorientation of the norms of sovereignty towards "the responsibility to protect", i.e. the assertion that, although state sovereignty provides recognition and international rights, it also entails the state's responsibility to provide security within its borders to its own citizens. Failing this, members of the international state community have the right, indeed in certain circumstances the responsibility, to intervene to protect the safety of populations in crisis, if necessary from the operations of their own governments.[20]

(d) The establishment of individual responsibility for war crimes committed in intra-state conflicts, in particular holding national political and military leaders responsible if they are judged to have fomented, authorized or stood by during atrocities in intra-state conflict.

Much of the credit for capturing and focusing world attention on this agenda is owing to a select set of norm entrepreneurs – the key voices for change coming from NGOs, non-major power states and within international institutions. Primary among them at present is UN Secretary-General Kofi Annan. Increasingly since 1999, his statements have come to advocate the notions that "state sovereignty, in its most basic sense, is being refined", that "states are now widely understood to be instruments in the service of their peoples, and not vice versa".[21] Annan's position, of course, is a delicate one, balancing the necessity of operating within the constraints of his office and sustaining the support of the United Nations' leading members against his entrepreneurial agenda for a reorientation of institutional priorities.

Initial norm entrepreneurial leadership was provided outside the United Nations, indeed in reaction to the United Nations' failure and with the aim of circumventing the United Nations' stymied decision-making. This leadership came from the foreign ministers and key political individuals in the smaller and middle powers. Thus, individuals including Gareth Evans (Australia) and Lloyd Axworthy (Canada), through the force of their own personalities and the energies of their countries' foreign services, in tandem with activist NGO communities, not only coined and advanced the concepts noted above, but were instrumental in creating initiatives around conflict diamonds, the protection of civilians and the plight of child soldiers.

It would be a mistake, however, not to acknowledge indications of change within the United Nations itself. A key indicator is the Security Council's interpretation of what constitutes a threat to international peace and security and, in turn, its authorization of the use of force in peace operations. In numerical terms, there has been a remarkable increase in the Council's willingness to invoke Chapter VII.[22] What is more significant is the changing definition of what the Council counts as a threat to international peace and security. As early as 1991, when first confronting Saddam Hussein, the Council was prepared to regard the repression of civilians as creating a threat to regional/international peace and security.[23] Since 1992 (Somalia), the protection of humanitarian personnel has become an almost standard consideration in invocations of Chapter VII. And, with the Sierra Leone crisis of 1999, the Council explicitly included the protection of civilian populations under threat as a critical component of its mandate for the forces authorized to intervene. The Council has abandoned any geographical requirement that a situation constitute a threat to "international" security. Particularly when the spectre of spillovers of refugee populations has loomed, the Council has been quite quick to authorize a Chapter VII response to a regional conflict and, more recently, to intra-state situations as well. The protection of refugee populations and the management of large internally displaced populations have become central components of many of the past decade's peace operation missions.

Thus, David Malone, one of the Council's most astute observers, concludes that the Council has "proved highly innovative in shaping the normative framework for international relations".[24] Although not explicitly characterizing its activities as advancing "human security" per se, the Council clearly has taken substantial steps towards establishing the norm of protection of civilians at risk in conflict situations. For example, despite China's extreme sensitivity to principles of state sovereignty, it has facilitated UN-authorized humanitarian intervention in circumstances involving failed states, e.g. Somalia and, more recently, the Democratic Republic of Congo.

Still, a caveat regarding the role of the United Nations is necessary. Over the past decade and a half, the tendency of states, NGOs and associated norm entrepreneurs has been to circumvent rather than to engage the United Nations. These strategies have taken two forms: on the one hand, multilateral actions to create new mechanisms that will institutionalize new regimes around revised norms; and, on the other hand, actions by states or coalitions of states to use force without first seeking the authorization of the Security Council. The first strategy is typified by the process, spearheaded by the Canadian government in coordination with key NGOs, to establish the Ottawa Convention on the banning of anti-personnel landmines,[25] as well as the subsequent move to create the International Criminal Court. The second strategy is typified by US actions concerning Kosovo and Iraq. It is ironic to note that both Kosovo and, in retrospect, Iraq have been justified as necessary responses to "human security" crises in contexts where the United Nations was seen to be paralysed.

In sum, there is evidence to support the argument that fundamental change has been set in motion, in particular that "the dominant moral discourse about humanitarian action has changed". However, the tensions remain, and the issues are not settled. Thus, although one can conclude that a "humanitarian impulse" certainly guides the Security Council's actions on matters of peace and security, this cannot be characterized as a "humanitarian imperative".[26] Indeed, in Adam Roberts' words, "all attempts to reach an agreed doctrine favoring humanitarian intervention have failed".[27]

The United States: Leading state and norm entrepreneur

The structural logic of US systemic dominance

The extent to which the United States now holds its place as the dominant global power requires no rehearsal. For many analysts, this structural fact is sufficient to explain the US attitude towards cooperation with other states and in international organizations such as the United Nations. As Ikenberry puts it, "[t]he simplest explanation for the new unilateralism is that the United States has grown in power during the 1990s, thereby reducing its incentives to operate within a multilateral order".[28] Today, one also finds this structural realist logic combined with the arguments of US historical exceptionalism and the nationalist imperatives of US domestic politics in times of crisis, both reinforcing a "go it alone" attitude, and at times a triumphalist attitude, towards international affairs.[29]

How should one interpret the key events that have placed the United States in this position of hegemonic dominance? The end of the Cold War in 1989 was a "great event", a systemic transformation in the sense that Gilpin, Waltz and others envisage a reordering of a dimension that alters prior rationales and patterns of international interaction. Two years later in 1991, with the United States' rapid rejection of Saddam Hussein's takeover of Kuwait, the supremacy of US military power was made very apparent, demonstrating that Washington requires no allies to project its military agenda effectively anywhere in the globe when it so chooses.

The events of 2001, however, were of a different order and have had profoundly different impacts. First, the attack on the US homeland caused a shift in the national psyche, i.e. an ideational transformation. Of equal import, the attacks marked a change in the structural order of the international system as well. They brought home the realization that the threats presented by non-state, terrorist actors could not be addressed through traditional patterns of inter-state security relations. In effect, when confronted by actors who cannot be constrained through "normal" patterns of relations, the logic of the "institutional bargain" to attain security by and for states breaks down. In particular, the capacities of the lead or leading states in the system no longer provide the advantages and leverage necessary for the logic of structural realist arguments to apply.

Rather than establishing any new pattern in the international order, the Iraq war of 2003 instead should be viewed as reinforcing trends and highlighting paradoxes set in motion over the previous half-decade. The Iraq war was not a surprise; Saddam Hussein's time in power was destined to be short after President G. W. Bush assumed office. Nor was the immediate outcome unexpected.

The election of George W. Bush in 2000 and the events and aftermath of 9/11 are both, in retrospect, more significant benchmarks. The former brought to power in Washington a regime motivated by an ideological agenda, an exceptionalist mentality and a conviction that security is achieved and sustained through military superiority. The latter event traumatized the American people, transformed their view of a world that they had previously largely ignored and, in turn, facilitated their support for a national security agenda couched in terms of a "war on terrorism". It is these *ideational* forces that are central to understanding the United States' increasingly controversial contesting of international norms.

The United States as norm entrepreneur

The contemporary attitude of the United States concerning the achievement of its own security and the utility of multilateral cooperation in attaining it is not preordained by its position of global dominance. It is instead the reflection of the role of its élite political leadership in attempting to reshape the global security architecture according to norms and principles congenial to its world view. This is not a new phenomenon, either in the historical past – one need only recall Woodrow Wilson or Franklin Roosevelt – or in the past decade. Thus, the Bush Sr administration was motivated by an effort, albeit frustrated, to establish "a new world order", one involving leadership in international institutions, particularly through the United Nations. Bill Clinton, although attempting to distinguish himself from this predecessor by limiting deployment of US forces abroad, was in turn characterized as advancing "assertive multilateralism".[30]

These administrations, like their predecessors since World War II, to a greater or lesser extent all articulated a US role of leadership premised on supporting the central multilateral economic and social institutions of the system, in effect providing public goods, exercising self-restraint and accepting short-term losses in anticipation of the longer-term benefits derived from cooperation. Established norms of sovereignty and a collective response to threats to international peace and security were thus sustained for almost half a century.

This did not mean that the United States was not a self-interested player, or for that matter not a dominant actor, in the international system. However, the bottom line was that Washington, although articulating its exceptionalism especially concerning subordination of its national jurisdiction to international institutions, remained in principle committed to principles of multilateralism (e.g. diffuse reciprocity). What is unique about the current US leadership is its apparent disavowal of these principles and its efforts to redesign an international systemic order, centred on itself, that operates according to different norms. In this sense, George W. Bush and influential administration figures such as Rumsfeld, Wolfowitz and Cheney need to be recognized as norm entrepreneurs. The tensions occasioned by this administration's actions – most notably its decision to depose Saddam Hussein without seeking the legitimation of the UN Security Council, but including its record of withdrawal from, vetoing, ignoring and failing to support international agreements – are symptoms of the campaign by norm entrepreneurs dedicated to bringing about change.

Most frequently the United States is characterized as a unilateralist, opposed in principle to operating through multilateral channels. This line of argument is misconstrued. It fails to take into account the sophistication of the strategy of change orchestrated by the Bush team. What is overlooked in the discussion of US unilateralism, and has been highlighted by the Iraq war, is the effective employment of multilateral strategies by the United States to further its goals. The United States' *unilateralism* is seen through its agenda-setting capacity. Its *multilateral* capacities are demonstrated through its effective use of persuasion, manipulation or coercion of other states and institutions in order to accomplish its goals.

In this sense, the United States has proved to be an adept and effective multilateral player. Whereas it seeks to avoid any multilateral institution that could constrain its behaviour – the Iraq war providing convincing evidence that Washington will not allow itself to be hindered by any institution with a consensus decision-making requirement (including the North Atlantic Treaty Organization) – the United States seeks to orchestrate and operate with ad hoc coalitions of like-minded states. As Rumsfeld has declared at home and admonished US allies abroad (including NATO partners), "The mission [read, as defined by the United States] must determine the coalition, and the coalition must not determine the mission."[31]

Since 9/11, the United States has in fact expanded both its bilateral and its multilateral activities. One need only point to the "coalitions of the willing" mobilized for the wars in Afghanistan and Iraq, the numbers of states on side for the missile defence programme, or the increasing numbers ready to participate in the Proliferation Security Initiative.

Where matters come to a head is over the distinction between two contrasting normative premises, those of ad hoc multilateralism and those of institutionalized multilateralism. The former, as espoused by the Bush administration, envisages the formation and employment of multilateral institutions simply as strategies to advance the immediate needs of the United States (and any other states that happen to have similar interests) on an ad hoc basis. The norms involved "rely on the sovereign accountability of states instead of strategies to limit sovereignty". There is a preference for "functional institutions that produce concrete results instead of symbolic measures that might rally more support for an ideal". The latter are viewed as "indulgences" that cannot be afforded.[32] In essence, these norms hearken back to a structural realist, rationalist, Westphalian order, in sharp contrast to the norms and institutional forms of multilateralism being advanced by others in the contemporary international context.[33]

An uncertain future

The United States: Prospects for change and continuity

"When it comes to our security ... we really don't need anybody's permission." (George W. Bush)

"We're so multilateral it keeps me up twenty-four hours a day checking on everybody." (Colin Powell)[34]

It is too early to assess the success of the norm entrepreneurship of the contemporary US administration. There are sharp divisions in the United States even within the high levels of the bureaucracy and the political élite. Joseph Nye, among others, has referred to

the administration [being] deeply divided between those who want to escape the constraints of the post-1945 institutional framework that the United States helped to build and those who believe the US goals are better achieved by working within the framework. The neoconservative "Wilsonians to the right" and the "Jackson unilateralists" ... are pitted against the more multilateral and cautious traditional realists.[35]

Already observers are suggesting that the hard lessons that the United States is learning in Afghanistan and Iraq are tempering its harsher rhetoric and introducing nuance into its attempts to orchestrate effective multilateral support for its policies. That being said, it would be optimistic to assume that any subsequent administration in Washington is going to dramatically alter key premises of the United States' post-9/11 approach to advancing its national security agenda. For the foreseeable future, the "war on terrorism" will remain the central pillar of US foreign policy, the asserted right of pre-emptive attack against perceived imminent threats will not be revoked, and the United States will not restrict the pursuit of its interests by participating in any multilateral security forum requiring decision-making by consensus.

The challenges to international norms of sovereignty and multilateralism may diminish in the short term, but they will not disappear.

The larger picture and the longer term: A global public goods dilemma[36]

The prosecution of the Iraq war and the subsequent US manoeuvring to hand on post-conflict responsibilities and costs call into question the viability of the framework of global and regional multilateral institutions. However, the United States is not alone in this regard. One can cite an increasing tendency for states (a) to define their commitments to international regimes and institutions on the basis of their short-term national interest priorities, (b) to abandon institutional frameworks when they do not produce results useful to them, and (c) to avoid establishing any new multilateral institutions, favouring instead short-term, single-purpose coalitions of interested states. Statements such as the following (by the Australian foreign minister) are illustrative:

Some multilateral institutions will remain important for our interests. But increasingly multilateralism is a synonym for an ineffective and unfocused policy involving internationalism of the lowest common denominator. Multilateral institutions need to become more results oriented if they are to serve the interests of the international community.... We are prepared to join coalitions of the willing that can bring focus and purpose to address the urgent security and other challenges we face.[37]

Such attitudes obscure a larger and more significant matter, namely that the provision of international institutions constitutes a set of public goods – public goods that are critical to the sustained stability of the international and regional security orders. Policies of "instrumental multilateralism", if practised by all states or by the most influential states, will inevitably erode these core foundations. So too will policies of "a la carte multilateralism", i.e. the arbitrary picking and choosing among international regimes or among the components of international regimes to suit immediate national interests.

The historical record suggests that such policies are short-sighted and ultimately place greater burdens on the international community. The frameworks of international and regional norms and institutions required to ensure peace and stability are delicate mechanisms. They can and should evolve as new circumstances dictate, and the present is indeed a moment when important changes are warranted. However, creating international and regional security architectures is an onerous task. In order to assure the longer-term provision of these essential international public goods, the major power must itself exercise positive leadership and be willing to absorb disproportionate costs of institution-building and maintenance. Whether or not, and how, this leadership will be taken up remains an unanswered question in the ongoing aftermath of the Iraq war.

Notes

I acknowledge the support for research and writing of the Social Science and Humanities Research Council of Canada and the Security and Defence Forum programme of the Centre of International Relations, University of British Columbia. Erin Williams and Ana-Marie Blanaru, Department of Political Science, UBC, provided excellent research assistance; Kal Holsti helped to refine key arguments. The views expressed are mine alone.

1. Thus, in terms of a theoretical point of view, this chapter is self-consciously written from what international relations theorists have labelled a constructivist perspective, whose key insight is captured in the title of Alexander Wendt's 1992 article "'Anarchy Is What States Make of It': The Social Construction of Power Politics", *International Organization*, Vol. 46 (1992), pp. 391–426.

2. As Ikenberry makes clear, there are more than two perspectives on the formation and operation of international institutions among students of international relations. Furthermore, along the lines of his own arguments, when tackling the emergence of specific institutions at a particular historical juncture, a synthesis of elements of different prototypical models provides the most satisfactory explanation. See G. John Ikenberry, *After Victory: Institutions, Strategic Restraint, and the Rebuilding of Order after Major Wars* (Princeton, NJ: Princeton University Press, 2001).

3. G. John Ikenberry, "State Power and the Institutional Bargain: America's Ambivalent Economic and Security Multilateralism", in Rosemary Foot, S. Neil MacFarlane and Michael Mastanduno, eds, *US Hegemony and International Organizations* (Oxford: Oxford University Press, 2003), pp. 49–72, at p. 50.

4. In his study of the formation of international institutional orders, Kalvei Holsti focuses more on the role of the "concert" of major powers and less on the determinative influence of a single major power. See Kal Holsti, *Taming the Sovereigns: Institutional Change in International Politics* (Cambridge: Cambridge University Press, 2004).

5. See Ikenberry, *After Victory*.

6. See Thomas Biersteker and Cynthia Weber, "The Social Construction of State Sovereignty", in Thomas Biersteker and Cynthia Weber, eds, *State Sovereignty as Social Construct* (Cambridge: Cambridge University Press, 1996), pp. 1–22; and Christian Reus-Smit, "The Constitutional Structure of International Society and the Nature of Fundamental Institutions", *International Organization*, Vol. 51 (1997), pp. 555–590.

7. These two approaches to thinking about international institutions also embody distinctive interpretations of multilateralism. On the one hand, multilateralism can refer to the "coordination of relations" among two or more states, varying according to the level and extent of coordination. Alternately, multilateralism can be viewed as involving adherence to and advancement of certain norms – procedural norms, normative principles of conduct and expectations of longer-term cooperation (diffuse reciprocity). On the former, see John Ikenberry, "Is American Multilateralism in Decline?", *Perspectives on Politics*, Vol. 1 (2003), pp. 534–550; for the latter, see John Ruggie, "Multilateralism: The Anatomy of an Institution", in John Ruggie, ed., *Multilateralism Matters: The Theory and Praxis of an Institutional Form* (New York: Columbia University, 1993), pp. 3–48; and Brian L. Job, "Matters of Multilateralism: Implications for Regional Conflict Management", in David Lake and Patrick Morgan, eds, *Regional Orders:*

Building Security in a New World (University Park, PA: Penn State University Press, 1997), pp. 165–191.

8. Kal Holsti, *Peace and War: Armed Conflicts and International Order, 1648–1989* (Cambridge: Cambridge University Press, 1991).

9. Thus, for Kenneth Waltz, the logic of the post–Cold War power distribution dictated that Japan and Germany should aspire to become nuclear powers. See "The Emerging Structure of International Politics", *International Security*, Vol. 18 (1993), pp. 44–79.

10. See Mathew Evangelista, *Unarmed Forces: The Transnational Movement to End the Cold War* (Ithaca, NY: Cornell University Press, 1999).

11. Successful norm entrepreneurship also requires opportunistic timing and coordinated strategizing. The "cycle" of norm change is discussed in detail in Martha Finnemore and Kathryn Sikkink, "International Norm Dynamics and Political Change", *International Organization*, Vol. 52 (1998), pp. 887–917; Margaret Keck and Kathryn Sikkink, "Transnational Advocacy Networks in International Politics: Introduction", in *Activists beyond Borders: Advocacy Networks in International Politics* (Ithaca, NY: Cornell University Press, 1998).

12. See Inis Claude, *Swords into Plowshares* (New York: Random House, 1983).

13. Monty G. Marshall and Robert Ted Gurr, "Peace and Conflict 2003: A Global Survey of Armed Conflicts, Self-Determination Movements, and Democracy", College Park, MD: CICDM, University of Maryland, 2003.

14. Indeed, the Council had become largely moribund in this regard, having not authorized a single mission between 1978 and 1988, in effect stymied by major power interests in Afghanistan, southern Africa, Southeast Asia, and so on.

15. See Brian L. Job, "The UN, Regional Organizations, and Regional Conflict: Is There a Viable Role for the UN?", in Richard Price and Mark Zacher, eds, *The United Nations and Global Security* (New York: Palgrave-Macmillan, 2004).

16. See Fen Hampson, *Madness in the Multitude: Human Security and World Disorder* (Don Mills: Oxford University Press Canada, 2002).

17. A key early statement is David Baldwin, "The Concept of Security", *Review of International Studies*, Vol. 23 (1997), pp. 3–26.

18. William T. Tow and Russell Trood, "Linkages between Traditional Security and Human Security", in William T. Tow, Ramesh Thakur and In-Taek Hyun, eds, *Asia's Emerging Regional Order: Reconciling Traditional and Human Security* (Tokyo: United Nations University Press, 2000), pp. 13–32.

19. Kofi A. Annan, "Two Concepts of Sovereignty", *The Economist*, 18 September 1999.

20. The "responsibility to protect" was coined by Francis Deng, referring initially to the responding to the plight of refugee populations. However, it is the *Responsibility to Protect* report by the International Commission on Intervention and State Sovereignty (Ottawa: International Development Research Centre, December 2001) – a norm entrepreneurship initiative of the Canadian government, the UN Secretary-General, several large foundations and like-minded notable persons – that has placed this concept at the heart of contemporary discourse on international security. The report has had a significant impact; notably, the 2004 UN High-level Panel Report adopts both the language and the logic of the "responsibility to protect".

21. Annan, "Two Concepts of Sovereignty".

22. Wallensteen and Johansson provide a detailed charting of this dramatic increase in the Council's invocation of Chapter VII, in their "Security Council Decisions in Perspective", in David Malone, ed., *The UN Security Council: From the Cold War to the 21st Century* (Boulder, CO: Lynne Rienner, 2004), pp. 17–33. They note (p. 19): "Ninety-three per cent of all Chapter VII resolutions passed from 1946 to 2002 have been adopted since the end of the Cold War."

23. See Joanna Weschler, "Human Rights", in Malone, ed., *The UN Security Council*, pp. 55–68, at p. 57.
24. See Malone, ed., *The UN Security Council*, p. 9.
25. Maxwell A. Cameron, Robert J. Lawson and Brian W. Tomlin, eds, *To Walk without Fear: The Global Movement to Ban Landmines* (Toronto: Oxford University Press, 1998).
26. See Thomas G. Weiss, "The Humanitarian Impulse", in Malone, ed., *The UN Security Council*, specifically p. 46, and in general regarding this conclusion.
27. Adam Roberts, "The Use of Force", in Malone, ed., *The UN Security Council*, pp. 133–152, at p. 146. As concerns the *Responsibility to Protect* report, Roberts characterizes it as "an ingenious attempt at a reformulation of the question of humanitarian intervention, [with] so far little sign of states explicitly accepting such a responsibility".
28. Ikenberry, "Is American Multilateralism in Decline?", p. 537.
29. For an excellent treatment of these arguments, especially the notion of US exceptionalism, see Edward C. Luck, "American Exceptionalism and International Organization: Lessons from the 1990s", in Foot, MacFarlane and Mastanduno, eds, *US Hegemony and International Organizations*, pp. 25–48.
30. Ibid., p. 26, footnote 2.
31. "Secretary Rumsfeld Speaks on '21st Century Transformation' of U.S. Armed Forces (transcript of remarks and question and answer period)". Remarks as Delivered by Secretary of Defense Donald Rumsfeld, National Defense University, Fort McNair, Washington, D.C., Thursday, January 31, 2002; ⟨http://www.defenselink.mil/speeches/2002/s20020131-secdef.html⟩ (accessed 25 January 2006).
32. Philip Zelikow, "The Transformation of National Security", *The National Interest*, Vol. 71 (2003), pp. 17–28.
33. The argument that the United States is a contemporary norm entrepreneur could be challenged. First, one could point out that "international norms" must espouse universal content and universal applicability. That is, they must be seen by their advocates as being inclusive and reciprocal, neither enabling nor excluding only themselves. One could question whether, in this sense, the Bush administration seeks to advance norms or simply to justify specific self-interested activities. However, I argue that the United States sees itself and is seen by others as a norm entrepreneur, and that the signs are becoming more apparent as the second George W. Bush term unfolds. This does not imply that either consistency or universality is involved. One sees a combination of selective reliance upon very traditional interpretations of sovereignty and self-help with the advancement of principles of democratic empowerment and particularistic interpretations of "freedom". (I am indebted to Kal Holsti for pointing out the first argument.)
34. Bush's comment is from Dan Balz, "President Puts Onus back on Iraqi Leader", *Washington Post*, 7 March 2003, cited in Ikenberry, "Is American Multilateralism in Decline?". Colin Powell's statement is from "Remarks at Business Event", Shanghai, People's Republic of China, 18 October 2001, ⟨http://www.state.gov/secretary/former/powell/remarks/2001/5441.htm⟩ (accessed 25 January 2006).
35. Joseph Nye, "US Power and Strategy after Iraq", *Foreign Affairs*, Vol. 82 (2003), pp. 60–73, at p. 63.
36. These remarks are expanded upon in Job, "The Challenges of International Relations and International Regimes: Emerging Parameters of a New Regional Paradigm", 17th Asia Pacific Roundtable, Kuala Lumpur, 6–9 August 2003.
37. Alexander Downer, "Security in an Unstable World", speech to the Australian National Press Club, 26 June 2003.

5

The world says no: The global movement against war in Iraq

David Cortright

On 15 February 2003, in hundreds of cities across the world, an estimated 10 million people demonstrated against the looming US-led invasion of Iraq. It was the largest-scale single day of anti-war protest in human history. More than 1 million people jammed the centre of London in one of the largest demonstrations ever held in that city. More than 1 million marched in Rome, and huge throngs paraded in Barcelona, Berlin, Madrid, Paris, Sydney and dozens of other cities. An estimated 400,000 braved bitter cold in New York.[1] The people of the globe spoke out as never before in one unified voice against the planned attack against Iraq. "The world says no to war" was the slogan and the reality.

The 15 February demonstrations were the high point of a vast and unprecedented mobilization of public opposition to war. The Iraq campaign "was the largest antiwar movement that has ever taken place", according to Barbara Epstein.[2] In the course of just a few months, the anti-war movement reached levels of mobilization that, during the Viet Nam era, took years to develop. The Iraq movement was more international in character than any previous anti-war movement. Opposition to war emerged not just in the United States but literally all over the world, as action campaigns were coordinated internationally and demonstrators understood themselves to be part of a truly global struggle.[3] The movement represented a convergence of anti-war and global justice efforts into a common campaign against military-corporate domination.[4] It was an expression of what Stephen Gill has called "new ... forms of global political agency".[5] But the movement also emerged from more traditional peace and justice networks and relied extensively on the knowledge and resources of organizations and individuals with previous experience in anti-war action. It engaged religious communities, trade unionists, students, feminists, environmentalists, academics, business executives, artists, musicians and many more. The movement was built largely through the Internet, which served as the primary tool for developing and communicating strategies and actions, and which accounted for the movement's extraordinary capacity for organizing huge numbers of people at short notice with limited resources. The movement effectively utilized mass media communications. The war in Iraq and the international opposition to it were the dominant news story throughout the world for months, and anti-war activists found themselves in the unaccustomed position of being the centre of media attention. For the first time in history, observed writer Rebecca Solnit, the peace movement was portrayed in the media as "diverse, legitimate and representative", which was a "watershed victory" for the movement's representation and long-term prospects.[6]

A few days after the 15 February demonstrations, a *New York Times* reporter conferred "superpower" status on the anti-war movement. The huge anti-war demonstrations were indications, wrote Patrick Tyler, of "two super powers on the planet: the United States and world public opinion". The White House faced a "tenacious new adversary" which was generating massive opposition to the administration's war policy and had left the world's greatest power virtually alone in the international community.[7] Anti-war commentators quickly adopted the phrase and proclaimed their movement "the other superpower". Jonathan Schell wrote in *The Nation* of the movement's "immense power" in winning the hearts and wills of the majority of the world's people.[8] Even UN Secretary-General Kofi Annan used the phrase in referring to anti-war opinion.[9] A new form of global social movement had emerged, an unprecedented expression of collective consciousness and action bound together through the World Wide Web.[10] Although the movement was unable to stop the march to war, and did not prevent the re-election of pro-war administrations a year and a half later in the United States and Australia, it nonetheless exerted considerable international influence.

In this chapter, I comment upon the Iraq anti-war movement and its extraordinary development in the months leading up to the March 2003 attack on Iraq. I write as an active participant, one who was intimately involved in many of the activities described here. Mine is hardly a disinterested view, although I strive to uphold scholarly standards. I provide an overview of several different elements of the movement, giving special attention to several key dimensions – the role of Internet-based organizing, the movement's international dimensions, and its communications and message-framing strategies. I conclude with some reflections on the movement's overall impact.

Uniting for peace

In the United States, the anti-war movement was led by two major coalitions, United for Peace and Justice (UFPJ) and Win Without War. Both coalitions emerged in the late fall of 2002. UFPJ was quintessentially a grassroots activist coalition and its principal action strategy was to organize protest demonstrations. The coalition's first action was a call for nationally coordinated local actions on 10 December, which was Human Rights Day. More than 130 events took place that day all over the United States, generating substantial local and regional press coverage for the growing anti-war movement. United for Peace and Justice was the principal sponsor of the 15 February demonstration in New York, when an estimated 400,000 gathered on the city's east side.[11] UFPJ continued to organize protest actions until and after the war began. One of the biggest actions came in New York on 22 March. The demonstration had been announced a couple of weeks before but came a few days after the war began. The estimated crowd of 300,000 rivalled the turnout on 15 February. One of the principal UFPJ organizers, Leslie Cagan, recalled the thinking of many New Yorkers, like herself, who bristled at the Bush administration's manipulation of the city's suffering: "For those of us who lived through 9/11, there was a sense that we never wanted to see that kind of horror visited on other people, whether by a small group of terrorists or by the state terrorism of a military invasion."[12]

The Win Without War coalition was formed in parallel with United for Peace and Justice as a more moderate, mainstream committee of national organizations. Among the participating groups were the Internet giant MoveOn, Working Assets (a telecommunications company with hundreds of thousands of subscribers), True Majority (an Internet-based activist network created by ice cream entrepreneur Ben Cohen), the National Council of Churches, Sojourners, the United Methodist Church, Physicians for Social Responsibility, the Sierra Club, the National Organization for Women, and the National Association for the Advancement of Colored People. The coalition believed that the political message of the activist movement should emphasize alternative means of containing and disarming Saddam Hussein without war. They also agreed on the pressing need for an effective public relations and communications campaign to reach mainstream audiences.

Virtual organizing became the métier of the Win Without War coalition, as it mobilized the vast membership networks of its Internet-based groups and constituency organizations for coordinated lobbying and action campaigns. Its most ambitious effort was the "virtual march" on Washington on 26 February 2003. Citizens all over the United States phoned, faxed or e-mailed their elected representatives to oppose the march to war. All across Capitol Hill on 26 February, the phones and fax machines were jammed. Win Without War national director Tom Andrews estimated that more than 1 million calls, faxes and e-mail messages were sent. It was the largest one-day lobbying event in US political history. In the final weeks before the invasion, Win Without War launched an international petition to the UN Security Council that was signed by more than 1 million people in a matter of days. On the weekend of 15–16 March, the coalition worked with MoveOn to sponsor candlelight vigils around the world. More than 6,000 vigils took place in more than 100 countries that weekend. Once again, the world said no to war, this time in a prayerful plea at the last hour before the onset of military hostilities.

The role of MoveOn

Much of the success of Win Without War and the anti-war movement in the United States can be ascribed to the powerful impact of Internet organizing and to the role of MoveOn specifically. It was during the Iraq anti-war movement that the full range of possibilities for utilizing the Internet for social change organizing became evident. The global justice movement used the Internet effectively as a means of communication, coordination and education among decentralized networks of organizers around the world. To these functions, anti-war activists added new dimensions of Internet mobilization: the development of organized "membership" networks, the creation of "meeting tools" to facilitate coordinated local actions, and on-line fundraising. The result was an unprecedented capacity to raise consciousness and mobilize political action.

MoveOn was the pioneer and leading force in this Internet revolution. The group was formed in 1998 to stop the impeachment of Bill Clinton. It was the lead group within Win Without War and served as the backbone of the movement's most important organizing and communication efforts. In the six months leading up to the outbreak of war in March 2003, MoveOn's on-line membership, US and international, grew from 700,000 to approximately 2,000,000. Other electronically based networks also experienced extraordinary growth and activity during this period. True Majority was founded in June 2002 and grew rapidly as the anti-war movement emerged, reaching 100,000 members by the end of 2002 and 500,000 a year later.

When Internet organizing began, some sceptics questioned the value of a tool that kept activists glued to their computer screens. The very ease with which one could click and send off a message, sometimes to hundreds of recipients, seemed to cheapen the value of the effort. MoveOn and the other Internet-based activist groups recognized these limitations early on and devised methods of mobilization that significantly broadened the impact of e-mail activism. One important innovation was the use of the Internet to organize coordinated local meetings. Activists were encouraged to leave their computer screens and go out to meetings where they connected with other activists in their communities. MoveOn developed a meeting tool that organizer Eli Pariser termed "action in a box". Action campaigns were programmed so that respondents could be led easily through a series of prompts offering various venues and functions for action. An e-mail message from MoveOn would contain the call to action and, by clicking the appropriate icons, the respondent could be connected to other activists and could volunteer for various tasks, ranging from attending a meeting and sending an e-mail to Congress, to more ambitious duties such as coordinating a meeting, speaking in public and contributing funds. By segmenting lists according to location and interest, Internet organizers could use their membership base to sponsor highly particularized forms of action. Equally important in translating Internet communications into political power were the development and use of on-line fundraising. Just as on-line marketing has become increasingly significant in the commercial economy, Internet-based fundraising has rapidly become a vital source of income for social movements, non-profit groups and political campaigns.

Other organizations with more traditional membership bases also developed e-mail networks during the anti-war movement. The religious-based organization Sojourners saw its newly created Sojo list expand from 20,000 in the summer of 2002 to approximately 70,000 in March 2003. Peace Action, The Council for a Livable World and many other organizations also developed e-mail listservs and experienced growth in electronic membership. All of these groups used the Internet as a mechanism for political communication and fundraising. The use of electronic organizing and the overall growth of anti-war activism led to membership increases in most of the established peace organizations. Women's Action for New Directions, Peace Action and Physicians for Social Responsibility all reported 20 per cent increases in membership during the anti-war campaign.[13] The movement against war in Iraq thus became an opportunity for traditional peace groups to grow organizationally and financially.

The world speaks

Of the many extraordinary features of the anti-war movement, none was more remarkable than its international dimension. In nearly every country, opinion polls showed solid and sometimes overwhelming majorities against US-led military action in Iraq. In some countries, people considered George W. Bush more of a threat than Saddam Hussein to international security.[14] In dozens of countries national anti-war coalitions were created, encompassing a wide range of movements and organizations. The United Kingdom had the Stop the War Coalition, Italy Fermiamo la Guerra all'Iraq, Germany Netzwerk Friedenskooperative, Spain No al la Guerra. All the national coalitions set up websites that were linked to each other. Many adopted the same slogan and graphic symbol, a missile crossed out with the words "stop the war".[15]

The protests of 15 February 2003 were literally a global phenomenon, with reports of anti-war action that weekend in more than 600 cities. In London, the crowd set off from two separate assembly sites, pouring into and filling much of Hyde Park. More than 1 million people overflowed the city's centre.[16] Tens of thousands also marched in Glasgow, Dublin and Belfast. Rivalling the demonstration in London was a massive protest of perhaps 1 million people in Rome. The historic heart of the city, between the Coliseum and Piazza San Giovanni, was packed for hours by a slow-moving procession of protesters. Half a million people assembled in Madrid, and the crowd in Barcelona was estimated at 1 million. Smaller protests occurred in Valencia, Seville, Los Palmas and Cadiz. Half a million marched in Berlin, and crowds of 100,000 or more gathered in Brussels, Paris and Athens, with smaller protests in more than 100 other European cities. Over 100,000 demonstrated in Montreal, Toronto, Vancouver and other Canadian cities. Tens of thousands turned out in Mexico City, Rio de Janeiro, Montevideo and Buenos Aires. Several hundred thousand gathered in Sidney and Melbourne. In New Zealand, protests took place in Auckland, Wellington and more than a dozen other cities. Thousands marched in Tokyo, Seoul, Bangkok, Manila, Kuala Lumpur, Jakarta (the week before), Lahore, New Delhi, Calcutta and other Asian cities. Approximately 20,000 people marched in Johannesburg, Cape Town and Durban. In Damascus, some 200,000 demonstrated at the People's Assembly. Tens of thousands rallied in Beirut and Amman. Several thousand people, Jews and Palestinians together, marched in Tel Aviv. A few dozen brave souls even demonstrated in Antarctica.

More important than the number and extent of these demonstrations was their political impact. Opposition to war was especially broad in those countries where the government supported the US-led war effort (see Figure 5.1). In the United Kingdom, Spain and Italy, citizens said no while their political leaders were saying yes. In Spain and Italy, opinion polls showed more than 80 per cent of the public opposed to participating in the US-led war. In Poland, although there was little organized protest, over 70 per cent opposed participation in the war.

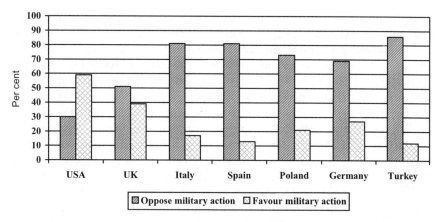

Figure 5.1 International anti-war opinion.
Source: Responses are from polling conducted by the Pew Research Center for the People & the Press, 10–17 March 2003. The Pew Global Attitudes Project, "America's Image Further Erodes, Europeans Want Weaker Ties: But Post-war Iraq Will Be Better Off, Most Say", 18 March 2003, ⟨http://www.people-press. org⟩ (accessed 13 November 2003).
Notes: Respondents in the United Kingdom, Italy, Spain and Poland were asked, "Would you favor or oppose [survey country] joining the U.S. and other allies in military action in Iraq to end Saddam Hussein's rule?" In the United States, the question posed was, "Would you favor or oppose taking military action in Iraq to end Saddam Hussein's rule?" In Germany and Turkey, respondents were asked, "Would you favor or oppose the U.S. and other allies taking military action in Iraq to end Saddam Hussein's rule?"

Just as the overall anti-war movement became internationalized to an unprecedented extent, so did the voice of religious opposition to war. Never before in history did so many religious leaders and organizations from around the world speak so forcefully against war. The most important voice was that of the Vatican, which repeatedly condemned the proposed invasion of Iraq and pleaded with world leaders to pursue diplomatic rather than military solutions. "War is always a defeat for humanity," Pope John Paul II told assembled diplomats during his New Year address in January. "War cannot be decided upon," he declared, "except as the very last option."[17] As the war began in March, the Pope urged people to continue standing against war. "It is ever more urgent to proclaim that only peace is the road to follow to construct a more just and united society."[18] National conferences of Catholic bishops in North America, Europe, Asia and Africa joined the Vatican in issuing statements against war. The deliberative bodies of many other religious communities around the world joined in this nearly universal faith-based outcry against war.

In Germany, anti-war sentiment played a decisive role in swaying the outcome of national elections. Social Democratic Chancellor Gerhard Schröder won a narrow come-from-behind victory in the September 2002 elections by emphasizing his opposition to war in Iraq. For months, Schröder had lagged behind in the polls because of widespread misgivings about his economic policies. As public alarm about the war spread, Schröder cobbled together a successful electoral strategy by consciously exploiting voters' anti-war sentiments and sharpening his criticism of US policy. One international news report quipped, "Schröder beats Bush in German election".[19] The vote not only kept a strongly anti-war Schröder in office, but also elevated the Green Party to new heights, further strengthening the position of Foreign Minister and Green Party leader Joschka Fischer. The election results reinforced international opposition to war because of Germany's position on the UN Security Council, and enhanced the influence of environmental and peace forces in German domestic politics.

Perhaps the most remarkable manifestation of anti-war sentiment occurred in Turkey, where a popularly elected parliament refused the Bush administration's request to use the country as a base and transit corridor for US invasion forces. The *Washington Post* called Turkey's rejection "a stunning setback" to the Bush administration's war plans.[20] Ankara's decision went against a tradition of decades of close military cooperation between Turkey and the United States. Turkish leaders also turned aside a huge package of financial inducements offered by Washington, including US$6 billion in direct grants and up to US$20 billion in loan guarantees.[21] The Turkish decision had a direct military impact. The United States had planned to deploy more than 60,000 troops in Turkey, including a strike force from the Fourth Infantry Division. The battle plan against Iraq called for a two-pronged attack from both north and south. US officials were so confident of Turkish cooperation that more than 30 military transport ships were on their way or already deployed off Turkey's Mediterranean coast as the decision was being made. Several hundred US support troops were in Turkey, renovating bases and ports in preparation for the invasion force. The Turkish parliament's last-minute rejection forced Pentagon planners to redeploy the Fourth Division and other troops to the south, creating a more complicated and difficult invasion scenario.

The rejection of war in Turkey came from a democratic, moderate Islamist government – precisely the kind of regime US officials claim to want for Iraq and other Middle East countries. The problem for US officials was that an expression of democratic sentiment meant rejection of American policy. Turkey's Justice and Development Party had won the November 2002 elections in part by appealing to popular opposition to

US war plans. A March 2003 poll by the Pew Research Center for the People and the Press measured anti-war opposition in Turkey at 86 per cent. Some 300,000 people demonstrated in Ankara as members of parliament gathered to vote on 1 March. The legislators were under enormous pressure, pulled by a powerful ally to provide military cooperation, pushed by an energized domestic constituency to represent the overwhelming popular rejection of war. It was a critically important moment for the young Justice and Development Party, which was trying to create a more democratic, yet Islamist, tradition in Turkish politics. When the parliamentary votes were tallied, the resolution to approve the US request fell three votes short of the required majority. Officials in Washington immediately demanded a revote, but Turkish leaders refused, fearing that an attempt to overturn the vote would bring down the government. The Turkish people and their elected representatives had spoken. The answer was no.

There were countless other global anti-war expressions. In Australia, the Senate voted to censure Prime Minister John Howard for agreeing to deploy troops to Iraq without parliamentary approval. It was the first no-confidence vote in the chamber's 102-year history. Australian opinion polls at the time showed 76 per cent of the public against participation in a war without UN backing.[22] In the national elections of October 2004, however, Australian voters gave Prime Minister Howard an unprecedented fourth term in office. In South Korea, Roh Moo Hyun won the presidency in December 2002, in part by riding a tide of anti-American sentiment. In his political campaign, Roh vowed to continue the conciliatory "sunshine" policy toward North Korea of his predecessor, Kim Dai Jung, rather than the confrontational approach favoured by the Bush administration. Roh's electoral victory was the third among long-term American allies based upon popular rejection of US foreign policy. In Pakistan, the elections of October 2002 showed a significant gain for pro-Taliban, anti-American religious parties. A group of six hard-line parties, campaigning on a platform that included sharp criticism of US policy, won a higher than expected number of seats in Pakistan's national assembly and gained a majority in the North-West Frontier Province near the Afghanistan border.[23] The election results were more anti-American than anti-war, but they were another sign of deepening political opposition to the United States around the world.

The significance of this pervasive anti-war sentiment for US policy can scarcely be exaggerated. The anti-war movement contributed to a major realignment of global public opinion. Former president Jimmy Carter wrote, "The heartfelt sympathy and friendship offered to America after the 9/11 attacks, even from formerly antagonistic regimes, has been largely dissipated; increasingly unilateral and domineering policies have brought international trust in our country to its lowest level in memory."[24] Washington's inability to win UN Security Council authorization for war undermined the legitimacy of American policy, and contributed to Turkey's rejection of US basing rights, which disrupted military planning. When the invasion began, no major government other than that of the United Kingdom agreed to participate. This added to the US military burden. In the post-war occupation, Washington's efforts to recruit a substantial international force were largely unsuccessful. As of December 2003, only 24,000 international troops were in Iraq, half of them from the United Kingdom, the rest consisting of modest contingents from Poland, Italy, Spain, Ukraine, Bulgaria and an array of smaller countries. Nor was Washington successful in gaining substantial financial support for Iraq's reconstruction. Having pushed ahead with the invasion against the advice of virtually the entire world, Washington was left on its own to attempt to deal with the violent and chaotic aftermath. The United States paid a high price for alienating international opinion and rejecting the global plea for peace.

The disastrous consequences of the occupation, combined with the war's unpopularity and lack of legitimacy, created additional political and military challenges for the United States. Spain withdrew its troops after the March 2004 election of the socialist prime minister, Jose Luis Rodriguez Zapatero. By the end of 2004, approximately half a dozen of the countries previously participating in the US-led coalition also withdrew their forces. In Ukraine, reform candidate Viktor Yushchenko won the December 2004 election on a platform that included a pledge to withdraw Ukraine's 1,600 troops from Iraq. The task of maintaining the occupation against fierce resistance and amidst widespread chaos thus remained primarily a US and UK burden.

Media communications

The Iraq anti-war movement featured the largest, most sophisticated and most successful media communications effort in the history of the peace movement. Anti-war movements traditionally have suffered from poor media relations. As Todd Gitlin and others have observed, peace activists have been slow to appreciate the enormous significance of media communications for social change. In recent decades, however, peace and justice activists have come to recognize the power and influence of the media. They have seen how communications strategies are becoming the dominant factor in shaping political discourse and swaying political opinion. When the debate over war in Iraq began, many activists were determined to mount an effective public relations and media communications campaign.

The 15 February demonstrations in the United States and around the world were enormously successful in attracting media coverage of the anti-war movement. The demonstrations that day were the lead story in practically every broadcast and print news source in the United States and in much of the world. Never before had the peace movement attracted so much press coverage. The image of the anti-war movement as a "superpower" was the direct result of those demonstrations and the resulting media coverage. The demonstrations conveyed a simple "no to war" message that was easily understood and resonated well with world opinion. The actions of the women's organization Code Pink, although much smaller in scale than the United for Peace and Justice demonstrations, were also successful in generating favourable media coverage. By appropriating feminist language and symbols, and by employing disruptive theatrics, Code Pink activists attracted considerable press attention and helped to frame opposition to war as a special concern of women.

Win Without War was specifically created as a vehicle for media communications. The coalition placed a great deal of emphasis on the framing of its message and the maintenance of a sustained and disciplined press operation. From the outset, Win Without War sought to portray itself as mainstream and patriotic. By framing its message in patriotic terms, Win Without War sought to capture the flag and thereby inoculate itself against the usual charges of aiding the enemy. The coalition, and many others in the anti-war movement, explicitly condemned the policies and rule of Saddam Hussein, and supported vigorous inspections and containment as means of countering the Iraqi military threat. The coalition expressed full support for the international campaign against terrorism, although it was careful to avoid any specific reference to or support for the administration's "war on terror" (so as not to reinforce Bush's militarized metaphor and policies). Through the framing and delivery of these patriotic messages, Win Without War sought to reach the political mainstream and effectively contest the Bush administration's case for war.

The Win Without War coalition name was itself a form of message framing. The phrase was alliterative and easy to express. It conveyed a positive theme (everyone wants to "win") without the negativity of being "against" war or the military. Yet it was specific about seeking a solution "without war", thus marking a clear break with the position of the Bush administration. The title implied support for constructive alternatives to war, such as vigorous UN weapons inspections and continued containment. It avoided the ambiguity and negative connotation that some people, still influenced by Cold War misconceptions, associate with the traditional "peace" movement. The Win Without War name projected a new, proactive image for the anti-war movement. It was both message and sound bite, and it became a brand that was the most widely communicated message of the anti-war movement.[25]

The Iraq anti-war movement was the most successful in history at media communications. Through the extensive use of the Internet, professional public relations services, paid newspaper and television advertising, and the participation of famous artists and musicians, the movement utilized the tools of mass communications to an unprecedented degree. More than a dozen full-page advertisements in the *New York Times*, hundreds of ads in local newspapers, hundreds of national and regional television ad placements, thousands of national and local television and radio interview programme appearances, and thousands of articles in national and local newspapers – all brought visibility and credibility to the anti-war message. The Win Without War media effort generated hundreds of millions of viewer impressions. This vast media communications campaign did not sway the unlistening Bush administration, but it significantly influenced public opinion.

Reflections

Despite the unprecedented scale and scope of the Iraq anti-war movement – the largest anti-war demonstrations in history, a campaign of global dimensions, a sophisticated and wide-reaching media effort – the Bush administration ignored the pervasive opposition to war and went ahead with its planned invasion. Given the administration's determination to remove Saddam Hussein by force, the movement probably had little chance of halting the march to war. Nor did the movement have much time to organize – less than six months from the time the major coalitions began to take shape in October 2002 until the onset of war in March 2003. The broad public opposition to war nonetheless had significant impacts. The administration's decision to take its case to the United Nations was a victory for the advocates of diplomacy in the United States and around the world. Hard-liners in the administration would have preferred to bypass the Security Council and proceed directly to military action, but the administration needed at least the appearance of seeking UN involvement to gain political legitimacy in Congress and elsewhere. Once the UN debate began, France, Russia and other countries were successful in forcing substantial changes in the draft resolution submitted by the United States and United Kingdom in October 2002. The resulting resolution in November, Security Council Resolution 1441, lacked the explicit authorization for military action that Washington and London had sought.

When the Bush administration returned to the Security Council in February 2003 to seek authority for war, it was decisively rebuffed. Not only France, Germany and Russia but six non-permanent members – Chile,

Mexico, Cameroon, Guinea, Angola and Pakistan – refused to support the US proposal. The opposition of the non-permanent members was especially significant, given their political and economic dependence on the United States. Washington made determined efforts to twist their arms, including diplomatic missions to each country, but to no avail. As Phyllis Bennis noted, the strength of worldwide anti-war sentiment prevented the Bush administration from gaining UN support for its planned invasion and forced the administration to abandon efforts to win UN endorsement.[26] As a result, the United States and the United Kingdom stood practically alone in their drive for war. The importance of this Security Council rebuff to the United States is enormous. It was, according to scholar Immanuel Wallerstein, "the first time since the United Nations was founded that the United States, on an issue that mattered to it, could not get a majority on the Security Council".[27] This was widely recognized as a humiliating political defeat for the supposed lone superpower. It represented a decisive loss of legitimacy and a fundamental weakening of US political power and prestige.

The interplay between the anti-war movement and the United Nations deserves special comment. Most UN officials and Security Council members were opposed to the war but were powerless to stop it. The UN Security Council by its very design is a captive of the permanent powers and, when its most powerful member is bent on military aggression, the United Nations has no capacity to prevent it. The most important power of the Security Council is its authority to confer international legitimacy. When it withholds consent, as it did in Iraq, it denies legitimacy. It was able to do so because of the worldwide anti-war movement. A creative dialectic developed between the Security Council and global civil society: the public opposition to war hinged on the lack of UN authorization; the objection of the United Nations in turn depended on the strength of anti-war opposition. The stronger the anti-war movement in Germany, France, Mexico and other countries, the greater the determination of UN diplomats to resist US pressures. The stronger the objections at the United Nations, the greater the legitimacy and political impact of the anti-war movement.[28] It was a unique and unprecedented form of global political synergy. By defending the United Nations, despite its many shortcomings, and insisting upon international authorization for the use of force, the peace movement helped to build the domestic opposition to war and strengthened respect for international law.

The dialectic between civil society and the United Nations is not without contradiction, however. As Waheguru Pal Singh Sidhu and Ramesh Thakur note, there is a disconnect between the rising role of civil society in recent decades and the continuing concentration of authority in the hands of nation-states and intergovernmental organizations. The domination of the state system at the United Nations significantly limits the influence of non-governmental actors. In some instances, government leaders attempt to use the United Nations instrumentally to shape domestic political dynamics. Some governments, such as those in Germany and France, have used diplomacy at the United Nations to appeal to anti-war opinion at home. Other countries, such as Australia, Italy and Japan, have cited international obligations to the United States and the United Nations to override domestic anti-war sentiments. Even when governments are highly attentive to public opinion, they are less likely to be swayed on matters of international policy than on issues of domestic policy. Anti-war movements face special challenges in attempting to exert political influence. Because national security is at stake, or is claimed to be, there is a greater tendency on the part of the public to give political leaders the benefit of the doubt. Citizens tend to be less well informed on international issues than on domestic issues. Foreign policy is usually less subject than domestic policy to democratic control. When foreign policy is mediated through international institutions, the challenge of exerting democratic influence is even greater.

The degree to which anti-war opposition weighed on the deliberations of the Bush administration is unknown, and may not be known until former officials write their memoirs. In the aftermath of the 15 February demonstrations, the President professed to be unmoved by the massive protests, saying that he would not decide policy merely on the basis of a "focus group".[29] Such denials of social movement influence are standard fare among political leaders who are the target of protest. During the Viet Nam era, President Nixon dismissed the huge Moratorium rally at the Washington Monument on 15 November 1969, claiming that he ignored the protest and was watching football on television. As Daniel Ellsberg later observed, however, the memoirs of Nixon and of his top aide H. R. Haldeman showed that the administration was deeply concerned about the Moratorium actions, and was forced to abandon its plans for a major military escalation against North Viet Nam for fear of sparking even greater protests.[30] Ronald Reagan and his advisers dismissed the nuclear freeze demonstrations and referenda of the early 1980s as "all sponsored by a thing called the World Peace Council"[31] (a false and absurd attempt to attack the movement as communistic). In fact, US public pressure during the 1980s derailed the MX missile system, blocked civil defence planning, persuaded Congress to halt funding for nuclear tests and forced the White House to begin negotiations with the Soviets that eventually led to significant arms reduction.[32]

One impact of the Iraq anti-war debate that has not been widely acknowledged was the strategic decision of the White House to justify its pre-planned war by emphasizing the supposed threat from Iraqi weapons of mass destruction. In a moment of unscripted candour after the war, Deputy Defense Secretary Paul Wolfowitz, a principal proponent of attacking Iraq, acknowledged that the focus on weapons of mass destruction was politically motivated. During an interview with *Vanity Fair* magazine, Wolfowitz stated: "The truth is that for reasons that have a lot to do with U.S. government bureaucracy, we settled on the one issue that everyone could agree on, which was weapons of mass destruction as the core reason."[33] This was an admission that the administration could not make an honest case for war and win the debate. Because opposition to war was so great, it was necessary to manipulate and deceive public opinion. By choosing to emphasize the weapons threat – disingenuously invoking fears of a nuclear mushroom cloud and chemical or biological attack – the administration focused the debate on issues it knew would be effective in mobilizing public concern. The tactic was successful in the short term, convincing many Americans that Saddam Hussein had deadly weapons poised to strike. But the strategy backfired when White House claims were exposed as lies – in part through the continuing efforts of anti-war groups.

It is too early to tell as of this writing how the crisis over the Bush administration's invasion and occupation of Iraq will unfold. The US military easily defeated the depleted and dispirited Iraqi armed forces, but the challenge of occupying and controlling Iraq turned out to be far more difficult. Many of the arguments made by the anti-war movement prior to the war were proven correct in its aftermath. The administration's deceit in justifying war set the context for the political problems the White House began to face afterwards. The anti-war movement's steady drumbeat about the lack of justification for war – the absence of a verified weapons threat in Iraq, the failure to demonstrate a link between Saddam Hussein and al-Qaeda – laid the groundwork for subsequent criticism of the Bush administration when in fact no weapons threat or terrorist connections were found. The post-war acknowledgements of faulty intelligence and flawed assumptions undermined confidence in the administration's foreign policy, especially its new doctrine of military pre-emption. The anti-war movement thus continued to have political influence even after the conflict was over.

The ways in which social movements influence policy are not always readily apparent. They often emerge in unanticipated form or in future impacts. Movements can win even as they lose. Although the anti-war movement did not succeed in preventing the invasion of Iraq, it helped to set the terms of the debate and exerted considerable influence on public opinion. The Bush administration rammed through its war policy, but it lost the larger and more important struggle for hearts and minds. The war was lost politically before it ever began militarily. The legitimacy of American leadership suffered grievous setbacks on the international level. Whether these developments will translate into a long-term loss for US militarism, and a concurrent increase in support for cooperative internationalism, is unknown. The answer will depend on whether the legacy of the international movement against war in Iraq is sustained and deepened in the years ahead.

Notes

1. Estimates of the numbers of demonstrators and anti-war events are drawn from the website of United for Peace and Justice, the largest grassroots peace coalition in the United States. See "The World Says No to War", 15 February 2003, ⟨http://www.unitedforpeace.org/feb15.html⟩ (accessed 24 November 2003). For newspaper accounts of the protests, see Angelique Chrisafis et al., "Threat of War: Millions Worldwide Rally for Peace", *Guardian* (London), 17 February 2003, p. 6; Glenn Frankel, "Millions Worldwide Protest Iraq War", *Washington Post*, 16 February 2003, p. A1; Alan Lowell, "1.5 Million Demonstrators in Cities across Europe Oppose a War in Iraq", *New York Times*, 16 February 2003, Section 1, p. 20.
2. Barbara Epstein, "Notes on the Antiwar Movement", *Monthly Review*, Vol. 55, No. 3 (2003).
3. Ibid.
4. Mark Levine, "The Peace Movement Plans for the Future", *Middle East Report*, July 2003, ⟨http://www.merip.org/mero/interventions/levine_interv.html⟩ (accessed 24 November 2003).
5. Stephen Gill, *Power and Resistance in the New World Order* (London: Palgrave, 2003), p. 218.
6. Rebecca Solnit, "Acts of Hope: Challenging Empire on the World Stage", *Orion*, 20 May 2003, ⟨http://www.oriononline.org/pages/oo/sidebars/Patriotism/index_SolnitPR.html⟩ (accessed 24 November 2003).
7. Patrick E. Tyler, "Threats and Responses: News Analysis; A New Power in the Streets", *New York Times*, 17 February 2003, p. A1.
8. Jonathan Schell, "The Other Superpower", *The Nation*, 27 March 2003, ⟨http://www.thenation.com/doc.mhtml?i=20030414&s=schell⟩ (accessed 14 September 2004).
9. Jeoffrey Nunberg, "As Google Goes, So Goes the Nation", *New York Times*, 18 May 2003, Section 4, p. 4.
10. James F. Moore, "The Second Super-Power Rears Its Beautiful Head", Berkman Center for Internet and Society, Harvard Law School, 31 March 2003, ⟨http://cyber.law.harvard.edu/people/jmoore/secondsuperpower.html⟩ (accessed 21 November 2003).
11. Levine, "The Peace Movement Plans for the Future".
12. Leslie Cagan, interview by author, 26 August 2003.
13. Based on my personal conversations with the directors of the three organizations – Susan Shaer, Kevin Martin and Bob Musil – in September 2003.
14. Glenn Kessler and Mike Allen, "Bush Faces Increasingly Poor Image Overseas", *Washington Post*, 24 February 2003, p. A01; CNN, "Poll: U.S. More a Threat Than Iraq", 11 February 2003, ⟨http://edition.cnn.com/2003/WORLD/europe/02/11/british.survey⟩ (accessed 19 November 2003).
15. Stefaan Walgrave and Joris Verhulst, "The February 15 Worldwide Protests against a War in Iraq: An Empirical Test of Transnational Opportunities", unpublished paper, University of Antwerp, 2003.

16. Crowd estimates in this paragraph are drawn from Bill Weinberg, "Antiwar around the World", Global Movement Against War: Taking it to the Streets, *Nonviolent Activist*, Vol. 20, No. 2 (2003). See also Norm Dixon, "The Largest Coordinated Antiwar Protest in History", *Scoop* (New Zealand), 20 February 2003, ⟨http://www.scoop.co.nz/mason/archive/scoop/stories/ed/fa/200302201002.43a56c8a.html⟩ (accessed 14 November 2003).

17. BBC, "Pope Condemns War in Iraq", 13 January 2003, ⟨http://www.news.bbc.co.uk/z/hi/europe/2654109.stm⟩ (accessed 24 November 2003).

18. CBC, "Pope Says War Threatens Humanity", 22 March 2003, ⟨http://www.cbc.cn/stories/2003/03/22/popewar_030322⟩ (accessed 24 November 2003).

19. Tekla Szymanski, "Schröder Beats Bush in German Election", *World Press Review*, 26 September 2002, ⟨http://www.worldpress.org/europe/741.cfm⟩ (accessed 19 November 2003).

20. Philip P. Pan, "Turkey Rejects U.S. Use of Bases", *Washington Post*, 2 March 2003, p. A1.

21. CNN, "NATO Approves Turkish Deployment", 20 February 2003, ⟨http://www.cnn.com/2003/WORLD/meast/02/19/sprj.irq.nato.turkey/index.html⟩ (accessed 19 November 2003).

22. BBC, "Australian PM Censured over Iraq", 5 February 2003, ⟨http://news.bbc.co.uk/2/low/asia-pacific/2727551.stm⟩ (accessed 19 November 2003).

23. *Guardian* (London), "Boost for Religious Parties in Pakistan Elections", 11 October 2002, ⟨http://www.guardian.co.uk/pakistan/Story/0,2763,810103,00.html⟩ (accessed 21 November 2003).

24. Jimmy Carter, "Just War – or a Just War?", *New York Times*, 9 March 2003.

25. The phrase was derived from the report by David Cortright, Alistair Millar and George A. Lopez, *Winning Without War: Sensible Security Options for Dealing with Iraq*, Policy Brief F5, October 2002, ⟨http://www.fourthfreedom.org⟩ (accessed 21 November 2003).

26. Phyllis Bennis, "Bush Isolated, Launches Terrifying Attack", *War Times*, April 2003, ⟨www.war-times.org/current/9art1.html⟩ (accessed 24 November 2003).

27. Immanuel Wallerstein, "U.S. Weakness and the Struggle for Hegemony", *Monthly Review*, Vol. 55, No. 3 (2003), p. 28.

28. I am indebted for this insight to Jack Odell, interview by author, 17 December 2003.

29. Quoted in Richard W. Stevenson, "Antiwar Protests Fail to Sway Bush on Plans for Iraq", *New York Times*, 19 February 2003, p. A1.

30. See the account of Daniel Ellsberg, "Introduction: A Call to Mutiny", in E. P. Thompson and Dan Smith, eds, *Protest and Survive* (New York: Monthly Review Press, 1981), pp. xv–xvi.

31. Quoted in Strobe Talbott, *Deadly Gambits: The Reagan Administration and the Stalemate in Nuclear Arms Control* (New York: Vintage Books, 1985).

32. See the summary of these impacts in David Cortright, *Peace Works: The Citizen's Role in Ending the Cold War* (Boulder, CO: Westview Press, 1993).

33. See the transcript of the Wolfowitz interview by Sam Tannenhaus of *Vanity Fair*, 9 May 2003, ⟨http://www.defenselink.mil/transcripts/2003/tr20030509-depsecdef0223.html⟩ (accessed 24 November 2003).

Part III

Perspectives from within the region

6

Iraq and world order: A Lebanese perspective

Latif Abul-Husn

Prelude

The purpose of this chapter is to explore the relationship of the Iraq crisis to the changing post–Cold War world order and its impact on Lebanon. I first deal with the US justifications for the invasion of Iraq in March 2003. I then look at the basic changes in the world order vis-à-vis US foreign policy options after 9/11 and the shift from a world order centred around the United Nations to one centred around and dominated largely by the United States. After assessing the proposed US democratization process in Iraq and beyond, I examine Lebanon's experience with consociationalism and power-sharing arrangements as a model for democracy in Iraq. Finally, I discuss the impact of the crisis on Lebanon's regional and international relations and the role played by international actors through the United Nations organizations.

The main argument of this chapter is that the United States is the superpower in this unipolar global system and is too great to be challenged by other states or non-state actors but not great enough to act alone in solving the emerging new problems.

The terrorist attack of 11 September 2001 on the twin towers of the World Trade Center in New York and on the Pentagon in Washington DC had an indelible impact on the US psyche. Prior to 9/11, the United States felt safe and secure within its borders and was confident that it could contain or deal with any threat in a variety of ways. After this attack, however, the administration quickly realized that terrorism and the proliferation of weapons of mass destruction constituted a credible and potentially devastating threat to the security of America. This prompted the United States to reverse some of its policy options and act swiftly, forcefully and decisively to dissipate the feeling of fear and insecurity among its people, thus forsaking much of its universally acclaimed values, such as the inadmissibility of intervention in the internal affairs of sovereign states and reverence for international law. The policy of containment gave way to the doctrine of preventive strikes at potential threats to US interests, and the support for international alliances gave way to a sort of unilateralism. Following the 9/11 attack, the urgent challenge for the United States became how to combat terrorism and proscribe the proliferation of weapons of mass destruction.

Combating terrorism and the dilemma of weapons of mass destruction

Iraq was accused of possessing and producing weapons of mass destruction (WMD). That was the major reason for going to war with Iraq in March 2003. The United States felt that the existence of such weapons in the hands of a "rogue state", such as Saddam's Iraq, posed a significant threat to the security and interests of the United States and Iraq's neighbours, meaning Israel and probably some Gulf states. An international process of inspection, monitoring, verification and destruction of such alleged weapons was set in motion. The inspection process, conducted by the United Nations, by the International Atomic Energy Agency (IAEA) and, later on, by the United States (in the aftermath of the occupation of Iraq) went on from 1991 to 2003,[1] but WMD were nowhere to be found. The eight years of inspection by the UN/IAEA between 1991 and 1998 yielded no empirical evidence of the existence of such weapons. The UN team announced later that it had "destroyed most, if not all, of Iraq's unconventional weapons and production facilities, and directly destroyed or monitored the destruction of most of its chemical and biological weapon agents".[2] Likewise, the United States Survey Group failed to uncover WMD, despite the free access it had to suspicious sites, a privilege denied to the UN/IAEA teams. In the light of these results, and faced with rather broad condemnation, the Bush administration embarked on a downward adjustment of its war goals as well as of its expectations of the inspectors' findings. The Bush administration shifted its proclaimed objectives from neutralizing a direct threat to the United States and the destruction of WMD to more contingent and perhaps less controversial issues such as: the failure of Iraq to comply with UN Security Council Resolutions 687 of 8 April 1991 and 1441 of

8 November 2002; freeing the people of Iraq from the brutality of a repressive regime (humanitarian intervention); and, lastly, establishing democracy in Iraq and beyond.

From the outset, public opinion in Lebanon and most of the Arab world was strongly sceptical of the US intentions and claims. The crisis brought to the forefront two main concerns: a growing anxiety over an unrestrained American power which might be challenged and eventually lead to a veritable "clash of civilizations", and the prospect of destabilization and regime changes in the region. It was emphatically believed that the United States had avaricious motives in Iraq. The war was not wholly about WMD and combating terrorism, or about the threat posed by Saddam Hussein to US security and world peace, or about his defiance of the United Nations, or about the desire of the United States to bring liberty and democracy to Iraq and the greater Middle East. It was widely suspected that the real motivation behind the war was the United States' desire to control the sources of energy[3] and to establish and maintain global domination.[4] The United States found a favourable target in Saddam's shunned and unpopular regime. Moreover, the US assessment of the WMD in Iraq was seen by the average Arab citizen as another example of US policy, which ignores Israel's production and stockpiling of such weapons as well as its stock of nuclear armaments. The argument abounds that, if the United States wants to make the world more secure, why not call for a nuclear arms free Middle East region, excluding no one.

On 20 March 2003, a US-led "coalition of the willing" invaded Iraq without the explicit authorization of the Security Council. This military invasion achieved a swift victory over Iraq. No one doubted that outcome. Iraq was an isolated, exhausted and demoralized regime and a state crippled by 13 years of economic and military sanctions. The compelling issue was whether the war was really necessary or justified and what would happen in the aftermath to Iraq and to the region. Europe was asymmetrically divided on the issue. The Arab world was numbed, unable to cope with the rationale and consequences of the war. In less than a month, Iraq was occupied, an oppressive regime defeated and deposed, the state institutions destroyed, the army of 400,000 disbanded, the ruling Ba'ath Party outlawed and persecuted, and society's centrifugal ethno-religious forces unleashed, although the petroleum industry was seemingly safe and well protected by the occupying powers.[5]

Nonetheless, the stated US policy remained unequivocal. It continued to assert that Saddam's WMD and his suspected links to al-Qaeda terrorists constituted a threat to the United States and to regional and world peace. However, when the combined UN/IAEA and US Survey Group inspection process failed to uncover any WMD, no credible links to al-Qaeda were apparent, and the US-led coalition's efforts to govern the country became unexpectedly costly and futile, a face-saving strategy, embracing the notion of liberty and democracy, became America's new rationale for waging war against Iraq.

The war on Iraq epitomized the US quest for centrality in world affairs and its desire to capture the "commanding heights" of the new world order and remain at its apex for the foreseeable future, thus denying the United Nations and any major power a vital role in shaping the international system. The world became polarized between power and legality.

Events at the end of the 1980s provided the United States with an opportunity to become the leader of a unipolar world. The collapse of communism, the disintegration of the Soviet Union and the disbanding of the Warsaw Pact left the United States as the only superpower. In addition, those events removed a major source of insecurity for the United States, enabling it to concentrate on two issues: serving democracy at home and nurturing its new unipolar status. The United States therefore felt that it could afford to disengage from certain international commitments and revert to a mild form of unilateralism, which its self-interest called for.

The post–Cold War order and the United States

Before 9/11 there were strong indications that US foreign policy was moving in the direction of disengagement from some of its major international commitments. The Bush administration rejected the verification protocol of the UN Biological Weapons Convention, the Kyoto Climate Change Protocol, missile conventions, and the International Criminal Court. The 9/11 attacks seemed to have motivated the United States to change course and embrace a more assertive security-centred foreign policy.

The 9/11 events prompted the Bush administration to make significant changes in its foreign policy options. The new course tilted towards unilateralism and was based on two principles: to "maximize America's freedom to act", and to use its strength to "change the status quo of the world".[6] To the neoconservatives of the Bush Jr administration, the "1990s were a decade of illusions in foreign policy. On September 11, 2001, this age of illusion ended. The United States asked its friends and allies to join in the fight against terror and discovered that ... those friends and allies were prepared to do little."[7] As for the United Nations' authority to maintain peace and order in the world, the neoconservatives believed that the United Nations ought to support the United States in its quest for security; otherwise, "we should formally reject the UN's authority over our war on terror".[8] High on the agenda of the neoconservatives was the doctrine of pre-emptive war and combating terrorism.

The doctrine of pre-emptive war as a tool for combating terrorism

Combating terrorism became a focus of US security concerns after 9/11. The war on Iraq was subsumed under this doctrine. Iraq was elevated to a principal target in the war on terrorism. The post–Cold War doctrine of deterrence was supplanted by the doctrine of pre-emptive war. The United States claimed the right to attack a country it identifies as its enemy or a possible launching pad for an attack on the United States, even before that country could harm the United States. The concept of self-defence (Article 51 of the UN Charter) was thus converted, according to this doctrine, into an offensive pre-emptive initiative. It is obvious that such a shift would terminate the consensus upon which the UN system of collective security rests. The Security Council refused to endorse direct pre-emptive military action against Iraq. Nevertheless, this doctrine "became the official strategy of the US",[9] supplanting the policy of containment, dual containment and deterrence. Major changes in the new world order provided the United States with a "menu" that was relatively free from the constraints that had usually affected its foreign policy options during the Cold War era.

The changing profile of the world order and its impact on the Iraq crisis

Specificities in the evolving world order have contributed to the Iraq crisis in a number of ways. First, the world order after the end of the Cold War itself acted as a spawning ground for the upsurge in centrifugal conflictual tendencies inherent in pluralist societies. Iraq's socio-political and ethnic structures are no exception. Second, the demise of the Soviet Union changed the international system from a bipolar to a unipolar system, depriving Iraq of possible Soviet intervention on its side, as might have occurred had the invasion taken place before 1989. Third, the United Nations, being the custodian and guarantor of world peace, was released from the shackles of Cold War superpower rivalries. The Iraq crisis offered the United Nations an opportunity to expand its role into the areas of deterrence and conflict prevention.

The Westphalian concept of sovereignty could not be utilized after the end of the Cold War as a shield to conceal a regime's oppressive policies. The changes in the world order that had an impact on the Iraq crisis can be summed up as: an end to bipolarity (in the demise of the Soviet Union

Iraq lost a staunch ally against the West); the petering out of superpower rivalry; an end to doctrines of containment and deterrence; a commitment to liberal democracy and an open market economy; a decline in the sanctity of state sovereignty; and an upsurge in ethno-national and religious conflicts. New concepts such as "combating terrorism", "preemptive war" and "global democratic revolution" were forced on the international system as the new framework for conducting international relations. However, the perception of these principles by world leaders was not uniform. The majority of international actors expressed unquestioning support for the United Nations in the face of the new challenges emanating from the war as well as from the evolving world order.

Challenges to the United Nations

The end of the Cold War and the demise of the Soviet Union provided the United Nations Organization with a significant opportunity to free itself from the shackles of superpower rivalries and veto exchanges in the Security Council. For almost 45 years the United Nations' capacity to take up the role that was intended for it in its Charter was curtailed by superpower rivalry. The upsurge in ethno-national conflicts and the disdain of major powers for involvement in their resolution unless they were directly affected provided the United Nations with an opportunity to retrieve the world's faith in its role. Changing attitudes toward intervention in domestic conflict and the desanctification of nation-state sovereignty gave the United Nations a wider margin in its efforts to fulfil its obligation to maintain peace and order in the world. Yet its effectiveness in settling and resolving some conflicts in the post–Cold War era was mixed – there were some successes (Namibia, Cambodia, East Timor, Mozambique) and some dismal failures (Somalia, Rwanda, Bosnia).[10]

The ideologically based distrust and hostility that marked international relations during the Cold War era undoubtedly had an impact on UN activities. The vetoes cast in the Security Council, reflecting the parochial interests of the major powers, rendered the United Nations powerless to deal with many of the conflicts around the globe.[11] As a result, only 13 peacekeeping missions were mounted between 1948 and 1989. As soon as the superpower rivalries vanished, however, the United Nations assumed a new prominence in world affairs and emerged as an indispensable instrument in conflict resolution and peacebuilding endeavours. Since 1990, its peace operations have vigorously expanded into new areas, such as conflict prevention and conflict transformation, peacemaking, peacebuilding and post-conflict peacebuilding, as well as peace enforcement.

The post–Cold War order brought about the end of superpower rivalry and the threat of nuclear confrontation, raising hopes that the world might, at long last, have entered an era of peace and tranquillity. Although the quest for peace and stability had been nourished by the demise of bipolarity, optimism soon faded as a series of events erupted around the world. Iraq invaded Kuwait in 1990 with the purpose of annexing it, the former Yugoslavia disintegrated in 1991, war broke out between Serbia and Croatia, Somalia engaged in a protracted internecine conflict that involved the major powers and resulted in thousands of casualties and fatalities, Rwanda succumbed to the nightmare of genocide, Cambodia's Pot Pol killed about 3 million of his citizens, and East Timor, Liberia, Sierra Leone and several other places were not spared the "butterfly effect" of conflict.

These were the testing grounds of the post–Cold War order. By failing to prevent or even to resolve these conflicts, the international community demonstrated that it had not yet developed resolution capacities in response to those deadly conflicts. The United Nations and its agencies were familiar with inter-state conflicts but not with the domestically based international conflicts that emerged after the end of the Cold War. Yet the United Nations was able to overcome this handicap in a short time. It soon acquired the knowledge and expertise that enabled it to play a central role in peacekeeping, peacemaking and post-conflict peacebuilding. This development was affirmed by the world leaders' decision at their summit meeting in September 2005, at the UN headquarters in New York, to recognize the need for a "peace-building commission" that would help countries after the termination of peacekeeping missions. This endorsement by the international community has seemingly bestowed on the United Nations a key role in preventive action.

In the aftermath of the war in Iraq, the US-led coalition failed to put in place a viable plan to proceed forward. The only place it could turn to for help was the UN body.[12] The UN record in resolving conflicts and its peacebuilding efforts in war-torn countries such as Mozambique, El Salvador, Haiti, Cambodia and East Timor are testimony to its relevance and credibility in handling such conflicts at that stage of their life cycle.

Meanwhile, the international community was pressing the United States to make the United Nations a full partner in the rebuilding efforts of the new order in Iraq. In the United States itself, leading opposition figures "demanded at once that the U.N. play a vital role in post war Iraq and rejected U.S. control of reconstruction or of the post-Saddam government".[13] Europe was vocal in its support for a vigorous and central role for the United Nations in the new Iraqi order. In a statement on 17 February 2003, 15 heads of state of the European Union reaffirmed their commitment to the United Nations and demanded a central role for the organization in the emerging post 9/11 international order.[14] Likewise, the League of Arab States, meeting at summit level in Tunisia on 16–17

May 2004, called for a central role for the United Nations in the transitional period, as well as in the political process that would lead to the termination of the occupation and the rebuilding of state institutions in Iraq.[15]

What role did the United Nations play before, during and in the aftermath of the war in Iraq? Two opposing views dominated perceptions of the UN role. The first, that of the United States, suggested that the United Nations was irrelevant not only because the Security Council failed to authorize the war but because the United Nations itself "is not some immemorial achievement of the human race".[16] The other view, advocated by most of the rest of the world, maintained that the United Nations had fulfilled its traditional role throughout the crisis, pointing to the fact that the Security Council was true to the goals of its Charter when it refused to authorize the US-led war because it could not reconcile the authorization to invade Iraq with the principles and goals of the Charter. The United States argued that elimination of WMD was a Security Council request (Resolutions 687 of April 1991 and 1441 of November 2002). Because Resolution 1441 fell short of automatic authorization for an enforcement intervention, the United States tried to secure a fresh resolution authorizing it explicitly to use force against Iraq, but abandoned its attempt after failing to obtain the required majority in the Security Council.[17]

What sort of a political system is expected to emerge in post-war Iraq? And what role will the United Nations earn for itself in building this system? After its failure to uncover any weapons of mass destruction in Iraq, the United States shifted its emphasis to democratizing the country along the principles of Western polyarchies. Its rationale is the much-applauded belief that democracies tend to be more peaceful, and "the more democratic [two states are] the less conflict between them".[18]

The US failure to uncover any WMD, whose discovery could have legitimized its invasion and occupation of the country, led the Bush administration to search for other justifications. It found its lost treasure in the concept of democracy and the rule of law. Assuming that "democracies do not go to war with each other", the United States had publicly declared that its interests would be best protected by the promotion of democracy in non-democratic states. The WMD crisis was morphed into a crisis of democracy in Iraq and beyond. Will democracy succeed in Iraq?

The transition to democracy in Iraq

What form might the new democracy conceivably take – a Western-centred liberal democratic majoritarian system in line with the democratization wave of the 1980s and 1990s; a consensual form based on power-sharing; or a democratic system that would give credence to the significance of Islamic political forms? The answer is rooted in Iraqi socio-political structures.

Iraq is a pluralist state encompassing several ethnic, sectarian, national and cultural groups – Arabs, Kurds, Turkmen, Armenians, Shiites, Sunnis, Chaldeans, Assyrians, Catholics, Orthodox, Jews and Yazidies. Each of these groups has demands on the political system. The Kurds wanted an "exit", whereas most of the others requested "access" to the vestiges of power and government rewards. They have cultural and religious concerns as well as material and political demands. Saddam Hussein's regime was not responsive to the demands of these groups, save for the Kurds, who in the 1970s were granted a form of autonomy that was reinforced after the 1990 Gulf war.

As a result of the US-led invasion and occupation of Iraq, Saddam's one-party state structure disintegrated and gave way to a multi-party system, spawning dozens of political, sectarian and ethnic parties and movements. The most enduring parties were those that had flourished in opposition in the autonomous regions and outside Iraq during the Saddam era, such as the Iraqi Islamic Party, the Islamic Al-Da'wah Party, the Supreme Council for the Islamic Revolution in Iraq, the Iraqi National Accord, the Iraqi National Congress, the Iraqi Communist Party, the Kurdish Democratic Party, the Patriotic Union of Kurdistan, the Iraqi Turkoman National Party, the Assyrian Democratic Movement and the Association of Muslim Clerics. Most of the other parties emerged after the removal of Saddam Hussein from power and the de-Ba'athification of the ruling party. With the exception of the Iraqi Communist Party, almost all of these groups were formed along ethnic, sectarian or nationalist lines.

These parties, groups and movements have diverse goals and agendas, but they are all vying for a share of power. The struggle to forge a new identity for the emerging political system in the wake of the fall of Saddam Hussein provided these groups with the opportunity to assert their own identities and the interests of their communities in the new political system. Political divisions and cultural cleavages among those groups are not new. The Sunni Arabs had dominated the political landscape in Iraq since the country's independence in 1932. Their hegemonic position was reinforced by the Saddam regime and his Ba'ath Party. The Sunnis of Iraq comprise around 32 per cent of the population, compared with the Shiites who comprise 62 per cent. Most of the component communities of Iraq have conflicting visions about their role in the post-Saddam political system. Sectarian tension ebbs and flows between the Sunnis and Shiites. Moreover, communal tension is evident between the Shiites and the

Kurds of northern Iraq over the spoils of the new Iraq. The Chaldeans and the Assyrians are demanding official recognition of their political and cultural identities and interests. However, this tension has not yet degenerated into a dissociative and disruptive inter-group conflict. The reality that foreign occupation was likely to persist until a stable political system emerged provided an incentive to these groups to forge a consensus that would overcome conflicting goals and cross-cutting interests. Hostilities are still mostly directed at the forces of occupation but, once the occupation ends, the conflictual tendencies inherent in the social structure could erupt and escalate into a deadly inter-group conflict and possibly civil war.

There is a strong indication that the major political trends in Iraq today are ethno-religiously based. The armed resistance to occupation is predominantly Sunni; the demand for a democratically elected government is basically a Shiite desire; federalism is a Kurdish demand and strategy. The question is, what kind of a political system can accommodate these contradictory demands and national aspirations and address the grievances of the component communities of Iraq? The Kurds have already obtained an autonomous status within the Iraqi political system and achieved a veto power in the Interim Constitution, which was confirmed in the permanent charter of the new republic.

The United States' democratizing initiative was intended to commence in Iraq and be railroaded through to other Middle East countries, including Iran, Pakistan and Afghanistan. This initiative sets out President Bush's vision for political, economic and social reform in the greater Middle East following the overthrow of Saddam's regime. The fact that it was floated without consulting the Arab leaders in the region made this new US strategy susceptible to rejection by the countries concerned. It has been interpreted as "another attempt by the US to impose its will on the Middle East".[19] Questions were raised about how and by what authority the United States could endow itself with the moral authority to change regimes in the Middle East and elsewhere. Nevertheless, the initiative seems to have moved the region in that direction. Arab leaders pledged at their summit in Tunisia in 2004 to move with the times and renew their efforts to build their own brand of home-grown democracy.[20] For many in this region, the demand for democracy is long overdue, but the question is whether Arab civic and political culture is ready for this move. There also remain the serious questions of how democracy can be woven into the fabric of the Islamic faith and what form it might take.

Creating a democratic system out of the remnants of a totalitarian state faces many challenges, the most significant of which are: an absence of political prerequisites such as a competitive party system, interest groups, an independent judiciary, a free press and a vibrant civil society; a debilitated bureaucracy; a disbanded army; and a tribal social structure that is unlikely to find expression in a Western-style democratic system. On the other hand, owing to its abundant natural resources, Iraq does not face similar challenges in building sustainable economic development.

Nevertheless, the United States has embarked upon a process of rebuilding the constitutional-institutional structure of Iraq along the main lines of pluralist Western democracies. To harness the inherent pluralist tendencies in Iraqi society, long subdued by the oppressive regime of Saddam Hussein, a temporary power-sharing arrangement was enshrined in the Interim Constitution (Law of Administration for the State of Iraq for the Transitional Period) of 8 March 2004. An Interim Governing Council was created composed of representatives of the main component communities of the country. Its membership reflected the numerical weight of each community.

Two encouraging signs of democracy-building have emerged from this: a spirit of concordance among the Shiite majority, the Sunni minority, the Kurds and other minority groups, and tacit consent for the role of Islam in the new democracy. Moreover, the Interim Constitution reconciled the basic principles of liberal democracy with the basic tenets of Islam. However, the main divisive issue in Iraq was never Islam but federalism and ethnicity. The new constitution acknowledges the saliency of ethnicity at the expense of Iraq's Arab identity, and promotes federalism as a solution to Iraq's religious and ethnic divisions. The notion of national unity is conspicuously lacking. The new constitution was approved despite overwhelming opposition from the Sunnis, who, in contrast to minority groups elsewhere, would prefer a centralized state. The Sunni community has already expressed its strong reservations about the devolution of power and resources to the other two main communities – the Kurds and the Shiites; indeed, the Shiites are seeking to create autonomous provinces as in Kurdistan. This is not a recipe for democracy; rather it may be a prescription for the dissolution of Iraq.

Federalism does not always provide an adequate mechanism for conflict management. The inherent conflictual tendencies of Iraq's social structure were aggravated rather than contained and managed by the constitution. Regions are to have their own armed forces, and new oil fields will be controlled by the regions. The Kurds' constitution can override that of the central government, thus putting them beyond the reach of the Supreme Court. Women's rights are not uniform throughout the country. The new constitutional framework does not provide the competing communities with common grounds on which to build their democratic aspirations or create conflict resolution safeguards that could guarantee stability and communal peace in the country.

The road to a stable democracy is still a very long one. The absence of a participatory political culture that could uphold democratic rule does not augur well for the future of democracy in Iraq. Moreover, civil society organizations need time to emerge and mature. There is no doubt that political parties and mass media have mushroomed since the defeat of the authoritarian regime, but will they persist long enough to make an effective contribution to the political culture? The rebuilding of a civic culture may be illustrated by examples from Russia, Germany and Italy. It took about 15 years after the collapse of fascism in Italy and Nazism in Germany to build a participatory culture in these two countries. In Russia, over 43 political parties competed for elections in 1995. Only six of them won seats in the parliament.

The transition to democracy in Iraq is contingent upon the restructuring of the social and political structure of the country. This means that the state must redefine itself as the political expression of a multi-ethnic and religious nation, and develop new bonds of loyalties to the state. The defunct Ba'athist regime's boundless might had generated an illusion of monopoly and immortality. The people were numbed and content to be used as fodder for a leviathan regime.

Although civil society can serve as a context for the process of democratization, the success of this process depends on effective leadership and international support.[21] Publicly accountable leaders who can inspire and motivate, and an institutional mechanism through which they can be removed, are needed for the post-Saddam era. In the restructured political system, there is a need for a leader who can cope with the breakdown of the Ba'athist regime and the old moral certainties and lead the country through the expected changes in the Iraqi socio-political structure as a result of democratization.

Given the lack of integrative mechanisms and conflict resolution practices in the new constitution, compounded by a feeble participatory political culture and an ineffectual leadership structure, the decision makers in Iraq and the architects of its new political order might find it appropriate to look closely at Lebanon's experiment in conflict resolution and nation-building.

An alternative road: Consociational democracy – Lebanon's experience

Lebanon is a composite of several religious and ethnic communities, both large and small, organized hierarchically within the confines of a political system that maintains sectarian identification. Since the mid-nineteenth century, the relationship between these communities has oscillated between cooperation and conflict. The political significance of these groups lies in the role they play as social organizations through which political security can be achieved. They have evolved over the years into semi-autonomous socio-political communities with distinctive political and administrative functions. This distinctiveness is evident in the power-sharing arrangement upon which Lebanon's political order rests and in the country's civil status law.

Iraq's social structure has many similarities to and equivalences with the Lebanese social structure. It is similarly divided and segmented and harbours similar conflictual (although more violent) tendencies among its ethno-religious and national component groups. However, the conflict process in Iraq took a different direction from that in Lebanon. Since its independence, Iraq had experienced a chain of violent revolts and revolutions that engulfed almost every ethnic, sectarian and minority group. Societal peace and political stability in Iraq were maintained through the exercise of a totalitarian rule in which ethnic, sectarian and nationalistic feelings were brutally suppressed.

Lebanon's political system has manifested and maintained a reasonably acceptable level of stability that could lend itself to consociational explication. Back in 1864, Lebanon's major communities agreed to share power. Since then, this arrangement has become the modus operandi of the evolving political order in Lebanon. It provided the country with almost 100 years of stability and communal peace before the power-sharing arrangements of consociationalism broke down in the mid-1970s, for a variety of reasons. Some of the causes were rooted in the power-sharing practices themselves and some were the result of external influences and pressures. In 1990, consociationalism was resurrected and reintroduced into the political system, thus restoring the balance in communal entitlements. A long-term remedy to a pluralist conflictual structure was revived.

Power-sharing practices may not be appealing to the minders of the new Iraq. It is assumed in the West that Arab countries are in need of strong government authority, "yet what is needed in Iraq to come into being, as Lebanon has proven, is a system based on communal compromise and state authority that merely manages, monitors and regulates centrifugal forces in society without stifling them".[22]

The reverberations of the Iraq crisis have been felt in almost every corner of the globe, but mostly by the countries of the Middle East. Lebanon, being an integral part of the Arab world, was affected by the crisis in the same way as a set of billiard balls are affected by a hit from a moving ball on a pool table. Moreover, the nature of the interaction and the degree of interdependence existing between Iraq and its neighbouring countries make it possible that this crisis might set off a chain of events throughout the region. The effect of the Iraq crisis and its aftermath on relations between Lebanon and Syria is discussed next.

The impact of the Iraq crisis on Lebanon's regional and international relations: Syria's legacy in Lebanon

Relations between Syria and Lebanon are rooted in geographical proximity and historical and cultural bonds. Both countries were placed under the French mandate in the early 1920s and both gained their independence in the mid-1940s. Until 1949 both countries had a joint central bank, one currency, one customs union, one railway administration, a common labour market and a coordinated foreign policy. In 1951, these institutional ties were completely severed and each country sought to develop its own independent infrastructure and its own domestic and foreign policy. Lebanon retained a liberal democratic multi-party political system, whereas Syria experienced a succession of military coups that transformed it into a centralized state dominated by the Ba'athist Party.

Regional variations, the Arab–Israeli conflict and centrifugal domestic pressure all had an adverse impact on Lebanon. In 1975, communal conflict broke out. It lasted for 15 years, brought the country to a standstill, exacted an expensive toll on civilian society with significant loss of life and major destruction of the socio-political structure, and brought all nation-building efforts to a halt.

At the request of the then president of the republic of Lebanon, and with the tacit approval of the major powers, Syria intervened at a very early stage of the conflict. Its intervention progressed from mediation to full participation, assuming the maximum degree of involvement, both militarily and politically, depending on the ebb and flow of the conflict.

The termination of hostilities came about with the conclusion, in 1989, of an inter-communal peace settlement, known as the Taiff Accord, brokered by the Arab League. But Syrian involvement and military presence in the country persisted unabated, until its forced withdrawal from Lebanon in April 2005.

The Iraq crisis increased the focus on Syrian intervention in Lebanon and raised the degree of anxiety of the United States about Syria's support of the insurgency in Iraq. This concern prompted the US Congress to pass a law in December 2003 called the "Syria Accountability and Lebanese Sovereignty Restoration Act 2003", requesting Syria to "end its occupation of Lebanon" and cease "undermining US and international efforts with respect to the stabilization and reconstruction of Iraq". Pursuant to this Act, President Bush signed an Executive Order imposing limited sanctions on Syria for failing to comply with it. Furthermore, in September 2004, the United States co-sponsored Security Council Resolution 1559 with France. This requested Syria, without actually naming it, to withdraw its troops from Lebanon, to stop interfering in Lebanon's internal affairs and to cease its aid to Hezbollah, also without specifically naming it. Supporters of the Syrian presence in Lebanon denounced this resolution, but opponents hailed it as the beginning of the end of Syria's involvement in Lebanese affairs.

Despite mounting domestic and international pressure for a Syrian withdrawal from Lebanon, the Syrian government refused to relinquish its role in Lebanon. On 14 February 2005, a former prime minister of Lebanon, Rafiq Hariri, an opponent of Syrian involvement in Lebanon's affairs, was brutally assassinated, along with an accompanying former minister, a member of parliament and 18 other people, by a massive explosion as he drove along the Beirut seafront district. Many Lebanese were quick to blame the assassination on Syria. Hariri's relationship with the post-Hafez al-Assad Syrian regime was, at the time, at its lowest. He was seen by the new Syrian leadership as an obstacle to its continued influence in Lebanon. The schism in the relationship between Hariri and the Syrian leadership reached its climax when Hariri tried to resist Syria's pressure to amend the Lebanese constitution to allow the extension of the term of office of the pro-Syrian president of the Lebanese Republic.

The assassination sparked a series of street protests and organized demonstrations in Beirut and other cities in Lebanon, as well as among some of the Lebanese immigrant groups in major cities of the world. The protestors demanded to know who had planned, ordered and carried out the assassination. The largest of these demonstrations was held on 14 March 2005. Over 1 million people from all sects, political affiliations and regions converged on Martyrs Square in Beirut's city centre, demanding to know who killed Hariri and requesting Syria to withdraw its troops from Lebanon. The demonstrations, dubbed the "Cedar Revolution", captured the interest and concern of the international community and forced the Syrian-backed Lebanese government to resign and eventually led to the withdrawal, in April 2005, of Syrian troops and their security agencies from Lebanon.

The assassination had far-reaching consequences for Syria. It triggered an international campaign against the Syrian presence in Lebanon. The United States and France were in the forefront calling for Syrian withdrawal from the country. At the request of the Security Council, the UN Secretary-General sent a three-man fact-finding mission to Lebanon with a mandate to enquire into the causes, circumstances and consequences of the assassination. The team was led by Ireland's deputy police commissioner, Peter Fitzgerald. It spent one month in Lebanon investigating the assassination. The ensuing report concluded that "the Lebanese security services and the Syrian Military Intelligence bear primary responsibility for the lack of security, protection, law and order in Lebanon".[23] However, the Fitzgerald investigation did not establish the direct culpability of Syria, although it pinned on it the primary responsibility for the political tension that preceded the assassination. The report stated clearly that "this atmosphere provided the backdrop for the assassination of Mr. Hariri".[24]

The Fitzgerald fact-finding mission recommended the establishment of an international independent investigation team with executive authority to carry out interrogations to find out who planned, ordered and executed the killing of Mr Hariri.[25] Based on Fitzgerald's recommendation and approval by the Lebanese government, the Security Council, in Resolution 1595, established an International Independent Investigation Commission, headed by the German prosecutor Metlev Mehlis, with the mandate to "assist the Lebanese authorities in their investigations of all aspects of the assassination of Hariri, to help identify perpetrators, sponsors, organizers and accomplices".[26]

Investigations by the Commission were conducted in Lebanon and Syria. As a result, the chiefs of the four security services in Lebanon were detained and charged with complicity in the planning of the assassination. The investigation in Syria has not gone that far yet. Nevertheless, the Commission's intermediate report on its findings pointed explicitly to the involvement of Syrian intelligence services, together with their Lebanese "hosts", in the assassination of Hariri. It was felt throughout Lebanon that the UN involvement in the investigation gave the process credibility and reassured the Lebanese that they were not being left to their fate.

A succession of developments followed the withdrawal of Syrian troops from Lebanon. Free parliamentary elections were held a month later in which 60 deputies out of 128 (46 per cent) entered parliament for the first time. Hariri supporters, spearheaded by his son, won a majority of seats in parliament. A new government headed by a former minister of finance and staunch Hariri loyalist was formed. A former prime minister, General Michael Aoun, a dedicated foe of Syria, returned to Lebanon from his 15-year forced exile in France and was elected to parliament. The imprisoned leader of the Lebanese Forces militia was pardoned and released from prison. Yet these developments failed to restore law and order in the country. On the contrary, the security situation deteriorated dramatically. Several bomb explosions in Beirut, caused by as yet unknown perpetrators, have killed innocent victims, including mainly anti-Syrian spokespeople, and instilled fear in Lebanese society.

Following these developments, the international community, spearheaded by the United States and France, pooled its resources to help Lebanon reconstitute itself and revitalize its security and political system without Syrian intervention, for the first time in 29 years. To some Lebanese politicians this change represented a switch from Syrian tutelage to Western custody. Lebanon was drawn incrementally away from the Syrian sphere of influence into the US-dominated international system via the UN order.

However, the UN role was not totally passive or reflexive. The Security Council adopted four resolutions in support of Lebanon's freedom, integrity and political independence: 1559 (2004), 1595 (2005), 1636 (2005) and 1644 (2005). Moreover, the Secretary-General commissioned three missions to Lebanon to monitor progress in the implementation of these resolutions.[27]

Conclusion

The Iraq crisis changed the political landscape in the region in four different ways. First, it brought US military might and political influence to the heart of the Middle East. Second, it provided the United States with an opportunity to promote and spread democracy in the region, beginning with Iraq. Third, it aided the emergence of a new regional order in which power and influence were redistributed among the states of the region in a way that allowed Lebanon to opt out of Syrian domination, though at a high cost. Fourth, Syria's position in the power hierarchy of the Middle East was significantly diminished, mainly owing to its opposition to the US-led invasion of Iraq (unlike in the previous Gulf war) and its loss of influence in Lebanon.

The high-cost US intervention in Iraq has revealed not so much US power as its limits. Peace, stability and democracy in Iraq and beyond have not happened yet. The dilemma facing the United States is best portrayed by Henry Kissinger: "what is new about the emerging world order is that, for the first time, the United States can neither withdraw from the world nor dominate it."[28]

Notes

1. Following the conclusion of the Gulf war in 1991, UN Security Council Resolution 687 of 3 April 1991 directed Saddam Hussein to destroy his chemical and biological weapons and all equipment for developing nuclear capabilities, and to permit UN/IAEA inspection teams to monitor, verify and destroy all WMD. The inspection process was terminated in 1998. In November 2002, Iraq submitted to a more intrusive inspection regime stipulated by Security Council Resolution 1441, dated 8 November 2002, and carried out by the United Nations Monitoring, Verification and Inspection Commission. A month later, Iraq submitted its report on the destruction of its WMD in a 12,000-page document. The United States rejected the report and tried to obtain from the Security Council a fresh resolution authorizing enforcement action against Iraq. The Security Council was unwilling to grant such authorization. The United States, together with the United Kingdom and a few other countries, launched Operation Iraqi

Freedom on 20 March 2003. It took only three weeks to topple Saddam's regime and occupy the country. The United States installed its own inspection team (the US Survey Group), which consisted of 1,500 inspectors working independently from the UN/IAEA team.

2. Jessica Mathews, "What Happened in Iraq: The Success Story of the United Nations Inspection", a keynote address at the International Peace Academy Conference, 5 March 2004.

3. Dan Morgan and David B. Ottaway, "In Iraq War Scenario, Oil Is Key Issue", *Washington Post*, 15 September 2002.

4. Geoff Simons, *Future Iraq: U.S. Policy in Reshaping the Middle East* (London: Saqi Books, 2003), pp. 313–317.

5. Ibid., pp. 255–267.

6. Ivo H. Daalder and James M. Lindsay, *America Unbound: The Bush Revolution in Foreign Policy* (Washington DC: Brookings Institution Press, 2003), p. 13.

7. David Frum and Richard Pearl, *An End to Evil: How to Win the War on Terror* (New York: Random House, 2003), p. 235.

8. Ibid., p. 271.

9. Clyde Prestowitz, *Rogue Nations: American Unilateralism and the Failure of Good Intentions* (New York: Basic Books, 2003), p. 273.

10. For a detailed analysis of the causes of failure of these missions, see Boutros-Boutros Ghali, *The Unvanquished: A U.S.-U.N. Saga* (New York: Random House, 1999).

11. United Nations Secretary-General, *An Agenda for Peace – Preventive Diplomacy, Peacemaking and Peacekeeping* (New York: United Nations, 1992).

12. "Searching for an Exit", *The Age* (Melbourne), 10 April 2004.

13. Noam Chomsky, *Hegemony or Survival: America's Quest for Global Dominance* (New York: Metropolitan Books, 2003), p. 142.

14. *New York Times*, 19 February 2003.

15. League of Arab States, *Final Communiqué of the Summit Meeting*, Tunisia, 16–17 May 2004.

16. Frum and Pearl, *An End to Evil*, p. 272.

17. United Nations Security Council Resolution 487 of 1981.

18. Bruce Russett, *Grasping for the Democratic Peace: Principles for a Post-Cold War Order* (Princeton, NJ: Princeton University Press, 1995), p. 86.

19. Rupert Cornwell, "U.S. Angers Allies with New Middle East Plan", *Independent.co.uk*, 28 February 2004.

20. League of Arab States, *Final Communiqué*.

21. Poland was an exception in that the main engine of political transformation in Poland was the leadership of Lech Walesa and his trade union, Solidarity, combined with the help of the Church, not civil society organizations.

22. Michael Young, "Defend Lebanon's Consociational System", *The Daily Star* (Beirut), 30 December 2003.

23. Peter Fitzgerald, *Report of the Fact-Finding Mission to Lebanon Inquiring into the Causes, Circumstances and Consequences of the Assassination of Former Prime Minister, Rafik Hariri*, 25 February–24 March 2005, p. 2.

24. Ibid., p. 20.

25. Ibid.

26. Security Council Resolution 1595, dated 7 April 2005.

27. Security Council Resolution 1559, dated 2 September 2004, calls for the "strict respect of the sovereignty, territorial integrity, unity and political independence of Lebanon under the sole and exclusive authority of the Government of Lebanon throughout Lebanon". It calls also for the withdrawal of all foreign forces from Lebanon and the dis-

banding and disarming of the Lebanese and non-Lebanese militias. Resolution 1595 of 7 April 2005 establishes an International Independent Investigation Commission to assist the Lebanese authorities in their investigation of the assassination of former Prime Minister Rafiq Hariri in Beirut on 14 February 2005. Resolution 1636 of 31 October 2005 endorses the Commission's intermediate report and insists that Syria "not interfere in Lebanese domestic affairs ... [and] refrain from any attempt aimed at destabilizing Lebanon". This resolution was adopted under Chapter VII of the UN Charter. Resolution 1644 demands that Syria respond "unambiguously" to the Commission's investigation and "implement without delay any future [relevant] request of the UN International Independent Commission". It further extends the probe for an additional six months, and authorizes the Commission to extend its technical assistance to the Lebanese authorities in their investigations of terrorist acts that followed Hariri's assassination.

The Secretary-General mandated three senior UN envoys to deal with the evolving Lebanese–Syrian conflict: Geir Pedersen, his Personal Representative for Lebanon; Terje Roed-Larsen, his representative for compliance with Security Council Resolution 1595; and Alvero de Soto, the UN Special Coordinator for the Middle East peace process.

28. Henry Kissinger, "The New World Order", in Chester A. Crocker and Fen Osler Hampson with Pamela Aall, eds, *Managing Global Chaos: Sources of and Responses to International Conflict* (Washington DC: United States Institute for Peace, 1996), p. 174.

7

Iraq and world order: A Turkish perspective

Ayla Göl

Introduction

Since the collapse of the Soviet Union, the United States has become not only a supreme power as a result of its unchallenged military, economic and cultural dominance but also an arrogant power set upon redesigning the world according to its own neoconservative image. The end of the Cold War changed the tacit agreement between the two superpowers on spheres of influence in the Balkans, Central Asia, the Caucasus and the Middle East, which brought new structural and normative challenges to global and regional orders. Establishing order in the post–Cold War Middle East remains the most challenging task for the international community, which was misinformed about two issues. There were claims, on the one hand, about the existence of weapons of mass destruction (WMD) in Iraq and, on the other, about an assumed link between the Iraqi government and al-Qaeda. However, the overthrow of Saddam Hussein's regime was not based on an international norm of humanitarian intervention. Even before the UN observers declared in their final report in October 2004 that there were no WMD, many scholars had questioned the legality and legitimacy of the war in Iraq, as David Krieger, Ramesh Thakur and Nicholas Wheeler discuss in this volume.

The 1991 Gulf war was the first example of a new world disorder in the Middle East, which put Iraq on the agenda of the post–Cold War era. Developments in northern Iraq in the 1990s left Turkey as one of the key countries in the region. It had mixed and somewhat conflicting interests and had to balance its US alignment and Middle Eastern policies. Thus, the main arguments of this chapter are threefold: to examine to what extent Turkey's Middle Eastern policies converge with the emerging US-dominated world order; to explain why Ankara's rapprochement with Iran and Syria took shape around the Kurdish issue independently from Washington's regional policies; and to discuss how Turkey's bid to achieve European Union (EU) membership influenced its policies towards the Middle East. After examining the structure of world order and the US hegemony in relation to the "Iraq crisis", I explain why Turkish and American interests diverged on the future of Kurds in northern Iraq, the rise of Islamism and terrorism, and cooperation with Iraq's neighbours – Syria and Iran. I then focus on the European Union's emphasis on the new unconventional security challenges as cross-border issues and the importance of trans-regional cooperation between Europe and the Middle East. Lastly I critically explore the new dimensions of the search for world order through a transition to democracy in the Muslim world, beginning with Iraq in the Middle East. In particular, the legitimacy of a "so-called" broader Middle East initiative is questioned, by comparing it with the Turkish experience of nation-building and the case of Afghanistan.

The US hegemony and world order

When President George W. Bush declared war against Iraq as the central front of the US war on terrorism there was no question in his mind that Saddam Hussein had links to al-Qaeda and possessed WMD. No evidence of WMD was found by the UN inspectors nor has the link between al-Qaeda and the Baghdad regime been proven since the removal of Saddam Hussein from power. The Bush administration dismissed the importance of international legitimacy based on the UN observers' reports and the UN Security Council's resolutions and acted unilaterally according to its own interests.

From the outset there were strong anti-war campaigns warning that the US-led occupation of Iraq would bring a long period of chronic instability. But Washington claimed that changing Saddam Hussein's authoritarian regime would bring a transition to democracy with a "domino effect" in the Middle East. There was no forward planning about who the US-led coalition would transfer power, authority and sovereignty to after removing Saddam. As Bush stated at the beginning of the war, Washington's primary concern was to secure Iraqi oil production against sabotage or attacks by Saddam's forces.[1] This concern was perceived as Washington's intention to establish long-term military bases in order to exploit Iraq's vast energy resources rather than to bring democracy to the Iraqi people.

With the US-led occupation of Iraq in March 2003 and its aftermath, the Bush administration lost its legitimacy and credibility in the post-Cold War order. The human rights scandals in the Abu Ghraib prison in April 2004 forced the Americans to see their powerful image from the perspective of Islamic public opinion. The scandals proved to the American public and the international community that the war in Iraq was wrong and questioned the legitimacy of Washington's engagement in the Middle East. More importantly, they destroyed the last element of trust in the US commitment to build democracy in the Middle East as a model for socio-economic and political transformation in the Islamic world. As Amin Saikal argues in Chapter 11, Muslims have a very poor image of the United States as a power dedicated to democratic and human rights causes. In reality, US "domino democratization" has fallen in the opposite direction ("domino terrorization") of anti-American sentiment and distrust in the region, as we are witnessing now. The US invasion of Iraq created a power vacuum that became the lure for fundamentalist terrorists in the region.

Why did the Turkish parliament reject Turkey's involvement?

Turkey had been a trusted strategic partner of US administrations in the region ever since it became a member of the North Atlantic Treaty Organization (NATO) in 1952. On 1 March 2003, when the Turkish parliament voted not to permit the deployment of US troops from Turkish territory to attack Iraq, the trust between the two states was damaged. Ironically, this time democracy was at work in its peculiar Turkish style. The elected members of the parliament acted in accordance with public opinion against the closed-door policies of Ankara and Washington. An overwhelming 94 per cent of Turkish people, as well as the military and the Turkish president, Ahmed Sezer, opposed the US-led war in Iraq on the following grounds.[2] First, the Turkish military élite was concerned about the possibility of Iraq's disintegration. A perceived US failure in rebuilding a united Iraq or a religiously provoked civil war in Baghdad would bring instability to Turkish borders. Second, the Turkish president based his opposition on the legal grounds that the Turkish constitution required international legitimacy. Third, Turkey faced a series of Kurdish refugee flows and serious economic losses after 1991. Some members of the government, including Prime Minister Recep Tayyip Erdoğan, thought that these problems would reoccur.[3] Fourth, the Turkish public expressed Islamic solidarity with the innocent Iraqi people and felt deeply insulted by the caricaturized image of Turks as greedy oriental bazaar dealers trying to profit from the situation.

Despite continuing opposition, US pressure via economic deals forced the Turkish parliament to authorize the government to send troops to Iraq in October 2003. In order to justify the Turkish involvement to the public, both the government and the military emphasized Turkey's duty on humanitarian grounds to protect the rights of Turkmen and to help the Iraqi people, though their real concern was not to be left out at the negotiating table when Iraq's future was discussed. The new decision was not welcomed by the Iraqi Governing Council (IGC) and in particular by Kurds in northern Iraq. The IGC's opposition, in fact, enforced the image of the new Turkish government of the Justice and Development Party (*Adalet ve Kalklnma Partisi* – AKP) as the first Islamic party in power, in the eyes of domestic public opinion, when it suspended its reluctant decision to join a Western coalition against its Muslim neighbour.[4]

Two weeks later, Turkish society was shaken by terrorist attacks in Istanbul on 15 and 20 November.[5] For Turks, the attacks in Istanbul had a specific meaning in terms of punishing their adherence to secularism and the Turkish state's Western orientation, which manifested itself as a strategic partnership with the United States after World War II and a desire to join the European Union since 1963. Turkey's place in the international system has been unresolved since the modernization policies of the Ottoman Empire. On the one hand, owing to its Muslim population, Turkey has never been identified as a European state; on the other, Turkish modernity and secularism have been criticized by Muslim countries since the abolition of the Caliphate in 1924. The Abu Hafz al-Masri Brigades, a group linked to al-Qaeda, claimed responsibility for the attacks and accused Turkey of joining "the Crusader Atlantic alliance" against the Islamic world. A statement on the Al Mujahidoun website warned Turkey to withdraw its soldiers from Afghanistan, to stop relations with Israel and not to join the US-led occupation of Iraq.[6]

Both the opposition from the IGS to Turkey's involvement and the terrorist attacks in Istanbul draw attention to Turkey's role in the disorder in the aftermath of 11 September 2001. In Washington, some policy makers argued that the attacks in Istanbul reinforced Turkey's relevance as a "model" of liberal democracy and moderate Islam for other Muslim countries. The US government has always emphasized the importance of a democratic and secular Turkey and has rarely criticized the military coups and the role of the Turkish army in politics. Contradictorily, the reaction against the American desire to promote Turkey as a "model" came from Turkish military circles whereas some among the right-wing and pro-American élite supported the idea. The deputy chief of the Turkish General Staff, Ilker Başbuğ, stated that Turkey had no intention of being a "model" for moderate Islam as promoted by the US administration. He argued that the fundamental characteristics of the Turkish Republic were defined in the 1982 constitution: it was to be a democratic, secular and social state governed by the rule of law, which implies an incompatibility with Islam.[7] Turkish military and secular circles are sceptical about what "moderate" Islam means in relation to "secularism" and about Turkey's role in the new US broader Middle East initiative, as I will discuss later.[8] Despite US support for Turkey's EU membership and the Baku–Tbilisi–Ceyhan pipeline project to transfer Caspian oil to world markets via Turkey, clear signals of a growing tension between Ankara and Washington emerged after the 1991 Gulf war.[9] The next section explains why Turkish regional interests diverged from those of Washington on the following issues: the Kurdish issue, the rise of Islamism and the war on terror, and relations with Iran and Syria.

Divergence of interests between Ankara and Washington in the Middle East

Turkey's relations with the Middle Eastern states have been determined and constrained by two threat perceptions. The first challenge was the rise of Kurdish nationalism, perceived as a threat to the Kemalist state ideology, which aims to preserve Turkish national unity through territorial integrity. The second was the growth of *"irtica"* (reactionary Islam), which poses a threat to the secular character of the Turkish state. Subsequently, when terrorist activities became the modus operandi of both Kurdish nationalism and Islamic fundamentalism, this created an *idée fixe* of a Turkish security paradox that has been shaping Turkish domestic and foreign policies since the 1980s.

The future of Kurds in northern Iraq

After the 1991 Gulf war, preventing the establishment of an independent Kurdish state in northern Iraq became a major foreign policy aim for Turkey. American and Turkish security interests first diverged on this issue: for the United States, Saddam Hussein's regime remained the primary threat to Washington's interests in the region; for Turkey, the establishment of a federal or even an autonomous region for the Kurds was perceived as a real threat to its national security.

The Kurdish issue has both regional and international dimensions that contribute to the complex nature of the Middle Eastern state system. After the collapse of the Ottoman Empire in 1918, Kurds became the largest stateless nation, occupying the borders of Turkey, Iraq, Syria and

Iran. Many scholars argued that an independent Kurdish state was unlikely unless there was a major disruption of the existing state system in the region. The overthrow of Saddam Hussein radically upset the regional dynamics and could have given Turkey the opportunity of independent military intervention in Iraq in order to determine the future of Iraqi Kurds. American politicians and the international media speculated on this possibility, given the fact that Turkish military forces had declared that the future establishment of a Kurdish state or federal region that included Mosul and Kirkuk would be a *casus belli.*

Between 1991 and 2003, the Kurds were very close to establishing an independent state in Iraq or, at least, an autonomous entity federated with the rest of the country. A de facto Iraqi Kurdish state was established when elections were held in May 1992. The Kurdistan National Assembly (KNA) and the Kurdistan Regional Government (KRG) were created within which the Kurdish Democratic Party (KDP), led by Masud Barzani, and the Patriotic Union of Kurdistan (PUK), led by Jalal Talabani, represented the Kurds. This Kurdish entity was protected by the so-called "Kurdish safe haven" and the "no-fly zone" in northern Iraq under Operation Provide Comfort (OPC), which was intended to provide security and humanitarian assistance to refugee camps along the Turkish border. The safe haven was supported economically by the UN Oil-for-Food programme until the removal of Saddam Hussein.[10]

Turkey has accordingly been evaluating and adjusting its foreign policy goals since the Gulf war. In the first place, Turkey consistently opposed the creation of an independent Kurdish state or an Iraqi federal unity. In particular, it did not want the oil-rich cities of Mosul and Kirkuk to be ceded to an autonomous Kurdish federal unit. According to Ankara, an independent Kurdish state benefiting from the economic income of these cities' oil revenues had the potential to be a prosperous example for Turkey's Kurds. Secondly, if a permanent Kurdistan federal region were created, Ankara was concerned that the rights of Turkmen should be protected by the establishment of a Turkmen federal unit to include the cities of Mosul and Kirkuk.

Furthermore, Ankara implemented a contradictory policy that the Iraqi Kurdish authority had to be kept strong enough to be able to prevent activities by the PKK (*Partia Karkaren Kurdistan* – Kurdistan Workers' Party) in the region while at the same time kept weak enough to prevent the creation of an independent Kurdish state.[11] Turkish military forces did not hesitate to cross the Iraqi border and enter the no-fly zone in 1995 and 1997 in order to attack the PKK camps in northern Iraq.

Turkey also had to come to a tacit agreement with the United States that Washington would not criticize Turkish military incursions if Ankara permitted the continuation of Operation Northern Watch (as OPC was renamed in 1997), despite the fact that the Turkish military élite regarded the OPC/ONW with suspicion as part of US plans to establish a Kurdish state at the expense of Turkey's territorial integrity.[12]

Finally, Ankara was also sceptical about Washington's reluctance to clamp down on the PKK. Despite the arrest of PKK leader Abdullah Öcalan in February 1999, the PKK/KADEK is still perceived as a threat to Turkish national security. The second conflict between Ankara and Washington was a result of this different threat perception, and of the definition of terrorist organizations and the war on terror.

The rise of Islamism and terrorism

According to Ankara, the US government clearly differentiates al-Qaeda and Ansar al-Islam from other terrorist organizations that are perceived as a threat to the national interests of other states under the rubric of the global war on terror. The Turkish state has been suffering from terrorism through bomb attacks by Islamic groups against the secular Turkish élite since the 1980s. In the early 1990s, a new terrorist group, the Turkish Hizbullah, particularly targeted the Kurdish cities of south-eastern Turkey and killed PKK supporters. The government remained silent in the face of accusations that there were no official investigations and that its security forces were making use of terrorist organizations such as the Turkish Hizbullah and IBDA-C as counter-terrorist groups.[13] When the leaders of the Turkish Hizbullah were captured in a series of security operations in January 2000, it was stated that the goal of this terrorist organization was to introduce an Islamic state based on the Iranian model.[14]

Whereas the relationship between Kurdish terrorism, Islamism and counter-state policies had been criticized in Turkish internal affairs, it was interpreted differently in Turkey's relations with the United States. For the Turkish military and political élites, Washington's war on terror seemed to be based on a double standard, which ignored Turkish interests. For Ankara, the overlap between the Kurdish nationalists and Islamists was in the use of terrorism that had cross-border dimensions. For the United States, its war on terrorism was linked to the "axis of evil", which had to be combated in order to prevent the provision of WMD to terrorists. After Iraq, North Korea and Iran would be next in line to be dealt with to make the world more secure. Clearly, US hegemonic designs would not coincide with Turkish national and regional interests. Ankara was concerned that the military intervention in Iraq should not be extended to Iran and Syria, as implied in US policy makers' indecisive statements.

This gave rise to the third conflict of interest between Ankara and Washington in the US-led world order. Turkey aimed to adopt a cooperative approach to its neighbours, determined by the divergence of its interests from those of the United States as regards the future of Iraqi Kurds and the rise of Islamic terrorism. Syria and Iran shared the Turkish fear of an independent Kurdish state at the cost of rearranging their territorial borders and the possibility of long-term US military establishment in the region, and this led to a new rapprochement between these three states. The development of Ankara's relations with Tehran and Damascus was the cause of the third conflict of interests between the Turkish and US governments.

The Turkish rapprochement with Syria and Iran

Traditionally, Syria and Iran were perceived as enemies by Ankara for historical and ideological reasons. Turkey accused Syria of giving active support to separatist PKK activities and likewise Iran of supporting Islamic fundamentalist groups since the 1980s. In the early 1990s, Turkey and Iran represented two contradictory models for post-Soviet republics in Central Asia. In the mid-1990s, the rivalry between the two states intensified over the transportation of Caspian, and particularly Azerbaijani, oil resources. Therefore, the evolution of relations from conflict to cooperation between the three states was difficult and experienced a series of crises between 1993 and 2003.

The first sign of a rapprochement between Ankara and Damascus was in 1993 when both sides signed a security protocol regarding the PKK and other terrorist organizations that were against Turkish national interests. For the first time, Syria recognized the PKK as a terrorist organization and promised not to provide a base for its activities. Two years later, in August 1995, the Turkish, Iranian and Syrian foreign ministers came together and expressed their displeasure at not being invited to attend the Kurdish Conference held on 23 July in Paris, although officials from the United Kingdom, France and the United States attended. When the US government brought the KDP and PUK leaders, Barzani and Talabani, together in Washington in September 1998 to promote a commitment to a federative Kurdish political entity in Iraq, Ankara felt that it had been left out of the final decisions in its own backyard. Consequently, Ankara's decision to establish good neighbourly relations with Damascus and Tehran was shaped by the Kurdish issue and implemented independently from US policies.

A major crisis occurred between Turkey and Syria in November 1998 when Ankara threatened Damascus with military intervention if the PKK leader, Öcalan, was not expelled. Interestingly enough, after the presidential election victory of the moderate Khatami in 1997, it was Iran that contributed to mediation of the Turkish–Syrian crisis. The Iranian foreign minister, Kamal Kharrazi, reportedly brought initial word to Ankara that Damascus was ready to end its support for the PKK and expel Öcalan.[15] The capture of Öcalan in February 1999 was a turning point in Turkish relations with Syria, which gained a new momentum with Bashar al-Asad's accession in 2000. Meanwhile, the extension of EU candidate status to Turkey in December 1999 by the Helsinki European Council had important impacts on Turkish relations with Syria and Iran. Ankara favoured cooperation with its neighbours because it began to regard security as a cross-border issue. Thus, one of the main arguments of this chapter is that Turkey prioritized its relations with Europe over its relations with the United States. The Turkish decision to avoid involvement in any conflict in the Middle East and in the military intervention in Iraq reflects Ankara's determination to fulfil its EU candidacy expectations. The direct impact of relations between Turkey and the European Union on Ankara's foreign affairs was the change in policy from conflict and containment to active cooperative engagement in the region.

Cross-border issues and trans-regional cooperation between Europe and the Middle East

The European Union has been critical of Turkey's proximity to the Middle East and regarded it as a source of instability at the margins of Europe. Neither policy makers nor public opinion in Europe want the European Union to have a real border with the Middle East, where it might become directly involved in conflicts in Syria, Iraq and Iran. This perception was intensified by the unconventional security challenges arising from the post-9/11 disorder. Both European and Middle Eastern states are aware of the relationship between terrorism and the black market economy in Europe, Central Asia and the Middle East, and Turkey is at the centre of this trans-regional link. Turkey's priority of initiating regional cooperation with the particular aim of controlling these problems is a reflection of Turkish–EU relations. In the past, Turkey followed a "de-Middle Easternization" of its policies and identity and favoured "Europeanization" in order to be regarded as part of the West.[16] However, post–Cold War and post-9/11 conditions have brought new challenges to regional dynamics both in Europe and in the Middle East.

Unconventional security challenges

Turkey shares EU concerns that terrorism, drug trafficking, money laundering and non-narcotics smuggling are cross-border issues and that trans-regional cooperation is necessary to fight them. Whereas Turkey is seen as a "danger zone" from EU members' perspective, an unstable Iraq is considered to be the real danger for the Turkish, Syrian and Iranian governments. The latter perceive northern Iraq, where the black market economy is in operation, as a crucial transfer link to Europe through Turkey and to Central Asia through Iran.[17] Although the EU perspective forces Turkey to be more actively engaged in addressing these issues in a wider regional context, its "national security paradox" establishes a link to the economic dimension of the Kurdish issue within this framework. The economic development of the Kurdish regions of Turkey, Syria, Iran and Iraq would help to improve the basic living conditions of Kurds and reduce their socio-political alienation from central governments. Such development could also attract foreign and international investors' attention not only to the oil- and gas-rich Iraqi Kurdistan but also to underdeveloped areas in the region where the Kurds are strongly represented.

The exchange of high-level official visits between Ankara, Damascus and Tehran in January and February 2004 indicated the beginning of a rapprochement based on common economic and political interests among Iraq's neighbours. Ankara was assured by Damascus and Tehran that they would not permit any terrorist activities against the Turkish state's security in their territories.[18] The Turkish foreign minister, Abdullah Gül, stated that ongoing conflicts and instability were major obstacles to the economic development of the Middle East and that regional cooperation could be developed to overcome such difficulties. Turkey's membership in the European Union would be beneficial to both Europe and the Middle East. According to Gül, Turkey's neighbours communicated to Ankara that its EU membership would increase stability and economic welfare in the region. Turkey's membership would also contribute to the European Union's role of challenging the US hegemony and establishing stability in Iraq, as defined in the EU Strategy Document.[19] In June 2004, the European Commission proposed to undertake multilateral action in Iraq for its immediate future, the post-election period and its medium-term development, all of which were defined as the new EU strategy for Iraq. The following three medium-term objectives were suggested: "the development of a stable and democratic Iraq; the establishment of an open, stable, sustainable and diversified market economy; Iraq's economic and political integration into its region and the open international system."[20]

Ankara also has the potential to ease tensions between its neighbours and with the United States. In particular, Syria and Iran fear Washington's future plans, wondering whether they will be the next front in the US war on terrorism. Turkey expressed its concern earlier than the

United States about the Iranian nuclear programme and Syrian missile capabilities, as well as their possession of WMD on its borders. The next section explains how Turkey's aim to join the European Union influenced Turkish perceptions of its own role in the region. In particular, the nature of Turkey's relations changed from conflicting interests to co-operation and dialogue with regional states.

The European regional order as a model for the Middle East

Despite the high expectation in US circles and among Iraqi Kurds that Turkey might independently intervene to occupy northern Iraq, Turkish "military intervention" never materialized. Turkish policy makers were determined not to compromise the 40-year pro-EU policy with an irrational military adventure. Rather than using force, Turkey initiated a search for diplomatic and peaceful solutions. The first summit of the foreign ministers of Iraq's neighbours and regional states was held in January 2003, and the fifth summit took place in Kuwait on 15 February 2004, involving Turkish, Egyptian, Jordanian, Saudi, Iraqi and Kuwaiti foreign ministers. At this summit, Gül came up with a new suggestion that the Middle Eastern states should follow the example of European unification and that this intention should be brought to the attention of the Security Council's permanent members through the mediation of UN Secretary-General Kofi Annan.[21]

Turkey adopted the EU stance on Iraq, which prioritizes the following five issues: the international community has a major contribution to make in the shaping of the future of the Iraqi people; the European Union encourages the United Nations to play a central role in the process restoring Iraqi sovereignty; the European Union suggests that Iraq's neighbours should support stability in Iraq and the region; the European Union reaffirms its own commitment to the political and economic reconstruction of Iraq and welcomes the participation of international financial institutions; and, finally, "as part of the process of regional security and stability the EU reaffirms its commitments to bring the Israeli-Palestinian peace process to a successful conclusion through the implementation of the steps foreseen in the Quartet's [the European Union, the United States, the United Nations and Russia] roadmap, keeping within established timelines."[22]

The Turkish, Syrian and Iranian foreign ministers reached a common policy on the future of Iraq as an independent nation-state based on territorial integrity and political unity rather than an ethnically or religiously defined federal unity.[23] The three states declared their commitment to a democratic and stable Iraq on their borders.[24] They also clearly echoed the EU position that the United Nations must play a central role in transferring full sovereignty to the Iraqi people. Turkey prioritizes the use of diplomacy in international organizations, such as the Organization of the Islamic Conference (OIC) and NATO, over unilateral action. The sixth summit of the foreign ministers of Iraq's neighbours and regional states took place within the framework of the thirty-first OIC meeting in Istanbul on 14–16 June 2004. The Iraq crisis, the Israeli–Palestinian conflict, international terrorism and the broader Middle East plan were among the main issues on the broader agenda of the OIC, and the Turkish president emphasized the importance of democracy for regional development and stability.[25] Furthermore, at NATO's Istanbul Summit on 28–29 June, NATO members agreed on three "soft power" initiatives in order to have a greater presence in the region (as Fred Tanner explains further in Chapter 20).

According to a Turkish foreign ministry statement, Turkey's Iraq policy is based on the idea that "the independence, territorial integrity, sovereignty and national unity of Iraq" should be preserved through internationally recognized norms. Moreover, the determination of Iraq's future is up to the free will of the Iraqi people and Iraq's natural resources must belong to them.[26] Turkish decision makers are probably using the European Union and multilateral forums as a means to justify their active engagement in the region without sacrificing the US partnership. Syria and Iran seem to be in accord with these Turkish views in order to prevent US military intervention in their countries that would further destabilize the Middle East.

Building democracy and stability in the Middle East

Since the US-led occupation of Iraq, current political and academic debates are focused on whether or not democracy can be imposed by external force. At the G-8 summit meeting in Georgia on 9 June 2004, George W. Bush launched a broader Middle East initiative without actually calling it that.[27] This "initiative" aims to promote "Western-style" democracy throughout the Middle East (including non-Arab countries such as Afghanistan, Iran, Israel, Pakistan and Turkey) and North Africa, encourages greater NATO involvement in Iraq and proposes a resolution to the Israeli–Palestinian conflict. Opposition came from President Chirac of France, who joined the Arab world in deriding the initiative.[28]

The legitimacy of a so-called broader Middle East initiative

Even before the initiative was launched, there were already strongly critical voices in Western and Arab countries. The initiative was seen as a priority objective of US domestic policy directed at influencing the US election in November 2004 and was presented as a major goal of US foreign policy and its war on terrorism. President Chirac's opposition at the 2004 G-8 summit echoed existing criticisms on three issues. First, the initiative would be counterproductive if it became another US-dictated solution that failed to consult and cooperate with regional states and societies. There is no ready-made formula for democracy that is instantly transposable from one country to another and there is no single "Western-style" democracy. Second, the Palestinian–Israeli conflict had to be the main concern in a search for democratization and stability in the region. To clear the path for this, the United States must drop its absolute support for Israel. Third, the Bush administration's high expectation that such an initiative could contribute to the transition to democratization and produce secular, modernized and pro-Western systems was misleading. Any such attempt would be regarded as the imposition of Western values on Arabic and Islamic cultures. If the US administration does not change its position on these three issues, it will certainly be disappointed in its expectations that Iraq will establish a nascent democratization in the region.

Turkey's position on the future of the Middle East as part of the US-determined world order is very clear: internationally recognized norms must be the basis for facilitating permanent peace and stability in the region, within which the Israeli–Palestinian conflict is the first obstacle to be overcome. Turkey, as the one regional state that enjoys the trust and confidence of both the Palestinians and the Israelis, is willing and ready to mediate to put the peace process back on track.[29] After the beginning of the Arab–Israeli peace process in 1991, Turkish governments established relations with Israel based on strategic and economic interests without provoking a rupture in Turkey's relations with the Palestinians. Although the Turkish–Israeli Security Agreement of 1996 complicated relations with the Arab states, it now serves Turkey to be a mediator between the two sides. Syria supports Turkey's role as a mediator between Israel and the Arab states.[30] Israel has also made it clear to Ankara that it favours the territorial integrity and political unity of Iraq and values its relations with Turkey.

Furthermore, Turkish policy makers have argued that US initiatives that aim to bring democracy and stability to the Middle East must take into account the political culture of the region and should prescribe gradual and evolutionary change.[31] The Turkish experience itself proves that democratization is a complex and long process, which unfolds differently in different countries based on specific socio-historical, political and economic factors. The Turkish case is by no means a "blueprint" or a "model", as presented by the US administration, but it does offer a historical experience from which important lessons can be drawn for Muslim societies.

The Turkish experience in nation-building

The US administration's emphasis on democracy and nation-building misleadingly equates nation-building with state-building. In Iraq, the issues are primarily about state-building, ranging from security challenges to the transfer of full sovereignty to a legitimate government. As long as Islam serves as the source of sovereignty and collective identity, the relationship between Islam and nation-state-building deserves careful reconsideration rather than Islam being presented as incompatible with modern Western values and institutions. This is where the Turkish experience with nation-state-building becomes crucial for correctly understanding this complex process.

As the first Islamic society to experience a democratic transformation, Turkey has gone through a series of crises, which are to a certain extent still unresolved and relevant to the current problems in the Islamic world. There are four major issues. First, the relationship between Islam and secular nationalism is intriguing: Islam has served as a source of national integrity in Turkish society despite the attempts of modern state builders to remove religion from the political discourse. The majority of Turkish people still describe themselves as Muslims, although in a modern and Europeanized manner. A second issue is the role of the military in politics: Turkey had three military coups and the role of the Turkish army as the guardian of secularism is not an appealing model for Western democratization. Third, Turkey has a strong state tradition, which is interrelated with the protection of secularism. The Turkish state synthesized Islam with secularism in a paradoxical way. Although secularism became a modernist and "didactic" ideology, which teaches and promotes a modern way of life, the Turkish state did not renounce Islam, but kept it under constant review and control.[32] Fourth, the tension between the secular character of the state and the Islamic identity of society in Turkey leads to serious concerns in the West. It is not surprising that Turkey has never been regarded as a European state. Turkey's EU candidate status has become a saga since Turkey first applied in 1964. Ironically, Turkey is not considered part of the Arab world either since it abolished the Caliphate in 1924. However, the Turkish success in constitutional and parliamentary governance proves that Islam is compatible with Western democracy and, like any other religion, should not be mystified.

The most important historical lesson to be drawn from the Turkish experience is that the solutions to these problems were not imposed on Turkey by external powers. On the contrary, the Turkish people decided on their own future in the face of the imperialist designs of Western powers at the beginning of the twentieth century.[33] It seems that we are witnessing similar transition processes in Afghanistan and Iraq at the beginning of the twenty-first century. Paradoxically, however, the process of nation-building is being imposed on them by external powers.

In Afghanistan, after the Taliban regime was overthrown in 2001, the first national elections took place on 9 November 2004 as prescribed by the UN Security Council. Amidst allegations of corruption and bribery, some commentators argued that the Bush administration, the United Nations and the international community had unnecessarily rushed the elections when the country was not ready. The key issue was whether this democratic move would be followed by local and regional parliamentary elections in April 2005. They did take place as planned, but we still do not know what the country's future will bring. Both pre- and post-election developments reveal the sharp contrast between the US-designed plans and the reality of societal factors and tribal structures.

Turkey actively engaged in the reconstruction of Afghanistan through multilateral efforts under the international legitimacy of the UN International Security Assistance Force (ISAF) and NATO. The major challenge these organizations had to face was to prevent conflict between the interim government of President Hamid Karzai, tribal forces and the war lords, who have their own small armies. The ISAF and NATO forces were relatively successful in establishing order in Kabul, but they have not been able to extend this tenuous stability to the rest of Afghanistan. The United States failed to recognize the existence of the strong tribal system, which began operating within the US-created power vacuum, and the fact that the construction of state institutions to provide for the security and safety of the country would take longer than planned. The Afghan example demonstrates that the main obstacles to the transition to democracy and stability are not only the reconstruction of infrastructure and institutions to improve people's daily lives in health, education and employment but also the creation of a national consciousness to strengthen a people's unity.[34] When the Bush administration decided to intervene militarily in Iraq, Paul Wolfowitz argued that it would be easier in Iraq than it had been in Afghanistan.[35] How wrong he was.

Since the US-led occupation of Iraq in March 2003, the country has become a new battlefield between Sunni and Shiite sectarian forces. Nobody knows how many Iraqi civilians have lost their lives – the numbers range between 30,000 and 100,000 depending on the source. The price of the transition to democracy seems to be rather high in Iraq.

The transitional period began with the formation of a fully sovereign Iraqi Interim Government (IIG), which took power on 28 June 2004 in accordance with the Coalition Provisional Authority (CPA) Law of Administration. The first election took place on 31 January 2005 to establish the National Assembly, which led to the formation of the Iraqi Transitional Government.[36] The IIG had been established on 1 June 2004 and then was given international legitimacy by the UN Security Council on 8 June 2004. Resolution 1546 looked forward to "the end of the occupation and the assumption of full responsibility and authority by a fully sovereign and independent Interim Government of Iraq", which led to the dissolution of the CPA.[37]

The United States first decided that the interim constitution would be drafted by a committee, hand-picked by the US-appointed Iraqi Governing Council (IGC). This decision was challenged by the *fatwa* of Grand Ayatollah Ali al-Sistani that any constitution-making committee had to be elected. Washington conceded to that criticism and called for direct elections to a constitutional assembly in January 2005. Despite serious delays to the August 2005 deadline, this newly elected assembly drafted a constitution that was approved by a public referendum held on 15 October 2005.[38] The results of the referendum were announced and approved by the United Nations on 25 October 2005.[39]

The main bones of contention in drafting the Iraqi constitution were the issue of federalism and the role of Islam in legislation. The Sunnis – the second-largest grouping in Iraq and the dominant group under Saddam Hussein's regime – do not want federalism, which would break up Iraq and deprive Sunnis of the country's oil wealth. The autonomous Kurdish area in the north and the self-ruled Shiite region in the south are the oil-rich areas of Iraq. Sunnis had boycotted the election in January 2005, but they realized that this allowed the Shiites and the Kurds to gain an overwhelming majority and shape the constitution. Three Sunni parties – the Iraqi Islamic party, the Iraqi National Dialogue and the General Conference for the People of Iraq – announced that they had formed an alliance to participate in the parliamentary elections on 15 December 2005.[40] The Shiite-led United Iraqi Alliance (UIA) won the vast majority of seats in parliament but failed to obtain an absolute majority. While the main Kurdish Alliance lost few seats, Sunni Arab parties increased their representation in comparison with the January 2005 elections.[41] In February 2006, the UIA voted for Ibrahim al-Jaafari as prime minister, with the task of forming Iraq's first independent government since the removal of Saddam Hussein in 2003. Al-Jaafari's task is a very sensitive and difficult one in view of the need to maintain the balance between the Shiite, Sunni and Kurdish factions in order to stabilize the country. The existing constitution created a weak central government and caused sectarian tensions among Iraqis. In particular, Sunnis are extremely concerned that federalism would give Shiites and Kurds too much power as well as control of Iraqi oil resources, and they want to endorse changes in the Constitution. The tensions between Islamists and secularists and sectarian factions are the main challenges that the new government has to resolve, notwithstanding the requirement to promote democracy and security in the country.[42] Iraq's actual transformation to democracy began in December 2005 and it will not be an easy process. The following few years, if not decades, will prove how difficult it will be, as we know from developments in Afghanistan. The developments following the US-manoeuvred regime changes in both these countries demonstrate that the promotion of liberal democracy and nation-building in Islamic societies is a very complex and difficult task.

Conclusion

Three important conclusions emerge from my analysis in this chapter, which reflect the Turkish perspective on the future of Iraq, regional stability and the US unipolar concert. First, the US-led military intervention in Iraq has resulted in an unstable and insecure Iraqi society, which is potentially dangerous for the whole Middle East. The successful rebuilding of a viable Iraqi state will depend on gaining international legitimacy and regional cooperation. The new Iraqi government must obtain international legitimacy through the multilateral efforts of the United Nations, the European Union, NATO and OIC members, as well as Iraq's neighbours. Such a broad international legitimacy might help to change the Iraqi people's cynical perception that the overthrow of Saddam Hussein's regime was part of the United States' hegemonic designs. Second, as in Afghanistan, the institutional reconstruction of Iraq must be supported by a nation-building process that appeals to both Sunnis and Shiites. The Turkish foreign minister, in cooperation with his Syrian and Iranian counterparts, has expressed Turkey's preference for a sovereign Iraqi nation-state rather than an ethnically or religiously defined federal unity. In the light of Turkey's candidacy for the European Union, Ankara has adopted EU policies on the future of Iraq rather than US-determined policies. Third, the current insurgency in Iraq confirms that the legacy of anti-imperialism runs very deep in the Middle East and frustration with the post-intervention chaos can easily turn into "anti-Western" (particularly anti-US and anti-UK) feelings and movements. If the West wants a secure Middle East and world order, regional peace and stability can be achieved only by recognizing the innate legitimacy of indigenous people to determine the future of their own societies without hegemonic interference.

Acknowledgements

I would like to thank and acknowledge the support of the Department of International Relations, the London School of Economics and Political Science and the Department of International Politics, University of Wales, Aberystwyth. In addition, Martha Mundy, of the Anthropology Department of the LSE, and Amin Saikal, of the Australian National University, were very constructive in their criticisms and comments. I am grateful to Derya Göçer for her efficient research assistance, and also to Cathy Suzuki for valuable help. Finally, I wish to thank the anonymous referees for their constructive comments and criticisms.

Notes

1. "President Bush Discusses the Iraqi Interim Government", White House Press Release, 1 June 2004, ⟨http://www.whitehouse.gov/news/releases/2004/06/20040601-2.html⟩ (accessed 8 March 2006).
2. Justus Leicht and Peter Schwarz, "Turkish Parliament Votes down US War Plans", 4 March 2003, ⟨http://www.wsws.org/articles/2003/mar2003/turk-m04.shtml⟩ (accessed 8 March 2006).
3. "Erdoğan Washington Post'a yazdı: Kuzey Irak güvenliğimiz için kritik", *Milliyet*, 21 April 2003, ⟨http://www.milliyet.com⟩.
4. The AKP won the elections in November 2002 with 34.2 per cent of the total votes and 363 of the 550 seats in the Turkish Grand National Assembly. The AKP became the first non-coalition government for 15 years.
5. On 15 November 2003, bombs exploded in front of two synagogues and then two more devastating blasts at the British Consulate and the HSBC bank buildings followed on 20 November. "Duaya Bomba", *Hürriyet*, 16 November 2003; "El Katil", *Hürriyet*, 21 November 2003.
6. "Al-Qaida Statement: The Cars of Death Will Not Stop", *Guardian*, 21 November 2003, p. 4.
7. "Başbuğ: ABD PKK'ya karşı somut adım atmalı", *NTVMSNBC*, 19 March 2004, ⟨http://www.ntvmsnbc.com⟩.
8. Hasan Pulur, "Törpülenmiş Laiklik", *Milliyet*, 8 April 2004.
9. Ayla Göl, "The Politics of the Baku-Tbilisi-Ceyhan Pipeline: Turkish Foreign Policy towards the Caucasus", paper presented at the Association for the Study of Nationalities 9th Annual World Convention, Columbia University, New York, 15–17 April 2004.
10. The creation of no-fly zones, whereby Iraqi planes were not allowed to fly north of the 36th parallel or south of the 32nd parallel, relied on UN Security Council Resolution 688 of 1991. The Oil-for-Food programme was established by US-proposed Resolution 986 in 1997.
11. The PKK was established in 1974 and launched its first terrorist attack in 1984. The party changed its name to the Kurdistan Freedom and Democracy Congress (KADEK) in order to disassociate itself from PKK's terrorist stance. In November 2003, KADEK was replaced by the Kurdistan People's Congress (Kontra-Gel) to indicate its new democratic character and declared ceasefire. However, Turkish politicians and the media still refer to this organization as the PKK or the PKK/KADEK.

12. Kemal Kirişçi, "Turkey and the Muslim Middle East", in Alan Makovsky and Sabri Sayari, eds, *Turkey's New World: Changing Dynamics in Turkish Foreign Policy* (Washington DC: Brookings Institution, 2000), p. 45.

13. "What Is Turkey's Hizbullah?", A Human Rights Watch Backgrounder, 16 February 2000, ⟨http://hrw.org/english/docs/2000/02/16/turkey3057.htm⟩ (accessed 2 March 2006); see also *Turkey: Human Rights Watch World Report 2000*, ⟨http://www.hrw.org/wr2k/⟩ (accessed 8 March 2006).

14. "Istanbul Police in Islamist Shoot-out", 18 January 2000, ⟨http://news.bbc.co.uk/1/hi/world/europe/607729.stm⟩ (accessed 8 March 2006).

15. Barçın Yınanç and Seval Çevikcan, "Harrazi eli boş geldi", *Milliyet*, 10 October 1998.

16. Olivier Roy, "Turkey – A World Apart, or Europe's New Frontier?" in Olivier Roy, ed., *Turkey Today: A European Country?* (London: Anthem Press, 2005), p. 24.

17. Ian O. Lesser, "Beyond 'Bridge or Barrier': Turkey's Evolving Security Relations with the West", in Makovsky and Sayari, eds, *Turkey's New World*, p. 211.

18. "Hatemi'den güvence: Düşmanlarınız topraklarımızı kullanamaz", *Milliyet*, 11 January 2004; and "Türkiye-Suriye ilişkisi tırmanşta", *NTVMSNBC*, 6 January 2004.

19. "Turkey and the Middle East: An Interview with Turkish Foreign Minister Abdullah Gül", *Insight Turkey*, Vol. 6, No. 1 (2004), p. 29.

20. "Iraq–EU Relations: A Strategy for the Medium Term", European Commission Press Releases, IP/04/723, 9 June 2004, ⟨http://europa.eu.int/rapid/pressReleasesAction.do?reference=IP/04/723&format=HTML&aged=0&language=en&guiLanguage=en⟩ (accessed 2 March 2006).

21. "Ortadoğu Birliği için ilk adım atıldı", *Milliyet*, 16 February 2004.

22. "Text: EU Declaration on Iraq", *Guardian*, 17 April 2003.

23. "Turkey and the Middle East: An Interview with Turkish Foreign Minister Abdullah Gül", p. 26.

24. "Ankara-Şam ilişkilerinde yeni dönem", *NTVMSNBC*, 7 January 2004.

25. "Sezer: Demokratikleşin", *Milliyet*, 15 June 2004.

26. Turkish Ministry of Foreign Affairs, "Outline: Turkey's Iraq Policy", 21 March 2003, ⟨http://www.iraqwatch.org/government/Turkey/turkey-mfa-iraqpolicy-032103.htm⟩ (accessed 2 March 2006).

27. "Bush: Our Middle East Mission Has Just Begun", *Guardian*, 10 June 2004, p. 1.

28. L. Elliot and D. Teather, "Chirac Derides Push for Democracy", *Guardian*, 10 June 2004, p. 1.

29. "Turkey and the Middle East: An Interview with Turkish Foreign Minister Abdullah Gül", p. 25.

30. *Milliyet*, 19 February 2004.

31. "Turkey and the Middle East: An Interview with Turkish Foreign Minister Abdullah Gül", p. 29.

32. Ernest Gellner, *Muslim Society* (Cambridge: Cambridge University Press, 1981), p. 68.

33. Ayla Göl, "The Place of Foreign Policy in the Transition to Modernity: Turkish Policy towards the South Caucasus, 1918–1920", PhD thesis, University of London, London School of Economics and Political Science, 2000, pp. 269–271.

34. Anatol Lieven, "Don't Forget Afghanistan", *Foreign Policy*, No. 137 (July/Aug 2003), p. 54.

35. Charles V. Pena, "Iraq: The Wrong War", *Insight Turkey*, Vol. 6, No. 1 (2004), p. 31.

36. "Coalition Provisional Authority, Law of Administration for the State of Iraq for the Transitional Period", 8 March 2004, ⟨http://www.cpa-iraq.org⟩.

37. Security Council Resolution 1546 on the situation between Iraq and Kuwait, UN Doc. S/RES/1546 (2004), 8 June 2004, pp. 1–2, ⟨http://daccessdds.un.org/doc/UNDOC/GEN/N04/381/16/PDF/N0438116.pdf?OpenElement⟩ (accessed 2 March 2006).

38. "23 Dead as Shia and Sunni Militia Clash after Raid to Free Hostage", *Guardian*, 28 October 2005.
39. Jonathan Steele, "Iraqi Constitution Yes Vote Approved by UN", *Guardian*, 26 October 2005.
40. Ewen MacAskill, "Sunnis Form Alliance to Fight Election", *Guardian*, 27 October 2005.
41. "Iraqi Shias Win Election Victory", *BBC News*, 21 January 2006, ⟨http://news.bbc.co.uk/1/hi/world/middle_east/4630518.stm⟩ (accessed 8 March 2006).
42. Michael Gregory, "Shi'ite Division May Hamstring Iraq Prime Minister", *Reuters*, 16 February 2006, ⟨http://today.reuters.co.uk⟩.

8

Iran's assessment of the Iraq crisis and the post-9/11 international order

Anoushiravan Ehteshami

Introduction

At least since the early 1970s Iran has been regarded as an important regional player; prior to that it had managed to accumulate considerable strategic value as a weighty pawn in the Cold War chessboard that straddled much of Asia and Europe. But it was the 1979 Islamic revolution that made Iran stand out on the international scene. After the overthrow of the Shah by a coalition of Islamist, liberal and radical forces, Iran emerged as a defiant, fiercely independent, proactively religious, and non-aligned power. Since then, as James Piscatori has noted, there has rarely been a period that "Iran escaped the attention of the world's foreign offices, press, and academic experts on the Middle East and Islam".[1] Dramatic developments in Iran and notable adjustments to its international relations since the late 1980s and the end of the bipolar world have ensured that Iran remains the country to watch and, for other actors in the international system, a growing force to reckon with. However, despite its revolutionary zeal and a reputation for non-conformity and defiance since the revolution, it can be argued that revolutionary Iran has always been a "rational actor" in the classic realist mould. Even some of its excesses can be seen as calculated risks or opportunist responses to difficult situations. Looking back at the post-Khomeini era, one cannot help but be struck by how "normal", largely non-aggressive and pragmatic Iran's foreign policy has been since 1989. The roots of this transformation in Iran's international relations must be found in Iran itself, but it also has much to do with Tehran's calculations about its standing in a changed regional and international environment since the end of the Cold War. So much so, that Iran is now fully engaged in the international system and is playing the more assertive role expected of a regional middle power in the Middle East and North Africa.

For centuries, geography has played a key part in informing Iran's foreign policy. An ancient landmass empire on the Eurasian crossroads, the modern state's regional ambitions extend to much of West Asia. In Iran's case, geography has acted as a single force with two countervailing tendencies. On the one hand, it has facilitated the spread of Persian influence in Asia, and on the other it has exposed Iran to great power rivalries and diplomatic machinations by out of area states. Historically, fears and perceptions of foreign interference have formed the basis of Iranian nationalism. Iranian nationalism, furthermore, has for generations been intertwined with the issue of ensuring Iran's territorial integrity, which in turn has created what Fuller calls "an intensely Irano-centric" view of the world. As he says, in this land "history itself is in part a product of classical geopolitical factors".[2] Geopolitics, therefore, has had, and continues to have, a special place in Iran's conception of its role, and as such must be given a special place in any analysis of Iranian foreign policy.

Iranian perceptions of their environment and historical fears of outside interference were partly responsible for the evolution of the "negative balance" doctrine that at times formed the basis of Iran's pre- and post-revolution foreign policy.[3] The same views have also informed the fierce struggle in Iranians for independence (esteqlal) – both political and economic – from foreign powers. Thus, one of the main battle cries of the revolution was "Esteqlal, Azadi: Jomhouri Eslami" (Independence, Freedom: Islamic Republic), purposefully placing independence as the precondition for the long-cherished goal of freedom. Thus, the attainment of full sovereignty and control over Iran's destiny has for many decades been both a popular and an élite sentiment.

The drive towards regional supremacy has been a feature of Iranian foreign policy. Because of its long history and its geography, Iran sees itself as uniquely qualified to determine, at the very least, the destiny of the Gulf sub-region. Furthermore, it sees itself as one of only a handful of "natural" states in the Middle East, which, by virtue of being an old and territorially established civilization (based around the notion of "Iran-zamin" or a Greater Iran), can and should have influence beyond its borders. Mohammad Reza Shah's long reign was full of evidence of this tendency in Iranian élite thinking after 1953, particularly in the 1970s.[4] Throughout the latter decade Iran strove to become the Gulf region's premier military power and aimed to become the main pillar of the Western security system in the Middle East – to resume, as the Shah himself put it, Iran's "historic responsibilities".[5]

Since 1979, where geopolitics has mattered, Iran has added a religious dimension to its projection of power. Over time, this new factor has formed an extra layer over the deeply felt territorial nationalism of the state. Since the revolution, Islamic issues have emerged to influence Iran's regional profile and its policies towards many of its neighbours. Iran's post-revolution posture has also been affected by what could be called the geopolitics of Islam. In the first instance, Tehran's Messianic Shiism of the early 1980s posed a direct challenge to the regional status quo and the political integrity of Iran's Arab neighbours. In making explicit its demand to speak in the name of Islam, Tehran's revolutionary leaders caused noticeable tensions in the country's relations with Saudi Arabia and other influential Islamic actors in the Muslim world. Today, it is again the geopolitics of Islam that is affecting Iran's world view and its relations with its neighbours.

At the same time, Iran's stand vis-à-vis the Soviet occupation of Afghanistan in the 1980s and Moscow's treatment of its own Muslim population added a religious dimension to Iranian–Soviet relations during the Cold War. Additionally, implicit and explicit support for the growing number of Islamist movements in Afghanistan and elsewhere in the Middle East became a fixture of Iranian foreign policy in its inter-state and sub-state interactions.

In the 1990s, despite a more integrationist and non-ideological foreign policy, Tehran tried to keep pace with the politicized Islamic groups in the Arab world and was active in showing support for Hezbollah in Lebanon, the Front Islamique du Salut (FIS) in Algeria, the Turabi regime in Sudan, Hamas and Islamic Jihad in Palestine, the Muslim Brotherhood in Jordan, the al-Nahda party in Tunisia, and the Jihad group in Egypt. Further afield, Tehran has been quite content to allow itself to be portrayed as a supporter of Islamist movements of all denominations (for example, the Islamic MORO movement in the Philippines in the 1980s and the Bosnian Muslims in the 1990s). One can deduce from Tehran's behaviour that the overt use of Islam, or at least of Islamic symbols, remains a feature of the country's conception of its role. Islam's place in Tehran's formulation of policy and strategic aims has caused serious rifts in – and continues to complicate – its relations with a number of the Sunni-dominated, largely secular-led, Arab states around it. Iran's Islamic revolution and the Iranian leadership's call for Islamic uprisings may have found sympathetic ears in many Arab and Muslim societies in the 1980s, but this call also reinforced Arab élite suspicions of Iranian intentions and encouraged their cautious policies towards Tehran. The "blockage" really only began clearing towards the end of the 1980s, thanks to several developments: the end of the Iran–Iraq war, the rise of a more pragmatic leadership in Iran, the growing importance of oil politics, the Kuwait crisis, and Iran's post–Cold War bridge-building regional strategy. Nonetheless, Iran retains a strong Islamic dimension in its external profile. However, it is fully aware of its fairly small international Shiite base compared with the majority Sunnis who populate many of the Arab and non-Arab states in Asia and North Africa. As such, Tehran treads carefully in inter-Islamic disputes. Although it branded the Taliban as "barbaric", for example, it did not openly attack Pakistan, Saudi Arabia and the United Arab Emirates as the Taliban's key supporters. Moreover, as the only Muslim country dominated and ruled by the Shiite minority sect of Islam, Iran plays on the bigger, pan-Islamic issues in its inter-Islamic relations.

Post–Cold War regional politics: 1990–2001

The end of the Cold War has brought to the fore the importance of the "three Gs" in Iran's foreign relations: geopolitics, geostrategic instabilities, and globalization. With over a decade of the post–Cold War order behind us, Iran is still trying to come to terms with the systemic changes that took place between 1989 and 1991, and in this endeavour is struggling to find its natural place in the increasingly interdependent and globalized international system. For Iran, the 1990s ushered in a new and highly unpredictable era. Since the late 1980s, Tehran has been compelled to function as much as possible within the new international system, which witnessed not only the end of the Cold War and the demise of the Soviet superpower, but also the emergence of the United States as the undisputed extra-regional power in the Middle East.[6] With ethnic resurgence becoming the order of the day in the post–Cold War international situation and with nationalist movements successfully evolving from insurgencies to territorial states, concern about Iran's territorial integrity has also been heightened. Fear that secessionist movements in Iran and on its borders could be used by outside powers to destabilize the country and the regime has struck a chord with Iranian Islamists and nationalists alike.

At least two schools of thought about the new international system have prevailed in Iran.[7] One school welcomes the changes that have occurred in the international system since 1989. Proponents of the "positive" school hold that, with the demise of the Soviet Union and with greater prospects for manoeuvrability as a result of the ending of the Cold War and the strategic competition between Moscow and Washington in regions such as the Middle East, Iran could emerge as a more independent and powerful regional power. In the absence of superpower pressures, Tehran would be better placed to create a new regional order in which Iran would hold the balance of power. In this situation, power derived from a combination of the Islamic revolution, a sound and pragmatic foreign policy and the country's hydrocarbon wealth could enhance Tehran's ability to influence regional developments more fully and directly. Tehran should therefore grasp the nettle and adopt a proactive strategy in the Middle East and in the Asian territories of the former Soviet Union. To do this successfully, Tehran would need to deepen its existing regional alliances and create new ones. Proponents of this school also argue that continuing competition between the United States, the European Union and Japan over the resources of the Persian Gulf, Central Asia and Azerbaijan will inevitably generate new rivalries at the international level, which, with careful planning, Tehran will be able to exploit at the regional level. In other words, they believe that, although the old "negative balance" arguments may no longer apply, continuing rivalries at the international level will, in the medium term, allow Iran to apply the same model to the new situation, securing independence of action and enhancing its room for manoeuvre.

The second school views the end of the Cold War and the demise of the USSR with deep anxiety. The "negative" school worries that Iran will no longer be able to rely on the tried and tested strategy of the negative balance between Washington and Moscow, fearing that Iran is being sidelined. With the superpower competition in effect now over, Iran has become less valuable strategically to the superpowers. It no longer has any value to the West in terms of "containing" the Soviet threat to vital Western interests in the Middle East. Moreover, because there appear to be no external checks on US power in the Middle East, the United States will inevitably increase its pressure on regional states such as Iran that manage to function outside of its sphere of influence, and perhaps on those with the potential to undermine its vital interests in the Persian Gulf sub-region and the rest of the Middle East (particularly in the Arab–Israeli arena). Even in Central Asia and the Caucasus, the proponents of this school argue, Washington is bent on "freezing" Iran out. Elements in this school also maintain that it is wrong to assume that, in the new world order, the hydrocarbon needs of the Western countries will lead to competition over control of these resources. Far from competing for control, the West will probably unite to prevent the monopolization of these resources by any local power unfriendly to the West.

So, if we are to find a general foreign policy strategy for Tehran in the post–Cold War era, it would have to be based around the notion of "both

North and South", which Ramazani popularized in 1992.[8] On the one hand, Iranian strategy needs to develop techniques to exploit the growing gap between the United States and its European allies and Japan over regional and international economic issues as a way of blunting the US-imposed sanctions on the country. Tehran's strategy also seeks to attract non-US Western capital into the country, in an attempt to draw closer to Washington's economic competitors, be they its global strategic partners or rivals.

Thus, since 1997, wherever possible Tehran has tried hard to mend its diplomatic and political bridges and fences in order to enhance its economy and create the conditions for prosperity. Indeed, in many ways President Khatami's administration has made a virtue of Iran's economic ills to argue for more drastic political reforms and the opening up of all sectors of the economy to foreign investment.

Iran and 9/11: Sympathy from above, grief from below

The terrorist attacks of 11 September 2001 shocked Iranians as much as anyone else, and resulted in a strong outpouring of support for the United States from below and expressions of sympathy from the Iranian leadership. Within hours of the attacks, in a statement read out on national television, President Khatami said: "I condemn the terrorist operations of hijacking and attacking public places in American cities which have resulted in the death of a large number of defenseless American people."

More broadly, however, expressions of sympathy were articulated in narrower terms. A senior cleric, Ayatollah Mohammad Emami-Kashani, said on 14 September that the attack against America was "heart-rending ... Everyone condemns, denounces and is saddened by it." However, he added that "Israel and the usurper Zionist regime are the number one state terrorists". "They are causing havoc like this ... America itself, the White House and the prevalent policy in the United States, most of which is in the hands of the Zionists – they condone these crimes which are perpetrated here and there".[9] Presidential Adviser Mohammad Reza Tajik, although condemning the terrorist attacks, warned in the same vein that "the rightists and the American and Israeli Zionists will take great advantage of this situation and will attempt to materialize their objectives and interests" in its aftermath.[10] Most Iranian officials balanced their condemnation of the terror attacks with references to the United States' regional policies and its apparent condoning of Israel's aggressive behaviour. Foreign Minister Kamal Kharrazi was not alone when on 13 September he publicly accused Israel of exploiting the attacks to cause problems in the Middle East. The pro-Khatami Islamic Iran Participation Party also openly criticized the Bush administration for "staunchly supporting the biggest state sponsor of terrorism in the world, Israel".[11]

The national press, particularly the right-leaning publications, adopted a similarly sceptical line. The English-language *Tehran Times* chose the headline "Paying the Price for Its Blind Support of the Zionist Regime" for its post-9/11 front page.[12] The daily *Kayhan* followed suit, saying in its editorial that the attacks "were the natural results of countless crimes which the United States, its Zionist masters, had carried out throughout the world". The managing editor of the prominent conservative newspaper *Resalat* stated in an interview that the "extent of these attacks shows that they were masterminded by elements inside the American intelligence and security apparatus".[13] In a perplexing argument, which was in fact consistent with the theme of conspiracy theories doing the rounds in Tehran and other capitals in the region, Taha Hashemi, managing editor of the conservative *Entekhab* newspaper in Qum (the Iranian Shiites' holy city), suggested that "the transfer of the centre of world attention from the [Palestinian] occupied territories to America was the objective pursued by the perpetrators of these attacks and explosions".[14] The Tehran-based Association of Muslim Journalists expressed its sympathies on 18 September, but went on to claim that "firm evidence" existed that proved that the terrorist attacks "could not have been designed out of the US security system and without aid from individuals inside the system".[15] As if on cue, in a report broadcast on 19 September, national television alluded to the findings of a news report that had claimed that the thousands of Jews who worked in the World Trade Center "had all decided to take a day off on 11 September", saying that "there were no Jews among those who were killed".

Such official responses to 9/11 stood in sharp contrast to the outpouring of sympathy from civil society and grassroots organizations. One of the most dramatic signs of public sympathy with the United States was the minute's silence held at a World Cup qualifying match on 14 September in Tehran, which had been preceded by a candlelight vigil in a northern Tehran public square the previous night. A second candlelight vigil on the 18th drew an even larger crowd, despite the banning of the event by the interior ministry. Students, who had always been the backbone of President Khatami's reform movement, strongly condemned these acts of terrorism and proclaimed 9/11 a "day of horror".[16] Most strikingly of all, the Deputy Chief of the Tehran Fire Department publicly declared his support for his US counterparts and revealed that many of his personnel had volunteered to go to New York to help. Tehran's Mayor Morteza Alviri and Municipal Council head Mohammad Atrianfar also went public with their sympathies and sent a letter to New York's Rudy Giuliani, stating that "Tehran's citizens express their deep hatred of this ominous and inhuman move, strongly condemn the culprits and express their sympathy with New Yorkers".[17] Reformist parliamentarian Ahmad Burqani became the first official to visit the US Interest Section at the Swiss Embassy in Tehran on the 17th to sign the book of condolences.

To explain the contrast between the two levels of reaction requires us to focus on the troubled relationship between Tehran and Washington since 1979 and the Iranian government's constant fears of active US opposition to the Islamic regime. Over the years these fears have cemented and the two sides stand far apart from each other, despite sharing many strategic concerns such as instability in Afghanistan and Iraq, al-Qaeda terrorism, narcotics trafficking, and the spread of radical Islam in Central Asia. Today, the two see each other as regional rivals bent on compromising the other's standing.

The Iranian people, by contrast, view the United States as an imposing power that could be used as a partner of reform. There is much affection for US political and social values in Iran, and the United States is respected for its ability to confront challenges head on. But, having said that, Iranians also have fears about US action and its ability to destabilize the geopolitical situation on Iran's doorstep. Moreover, being largely nationalist in outlook, the people resent any US action that seeks to "contain" Iran or to trim its regional influence. What had been a love–hate relationship for too long was complicated by 9/11. Although the terror attacks struck a chord with the humanity of Iranians at all levels, they failed to ignite a willingness in either Iran or the United States to make a fresh start. Indeed, the "axis of evil" State of the Union address by President Bush in January 2002 did much to undo the goodwill generated by the tragedy of 9/11 and helped to convince Tehran that the United States intended to capitalize on 9/11 to target Iran, Iraq and North Korea as the three rogue states to be countered. From the moment (in the summer of 2002) that regime change in Iraq emerged as a major US foreign policy objective, Tehran began to see itself in a short queue of regimes to be targeted by Washington. The start of the war against the Ba'athist regime in Iraq in March 2003 was the signal to Tehran that the containment strategy of the Clinton era had now given way to active opposition to two northern Gulf neighbours by the Bush administration.

In sum, Washington had set itself the military aim in the 1990s of isolating Iraq, with the strategic option of overthrowing the Ba'athist regime. But it took a new Republican White House and the events of 11 September 2001 finally to push the United States towards the adoption of the military option. In normal circumstances Iran would have welcomed any effort to remove the Iraqi regime, but Tehran was unprepared to lend any direct support to the United States' effort. The reason was simple and understandable: Iran itself was in the containment zone with Iraq. Why should it strengthen the isolation of Iraq when that isolation squeezed Iran as well? As dual containment faded away with the departure of the Clinton administration, Tehran had hoped that a better working relationship could be established with the new Republican White House. Despite some evidence of flexibility on both sides, however, Iran's anxiety was again heightened in 2002, when it found itself portrayed by a new US president as Iraq's bedfellow, this time in a new "axis of evil".[18] The difference in emphasis was a significant one. Whereas the containment policy had sought to isolate Tehran and curtail its regional influence, the new "axis" doctrine more directly targeted specific ruling regimes as "evil" powers and therefore, Iran calculated, potentially subjected the leadership to direct US pressure.

With the Taliban removed from Afghanistan and Iran's northern borders relatively quiet, Iraq would naturally have emerged as the most immediate security concern for Tehran. In the run-up to the war, Tehran seemed to consider it prudent to keep all its options open and follow a unilateralist policy on Iraq, declaring its policy to be "active neutrality". It is interesting that the Iranian foreign minister summarized Tehran's position to the Iranian parliament as "neutral but not indifferent".

Iran and the Iraq crisis

Iran and regime change in Iraq

The new Persian year of 1382 started on 21 March 2003 with two overwhelming pressures influencing every aspect of decision-making in Iran. The first pressure was a product of the bruising political battles at home, which had over the previous year acquired a "civilizational" dimension in terms of a growing clash of values and political outlook between the country's two main political factions. The reformist camp's disenchantment with the conservative establishment had increasingly manifested itself in their more daring, and sometimes rather far-fetched, demands for faster introduction of reforms in the economy and an overhaul of the constitution and the national institutions of power so as to transfer the locus of decision-making to the elected officers of the republic. As war clouds gathered over the Persian Gulf in late winter 2003, the battle between Iran's main two factions was raging in the corridors of power in the Majlis (parliament) and the various ministries and between the executive branch and its supportive Majlis allies and the 12-man Council of Guardians (CG). The Council of Guardians was entrusted by the constitution with the vetting of candidates for political office, and of every piece of legislation for compatibility with Islamic law and values, and of course with the Iranian constitution itself. In Iranian year 1381, the CG had already refused to approve several pieces of important legislation from the Majlis, including two pieces legislation proposed by President Khatami that were designed to increase the authority of the president. The Majlis had already passed these and was pressuring the CG to approve them when the domestic political wrangling was overshadowed by concerns about Iraq and the launch of Operation Iraqi Freedom on the eve of the Persian new year.

The Iraq war proved to be a mixed blessing for Tehran.[19] Although the Coalition's action to unseat the Iraqi dictator was effectively removing a deep and painful thorn from the side of Iran, Tehran was nonetheless disturbed to find the United States a powerful resident force in both Afghanistan and Iraq. Furthermore, the liberation of the Iraqi Shiites would inevitably directly affect the policy cleavages in Iran's own unique Islamic political system. Najaf's traditional opposition to the mixing of religion and politics was by February 2004 also providing considerable intellectual support for those forces in the Iranian power structure who now openly questioned the prudence of religious-political authority being monopolized in the hands of the Faqih (the "Leader", the just jurist) and a small group of his trusted allies in the CG, the judiciary and the security forces, and the Expediency Council headed by the powerful figure of the two-term former president, Hashemi Rafsanjani. One of the clerical members of the CG, Ayatollah Momen, had effectively closed the door on the reformist camp, which had been hoping to compete in the February 2004 parliamentary elections, by announcing in September 2003 that none of the signatories of a highly critical letter to Ayatollah Khamenei (the Leader of the Islamic Republic), complaining about the regime's repressive tendencies, would be allowed to enter the race for the Seventh Majlis elections. The signatories of the letter were all reformists, many of them prominent members of the pro-Khatami camp. In the event, over 2,500 hopefuls were barred by the CG in January 2004 from standing as parliamentary candidates, which effectively and emphatically tilted the balance in favour of the conservative camp. Thus, the conservatives were able to secure a substantial majority of over 160 seats out of 290 in the Seventh Majlis. Their number in the Sixth Majlis had been fewer than 60.

The war and its aftermath

As already stated, regime change in Iraq proved to be a bittersweet experience for Iran. From the sidelines, it saw its bitter enemy in Iraq reduced to a pulp at the hands of an even bigger potential enemy (the United

States). Tehran's more immediate concerns lay not with Iraq, therefore, but with Washington's intentions toward the Islamic Republic itself. The view has persisted in Tehran – as indeed it has in Damascus, Riyadh and even Cairo – that Iran is the next target on the US hit list. Accordingly, going by past performance, it is to be expected that Tehran would be fully preparing itself for the possible outbreak of hostilities either with the United States itself or with its designated allies in the region.

From the perspective that Iran is next, Tehran sensibly regarded Iraq as its first line of defence and thus looked for ways of preventing the United States from finding the time or opportunity to secure decisive control of it. One strategy entailed keeping Washington fully occupied in Iraq by flexing Tehran's muscles through Iraq's large Shiite constituency. Indeed, since late March 2003 Tehran has been an active player in the shaping of the Iraqi Shiite debate and its policy alternatives with regard to the election of a sovereign Iraqi government in 2005.[20] This has proved to be a risky strategy for Tehran to follow, however, for three main reasons.

First, any obvious exercise of influence in Iraq made it easy for Washington to accuse Iran of meddling in Iraq's internal affairs and to expose it to even more US pressure. Second, even if Iran pursued this course, Iraq's diverse Shiite population would not necessarily listen to it. Indeed, Iraq's Shiites form many communities and speak with several, often competing, voices – sometimes tribal, other times religious. To many Iraqi Shiites, Najaf, in Iraq, is the seat of Shia learning (and power) – not Qum, in Iran. At the same time, however, while Saddam Hussein was busy dismantling the Shiite seat of learning in Iraq, he was in practice strengthening the Iranian Shiite élite and the place of Qum as the guardian of the Shiite world. Indeed, as many Iraqi Shiite leaders actually took refuge in Iran it was possible for Iranians to claim that Ayatollah Khomeini's doctrine of political Islam was dominant in Shia Islam and not the traditional "quietist" school long advocated in Najaf, which firmly believed in a clear separation between politics and religion and between religious and political authority. It can be argued that this pendulum may have begun to swing towards Najaf (and Karbala) again since the fall of Baghdad. With Iraq free of direct political control by the United States since June 2004, there is every chance that this process will accelerate, slowly "marginalizing" Qum. Furthermore, having just shaken off the shackles of Saddam's regime, the Iraqi Shiite community is clearly unwilling to take kindly to Iranian dictates. An indiscrete Iranian attempt to assert authority in Shiite Iraq, therefore, could easily cause both Tehran and Qum much loss of prestige as well as influence in Shiite communities in the wider Arab world, suffering a backlash from the very forces it aims to rally.

Finally, and perhaps most important of all, the liberation of the Iraqi Shiites is likely to further deepen the policy and doctrinal cleavages in Iran's own unique Islamic political system. In a country where both influence and political power are derived from religion and the religious hierarchy, where Tehran and Qum stand united only through the mainte- nance of the Velayat-e Faqih system (rule through a clerical system of jurisprudence in which a senior cleric acts as the spiritual leader of the Islamic state), a new and powerful source of religious authority beyond Tehran's control, in Grand Ayatollah Sistani for example, could act as a lightning rod, seriously testing the doctrinal basis of a regime founded on a fairly narrow interpretation of Shiite thought. The rise of Najaf, there- fore, will not only challenge Qum and give Arab Shiites a bigger say in Shia affairs (from Lebanon to Yemen in the Arab world, and from Azerbaijan to India in the non-Arab Shiite communities), but also raise considerable intellectual support for those forces in the Iranian power structure who now openly question the prudence of religious-political au- thority centralized in the hands of the Faqih (the "Leader", the just ju- rist) and a small group of his trusted allies in the Guardian Council, the judiciary and the security forces, and the Expediency Council.

Saddam's fall has thus directly affected factional rivalries in Iran. Some elements in Iran have pointed to US behaviour in Iraq – the imposition of a US political model on a Muslim state, the establishment of military bases and the control of Iraq's oil wealth – as well as the expansion of military facilities in the small Gulf Arab states of Bahrain and Qatar and the perceived encirclement of Iran through an elaborate network of alli- ances as justification for encouraging some Iraqi Shiite forces to assist Tehran in extending its power in Iraq by infiltrating the emerging post- Ba'athist polity. Tehran does have several potentially powerful allies among Iraqi Shiites, notably al-Hakim's Supreme Council for Islamic Revolution in Iraq (SCIRI) and the well-established Islamist al-Da'wah Party, both of which are armed and have an influential political role in the new domestic balance of forces in Iraq. It should also be noted that Tehran has been heavily engaged in providing military training for SCIRI as well as the well-established Patriotic Union of Kurdistan and the al- Da'wah Party. An interesting possibility is that continuing Iranian con- tacts with SCIRI could have a reverse effect on the Iranian élite and help in bringing Iraqi Shiite influences into Iran and encourage fresh thinking on Shiite issues, thereby endangering the semi-unity of the reli- gious establishment in Iran over matters of state (the future role of the Faqih, the future role of the clergy in the day-to-day running of the coun- try, the curtailment of the Faqih's constitutional powers, relations with the United States) and national political issues (the distribution of power between the three branches, social and political reforms, press freedom, the organization of political parties). As a new leadership emerges in SCIRI and as its new leaders get embedded in Iraq itself, however, Tehran's grip over this organization will continue to loosen, particularly since SCIRI's leadership has had to strike a series of compromises with the emerging Iraqi leadership in order to ensure that it will remain a force in the evolving post-Saddam power structures.

Some in Tehran are deeply worried about developments in Iraq and the domestic and foreign policy consequences of manipulating Iraq's large Shiite constituency for narrow political ends, and they counsel caution. Far from seeking to meddle in Iraq's internal affairs, they desire to protect Qum's place as the beating heart of Shiism. They also wish to use the opportunity afforded by Saddam's overthrow to deepen relations with the countries of the Gulf Cooperation Council (GCC). The end of Saddam's regime has removed a rigid barrier to closer Iranian links with the GCC states. Tehran no longer has to worry about the GCC states keeping their distance for fear of Iraqi pressure; and the fall of Baghdad has allowed the emergence of the "Shiite" issue into the open. The fears expressed in 1991 that the removal of Saddam Hussein would somehow lead to the rise of an Iranian-controlled Shiite-dominated state in Iraq have not been realized and, rather than the Shiite dimension of Iraqi society being seen as a direct security threat, it is part of the reality of the country. The Shiites no longer stand in the way of closer relations between Tehran and the GCC states; indeed, with every act of violence in Iraq, suspicion of the Shiite factor has continued to grow in the Arabian Peninsula. In theory, US removal of the Ba'athist regime in Iraq has allowed Arab Shiites in that country to make their presence known and Iran no longer has to fear negative fall-out in the Arab world of its own Shiite identity or of close association with this community across the Arab world.

Inter-Shia politics

As already noted, Iraq has the potential to become a domestic force in Iranian politics and in the changing contours of political Islam. Because of the role of the United States there and the huge Shiite factor, domestic developments in Iraq have a direct bearing on Iran's own political system. As already mentioned, with regard to Shiite interpretations of relations with the state for example, Iran may find a rival in Najaf. Furthermore, the complex Qum–Tehran–Najaf relationship needs untangling before Iran can formulate a clear strategy towards its neighbour. Yet Iran still has to treat Iraq as an independent factor if it is to produce a coherent strategy towards it. Can it do so if its policy makers find themselves caught at the intersection of the two variables of domestic and foreign policy over Iraq? Only careful planning by Tehran can offer it a way out of this complex matrix, but I suspect that that can happen only if Tehran is finally able to develop a mutually beneficial relationship with Baghdad's new rulers, as well as with Iraq's modern "political agent", the United States. Although the former may already be on the cards, the latter will certainly have to await the outcome of the presidential races in both the United States and Iran.

On another front, the political voice of Iraq's Shiite communities has mobilized a violent backlash among Salafis. Salafis despise Shiites as much as they hate the United States. Many see the United States' intervention in Iraq as part of a bigger conspiracy to promote the "heretical" Shiites against the larger Sunni Arab states and communities as a way of strengthening its control of Arab Muslim lands and resources. The Iraq war, therefore, has changed the character of political Islam itself and, very broadly speaking, has separated it into the Salafi/al-Qaeda and Shiite camps. The war, furthermore, may well have unleashed much wider and deeper inter-communal strife in the Muslim world between the majority Sunnis and the minority Shiites. The ugly manifestations of this division have already been in evidence in Afghanistan, Pakistan and India but, with Iraqi Shiites now free to enter the fray, the front-line of this struggle will have widened and deepened to encompass the Levant and South and West Asia, locations in which the West has many vital interests to protect.

Although political Islam will remain a force to be reckoned with in the next generation, it will increasingly become a divided force (between its Salafi and Shiite varieties) and will, as a consequence, turn on itself as frequently as it targets the West.

Iraq and Iranian domestic politics

The Iranian political élite is totally fragmented and factionalized. Factionalism as a system affects every aspect of public policy in Iran, and its impact on foreign policy cannot be over-emphasized, particularly as factional and individual rivalries feed directly into policy decisions. Furthermore, with the domestic arena becoming rather overcrowded and avenues for critical debate more tightly controlled, factions seem increasingly to articulate their distinctive positions on domestic and related issues in foreign policy terms. The debate takes place in the context of efforts to "save" the revolution and the "*nezam*",[21] but the proposed strategies for doing so are widely divergent. For many of the reformists, for example, restoration of relations with the United States is vital for renewal at home,[22] whereas for the more conservative forces even mentioning relations with the "great satan" is tantamount to treason.[23] The two major camps, around which gather numerous other groups and influential personalities, often quote the founder of the Islamic Republic, Ayatollah Khomeini, in support of their own position, which further confuses the picture, or they try and chart their own strategies for ascendancy in the power struggle at home in terms of Ayatollah Khomeini's deeds at times of crisis. All the while the factions are using foreign policy as a tactical weapon for warfare at home, and this is where the Iraq factor comes in.

The invitation in February 2004 by a group of Iranian political dignitaries to Grand Ayatollah Ali al-Sistani of Najaf to intervene in his home land's parliamentary electoral process is indicative of the evolving complexity of the Qum–Tehran–Najaf triangle. In their letter, the 400 signatories requested that Ayatollah Sistani express a view on the "massacre of democracy and the transformation of [the 2004] parliamentary elections into a mere stage play". They further state:

"We have followed with appreciation your courageous positions in calling for the holding of free, fair, and direct elections in Iraq, where the population did not have, until the fall of the Ba'ath regime, the right to own a shortwave radio. That is, holding free elections that can escape foreign influence is a difficult matter if not an impossible one. Nevertheless, your Excellency is insisting that the first and last word in the matter of choosing rulers and representatives belongs to the Iraqi people. How wonderful it would be if your Excellency would express your opinion regarding the farce that some in your native land of Iran are attempting to impose on its people, who are wide awake, under the rubric of "elections". Najaf has always been a support for freedom lovers in Iran ... Without their famous fatwa, the people would not have been able to bring down the tyrant Muhammad Ali shah [in the 1905 constitutional revolution].[24]

Thus, owing to the presence of the deep-rooted trans-border Shiite network, what passes for domestic politics in post-Saddam Iraq also passes as part of the domestic politics of Iran, and vice versa. Reformation in Iraq will have a direct knock-on effect on Iran's own political system and, if security in Iraq can be achieved, then political changes there will spur on Iran's own reformers in their endeavours to democratize the Islamic Republic. By the same token, continuing insecurity in Iraq will help to strengthen the hand of the hard-liners in the regime and help their efforts to consolidate their grip on the legislative, executive and advisory bodies of the Islamic Republic.

Security as a prime driver

Although Tehran is fully cognizant of the geopolitical opportunities the emerging regional order may present, it is at the same time mindful of the constraints slowly but surely being imposed on its orbit of influence. In Afghanistan, for example, it is delighted to see the back of the Taliban, but it is no longer a direct pillar of stability there. It should be recalled that, during the dark years of Taliban rule, Iran steadfastly supported the Northern Alliance, which in the end emerged as the military spearhead of the anti-Taliban campaign in that country. Without Iranian support in the 1990s, the United States and the United Nations would not have had the option of using a local force against the Taliban and al-Qaeda. Yet Tehran feels exposed to developments in Afghanistan and worries that the US presence there could undermine Iran's deep-rooted influence in that largely Persian-speaking country. Weakness in Afghanistan has a direct bearing on Iran's relations with Central Asia too, in particular with its poorest and only Persian-speaking country, Tajikistan. US military encirclement, from Tehran's perspective, is being underpinned with subtle barriers being erected between Iran and its traditional spheres of cultural influence in West Asia. It should not be surprising then to see a siege mentality taking root there.

In Iraq, Iran is being portrayed as part of the post-Saddam problem rather than as the solution it had hoped to be. Having borne the brunt of Saddam's brutality in an eight-year war with his regime, having provided shelter for well over 500,000 Iraqi refugees, having followed the UN line on Iraq since 1990, having not meddled in Iraqi domestic politics for all this time, it is less than satisfying to the Iranians now to be cast as the chief villain in Iraq. But Iran's concerns about post-Saddam Iraq are far greater than addressing an image problem. Broadly speaking, Iran's issues in Iraq can be divided into two groups: internal Iraqi politics; and the impact of Iraq's future foreign, security and economic policies on Iran and the rest of the Persian Gulf. With regard to the former, three issues are of importance: the future character of the state of Iraq, the role of the Shiite forces there, and the impact of political developments in Iraq on Iran itself. Although the prospect of the return of the monarchy remains rather dim, the need for Tehran to define a relationship with a secular-leaning republican or monarchical ruling regime in Iraq is unlikely to disappear any time soon.

If, however, Iraq remains an Arab republic, then Iran should expect that the Shiites will be given a seat at the centre of power in the country. But which Shiite groups are in a position to negotiate a deal with the United States and the other Iraqi parties, and which ones should Iran promote in the context of its wider concerns there? For example, will the Supreme Council for Islamic Revolution in Iraq, which was founded in Iran in 1980, continue to present a credible force for Tehran to rely upon? If SCIRI fails to become a major force in the new Iraq, should Tehran abandon its own child and seek other alliances with the multitude of Shiite personalities and organizations (Hojjatoleslam al-Sadr, for example)? Whether it could do so without disrupting its relations with the far more important force of Grand Ayatollah Sistani is certainly in doubt. Can it indeed afford to tie its fortunes publicly to any Shiite force whose prospects in post-Saddam Iraq would appear less than clear? The volatility of the Iraqi political order, therefore, is a substantial security and foreign policy challenge for Tehran.

Although no one in Iran bemoans the fall of the Ba'athist regime in Iraq, there are those in the Iranian élite who do miss the large degree of continuity, predictability and, dare I say, stability that Saddam Hussein had brought to Iraq's post-war relations with its neighbour. Tensions between the two countries during the July–August 2004 crisis in Najaf exemplify the problem for Tehran. For all the declarations of friendship between the two sides and Iran's continuing expression of support for the post-Saddam Iraqi leadership, it was Iraq's interior minister himself, Falah Hassan al-Naqib, who in mid-July accused Iran of involvement in unrest in Iraq, and the Iraqi defence minister, Hazim Sha'lan al-Khuza'i, accused Iran of "blatant interference" in Iraq's internal affairs.[25] The Governor of Najaf, Adnan al-Zurufi, said on 8 August that "there is Iranian support for al-Sadr's group, and this is no secret. We have information and evidence that they are supplying the [Imam] Al-Mahdi Army with weapons and have found such weapons in their possession".[26]

Tehran was quite taken aback by the forcefulness of these attacks from senior Iraqi officials, and in frustration warned that "Iraqi officials have just begun working and need to be cautious … [as their remarks will] have serious legal and political consequences" for relations between Iran and Iraq.[27] *Jomhuri-yi Islami*, an influential hard-line newspaper, stated in an editorial (8 August) that the interim government was a "cast of hand-picked actors". The next day, it opined that the Najaf crisis was a "premeditated conspiracy to eliminate the forces of resistance" in Iraq: "the time [has] come for us to get up and go after the crown of Islam, the very existence of the Shi'a, and the national interests of the Islamic Republic of Iran."[28] The Shiite file in the hands of the hard-liners could spell disaster for the moderate camp in Iran, further testing its relations with the West (notably the European Union, which is being strained by Iran's activities in the nuclear field), and adding to Iran's problems with Iraq and with Baghdad's Western backers.

So, as we see, for all its purported influence in Iraq and its desire to intervene, Iran seems to have little choice but to sit on the sidelines while Iraq's future is being determined by other interlocutors. It also has to adopt an arms-length position for the further reason that it cannot afford to be seen meddling in Iraq's internal affairs, even though it has a direct and immediate interest in Iraq's future. Although it clearly wishes for a democratic and open Iraq, it still has a host of important and tangible issues that it needs to discuss with any future Iraqi government. Its list of concerns includes: a final agreement on a border treaty with Iraq, war reparations (Iran is claiming some US$100 billion from Iraq), the settlement of the PoW issue, the release of several Iranian officials and a diplomat who were kidnapped in Iraq in 2004, and the future of the anti-Tehran Mojahedin-e Khalq Organization based in Iraq. Iraq, on the other hand, wants its 100+ military aircraft returned, it wants to manage the border so that insurgents cannot enter the country from Iran, and it wants Iran to stop using geography as a lever in its relations with Iraq. Baghdad is also loathe to see its relations with its Arab neighbours dictated by the inter-Shia debates or by its relations with Iran.

Iraq's external policies will also affect Iranian security thinking. A first concern is whether Baghdad will become a future ally of the United States in the region, open ties with Israel and act as Washington's strategic partner in the region. The US–Iraqi partnership could in fact resemble the Iranian–US partnership of old during the Pahlavi era. A stable Iraq could act as a security guarantor of Western interests in the Persian Gulf as well as the wider Middle East. Iraq's oil could underpin the relationship and enable Baghdad to build a strong, US-supplied military machine that could, in conjunction with the United States' other Gulf Arab security partners, resurrect the old "twin pillars" security umbrella first introduced by President Richard Nixon in the 1970s. Iran would then find itself on the margins of an imposed security structure in a region that it regards to be of vital importance to its prosperity and survival.

Secondly, Iran and its Gulf Arab neighbours are busy assessing the long-term geo-economic consequences of oil-laden Iraq returning to the market (and the Organization of Petroleum Exporting Countries – OPEC) as a big producer and no longer constrained by quota restrictions and political obligations towards its neighbours. Assuming that its oil output can stabilize, Iraq's unbridled export of oil in the next decade could bring havoc to a finely balanced and carefully managed international oil market. Iran will stand to lose if Iraqi action suppresses the price; Iran's influence in the market will also be dealt a blow if Iraq emerges as one of OPEC's primary producers. Once its production capacity is enhanced, with its massive reserves it could easily compete with Saudi Arabia on price and replace Iran as OPEC's other main producer. Iran's political vulnerabilities with regard to Iraq will then be multiplied to include the oil factor in their bilateral equation.

Iran and the post-9/11 international order

The paradox for Iran as it adjusts to the reality of US pre-eminence in the post-9/11 international order is that, although its own role is enhanced in geopolitical terms, the very fact that it has emerged as a big player also exposes it to greater external pressures and, in particular, much US scrutiny. The post-9/11 order, therefore, has been both good and problematic for the Islamic Republic. Enemies on its two longest land borders have been destroyed since 9/11, but at the same time the US military and political presence in West Asia has increased exponentially. Even fears about Iraq's WMD capabilities were reduced to dust in the course of the 2003 war, but Tehran's own activities in the nuclear field have come under much greater international attention since then. Although Iran finds itself as an ally of the West in the anti-Salafi Islam struggle, it remains on the United States' list of terrorist states by virtue of its close association with the Hezbollah organization in Lebanon and its support for Palestinian groups.

It is in the context of Iran's complex position in the 9/11 international order that Iranian national security debates and its various military and civilian nuclear programmes crystallize.

National security and Iran's nuclear programme

Since the introduction of the Clinton doctrine of "dual containment" of Iran and Iraq in 1993, the United States and the 15-member European Union have had their differences over Western policy options towards these oil-rich neighbouring states. Owing to a set of complex reasons, "dual containment" did not encourage the emergence of a partnership between Tehran and Baghdad. Nonetheless, both countries were from the mid-1990s heavily engaged in courting European countries (including Russia) as a means of bending the containment barrier. They also banked on winning European support through successfully exploiting potential transatlantic rifts over President Clinton's Gulf policy. In the aftermath of President George W. Bush's "axis of evil" State of the Union address in January 2002, which placed both Tehran and Baghdad on notice, it is fair to say that neither Iran nor Iraq has managed successfully to use the European Union as a protective shield against the United States. Furthermore, Operation Iraqi Freedom and the fall of the Iraqi Ba'athist regime in April 2003 provided sufficient evidence for the European powers that Washington was prepared to engage in costly and sustained military campaigns if it felt that such actions were an effective preventive national security measure. Recognition of the United States' ability and willingness to act without the consent of the international community encouraged a meeting of minds between Tehran on the one hand, which had only just managed more ably to resist the United States' political, diplomatic and economic pressures, and the European Union on the other, which was struggling very hard to mend bridges at the heart of the Union following the very public and sustained opposition of Germany and France to the US/UK-led war in Iraq. In the charged diplomatic atmosphere following the failure of UN debates on Iraq, both Iran and the European Union had much to gain from making the European Union's "constructive engagement" dialogue with Tehran a higher priority. Tehran could try to engage Europe against the United States; the European Union could claim to be taking direct and effective action to bring Iran into line without the need for the threat of force. The ability in October 2003 of the EU trio of Germany, France and the United Kingdom to convince Iran to give a full account of its nuclear programme before the 31 October deadline set by the board of the International Atomic Energy Agency (IAEA), to halt its uranium enrichment activities and to bring its entire nuclear activities under the IAEA regime of snap actions was portrayed by both sides as a victory for dialogue over the threat or use of force. The onus now was on Tehran and the European Union to convince a sceptical United States that the agreement reached in Tehran on 21 October between the trio's foreign ministers and the Iranian government, through the office of its National Security Council, was comprehensive and robust enough not to require a referral of the Iranian case to the UN Security Council for a fuller discussion. The latter option had been the United States' preferred route of dealing with Iran since 2002, when revelations about its apparently clandestine nuclear activities had begun to surface.

Although Brussels and Washington approached Iran differently, Tehran was left in no doubt that, in the aftermath of the Iraq war and the North Korean nuclear stand-off, both sides of the Atlantic took Iran's nuclear programme extremely seriously and were dismayed by the direction of its activities. Even Moscow, the supplier of Iran's nuclear power plants, entered the fray by expressing concern about the nature of the ongoing nuclear research in Iran. Moscow publicly urged Tehran to sign the Additional Protocol to the Treaty on the Non-Proliferation of Nuclear Weapons (NPT). In a blunt warning, Russia also stated that it too would not tolerate a state with nuclear weapons in West Asia, on its own door-step.

The programme itself has become much more public since 2002, when a string of revelations forced the Iranian authorities to acknowledge that they had in fact sought enrichment facilities, separating units and nuclear weapons designs.[29] It was announced by the Iranian authorities in early 2003 that Iran's nuclear programme aimed "to complete the circle [cycle] of fuel for plants for peaceful purposes". The head of the country's atomic energy programme, Mr Aqazadeh, declared on 10 February 2003 that his agency had begun work on a uranium enrichment plant near the city of Kashan (the Natanz site), stating that "very extensive research

[had] already started". The fuel would come from the brand-new Uranium Conversion Facility built in the industrial city of Isfahan. Mr Aqazadeh added that the Isfahan plant was to be complemented with another facility for producing uranium fuel casings. International concerns about Iran's nuclear ambitions were further heightened by these announcements, particularly as only a day earlier Tehran had announced that it had successfully extracted uranium and was planning to process the spent fuel from its nuclear facilities within the country. The Iranian president himself appeared on national television on the anniversary of Iran's Islamic revolution in February to congratulate his countrymen on their nuclear achievements, enumerating their research successes and then underlining the statements already made by the head of the Iranian atomic energy programme.

The IAEA, of course, which was already under severe pressure for its failures in Iraq and North Korea, immediately entered the debate. Of further concern to the IAEA at this time were the sites being developed in the cities of Natanz and Arak, of whose existence the agency had first learnt through intelligence sources and not the Iranian authorities themselves. Iran's late notification of the two sites to the IAEA, though legal under the NPT terms, reached the Vienna-based organization only in September 2002, a month after an opposition group had published details of the facilities. The revelations showed that the underground site near Natanz would house Iran's main gas centrifuge plant for enriching uranium for use in reactors, while the Arak facility would produce heavy water, an essential ingredient for plutonium production. The IAEA's February 2003 inspection of Natanz revealed that Iran not only had been able to develop and advance the Pakistani-supplied technology to assemble and "cascade" 160 centrifuge machines, but had assembled a sufficient quantity of parts for installing a further 1,000–5,000 centrifuge machines between 2003 and 2005. Natanz, Iran has told the IAEA, has been designed to produce low-enriched uranium for Iran's planned expansion of nuclear power plants, and is therefore unable to generate weapons-grade highly enriched uranium. The scientific community, however, is concerned that the depth and extent of the Natanz plant implies a far more ambitious project. From the US perspective, of course, Iran's intention to process and complete the nuclear fuel cycle would have only one purpose: to develop nuclear weapons.

We now know that Libya's secret negotiations with London and Washington over the abandoning of all of its WMD activities also yielded much valuable information about Iran's secret nuclear programme, shedding more light on the nature of its clandestine links with Pakistan and North Korea and the murky nuclear trade across Asia. It had thus emerged by late 2003 that Iran had established a multiple programme of research and development, based around a strategy of flexible acquisition.

Prior to Iran's 2003 revelations, it had been surmised that Iran was secretly pursuing the development of a nuclear weapons option in parallel with its IAEA-registered nuclear research and power-generation programme. The argument at the turn of the century was about "when" Iran might be able to acquire and deploy home-grown nuclear weapons and not "if". In Tehran itself, however, the inter-élite discussions about Iran's nuclear options entered the public arena much later than in the West, namely in the course of the IAEA's high-profile engagement of Tehran from early 2003.

In Iran itself, the nuclear debate has tended to cut across factional lines. Conservative elements make the argument against the possession of WMD, whereas some reformers passionately argue in favour of developing a nuclear weapons option as Iran's right and a national security imperative. In broad terms, five principle arguments have been circulating in Iran. The first argument has been rooted in the rights and responsibilities of sovereign states signatories to the NPT. As a loyal member, some circles argue, Iran has never violated the terms of the NPT, but it nonetheless wishes to take maximum (and legitimate) advantage of the opportunities that the NPT offers the member states to acquire nuclear technology and know-how for peaceful purposes. Iran, the argument goes, should take full advantage of its NPT regime membership. Others argue that the costs associated with nuclear research are so great that Iran should not even enter this field. In addition, there are environmental issues to consider and the fact that, by building nuclear facilities, Iran will create more strategic targets for its adversaries to strike at.

The second argument pertains to the prestige of being a nuclear state. The proponents of the nuclear option argue that, for Iran to be taken seriously as a dominant regional actor, it must be seen to have an extensive nuclear R&D programme, even though in practice it may not be translating its research into practical use. Pointing to the examples of North Korea, Pakistan and India, it is said that these countries have become immune to US aggression thanks to their nuclear weapons capabilities. The opponents of this view argue that the Soviet and North Korean examples show not only that the technological spin-offs from nuclear research are minimal, but that any advances in this field will inevitably occur at the expense of another, probably vital, civilian sector. For middle-income countries such as Iran, the means of recouping the costs of nuclear research through technological spin-offs simply do not exist; in particular, since the majority of Iran's experienced scientific community reside overseas, how are the benefits of such highly sensitive research to have the proposed national impact?

The third argument for developing a nuclear option is rooted in the geopolitical insecurity paradigm. Members of both main factions argue that Iran's neighbourhood is insecure and inter-state relations uncertain. With Israel and Pakistan in possession of nuclear weapons, it would make strategic sense for Iran at least to develop the option, if not actually to declare itself as a nuclear weapons state. However, the dangers of a nuclear arms race developing as a consequence of Iran's decision are acknowledged by the pro-nuclear camp. Others argue that, because Iran does not face any existential threat to itself, and indeed its borders have been breached only once over the past 200 years (in the 1980–1988 Iran–Iraq war), there can be no conceivable justification on security grounds for Iran's possession of such evil weapons. With the Iraqi threat now practically removed, Iran no longer has any natural enemies to warrant the development of nuclear weapons.

The fourth argument is closely linked to the above and is found in territorial nationalist debates in Iran. In the post–Cold War, post-9/11 era, Iran's independence and its sovereignty can be guaranteed only through the possession of such powerful weapons as nuclear-armed missile systems. Without such a capability, Tehran will always be open to threats from the United States and other states with aggressive intent towards it. The opposite camp argues that there is no evidence to suggest that Iran will be more secure as a consequence of nuclearization, that the United States will change its policies towards the Islamic Republic, or that the regional countries themselves will submit to Iran's will. If anything, even some advisers to the president have suggested that the deployment of nuclear weapons by Iran will adversely affect its relations with all of its neighbours, including Russia. Also, they claim, nuclear weapons deployment could encourage militarization of the polity and more adventurism in Iran's foreign relations.

The final argument relates to the national resources issue. The proponents of total freedom of action for Iran in all fields of nuclear research and technological development argue that completing the fuel cycle would allow the construction of several nuclear power stations without complete dependence on outside suppliers. It is claimed that such action will secure an endless supply of energy for future generations. The opponents of this view point to the start-up costs of such a huge programme, as well as to its maintenance and periodic modernization expenses. A country endowed with some of the largest gas deposits in the world will find it hard to convince the international community that its interest in nuclear technology is to secure badly needed energy supplies.

A geopolitical endgame?

These nuclear debates do not seem to have reached a conclusive point in Iran, and the outcome will depend as much on the balance of power between the various factions and the nuclear schools of thought, as on how the West reacts to Iran's nuclear ambitions. A glimpse of the balance of arguments on the pace of Iran's nuclear programme was gleaned by the IAEA board of governors' resolution of 13 March 2004 in which Iran was criticized for the fact that its October 2003 declarations "did not amount to the complete and final picture of Iran's past and present nuclear programme considered essential by the board's November 2003 resolution". The IAEA expressed particular concern regarding Iran's advanced centrifuge design, its laser enrichment capabilities and its hot cells facility at its heavy-water research reactor. The Iranian expression of outrage at all levels of its leadership at the resolution and the calls from the leadership of the Islamic Revolution Guards Corp for Iran to withdraw from the NPT altogether were soon tempered with a more conciliatory line that Iran remained committed to the agreements reached with the EU trio's foreign ministers. They in effect had become the guardians of Iran's relationship with the IAEA – a position that none seems to want, let alone enjoy.

However, because the resolution also praised Iran for its cooperation and openness, it proved very difficult for the US administration to pull Iran in front of the Security Council for its nuclear indiscretions. Furthermore, the United States needs Iranian acquiescence for its presence in Iraq and Afghanistan, and Washington increasingly needs the European Union for its post-occupation plans in Iraq (and also post-election Afghanistan), so it was unable to escalate the concerns over Iran's nuclear ambitions into a general crisis at this stage.[30] Apart from its own unilateral condemnation of Tehran, it was hard to see as the crisis unfolded how the United States could do more than ensure that the European Union and the IAEA continue to prise open Iran's nuclear secrets while pressing it to comply with its NPT obligations without delay. This may well prove to be the United States' only realistic option in the medium term, but this is not a position with which it can be content if Tehran does not yield to international pressure.

The intensity of debates about Iran's national security, its defence priorities and even the organization of its military forces is symptomatic of a wider concern arising from the rapid changes that have occurred in West Asia since 1989. The Soviet withdrawal from Afghanistan in 1989 was the start of a rapid process that not only ended the bipolar world in which Iran thrived but changed beyond recognition the geopolitics of West Asia. Over a short period of time, the United States emerged as the dominant force in politico-military and economic terms in the new post–Cold War order, building on the ashes of the Soviet super-state and the Warsaw Pact an extensive range of local partnerships in key regions of the world. In the aftermath of the 1991 war for the liberation of Kuwait, it also consolidated its position as the Middle East's premier power. US-induced regime change in Afghanistan and Iraq in the wake of 9/11 and growing US sensitivities about Iran's regional role have added new layers of concern to Tehran's anxieties.[31] Iran has had only a decade to absorb the impact of the end of the bipolar order, and is still debating how to adjust to the geopolitical implications of a US-dominated post–Cold War order. Yet, by early 2002, Iran had to take immediate stock of a potentially even bigger upheaval in the international system – the direct and indirect costs of a post-9/11 international order in which the US presence in the area would be even greater and possibly more long term. Despite the advantages for Iran of US military interventions in Afghanistan and Iraq (two of its traditional spheres of influence), the country's leadership has had to balance such benefits against the real threats to Iran that US action in Iran's immediate neighbourhood could pose. As we have seen, despite its consummate efforts to chart a truly independent line in its foreign affairs, for the first time in over a century Iran seems to have little say, let alone control, over developments, or the direction of events, in West Asia. The absence of control over developments around it merely helps to exacerbate Tehran's anxieties about the regime's own future. This anxiety has in turn heightened the country's security dilemmas, as shown in its nuclear debates. Adopting a longer-term view, however, it is ironic that the removal of the Soviet superpower from its northern borders in 1991 and of the threats emanating from the Taliban and Saddam Hussein in 2001 and 2003, respectively, has not only made Iranians feel less safe at home but actually deepened the sense of siege in Tehran. In Iran at least, the volatility of the post-9/11 international order resonates strongly at home, both in its inter-factional relations and in its domestic agenda-setting. But it is in the foreign policy realm that the post-9/11 order has fundamentally affected this ancient country's ways of interaction, and also its established relations, with its immediate hinterland. With the West Asian ground now likely to be shifting under the feet of its states for some time to come, Iran is set to continue the long cycle of geopolitical recalculations it has been making since 1989 before it can discover again a natural posture for itself in this volatile but strategically significant part of the international system.

Notes

1. James Piscatori, "Foreword", in Anoushiravan Ehteshami and Manshour Varasteh, eds, *Iran and the International Community* (London: Routledge, 1991), p. ix.
2. Graham E. Fuller, *The "Center of the Universe": The Geopolitics of Iran* (Boulder, CO: Westview Press, 1991), p. 2.
3. For discussion of the negative balance concept, see Rouhollah K. Ramazani, *Iran's*

Foreign Policy: A Study of Foreign Policy in Modernizing Nations (Charlottesville, VA: University of Virginia Press, 1975).

4. See Hossein Amirsadeghi, ed., *The Security of the Persian Gulf* (New York: St Martin's Press, 1981).

5. Shahram Chubin and Sepehr Zabih, *The Foreign Relations of Iran* (Berkeley, CA: University of California Press, 1974), p. 214.

6. Akbar Mahdi, "Islam, the Middle East, and the New World Order", in Hamid Zangeneh, ed., *Islam, Iran and World Stability* (New York: St Martin's Press, 1994), pp. 75–96.

7. For a more detailed discussion of Iranian perspectives on the "new world order", see Raymond A. Hinnebusch and Anoushiravan Ehteshami, eds, *The Foreign Policies of Middle East States* (Boulder, CO: Lynne Rienner, 2002).

8. Rouhollah K. Ramazani, "Iran's Foreign Policy: Both North and South", *Middle East Journal*, Vol. 46, No. 3 (Summer 1992), pp. 393–412.

9. Islamic Republic News Agency (IRNA), 14 September 2001.

10. Reports by the Islamic Students' News Agency (ISNA), 12 September 2001.

11. IRNA, 12 September 2001.

12. *Tehran Times*, 12 September 2001. The paper editorialized that, "[w]hen a government is prepared to go against all internationally accepted principles in its support of a racist and criminal regime, it cannot expect to escape unscathed".

13. Morteza Nabavi gave this interview to ISNA, 14 September 2001.

14. *Entekhab*, 13 September 2001.

15. IRNA, 18 September 2001.

16. *Radio Free Europe/Radio Liberty (RFE/RL) Iran Report*, Vol. 4, No. 35, 17 September 2001.

17. *RFE/RL Iran Report*, Vol. 4, No. 36, 24 September 2001.

18. Mahan Abedin, "Iranian Views of Regime Change in Iraq", *Middle East Bulletin*, Vol. 4, No. 11 (November–December 2002).

19. Jon B. Alterman, "Not in My Backyard: Iraq's Neighbors' Interests", *Washington Quarterly*, Vol. 26, No. 3 (Summer 2003), pp. 149–160.

20. According to some Arab sources, "[t]he yellow Iranian birth certificates [issued by Iranian consulates in Karbala and other cities] bear witness to the fact that those Shia who dream of ruling Iraq are more Iranian than Iraqi". See *The Daily Star*, 24 March 2003.

21. "*Nezam*" encompasses the ruling élite and its social allies and beneficiaries, as well as the broader post-Pahlavi state and government structures.

22. In May 2003, for example, a large group of parliamentarians again called for the restoration of relations with the United States. In an open letter signed by 153 deputies in the 290-seat Majlis and read out in the chamber, the parliamentarians stated that Iran was in "a critical situation" and "following the installation of American forces in Afghanistan and the occupation of Iraq, the threat has arrived at our borders" (*Daily Telegraph*, 9 May 2003).

23. Elements of both camps have also argued that Tehran would be in an exceptionally weak bargaining position if it suddenly proposed talks at the height of the United States' influence in the region (*Mardom Salari*, 19 April 2003).

24. A translation of the original 1 February 2004 *ash-Sharq al-Awsat* article is available at: ⟨http://www.juancole.com/2004_02_01_juancole_archive.html#107596823435980037⟩.

25. Al-Khuza'i also said on 9 August that "[w]eapons manufactured in Iran were found in Al-Najaf in the hands of those criminals, who received these weapons from the Iranian border". He accused Iran of being Iraq's "first enemy", in the same interview with Abu Dhabi-based Al-Arabiyah television.

26. *RFE/RL Iran Report*, 17 August 2004.

27. Remarks made by the Iranian foreign ministry spokesman Hamid Reza Assefi. See

RFE/RL Iraq Report, 22 July 2004. Iraqi Foreign Minister Hoshyar Zebari told the *Sunday Telegraph* (4 July 2004) that as many as 10,000 foreign spies had entered Iraq since May 2003.

28. *RFE/RL Iran Report*, 17 August 2004.

29. Robert J. Einhorn, "A Transatlantic Strategy on Iran's Nuclear Program", *Washington Quarterly*, Vol. 27, No. 4 (2004), pp. 21–32.

30. According to Seymour Hersh: "Iraqi Shiite militia leaders like Moqtada al-Sadr, the former American intelligence official said, are seen by the Israeli leadership as 'stalking horses' for Iran – owing much of their success in defying the American-led coalition to logistical and communications support and training provided by Iran. The former intelligence official said, 'We began to see telltale signs of organizational training last summer. But the White House didn't want to hear it: "We can't take on another problem right now. We can't afford to push Iran to the point where we've got to have a showdown."'" See "PLAN B: As June 30th Approaches, Israel Looks to the Kurds", *New Yorker*, 28 June 2004.

31. In the words of Afrasiabi and Maleki, Iranians were "unprepared for the massive change – indeed a revolution – in the security environment around Iran wrought almost overnight in the aftermath of the 11 September atrocities". Kaveh Afrasiabi and Abbas Maleki, "Iran's Foreign Policy after 11 September", *Brown Journal of World Affairs*, Vol. 9, No. 2 (Winter/Spring 2003), p. 255.

9

The Iraq crisis and world order: An Israeli perspective

Mark A. Heller

The international system after the war in Iraq

The decision-making process leading up to the war in Iraq, as well as the course of the military campaign itself, seemed to reinforce the argument that the United States, in the aftermath of the Cold War, was both willing and able to pursue an essentially unilateralist foreign policy. Both proponents and critics of US behaviour posited the proposition that the collapse of the Soviet Union had removed the only real constraint on America's ability to act as it saw fit and that, henceforth, the only variable in determining whether or not the international system would impinge on US decisions would be the ideological predilections of the US government. In other words, the Iraq crisis (or at least part of it) seemed to validate the notion of emerging unipolarity in the international system.

The aftermath of the war in Iraq seemed to reinforce the argument that the United States was, after all, unable to promote its foreign policy objectives without reference to the rest of the world. Both proponents and critics of US behaviour posited the proposition that the growing chaos in Iraq following the stage of active hostilities and the United States' difficulties in mobilizing the legitimacy and resources needed to deal with it underscored the continuing dependence of the United States on international institutions and procedures. Hence the need to restore the "multilateral imperative" in US foreign policy. In other words, the Iraq crisis (or at least part of it) seemed to validate the notion of persistent multipolarity in the international system.

The central argument of this chapter is that, although both hypotheses contain important insights, both also exaggerate the extent to which the international system is evolving and both fail to capture the nuances of a more complex reality. Instead, the Iraq crisis demonstrates that, though US pre-eminence is both unprecedented and undeniable, major constraints still operate on US policy, and that the term that best captures this complex reality is "uni-multipolarity".[1] This reality is unlikely to change in any foreseeable circumstances, certainly not before profound changes are made in the character of international organizations and international law. Finally, I argue that this is a reality to which Israel, as a small power with little influence on the structure or norms of the international order, must adapt itself but with which it is, for a variety of reasons, rather comfortable.

The United States in the international system

The most salient feature of the current international system is the overwhelming pre-eminence of the United States, particularly in the military sphere. In terms of its ability to generate military power and project it abroad, the United States has no rivals and practically needs no partners. Indeed, the current gap in military capabilities between the leading actor and all others probably exceeds anything at least since the time of the Roman Empire. For example, the United States already spends more than twice as much on military procurement as does the entire European Union. Moreover, every indicator suggests that the military divide between the United States and the rest of the world will only grow in the foreseeable future. US investment in military research and development (R&D), particularly in exotic areas such as cybernetics and nanotechnology, far outstrips that of any other country or probable coalition of countries; it is more than four times the total R&D investment of all EU members. This virtually ensures that the United States' technological advantage will only increase in the coming years.

Of course, the United States' pre-eminence does not derive solely from its military power. The United States is also the largest single-country economy and consumer market in the world, making it the premier target for exports of most other countries. Compared with its nearest putative rival – united Europe – its economy has grown faster during periods of expansion and declined more slowly during periods of contraction. Its population is younger and growing, whereas that of Europe is ageing and dwindling. It is the largest underwriter of higher education and of public and private sector scientific and medical research and development, and it is the biggest source of technical innovation. It is even the greatest producer and exporter of mass culture, ranging from literature and film to pop music and junk food.

None of this means that US pre-eminence is permanent. But it does mean that the United States, for the foreseeable future, will truly qualify as what former French Foreign Minister Hubert Védrine once termed the "hyper-power". And it does mean that the current international system is as close to being structurally unipolar as any that has ever existed.

Constraints on US power and the need for partners

Nevertheless, the exercise of US power, even military power, is not un-constrained by other actors in the international system. For one thing, the United States, unlike previous international hegemons, is a democracy. Executive decision-making processes are influenced by public opinion and legislative action, one determinant of which is the perception of legitimacy. Part of that depends on the support or at least tacit approval of other international actors, which is why the United States stressed so strongly that it was acting in Iraq with a "coalition of the willing", even if coalition partners were actually dispensable for military operations (as they were in Kosovo, where the United States, under a different administration, operated without UN authorization but under the cover of NATO). As a result, the rest of the international system, even if it cannot directly prevent the use of US force, can indirectly constrain it by providing input into the domestic US debate.

The willingness of other actors to support or object to US action is conditioned not only by their material stakes in the issue at hand, but also by their general level of comfort or discomfort with US pre-eminence in global affairs. Historically, the emergence of such hegemonic power has prompted others to try, almost instinctively, to mobilize balancing or countervailing power, if not alone then through the building of counter-coalitions. The combination of resentment, envy and fear that explains this instinct was given expression in one of French President Jacques Chirac's explanations for his opposition to the use of US force in Iraq: "Any community with only one dominant power is always a dangerous one, and provokes reactions. That's why I favor a multipolar world, in which Europe obviously has its place."[2]

A second constraint concerns the sorts of security threats that military force is intended to address. US military power is undoubtedly sufficient to deter or defeat any traditional, state-based military threat to itself or its allies. Since the end of the Cold War, however, the United States has increasingly broadened the definition of its threat agenda to include, and in fact emphasize, threats of terrorism by non-state actors and state supporters of terrorism and the proliferation of weapons of mass destruction (WMD) to "rogue states" and terrorists. The applicability of military power to these sorts of threats is far more problematic.

Non-state actors, even in an era of cybernetics and virtual reality, need to occupy some physical space in order to plan, train, equip, finance and launch operations. That physical space exists within the frontiers of states, and terrorists can freely use it only if governments support or tolerate their presence or else are unable to assert control of the territory nominally under their jurisdiction, e.g. in "failed states". In some circumstances, military power can be applied to contain or eliminate state supporters of terrorism or else take control of failed states. That is what the United States did in Afghanistan and also (as at least part of the rationale for war) in Iraq. But, even in these circumstances, the use of military force is politically feasible only if some degree of legitimacy has been established through a prior effort to address the threat through methods short of war and a successful search for some degree of approval by other international actors. Such preconditions do not mean that the United States will subordinate its own assessment of when all means short of war have been exhausted or that it will accept that only institutionalized bodies such as the United Nations or the European Union can confer the "seal of approval". But they do constrain the extent to which the United States can act militarily in a truly unilateral fashion.

Thirdly, to be effective, counter-terrorism measures short of war depend in large measure on international cooperation. In assessing and evaluating information about the capabilities and intentions of terrorists and state sponsors of terrorism (and especially in tapping human intelligence), in tracking and controlling the movement of suspect individuals, suspect funds and suspect materials and components, in police operations and in judicial proceedings, US security agencies have no choice but to rely on cooperation with their counterparts in other countries.

Finally, and most critically, US military preponderance is not easily adapted to dealing with what are increasingly seen as the "root causes" of the international terrorist threat – the conditions of political, economic and social dysfunction that create both a large corps of highly motivated terrorists and an even larger corps of supporters and sympathizers who provide the material infrastructure and psychological foundation for terrorists. Particularly since 11 September 2001, the US administration has focused on the nexus between terrorism/WMD proliferation, on the one hand, and the lack of political, economic and social freedoms among those posing the chief threats, on the other. What this logically implies is an essentially subversive foreign policy to promote the liberalization of political and economic systems in the developing world.

In one sense, there is nothing new about this. The United States and most European countries have for decades been ostensibly committed to development and modernization in developing countries, and they have also gone through spasms of commitment to the promotion of human rights. Indeed, the European Union actually preceded the United States in appreciating the security threat stemming from political repression, economic regression and social stagnation in neighbouring areas. That appreciation gave rise to the Euro-Mediterranean Partnership (EMP), an initiative undertaken by the European Union in 1995 to promote democratization, civil society and human rights in the Mediterranean through dialogue and economic incentives, including a Euro-Mediterranean free trade area.

What seemed different about the post-9/11 US approach, therefore, was not the mere conviction that the ills associated with the failure to move the modernization project forward – ills vividly documented by the 2002 and 2003 Arab Human Development Reports of the United Nations – constituted a direct threat to its national security. Instead, it was the apparent determination to push the modernization project with greater vigour, even if that meant no longer working only with existing regimes but also working against them. In other words, the United States apparently concluded that it could no longer rely on inducements such as security support and economic assistance to elicit greater domestic liberalization, but that it needed to apply some degree of coercion and run the risk of confrontation with authoritarian regimes, even those otherwise deemed "friendly" or "moderate".

Yet, outside of the military sphere, it will be very difficult for the United States alone to make coercion truly effective. This is not because the United States lacks non-military instruments of its own. After all, US diplomatic and economic levers are not inconsequential, and the costs of defying strong US preferences cannot be airily dismissed. But these instruments do not begin to "dominate the market" in the same way that US military power does. Consequently, the threat of US political and economic sanctions, unless coordinated with a critical mass of other international actors, cannot have the same impact. In short, non-military unilateralism by the United States is even less feasible than is military unilateralism.

Besides, embarrassing revelations about the intelligence assessments and decision-making processes leading up to the war in Iraq, together with the obvious complications and costs of arranging a viable post-war order in Iraq, suggest that Iraq, rather than serving as some kind of precedent or template for future action, will actually turn out to be *sui generis*. This does not mean that limited operations ("surgical strikes") are precluded. But it does mean that the credibility of future military unilateralism on a very large scale, even under the cover of "coalitions of the willing", has been undermined for the foreseeable future, and the United States will need the support of others even more than it did before – as evidenced by the efforts of the US administration to enlist multilateral support for its ongoing state-building operations in Iraq and for efforts to contain Iran and roll back North Korean nuclear programmes. In short, the international system remains multipolar in many important respects.

Building a coalition on the Middle East

Both the need for cooperation with others and the difficulty of obtaining it will almost certainly be most evident with respect to the Muslim world, especially the Middle East. The need stems from the fact that this is where the greatest socio-economic dysfunction is found and from where the greatest new security threats emanate. By nearly all indicators of political and economic openness, the Middle East lags behind most other regions of the world. With a few notable exceptions, almost all the remaining authoritarian governments and state-controlled economies are concentrated there. Again with a few exceptions, it is also the region that generates the most intense concerns about proliferation of weapons of mass destruction and long-range delivery systems, where the most virulent anti-Western sentiment is cultivated, and from which the most numerous and destructive perpetrators of terrorism draw their support, inspiration, financing and recruits.

The difficulty of securing international cooperation stems from the fact that this is also where other major international actors find the greatest opportunities to assert their independence from the United States and the fewest reasons to align themselves with it in pursuing confrontational policies with local regimes. To some extent, this is merely a local/regional manifestation of the general aversion of other states and international organizations to being seen as accomplices or tools of a United States suspected of hegemonic aspirations. Most other international actors, especially in Europe, do not share the US view that coercion can be a legitimate instrument of foreign policy, except in direct self-defence (however slippery that principle may be when their own vital interests are threatened).

However, there are also specific reasons why other actors will be reluctant to alienate regional governments and vocal publics in Arab or Muslim countries. These include dependence on oil, the absence of visible and effective liberal opposition movements in most of these countries and sensitivity about participating in what will inevitably be described by the targets of US-led action as an anti-Muslim or anti-Arab crusade.

This latter consideration is particularly compelling in countries with large Muslim minorities.

Both the general and the specific reasons have particular resonance in Europe, especially in some of the larger countries where participation in US-led enterprises is believed to compromise independent stature in global affairs, and in Russia. Many Europeans believe that they have an even greater stake in Middle Eastern/North African/Mediterranean affairs than does the United States because of geographical proximity, closer economic links (including a larger share of Middle Eastern import markets, which they are reluctant to lose, and greater dependence on Middle Eastern sources of energy, which they are reluctant to jeopardize) and a larger domestic Muslim/Arab population. They also believe that they have a better understanding of these regions because of longer – if not always happier – experience dealing with former colonies. Some of them even claim a more nuanced appreciation of terrorism owing to longer exposure to it at home. For these reasons, several European countries have invested considerable diplomatic resources in the region, and the European Union as a whole has made the Middle East the centrepiece of its Common Foreign and Security Policy.

This means that it will be difficult for the United States to assemble broad coalitions to promote US-defined solutions to various challenges. In the most extreme cases involving large-scale military intervention, that does not necessarily pose a problem insofar as the conduct of military operations is concerned, since US power alone may be sufficient to eliminate hostile regimes in "rogue states" or, where regimes barely function, to take physical control of "failed states" (or parts of them).

But if the purpose afterward is to transform the societies that harbour terrorists and/or weapons of mass destruction, then there must be sustained follow-up in the form of humanitarian assistance, peacekeeping, law enforcement, the entrenchment of political institutions and the propagation of different political values – in short, "nation-building". US military forces are not trained or equipped for these sorts of tasks. Nor are they particularly eager to undertake them. It is not clear that any externally sponsored project in nation-building can ever really succeed anywhere. But the indications from Afghanistan as well as from Iraq make it clear that, for the project to have any chance of success, structures, skills, resources and experiences are needed that the United States, alone, does not possess in sufficient quantities. In other words, for a military action, even a unilateral one, to accomplish its political purpose, the United States will need to mobilize the willing involvement of other states and international organizations, including the United Nations.

In any case, the aftermath of the war in Iraq reinforces the expectation that this sort of exercise will not be repeated any time soon. And the need for international cooperation is even more apparent in less extreme and less unlikely situations, where the purpose is not to replace a regime or to create one where it in effect does not exist, but rather to influence the domestic and international behaviour of functioning regimes. This might imply diplomatic and/or economic sanctions (for example, boycotts or embargoes). Here, too, the United States has the greatest capacity to act, and it is rarely possible for any other individual country to step in and fill whatever diplomatic, economic or security role the United States plays; it is precisely the expectation of US leadership that usually prompts the rest of the so-called "international community" to respond to every problem by asking Washington, "What are you going to do about it?" But it is also rarely possible for the United States, acting alone, to apply enough pressure to bring about change in the behaviour of regimes, particularly when that change represents a threat to the long-term survival of a regime. For such pressure to be effective, it must encompass a critical mass of other diplomatic and/or economic actors, so that any remaining cracks in the wall of containment are not wide enough for regimes to wriggle through.

The problem is that sanctions almost always also imply some diplomatic and/or economic costs to the states that apply them, or to important domestic elements within those states, and they almost always provoke opposition on humanitarian grounds because they punish innocent civilians more than the government they are intended to target. Even the post-1991 sanctions regime against Iraq, which enjoyed indisputable international legitimacy, was not immune to these sorts of counter-consideration, which manifested themselves in the distortions of the "Oil-for-Food" programme.

Given the nature of vested economic interests and domestic political calculations, any future call for sanctions against other Muslim or Arab states is likely to elicit even less cooperation and compliance. And given the fact that Europe, not the United States, is the largest trading partner for most states in the region, any refusal to exercise potential European leverage will constitute a particularly wide crack in any wall.

Finally, even the mildest form of US coercion – assistance made contingent on compliance with donor-defined criteria – cannot be effective if it is only unilateral. There is a whole range of performance standards that do not immediately produce democracy but do pose longer-term threats to the viability of authoritarian systems. Some of these are explicitly political, such as independent judiciaries, tolerance of civil society, a free press and the uncontrolled movement of ideas. Some are implicit in economic restructuring, such as financial transparency, the sanctity of contracts, campaigns against corruption and the reduction or elimination of monopolies, licensing arrangements, indirect taxes and other controls on the movement of people, goods, services and capital. But all of them go to the heart of how bureaucratic-patrimonial regimes survive. The European Union made an effort to promote some of these standards in the EMP through a variety of inducements, but it never threatened to withhold these "carrots" in the event of failure to comply. Nor did its individual members make their own assistance programmes contingent on conformity by regional recipients with their standards of governance. In part, they probably hoped that any incidental economic improvement would reduce the pressures causing illegal immigration into Europe. In part, they were responsive to complaints that such action would constitute unwarranted interference in domestic affairs and contempt for the sovereign rights of recipient states. By and large, US policy in the past operated in a similar manner. But even if post-9/11, post-Afghanistan, post-Iraq thinking augurs a change in US behaviour in this regard, that change cannot have a truly decisive impact unless it is simultaneously implemented by a sufficient number of other providers of financial, technical and/or security assistance – and resistance to that sort of coordinated implementation has already compelled the United States to water down its more ambitious plans for a "Greater Middle East Initiative" and make do, instead, with yet another set of anodyne aid programmes of the sort that have failed, in the past, to produce significant transformation in the economics or politics of the region.

Uni-multipolarity in the international system

All in all, the implications of these conflicting impulses are clear. In the international system, the United States is not even "first among equals" because there are no presumptive equals. Instead, it is the pre-eminent actor in almost every respect, particularly in respect of military power. As a result, it has the capacity, along with the will, to act unilaterally when it feels that its vital interests are threatened. And it certainly has the capacity to resist demands by others eager to constrain it in the hope of transforming the international system into a kind of European Union writ large, in which some components of identity and sovereignty are transferred to supranational institutions, all disputes are settled peacefully on the basis of supranational consensus or international law defined by multilateral consultation and negotiation, and force (except in totally unambiguous and highly unusual instances of self-defence against direct aggression) is effectively banished from the repertoire of foreign policy.

At the same time, however, US power alone is far from sufficient to accomplish ambitious goals of conflict resolution between states and of political and social transformation within states that are the source of the most palpable political-security threats. To act effectively against these threats, the United States will need to convince others of the nature and immediacy of these threats and of the legitimacy of the actions it proposes to take against them. "Others" does not necessarily mean global or even regional institutions and organizations. There can be no delusion about the near impossibility of mobilizing universal support based on general principles for anything the United States wishes to do anytime or anywhere (especially in the Middle East). Nor is it likely that the United States will agree to condition its policy on such support and thus find itself in a situation of Gulliver-like paralysis, much less act in ways it finds distinctly repugnant. For example, it is highly unlikely that the United States will accede to entreaties by others to pressure Israel into conceding Arab demands. In this sense, exhortations that the United States confine itself to the use of "soft power" and subordinate its foreign policy to the strictures of international law and organizations such as the United Nations are highly unrealistic.

This reality will not change, regardless of the party in power, at least until international law and international organizations are themselves reformed in a manner that reflects the realities of international politics rather than the platitudes of international diplomacy. International law needs to address illusions about the rule of law in lawless environments and about the problem of effective immunity for non-state actors or rogue states that operate outside its confines. Most importantly, it needs to confront the absurdity of granting terrorists and their state sponsors and apologists a seemingly legitimate role in the elaboration, interpretation and enforcement of the law; in properly functioning legal systems, they would be recused on grounds of clear conflict of interest. And international organizations need to address the incongruities of a system still formally based on the legal fiction of sovereign equality, as conceived at Westphalia more than 350 years ago, without regard to the normative content of the system or the character of its members. Under current operating rules, institutions such as the General Assembly and the UN Commission on Human Rights are often dismissed because they resemble the proverbial hen house guarded by the foxes.

It would be wrong to attribute this approach only to the so-called "neoconservatives" in the current US administration. The goal of disseminating the United States' core values and the inclination to act unilaterally are persistent themes throughout US history; the dedication to spreading democracy was associated with Woodrow Wilson, perhaps the US president most often seen as a liberal internationalist.[3] But, unless the United States actually builds the capacity to impose its will on the entire world (which is improbable) or retreats, once again, into isolationism (which is only slightly less improbable), it will have to engage in a continuous process of building ad hoc coalitions with like-minded partners. And building a sufficient base of international sympathy and support inevitably means some dilution of or compromise over US preferences, not just on the immediate issue at stake but also, perhaps as part of a trade-off, on other specific issues or general matters such as environmental codes of conduct or universal criminal jurisdiction.

As a result, US policy, though probably impelled by an underlying unilateralist impulse, will necessarily include elements of substantial multilateralism. This simply reflects a distribution of power dictating an international system that is neither truly unipolar nor truly multipolar, but rather some kind of hybrid that might be termed uni-multipolarity. Still, the engine at the centre of this variable global geometry is the United States, and the primary authority and responsibility for determining its success or failure will remain in US hands for a long time to come.

The implications for Israel

Since its creation, Israel has seen itself as a small power in a hostile environment, outnumbered and out-resourced both materially and diplomatically by those arrayed against it. As such, it cannot presume to shape the world order but must instead adapt itself to it. More to the point, it has always striven to make sure that it has the support and understanding of at least one of the major powers. In the first decade or two of the Cold War, the range of powers willing and able to fill this role was somewhat broader than it subsequently became. Both France and (to a lesser extent) the United Kingdom occasionally offered material and diplomatic backing at a time when the vestiges of empire still endowed them with great power status. Indeed, France was Israel's major foreign partner and virtual ally from the mid-1950s to the mid-1960s, when the convergence of interests that brought the two countries together cracked following Algerian independence. By that time, however, both European powers had reconciled themselves to the retreat from empire and (with greater or lesser enthusiasm) to the reality that they could no longer aspire to the role of global power.

That left only the United States and the Soviet Union, and the Soviet Union was not a viable option. It is true that in the very early years of Israel's independence, when socialist parties were still strong and not yet ideologically disillusioned, there were prominent voices in the Israeli political system calling for the country to align itself with the "progressive camp" in the world; in 1953, the day after Stalin died, the newspaper of Mapam (a self-proclaimed Marxist party in the governing coalition) declared that the "light of the earth" had gone out. However, it was already clear since the time of the Korean war that Israel, as a whole, had made a strategic choice in favour of the West. For the most part, this was because of a range of normative, cultural and economic affinities. But it was also the case that the Soviet Union had disqualified itself in Israeli eyes, both because of a resurgence of government-inspired anti-Semitism at home and because Soviet foreign policy, in its pursuit of "anti-imperialist" partners in Africa, Asia and Latin America, had dedicated itself to cultivating "progressive" Arab regimes. As a result, the Soviet Union was unavailable, whatever Israeli preferences may have been, and, despite some early frictions in the US–Israeli relationship, the United States became the default option when it began to make itself available as a strategic ally for Israel from the mid-1960s onward.

This fundamental need to maintain a close, cooperative relationship with the United States runs like a thread through the history of Israeli foreign and security policy for the past four decades and explains, in particular, Israel's response to the Iraq crisis both before and after the stage of active hostilities. In the period leading up to the beginning of the campaign, Israel modulated its posture of non-involvement to take account of US political needs, to the point where Cabinet ministers – apart from the foreign affairs and defence ministers – were essentially issued with "gag orders" by the prime minister. The basic message was that Israel was neither opposed to the war (unlike many other US allies, Israel could not possibly risk alienating the administration) nor in favour of it (lest that compromise the US search for coalition partners and intensify resistance in the Arab/Muslim world). In fact, to the extent that the public posture indicated some ambivalence, that accurately reflected real sentiment.

On the one hand, Israel had no particular reason to feel at all solicitous of Saddam Hussein. Indeed, it had a long score to settle with him, stretching back through his active support of Palestinian terrorism (the US$25,000 reward paid by the Arab Liberation Front to families of suicide-bombers), through the gratuitous launch of 39 Scud missiles on Israel during the first Gulf war of 1991 and the dispatch of an Iraqi expeditionary force to the Golan Heights in 1973, all the way to the public hanging of Iraqi Jews in 1968/1969. On the other hand, Saddam Hussein contained "in the box" was seen to be less dangerous than Saddam Hussein placed in a position where he had nothing left to lose. The reason for this calculus has to do with the fact that, apart from the question of missiles and weapons of mass destruction, Iraq had already disappeared as a strategic actor as far as Israel was concerned. Following Operation Desert Storm, Iraq had lost whatever capacity it previously had to contribute a significant expeditionary force to any eastern front, a scenario that had become even more remote after the Jordanian–Israeli Peace Agreement in 1994. And Saddam's contributions to the Palestinian capacity to threaten Israel, although perhaps of some propaganda value to him, were ultimately marginal. Even without Iraqi subsidies, there was no lack of motivation by suicide-bombers to blow themselves up, and all the rest was little more than sound and fury. Saddam's much-vaunted million-man "Jerusalem army", for example, was known to be a hollow shell. Consequently, Saddam hardly inspired more fear among Israelis in this respect than he did hope among thoughtful Palestinians.

However, Saddam's missiles and WMD were a rather different matter. For the most part, Israeli pre-war intelligence assessments conformed to those of the United States and the United Kingdom, and any analysts who may have had reservations about these assessments were reluctant to express them, primarily because of the professional (and self-protecting) bias in favour of worst-case analysis. The operating assumption was that Iraq retained or had reconstructed a small number of usable delivery systems and perhaps some WMD warheads – chemical and biological if not nuclear. The missiles themselves were not of overwhelming concern if armed with conventional warheads, since even those not intercepted could do only a minimal amount of damage. But the presumed WMD warheads were a different matter. As long as Saddam stayed contained or subject only to the kind of attack that preserved the possibility of his political and personal survival, it was felt that the threat of further escalation, including Israeli retaliation, could deter him from using WMD. But the worst-case scenario, which most preoccupied defence planners and analysts, was one in which he was left with no prospect of survival and might lash out in sheer vengefulness or in a final effort to secure his historical reputation. In other words, Israel believed that it had more reason to fear forcible regime change in Iraq than a perpetuation of the status quo. For this reason, although Israel would shed no tears over Saddam's demise and could not, in any case, express any reservations about what the United States was determined to do, it was far less enthusiastic about the war in Iraq than was portrayed by those eager to depict the war as some kind of US–Israeli conspiracy or even an Israeli objective foisted on an unwitting US administration.[4]

Israel's margin of manoeuvre is similarly constrained in the post–Cold War uni-multipolar world order that persists after Iraq – not that this is a particularly uncomfortable system in which to operate. After all, Israel benefits from a very intimate relationship that transcends party lines in the United States and extends beyond the executive branch into Congress and public opinion. This relationship is underpinned by a set of shared values as well as shared perspectives on issues that are of greatest concern to Israel, such as terrorism, the proliferation of weapons of mass destruction, rogue states and manipulation by adversaries of international organizations and international law. At the same time, there is a prudential reluctance to put all its eggs in the same basket, and Israel would certainly prefer to diversify its foreign relations "portfolio" to the extent that is possible. Indeed, it has invested considerable resources in cultivating other, rising powers, such as China, India, Russia and Turkey, in addition to Europe. This diversification is reflected in patterns of foreign trade, including defence-industrial trade. In the current and foreseeable circumstances, however, these other powers are not as available, attractive or reliable as partners in the political-security domain. Furthermore, even if the gap in political-security "weight" separating them from the United States were smaller, the political cost of pursuing a closer partnership with them would in some cases be unacceptably high – either because of the political conditions attached or because of the opportunity cost incurred by alienating the United States. The former consideration applies in particular to Europe; the latter applies to China (as evidenced by the Israeli decision, under intense US pressure, to cancel a sale of the Falcon airborne warning-and-control system).

All in all, Israel has no particular reason to find intolerable a uni-multipolar world order in which the "uni" part is its closest ally and strongest supporter. Since it is too small to have any significant impact on the way the international order has evolved or is evolving, this is almost certainly as much a function of good luck as of good planning. In this case, however, the result is more important than the cause.

Notes

1. Mohammed Ayoob and Matthew Zierler use the phrase "unipolar concert" to describe essentially the same phenomenon in their contribution to this volume (Chapter 3).
2. Interview in *Time Magazine*, 24 February 2003.
3. Melvyn P. Leffler, "Bush's Foreign Policy", *Foreign Policy* (September/October 2004), pp. 22–23.
4. Even the most critical analyses of exaggerated Israeli intelligence assessments of Iraq's pre-war capabilities acknowledge that Israel had consistently stressed, in dialogues with US counterparts, that the Iraqi threat was under control and that the Iranian threat was far more serious. However, "[o]nce the Bush administration decided to take action against Iraq, it was more difficult for Israel to maintain its position that dealing with Iraq was not the highest priority". Shlomo Brom, "Israeli Intelligence on Iraq: An Intelligence Failure?", *Strategic Assessment*, Vol. 6, No. 3 (November 2003), pp. 15–16.

10

Egypt and the Iraq war

Ibrahim A. Karawan

As in the rest of the Arab world, the tendency in Egypt was to see the US military intervention in Iraq not just as one more Western intervention in the region, but as a manifestation of a restructuring of the international system to enforce a world order led by the United States, with the Middle East considered as the launching pad of such global alteration. Political activists and analysts alike in Egypt argued that the aggregate power of the United States, reflected in its massive military strength, economic wealth, technological edge and political leverage, gives it a decided superiority that all other states and international institutions cannot match or effectively block.

The 1991 war in the Gulf was an early attempt by the United States to project its newly acquired power against Iraq to liberate Kuwait from occupation while the Soviet Union was in the process of rapid disintegration. The US military intervention, with the objective of changing the regime in Iraq under the banner of strategic pre-emption and outside the scope of international legitimacy, was seen by Egyptian observers as a full-blown design to reshape the region and a message to the rest of the world that the United States' predominance had become a fact of life and a strategic reality.

In mapping its policy options with regard to the Iraq war in 2003, the Egyptian regime was caught between the requirements of its role as a regional actor striving to exercise influence in the Arab world and the imperatives of its close relations with the United States as a predominant arms supplier, a major aid donor, a political backer and a strategic partner since the late 1970s. In addition, the regime had to consider its domestic political climate, in which an attentive public had become increasingly anti-American owing to the Palestinian–Israeli conflict, the tensions in the Gulf and the growth of sentiments associated with political Islam in society at large.

This chapter will examine the interaction of these factors and how they shaped Egyptian perceptions of the US military intervention in Iraq and the implications for Egyptian policy toward the Iraq war. In addition, it will analyse the debates that emerged in Egyptian society regarding the impact of the war on the international order and the desirable and feasible options available to the current Egyptian regime concerning the roles of both the United States and the United Nations in the Middle East. For the Egyptian regime, addressing all these considerations is like balancing on a tightrope between the regime's reluctance to take any radical position that could disrupt its relations with the United States and its preference for an active role by the United Nations and its system of collective security. According to Egyptian President Hosni Mubarak, Egypt can never lose sight of its main priority – "[p]rotecting the home front from the repercussions of this war and rais[ing] high the banner of Egyptian national security ... Egypt's position was, and still is, in opposition to this war and it will not take part in military operations against brotherly Iraq."[1]

A US-dominated world order?

Whereas some political actors in Egypt saw the US hegemony as an inescapable strategic reality, others maintained the belief that strategic realities can be reversed by acts presumed to cement such realities, as the 2003 war in Iraq was supposed to do. For the latter, the basic issue was not whether US policy makers wanted to establish a position not just of primacy but also of global dominance. Rather, it was whether US economic and political conditions at home could make it possible to have a sustained and coordinated pursuit of such hegemonic designs. Large-scale and protracted conquests, such as the one that the United States launched in Iraq, tend to be especially costly in economic, human and political terms. In that sense, the Iraq war in 1991 was not a representative example but a deviant case from which it is not possible to assess the future course of US behaviour in the post–Cold War era.

The optimists in this Egyptian debate believed that a preponderance of military power does not translate automatically into an effective exercise of leverage. In other words, the possession of immense power measured in material resources does not necessarily translate into power as influence and leverage. Usama al-Baz, a senior foreign policy adviser to President Mubarak, is an advocate of the notion that the international system has been moving toward multipolarity. Although US military power appears to be expanding, the political utility of reliance on military power is in a state of relative decline. Such power, according to al-Baz, is no longer the primary currency in international politics because the financial costs of large-scale and prolonged military intervention have become burdensome, even for the mightiest military powers. Domestic factors in such countries, including the United States, deserve more analytic attention.

Thus, from such a perspective, foreign policy predicated on the assumption of an unchallenged US hegemony would be problem ridden because the international realities are more complicated than suggested by the logic of a fleeting "unipolar moment". Not only is the international system in transition, but the choices made by regional actors can also play an important role in shaping policy outcomes. It may be instructive, for instance, to refer to how two Middle Eastern states, Iran and Syria, took advantage of the US stalemate in Iraq to enhance their bargaining positions in relation to the United States, despite the decisive power asymmetry between each country and the United States.

Other examples of the perceived limits of structural factors in determining the positions of states in conflict areas and of the argument that US dominance is not necessarily compelling may be seen in the following:

1. Turkey's rejection of deployment by the United States, another NATO member, through its borders with Iraq, despite US power, was a sign that political reform may not necessarily produce outcomes that are favourable to or congruent with US policies or élite preferences.

2. Despite Saudi Arabia's strategic reliance on the United States, its leadership decided, owing to public opinion among other factors, to limit US military access to some of its most sophisticated and strategically located airbases.

3. Although the United States refused to rule out any significant European role at the beginning of the armed intervention in Iraq, the growing difficulties faced by the United States seem to have convinced its leaders to seek incremental rapprochement with Europe, as much as possible, in order to increase the chances of multilateral action.

4. The previous point applies also to the case of the United Nations in Iraq, particularly concerning the elections in that country, whose legitimacy required going beyond US unilateral action and legitimizing and accepting the role of the United Nations.

5. The same asymmetry exists in Iran's relations with the United States, although US policy makers must take into account the economic and political price that society and its élites may be willing to pay for exter-

nal involvement where the immediate security interests of the dominant power are not directly at stake.

Egyptian commentators in *Al-Ahram* newspaper entertained the hope that opposition to US policies in Iraq on the part of many European states, particularly by France and Germany, would constrain the United States and influence the shape of the post-war settlement. They took note in particular of the statements made by President Chirac at the meeting of the heads of European states and governments in Brussels at which he announced that "France will not accept any UN resolution legitimating the military intervention and giving the Anglo-American belligerents the right to administer Iraq [after the end of hostilities]".[2]

Challenges to the UN role

Viewed from Cairo, once more, international crises such as that in Iraq since 2003 have resulted in a situation in which the Middle East has emerged as the region where the features of the world order at large have manifested themselves most clearly. Before that, and going back to the post-1956 war era, the parameters of the bipolar world were very obvious. In the 1973 war, the features of conflict management under conditions of détente between the superpowers were demonstrated. By 1991 in the Gulf, the characteristics of the new world order were beginning to take shape.

From this perspective, the war against Iraq has reflected both the US drive toward dominance and opposition to US hegemony through the efforts of France, Germany, Russia and China. Put differently, the United States led a military intervention in Iraq with no regard for international legality, and the aforementioned powers mounted a political and diplomatic campaign to, in effect, isolate United States policy and place greater reliance on the United Nations.[3] That diplomatic and political campaign was influenced by the assertiveness of civil society organizations against the United States' campaign in Iraq. The international rift between the major powers reflects a certain rivalry over "status" and a sense of efficacy more than it reflects primarily any differences over the well-being or welfare of the Iraqi people.

With regard to the role or weight of the United Nations, many analysts in Egypt worried that tensions between the veto-holding members of the Security Council over the US intervention and the prolonged war in Iraq might end up reducing or dooming the international organization to a state of irrelevance. US President George W. Bush argued during the crisis that the United Nations would face serious risks if it failed to live up to its responsibilities and to act against the Iraqi threat. This threat evoked the precedent of US military intervention in the Balkans without the backing of the United Nations.

For many concerned Egyptian analysts, despite the imperfections of the United Nations, a world without it would be a world of anarchy and unpredictability as well as instability.[4] The United Nations has been active in arenas other than Iraq, and an initial US–UK monopoly over the situation in Iraq should not necessarily indicate the demise of the United Nations and its role in the domain of international security. Before Iraq, in Afghanistan, Somalia, Lebanon, Cambodia, Mozambique and Angola, the United Nations was not simply a helpless actor manipulated by the United States, and it should not be expected to go down the path of the League of Nations. Advocates of such perspectives in Egypt argue along the lines of former UN Secretary-General Hammarskjöld that the main task of the United Nations is not to turn the world into a paradise but to prevent it from becoming a living hell. It is in that sense that the United Nations is still relevant, at least in depriving those who resort to military pre-emption of international legitimacy.[5]

Serious worries about the viability and effectiveness of the United Nations, particularly the Security Council, continue to be expressed in Egypt and the Arab world. The decision of the United States under the George W. Bush administration ultimately to ignore the Security Council and resort to the use of force after it had become clear that it was unlikely to win in Security Council deliberations and rally a simple majority of Council member states in support of a war resolution has not only weakened the international legitimacy of the US military intervention in Iraq but also weakened the effectiveness of the United Nations and its role in the field of international security. A paradigm that legitimizes the use of force to settle political scores may create precedents that could replace the UN advocacy of the peaceful settlement of international disputes.[6]

The conflict and war in Iraq have posed significant challenges to the authority of the United Nations, and the future of world governance as a whole came to be at the mercy of the way in which the US administration reacted to the situation in the Gulf and to international terrorism. "By insisting on using force outside the United Nations system, it made clear that the multilateral control on the use of force which has been the hallmark of world order since 1945 no longer held."[7] This was demonstrated by the policy prescriptions put forward in September 2002 by the *National Security Strategy of the United States of America*, which advocated the resort to unilateral pre-emption if deemed necessary by the United States to stop so-called rogue states and their terrorist clients threatening the United States and its allies. According to this doctrine, the United States must forestall or prevent these hostile acts and, if necessary, resort to pre-emptive military reaction regardless of the availability of international backing and without any recourse to collective security under the United Nations.

In the case of Afghanistan, the UN endorsement of military action by the United States was rather tacit. In the case of Iraq, as Egypt saw it, the United States obtained neither implicit nor explicit endorsement by the international organization. That is why, when military action was imminent, the United States and the United Kingdom decided not to seek UN approval because it was clear that such approval would not be forthcoming, even from countries with which the two states had historically had close relations. The fears expressed in Egypt were that the United States' behaviour might provide a precedent or lead to a contagion effect among other powers in the name of averting attacks or threats, whether conventional, by terrorist groups or by weapons of mass destruction. These fears implied greater tension, arms races and an unbridled resort to power in the absence of another superpower that could stand up to the supremacy of the superpower at the top of the pyramid of the international system.

Despite the superiority of the United States in terms of its vast power capabilities, much about the future of international order may depend on how it manages its resources and avoids what may be characterized as the temptations of excessive unilateralism as well as overextension. According to the prominent Egyptian writer and political activist, Mohamed Sid-Ahmed, "[t]his seems to be the challenge that will determine the future of our world".[8]

According to this view, US policy on Iraq benefited from an ambiguity in Security Council Resolution 1441, similar to the one that afflicted Resolution 242 on the Middle East settlement. Whereas some thought Resolution 1441 required the United States to obtain yet another decision from the Security Council to authorize the use of force against the Iraqi state, the Bush foreign policy and national security team insisted that it was required only to "consult" with members of the UN Security Council before unleashing its own massive military intervention, and had no obligation to seek a second resolution by the Council or to get its endorsement. Because Security Council resolutions are sometimes passed as a result of complex compromises, their inconsistencies and ambiguities may gloss over sharp differences among states, as was the case in Resolution 242, which was not implemented because of such ambiguities.[9]

As a result, the view from Cairo is that, far from containing terrorism, the war in Iraq has made the country a haven for a number of transnational terrorist groups, which have expanded their activities under the conditions of anarchy prevailing at least in certain parts of Iraq. Egyptian policy makers and analysts tend to conclude that there is thus little likelihood of serious reconstruction in Iraq in the short run. In fact, since the

US intervention Iraq has become a centre of terrorism and the offices in the UN compound in Baghdad have come under violent attack by terrorist groups. Thus, the security of UN personnel was compromised further at a time when more members of the "coalition of the willing" were expressing interest in reducing, if not eliminating, their military presence and role in Iraq and other countries were continuing to refuse to deploy their troops to Iraq as long as these troops were not under the command and direction of the United Nations.[10]

According to foreign policy adviser al-Baz, a political solution in which the United Nations would play a major role was the only realistic and prudent way to deal with the Iraq issue. Before the 2003 war, al-Baz argued that Iraq had to be dealt with along the lines stipulated by international law, that international inspectors of weapons of mass destruction should be allowed to pursue their comprehensive inspection unhindered, and, finally, that any US military action should be decided upon only with an international consensus through the United Nations.[11]

Less than a year later, al-Baz acknowledged the complex balancing act in which the Egyptian regime was forced to engage. On the one hand, with the objective of ensuring Iraq's compliance with its commitments to eliminate weapons of mass destruction, Egypt was in favour of persuading the United States to act within the boundaries of international legitimacy and secure solid international backing to make sure that the stability and territorial integrity of Iraq itself would not be compromised. On the other hand, Egypt did not want the United States to get involved in a military and political quagmire in Iraq. Since Egypt's leadership was aware that the United States was not likely to rule out military options, Egyptian policy as expressed by al-Baz was that the United States should have allowed enough time to examine and assess all possible policy options before embarking on any military action in Iraq, particularly given the escalation of anti-US feelings in the Arab world. After all, the Middle East had witnessed greater instability since 11 September 2001, and any large-scale military action by the United States was likely to increase regional instability, radicalism and unpredictability, well beyond Iraq and its ethnic and religious divisions.

To avoid such destabilizing spillover effects, Egypt proposed an open discussion or exchange of views between the United States and Egypt, with the participation of other Arab countries, possibly including Jordan, Saudi Arabia and Morocco. Such discussions would have extended to examining how to put the stalemated Palestinian–Israeli peace process back on track and break the vicious cycle between the parties by holding them accountable. As al-Baz put it, Washington had to become politically engaged in this process instead of leaving the escalating crisis simmering on the so-called back burner. Otherwise, the radical elements working against peace in the region might become stronger. Europe, the United Nations and the United States could play a role in implementing the road map to peace and thus avoid a risky regional outcome.[12]

The demise of the Arab order

It was not just global diplomacy that failed to find a peaceful way out of the crisis over Iraq and its rapid acceleration into a full-fledged war; diplomacy at the regional and Arab levels also failed to identify a viable political alternative to US-led military action against Iraq in March 2003. Perhaps the most striking illustration of that failure occurred when the Sharm el-Sheikh Arab summit decided to assign a high-level Arab delegation that included five foreign ministers and Amr Moussa, the Secretary General of the Arab League, to hold talks with top-ranking US and Iraqi officials to identify a possible solution to the crisis. However, the delegation was not received by either US officials or their Iraqi counterparts and, thus, the mission was terminated with no result. As Salama A. Salama of *al-Ahram* pointed out, "Given the pressing nature of the timetable, one cannot quite allay the suspicion that the [Arab] summit [in Sharm el-Sheikh] is nothing but an exercise in passing the buck. It will have no effect because it is not intended to have one."[13]

It is possible to argue that the US side was not prepared to give this delegation any guarantees that military action by the United States was not imminent, and Iraqi officials would not, and possibly could not, discuss with the Arab delegation anything pertaining to the potential exile of Saddam Hussein and his sons from Iraq. Whatever the reasons, the coalition represented by the Arab League was not even remotely able to persuade either side to modify the fundamentals of its position. The failure of this delegation to meet anyone on either side of the crisis might have been a slap in the face of Arab diplomacy and a sign that the diplomatic route as a whole was increasingly perceived as superfluous in making a difference to the course of the crisis that was intensifying in the region.[14]

It is important to recall here the argument by Roger Owen that, "[a]t previous times of crisis or change within the international system, a stock Arab reaction has been to call for a united response to the challenge they face".[15] In most cases, however, a collective Arab response has never materialized. The threat was not really seen as a collective one, and some Arab states had provided their own military facilities for use by US forces. This explains some states' preference, while a divided Arab world dithered over what it was permissible to denounce, for bilateral arrangements with the United States and under its security umbrella, regardless of what they said in their media. Perhaps that is why some pan-Arabist circles describe their vulnerable position with terms such as *in'idam al-wazn* (weightlessness), *tahmish* (marginalization), *ma'zaq* (predicament), and *azmah-karethah* (crisis disaster).[16]

As a result, the Arab system was not able to make a difference to the mother of all Arab causes, namely the Palestinian issue vis-à-vis Israel, let alone the case of Iraq being attacked by the United States. In practice, Arab state preferences have taken precedence over all pan-Arabist claims. Egypt's prominent writer Mohamed H. Heikal attributed the erosion of the pan-Arabist camp and the weakening of the Arab world to the dramatic defection of Egypt from the Arab coalition and its disengagement from the Arab–Israeli conflict.[17] It is not self-evident, however, that Egypt had the ability to maintain the struggle for ever or that a consensus on its leadership had existed at the Arab level. It is more likely that the state of fragmentation in the Arab order made it even more difficult for Arab states to cope effectively with the Iraq war.

It was Robert Fisk of the UK newspaper *The Independent* who popularized the question during the Iraq war: "What on earth is it with the Arabs?" While millions of protesters marched in Europe and Asia against the looming war in Iraq, Arab capitals were indeed largely quiet in what was described as a "deafening silence".[18] One Arab intellectual argued that the Arabs are in fact torn between authoritarian regimes that lack the political power to express their national will and aspirations positively, and a superpower that wants to implement its control over the region. In the words of Talal Salman, editor of *al-Safir* newspaper,

It is a sad reality that people around the world were able to express their views on the Iraq crisis while all of us took refuge in silence. [Many] regimes in the Arab world believe they can buy their survival from the United States by discreetly agreeing to American plans, while publicly denouncing the U.S. and suppressing all forms of public resentment.[19]

This is, of course, related to what has come to be known as the role of the Arab street in constraining the foreign policies of its current political regimes.[20]

Egyptian state strategies

It was not particularly difficult for the Egyptian state to contain the small demonstrations against the US military intervention in Iraq that erupted in Cairo and other large Egyptian cities. In Egypt and other Arab countries there was an expectation that, even in any relatively small demonstrations and riots against the Iraq war, opposition movements would seize the opportunity to benefit from coverage by news media and satellite television stations to mobilize support among intellectuals and in the street. Arab satellite TV stations have influenced the perception of viewers in Egypt and in other Arab countries. Perhaps no previous war has been so extensively covered by various news sources around the clock. In Egypt, the anti-riot police forces backed by armoured personnel carriers were mobilized to prevent and deter potential demonstrators. Thus, while the opposition wanted to use the Iraq war to discredit the regime, policy makers made sure there were adequate coercive instruments to contain the challenges posed by Islamist, Nasserite and leftist opposition groups, who were shouting such things as "We won't bow, we won't bow, we are sick of the quiet voice", and "Build more prison cells, tomorrow the revolution will come and leave no one".[21]

Many political activists in Egypt were arrested for their activities against the war in Iraq, and their cases were supported by groups such as Human Rights Watch, the Egyptian Organization for Human Rights and the Egyptian Press Syndicate. In these instances, condemnations of the war and of state repression, as well demands for political reform, political liberalization and cancellation of the emergency laws, were packaged together in the demand, "No to war ... No to tyranny".[22]

Repression was not the only means through which the Egyptian state tried to cope with the situation. President Mubarak called for an urgent Arab summit meeting in Sharm el-Sheikh saying, "We must show our people that we are making an effort to stop the war." As Ahmed Maher, Egypt's foreign minister, made clear, "There is anger on the streets because there is a feeling that Muslim countries are under attack."[23] The official media were allowed by the state to take militant positions that might be even more extreme than the positions taken by opposition newspapers during the war in terms of denouncing the US policy of force in Iraq. The ruling National Democratic Party organized Egypt's largest rally against the war, with probably 600,000 protesters taking part. As in other Arab countries, the regime proved able to co-opt the street, even to emasculate the protest, and make its citizens watch the war on television.

Thus, little threat to regime security has materialized. Regimes had enough time and resources to take steps to maintain political control, including occasional talk about reform, which, according to officials, has to come from within and not from outside, to be incremental not radical, and to be consistent with Arab cultural specificity. The Egyptian state also engaged in a few symbolic acts as manifestations of gradual reform, such as abolishing law no. 105 regulating state security courts and establishing a national council for human rights.[24] The top priority of the regime, however, is to weaken any opposition movement that might translate frustration in Egyptian society into organized political action.[25]

Notes

1. Nevine Khalil, "Walking a Tight Rope", *Al-Ahram Weekly*, 2 April 2003.
2. "France to Resist US Plans for Iraq", *Al-Ahram Weekly*, 27 March 2003.
3. Osama El-Ghazali Harb, "As Another World Emerges", *Al-Ahram Weekly*, No. 626 (20–26 February 2003). For the explanations given by Mohamed Hassanein Heikal of the US policy in Iraq, see Amira Howeidy, "Heikal's Dream", *Al-Ahram Weekly*, No. 607 (10–16 October 2002).
4. Nyier Abdou, "As the World Turns", *Al-Ahram Weekly*, No. 629 (13–19 March 2003).
5. Abdel-Alim Mohamed, "A Matter of Relevance", *Al-Ahram Weekly*, No. 632 (3–9 April 2003).
6. Ayman El-Amir, "A World United against War", *Al-Ahram Weekly*, No. 630 (20–26 March 2003).
7. "The Death of the UN", *Al-Ahram Weekly*, No. 631 (27 March–2 April 2003).
8. Mohamed Sid-Ahmed, "Challenging America's Hyperpowerdom", *Al-Ahram Weekly*, No. 640 (29 May–4 June 2003).
9. Mohamed Sid-Ahmed, "Degenerating into Chaos", *Al-Ahram Weekly*, No. 653 (28 August–3 September 2003).
10. Ibid.
11. Nevine Khalil, "The Rules of the Game", *Al-Ahram Weekly*, No. 609 (20–26 June 2002).
12. Osama al-Baz, "Special Policy Forum Report: Iraq and the Middle East – A View from Cairo", Washington Institute for Near East Policy, *PolicyWatch*, No. 711 (13 February 2003).
13. Salama Ahmad Salama, "Passing the Buck", *Al-Ahram Weekly*, No. 626 (20–26 February 2003).
14. Abdel-Moneim Said, "A Problem with the World", *Al-Ahram Weekly*, No. 613 (21–27 November 2002).
15. Roger Owen, "A New Post-Cold War System?" *Middle East Report*, Vol. 23, No. 5 (September–October 1993), p. 3.
16. Ibrahim Karawan, "Arab Dilemmas in the 1990s: Breaking Taboos and Searching for Signposts", *Middle East Journal*, Vol. 48, No. 3 (Summer 1994), p. 441.
17. Amira Howeidy, "Heikal's Dream", *Al-Ahram Weekly*, 10–16 October 2002.
18. Omayma Abdel-Latif, "Arab Apathy", *Al-Ahram Weekly*, No. 627 (27 February–5 March 2003). See also Hassan Nafaa, "End of the Arab Order?" *Al-Ahram Weekly*, No. 631 (27 March–2 April 2003); Jim Lobe, "Arab Public Opinion Deeply Ambivalent about U.S.", *Inter Press Service*, 9 October 2004; Marc Lynch, "Taking Arabs Seriously", *Foreign Affairs*, September/October 2003; and Shibley Telhami, "Double Blow to Middle East Democracy", *Washington Post*, 1 May 2004, p. A21.
19. Abdel-Latif, "Arab Apathy".
20. Asef Bayat, "The Street and the Politics of Dissent in the Arab World", *Middle East Report*, Spring 2003; Hossam el-Hamlawy, "Closer to the Street", *Cairo Times*, 6–19 February 2003; and Sherine Bahaa, "Arabs Show Their Rage", *Al-Ahram Weekly*, No. 631 (27 March–2 April 2003).
21. Amira Howeidy, "Where Did All the Anger Go?", *Al-Ahram Weekly*, No. 626 (20–26 February 2003); and Paul Schemm, "Egypt Struggles to Control Anti-War Protests", *Middle East Report*, 31 March 2003.

22. International Crisis Group, *The Challenge of Political Reform: Egypt after the Iraq War*, Middle East Briefing, Cairo/Brussels, 30 September 2003; Mohamed Sid-Ahmed, "No to War ... No to Tyranny", *Al-Ahram Weekly*, No. 627 (27 February–5 March 2003); Mona El-Ghobashy, "Egypt's Summer of Discontent", *Middle East Report*, 18 September 2003; and Tamir Moustafa, "Protests Hint at New Chapter in Egyptian Politics", *Middle East Report*, 9 April 2004.

23. Nevine Khalil, "End of the Road", *Al-Ahram Weekly*, No. 628 (6–12 March 2003). See Jonathan Schanzer, "The Arab Street and the War: Are Regimes in Control?", Washington Institute for Near East Policy, *PolicyWatch*, No. 729 (21 March 2003).

24. Ibrahim Karawan, "Security Sector Reform and Retrenchment in the Middle East", in Heiner Hanggi and Theodore H. Winkler, eds, *Challenges of Security Sector Governance* (Munster: LIT Verlag, 2003), p. 258.

25. See the statements by Issam El-Erian, member of the Shura Council of the Muslim Brotherhood, in Omayma Abdel-Latif, "Preemptive Containment", *Al-Ahram Weekly*, No. 620 (9–15 January 2003). See also a comprehensive analysis in Ahmed Abdalla, *Egypt before & after September 11, 2001: Problems of Political Transformation in a Complicated International Setting*, Doi-Focus, No. 9 (March 2003); and see also Amr Hamzawy, *The Continued Costs of Political Stagnation in Egypt*, Democracy and Rule of Law Project (Washington DC: Carnegie Endowment for International Peace, February 2005).

11

Reactions in the Muslim world to the Iraq conflict

Amin Saikal

The public reaction to the Iraq war and occupation has been one of almost universal opposition in the Muslim world, and has extended to non-Muslim minorities, especially within its Arab domain. With the exception of the oil-rich mini-states of Kuwait and, to some extent, Qatar, as well as Afghanistan, leaderships of all Muslim countries have either condemned or criticized military actions against Iraq. They have called for the withdrawal of occupying forces and for UN supervision of Iraq's transition, empowerment of the Iraqi people to run their country and restoration of Iraq's independence and sovereignty. Further, they regard the invasion of Iraq as being against the better judgement of the UN Security Council, a defiance of international law and a serious threat to regional stability and international order. In this, they have reflected the mood of a majority of their populations, which, according to various pre- and post-war public opinion surveys by Gallup and other agencies, have been anti-war and anti-American.

This, however, should not hide the diversity of views and attitudes that have emerged at the levels of élites as distinct from the masses, and of public as distinct from private circles. While publicly emphasizing an accord between their policy stand and the attitudes of a majority of their subjects in common opposition to the US-led military actions, at the private level many regimes have nonetheless either acquiesced in US actions or supported them. In this, they have given effect to different and shifting "national interests", geopolitical circumstances and political preferences, as defined by rulers of the day. Two bodies that have actively sought to articulate a collective position on behalf of Arabs/Muslims are the League of Arab States (or simply the Arab League) and the Organization of the Islamic Conference (OIC), which includes all Arab League member states. Yet what these bodies have articulated has provided little insight into the policy approaches of the individual member states. The rhetorical or public face presented by them has been as lacking in political credibility as have the organizations themselves.

This chapter has three specific objectives. The first is to survey élite positions in the Muslim world. The second is to assess the collective positions articulated by the Arab League and the OIC and the private position of some of the key Muslim regimes and their diverse dependence on and vulnerability to Washington. The third is to evaluate various clusters of attitudes at the popular level and the representativeness and effectiveness of these positions as expressions of a general popular Muslim perception of the Iraq conflict and the United States.

Élite attitudes

Any discussion of Muslim attitudes to the Iraq conflict must be qualified by three observations at the outset. One is the prevalence of political authoritarianism and societal illiberalism and the consequent schism between state and society in the Muslim world.[1] This has engendered a distinction between what the élites publicly say and what they privately do, and what the masses aspire to do and what they are able to achieve in the formulation and conduct of both domestic and foreign policy in most Muslim countries.[2] Another is the varying degrees to which these countries are vulnerable to US power and influence and can shape their policy priorities and actions in response to this vulnerability. The third is the ability of rulers to strike a balance between the demands of the geopolitical circumstances of their countries and the extent to which they can respond to the need to maintain the United States' favours.

Authoritarianism has produced inherently insecure rulers in most Muslim countries. A majority of them lack direct public mandates and popular legitimacy, making them feel insecure in relation to their own people and to one another.[3] As a result, many have found it imperative either to secure or to be very mindful of an external source of support, and to take this into account as a major determinant in defining their national interests. Since the end of the Cold War and the collapse of the Soviet Union in 1991, US power has become more than ever attractive in this respect. Yet dependence on the United States has also meant vulnerability to US pressure and dictates in one form or another and the necessity to behave in such a way as not to lose Washington's support.

Meanwhile, despite their authoritarian aloofness from the public, the rulers have found it incumbent to impress upon their publics that they are not "stooges" of the United States and are responsive to their moods and expectations when it comes to the issue of wider Muslim solidarity. There is a felt need to insist to their domestic audience that their individual policy behaviour and promotion of national interests are conditioned not exclusively by their need for regime preservation but also by the dictates of public aspirations. As a consequence, regimes in most key Muslim states from Morocco, Egypt, Jordan and Saudi Arabia and its partners in the Gulf Cooperation Council (GCC) to Pakistan have walked a tightrope to strike a balance between what is demanded of them to create at least an appearance of domestic legitimacy, and what is required of them in pursuit of cooperative relations with Washington.

With the exception of Kuwait, where both the state and a majority in the society have been in favour of US-led military actions, and Afghanistan, where the Karzai government is totally dependent on the United States for its survival, all other Muslim governments – whether generally friendly or adversarial towards the United States – have publicly opposed, though in various degrees, the military campaign and called for an immediate halt to hostilities and withdrawal of foreign forces, as well as for UN involvement in Iraq. For example, even three of the United States' allies, the Egyptian, Saudi and Pakistani regimes, voiced some very harsh criticisms of Washington. Egyptian President Hosni Mubarak went as far as to warn Washington that its military actions could produce hundreds more bin Ladens and widen rather than diminish the threat of international terrorism – a warning that was echoed in different ways by many other Muslim government leaders. President Musharraf of Pakistan refused to declare his hand on behalf of Pakistan as a non-permanent member of the UN Security Council (2002–2003) in support of a military campaign, and firmly cautioned against its destabilizing consequences. The Saudi leadership, despite being the United States' longest-standing Arab Islamic ally, not only expressed open opposition to military action but also publicly announced a refusal, contrary to its position during the Gulf war of 1991 over Kuwait, to make Saudi territory and facilities available to be used for the invasion of Iraq. This was also the position that was reflected in the official statements and final communiqués of four major Arab League and OIC summit meetings held shortly before the Iraq war and after it.

The Arab League and the OIC

Prior to the invasion, the Arab League's Secretary General, former Egyptian foreign minister Amr Moussa, raised serious alarm about the impending invasion. He called for rapid international and Arab action to stop it. He reiterated resolutions issued on 1 March 2003 by the Arab summit held in Sharm el-Sheikh that rejected the use of military force against Iraq, or for that matter any Arab country, and emphasized the imperative that there should be no Arab participation in these attacks. He drew attention to the lack of UN backing for the invasion and therefore the illegality of the action.[4] To reinforce this position, an emergency Arab League meeting was called for 22–25 March 2003. In the end, despite Kuwait's serious objections, the meeting issued a resolution condemning "the US–British military aggression on Iraq – a member state of the United Nations and of the League of Arab States". It deemed the "aggression" in "violation of the Charter of the United Nations and of the principles of international law, a deviation from international legality and a threat to international security and peace". It also called "for the immediate and unconditional withdrawal of US–British forces from Iraqi lands, and for making them accountable for the financial, moral and legal liabilities of this military aggression".[5]

The OIC adopted a similar policy line. In its pre-war summit on 6 March 2003, its 57 member countries essentially decided on a position that was in full agreement with that of the Arab League. It declared its "total rejection of any strike on Iraq and any threat to the security of any Islamic state", and called on Muslim countries "to refrain from taking part in any military action targeting the security and territorial integrity of Iraq or any Muslim nation". It also rejected the US vision of reshaping the Middle East and any US attempt to "impose change in the region and interfere in its internal affairs".[6] It reiterated the need for a peaceful resolution of problems with Iraq. Similarly to the Arab League, the OIC reinforced its assertions by making it clear that the UN Security Council had not authorized military action against Iraq nor could such an action be justified under international law. The OIC also, again like the Arab League, appealed for the problems with Iraq to be resolved within the UN framework.

As soon as the Iraq war commenced, the OIC joined forces with the Arab League to call a special meeting of the UN Security Council to halt the military conflict. In the OIC's subsequent meetings in Doha, Tehran and Kuala Lumpur over the next year, it reaffirmed its opposition to Iraq's occupation, with a call for the withdrawal of foreign forces in favour of the United Nations' taking over the administration of Iraq's transition and restoration of Iraqi sovereignty.

Yet neither the Arab League nor the OIC proposed any practical measures to enforce their resolutions or achieve their declared objectives. They contented themselves with hollow appeals to the occupying powers and the United Nations, while knowing that their calls would fall on deaf ears. The problem with the Arab League and OIC positions from the start was two-fold. First, these organizations arose in 1945 and 1969, respectively, in response to a need of many Arab and Muslim leaders to show a semblance of unity based on shared, intertwined factors of Arabism and Muslim identity against challenges from inside and outside their domains. However, in the absence of concrete common political principles, ideological values and mechanisms and instruments of policy enforcement to bind them together, they have had little on which they could rely to enable them to elevate themselves beyond formulating a collective position to give practical expression to that position on vital foreign policy issues.

During the Cold War, when most of the OIC members joined the Non-Aligned Movement from the late 1950s and 1960s, they were in practice haunted by and divided over a variety of questions, ranging from what to do with the Palestinian problem and how to protect themselves against rival major powers to how to deal with the challenges of modernization versus traditionalism. As it turned out, they dissipated most of their energy and resources on defending themselves against one another and securing the favours of one superpower against the other, rather than forging a united front in world politics. The disintegration of the Soviet Union and the end of the Cold War did not bring any major change in this respect. If anything, the constraint of the politics of global bipolarity was lifted, enabling OIC members to become more daring and competitive against one another in search of security in a world dominated by one superpower – the United States. The deference of their regimes to the power and influence of the United States did not allow most of them to reconcile their private positions with their public rhetoric on many issues, including, most importantly, the latest Iraq conflict.

The meetings of the League and the OIC prior to the invasion of Iraq were marred by fundamental disputes between Iraq and Kuwait. Small but oil-rich Kuwait constantly accused Iraq of threatening its sovereignty and independence, based on Iraq's past claims on Kuwait and its 1990 invasion. On the other hand, Iraq persistently painted Kuwait as a bridgehead enabling the United States to achieve its "imperialist designs" against Iraq and for that matter the Arab nation and Muslim world, and pressured other participants to side with it. The acrimonious exchanges between the two degenerated into a circus at the early and late March 2003 meetings of the League and the OIC. Whereas Saudi Arabia and other oil-rich GCC members backed Kuwait and used their oil muscle to influence others to do the same, other participants walked a tightrope with a view to not being seen either as upholding Iraq's position or as offending the United States and its GCC allies.[7]

The charade behind that meeting was typical of many other meetings of the two organizations following the invasion of Iraq. The outcome of the meetings was always a compromise between pro-US and anti-US elements, with a number of other members, including those with strong nationalist or pro-Arabist or pro-Islamist leanings, finding themselves with the awkward task of maintaining and projecting the image of unity to the outside world. Even when finally the League and the OIC found it necessary to invite the representative of the US-appointed Iraqi Interim Governing Council and its successor, the Iraqi Interim Government, to take up the Iraq seat from 1 June 2004, the struggle between those opposing and those supporting a dominant US role in the Arab and Muslim worlds underlined the ineffectiveness of the League and the OIC. Although their members have publicly adopted a common position, in private those members have had little hesitation in undermining that position by pursuing policy actions beneficial to their individual interests.

Élites' private positions

The very leaders who publicly levelled serious criticism at the United States assured Washington in private that, as many in the Bush administration have claimed, they would do nothing to hinder or cause difficulties for the United States in achieving its objectives. All of them have used repressive measures wherever required to control anti-war dissent and active opposition in their countries. No leaders were more assertive in this respect than those of Egypt, Saudi Arabia, Pakistan and Jordan. This was true even in the case of the government of the Islamic Republic of Iran – a staunch opponent of the United States in the Muslim world. Tehran, of course, was not guided by a politics of dependence on the United States but rather was induced by strategic considerations to do whatever was feasible to avoid becoming a direct target of the United States and to exploit the unprecedented opportunities opened up to Iran by the US fixation on the Saddam Hussein regime. Iran adopted the position that, although it was opposed to US-led military action, it had deeper grievances against Saddam Hussein and therefore it would not stand in the way of the United States toppling the Iraqi dictator.

While talking of a united opposition to military actions, for example, the governments of the United Arab Emirates, Bahrain, Qatar and Oman, as well as that of Saudi Arabia, were concurrently making their territories and facilities available for use by the forces of the United States and its allies. Of course some of them did so more than others, although none of them to the extent of Kuwait, Qatar and Bahrain. If it had not been for the assistance of these states, the United States and its partners in the "coalition of the willing" would have had enormous difficulty in launching and prosecuting the war successfully. This was particularly so in view of the fact that a conflict in Muslim Turkey between its government, which was willing to fulfil Turkey's alliance obligations towards the United States and keen to use US leverage to support other foreign policy interests, and its people, an overwhelming majority of whom opposed any participation in the war, caused such political consternation and delay as to prevent Turkey from serving as the northern launch pad for the US attack on Iraq.

Popular sentiment

This élite duplicity has not been representative of the popular reaction, under both religious and nationalist impulses, to the invasion and occupation of Iraq. Based on various public opinion surveys,[8] a majority of citizens in the Muslim world have been scornful of the invasion and what has transpired in Iraq since then. Saddam Hussein's dictatorship, which was courted as an ally by the United States in the 1980s, enjoyed little popular support in Iraq and the Muslim world, given its brutal and secular nature. However, most Muslims have rejected Washington's approach to solving the problem as two-faced and irresponsible. They easily recall that it was the United States that left Saddam Hussein in place in 1991, knowing full well that he would continue to brutalize the Iraqi population. They realize that, when Saddam Hussein used weapons of mass destruction against his own people, the US administration knew what was happening but did nothing major to prevent it. They are suspicious of the reasons for which the United States and its largely Anglo-Celtic allies (the United Kingdom and Australia) took it upon themselves to secure the removal of that regime by military means. The failure of the occupying forces thus far to substantiate their original justification for war by proving that Saddam Hussein's regime possessed dangerous weapons of mass destruction[9] or had aided international terrorism has reinforced their belief that the war and the occupation have been part of a wider strategy to remake the Middle East in the image of the United States and its allies and to marginalize political Islam in world politics.

They are pained by the fact that, in demolishing Saddam Hussein's regime, the United States and its coalition of the willing also destroyed the state in Iraq, with no appropriate plan for post-war management of the country. Although shedding no tears over Saddam Hussein's departure, like many in the rest of the world they are appalled that a devastating war was imposed on the Iraqi people at the cost of thousands of civilian casualties and infrastructural and historical destruction for what they see as economic and geostrategic reasons. The sight of the sadistic humiliation and even death of randomly rounded-up Iraqi prisoners by US forces at Abu Ghraib prison has made an indelible impact and shaped their perceptions of the United States and its allies for years to come. The apology by President Bush to the abused prisoners, their families and the Iraqi people has done little to make a difference in this respect. The events have resonated so badly with Arabs and Muslims that most of them no longer believe what the United States says or does. They now have a very poor image of the United States as a power dedicated to democratic and human rights causes, and see the US promise of democracy as nothing more than a gimmick.[10]

This impression has been reinforced by the upsurge of violence and the US application of disproportionate force against resistance fighters at the cost of thousands of civilian lives and massive destruction of property in Fallujah, especially in April 2004. The same happened in one form or another in the following two months in the Shiites' holiest cities, Najaf and Karbala, where a number of mosques were either destroyed or damaged as a result of US shelling. The anti-US resistance has been only too happy to foster this situation for its own political objectives, both within Iraq and in the wider Arab and Muslim world. It has constantly sought opportunities to weaken domestic support for the United States and its Iraqi allies and, by exhausting popular patience with the US role, to build momentum behind a reassertion of anti-US Iraqi nationalism.[11]

Playing into that agenda, Washington has persisted in its efforts to influence in its favour the outcome of the democratic processes that it has put in place in Iraq. US Secretary of Defense Donald Rumsfeld has all along been opposed to the emergence of an Islamic government as a democratic outcome. To many Muslims this is a gratuitous provocation, almost as offensive as Rumsfeld's early description of the chaos and insecurity that had followed the war as "a little bit of untidiness" and of Israel's occupation of Palestinian lands as "the so-called occupation".[12] Many Iraqis and their Arab/Muslim counterparts do not believe the United States has the ability and willingness to generate anything more than a US puppet administration. They are even highly suspicious of the Iraqi elected government under Prime Minister Ibrahim al-Jaafari and President Jalal Talabani as little more than a government dependent on the United States for its survival and therefore vulnerable to American dictates.

A view that seems to have gained hold among Muslims around the world is that the US policy approach to the management of post-war Iraq has been to maximize the regional dominance of the United States and of Israel. Many Arabs and Muslims have viewed the war as a gross exploitation of the post-9/11 global sympathy for the United States and as part of a strategy to enable a small group of neoconservatives and "born again" Christians in the Bush administration to achieve their "power reality" goal of wider domination.[13] The war has reminded them of the long centuries of European colonization of much of the Muslim world, and prompted them to regard it as imperialist and anti-Islamic. In addition, the war has played into the hands of the radical and neo-fundamentalist forces of political Islam and galvanized support for them even among those for whom Islam is essentially a faith and a form of identity rather than an ideology – a development that Osama bin Laden and his operatives would celebrate. This is a most unfortunate development because, if the West wants to build bridges of understanding, it will need to engage the Muslim mainstream.

Of course, these views are not expressed uniformly in the Muslim world. They represent the convergence of positions articulated primarily by four different but at the same time politically and ideologically overlapping active clusters across the Muslim domain. To understand this, it is desirable to look at each of these clusters and the degree to which their positions have converged in reaction to the Iraq conflict, while bearing in mind that each cluster's position can be treated only as indicative of a broad attitude.[14] A considerable degree of overlap and variation exists between and within each of the clusters, largely because of the wide range of cultural, political and religious diversity within the Muslim world and in some cases within each Muslim country.

The first cluster comprises moderate Islamists who uphold Islam as a dynamic ideology of political and social transformation and a meaningful ideology of opposition to authoritarian regimes at home, but reject any form of violence as a means to achieving such objectives, unless their religion, life and liberty at either the individual or the societal level are seriously threatened or invaded. On the whole they subscribe to what has been termed "Islamic liberalism" and adhere strictly to the Islamic command, as enshrined in the Qur'an, that there is no compulsion in religion. They operate mainly within loose organizations, informal small groups or at individual levels. Many Muslim intellectuals and informed Muslims fall into this category. They rejected the 11 September attacks as unacceptable, and were pained to learn that Osama bin Laden and his al-Qaeda were responsible for them. They have dissociated Islam from extremism and are appalled by those who have presumed to act in its name to take innocent lives, whether at home or abroad, and thereby place Muslims everywhere under siege. They reject extremist impositions on the Muslims over whom Islamist regimes have managed to gain control, such as the people of Afghanistan during the Taliban rule. More importantly, they regard the 11 September events as providing a dangerous incentive to the United States and its allies to expand and deepen US dominance in the Muslim world and to marginalize defiant political Islam more than ever before.

They stress the value of peaceful, evolutionary change and want to work within existing national and international structures to bring about structural change. They are open to modernity, believe in the inevitability of progress, are well disposed to interfaith dialogue and have no aversion to utilizing Western knowledge and achievements to benefit their societies within a globalized world. Yet they simultaneously criticize the United States and some of its allies for not making the necessary efforts to develop a better understanding of Muslim faith, norms, values and practices and to build solid bridges of understanding for mutually rather than unilaterally beneficial relationships. Their attitude towards the United States and its Western allies is one of affection and despair: they are keen to benefit from Western education, technology and institutions, and to secure access to Western countries as both migrants and visitors, but they are critical of Western policy behaviour towards the Muslim world and of arrogant claims of supremacy over Muslims. In Islamic terms, the moderate Islamists are on the whole *ijtihadi* – creatively interpretive of Islam, with a dedication to renewal and reform as the best means to achieve salvation and prosperity.

Yet many of these moderate Islamists have found US behaviour in relation to Iraq unjustifiable and the conduct of the war on terror to be pointedly anti-Muslim, with the two interactively being detrimental to Muslim causes. If in the past they looked to the United States as a source of support for reforming and democratizing their societies, they are now disillusioned with the United States. The US policy actions have put them on the defensive, prompting some of them to become amenable to anti-US Islamic resistance. They no longer find themselves in a position to play a determining role in the politics of their countries and the conduct of relations with the United States and its allies. Their voices are drowned out in favour of their radical counterparts. Important casualties of this development have been the moderate, reformist Islamists, who were until recently led by former President Mohammad Khatami in Iran, and who until the start of the Iraq war had succeeded in moderating the excesses of their conservative Islamist opponents and in restraining them from pursuing their anti-US foreign policy agenda. The Iraq war and its consequences weakened the position of the reformists, enabling their hard-line opponents to outmanoeuvre them in the February 2004 parliamentary election and substantially to reduce their political influence. With the hard-line Islamist Ahmedi Nejad winning the presidential election in mid-2005, the reformists are now badly marginalized in Iranian politics.

The second cluster comprises radical Islamists, who are again diverse in their ideological disposition and modus operandi and share some of the platform of their moderate counterparts, especially in adhering to the fundamentals of Islam. However, they differ from the moderates in their puritanical disposition and orthodox political and social operations. They want the sharia (Islamic law) instituted as the foundation for the operation of the state. They view political and social imposition and the use of violence in certain circumstances as legitimate means to protect and assert their religion and religious-cultural identity and to create the kind of polity they deem Islamic. They are not necessarily against modernity, but they want to ensure that modernity and all its manifestations are adopted in conformity with their religious values and practices. They are prone to act radically to redress perceived historical and contemporary injustices inflicted upon Muslims by outsiders, but do not necessarily extend this to similar injustices committed by Muslim against Muslim. They challenge outside powers and their own governments for either being under the influence and control of those powers or failing to respond effectively to the domestic and foreign policy problems facing the Muslim world. They hold the West, and the United States in particular, responsible for the political, social and economic plight and cultural decay of Muslims everywhere and for the damage inflicted upon Muslims by European colonization and post-1945 US domination of most of the Muslim domain. They have often functioned more successfully in opposition than in power. They characterize violent Muslim actions against the United States and its allies as legitimate responses to US behaviour.

Radical Islamists view the United States as their most dangerous enemy, not only for backing Israel's occupation of Palestinian lands, most importantly East Jerusalem, but also for propping up corrupt and dictatorial regimes in many Muslim countries, which they maintain the United States does in order to keep the Muslim world backward and to ensure US hegemonic dominance in world politics. They consider much of what has become an international crisis since 11 September to be a deliberate strategy by hard-core realists of the Cold War era and "born again" Christians, who they believe now dominate the Bush administration and who want to replace the Soviet Union with Islam as the enemy. Their views are often marked by intense hostility to Jews (while insisting they have no quarrel with Judaism). Many among them regard the United States and the civilization for which it stands as demeaning and repugnant to Islam and the Islamic way of life. They have pointed to the US military involvement in Afghanistan and the occupation of Iraq as clear evidence of the United States' hostility towards not just Muslims but also Islam per se. From their perspective, the battle for the future of relations between Islam and the West, more specifically the United States, is now fought on several fronts, but none as important as those of Iraq and

Afghanistan. They would regard a defeat in either of these two countries as a major strategic setback for the world of Islam. In this, they essentially mirror the position of the United States and its allies, which have claimed, in UK Prime Minister Tony Blair's words, that Iraq will determine the future of relations between the West and the Muslim world. In Islamic terms, they are more *jihadi* (in the combative and assertive meaning of the term) than *ijtihadi* (creatively interpretive) in their approach to societal reconstruction and foreign policy. Al-Qaeda and Jama'a Islamiya are examples that essentially belong to this category.

The third cluster consists of neo-fundamentalists or those who adhere to a strict, literal interpretation of Islam. What matters to them most is the text rather than the context. Although diverse streams exist, on the whole they tend to be far more puritanical, sectarian, self-righteous, single-minded, discriminatory, xenophobic and coercive in their approach than the radical Islamists. They apply violence as a means not only to bring change but also to govern. In this sense, they are not much different from a variety of Marxist-Leninist totalitarian groups in the course of modern history. Their understanding of religion is basic, and they are generally poorly educated but highly socialized in a particular religious setting. They are often popularly described as extremists or ultra-orthodox traditionalists. A good example of them was, and still is, the Taliban group. Given the overlap between neo-fundamentalist and radical Islamist views, there have often been links between the two, with radical Islamists using the neo-fundamentalists for human resources, protective purposes and outreach activities, including armed or terrorist operations. This was the nature of relations between the Taliban, an example of a neo-fundamentalist group, and al-Qaeda, a radical Islamist group. The Muslims in this cluster are prepared to go to any lengths to achieve what they consider to be "Islamic martyrdom" in defence of Islam and an Islamic way of life. They are driven by religion rather than politics, and many of them, together with some elements of radical Islamists, form the core of what have become known as Jihadis. They have welcomed the opening of Iraq as another theatre of conflict in which they can engage the United States and its allies on Muslim soil and on their terms.

The fourth cluster consists of radical secular Arab/Muslim nationalists, whose goal is a reformation of their societies, free from domination by foreign, especially US, imperialism in one form or another. Although many radical nationalists are guided by a mixture of secular and religious ideologies, most of them share a strong sense of commitment to their individual national identity and independence, as well as the concepts of pan-Arab and pan-Muslim unity. They range from radical Arab nationalists of the Gemal Abdul Nasser and Saddam Hussein eras to the active Iranian, Pakistani, Malaysian and Indonesian patriots of today. Similar to radical Islamists, they have viewed the United States as hegemonic. They share the other clusters' views of the invasion and occupation of Iraq and are equally determined to counter the occupation and US hegemonic operations in the wider Muslim world whenever the opportunity presents itself.

These four clusters have constituted a cross-section, collectively synthesizing the dominant attitude towards the Iraq conflict within the Muslim world. This attitude appears to resonate well with grassroots networks at village and madrasa levels, whose knowledge of Islam is generally basic. They essentially follow Islam as a faith, and can be apolitical or political, depending on whether or not they feel their faith and way of life threatened by hostile forces. Many of them are potential foot-soldiers of Islam, vulnerable to manipulation by radical Islamists, neo-fundamentalists and radical nationalists. They are often incapable of forming their own opinions about major political issues and events of the day, and remain very much at the mercy of what they learn from or are offered by the politically more informed and judgemental Islamists and nationalists. They constitute the bulk of ordinary Muslims, who if left alone could well remain preoccupied with their daily lives, especially in poor countries. However, in certain circumstances they can be galvanized and mobilized by Islamists and nationalists, whether they live in poor suburbs or in the countryside of Egypt or Pakistan. The plight of Muslims at the hands of "foreigners", whether in Iraq or Palestine, can rouse them to action.

The most dangerous outcome of the Iraq conflict is that it has not only galvanized the politically and religiously active segments across the Muslim world, but also provided a majority of Muslims with a common factor of convergence in their views. If, in the past, it was only the radical Islamists and nationalists who harboured resentment of the United States and its allies, since the advent of the Iraq conflict this resentment has found wider support and acceptability among all social strata in the Muslim world. Unless this trend is reversed by the United States and its allies in such a way as to regain credibility and trust among Muslims, the future of relations between the two sides looks bleak for years to come.[15] Of course, the United States could start the process by developing a political strategy in which it could reconcile its interests with those of the rest of the world. Rather than making facile comments such as "we are hated for who we are and what we stand for", Washington and its allies have to become more sensitive in the conduct of their relations with the Muslim world – acknowledging and rectifying past fundamental mistakes, including the invasion of Iraq and biases towards Israel over the Palestinian problem. Having Muslim governments on side is not the same as winning the minds and hearts of Muslims.

Notes

1. For a detailed discussion, see Fareed Zakaria, *The Future of Freedom: Illiberal Democracy at Home and Abroad* (New York: W. W. Norton, 2003), Chapter 4.
2. For a detailed critical discussion, see Robert Bowker, *Beyond Peace: The Search for Security in the Middle East* (Boulder, CO: Lynne Rienner, 1996), pp. 24–28.
3. See Amin Saikal, *Islam and the West: Conflict or Cooperation?* (London: Palgrave Macmillan, 2003), Chapter 5.
4. *The League of Arab States – Press Release*, 21 March 2003.
5. *League of Arab States Resolution – Press Release*, 25 March 2003.
6. "Islamic Nations Totally Reject Iraq War", *Al-Jazeera, News*, March 2003.
7. For a sample of analyses on the subject, see "Arab League Meet Will Not Help Baghdad, Says Analyst", *Gulf News*, 22 February 2003; Mohammed Sid-Ahmed, "The Future of the Arab League", *Al-Ahram* (Weekly), 15–21 March 2003; Waseem Shehzad, "OIC Fiasco Exposes Arab Rulers' Divisions and Impotence", *Muslimedia International*, 16–31 March 2003; Mushahid Hussein, "OIC Proves to Be a Damp Squib", *Gulf News*, 22 October 2003.
8. See Jim Lobe, "Gap Grows between U.S., World Public Opinion", *Inter-Press Service*, 16 March 2004; Shiibley Telhami, "Arab Public Opinion: A Survey in Six Countries", *San Jose Mercury*, 16 March 2003; Susan Page, "Poll: Muslim Countries, Europe Question U.S. Motives", *USA Today*, 24 June 2004; "Poll: Majority of Muslims Think U.S. 'Ruthless', 'Arrogant'", *IslamOnline*, ⟨http://www.islamonline.net/english/News/2002–02/27/artucke05.shtml⟩, 24 June 2004.
9. See Joseph Cirincione, Jessica T. Mathews and George Perkovich, *WMD in Iraq: Evidence and Implications* (Washington, DC: Carnegie Endowment for International Peace, 2004).
10. For details, see *BBC News World Edition*, 6 May 2004.
11. Scott Ritter, "Saddam's People Are Winning the War", *International Herald Tribune*, 22 July 2004. On the issue of Iraqis' distrust of the United States and its allies, see Thomas E. Ricks, "80% in Iraq Distrust Occupation Authority", *Washington Post*, 13 May 2004.
12. *United Press International*, 28 August 2002.
13. This is also a central argument in Richard A. Clarke, *Against All Enemies: Inside America's War on Terror* (New York: Free Press, 2004).
14. For a detailed discussion of these clusters, see Saikal, *Islam and the West*, pp. 19–23.
15. For a US perspective from inside the US administration, see Clarke, *Against All Enemies*, Chapters 10–11.

Part IV

External actor perspectives

12

The United States and the United Nations in light of wars on terrorism and Iraq

Jane Boulden and Thomas G. Weiss

The United Nations (UN) is predicated on the support of key member states, but divisions over actions by the United States in Iraq have thrown a monkey wrench into the multilateral machinery. Our purpose is to examine how the United Nations has dealt with terrorism, how the advent of US power and foreign policy under the George W. Bush administration has affected the United Nations, and how these two issues, together, have affected the world organization and its future. Our assumption is that the United Nations' responses, as well as the impact of terrorism itself, have significant unexplored implications for international society. Like virtually every issue on today's UN agenda, the analysis requires an understanding of Washington's love/hate relationship with the world organization. In addition, we probe the implications for the future of the United Nations at a time when the prelude to and aftermath of the war on Iraq have raised questions about its relevance.

The Iraq crisis – both the conduct of the war outside of the Security Council and the blowback afterwards – has had a clear negative impact in the short run on the existing UN-centred world order. The re-election of George W. Bush in November 2004 augured poorly, according to conventional wisdom, for multilateralism. Paradoxically, the history of the world organization's efforts to address terrorism, especially after the attacks of 11 September 2001, hold the potential to re-knit the fabric of relations between the United Nations and the United States. That conclusion is preceded by an overview of UN action on terrorism;[1] the impact of 9/11; the roles of the Secretary-General, the Counter-Terrorism Committee (CTC) and the 2005 UN World Summit; the role of other actors and factors; and the implications of Iraq.

Overview of UN action on terrorism

The combined effects of the politics of the Cold War and of the Middle East meant that the Security Council was unable to address the issue of terrorism when it surged in the early 1970s.[2] Beginning in 1972 after a request from the Secretary-General, the General Assembly – primarily through the Sixth Committee – worked to negotiate a series of international conventions under the heading "measures to prevent terrorism". In taking up the issue, however, the Assembly found itself embroiled in how to define the term itself. At the heart of the brouhaha was the argument that, in struggles for liberation from a colonial or repressive regime, terrorism was acceptable, or at least should not be criminalized.

The General Assembly set aside the effort to define the term, and by extension a judgement about possible motivations for terrorism, and focused instead on imposing limits on various methods. The legal conventions established by the Assembly currently number 13. The prohibitions include hijacking, interfering with the safe operation of an aircraft, seizing offshore platforms and ships on the high seas, hostage taking, deliberately damaging public buildings and spaces, and the acquisition of radioactive material.[3]

The end of the Cold War created an opening for change. In 1991 the rubric under which the General Assembly pursued terrorism changed from "measures to prevent" to "measures to eliminate" terrorism – a reflection of a growing sense that the tactic itself was unacceptable, whatever the motivations. Two years later, the Third Committee began work on human rights and terrorism, focusing on the need to protect the rights of both the perpetrators and the victims. In 1997 the General Assembly completed the Convention for the Suppression of Terrorist Bombings; in 1999 the Convention for the Suppression of the Financing of Terrorism; and in April 2005 the Convention for the Suppression of Nuclear Terrorism.

Reflecting its wide conception of terrorism and its implications, in 1996 the General Assembly established an ad hoc Committee on Terrorism whose task is to work to plug the gaps between existing conventions through the development of a comprehensive convention on international terrorism. The ad hoc committee's work on the convention and a high-level conference has long been impeded by the absence of a definition.

The Security Council's first concrete response to terrorism came in

1992 when it sought to compel Libyan compliance with the criminal investigation relating to the bombings of the Pan Am and UTA flights, in 1988 and 1989 respectively, and end Libyan support of terrorism more generally.[4] In the absence of Tripoli's cooperation, the Security Council moved, in March 1992, to impose economic sanctions on Libya, strengthening them later by Resolutions 731, 748 and 883. The Council responded similarly for the Sudan in 1996, calling on the government to extradite the suspects in an assassination attempt on Egyptian President Hosni Mubarak, and then imposing sanctions when Khartoum failed to do so in Resolutions 1044, 1054 and 1070. In response to the bombings of US embassies in East Africa, Council members imposed sanctions against the Taliban regime in Afghanistan, increasing their strength and scope over time through Resolutions 1267 and 1333. In this last instance, in order to oversee the sanctions process and ensure that it was being adequately implemented, in July 2001 Security Council Resolution 1363 created a committee to monitor the sanctions process.

The General Assembly thus dealt with terrorism overall by establishing international rules and norms about what kind of behaviour was and was not acceptable. By contrast, the Security Council responded to specific events with concrete measures on a case-by-case basis. The focus of both was on the state as a source of and a solution to the problem.

Signs of a shift in the division of labour appeared in 1999, when the Security Council passed Resolution 1269 dealing with terrorism as a general issue and condemned "all acts, methods and practices of terrorism as criminal and unjustifiable, regardless of their motivation" and called on states to take a series of measures to prevent and suppress terrorist acts and deny safe haven to those planning them. The resolution was notable because motivation was not an attenuating factor, and the Security Council was responding to terrorism as a global phenomenon.

9/11

Neither terrorism, nor its manifestation in the form of al-Qaeda, was unfamiliar territory when the tragic attacks took place against US territory on 11 September 2001. The Security Council met the following day and with remarkable unanimity and speed passed Resolution 1368, recognizing the "inherent right to self-defence" as a legitimate response. Shortly thereafter, it moved further to establish a wide-ranging set of requirements to be undertaken by states in order to suppress and hinder terrorist activity. Resolution 1373 requires states to undertake a variety of national measures to suppress financing and to ensure non-support for terrorist activity, as well as such cooperative international measures as exchanges of information and early warning. In order to monitor the implementation of these measures, the resolution also established the Counter-Terrorism Committee.

This latter resolution marks a turning point in the Council's approach to terrorism. Building on the earlier Resolution 1269, the provisions of 1373 bring the Security Council firmly into the General Assembly's traditional realm of dealing with terrorism as a general phenomenon, using the mechanism of the state to prohibit, suppress and hinder terrorist activity. In addition, this resolution makes such actions legally binding on all states even while many had failed to sign or ratify the General Assembly's recommended conventions. In case there was any doubt that terrorism was firmly on the agenda, in November 2001 Security Council Resolution 1377 declared that terrorism constitutes "one of the most serious threats to international peace and security".

Read together with the earlier self-defence resolution, the Council's new approach reflected a remarkable dichotomy. Although Resolution 1368 recognized the inherent right to self-defence, it made no attempt to articulate what that meant. Article 51 of the UN Charter provides for the right to individual and collective self-defence, but only until the Security Council has taken the measures necessary to maintain international peace and security. Neither the resolution itself nor subsequent Council statements or activity, however, give any indication that such action was forthcoming. The recognition of self-defence, therefore, represents a virtual *carte blanche* for the use of force by the United States.

Moreover, instead of the 13 international treaties that bind only those states that accede to them, Resolution 1373 creates uniform obligations for all member states and establishes a committee to ensure their implementation. At the same time, therefore, that the Security Council is absenting itself from an oversight role with respect to the use of force in fighting terrorism, it is inserting itself in a significant way into state-based activity by creating international law.

The evolution continues: The Secretary-General, the CTC and the 2005 World Summit

The attacks of 11 September prompted Secretary-General Kofi Annan to enter the fray. Shortly after airplanes destroyed the Twin Towers and part of the Pentagon, he established a working group to examine the implications for the United Nations and recommend how the world organization might best address terrorism. The Policy Working Group on the United Nations and Terrorism advocated an overarching approach with three components: to dissuade disaffected groups from embracing terrorism; to deny groups or individuals the means to carry out such acts; and to work to sustain international cooperation.[5]

With the United Nations sidelined in the war against Iraq, everyone was unhappy – the United Nations could not impede US hegemony, and it could not approve the requisite action against Saddam Hussein. In the midst of the crisis about intervention in Iraq, the Secretary-General indicated that the United Nations was at a "fork in the road ... no less decisive than 1945 itself, when the United Nations was founded".[6] Annan asked 16 former senior government officials – the High-level Panel on Threats, Challenges and Change (HLP) – to describe what ailed the United Nations and propose a way forward. Among its shopping list of 101 recommendations on virtually every topic on the United Nations' agenda, the blue-ribbon panel's December 2004 report, *A More Secure World*, outlined a useful strategy based on dissuasion, measures to counter extremism and intolerance, the development of better counter-terrorism instruments in the context of human rights requirements, strengthened state capabilities, and control of dangerous materials.[7]

While reaffirming the approach in place at the United Nations, the HLP emphasized the extent to which the absence of an agreed definition of terrorism hampered progress. It argued that a definition should be agreed in the General Assembly, "given its unique legitimacy in normative terms", and suggested that a definition of terrorism should recognize that the use of force against civilians constitutes a war crime or crime against humanity. The panel proposed "a description of terrorism as 'any action, in addition to actions already specified by existing conventions ... that is intended to cause death or serious bodily harm to civilians or non-combatants, when the purpose of such an act, by its nature or context, is to intimidate a population or to compel a Government or an international organization to do or to abstain from doing any act'".[8]

There always have been two main sticking points relating to defining terrorism. The first was captured by the expression "your terrorist is my freedom fighter" – that is, many developing countries justify armed violence by those fighting for national liberation. The second was whether "state terrorism" should be included in any definition agreed by the vast majority of member states – for many, the use of force by Israeli and, more recently, US forces is mentioned in the same breath as suicide-bombers.

The HLP confronted these traditional stumbling blocks: "Attacks that specifically target innocent civilians and non-combatants must be condemned clearly and unequivocally by all."[9] The Secretary-General supported this in his own document for the Summit by stating that "the proposal has clear moral force".[10]

The World Summit's final text failed to define terrorism, but for the first time in UN history the assembled heads of state and government issued an unqualified condemnation.[11] They agreed to "strongly condemn terrorism in all forms and manifestations, committed by whomever, wherever and for whatever purposes".[12] The final text eliminated earlier and clearer language that targeting civilians could not be justified, in exchange for dropping an exemption for movements resisting occupation. On balance, the Summit adds momentum to the Secretary-General's evolving counter-terrorism strategy. Whether or not it is signed, sealed and delivered anytime soon or whether the General Assembly "concludes a comprehensive convention on international terrorism" within a year as hoped, the Summit's clear condemnation of violence against civilians is a step forward. It has ethical content, contains the basis for a convention and places the United Nations near the centre of the fight against terrorism.

In brief, the United Nations' response to terrorism has evolved considerably from the early 1970s. During three decades, the General Assembly has generated 13 legal conventions focusing on prohibiting and inhibiting various terrorist forms of attack and support. By contrast, the Security Council did not begin to deal with the question until the early 1990s, and then it took a case-by-case approach to de-legitimize state support for terrorism and to compel states sponsoring terrorism to comply with national and international requirements. Terrorist activity, especially the attacks on the World Trade Center in 1993 and on US embassies later in the 1990s, catapulted the Security Council, under Washington's impetus, into the terrorism realm at a time when the end of the Cold War made agreement more plausible than it had been earlier. It also eventually prompted the Security Council to address terrorism in a more comprehensive manner, a foundation used to construct its post-9/11 strategy.

The Security Council has overtaken, although not eliminated, the General Assembly's role, but the latter remains crucial as the follow-up to the World Summit suggests. If the views of the world organization's entire membership are considered important to the development of international order, the codification of emerging norms should take place in a forum with a comprehensive view. A counterbalance is necessary to offset concerns about Western-centric emphases in the Security Council, which predictably were not changed by the Summit.[13] But the overall impact on this score is mixed, and acceptance and adherence to the conventions remain a struggle.[14]

The Security Council's record is also chequered. Arguably, the sanctions strategy had some impact against Libya and the Sudan – both eventually found a way to hand over suspects and meet the demands to comply with legal processes. But there was little such progress with the Taliban and al-Qaeda prior to 9/11, and Security Council actions up until that point clearly had no impact on al-Qaeda's ability to launch its lethal attacks of September 2001.

A more significant development was the establishment of the CTC. Formed to monitor the implementation of Resolution 1373, it has become an integral part of the United Nations' terrorism strategy. All 15 Security Council members take part, and three sub-committees undertake to analyse reports provided by member states. This process is supplemented by routine advice and assistance from outside experts, an important first in Security Council work. The CTC also consults with regional and other international organizations in order to facilitate greater cooperation. Early in its mandate, the CTC determined that the tasks required of member states were taxing. Through Resolution 1377 in November 2001, it began an assistance role, providing support in the form of advice, experts and technical cooperation to those states in need.

The CTC does not deal in policy, and its mandate is solely to monitor and facilitate the provisions of Resolution 1373. Its first chairman, the United Kingdom's Permanent Representative Sir Jeremy Greenstock, stated that the CTC's purpose is to "monitor, to be analytical, and to report facts to the Security Council for consideration".[15] In addition to establishing and overseeing support for member states in need of assistance – a major undertaking, especially for a committee that is an ad hoc creation and continues to work on the basis of 90-day work plans – during 2004 the Security Council worked to "revitalize" the CTC's work by strengthening its capabilities. In March 2004, Security Council Resolution 1535 approved a new structure, establishing a Counter-Terrorism Executive Directorate, whose executive director is appointed by the Secretary-General and is based in the secretariat.

Other actors, other factors

In addition to Resolutions 1368 and 1373, the Security Council continued to isolate and restrict al-Qaeda by using financial sanctions and controls as well as limitations on travel. In January 2004, the Council passed Resolution 1526, requiring states to impose further financial and travel restrictions on al-Qaeda members and others connected with them, and asking the Secretary-General to appoint an analytical support and sanctions monitoring team for an 18-month period. More than a year later, in July 2005, the Council moved again in Resolution 1617 to strengthen the process by clarifying the listing process for those subject to restrictions. These provisions not only strengthen the existing restrictions but do so by enhancing the United Nations' ability to ensure their implementation.

The savage September 2004 attack on a school in Beslan, in the Russian Republic of North Ossetia, prompted a Security Council reaction, giving more impetus to the CTC's task expansion. Russia proposed that the Council develop a list of terrorist individuals and groups beyond al-Qaeda and the Taliban, who could be made subject to sanctions and other restrictions. Rather than create a list, the Security Council agreed, in Resolution 1566, to establish an internal working group to examine "practical measures to be imposed upon individuals, groups or entities" associated with terrorist activities. Less comprehensive than Russia would have liked, it nonetheless paves the way for expanding the terrorist groups and individuals subject to council scrutiny.

The working group is in addition to another Security Council committee established in April 2004 by Resolution 1540. Prompted by a growing concern that terrorists might acquire and use weapons of mass destruction (WMD), this resolution requires member states to establish appropriate national legislation to ensure domestic control over nuclear, chemical and biological weapons – including border, export and transhipment controls as well as physical protection measures and accountability procedures for existing materials. The resolution also establishes, for a two-year period, a committee to oversee and assist member states in the implementation of these provisions, using outside expertise where desirable along with consultation and cooperation with the CTC and the al-Qaeda sanctions committee.

The United Nations' position on terrorism can be characterized by three linked concepts: evolution, institutionalization and proliferation. The approach has evolved from General Assembly-centred efforts to establish legal limits on terrorist methodologies to one in which terrorism is treated as a global security concern requiring Security Council-led responses. Instead of recommendations from the Assembly, there are obligations from the Council. In the process, both have established a number of working groups and committees to consider various nuts-and-bolts aspects of the problem. Although these mechanisms are ad hoc, the consolidation of the CTC and the nature of the tasks together mark a process of institutionalization in the context of a proliferation of actors, both state and non-state. Indeed, even as the 2005 World Summit was unable to agree on a definition of terrorism, the Security Council met on the Summit's first day at the level of heads of state and passed Resolution 1624, calling on states to work to make incitement to commit terrorism illegal and handing the CTC yet another task that required reporting progress within a year.

September 11 brought about a determined change as well as an intensity in the Security Council, whose resolutions, declarations and presidential statements show a remarkably consistent and collective leadership. As impressive as this review sounds, and as important as these developments are, the Security Council's debates and actions are missing two elements: limits or qualifications for responding to terrorism; and the legitimacy of the Council, and by extension of the United Nations, to act on these matters.

Much of the United Nations' response is about process – committees, reports, lists, cooperation and consultation. None of it involves consideration of the questions of how or whether to address root causes[16] or of the legitimacy and adequacy of force as a response to terrorist events. An avoidance of judgement of state responses to terrorism is not new – just as the Security Council was unable to deal with terrorism prior to the end of the Cold War, it was also unable and unwilling to address the nature of state responses to attacks.[17] One shift after 9/11 is that UN responses consist of a more vocal concern that international commitments to human rights be respected. Almost every Security Council resolution now contains within it, as did the final declaration by the 2005 World Summit, this reminder. By contrast, the question of how to deal with the use of force in counter-terrorist operations remains unaddressed.

The fact that the United States has a *carte blanche* in Afghanistan, whereas others are required to play by the rules, has had a negative impact on the credibility of the Security Council. Washington has to do more than give lip-service to the needs of others. Unless the United States is prepared to bend on occasion and contribute to solutions for priority problems of other regions and countries, the latter are unlikely to sign on when their helping hands are necessary for US priorities. This realization has yet to dawn fully on the Bush administration, whose standard operating procedure is that the United States leads and other countries either follow or get out of the way. Will this continue? We come back to this question after examining developments in Iraq with especial relevance in the United Nations' consideration of what Brian Urquhart speculates could be "the mother of all poisoned chalices".[18]

The implications of Iraq

The impact of Iraq is intimately related to the American role on the world stage and the United Nations' record, and these variables circumscribe the world organization's future prospects.[19] Terrorism and Iraq, issues that have constituted the two most significant threats to the United Nations in recent years, exist in apparent isolation from each other. This is in spite of the efforts – exposed as false by government investigations in both the United States and the United Kingdom[20] – of the Bush administration to point to a link not just between Iraq and terrorism and the existence of WMD, but between Iraq and 9/11. Most of the rationale for action in Iraq, at least as it occurred at the United Nations, focused on WMD and the need to prove the world organization's mettle by enforcing Iraq's compliance with Security Council resolutions. President Bush, for instance, warned listeners at the 2002 General Assembly: "We created the United Nations Security Council so that, unlike the League of Nations, our deliberations would be more than talk. Our resolution would be more than wishes."[21]

US power poses a significant challenge to the type of multilateralism represented by the United Nations at the beginning of the twenty-first century. Bipolarity gave way to what was supposed to be US primacy, but the sheer size and scope of US power makes "primacy" a vast understatement. Scholars speculate about the nuances of economic and cultural leverage resulting from US soft power,[22] but the hard currency of international politics undoubtedly remains military might – which was dramatically illustrated by Washington in Kosovo, Afghanistan and Iraq. Before the wars on terrorism and Iraq, Washington was already spending more on its military than the next 15–25 countries (depending on who was counting); with additional appropriation for Afghanistan and Iraq, the United States now spends more than the rest of the world's militaries combined.[23] Yet Iraq suggests the limits of US military power. The costs of trying to pursue a policy of primacy instead of selective engagement are having an impact, even in Washington.[24]

Ironically, our discussion thus far gives no indication of the Iraqi debate having had a significant impact on the United Nations' terrorism efforts. In fact, the continued ability of the Security Council to agree on terrorist-related measures, and to do so with unanimity, is especially notable after the Iraq trauma. There thus appears to be a shared sense of a global threat and an urgency that could be built upon.

And yet another side of the equation is critical. The end of the Cold War and the willingness to engage the United Nations on security issues made Council action on terrorism possible. There is no question that the driving force was the United States, and this reality provides a possible link between Iraq and terrorism because events there may influence the world organization's counter-terrorism efforts. In August 2005, Security Council Resolution 1618 condemned a series of attacks in Iraq as "terrorist acts", especially those resulting in the deaths of employees of the Independent Electoral Commission and 32 children. Such acts fall well within the World Summit's conception of terrorism and the wording of previous Council resolutions. In this sense, the situation in Iraq links terrorism and Iraq in an unanticipated but unequivocal way. If the situation continues to worsen, the United Nations, already increasingly involved in Iraq through the electoral process, may find itself drawn more deeply into the terrorist side of the equation.

Conclusion

Conventional wisdom now holds that terrorism and the attacks of September 2001, mixed with US power, changed international relations irreversibly. The establishment of the High-level Panel was to help determine a future course of action for the world body, but the none-too-hidden agenda was how to engage the United States.

The existence and viability of Iraq's transitional government after the January 2005 elections and the October 2005 consultations on a new constitution depend largely on the United Nations, whatever the rhetoric from Washington. No US administration will permit the Security Council, or any other part of the UN system, to stand in the way of its pursuit of its perceived vital interests. At the same time, the Council and the UN system as a whole often serve US national interests and give the United States cause to proceed cautiously and with international acquiescence, if not jubilant support. Depending on the issue, the stakes at hand, the positions of other potential allies and the plausibility of collective action, the United States is unlike any other state in that it has the power to act either unilaterally or multilaterally.[25] As the Bush administration discovered, however, "even imperfectly legitimated power is likely to be much more effective than crude coercion".[26]

In light of the sobering experience in occupied Iraq, perhaps the United Nations will become more appealing to Washington.[27] There are numerous other examples of shared interests, which most certainly include fighting terrorism along with confronting the global spectre of infectious diseases (HIV/AIDS, Ebola, and SARS), pursuing environmental sustainability, trade and development, monitoring human rights and criminal tribunals, humanitarian intervention, as well as pursuing weapons inspections and a host of other tasks in post-conflict reconstruction in Iraq and elsewhere. Facing a hurricane-induced crisis at home and plummeting popularity, President Bush's annual address in New York – this time to the presidents, prime ministers and monarchs at the September 2005 World Summit – mentioned these very issues and reflected a broader vision of security threats and the role of the United Nations than in previous years.[28]

The unfortunate reality of power means that, if the United Nations and multilateral cooperation are to flourish, the United States as the globe's remaining superpower must be on board. The record of the Bush administration gives pause, amounting to what K. J. Holsti has summarized as "major assaults on [international] community projects".[29] The list is long, including in addition to the war in Iraq: abrogating the Anti-Ballistic Missile Treaty; withdrawing from the draft protocol for verification of the Biological Weapons Convention and from the Kyoto accords on global warming; subverting the International Criminal Court; rejecting the Comprehensive Nuclear Test Ban Treaty; failing to sign the Convention on the Rights of the Child; and resorting to predatory trade practices. And the achievement of a final document at the World Summit can in some ways be characterized as having come about in spite of rather than because of the United States and the presence of the new conservative firebrand, Ambassador John Bolton.

The crying need to re-engage the United States at the United Nations is certainly not the only prerequisite if the world organization is to move from under the dark cloud of the oil-for-food scandal and overcome the accumulated effects of its own post–Cold War record. Although this is often overlooked as a priority, it is necessary to re-engage the rest of the membership as well. The United Nations' fundamental inequality and concerns about Western-centric abuse or at least double standards in pursuing its goals, and the resulting perception of diminished credibility and legitimacy have all served to affirm many member states' worst suspicions about the United Nations. The events surrounding Iraq have deepened that foreboding.

The terrorism-related structures and activities at the United Nations cry out for coordination. The new tendency of the Security Council to create resolution-specific committees, although intended to contribute to greater focus and efficiency, may represent a dispersal of effort. In conjunction with General Assembly activities, such growth raises questions about the need for centralized direction. To draw the effort together in a way that moves beyond process and into the realm of normative and practical achievement requires leadership – here there is a role for the next Secretary-General and Washington.

Terrorism and UN responses to it reveal and accentuate the implications of the post–Cold War trend toward a system in which the preponderant power of the United States – militarily, economically and culturally – is ever more striking. If the United Nations makes a difference to issues high on the list of US priorities, the world organization becomes a more essential institution. This does not mean becoming a rubber stamp or a cipher, but it does mean making a difference on priorities for Washington.

It is difficult to underestimate the impact of Iraq on the United Nations. Its implications run like a fault-line through the world organization's normative structure. And recent events, rather than working to seal the fault-line, have opened it into a threatening chasm. The consequences of Iraq may yet widen it beyond repair, but there are some grounds to argue that the United Nations' response to terrorism and the way that it may develop hold the potential for bridging the divide.

It is often the shadow of a darker threat that prompts a new vigour and willingness to work together. The precise influence of Iraq on the United Nations and on the broader rules of international order and society that it seeks to uphold has yet to be fully measured. But the impact of terrorism left unaddressed is potentially far greater. The need to deal with this scourge is compelling, both in terms of domestic political support in the West and in terms of real security, presenting both the United States and other member states with not just an opportunity but a necessity to work together. The existing UN efforts on terrorism represent a starting point, and member state involvement may generate new momentum and legitimacy for the world organization.

This is an immodest goal now that the champagne flutes have been stored after the United Nations' sixtieth anniversary celebrations.

Notes

1. The argument draws upon Jane Boulden and Thomas G. Weiss, eds, *Terrorism and the UN: Before and After September 11* (Bloomington: Indiana University Press, 2004).
2. An exception was Security Council Resolution 286, adopted by consensus in 1970, calling on states to take measures to prevent hijackings.
3. For details of the General Assembly's role, see M. J. Peterson, "Using the General Assembly", in Boulden and Weiss, eds, *Terrorism and the UN*, pp. 173–197. For a listing of the terrorist conventions, see ⟨http://untreaty.un.org/English/Terrorism.asp⟩; and for the General Assembly resolutions, see ⟨http://www.un.org/terrorism/res.htm⟩.
4. For details of the Security Council's role, see Chantal de Jonge Oudraat, "The Role of the Security Council", in Boulden and Weiss, eds, *Terrorism and the UN*, pp. 151–172.
5. *Report of the Policy Working Group on the United Nations and Terrorism*, UN Doc. A/57/273–S/2002/875, 6 August 2002.
6. The Secretary-General's Address to the 58th Session of the UN General Assembly, New York, 23 September 2003, UN Doc. A/58/PV.7, p. 3.
7. *A More Secure World: Our Shared Responsibility. Report of the Secretary-General's High-level Panel on Threats, Challenges and Change* (New York: United Nations, 2004), paras 145–164.
8. Ibid., paras 163–164.
9. Ibid., para. 161.
10. Kofi Annan, *In Larger Freedom: Towards Development, Security and Human Rights for All*, UN Doc. A/59/2005, 21 March 2005, para. 91.
11. For an evaluation of this and other issues from the World Summit, see Thomas G. Weiss and Barbara Crossette, "The United Nations, post-Kofi Annan", in *Great Decisions 2006* (New York: Foreign Policy Association, forthcoming).
12. *2005 World Summit Outcome*, UN Doc. A/60/L.1, 15 September 2005, para. 81.
13. See Thomas G. Weiss and Karen Young, "Compromise and Credibility: Security Council Reform?", *Security Dialogue*, Vol. 36, No. 2 (June 2005), pp. 131–154; and Thomas G. Weiss, *Overcoming the Security Council Impasse: Envisioning Reform*, Occasional Paper 14 (Berlin: Friedrich Ebert Stiftung, 2005).
14. Few states have ratified the three earliest conventions: 25 for the 1973 Convention on the Prevention and Punishment of Crimes against Internationally Protected Persons, including Diplomatic Agents; 39 for the 1979 International Convention against the Taking

of Hostages; and 58 for the 1997 Convention for the Suppression of Terrorist Bombings. The 1999 Convention for the Suppression of the Financing of Terrorism has 117 ratifications.

15. See Press Briefings by the Chairman of the CTC, 19 October 2001, ⟨http://www.un.org/Docs/sc/committees/1373/briefings.html⟩.

16. See Rama Mani, "The Root Causes of Terrorism and Prevention", in Boulden and Weiss, eds, *Terrorism and the UN*, pp. 219–241.

17. Edward C. Luck, "Tackling Terrorism", in David M. Malone, ed., *The UN Security Council: From the Cold War to the 21ˢᵗ Century* (Boulder, CO: Lynne Rienner, 2004), pp. 85–100.

18. Brian Urquhart, "The United Nations Rediscovered?", *World Policy Journal*, Vol. 21, No. 2 (2004), pp. 1–2.

19. For additional material with specific reference to US domestic and foreign policy, see Thomas G. Weiss, Margaret E. Crahan and John Goering, eds, *Wars on Terrorism and Iraq: Human Rights, Unilateralism, and U.S. Foreign Policy* (London: Routledge, 2004).

20. *Comprehensive Report of the Special Advisor to the DCI on Iraq's WMD*, 30 September 2004 (report by Charles Duelfer), ⟨http://www.cia.gov/cia/reports/iraq_wmd_2004/⟩; and *Review of Intelligence on Weapons of Mass Destruction* (the "Butler" report, chaired by Rt. Hon. Lord Butler of Brockwell), 14 July 2004, ⟨http://www.official-documents.co.uk/document/deps/hc/hc898/898.pdf⟩.

21. "Address by Mr. George W. Bush, President of the United States of America", UN General Assembly, 57th Session, 12 September 2002, UN Doc. A/57/PV.2, p. 6.

22. See Joseph E. Nye, Jr, *The Paradox of American Power: Why the World's Only Superpower Can't Go It Alone* (New York: Oxford University Press, 2002).

23. "Last of the Big Time Spenders: U.S. Military Budget Still the World's Largest, and Growing", Center for Defense Information, Table on "Fiscal Year 2004 Budget", based on data provided by the US Department of Defense and International Institute for Strategic Studies, Washington, D.C., ⟨http://www.cdi.org/budget/2004/world-military-spending.cfm⟩.

24. Barry R. Posen, "Command of the Commons: The Military Foundation of U.S. Hegemony", *International Security*, Vol. 28, No. 1 (2003), pp. 5–46.

25. See Stewart Patrick and Shepard Forman, eds, *Multilateralism and U.S. Foreign Policy: Ambivalent Engagement* (Boulder, CO: Lynne Rienner, 2002). A companion volume of non-US reactions is David M. Malone and Yuen Foong Khong, eds, *Unilateralism and U.S. Foreign Policy: International Perspectives* (Boulder, CO: Lynne Rienner, 2003).

26. Andrew Hurrell, "International Law and the Changing Constitution of International Society", in Michael Byers, ed., *The Role of Law in International Politics: Essays in International Relations and International Law* (Oxford: Oxford University Press, 2000), p. 344.

27. See Mats Berdal, "The UN Security Council: Ineffective but Indispensable", *Survival*, Vol. 45, No. 2 (2003), pp. 7–30; Shashi Tharoor, "Why America Still Needs the United Nations", *Foreign Affairs*, Vol. 82, No. 5 (2003), pp. 67–80; and Madeleine K. Albright, "Think Again: United Nations", *Foreign Policy*, No. 138 (2003), pp. 16–24.

28. "Statement of H.E. George W. Bush, President of the United States of America, 2005 World Summit, High Level Plenary Meeting, September 14, 2005", ⟨http://www.whitehouse.gov/news/releases/2005/09/20050914.html⟩.

29. K. J. Holsti, *Taming the Sovereigns: Institutional Change in International Politics* (Cambridge: Cambridge University Press, 2004), p. 316.

13

Baghdad to Baghdad: The United Kingdom's odyssey

A. J. R. Groom and Sally Morphet

The United Kingdom and Iraq until 1990

In the nineteenth century the United Kingdom wished to maintain the viability of the Ottoman Empire to block the expansion of Russia from the Black Sea to the Mediterranean. At the same time, the United Kingdom was gradually establishing control over various political entities in the Gulf as part of its strategy to safeguard the links with India. The Empire was crucial in deciding UK policy.

The Ottoman Empire entered World War I in alliance with the central powers and, as such, was coveted for UK imperial expansion as well as an enemy.[1] A British-led force, mainly of Indian troops, landed in Basra and fought its way north to Baghdad. Politically, the United Kingdom combined with the French to dismember parts of the Ottoman Empire through the Sykes–Picot agreement. The United Kingdom was finally awarded Palestine, Trans-Jordan and Iraq as Class A mandates of the League of Nations. Oil was a factor in the case of Iraq, as well as in neighbouring Iran, and Palestine was to defend the flanks of the Suez Canal. But all was not well since the UK government had been persuaded by Zionists to offer a "national home for the Jews" in Palestine. It soon became clear that this could not be achieved without harming the interests of the indigenous inhabitants of what was to become Palestine.

In Iraq, matters were not much better. It was made up of three Ottoman *vilayets* and there were local aspirations to add a fourth, namely Kuwait, which, the British considered, should be a linchpin in the Gulf. Iraq

217

was ultimately an invention of Winston Churchill in his role of Secretary for the Colonies. But Iraq was made up of unwilling people. The Kurds, who had been promised but then denied their own state, rebelled. The Turks felt thwarted by the loss of the northern towns of Mosul and Kirkuk, which dominated the northern oil fields, and, in the south, the Shiites found themselves under a Sunni Hashemite monarchy very dependent upon UK power. Throughout the region, indigenous peoples did not wish to swap Ottoman domination for colonial control by the United Kingdom, with its aerial colonial policing, France, Italy or the United States.

In 1932 Iraq became independent and a member of the League of Nations. UK control in the Middle East was fragile, particularly in Palestine as well as in Egypt. World War II gave a new opportunity to those who wished to challenge UK power: in Iraq there was an unsuccessful pro-Nazi revolt. In the 1950s, a two-way struggle evolved between the United Kingdom and the nationalists on the one hand and between Ba'athists and Nasserites on the other. The United Kingdom failed to win US support and was able to count only on France, Israel and a few Commonwealth countries in the disastrous Suez crisis in 1956. The United Kingdom's attempt to form an alliance (the Baghdad pact) in the northern tier of the region, as a buffer against Soviet expansion southwards, failed when Iraq pulled out following the assassination of the king in 1958. Iraq was subsequently governed by a succession of dictators, of whom Saddam Hussein was but one of the longest-serving and most brutal.

Similarly the United Kingdom lost power through the nationalization of UK oil interests in Iran by Prime Minister Mossadeq in 1951. The Labour government of Prime Minister Attlee seriously considered retaking the installations by military force. Nevertheless, in connivance with the CIA, Mossadeq was eventually overthrown and the Shah reinstated with full political power as a pro-Western leader, as an instrument not so much of UK hegemonic control as of the United States. Here as elsewhere, the United States was establishing itself as the principal hegemonic power in the region. Iraq was a key state both in the expansion of UK power in the region as well as in its decline and ultimate collapse.

The independence of Kuwait in 1961 reopened the question of Iraq's claim. The United Kingdom redeployed troops to Kuwait as an emergency protection force. The force was subsequently withdrawn and replaced by troops from Saudi Arabia and Egypt under the auspices of the Arab League. Kuwait was generally recognized as an independent state and the issue went into abeyance until 1990 without being resolved.

UK power continued to wane in the Gulf, although the UK Defence White Paper of 1966 claimed that the United Kingdom's front-line stretched from the Himalayas to Suez. The UK Labour government had, nevertheless, to withdraw from east of Suez after the collapse of sterling. Once this had been accomplished by the early 1970s, the question arose of who would fill the vacuum. Quietly behind this, the United States began to establish itself, not just in its traditional fiefdom, Saudi Arabia (unaccountably it did not try to change the Wahabist teachings), but also in the Gulf and in support of the Shah in Iran. But the lid was blown off in the late 1970s when the Shah was forced into exile and the Ayatollah Khomeini returned from his exile. After such a momentous change, Iran's neighbours, as well as the United States and the Soviet Union, feared for their fiefdoms in various parts of the world as Iran's proselytizing revolutionary Shiite government began to try to exert its power throughout the region.

In this context, and aggravated by recurrent local problems such as control of Shatt-al-Arab and the Kurdish question, Iraq invaded Iran in September 1980. The main external actors – the United States, France and the Soviet Union – wished to put a *cordon sanitaire* around a revolutionary Iran while not wishing to see Iraq win the war, since it would then be in a position to control the Gulf and threaten Saudi Arabia's political stability. In short, balance was the name of the game and a bloody deadlock was the outcome.

The impasse was broken in terms of international diplomacy when President Gorbachev's fears about the overstretching of the Soviet Union's international commitments in Africa and Latin America meant that he viewed the United Nations more positively. Western ministers were eventually won round by his repeated positive gestures. The French and UK ambassadors to the United Nations took the initiative to bring about cooperation between the permanent five members of the Security Council (the P-5) on a regular basis through a UK-hosted tea party in the autumn of 1986. This led to a series of informal meetings, the first fruit of which was the drafting of what became Security Council Resolution (SCR) 598 on the ending of hostilities between Iran and Iraq. The terrible war came to an end and Saddam Hussein found himself neither victorious nor defeated but with enormous political, economic and social burdens.

The United Kingdom and Iraq, 1990–2001

On 2 August 1990, Iraq invaded and shortly thereafter annexed Kuwait.[2] Within six hours the Security Council met and passed SCR 660 condemning the invasion, and followed this four days later with SCR 661, applying economic sanctions to Iraq. UK Prime Minister Thatcher gave strong support to President Bush in the United States to ensure that he did not "wobble". Thereafter, the UK and US governments worked in close accord. There were a number of observable patterns in the diplomacy of the P-5 in the Security Council. Although the lead was normally taken by the US government, this was almost invariably in close consultation with the British. Indeed, on some resolutions the United Kingdom played the leading role. These were the main activist states, although the French role was crucial: as the French aligned themselves increasingly strongly with the British and the Americans, then any proposal that had the support of the three was usually able to elicit support from the Soviet Union and China, even though China was on the whole cautious and more inclined to abstain.

There is some evidence to suggest that, in the early days, the United States and the United Kingdom were prepared to act against Iraq outside the framework of the United Nations if necessary, and the early resolutions were shaped to permit this. However, it was realized that legitimacy for military operations was essential and therefore the United Kingdom and the United States became ever more concerned to develop maximum support in the Security Council for the possible use of force. Insofar as the practical elements of this were concerned, the British, Americans and French were determined that forces should not be placed under United Nations' command and the resolutions on military action, in particular SCRs 665 and 678, reflected this. The Soviet Union wanted to work to the letter of the UN Charter, even though the Military Staff Committee had never been used, but in the end it gave way because it was not providing troops. The phrase "all necessary means" was used in SCR 678 in order to placate Soviet susceptibilities and the USSR voted in favour and China abstained. Although the operation was not a NATO one, it took advantage of NATO experience.

In the actual fighting, the overwhelming military effort was by the United States. The only other significant elements were those provided by France and the United Kingdom. At the end of the operation, the United Kingdom played a major role in drafting the Chapter VII demands on Iraq in SCR 687. A French initiative, SCR 688 of April 1991, was also significant. It stated that the oppression of Iraqi civilians and especially the Kurds by their own government had "consequences ... which threatened international peace and security in the region". SCR 688 (not a Chapter VII resolution, but in its shadow) was used to justify international intervention in Iraq to defend the Kurds. This led to a limited and short intervention by UK, French and US troops in the north and then to the establishment of a no-fly zone in which the three countries' air forces regularly patrolled the region to ensure that there would be no intervention by Iraqi military forces. However, SCR 688 was not evoked at that time to enable the allies to provide air cover and protection for the Shiite population of the south, who had been brutally crushed by the Iraqi military following an uprising at the end of the military operations – in short, the Kurds were protected and the Shiites were not.

Air patrols in the north continued and were extended to the south by the United States and the United Kingdom in the 1990s. At this point the French withdrew from the operation and the P-5 were beginning to split ever more ominously between the activist British and Americans and the French, Russians and Chinese. The latter began to see sanctions as much a part of the problem as of the solution since they were causing immense hardship to the Iraqi population. The Iraqi regime, on the other hand, was literally getting rich through sanctions. There were also differing interpretations about the extent to which Iraq had conformed to the draconian requirements for disarmament. The French, Russians and Chinese were beginning to look to the period beyond the aftermath of the war and SCR 687, whereas the British and Americans were insistent that Saddam Hussein must complete the requirements in SCR 687 in a cast-iron manner. Even when Saddam Hussein did move towards fulfilment, it was not beyond the United States, in particular, to move the goalposts. The application of the no-fly zone in the south signified the growing isolation of the United Kingdom and the United States.

The no-fly zone reached almost to Baghdad and its purpose was to make the Iraqi use of air power more difficult because its major bases were in the south. From 1997 onwards this gave rise to two cat-and-mouse games between the British and Americans and Saddam Hussein. First, missiles were launched both as a sign of intent and as a punishment when the two Western powers considered that there had been major violations of disarmament procedures. Secondly, UK and US planes destroyed ground installations if the Iraqis adopted "provocative" defensive procedures. These incidents increased in tempo so that by the early 2000s the number of bombs dropped on Iraq was greater than had been dropped in the Kosovo war. Historical analogies with UK aerial participation in the 1920s were clearly evident. Thus, as the new Bush administration took office in January 2001, Iraq was firmly on the international agenda for military, political and humanitarian reasons.

The operation to enforce the withdrawal of Iraq from the occupation and annexation of Kuwait was as near a textbook example of collective security at work as we are likely to see. It also stimulated a wide range of activities by the international community, usually through the United Nations, in a significant range of disputes. These were often of an internal nature and had flared up after the ending of the Cold War and the disintegration of the Soviet Union. In many of these the United Kingdom played a major role. The case of Kosovo, in particular, raises important questions for the intervention in Iraq.[3] The operation in Kosovo undertaken by NATO forces did not have a resolution from the UN Security Council as a basis. It was therefore illegal, although arguments were made that the series of resolutions in the Council created a logic that was not crowned by the equivalent of SCR 678 only because of the likely obstructionism of Russia and China in the Security Council. Given the role that Russia played subsequently in ending the Kosovo crisis, it is at least thinkable that, with more time and better diplomacy, Russia would have agreed to a Kosovo intervention, in which case China might again have abstained. This suggests there was a different dynamic in operation.

In 1990 and 1991 there was a clear violation of the UN Charter by Iraq in an international dispute, whereas in Kosovo there was an internal dispute in which the disputants were both, according to UN resolutions, guilty of abuses of human rights and terrorist activities. What is more, UK Prime Minister Tony Blair gave every indication of being on a mission to "get" Milosevic.[4] It was a clear indication of Blair's willingness, as he himself stated later, to disregard certain Security Council resolutions if they did not suit him or were an affront to his values.[5] Even if we are to take the argument that the Security Council was blocked by a potential veto, there remained the Uniting for Peace Resolution. The Kosovo question could then have been taken to the General Assembly, where the necessary two-thirds majority might have provided some of the legitimacy that was lacking. Moreover, in working for a Uniting for Peace Resolution, the General Assembly has reasonably tight procedural rules, so the question would not be a long-drawn-out affair. The General Assembly cannot, however, authorize force. But, if the United States, the United Kingdom, France and other NATO allies had failed to get a resolution, then that would surely have been reason to think again about a policy and the bases upon which it had been built. The significance for UK policy is that a new proactive, morally driven, obsessed prime minister got away with it, along with his allies. Conviction politics had proved to be not only convincing but also effective. The lesson was not lost on a prime minister who managed to involve the United Kingdom in five wars in his first six years of office.

Back to Baghdad, 2001–2005

The Blair government's decision to go to war in Iraq created the biggest foreign policy and moral crisis since Suez. Fiercely held and strongly opposed positions have enveloped UK politics – domestic and foreign – almost throughout the period since 11 September 2001. As Blair noted, "No decision I have ever made in politics has been as divisive as the decision to go to war in Iraq."[6] This is reflected in the way that foreign policy made within the government, with its allies and at the United Nations was played in Parliament. There are further linkages: policy on Israel/Palestine and Afghanistan; legal issues; political investigations; military policy; and opinion polls. These linkages show that, given long-standing UK involvement in Iraq before and after its independence, and Iraq's own complexities, there are many UK perspectives on Iraq and its internal and external situation both regionally and globally.

The development of UK foreign policy on Iraq

The deliberate attack on the World Trade Center in New York and the Pentagon in Washington on 11 September 2001 just before the plenary debate in the UN General Assembly (GA), though not a new phenomenon, powerfully affected the United States. As Nicole Gnesotto has noted, the US reaction comprised "urgency, militarisation, and unilateralism" and the United States "made the fight against terrorism and the defence of its homeland absolute priorities".[7] Freedman suggests that 9/11 "changed the terms of the security debate by establishing the notion that potential threats had to be dealt with before they became actual".[8] Nevertheless, Blair is said, at that time, to have pressed the US administration not to attack Iraq and to focus on building an alliance against al-Qaeda and the Taliban regime in Afghanistan.[9] He first visited US President Bush at Camp David in February 2001, when they discussed weapons of mass destruction (WMD).[10]

Despite the resurgence of unilateralism, the United Nations was, as has often been the case, still used. Two SCRs on terrorism were passed in the aftermath of the September bombings and Bush spoke to the General Assembly in the November 2001 debate on terrorism, which also produced a further SCR on a global effort to combat it (all these were unanimous). The UK government was also influenced by 9/11 and revised its strategy towards the Saddam regime to one in which regime change became more prominent. Moreover, Bush referred to the "axis of evil" including Iraq in his State of the Union speech in January 2002.

After Blair's visit to Bush in Texas in April 2002, he said:

The moment for decision on how to act is not yet with us ... But to allow WMD to be developed by a state like Iraq without let or hindrance would be grossly to ignore the lessons of September 11th and we will not do it. The message to Saddam is clear: he has to let the inspectors back in – anyone, any time, any place that the international community demands. If necessary, the action should be military – and again, if necessary and justified, it should involve regime change.[11]

As the domestic debate on Iraq developed strongly over the summer of 2002, Blair promised to release a dossier on the subject. He considered that Iraq should be taken to the United Nations but only so long as it was "a way of dealing with the matter rather than a means of avoiding it".[12] Blair went to discuss the situation with Bush on the weekend of 7 September; in the GA plenary debate on 12 September, Bush then called for a new UN resolution or resolutions on enforcement of weapons inspection. "If the Iraq regime defies us again, the world must move deliberately, decisively to hold Iraq to account. We will work with the Security Council for the necessary resolutions. But the purpose of the United States should not be doubted. The Security Council resolutions will be enforced – the just demands of peace and security will be met – or action will be unavoidable."

Parliament was subsequently recalled to discuss Iraq issues on 24 September 2002. Blair released what became known as the "dodgy" dossier on the subject. He stated *inter alia* that the UN Secretary-General had decided to end negotiations on the admission of inspectors in July. On WMD he noted that the Joint Intelligence Committee (JIC), which considers UK intelligence overall, had concluded that Iraq had chemical and biological weapons and that Saddam had existing and active military plans for their use; they could be activated within 45 minutes, including against his Shiite population. Saddam was trying actively to acquire a nuclear weapons capacity. The dossier proved problematical for the government when much of it was found to contain quotations from an old PhD thesis – 53 Labour MPs rebelled.

Meanwhile, a long and difficult negotiating process led to SCR 1441 being adopted unanimously on 8 November 2002. Acting under Chapter VII, the Security Council decided that Iraq had been and remained in material breach of its obligations under relevant resolutions, in particular through its failure to cooperate with UN inspectors and the International Atomic Energy Agency. The resolution gave Iraq a last opportunity to comply with its disarmament obligations. The penultimate paragraph recalled that the Council had repeatedly warned Iraq that it would face serious consequences if it continued in violation of its obligations. The resolution may well have been deliberately ambiguous, providing "a legal safety valve which helps to buy time in the hope that the problems giving rise to its deployment can be addressed later, in circumstances more favourable to the continued rule of law – and to real diplomatic agreement".[13] Iraq subsequently allowed inspectors under Dr Hans Blix to return (before the end of November) and provided a declaration of its disarmament programmes (in December) as required by the resolution. It denied that it had a WMD capability.

In January 2003, Franco-German relations came into the Iraq orbit.[14]

Germany joined the Security Council as a non-permanent member on 1 January. France under President Chirac and Germany under Chancellor Schröder celebrated 40 years of reconciliation at Versailles later that month. There Schröder noted that close cooperation between France and Germany, particularly on an international level, was more important than ever. Their views were countered both by a pro-US declaration agreed to *inter alia* by prime ministers Aznar of Spain, Berlusconi of Italy and Blair and by a similar declaration by 10 Central and East European states. Meanwhile, US forces had been building up in the Gulf and UK Defence Secretary Geoff Hoon announced in January that 26,000 soldiers were to be deployed there (others had been sent in the previous autumn). Both the Foreign Secretary, Jack Straw, and the Prime Minister were of the view that, if Saddam complied, war was not inevitable, although they noted the official line that a second resolution authorizing war was preferable but not essential. In early February, Russia joined the group counselling against military action.[15]

On 31 January 2003 Blair flew to a difficult meeting at Camp David following talks in Washington between Secretary of State Powell and Straw. The coalition was said to need another six weeks to bring around public opinion. These actions were made more difficult by huge anti-war protests in Europe (4 million overall), including at least 1 million in London on 15 February. The protests were followed by a debate in the House of Commons on 26 February when 121 MPs voted against the war. Clare Short, the Development Secretary, subsequently threatened to resign and Robin Cook resigned on 17 March. Blix meanwhile reported to the Security Council in February and March and asked, *inter alia*, for more time; the inspectors had not found any WMD. It became more and more obvious that a second resolution on Iraq could not be agreed because the six non-aligned members of the Security Council (Angola, Cameroon, Chile, Guinea, Pakistan and Syria),[16] which wielded a collective veto, had not agreed to support such a resolution. Their determination was fortified by the knowledge that either France or Russia would use its veto. Nevertheless, on 7 March a second resolution was tabled by Straw giving Iraq 10 days to come into line; it was withdrawn on the 17th. Chirac had made it clear that, until Blix had been given reasonable time, he would veto a resolution although, if necessary, France was ready to take military action if Iraq did not comply.

Bush and Blair met in the Azores on 16 March 2003 with Spanish Prime Minister Aznar and Portuguese Prime Minister Baroso. On 18 March the House of Commons voted on the war: 139 Labour MPs rebelled, but this figure was not sufficient to stop the Prime Minister from gaining parliamentary backing for action. The war began on 20 March.

Linkages – Palestine and Afghanistan

A letter from former UK diplomats published in *The Times* (27 April 2004) noted, correctly, that the Israel/Palestine problem had poisoned relations between the West and the Islamic and Arab worlds for decades and referred to the new fact that the Prime Minister had, by following Bush and Sharon, "abandoned the principles which for nearly four decades have guided international efforts to restore peace in the Holy Land and which have been the basis for such successes as those efforts have produced". It ended, "there is no case for supporting policies which are doomed to failure". Palestine was mentioned only once in Blair's speech of March 2004 in his home constituency of Sedgefield, even though "the emotional thrust of the neoconservatives' campaign against Iraq was predicated more on the security needs of Israel which Saddam really threatened, than that of the US".[17] The Palestine problem cannot be settled by the United States and Israel. The rule of law and justice remains important.

Bush was much less interested than Blair in the long-term development of Afghanistan once both al-Qaeda and the Taliban had been removed,[18] notwithstanding the return of the warlords and flourishing drug production. This made it more difficult to engage in long-term well-considered nation-building.

Legal issues

In March 2003 the Attorney General, Lord Goldsmith, stated that the legal grounds for the United Kingdom's authority to use force against Iraq existed from the combined effect of SCRs 678, 687 and 1441.[19] SCR 678 had authorized force against Iraq and the ceasefire resolution SCR 687 had only suspended SCR 678's authority. A material breach of SCR 687 existed (as asserted in SCR 1441) because Iraq had not complied with its obligations to disarm. SCR 1441 had also not been complied with; this was a further material breach. Thus, authority to use force under SCR 678 had been revived. SCR 1441 had not intended a further SC resolution to authorize force. All it required was the reporting and discussion of Iraq's failures. A similar argument had been used by the UK government in the context of US/UK bombing of Iraq in Operation Desert Fox (1998–99).[20] The case made above was accepted by only a minority of UK legal experts.[21] The detailed advice to the government given by the Attorney General, a close friend of the Prime Minister, has not been revealed.

The Attorney General subsequently advised (on 26 March 2003) of the need for Security Council authorization for the coalition or the international community to establish an interim Iraqi administration to reform and restructure Iraq and its administration.[22] Iraq had become an amalgam of moral, political and legal argument. The Foreign and Commonwealth Office had been shaken by the resignation of the deputy legal adviser, Elizabeth Wilmshurst, a few days earlier. A previous legal adviser, Sir Frank Berman, has subsequently argued that the Blair government's action was illegal. Berman notes: "At the level of theory, a truly perpetual authorization to resort to force at the option of the authorized party would appear to be indistinguishable from the delegation away, if only in part, of the Council's 'primary responsibility' under Article 24 of the Charter."[23]

The essential concern of Lord Goldsmith's case was Saddam Hussein's possible non-compliance with the disarmament clauses of SCR 687 and his hindrance of full and complete inspection procedures – not regime change. There is a difference, too, between SCR 678, which stressed that "all necessary means" would be used if Iraq failed to comply with certain resolutions before 15 January, and SCR 1441, which used the phrase "serious consequences", with the possible implication that the Security Council might move on to "all necessary means" in the event of Iraq's non-compliance. This would depend on Blix's investigations and report to the Council. Many considered there was a need for a second Security Council resolution – the Blair government saw this only as desirable. The PM's Private Secretary wrote to Goldsmith on 15 March 2003 on the question of the existence of hard evidence of Saddam Hussein's non-compliance with SCRs 687 and 1441. He stated, "it is indeed the Prime Minister's unequivocal view that Iraq is in further material breach of its obligations, as in operative paragraph four of UN SCR 1441",[24] despite the fact (see below) that the Joint Intelligence Committee made no assessments of the Iraqi declaration after 18 December 2002. It would have been useful to know what aspects of this wide-ranging paragraph the Prime Minister thought were breached by Iraq: certainly Saddam Hussein's claim that he had no weapons of mass destruction was almost certainly correct.

Political investigations

Much of the political investigation that followed was concerned with whether the Prime Minister was correct at the time in his estimation of Saddam Hussein's behaviour and why the Blix investigation had not been given time to do its job. Military imperatives and the action policy of regime change argued otherwise. The investigations of Hutton, Butler and others have not concluded that the Prime Minister was deliberately leading the Attorney General astray, but the charge has not gone away. Butler actually notes "that despite its importance to the determination of whether Iraq was in further material breach of its obligations under Resolution 1441, the JIC made no further assessment of the Iraqi declaration beyond its *'Initial Assessment'* provided on 18 December [2002]".[25]

The House of Commons Select Committee on Foreign Affairs concluded, following the bombing of the UK consulate in Istanbul in November 2003, "that the threats facing the United Kingdom, both at home and overseas, in the war against terrorism have not diminished". In particular, "the war in Iraq has possibly made terrorist attacks against UK nationals and UK interests more likely in the short term".[26] Blair's period in office will be indelibly marked by the Iraqi affairs.

Military policy

The Ministry of Defence and the Prime Minister's office are said to have been at odds about the question of when to deploy UK troops, which arrived in the Gulf later than their US counterparts.[27] The former thought that earlier deployment would put more pressure on Saddam; the latter considered it might add to the opposition to the war in the United Kingdom. However, it was made abundantly clear by the UK military at the highest level that before they entered into military action they required cover both politically and legally. Politically, it was now necessary to have the agreement of the House of Commons to military action and for the action itself to be legal. As Air Marshal Sir Timothy Garden commented, "and this isn't just niceties anymore, of course, because now with the International Criminal Court a reality and the UK signed up to it, there is a need for UK military, particularly senior commanders, to be assured that what they are doing is covered".[28] They also need to be aware of the European Court of Human Rights. Abuses by UK soldiers of prisoners held under UK custody make these soldiers ultimately liable at both national and European levels.

A military imperative influenced events because of UK troops' difficulty in operating at full capacity and efficiency with the onset of summer heat. It became urgent to push Blix aside in order to deploy troops at an appropriate time. Moreover, many of the armed forces were reservists and to keep them in this high state of readiness away from home for long periods was politically damaging. Moreover, withdrawal would have handed Saddam Hussein a political victory and created a hole in US war plans at the last minute, thus aggravating the loss of the northern front because of Turkey's refusal to join the coalition. In the actual war, the UK contingent performed their tasks with reasonable efficiency although there was a string of complaints about the inappropriate supply of equipment and also about its reliability. As the UK contingent settled into the routine of pacification and peacekeeping in the Basra area, charges of abuse by UK troops were made – these are now going through legal processes.

Opinion polls

The differing perspectives of UK voters over intervention in Iraq were shown through the polls. The Guardian/ICM war tracker poll[29] from 25 August 2002 to 13 April 2003 asked the question: "Do you approve or disapprove of the military attack on Iraq to remove Saddam Hussein?" Of the 14 polls taken between August 2002 and mid-March 2003, all showed more support for the anti-war movement, except for the one following the Bali bombing in October. The peak was reached in February 2003 with the march against the war in London – 52 per cent of UK voters stated that they opposed the war.

The situation changed once the war had begun in March 2003. Four days later, opposition had reduced to 30 per cent from 44 per cent and the pro-war vote had gone up from 38 per cent to 54 per cent. A further ICM poll on 9 September 2004, however, found that 70 per cent of the respondents wanted a deadline set for the withdrawal of UK soldiers from Iraq (a similar poll in May 2004 had found that 45 per cent of voters wanted troops to remain in Iraq for as long as necessary).[30] A poll for *The Times* in January 2005 showed that fewer than 30 per cent believed the war was the right thing to do.[31]

Conclusions

It is hard not to see UK government policy on Iraq as anything other than the Prime Minister's policy. Blair was criticized in the Butler report for his method of taking decisions and for a misuse of the civil service.[32] Many of the decisions were taken with a small group of advisers. Blair appears autocratic in the way he overrides his party, the Cabinet and the public. He often targets individuals (Slobodan Milosevic, Saddam Hussein and Robert Mugabe) and seeks regime change through their removal. He seems to be driven by the need to do what he considers to be right, and he is willing to push international law and the United Nations out of the way if they impede his crusade. Nor is he above being economical with the truth. Although Blair has great belief in his own vision of the truth and considers himself a great persuader, when called upon to deliver the United Nations in support of the Bush–Blair drive for regime change through finding weapons of mass destruction in Iraq, he was not able to get a second resolution through the Security Council. Indeed, his only real influence on Bush seems to have been to cause the United

States to return to the framework of the United Nations, but this was only temporary. Nevertheless the problem has, once again, gone back to the United Nations through the need for international cooperation and UN legitimacy.

Blair had little political support among his colleagues for his Iraq policy. It would be fascinating to know whether he ever considered following Prime Minister Wilson's course over Viet Nam – that is, no military involvement. It has been widely bruited about that Foreign Secretary Straw had many misgivings. Defence Secretary Hoon was close to Blair, whereas Robin Cook and Clare Short both resigned. Other heavyweights such as Brown and Blunkett kept a very low profile on the issue of Iraq and only the Attorney General, Lord Goldsmith, could be trusted to support Blair, perhaps on the basis more of personal friendship than of legal conviction, although this is speculation. Nevertheless, despite resignations from the Cabinet and muted support from the rest, despite a divided political party and despite a largely hostile public opinion, Blair continued. Whatever the cost, the United Kingdom is now back in Baghdad, if only in the green zone, but there is no hint of an exit strategy other than the establishment of "democracy" in Iraq.

Blair seems to pursue a two-level policy. At one level he wishes to share in global management with the United States. He has embraced what General de Gaulle always suspected of the British, that they would choose the *grand large* over a full commitment to European questions. Yet, at another level, Blair is committed to the United Kingdom being at the heart of Europe. However, his policy on one makes the other more difficult and the split between the United Kingdom, on the one hand, and France and Germany (not to mention Russia and China), on the other, is clear. The United Kingdom has moved more into the European framework because of this split, particularly regarding European independence in defence matters, even in the face of stiff US opposition.[33]

Blair, like many others, takes a Western view of the Middle East, one that is closely allied to that of the US neoconservatives. He accepts that Israel, a nuclear power unharried by the West, should maintain many of its policies over Palestine and that it should add even more land to the 78 per cent it has occupied since 1948. He shares his oscillating views on the rule of law with his Israeli counterparts. The non-aligned states see this differently. At their summit in Kuala Lumpur in February 2003, they, as always, reiterated their support for the Palestine people and recalled that in 1948 more than half were uprooted and forced to live as refugees. They recalled Israel's foreign occupation of the remainder of Occupied Palestinian Territory, including East Jerusalem since 1967. They noted that the occupying power had systematically established and expanded settlements, reflecting a new and special form of settler colonialism. The

US entry into Iraq was predicated on the security needs of Israel.[34] Although many Western governments find it difficult to take this seriously, the need for real justice for the Palestinians unites the global South beyond its Arab and Islamic states. Perhaps Blair will recognize this in his forthcoming conference with the Palestinians in London or is this just doing Bush and Sharon's work of disciplining the new leadership to US–Israeli policy imperatives?

There is also the question of economic costs. Iraqi debts to the United Kingdom are, fortunately, modest. The United Kingdom is far behind Japan, Russia, France, Germany, Italy and the United States, to whom the Iraqis are most indebted. For them it is a question of billions, whereas for the United Kingdom it is a question of millions.[35] Nevertheless, the economic cost of the war is significant and victory was only an economic and political down payment. The United Kingdom is faced with continuing instalments of the cost of the occupation in what is really a second phase of the war. Moreover, the United Kingdom has not done well in gaining contracts, except, perhaps, in the slightly dubious area of security firms supplying personnel, who are, in effect, mercenaries.

The disenchanted UK public are not only concerned about the economic costs. They are losing trust in the political system. The UK public were strongly against the government's policy, and they have been ignored. This contributes significantly to the erosion of the legitimacy of the political system that is evident in many mature democracies where people consider that the electoral system is fair but that governments ignore their wishes once in office. Like Bush, Blair was able to push through his policies because there was no structured internal opposition. In the House of Commons, the main opposition was within the Labour Party since the Conservatives, who themselves were in disarray, largely supported Blair, and the only party that was strongly opposed to him was the Liberal Democrats. As a result, it was Blair versus the differing perspectives of the UK people, and the people so far have lost. The consequence is that, for the time being, the United Kingdom is firmly up the creek without a paddle.

Notes

1. For the history of Iraq, consult Christopher Catherwood, *Winston's Folly: Imperialism and the Creation of Modern Iraq* (London: Constable, 2004); Toby Dodge, *Inventing Iraq: The Failure of Nation Building and a History Denied* (London: Hurst, 2003); S. H. Longrigg, *Iraq, 1900 to 1950* (London: Oxford University Press, 1956); Pierre-Jean Luizard, *La formation de l'Irak contemporain* (Paris: Editions du CNRS, 1991); P. Sluglett, *Britain in Iraq, 1914–1932* (London: Ithaca Press, 1976); Charles Tripp, *A History of Iraq* (Cambridge: Cambridge University Press, 2002).

2. For an analysis of the 1990–1991 crisis and subsequent developments, see A. J. R. Groom and Paul Taylor, "The United Nations and the Gulf War, 1990–1991: Back to the Future", RIIA Discussion Paper No. 38, London, 1992; and A. J. R. Groom, Edward Newman and Paul Taylor, "Burdensome Victory: The United Nations and Iraq", Working Paper No. 163, Peace Research Centre, Australian National University, Canberra, 1996.

3. For an analysis of the Kosovo crisis from the UN perspective, see A. J. R. Groom and Paul Taylor, "The United Nations and Kosovo", in Ramesh Thakur and Albrecht Schnabel, eds, *The Kosovo Conflict* (Tokyo: United Nations University Press, 2000). For an analysis of Blair's policy, see John Kampfner, *Blair's Wars* (2nd edn, New York: Free Press, 2004), pp. 36–61.

4. Kampfner, *Blair's Wars*, p. 59.

5. See Blair's speech on global terrorism at Sedgefield, 5 March 2004 (*Guardian*, 5 March 2004).

6. Ibid., p. 1.

7. Nicole Gnesotto, "Reacting to America", *Survival*, Vol. 44, No. 4 (2002–3), p. 99.

8. Lawrence Freedman, "War in Iraq: Selling the Threat", *Survival*, Vol. 46, No. 2 (2004), p. 38.

9. Patrick Wintour and Martin Kettle, "Blair's Road to War", *Guardian*, 26 April 2003, pp. 12–15. This has been extensively used in this analysis.

10. Blair's speech at Sedgefield, p. 5.

11. *Guardian*, 26 April 2003, p. 12.

12. Ibid.

13. Michael Byers, "Agreeing to Disagree: Security Council Resolution 1441", *Global Governance*, Vol. 10, No. 2 (2004), p. 181.

14. *Guardian*, 26 April 2003, p. 14.

15. *Ibid.*, p. 12.

16. Mexico is not a member of the non-aligned movement, though it is an observer.

17. Kampfner, *Blair's Wars*, p. 215.

18. Ibid., pp. 129–151.

19. *Hansard* (Lords), 17 March 2003, cols WA2–3.

20. Lord Grabiner, QC, "After Iraq: The Fallout", a seminar report published by the law firm, Ashurst, London, 18 November 2003, pp. 32–33. See also Marc Weller, "The US, Iraq and the Use of Force in a Unipolar World", *Survival*, Vol. 41, No. 4 (1999–2000).

21. Richard Norton-Taylor, *Guardian*, 3 March 2004. See also Professor Philippe Sands QC, Memorandum on International Law and the Use of Force for the House of Commons Select Committee on Foreign Affairs, 1 June 2004.

22. Reported in *New Statesman*, 22 May 2003, p. 17.

23. Frank Berman, "The Authorization Model: Resolution 678 and Its Effects", in David M. Malone, ed., *The UN Security Council: From the Cold War to the 21ˢᵗ Century* (Boulder, CO: Lynne Rienner, 2004), p. 164.

24. *Guardian*, 15 July 2004.

25. Lord Butler, *Review of Intelligence on Weapons of Mass Destruction* (London: The Stationery Office, 2004), p. 155.

26. Select Committee on Foreign Affairs, *Foreign Policy Aspects of the War against Terrorism: Second Report, 2003–04*, HC81 (London: The Stationery Office, 2004), paragraphs 329 and 123.

27. *Guardian*, 26 April 2003.

28. Air Marshal Sir Timothy Garden in the seminar report published by Ashurst, p. 23.

29. *Guardian*, 26 April 2003.

30. Chris Marsden, "Britain: Iraq Debacle Deepens Crisis of Blair Government", World

Socialist Web Site, 24 September 2004, ⟨http://www.wsws.org/articles/2004/sep2004/blai-s24.shtml⟩, p. 1.
31. Peter Riddell, "Support for Iraq War at Its Lowest Level, Poll Says", *The Times*, 12 January 2005.
32. Lord Butler, *Review of Intelligence*.
33. See A. J. R. Groom, "Britain and Europe: Looking through the Defence Prism", *ARÈS*, Vol. 21, No. 54 (2005).
34. Kampfner, *Blair's Wars*, p. 215.
35. *Le Monde*, 23 November 2004.

14

Explaining France's opposition to the war against Iraq

Jean-Marc Coicaud, with Hélène Gandois
and Lysette Rutgers

Throughout the unfolding of the Iraq crisis in the early 2000s, France has been portrayed as an unrepentant anti-US country, a partisan of the status quo, a supporter of multilateral institutions and the international rule of law, and even, at times, a pacifist nation. Depending on the observer, the French stance on the issue has been regarded as irritating (indeed, deeply irritating for Washington) or commendable. As a result, two diametrically opposed images of France have emerged. One, which has been particularly virulent in the US media, has simply led to the vilification of France and its portrayal as either a traitor or a coward; the other has pictured France as a defender of the United Nations, international peace and international legitimacy. This black and white portrait does not match reality. The truth stands somewhere between these two extremes.

This chapter aims at providing an explanation of the French opposition to the war against Iraq in winter 2002 and spring 2003. In order to do so, we stress the fact that the 2002–2003 stalemate between France and the United States (and the United Kingdom) was not a one-off but, rather, is part of long-term trends and tendencies in French foreign policy. We therefore begin by outlining the core characteristics of French foreign policy. We then explain how the reasons at the heart of the French opposition to the war against Iraq, although neither totally egoistic nor completely altruistic, are part and parcel of its strategic vision of the world and the Middle East. Finally, we evaluate France's current position vis-à-vis Iraq, the Middle East and the United States, and touch upon how it is likely to evolve in the near future.

Core characteristics of French foreign policy

To gain an accurate picture of French foreign policy, it helps not only to be aware of its core values but also to have a precise idea of the mechanics of the decision-making process.

The essentials of French foreign policy

At the heart of French foreign policy are three basic elements: the national interest, an international projection of influence, and a commitment to the international order via a balance of power and the international rule of law. This, and especially the last element, leads French foreign policy to understand multilateralism in terms of multipolarity.

The primacy of national interest is the single most important factor. Like any other country, France has two major goals in the pursuit of its national interest: it tries to secure as many guarantees as possible to preserve its existence, nationally and internationally; and it seeks to define and bend the terms and modalities of its relations with other nations in ways favourable to its interest.[1]

The second characteristic of French foreign policy, the international projection of influence, has to be understood in connection with the fact that, for France, the time is long gone when it could envision its projection of power beyond borders as part of a hegemonic agenda – regional or global. No longer being able to shape the world, France has adopted the medium of influence as a second best to try to continue to have an international impact.

Not losing sight of the political, geopolitical, economic and security needs associated with its national interest, France seeks to have international influence by focusing on those regions in which it still counts. In this respect, the construction of the European community has increasingly become an essential concern for France since the 1960s.[2] Lately, this European focus has included following closely not only the evolution of the North Atlantic Treaty Organization (NATO) but also the emergence, since the signature in Maastricht in 1993 of the Treaty on European Union, of the Common Foreign and Security Policy (CFSP).

Beyond Europe, there are three other regions in which French foreign policy seeks to have a special influence: West Africa, North Africa and the Middle East. In West Africa and North Africa, France remains a significant actor (probably more in West Africa than in North Africa), able to be a decisive factor in many situations. In the Middle East, on the other hand, its influence, while continuing to be important, is more intangible. France has strategic (oil), commercial[3] and some military[4] interests in the region. However, its leverage in the Middle East is not comparable to its leverage in the regions where it exercises a prime influence.

The third element of permanence in French foreign policy is a commitment to multilateralism as a way of promoting a multipolar world and the politics of collective security that the United Nations represents. The French commitment to the United Nations, multilateralism and multipolarity cannot be separated from its equally important support for the balance of power. As a matter of fact, these elements have come to work together in French diplomacy.

Using the balance of power as a way to mitigate or hamper the overwhelming power of one country over others, in Europe or globally, has been one of the key concerns of France's diplomacy of the post–World War II era.[5] French presidents, starting with General de Gaulle and continuing with Georges Pompidou, Valéry Giscard d'Estaing, François Mitterrand and Jacques Chirac, have all, regardless of their political affiliation and beyond at times notable foreign policy differences, borne in mind the need to balance the global weight of superpowers. In times of bipolarity such as during the Cold War, France adopted a "middle of the road" position between the Soviet Union and the United States, while being at heart a close ally to the United States. Today, although continuing to see itself as a natural ally of the United States, it is eager to keep US power in check.

France initially approached multilateralism and the United Nations with scepticism, but over time its inclination to endorse multipolarity has worked hand in hand with a plea for multilateralism as well as for international security management via the United Nations. France's support for multipolarity and multilateralism became as much a matter of principle (with an international system in which agreed-upon regulations and initiatives play a significant role) as a question of realpolitik.[6] Moreover, the centrality of the Security Council gave France an international power that it could no longer claim on its own.[7]

The French foreign policy decision-making process

The French constitution makes the president of the Republic responsible for France's foreign policy.[8] The president has the prerogative of indicating what should be the main strategic directions of French foreign policy. It is then the responsibility of the minister of foreign affairs, monitored by the prime minister, to implement the foreign policy decided by the president. Of course, the reality of the decision-making process in French foreign policy is more complicated than is outlined in the constitution.

To begin with, the French president does not have *carte blanche*. The political and normative guidelines accumulated over the years by French diplomacy cannot be ignored. The president also has to take into account the various strategic political, economic and geopolitical interests that coalesce in French foreign policy at any given time.

In addition, to have the president outlining French foreign policy, and the minister of foreign affairs and the prime minister implementing it, works well when these actors belong to the same political majority. But conducting French foreign policy can become tricky when this is not the case. The tensions associated with "cohabitation" (during which the president is of one party and the prime minister and his government of another) serve as a case in point. The first cohabitation in 1986–1988, between the socialist President François Mitterrand and the right-wing Prime Minister Jacques Chirac, the second one in 1993–1995 between President Mitterrand and the right-wing Prime Minister Edouard Balladur, and the third one in 1997–2002 between President Jacques Chirac and socialist Prime Minister Lionel Jospin on a number of occasions generated turf wars between the president and the government over foreign policy questions.

Moreover, even in ideal political circumstances, the range of actors deciding and implementing French foreign policy goes beyond the president, the prime minister and the minister of foreign affairs and their respective staffs. French foreign policy is also the outcome of a process involving other ministries, including the ministry of defence and the ministry of economy, finance and industry. Furthermore, these institutional actors serve as the channels through which the concerns of the various public, semi-public and private sectors relevant to foreign policy are heard and taken on board.

Another feature that is worth underlining in relation to the foreign policy decision-making process is that French foreign policy is now "demilitarized". This certainly does not imply that the defence industry is an insignificant part of French foreign policy. After all, France is the third-biggest arms exporter in the world.[9] Nor does this imply that the French military establishment has no place in the institutional framework of French foreign policy, although it is hardly part of the decision-making process. The French military establishment is meant to have a say, but its input is quite minimal. Interestingly, this is somewhat similar to the situation in another permanent member of the UN Security Council, the United Kingdom. However, it is in sharp contrast to the situation of the three other permanent members of the Security Council – the United States, Russia and China. In these countries, beyond the differences in civil–military relations (and in the relations of political and military institutions), military actors, each in their own way, have an important voice in the foreign policy decision-making process.[10]

The road to war and the French attitude

These characteristics of French foreign policy serve as a backdrop for the analysis of the French position during the Iraq crisis. They certainly help us to understand the careful course that France tried to steer between the autumn of 2002 and the early months of 2003 between what it saw as the Scylla of an illegal and illegitimate unilateral American intervention, and the Charybdis of having to support a war that would lead it to be associated with a vilified image of the United States in Arabs' eyes.

Following the war against the Taliban regime in Afghanistan, the Bush administration pushed Iraq onto the international agenda and forced countries to take a stance on the threat it allegedly represented. From the start, France's reaction was uneasy. Certainly, on the occasion of the conference of French ambassadors held in Paris in August 2002, Foreign Minister Dominique de Villepin declared that Saddam Hussein's defiance of the international community was not acceptable. He suggested that France would not necessarily oppose the use of force if Iraq did not agree to comply with its disarmament obligations. But he also added that the international community should decide the measures to be taken through a collective process. More to the point, he stressed that no military action could be conducted without a Security Council decision.[11]

Later, in the autumn of 2002, President Jacques Chirac outlined a two-stage UN process to address the Iraq crisis. This process envisioned a first stage that would demand Iraq's compliance with a more rigorous weapons inspection regime. Upon failure by Iraq to comply, the second stage would request that the Security Council take action to deal with the problem.[12] President Chirac insisted as well on the fact that use of force was a possibility provided that it was decided by the international community on the basis of indisputable proof.

A key aspect of the French cooperation with the United States and the United Kingdom in the Security Council in the autumn of 2002 for the drafting and adoption of UN Resolution 1441 and the implementation of the inspection regime that followed was therefore France's firmness on the fact that the resolution on Iraqi disarmament and weapons inspections should not contain an automatic recourse to force. From a French perspective, the drafting and adoption of a UN Security Council resolution that did not contain an automatic recourse to force had the official merit of emphasizing the ultimate authority of the UN Security Council.[13] Less officially, it also had the advantage for France of denying Washington the right unilaterally to declare Iraq in non-compliance and thus the ability to go to war over Iraqi lapses. And it demonstrated to the

French public and the world at large that the international community was going the extra mile to avoid war. What all of this meant, however, was that the divergence of views between France and the United States (and the United Kingdom) was likely to create problems down the road over the threshold for compliance, how it should be interpreted and how the international community should act in the event of disagreement. This is exactly what happened.

Deep differences soon emerged in the interpretation of the text of Resolution 1441 regarding whether it authorized UN member states to use force against Iraq.[14] The French position was that Resolution 1441 did not contain the signal words "use all necessary means" which have traditionally been considered vital to a Security Council authorization of the use of force.[15] This interpretation was supported by the fact that representatives of all the members of the Security Council, including the United States and the United Kingdom, had publicly confirmed, at the time of its adoption, that Resolution 1441 contained no "hidden triggers" or "automaticity" with respect to the use of force.[16] But this did not exclude the United States from also envisioning acting unilaterally if it saw fit.[17]

Between December 2002 and March 2003, the accumulated evidence could not demonstrate in absolute terms the existence of weapons of mass destruction (WMD) in Iraq. Yet the Bush administration and Blair's government were adamant about going to war, no matter what.[18] And the more eager the United States and the United Kingdom were to act, the less France was willing to compromise and the more it became opposed to war. What had been envisaged by President Chirac as a possibility (the use of force) in the autumn of 2002 became an impossibility in March 2003. Ultimately, France gave more credit to Hans Blix and his inspectors' point of view than to the White House and Downing Street. The French government was not disputing the horrific nature of Saddam Hussein's regime. It simply felt that war against Iraq was not justified on the grounds of weapons of mass destruction.

In the end, France could not be convinced to give its support to a second resolution of the Security Council that would have justified the military intervention in Iraq. After it became clear that the second resolution would not get a majority, not to mention the French (and possibly Russian) veto, the United States, the United Kingdom and Spain decided to withdraw the draft.

Because of France's opposition, the war began two days later, on 20 March 2003, without UN authorization. In the aftermath of the war campaign, the French position remained the same: the war against Iraq was neither legal (it did not conform to international law) nor legitimate (it was based on shaky justifications).

Explaining the French opposition to the war against Iraq

The way in which the essentials of French foreign policy came together with the specific issues at the centre of the Iraq crisis is crucial for explaining, and understanding, France's opposition to the war against Iraq. This exercise identifies four explanatory factors: the support given by France to Iraq throughout the 1990s; the French vision of a multipolar and multilateral world; the French view on the use of force in Iraq and the Middle East; and France's assessment of the threat represented by Iraq and terrorism in general.

France's support to Iraq

The French opposition to the war should not have come as a surprise to the United States and the United Kingdom. It echoed what had been the attitude of France vis-à-vis Iraq since the end of the first Gulf war. Throughout the 1990s France was indeed quite supportive of Baghdad. In particular, over time France moved to a position in favour of the easing, if not the lifting, of the UN sanctions against Iraq.[19] This stood in sharp contrast to the US and UK positions, which were eager to nail Saddam Hussein's regime as much as possible.

The relatively lenient French position towards Iraq in the aftermath of the first Gulf war was principally fuelled by three considerations. First, France was willing to give Saddam Hussein the benefit of the doubt. This was in line with its longstanding support of his secular regime, which was a continuation of the strong links that France had cultivated with Baghdad since the 1970s, in part based on its somewhat republican nationalist ideology.[20] Second, there was the genuine belief that the UN sanctions were hurting Iraqi civilians far more than was Saddam Hussein's regime.[21] In this regard, Paris felt that, although the sanctions were crippling Saddam Hussein's efforts to rearm, there was no doubt that they were also worsening the already very low standards of living of ordinary Iraqis.[22] A third consideration was French economic interests in Iraq. These interests broke down into four elements: France's oil dependency on Iraq; the Oil-for-Food programme; oil concessions; and accumulated debt. As we are about to see, these considerations were not as important as is usually assumed.

French dependence on Iraqi oil, although significant, was far from being critical. In the early 2000s, France's imports of oil came primarily from Saudi Arabia (18.4 per cent), Norway (18.2 per cent), the United Kingdom (15.8 per cent), Iraq (8.9 per cent) and Iran (8.3 per cent).[23] Thus, although three of the five main providers of oil were Middle Eastern countries – Saudi Arabia, Iraq and Iran – accounting for 35.6 per cent of French oil imports, Iraq was only the fourth provider.

The contracts obtained by France through the UN Oil-for-Food programme starting in the second half of the 1990s were another aspect of French economic interests in Iraq.[24] Certainly, oil-for-food contracts went largely to France for a while. But in this area too the French interests should not be overstated. In 2001, France ranked eleventh in terms of these contracts, behind Egypt, Jordan, Syria, the United Arab Emirates, Turkey, Russia, China and India.[25]

The potentially lucrative oil concessions that would be granted to French companies should sanctions be lifted were another reason for France to want to proceed carefully with Saddam Hussein's regime. A final concern was the some US$5 billion debt accumulated by Baghdad over the years.

Needless to say, the fact that the Bush administration did not say what attitude it would adopt after the war on some of these issues (for instance, whether or not the Iraqi debts would be honoured), and whether or not France (and Russia) would be allowed to participate in the reconstruction of Iraq, did not encourage Paris to share the US and UK enthusiasm for war.

Iraq and France's vision of a multipolar world

Contrary to what Robert Kagan seems to argue, France does not shy away from the use of force when it deems it necessary.[26] Nor does it hesitate to deploy troops abroad. In 2004, for example, more than 40,000 French troops were stationed outside of mainland France, including 15,000 deployed under a national, European, UN or international mandate.[27]

Against this background, France did not entirely exclude, as a matter of principle, war as an option in the context of the Iraqi crisis. But, short of clear evidence of a threat, the US eagerness to launch a war against Baghdad was bound to make Paris uncomfortable. It was at odds with its favoured vision of a multipolar and multilateral world order in which the United States, while having a pre-eminent role, would still be constrained by international rules.

As the crisis unfolded within the UN Security Council, China and Russia failed to take the lead in challenging the United States and the United Kingdom, and France's emergence as the only real counter-voice was very much to its liking.[28] It demonstrated France's power of influence and also allowed it to mount a defence and illustration of its multipolar and multilateral vision of the world.

France and the use of force in Iraq and the Middle East

For France, the Middle East is a powder keg and one should tread with caution in order to preserve the stability of the region. In addition, the French view is that a cut and dried approach to the numerous problems and challenges facing the Middle East is counterproductive. Moreover, before the war, the French leadership continued to think that the central issue in the region was not Iraq but the Israeli–Palestinian conflict.[29] France was therefore deeply concerned about the prospect of using force in Iraq.

The use of force did not seem the best way to address the problems on the ground. In particular, French decision makers were highly sceptical that a regime change imposed from the outside would lead to a stable regime or that international security in the Middle East could be secured by war. Although no one in France really mourned the prospect of the fall of Saddam Hussein's dictatorial regime, the French government sensed that the Bush administration did not have a clear vision of what a post-Saddam Iraq would look like. As a former colonial power that had experienced failed attempts to govern countries from afar, France was doubtful that the United States, or anyone else for that matter, could successfully govern Iraq with a large occupation force.[30] France feared also that in the absence of such a military force, once war had taken place, a quick handover of authority to a new implanted Iraqi regime could fail, leading to internal conflicts over resources, ethnic and clan reprisals, if not intervention by a number of Iraq's neighbours. Post-invasion chaos could then constitute a fertile ground for terrorists.

To a certain extent, the French government was worried as well by the fact that an intervention in Iraq, particularly if it led to widespread Arab civilian deaths, could have spillover effects in France. It could provoke unrest among France's 4–6 million strong Muslim population (nearly 10 per cent of the population) and be exploited by fundamentalists. France did not want to give the Muslim world the impression that the "West" is opposed to "Islam".[31] It wanted to project an alternative vision of the West to the Arab and Muslim populations in the Middle East but also in Europe.

A different assessment of the threat posed by Iraq and terrorism

A final factor accounting for the French reluctance to go along with the United States and the United Kingdom was that France simply did not believe that Iraq and its alleged links with terrorism were much of a threat, regionally or globally. By the winter of 2002–2003 France had by and large come to the conclusion that the disarmament policies conducted under the UN inspection regime during the 1990s had worked: the Iraqi army had been reduced to about half its previous size; its conventional weapons were out of date; its missiles had been used and not replaced; and most of its arsenal of mass destruction had been destroyed by UN inspectors and various bombing campaigns.

In addition, it was clear to France that Saddam Hussein's regime was not popular. In the north of the country, the Kurds were in almost open revolt; in the south, the Shiite majority had long resented its exclusion from government. This made the Iraqi regime all the weaker internally and not in a position to be a major danger externally.

Furthermore, the French government thought that the links that the Bush administration claimed existed between al-Qaeda and Saddam's regime had no credibility. In this regard, the lack of evidence of terrorist activities in Iraq or of links with transnational terrorist organizations played into the hands of France's rather relaxed conception of the terrorist threat.[32] In France, as in other European countries, there was no sense of paranoia about terrorism and its Middle Eastern (and Iraqi) origins. Paris went along with the war against terrorism after the attacks of 11 September 2001; it was concerned about possible terrorist attacks; but it did not give them primary importance.[33]

On all these issues, the position of the French government was ultimately very much in tune with national public opinion.[34]

Evaluating the French position and the way forward

Was France right to oppose the war, and where does this position leave France, and the international community, in the future? We end this chapter by briefly offering some elements of an answer to these two questions.

When words are not enough

France proved itself expert at opposing the United States. But, overall, it is tempting to think that it failed to put forward a credible alternative to the course of action recommended by the United States and the United Kingdom vis-à-vis Iraq. It was all part of a pattern.

By the end of the 1990s and the early 2000s, it was clear that the sanctions regime and the no-fly zones imposed on Iraq could not last forever. Something had to be done. Moreover, the repressive nature of the regime, Saddam Hussein's propensity for aggressive behaviour internationally and his unwillingness to change his ways made it rather inconceivable to endorse the idea that he should remain in power. Yet, by simply favouring the easing and lifting of UN sanctions, France could not help but give the impression that it wanted to go back to "business as usual".

Later on, in the last months of 2002, the only reason the UN weapons inspectors had been allowed back into Iraq had been the pressure exercised by the United States at the UN headquarters and the fact that it had positioned its troops outside Iraq's borders. Rather disingenuously, France did not really give credit to Washington for this. Choosing to focus on those aspects of the Bush foreign policy that it saw as unpalatable and dangerous, France essentially limited itself to asking the United States to restrain its aggressiveness.

Finally, had Saddam Hussein managed to have the UN inspections drag on in 2003 with no decisive action taken by the international community (which was probably his intention), France was not in a position to use force. It had made no preparation for the deployment of troops in the event that the·use of force became necessary. Not being able to act rapidly, it would have had to rely on US power.

All this showed that, as the crisis unfolded and was approaching its "dénouement", France did not have a systematic alternative game plan for Iraq, with all the possible options envisioned, covered and prepared for. That was all the more unfortunate considering that, beyond opposing the US and UK urge to attack, there was a desperate need for a convincing, workable and reconstruction-oriented "plan B" for Iraq – one that would have triggered change in the country and the region while avoiding the launching of a full-scale war.

In its own way, the Iraq crisis thus epitomized the French reticence about change. For all its declared support for progressive values and calls for a more just international system, France tends towards the status quo. The main arena in which it can be considered a key promoter of change is the European one. Along with Germany, France has indeed proved to be a critical actor in the evolution of the European Union. It is at this level that it has focused its attention and exercised much of its muscle. But this is balanced by some reluctance to push forcefully for systemic change in the global realm.

France now lacks the political clout to engineer and see through sweeping changes in the international landscape that would be in line both with its national interest and with its preferred vision of the world. It is therefore inclined to stick to a conservative course (or to lean towards modest if not piecemeal global change). In the European theatre, this helps to explain why France was sceptical about the rapid dismantling of the Soviet Union and its European zones of influence, and about German reunification, and why it did not favour the breakup of the Federal Republic of Yugoslavia or the enlargement of NATO.[35]

The way forward

The aftermath of the Iraq war has been a bit of a rollercoaster for France. The more the situation in Iraq fulfilled the doomsayers' predictions, the more France's calls for prudence about going to war were vindicated. The more the situation seemed to unfold in line with the most optimistic of US plans, the more France's position was proven wrong.

After the United States had flatly rejected France's recommendation for strong involvement by the United Nations in the management of post-conflict Iraq, France made a point of refusing any deployment of its troops to help the Americans to contain the Iraqi insurgency. To be sure, the relatively successful election of 30 January 2005 put the French government in an awkward situation. France was caught between grudging acceptance of the poll and lingering indignation over how it came about. But the continued inability of the United States to bring security to Iraq and the proliferation of terrorist attacks are confirming the warnings expressed by France about the dangers of war.

The chances are that in the future the French attitude towards Iraq, the Middle East and the United States will be that, while continuing to give priority to solving the Israeli–Palestinian conflict by advocating Palestinian rights, France will not oppose US efforts in Iraq in order to improve the situation of the Iraqi people over time.[36] Favouring the preservation of the territorial integrity of Iraq and ensuring that its three main communities – Shiites, Sunnis and Kurds – are able to live together is part of this agenda. However, although France will support the United States, it will do all it can to hamper US efforts to build a stronghold in Iraq and an even stronger one in the region, with a view to providing a counterbalance to the US approach to the Arab world and terrorism as well as to defending its oil interests.

In the end, Paris will make efforts to bury past differences. Nevertheless, we have not seen the last of the tensions, distrust and suspicion between France and the United States over Iraq and the Middle East.[37]

Notes

1. See Lucien Poirier, *La crise des fondements* (Paris: Economica, 1994), Part I in particular.
2. See, for example, Frédéric Bozo, *La France et l'Alliance Atlantique depuis la fin de la guerre froide. Le Modèle gaullien en question (1989–1999)*, Cahier No. 17 (Paris: Cahiers du Centre d'Etudes d'Histoire de la Défense, 2001).
3. France's commercial exchanges with the countries of the Middle East are quite marginal compared with the overall volume of French trade.
4. France is not under any massive military threat from the Middle East.

5. Before the twentieth century, the balance of power (along with the quest for continental hegemony) was one of the defining elements of French foreign policy.
6. See Thierry Tardy, "France and the US. The Inevitable Clash?", *International Journal*, Vol. 59, No. 1 (Winter 2003–2004). Also, for a good explanation of what a multipolar international order means to French foreign policy see "Un après-guerre sans guerre: Nouvel ordre ou désordre internationale?", *La France et le monde*, AFRI – Annuaire Français de relations internationales (Paris: Editions Bruylant, 2000).
7. Wherever and whenever its interests are at stake and its power permits, France does not shy away from acting against UN principles. France's poor track record in Africa is one example among many of its foreign policy realism, and of the limits of its internationalism and solidarism. The minor place assigned to human rights issues in French foreign policy as a whole is another example.
8. Refer in particular to Article 5 of the Constitution, ⟨http://www.conseil-constitutionel.fr/textes/constit.htm⟩.
9. *Rapport au Parlement sur les exportations d'armement de la France en 2002 et 2003*, Ministry of Defence, Paris, 28 January 2005, ⟨http://www.defense.gouv.fr/portal_repository/817696033__0002/fichier/getData?_&ispopup=1⟩.
10. In the United States, recent examples of this phenomenon are General Colin Powell as Secretary of State in the Bush administration and General Wesley Clark, former Supreme Allied Commander of NATO, running for President in the 2004 Democratic primaries. In Russia, the key role of the army is linked to its communist past but has also come to the foreground recently with the war in Chechnya. See, for instance, Dmitri V. Trenin and Aleksei V. Malashenko, with Anatol Lieven, *Russia's Restless Frontier. The Chechnya Factor in Post-Soviet Russia* (Washington, DC: Carnegie Endowment for International Peace, 2004). For China, see David Shambaugh, *Modernizing China's Military. Progress, Problems, and Prospects* (Berkeley, CA: University of California Press, 2004), and *Chinese Military Power. Report of an Independent Task Force* (Washington, DC: Council on Foreign Relations, 2003).
11. Opening speech by Dominique de Villepin at the 10th Conference of Ambassadors, Paris, Centre des Conférences Internationales, 27 August 2002, ⟨http://www.info-france-usa.org/news/statmnts/2002/villepin82702.asp⟩. See also Dominique de Villepin, *Toward a New World* (translated from French, Hoboken, NJ: Melville House Publishing, 2004).
12. See, for example, the press conference given by President Chirac on 20 October 2002, on the occasion of the 9th Heads of State Francophone Summit in Beirut, ⟨http://www.elysee.fr/pres/iraq/ext201002b.htm⟩.
13. See the remarks of the French Permanent Representative to the United Nations, Jean-David Levitte, following the adoption of Resolution 1441 on 8 November 2002 (UN Doc. S/PV.4644, 8 November 2002, p. 5).
14. For an interesting analysis of the debates around the interpretation of Security Council Resolution 1441, refer to Michael Byers, "Agreeing to Disagree: Security Council Resolution 1441 and Intentional Ambiguity", in *Global Governance. A Review of Multilateralism and International Organizations* (Boulder, CO: Lynne Rienner, in cooperation with ACUNS and the United Nations University), Vol. 10, No. 2 (April–June 2004). For more on the issues of drafting and interpreting UN Security Council resolutions in the post–Cold War context, see Jean-Marc Coicaud, *Beyond the National Interest* (Washington, DC: United States Institute of Peace Press, forthcoming 2006), Chapter 3.
15. Paragraph 13 of Resolution 1441 mentions only that "the Council has repeatedly warned Iraq that it will face serious consequences as a result of its continued violations of its obligations". See UN Security Council Resolution 1441, UN Doc. S/RES/1441 (2002), 8 November 2002.
16. Refer in particular to the statement of the US Permanent Representative to the United

Nations, John Negroponte, on 8 November 2002: "As we have said on numerous occasions to Council members, this resolution contains no 'hidden triggers' and no 'automaticity' with respect to the use of force. If there is a further Iraqi breach, reported to the Council by UNMOVIC, the IAEA, or a Member State, the matter will return to the Council for discussions as required in paragraph 12" (UN Doc. S/PV.4644, p. 3).

17. John Negroponte again: "The resolution makes clear that any Iraqi failure to comply is unacceptable and that Iraq must be disarmed. And, one way or another, Iraq will be disarmed. If the Security Council fails to act decisively in the event of further Iraqi violations, this resolution does not constrain any Member State from acting to defend itself against the threat posed by Iraq or to enforce relevant United Nations resolutions and protect world peace and security" (UN Doc. S/PV.4644, p. 3).

18. For the attitude of the Bush administration, see Bob Woodward, *Plan of Attack* (New York: Simon & Schuster, 2004), and Stefan Halper and Jonathan Clarke, *America Alone. The Neo-Conservatives and the Global Order* (Cambridge: Cambridge University Press, 2004), Chapter 4, for example. For the United Kingdom, refer to John Kampfner, *Blair's Wars* (London: Free Press, 2004).

19. On UN sanctions against Iraq in general, see for instance Meghan L. O'Sullivan, *Iraq: Time for a Modified Approach*, Policy Brief No. 71 (Washington, DC: Brookings Institution, February 2001). For the French position on sanctions, refer for example to *Les propositions françaises pour l'Iraq*, 25 August 1999, ⟨http://www.diplomatie.gouv.fr/actual/dossiers/iraq/index.html⟩, or *Intervention publique du représentant permanent de la France aux Nations Unies*, New York, 26 June 2001, ⟨http://www.diplomatie.gouv.fr/actual/dossiers/iraq2/iraq260601.html⟩.

20. Dominique Moïsi, "Iraq", in Richard N. Haass, *Transatlantic Tension: The United States, Europe, and Problem Countries* (Washington, DC: Brookings Institution Press, 1999); Georges Corm, *Le Proche-Orient éclaté – II. Mirages de paix et blocages identitaires 1990–1996* (Paris: Editions la Découverte, 1997), pp. 35 and 55, for example. See also Jean-Pierre Chevènement, *Le vert et le noir: Intégrisme, pétrole, dollars* (Paris: Grasset, 1995). On 29 January 1991, Jean-Pierre Chevènement, at the time minister of national defence in the socialist government, offered his resignation to mark his opposition to the war against Iraq.

21. See, for example, the interview of the French minister of foreign affairs, Hubert Védrine, with *Al Hayat*, 1 August 2000, ⟨http://www.diplomatie.gouv.fr/actual/dossiers/iraq2/vedrinealhayat.html⟩.

22. On the effect of sanctions on the humanitarian situation in Iraq, refer also to David Rieff, "Were Sanctions Right?", *New York Times*, 27 July 2003.

23. These figures represented 1.9 million barrels per day of France's approximately 2 million barrels per day consumption. See *France Energy Profile*, February 2002, ⟨http://www.sce.doc.gov/documents/market_briefs/energy/pdf/france.pdf⟩. See also Jacques Beltran, "French Policy toward Iraq", *US-France Analysis Series* (Washington, DC: Brookings Institution, September 2002).

24. For an analysis of the Oil-for-Food programme, see for instance Paul A. Volker, Richard J. Goldstone and Mark Pieth, *Independent Inquiry Committee. The United Nations Oil-for-Food Programme, Interim Report*, 3 February 2005, Part II, Chapter 2 in particular, ⟨http://www.iic-offp.org⟩.

25. Beltran, "French Policy toward Iraq".

26. Robert Kagan, "Power and Weakness", *Policy Review*, No. 113 (June 2002), ⟨http://www.policyreview.org/JUN02/kagan_print.html⟩.

27. For further information, please refer to the website of the French defence ministry, ⟨http://www.defense.gouv.fr/ema⟩. The actions of French troops in Côte d'Ivoire also made the headlines in 2004.

28. Lilia Shevtsova is misled when she argues in *Putin's Russia* (Washington, DC: Carnegie Endowment for International Peace, 2003, p. 265): "I believe that Moscow – and not Paris, as many felt – played the determining role in deepening the schism in NATO by its choice in early 2003. I am convinced that if Putin have behaved like the Chinese leaders on the Iraq question – that is, taking a wait-and-see position – Jacques Chirac would not have been so active in his opposition".

29. France has been a long-time advocate of the existence of a Palestinian state alongside the Israeli state.

30. Gilles Kepel, *The War for Muslim Minds: Islam and the West* (Cambridge, MA: Belknap Press of Harvard University Press, 2004).

31. Stanley Hoffmann, "Out of Iraq", *New York Review of Books*, 21 October 2004.

32. There are four reasons for this. First, France does not see itself as particularly targeted. Second, France's foreign policy is not about trying to achieve absolute security against external threats, because France does not think that absolute security (the total absence of external threats) is either achievable or something to wish for. This attitude could be called "insecurity tolerance". Third, France does not believe that a foreign policy of military intervention is essential to ending terrorism. It is more inclined to think that the answer is to address the root causes of terrorism. Fourth, France is wary of giving the Arab masses the impression that the West is adopting policies of force. In its view, such policies are likely further to fuel their sense of historical humiliation. Moreover, the fact that Arab populations resent most of their local political leaders does not mean that they are eager to embrace foreign troops.

33. See, for example, Stephen F. Szabo, *Parting Ways. The Crisis in German–American Relations* (Washington, DC: Brookings Institution Press, 2004), pp. 67–74. For more information on the French perspective see Marc Perelman, "How the French Fight Terror", *Foreign Policy*, Web Exclusive, posted January 2006, ⟨www.foreignpolicy.com/story/cms.php?story_id=3353⟩.

34. "La Guerre en Irak inquiète les Français", poll conducted by Ipsos for *Le Monde* and *TF1* on 28 and 29 March 2003 among a representative sample of 948 people, ⟨http://www.ipsos.fr/CanalIpsos/articles/1095.asp⟩.

35. Bozo, *La France et l'Alliance Atlantique depuis la fin de la guerre froide*. See also *French Negotiating Style*, Special Report 70 (Washington, DC: United States Institute of Peace, 26 April 2001). Among other reasons for France's difficulty in being an engine of systemic change at the global level are a lack of a drive to act, of discipline and, perhaps paradoxically, of expertise (policy and academic) on a number of global issues.

36. On 22 February 2005, on the occasion of President Bush's visit to Brussels, it was announced that all 26 NATO countries would support the training of security forces in post-war Iraq, with France contributing one officer to help coordination at NATO's military headquarters in southern Belgium. In addition, France separately offered to train 1,500 Iraqi military police in Qatar and play a lead role in European Union efforts to train Iraqi judicial officials. "Bush Praises Modest Pledge from NATO on Training Iraqi Forces", *New York Times*, 22 February 2005.

37. See letter to the editor by Jean-David Levitte, France's ambassador to the United States, in the *Wall Street Journal*, following an editorial in the same newspaper ("Multilateralism à la française", Eastern Edition, 14 October 2005) dwelling on the placing under formal investigation in Paris in October 2005 of Jean-Bernard Mérimée, a former French ambassador to the United Nations, as part of a corruption enquiry into the UN-run Oil-for-Food programme in Iraq ("France Deservedly Proud of Its Decision on Iraq", 17 October 2005).

15

Iraq and world order: A Russian perspective

Ekaterina Stepanova

Russia's perspective on the Iraq crisis and its implications has to be put into the broader post–Cold War context. Since the end of the Cold War, perhaps no other major state had undergone changes as deep and profound as those experienced, both internally and externally, by post-Soviet Russia, which itself is partly a product of the end of the Cold War. Although this adaptation was painful, by the turn of the century Russia had by and large adjusted to its reduced global role and influence. It increasingly assumed what appeared to be its more natural role of a major Eurasian regional power, enjoying unique geopolitical and geo-economic conditions, concentrating on domestic development and modernization and acting as a predictable and international law-abiding partner in world affairs.

For much of the 1990s, though, Russia's international security agenda was overwhelmed by the need to manage the consequences of the collapse of the Soviet Union and to limit at least some of the damage caused by the West's consolidation of post–Cold War security gains, such as the eastward expansion of the North Atlantic Treaty Organization (NATO). It was not until the late 1990s that any coherent Russian foreign policy extending beyond post–Cold War "damage limitation" could be identified at all. For Russia, the completion of its own external adaptation meant the end of the period of post–Cold War damage limitation on its own side – something that, in Moscow's view, was not yet paralleled by adequate changes in the security perceptions, threat assessment, policy priorities and behaviour of its Western counterparts, as demonstrated by the 1999 NATO war against Yugoslavia.

Against this background, much as the 1991 war in the Gulf marked international changes associated with the end of the Cold War, the new US-led intervention in Iraq and its implications were viewed in Russia as one of the two major international developments (the other being the war on terrorism in the wake of the attacks of 11 September 2001) that formally concluded the post–Cold War era. For that reason alone, the 2003 Iraq crisis was bound to be seen as a landmark development by Russia, even if the extent of its broader transformative effect on the state of the "world order" remained questionable.

Indeed, the crisis in Iraq that was aggravated by the United States' direct military intervention in that country hardly led to any radical transformation of the international system, particularly in the sense of heralding the emergence of a "new world order". First of all, in the post-bipolar world, the international system may generally fail to meet the strict standards of a structured "order" similar to that associated with the Cold War era, and seems more likely to remain less structured and more susceptible to tension for a significant period of time. Secondly, although the crisis in Iraq had its own logic and a post–Cold War history of more than a decade, the US intervention in Iraq cannot be taken out of the broader post-9/11 context, particularly the global "war on terrorism".

The effect of the "war on terrorism" on world politics is not necessarily one of radical change either – rather, it can be more accurately described as a pendulum that further radicalized and accelerated some of the conflicting trends in international politics that were already in place. First, the rapid and unhindered US intervention in Afghanistan following the 9/11 attacks encouraged the George W. Bush administration to go to extremes in its unilateralist approach, and this later helped pave the way for its unconstrained intervention in Iraq. But the very same excesses of US unilateralism in turn provoked a swing in the other direction and accelerated a second major trend in world politics. The war in Iraq stimulated an unprecedented backlash worldwide (unparalleled in the post–Cold War years) and, rather than setting the dominant "Concert of Powers"[1] against the rest of the world, it polarized key members of the Concert on the unilateralism/multilateralism dilemma. Whereas the US-led intervention in Iraq served as the peak of the United States' "unipolar moment", sharp international disagreements over the war, the UN refusal to mandate it, and the mounting difficulties of occupation and post-war conflict management have all pointed in the opposite direction and challenged US unilateralism. There might have been few doubts about the US ability to win the war – almost any war – unilaterally, but the continuing crisis in Iraq most vividly demonstrates its inability to "win the peace" unilaterally and even the possibility of losing the peace altogether.

Although the Iraq crisis proved to be a serious test for US global security dominance, it is not yet clear whether the world's reaction to the US-led intervention and the coalition's failure to "win the peace" in post-war Iraq mean the beginning of the end of the United States' "unipolar moment" or simply drew its objective limits. The answer to that question goes to the heart of the unilateralism/multilateralism dilemma.

On the multilateralism side, in the context of the Iraq crisis the long-standing debate on the role of the United Nations in general and of the UN Security Council in particular acquired a new urgency and an almost metaphysical nature. The handling of the crisis aroused an exceptional level of pessimism, both outside and within the United Nations, and was seen by many as a failure of the UN system to solve the crisis by peaceful means, to reach an agreement among the key members of the Security Council in order to prevent the war and, ultimately, to stop the aggression. The very relevance of the United Nations in its current form had never been so seriously questioned. But the opposite view could also be argued for – namely, that the United Nations did in fact pass one of the most crucial tests in its history and that the UN system, and the Security Council in particular, did work in the sense that they did not approve an aggression and managed not to become associated with it, despite the position of two of the permanent members of the Council.

It need hardly be mentioned that the war against Iraq was seriously questioned on various grounds by much of the rest of the world outside the United States. The US-led intervention in Iraq drew objective limits to the "flexibility" of international law – limits that, if crossed, could even play against the sole remaining superpower. The main point of resentment was best summarized by Hans Blix, the UN chief weapons inspector, who stressed that even direct violations of the UN Security Council resolutions by Iraq did not provide sufficient grounds to legitimize the use of military force against that state.[2] However, just continuing to stress the illegal nature of the US-led intervention in Iraq scarcely adds anything new to the debate. Rather, it might be more productive to focus on how the crisis in Iraq could be managed in the realities of the present international system and on what the war and its aftermath tell us about the character and potential evolution of this system. This chapter will present Russia's perspective on these issues.

General framework for Russia's policy on Iraq

In the late 1990s and early 2000s, Moscow's approach to the Iraq crisis provided signs of a growing normalization of Russian foreign policy and reflected Russia's new role and place in the international system. There was nothing unique, for instance, about Russia's preference for solving the crisis by peaceful means and its strong opposition to US intervention in Iraq, which was undertaken without a UN Security Council mandate – a position that in many ways mirrored that of France and Germany. Having completed its external adjustment, the new Russia was no less interested in long-term cooperation with the United States than were the United States' major European partners and it acknowledged that the United States had certain unique global responsibilities as the world's leading power. At the same time, Russia contested any "excessive" global role and regional involvement for the United States, particularly in areas of special economic and/or political interest to itself. Although Russia joined its European partners France and Germany to form a political UN-centred "axis of peace" in the rift with the US–UK "axis of war", its reaction to the US intervention in Iraq remained reserved and far from hysterical (in some contrast to its reaction to the NATO war against Yugoslavia) and was driven less by anti-Americanism than by the need to bring the process back to the United Nations and the international legal context and to preserve the viability of the United Nations.

Prior to the US intervention in Iraq, the urgent need to adjust the international system to the realities of the twenty-first century had not only stimulated various proposals for UN reform, but also appeared to be at least partly met by supplementing the role of the United Nations with that of regional institutions as well as broader and less formal, but no less critical, arrangements such as the G-8. The United States' handling of the Iraq crisis, which bypassed both formal institutions (the United Nations at the global level, as well as regional security organizations) and informal international political mechanisms (G-8), proved to be not only illegal and illegitimate[3] but also inadequately reflective of the new global balance of powers, mistaking it for the United States' unchallenged "unipolar" moment. It also gave a new momentum to the "limited sovereignty" trend in post–Cold War global politics that emerged in the context of the humanitarian interventions of the 1990s. Russia had its own reservations about "limited sovereignty" as the new emerging principle of international affairs because it was bound to be applied mainly by the dominant Concert of Powers to weaker and more vulnerable states, such as the former Yugoslavia. In Moscow it was implied that, by granting the right to violate sovereignty for such benign purposes as humanitarian assistance and human rights protection, the international community de facto creates more favourable conditions for future violations of state sovereignty, particularly by the most powerful states, for much less benign reasons. In Russia's eyes, the illegal intervention by the United States in Iraq, driven by highly controversial motivations of self-interest, fully confirmed and reinforced these concerns. Moreover, such blatant violations of state sovereignty as this seriously compromised the idea of intervening in a state's internal affairs, even for allegedly benign purposes (for example, the idea of humanitarian intervention).

Both the US refusal to act within the existing international framework and the powerful blow to the concept of sovereignty dealt by the US intervention in Iraq pointed in the direction of change in the international system, which, given Russia's relative weakness, could be pursued only at the expense of its own national interests. In this context, preserving at least a minimum level of integrity and viability of the United Nations as the world's chief multilateral institution for managing international crises became for Moscow an interest in its own right to be pursued vis-à-vis the situation in Iraq. This explains why the UN system, and the Security Council in particular, remained Russia's natural framework of choice in dealing with Iraq and why the Security Council decisions became the minimum common denominator for all Russian policy discussions on Iraq and for all policy scenarios to be considered by Moscow.

More generally, Russia's strong preference for a multilateralist approach to Iraq was a logical progression and an integral part of its newly acquired role as a large regional power, strong enough to defend its sovereignty (owing to the remnants of its global past, such as its nuclear potential) but unable to exercise major influence on global politics or even to push forward its interests if challenged by the dominant concert of more powerful states. Russia's bilateral policy towards the United States at the time of the crisis and in its aftermath fully reflected these realities and was elegantly termed by Russian foreign policy experts a "responsible partnership" strategy.[4] This implied that Russia, acting as a partner of the United States, rather than a client or satellite, took responsibility for disagreeing with the use of force against Iraq in view of its adverse implications for the United States' own security and for global security. The same approach dominated Russia's behaviour in the UN Security Council: it was more important for Russia to warn the United States that it could use its veto power on Iraq (as Russian Foreign Minister Ivanov warned on 26 February 2003 in China) than actually to use that power.

In sum, Russia's foreign policy in general and on Iraq in particular had two dimensions or levels. The essence of the first dimension is that, at the level of the world order, the Iraq problem served for Russia as an indicator of the normative and structural changes in the international system, particularly through the prism of the US unilateralism – UN multilateralism dilemma. Although, internationally, Russia had some voice at this level as a permanent member of the Security Council, there was no way it could push forward its position if challenged by the dominant concert, as demonstrated by Russia's policy on Iraq throughout the 1990s. Russia could hope to make an impact on the decision-making process only if it acted in concert with at least some of the key members of the dominant Concert of Powers (for example, coordinating its position on the US intervention in Iraq with France at the Security Council).

Although UN-centred multilateralism remained the underlying framework that dominated Russia's public attitudes and foreign policy discourse, it could hardly explain all the nuances of Russia's practical policy and behaviour, in Iraq and elsewhere. This policy was increasingly shaped by the second, more practical dimension – the combination and interplay of at least two pragmatic trends. The first trend was the growing role of geo-economics in Russia's foreign policy. This trend has been further reinforced during President Putin's second term (2004–2008), with an even greater emphasis put on the "oil and gas factor" and on diplomatic support for the transnational projects of Russia's major corporations. The second trend was the emergence of Russia's new security agenda, with its focus shifting from the West to the South as the main source of potential threats and in particular with its new emphasis on anti-terrorism.

A certain gap between the normative and structural dimension of Russia's foreign policy, dominated by UN-centred multilateralism, and its more pragmatic interests and concerns did not necessarily mean, though, that they could not be congruent and even mutually reinforcing.

Russia's policy scenarios on post-war Iraq: Accommodation or non-association?

For those powers opposed to the US intervention, including Russia, there seemed to be two mainstream policy options or scenarios regarding the situation in post-war Iraq. Each had its own advantages and limitations.

The *accommodation scenario* implied cooperation with the US-led coalition, particularly on economic issues, and moderate concessions on the part of the occupying powers in the distribution of the Iraqi "oil pie" and in the role of the United Nations in post-war Iraq, in exchange for post factum de facto recognition of the US protectorate in post-war Iraq. The *non-association (keeping-the-distance) scenario* implied the need to follow the situation closely and to "wait and see" if, with time, the United States would become increasingly mired in its attempts to install a proxy regime in Iraq and to counter the mounting resistance movement and would become more willing to involve the broader international community in the "consequences management" process in Iraq, on UN terms and within the UN framework. One clear sign of the growing normalization of Russia's foreign policy had been that none of the more "extreme" scenarios – full acquiescence in the US pressure or, conversely, confrontation with the United States over Iraq – had been seen as an option to be seriously considered.[5]

At first, after the rapid US military victory and the demise of Saddam's regime in Iraq, a modification of the "accommodation" scenario appeared to emerge as a policy option for Russia. This scenario promised accommodation of at least some Russian economic interests in Iraq and thus appeared to be in line with the general primacy of geo-economics in Russia's foreign policy. Needless to say, Russia's economic interests in Iraq (under the Saddam government, contracts had been signed by more than 200 Russian firms,[6] including lucrative oil projects,[7] and repayment of Iraq's debt to Russia) were damaged by the war and occupation. The economic benefits of the lifting of sanctions, which could have improved the prospects of repayment of Iraq's debt to Russia, were completely overshadowed by the terms of the post-war economic game, which strongly favoured the coalition powers. Trade and market liberalization measures imposed on an economy weakened by a decade of sanctions, as well as putting the US-contracted firms in charge of reconstruction and depriving the Interim Government of Iraq of the right to cancel contracts negotiated by the coalition administration, facilitated US control of Iraqi national assets and, at best, left key foreign competitors a marginal economic role to play.

Russia hoped to limit the damage to its economic interests in Iraq by participating in some form in post-war reconstruction, oil exploitation and production, and so on. In return, Russia could offer little but accommodation of at least some of the United States' demands and concerns, particularly within the framework of the UN Security Council, such as a commitment not to contest the US leadership of a multinational security force to be mandated by the Council. Even then, Russian companies could hope to play only a marginal role in post-war Iraq. Although some of the secondary projects (reconstruction of electricity power stations, training Iraqi oil production experts, etc.) survived, LUKOIL's efforts to reactivate its US$3.7 billion project to develop one of the world's largest oil fields (Western Qurna-2) had little chance of succeeding[8] if they were not supported by the United States. In the circumstances, it appeared that one of the few available options for Russian business was to operate through structures affiliated with Western companies.

However, the pace of reconstruction was delayed by destabilization and the deteriorating security conditions in Iraq, which caused the main foreign critics of US policy, including Russia, to shift towards the "non-association" scenario. This scenario was not in conflict with Russia's geo-economic interests either. Russia is second only to Saudi Arabia as a crude oil producer, with daily production of 8.4 million barrels, and oil and gas account for 30 per cent of its overall exports. At that point, when the long-term nature of the rise in world oil prices was not yet clear, it was believed in Russia that, with sanctions lifted, reconstruction and modernization of the Iraqi oil sector would help bring world oil prices down.[9] This, in turn, could weaken the main basis of Russia's short-term economic stabilization and the Russian government's ambitious economic growth plans.

In fact, it was the deteriorating security situation in post-war Iraq that replaced sanctions as the factor limiting the flow of Iraqi oil to international markets and contributing to high world oil prices. Thus, the broader economic implications of the situation in Iraq might not have been that dramatic, at least for Russia's oil export sector, and some of Russia's economic losses in Iraq could be compensated for by overall financial gains from high oil prices. In the longer term, damage to Russian economic interests in Iraq could also be partly mitigated by granting Russian oil companies permanent access to the US oil market. More generally, it should be noted, though, that Russia's excessive dependence on oil exports has extremely mixed implications and "what is good for LUK-OIL" is not necessarily a priori "good" for the long-term modernization and development needs of the Russian economy, state and society.

Nevertheless, in purely pragmatic geo-economic terms, both political scenarios under consideration appeared to be equally acceptable to Russia. Moreover, Russia's limited political role and influence gave it the advantage of having to make relatively low-risk choices. This partly explains why Russia could never become the main driving force behind a push for one or the other scenario and tried instead to achieve limited political and economic goals, preferably by others' hands. All this demonstrated the extent to which Russia's policy towards post-war Iraq was circumstantial, reactive to developments on the ground, and permeated by a "wait and see" attitude: US success in post-Saddam Iraq would make Russia far more willing to close its eyes to the nature of the occupation regime, whereas a US quagmire would increase the incentives to follow the "non-association" scenario.

Another example of Russia's flexible "wait and see" attitude (which also characterized the policy on Iraq of many other external actors) was its position on the post-war interim political governance arrangements in Iraq. Although Moscow always insisted on the need to restore Iraqi sovereignty as soon as possible, its position on the US-sponsored "proxy" Iraqi Governing Council shifted from initial scepticism (up until the end of 2003) to "conditional" support from early 2004. After the radical Shiite insurgency against the coalition in April 2004, Russia intensified its calls for an international conference on Iraq, with the participation of all local political forces, including the "forces of resistance", representatives of the neighbouring states and the UN Security Council, to be convened as soon as possible (the idea was repeatedly dismissed by the United States).

Certainly, it would be an exaggeration to suggest that Russia's policy on Iraq was driven only by pragmatic concerns and was not guided by any broader strategic vision whatsoever. Rather, my point is to highlight a certain gap between Russia's broader "global order" concerns and its practical policy of pursuing more pragmatic, often purely economic, interests. By late 2004, the "accommodation" and "non-association" scenarios seemed to be reconciled in the form of a compromise policy, allowing accommodation of Russia's economic interests, while keeping a political distance from the coalition.

Politically, Russia's position on the nature of political governance in Iraq gradually became more substantive, with Russian officials stressing the fallacy of attempts to build the new state on the basis of ethnic and confessional principles.[10] Later, Russia even openly called for "a significant part of the armed Iraqi resistance to be brought into the process of creating a state", as well as for a timetable for the withdrawal of foreign forces from Iraq (as stated by President Putin in August 2005),[11] and in June 2005 Russian representatives established direct contact with one of the key Shiite opposition leaders, Moqtada al-Sadr.

Economically, in contrast, the Russian government took several accommodating steps towards the coalition powers, particularly the United States. Among other things, it agreed to sell part of its "strategic" asset LUKOIL to an affiliate of the fourth-largest US oil company, Conoco-Phillips.[12] This decision was apparently intended to regain access to at least some of the Russian contracts in Iraq, allowing LUKOIL and ConocoPhillips to start joint negotiations with the Interim Government of Iraq to unfreeze LUKOIL oil contracts in Western Qurna.[13] The deal might also have involved or at least was timed with Russia's promise to write off a substantial portion of Iraq's debt. In October 2004, Moscow confirmed to the International Monetary Fund and the World Bank that it was ready to support the French initiative to cut Iraq's debt by half,[14] and, in November, Russia joined the United States, Japan, European nations and other Paris Club donors in announcing that they would write off 80 per cent, or more than US$31 billion (€23.9 billion), of the debts Iraq owed them.[15]

In the end, Russia chose to follow a compromise scenario, aimed at securing at least some of its economic interests in relation to Iraq while avoiding any close or direct political association with the US policy on Iraq. This scenario was also in line with Russia's broader global vision based on the concept of multilateralism, which was still most fully, although imperfectly, embodied in the UN system. The war in Iraq and its consequences demonstrated Moscow's growing pragmatism, but also served as a litmus test of the limits of Russia's flexibility and highlighted Russia's non-negotiable "sacred cows". Even US success in post-conflict peacebuilding in Iraq would not have led Russia to stop criticizing, let alone to approve, the illegal military intervention. Any association with the United States' political role and military presence in Iraq would have involved serious political, legal and moral dilemmas for the Russian leadership and could have been interpreted, both internationally and, perhaps more importantly, domestically, as acquiescence in US pressure. Political non-association with the United States on Iraq was a popular public policy to follow in Russia, where the pro-Iraq and pro-UN approach enjoyed broad public support. According to a poll conducted in February 2004, most Russians viewed the war negatively as an aggression against the Iraqi people (62 per cent referred to it as "a crime against the Iraqi people"; 23 per cent, while supporting the need to get rid of Saddam Hussein, strongly disagreed with the methods used by the United States to achieve this goal; and only 4 per cent supported the US intervention); 69 per cent of respondents were confident that the United States would completely fail in Iraq. According to a September 2003 poll, most respondents thought that the main goal of the US intervention had been the need to control world oil prices (52 per cent) and the Persian Gulf region (27 per cent); far fewer people supported the view that the primary goal was the fight against international terrorism (12 per cent) and the search for WMD (10 per cent).[16]

In sum, the broader UN-centred multilateralist dimension does make a difference and can play a role in and even direct Russia's policy, particularly when the policy options dictated by more pragmatic interests involve similar or comparable gains and/or losses, as in the case of Russia's policy options vis-à-vis post-Saddam Iraq.

Iraq and the "war on terrorism": A view from Russia

For Russia, one of the most problematic aspects of the US intervention in Iraq (apart from concerns about the negative implications for the role of the United Nations) was its potential to deal a serious blow to the "international coalition against terror" and to stimulate a new upsurge of international terrorism. The most intriguing connection to be explored in this context is that between the war on terrorism and the crisis in Iraq. Whereas, prior to the US intervention, this connection had remained a virtual product of US official propaganda, it started to materialize in post-war Iraq.

One of the reasons Russia opposed the US intervention in Iraq in the first place was that it threatened to be counterproductive to anti-terrorist priorities and to provoke more terrorism, rather than lessen it. By turning a rogue state into a failed state, the United States replaced a rigid authoritarian secular nationalist regime that had harshly suppressed any form and manifestation of Islamist extremism with a weak proxy state that was fully dependent on the security support of the foreign forces, whose continuing presence on Iraqi soil remained the main factor stimulating the rise of terrorism in post-war Iraq and the Islamization of the resistance. The US presence in Iraq also strengthened the motivation of forces that were ready to employ terrorist means in the global fight against the United States and its allies and thus reinforced the war on terrorism and gave it a new self-created rationale.

Terrorism generated by the conflict in Iraq accounted for only part of the resistance activities (which also involved guerrilla attacks against coalition military targets) and the US intervention and post-war presence in Iraq initially stimulated mainly the import, rather than the export, of terrorism. But, as the conflict became protracted, terrorism increasingly served as a self-perpetuating mechanism for the re-escalation of violence, and the use of terrorist means by Iraqi groups appeared to become increasingly intertwined with transnational terrorist networks' activities.

The prospect of Iraq becoming a major rallying point for terrorists has been of deep concern to Russia, in terms of the country's broader security agenda as well as its anti-terrorism strategy and experience. For a decade, Russia was confronted with the challenge of terrorism generated by an armed conflict on its own territory and expressed growing concerns about terrorist threats to its neighbours in the Commonwealth of Independent States, particularly the Central Asian states. In this context, Moscow was alarmed that Iraq might become a hotbed of Islamist terrorism, located not far from Russia's own southern borders and emerging as a new potential trigger that could at any time reactivate the "southern arc of instability". Moscow was also worried about the damage dealt by the US intervention in Iraq to the integrity of the "coalition against terror" and to the new momentum of the post-9/11 cooperation between the United States and Russia on anti-terrorism, which was highly valued by Moscow (most obviously by providing a more favourable international context for its own operations in the North Caucasus). A combination of anti-terrorism priorities and broader security and political concerns provided an additional argument for Russia to support efforts to build a functioning and legitimate Iraqi state (as the most effective long-term anti-terrorist strategy for a semi-failed state), but also made Moscow more willing to accept the reality of the US-dominated security presence in Iraq.

The problem of terrorism generated by the US-led intervention in and occupation of Iraq was likely to become long term, and there was a growing need to think about potential ways of combining anti-terrorism with post-war reconstruction that might be utilized in future attempts to find a way out of the continuing Iraqi crisis. Russia's own hard and often flawed experience with anti-terrorism, particularly in dealing with a complex mix of domestic, conflict-generated resistance and international influences and connections, could provide some operational and strategic lessons for coping with terrorism in post-war Iraq.

As demonstrated by Russia's own experience of combining counter-insurgency and counter-terrorist operations, in a shaky post-war environment that might easily degenerate into a full-scale armed conflict, the range of the threats and of the security measures that need to be undertaken to meet these threats always goes beyond the terrorism/anti-terrorism dichotomy. From fighting an asymmetric war on its own territory, Russia knew the difficulty of reconciling tasks that are more specifically focused on and tailored to counter-terrorism needs (intelligence collection and analysis, carefully targeted and highly selective special and covert operations aimed, first and foremost, at the prevention and pre-emptive disruption of terrorist activities and networks) with more regular enforcement and policing measures, let alone with military/counter-insurgency operations emphasizing coercion and post hoc retaliation, often in the form of "collective punishment".

Because the US-led occupation of Iraq was to a large extent handled as a military affair, with elements of a massive counter-insurgency campaign, many, if not most, of the problems it raised, the operational tasks it posed and the methods that were employed (including high-altitude bombing of certain areas and long-range missile strikes, on the one hand, and massive "cordon and search" actions on the ground, on the other hand) had little to do with counter-terrorism in a more narrow sense. Coercive measures in general and "collective impact" measures in particular (such as closures and mopping-up *zachistka*-style operations, which have been increasingly employed by the US forces in Iraq) hardly serve and may even interfere with counter-terrorist goals when they are used as essentially punitive or retaliatory measures or as a substitute for other security activities, rather than as a highly selective tool, employed for a pre-defined period of time, in a limited area, based on very solid intelligence and for specific operational purposes.

There is little doubt that conflict-generated terrorism cannot be successfully countered at just the operational level. More fundamentally, the most effective long-term anti-terrorism strategy would appear to be restoring and strengthening state control or, in failed states, (re)building national state institutions and authority.[17] Russia's own experience with the process of building a functioning local administration in a chaotic war-torn area demonstrates that it involves many dilemmas, such as that between the more rigid security-oriented approach to institution-building, focused on centralization of power, strict hierarchies and formal institutional mechanisms, or a more flexible approach that might involve more informal and less centralized political arrangements. Other crucial dilemmas include the constant trade-off between the functionality and legitimacy of the administrative authority and an uneasy compromise among various institution-building agendas, which are often in conflict.

In this sense, post-Saddam Iraq is no exception. The threat of terrorism generated by the situation in Iraq cannot be written off until post-war Iraq fully overcomes regime collapse and ceases to be an externally imposed embryonic state, dependent on the presence of foreign forces for its security and lacking both functionality and legitimacy. In other words, the key to preventing Iraq from becoming a major source of international terrorism and extremism lies in the formation of functioning state institutions that enjoy not only formal UN recognition but also sufficient public legitimacy among the core political and regional ethno-confessional constituencies. Such a state is unlikely to emerge, let alone become consolidated, in the context of the United States' "divide and rule" policy, which implies a primary reliance on the relatively moderate Shiite political/religious forces and the Kurds, while alienating the Sunnis and the more radical Shiites and extending the coalition presence in Iraq indefinitely.

If any "post-post–Cold War" world order is on the horizon, its security contours are likely to be shaped by the dialectical interaction of two trends in international politics that both highlight the changing nature of global security threats but may point in different, if not entirely opposite, directions.

The first trend, most vividly exemplified by the situation in post-war Iraq, is represented by the growing demand for national, international and subnational actors capable of "winning the peace", in contrast to those best suited to the more traditional business of "winning the war". The crisis in Iraq has not merely defined the objective limits of US unilateralism but, perhaps more importantly, demonstrated the apparent failure of unprecedented military might unconstrained by international legal norms and of technological and economic superiority to achieve a just and durable peace after the war – a challenge no less ambitious and complex than, for instance, effectively countering international terrorism. The much-needed capacity to "win the peace" can be provided only by a combination of substantial economic resources and a spotless international reputation, including full respect for the basic tenets of international law (which does not preclude the further development and improvement of the existing international legal system). It is this capacity that may increasingly determine the ranking and clout of a particular state or an international organization in global politics.

The second trend manifested itself, above all, in the post-9/11 war on terrorism. Although this global campaign launched and led by the United States was based on a broad international consensus about the gravity of the new mega-threat to international security, it also reaffirmed the central role of the United States in the world system. Moreover, the excessive reliance on enforcement in general and on military force in particular appeared to be seen by the US leadership as the key to successfully winning the war against terrorism. Among other things, this trend was revealed in the way Iraq became forcibly intertwined with the war on terrorism as a direct consequence of the US-led intervention and occupation. That link is highly controversial. The dismantling of Saddam Hussein's "rogue" regime might have had a certain demonstration effect on other "rogue states", but on most other counts it appeared irrelevant, if not damaging, to anti-terrorism priorities. As demonstrated by the situation in post-war Iraq, turning rogue states into failed states leads to more rather than to less terrorism. Moreover, an upsurge in terrorist activity generated by the conflict in Iraq had every chance to be employed as an additional rationale for reinforcing the war on terrorism in its most militant form.

Against this background, how does Russia see itself in the world after 11 September and the intervention in and occupation of Iraq? More specifically, which of the two main new trends in global politics is likely to become a leitmotif of Russia's own strategic thinking and policy and decisively affect its behaviour on the world stage? It might well seem that the crisis in Iraq has pushed Russia in the "winning the peace" direction. However, even with its permanent seat at the UN Security Council and its traditionally strong opposition to the use of force to settle international disputes, Russia is unlikely to assume one of the leading roles in "winning the peace", for a number of reasons. Russia has only limited political leverage and interest in managing conflicts that do not directly affect its own national security, and it is still struggling with the task of solving a long-standing conflict on its own territory. It also lacks significant financial resources that could be directed to global conflict resolution and post-conflict peacebuilding purposes. Russia's limited capacity to gain high scores on the "winning the peace" scale may provide an additional rationale for the Russian leadership to seek a higher profile in the international arena through a closer association with the harsher forms of the US-led war on terrorism.

Notes

1. For more detail on the "Concert of Powers" concept, see Chapter 3 by Ayoob and Zierler in this volume.
2. Cited in *The Independent*, 5 March 2004.
3. See Chapter 23 by Krieger in this volume.
4. For a detailed discussion of the "responsible partnership" strategy, see records of a series of expert round tables on the subject held in Moscow in 2003: *Irakski krizis i stanovlenije novogo mirovogo poryadka: sbornik materialov* [The Iraq Crisis and the Making of the New World Order: A Collection of Materials] (Moscow: "Orbita-M" Publ. for Foreign Policy Planning Committee & Institute of Strategic Assessments and Analysis, 2004), pp. 174–293.
5. In public discussions, there certainly were some exceptions and a few opinions calling for more extreme policy choices were voiced. See, for example, a statement by the Yukos Oil Co. Institute for Applied Political Studies, calling for Russia's full acquiescence in US pressure and for it to join the anti-Iraq coalition: "Russia Has Already Lost the War in Iraq – It Has to Become Reconciled with the U.S.", Moscow, 31 March 2003.
6. According to the deputy chairperson of the Foreign Relations Committee of the Russian upper chamber of parliament (the Council of Federation), V. Iver, the losses of the Kama Automobile Plant (KAMAZ) alone exceeded €200 million (see *Irakski krizis i stanovlenije novogo mirovogo poryadka*, p. 234).
7. Russian companies (including Zarubezhneft, Alfa Eco, Machinoimport, and ACTEC) received about 30 per cent of oil sales under the UN humanitarian Oil-for-Food programme (1996–2002), worth some US$19.3 billion (see the Independent Inquiry Committee into the UN Oil-for-Food Programme, *Report on Programme Manipulation*, 27 October 2005, p. 22). Russian officials (as well as politicians and business leaders) deny the claims made by the authors of the report that Russian companies paid millions of dollars in illicit surcharges to Saddam Hussein's government on "Oil-for-Food" oil sales. See C. Bigg, "Russia: Oil-For-Food Corruption Report Leaves Russians Cold", *Radio Free Europe/Radio Liberty (RFE/RL)*, 28 October 2005; A. Nicholson, "Russians Say Volcker Report Based on Forgeries", *Moscow Times*, 31 October 2005.
8. In March 1997, LUKOIL signed an agreement with the Iraqi Ministry of Oil and Gas to develop Western Qurna-2 oil field on production-sharing terms. The agreement could not come into force, however, because Iraq remained subject to UN sanctions. Later, Saddam Hussein's government unilaterally denounced the agreement, claiming that the Russian side (constrained by UN sanctions) had refused to fulfil its obligations, whereas LUKOIL considered the agreement still to be in force.
9. With only one-third of its territory explored, Iraq already has known oil resources exceeding those of Russia and all other former Soviet republics, Mexico, the United States and Canada combined. At the same time, the costs of oil extraction in pre-war Iraq were 8–10 times lower than in Russia.
10. See an interview with First Deputy Foreign Minister Vyacheslav Trubnikov: "Yest' predel ustupkam Moskvy" ["There is a Limit to Moscow's Concessions"], *Nezavisimaya Gazeta*, 12 May 2004.
11. Quoted in "Putin Calls for Withdrawal Timetable for Iraq", *RFE/RL*, 19 August 2005.
12. In September 2004, Spring Time Holding Ltd, which was affiliated with ConocoPhillips, bought the former state-owned 7.59 per cent stake in LUKOIL for almost US$2 billion.
13. According to a preliminary arrangement, LUKOIL was to keep 51 per cent of the contract share and ConocoPhillips acquired another 17.5 per cent.

14. Cited in *Rosbisnessconsulting*, 2 October 2004. In addition to Iraq debt cuts, under the Paris Club terms, Russia had already agreed to write off 80 per cent of Afghanistan's US$10.5 billion debt (which would reduce the debt to US$2 billion), and in early 2006 expressed its willingness to go even further in helping settle Afghanistan's debt.

15. In April 2005, Russia went even further by announcing that it would sign an intergovernmental agreement with Iraq writing off 90 per cent of the nation's US$10.5 billion (€8.1 billion) debt to Moscow by the end of 2005.

16. Polls were conducted by the All-Russia Public Opinion Research Center (VTSIOM). Interestingly, a relatively high percentage of respondents (29 per cent) agreed that the United States had fought the war to defend democratic values. "VTSIOM: 62% rossiyan schitayut operatsiyu SShA v Irake prestupleniyem" [VTSIOM: 62 per cent of Russians Consider the US Operation in Iraq a Crime], *Rosbisnessconsulting*, 18 March 2004.

17. For more detail, see Ekaterina Stepanova, *Anti-terrorism and Peace-building during and after Conflict* (Stockholm: Stockholm International Peace Research Institute, June 2003), ⟨http://editors.sipri.se/pubs/Stepanova.pdf⟩.

16

Iraq and world order: A German perspective

Harald Müller

Introduction

The war in Iraq and its aftermath pose three powerful questions to all those thinking about the possibility and the shape of a world order in the era of undisputed US preponderance:

- What idea of order do the war in Iraq and the US administration's immediate post-war strategy stand for?
- What lessons do these experiences hold for this idea of order?
- Apart from this particular approach to order, what are the general requirements for world order in the present circumstances and how, if at all, can they be fulfilled?

This chapter attempts to answer all three questions from "a German perspective". The first section will explain what makes a perspective particularly German. Next, I analyse the neoconservative idea of order that finds vivid expression in US policy (before and after the attacks of 11 September), the 2002 *National Security Strategy of the United States of America*, and its implementation in Iraq. The handling of the Iraq crisis by the United Nations, which is often described as a "failure" that proves the organization's "irrelevance", is then narrated from the opposite perspective – as a success, proving the capability of the world community to tackle the extremely complex and difficult issue of dealing with "deviant behaviour" in the sensitive area of weapons of mass destruction.

After dealing with this telling historical example, and making deductions from the various experiences, I then put forward some propositions for what a world order in the present situation would require. I first look at these requirements from the perspective of a world whose parts are coming ever closer to each other through the growing interdependence of economies, the global environment, international security and global communications. I then try to understand the implications for order of the visible fragmentation into strong reassertions of particularistic futures (in the extreme form, militant "fundamentalisms"). I conclude that even vastly superior resources of power are not enough, in the circumstances, to ensure the power holders' desired outcomes, but that multilateral cooperation and strong legitimacy of, and broad participation in, world order are preconditions for achieving desired outcomes: order will function only if many actors know they have a stake in it.

This chapter does not deal with the intra-German debate on the Iraq war. The main reason is that there was not very much of a debate. Public opinion was opposed to the war throughout, with very large majorities, and these majorities cut across all parties. As a consequence, even the opposition did not support the war; the opposition candidate for the chancellorship, Mr Stoiber, even vowed at one point that he would not open German air space to allied aircraft supplying the war. Criticism of the government's position focused on procedure rather than on substance: that the Chancellor had announced his principled hostility to the war during a campaign speech in a public forum rather than in a private talk with the US President; that he had insinuated that the American ally was an "adventurer"; and that he had refused German support even in the event of a second UN resolution. The policy of the German–French–Russian axis was seen by staunch Atlanticists as strategic folly. In terms of direct support for the US–UK campaign, however, only a few lonely voices from the most conservative press or expert community bought US arguments about the danger from Iraq's (non-existent) weapons of mass destruction or the benefits that would accrue to the Middle East and the campaign against terror from a regime change in Iraq. The majority of the political élite and the public, in contrast, were deeply sceptical about these propositions. And this is about all one can say about the "German debate".[1]

What makes a perspective particularly German?

The "German perspective" is derived from Germany's post–World War II identity as a "civilian power".[2] After two catastrophic failures to achieve impregnable security for the German state in the centre of Europe by attempting to impose its superior military power on its neighbourhood, the collective creed of Germans became that national interests must be pursued by drastically different means. Germany became a promoter of multilateralism, binding itself willingly to organizations such as the North Atlantic Treaty Organization (NATO), the European Union, the Organization for Security and Co-operation in Europe and the United Nations. The transfer of some national sovereignty to these organizations, and through the instruments of binding international law, became instrumental to the realization of German national interests; in contrast to other middle and great powers, these self-binding and self-constraining moves were seen not as contrary to national interests and influence but as their best expression and as a particular, appropriate way to realize interests and to achieve influence.

It would be wrong to assume that this Germany is pacifistic. It contributed to NATO during the Cold War: 500,000 soldiers were permanently deployed in a strong, tank-heavy army that proved itself in countless manoeuvres as highly capable. After the end of the Cold War and a brief period of agonizing soul-searching, the constitutional court eventually decided that Germany could participate in multinational peacekeeping and peace-enforcement operations. The greatest number of German soldiers deployed abroad has been more than 12,000; in 2004, the number was between 8,000 and 9,000. The most contested operation was that in Kosovo, the only time when Germany joined military operations without a UN Security Council mandate. The government made it clear, though, that this was a singular exception, never to be repeated; German participation in any military action had to be, in principle, both multinational and in strict accordance with international law, that is, either in self-defence (including alliance defence) or mandated by the Security Council. In any event, the military instrument should be used only after all alternative ways to solve a conflict by peaceful means have been completely exhausted; in this reluctance the collective memory of the horrors of war, passed down from generation to generation, continues to make an impact.[3]

This perspective of international order based on multilateralism and international law, with the United Nations playing a central role, and of a continuing reluctance to use military instruments to achieve political goals except as an absolute last resort and in full accordance with the UN Charter, is what I would describe today as "the German perspective".[4] I fully share this perspective; and it is shared even by those who see a "normalization" in German foreign policy. This perspective was clearly in evidence in the Iraq case.[5]

Illusions of hegemonic order: Neoconservatives, the *National Security Strategy* and the Iraq war

The Iraq war was in itself an expression of a particular view of world order.[6] This world view has been developed by the neoconservative security community in the United States since the 1970s and found its first authoritative expression in the work of the Committee on the Present Danger, a conservative think tank that prepared the external policy of the Reagan presidency.[7] The first few years of the Reagan administration transferred some of this blueprint into reality, but it was soon undercut by Gorbachev's reforms in the USSR, which made a more accommodative US policy imperative (and preferred by the vast majority of the American people).[8] The first President Bush conducted a much more centrist policy from the beginning. In Defense Secretary Cheney's Pentagon, however, the more radical views still had a home, and the first draft for the Defense Planning Guidance of 1992 contained many elements that found their way into the 2002 *National Security Strategy*.[9] Other documents written by neoconservatives left no doubts about what the policies of a future government, led by them, would be.[10]

The terrorist attacks of 11 September 2001 gave the neoconservative members of the George W. Bush administration the opportunity finally to prevail over sceptics and traditional conservatives such as Secretary of State Powell and his deputy, Richard Armitage. However, the policy had been discernible earlier, notably in the refusal to engage in further arms control and the visible desire generally to avoid any entangling constraints by international law.[11] Retaining freedom of action for the United States is a very important part of this idea of order. The US role is to confer order by its sheer superiority in military and other resources and its determination to apply this power without hesitation. In this view, US hegemony is the best guarantee of a flourishing international system in which democracy and free markets expand; the spread of democracy and free markets, in turn, improve the prospects for stability and thereby lower the costs of hegemony, but never to the point where the United States would renounce its claim to superiority over all possible enemies.[12]

International law and organizations are, at best, helpful for upholding hegemonic order and, at worst, serious stumbling blocks that must be removed and deconstructed. Decision-making belongs to Washington; foreign participation is not desired and, if it must occur, it should be granted only to sympathetic governments in "coalitions of the willing" rather than to formal alliances or collective security institutions. The main danger to this order arises from rogue states with weapons of mass destruction or terrorists, or a combination of both. It is precisely to eradicate this lethal threat preventively, before it can achieve its evil goals, that US superiority, unilateralism and rapid and determined military action are required for both world order and US security.[13]

The Iraq war was a logical application of this strategy. Iraq, in the view of those who had been promoting the elimination of Saddam Hussein's regime for a decade, epitomized the threat to world order that US strategy was meant to address. The United States made a detour through the United Nations in order to support its best ally, UK Prime Minister Tony Blair, at home and if possible to garner the useful legitimacy that comes with a Security Council mandate. When the latter was not forthcoming, the resort to unilateral action was predictable. The work of the UN inspectors (successful, as we now know) was ignored, as was the wish of the vast majority of the Security Council (and of world opinion) to give the inspectors more time, as they requested.[14]

The war was a crushing success militarily, apparently confirming Americans' faith in the superiority of US arms as a source of order-making. The aftermath of the war, however, raises serious concerns that the neoconservative dream of hegemonic order will turn out to be a new "Proud Tower" illusion,[15] a pipe-dream that cannot be realized because its analysis and prescription badly misrepresent real-world conditions. The Iraqis did not take to the streets in their millions to greet the liberators with jubilation. The occupation forces failed badly in providing security on the ground and quickly restoring the basic infrastructure needed to make life bearable in a material sense. The disbanding of the army and police forces and the purging of Ba'ath Party officials from the civil service proved disastrous for internal order and had to be partially revoked after a few months. Divisions between and within the major ethnic and religious groups made political reconstruction unexpectedly difficult. Many of the exiles on whom the Pentagon had relied, especially Mr Chalabi, did not command much authority or credibility among the Iraqis who had been living under Saddam Hussein's rule for a quarter of a century. In contrast, the Shiite clergy emerged as much more powerful and better organized politically than the planners had anticipated. Instead of being a decisive victory in the "war on terrorism", the Iraq war attracted terrorists from around the Muslim world and made the country the world's most terrorist-targeted place. Desperately overburdened US soldiers looked in vain for strong reinforcements from abroad. The "coalition of the willing" remained too small to supply the necessary forces to grant the United States the desired relief and to stabilize Iraq by way of a much more substantial occupation. The United Nations, rudely pushed aside after the war, was called back to provide decisive services in the transfer of sovereignty to the Iraqis. This transfer was hastily brought forward in order to calm hostile feelings in the occupied country. Eventually, the impact on the military rank and file of two years of disparagement of international law and of describing the enemy as the embodiment of evil reared up with a vengeance in the ugly pictures from Abu Ghraib. It was at first denied then gradually recognized that what had happened there was the tip of the iceberg, the result of systematic rather than random violation of the very values on which the US image of world order is built.[16]

As a consequence of choosing the wrong blueprint, President George W. Bush and his collaborators have lost the world. Goodwill towards America, which reached an unusual high immediately after the attacks of 11 September, took an unprecedented dive to the lowest values ever measured in public opinion polls. Even in the most supportive population of the United Kingdom, US standing fell by 30 per cent. In the Arab world, supporters of the United States found themselves in a minority of less than 10 per cent; in US-friendly Jordan, anti-American feeling rose to an incredible 99 per cent. Osama bin Laden, whose political-fundamentalist utopia did not receive majority appreciation, did receive majority acclamation for his courage in taking on the superpower.[17] If the US government had wanted to attract support for its vision of order, it had failed as badly as it was possible to do.

Hopes for order: The Security Council, the United Nations Monitoring, Verification and Inspection Commission, and the lessons

Before I discuss the concept of order in a more fundamental way, I want to take a brief look at an alternative for creating order in the Iraqi case that was developed and temporarily applied but not completed. In autumn 2002, after years of vacillation and under the considerable pressure of the US threat to go to war, Security Council Resolution 1441 established a process that was designed to eliminate the anomaly that had reigned in Mesopotamia since 1999, a state of affairs that was in clear violation of and incompatible with armistice Resolution 687 of 1991, and the follow-up implementation Resolutions 705 and 717. The military build-up by the United States and the United Kingdom created the necessary persuasive force to induce Saddam Hussein to comply. Inspections began in December 2002, but encountered less than satisfactory Iraqi cooperation.

Cooperation improved after the harsh criticism contained in Hans Blix's report to the Security Council on 27 January 2003 raised the spectre of possible Security Council assent to the use of force. In February, Iraq consented to the destruction of the Al Samoud missile, which exceeded the permitted range of 150 km. Resistance to unobserved interviews of weapons experts by the inspectors ceased.

In March, Iraq showed a readiness to provide proof that all chemical and biological weapons had indeed been destroyed in 1991, as the Iraqis had long maintained. The United Nations Monitoring, Verification and Inspection Commission and the International Atomic Energy Agency produced a "cluster document" outlining the remaining unanswered questions and their interrelations and proposed a programme of action and a list of required Iraqi proofs that, in the course of about four months, would have provided the Security Council with a solid basis for a decision on further proceedings. When three members of the Security Council proposed a resolution mandating the use of force, based mainly on intelligence allegations that did not convince the other members (and were proved patently false after the war), the rest of the Council balked and opted for a continuation of the inspections, as requested by Hans Blix and Mohammed ElBaradei. The majority thus behaved completely rationally. If the minority had abided by international law and renounced the use of force at this point, this would have represented a remarkable and well-ordered functioning of international order as intended in the multilateralism project. Owing to the diligent work of the inspectorate, there was a viable alternative to coercive unilateral action, but it was not used because of ideological bias and misinformation.[18]

The meaning of world order: Peacefulness, stability, predictability, legitimacy

The term "order" can be used in two ways.[19] As a tool of positivism, it can serve to describe the discernible structure emerging from the fixed attributes of a given system and of repetitive, regular processes that take place without major disruption.[20] The decisive criterion for order is thus long-term stability, including some resilience in the face of minor disruptions. A given order may nevertheless end; anarchy and anomie may ensue, from which a new order may then emerge in the future.[21]

The second use of the term has normative connotations. It defines the conditions that must be fulfilled for order to endure for the foreseeable future. In this situation, stability itself might be a treacherous pretence, masking the forces of destruction growing underground, as in a boiler without a safety-valve. Peacefulness is thus a necessary qualifier for stability. The stability must be such that most world actors capable of disruption are motivated to renounce attempts at violent disruption because they are sufficiently satisfied with the status quo. If they are not satisfied, they must have sufficient prospects of improving their lot in the future to keep them quiet, or else emergency measures must exist, with sufficient consent among the majority to apply them in crises, to make attempts at disruption futile. In this normative sense, order transforms into the "good order" that has been the subject of moral and political philosophy since ancient times.

Order, as I have said, is linked with time. The longstanding existence of a particular structure and of processes that have become routine creates the reassurance that the future will not be too dissimilar from the present and that changes can be predicted with some reliability to remain within sustainable limits. Stable expectations exist for the behaviour of most other actors. Although this criterion would be met in a balance of power system – where balancing and bandwaggoning are predictable types of behaviour given certain distributions of power among the actors[22] – a normative understanding of order would aim at conditions in which the impacts of the security dilemma would be mitigated. Not only should behaviour be predictable, but it should be ensured that the predictable behaviour by all actors (or at least most of them) is in line with the security needs of all others (or at least most of them).[23]

Lastly, the order should enjoy the support and commitment of most of its members. Such support is the basic condition that ensures stability over time and a broad enough consensus to deal with the deviant behaviour of individual challengers in any political system, whether national or international.[24] This requires that the order is seen as legitimate by most. Legitimacy, in turn, has an input and an output side. On the input side, it requires that there is a fair opportunity to participate in the decision-making processes whose results impact on the actors. On the output side, the distribution of values emerging from these decisions should be reasonably fair, or at least seen as such by most of the actors.[25]

The requirements for global order

Globalization and interdependence

We are living in an age in which the ties of interaction between distant places have become more substantial than at any time in world history. Globalization is the name for this process and, even though it affects different sites with varying intensities, it has become clear over the past 20 years that there is little chance of escaping these external influences over which little control exists. Obtaining the values we desire depends on the contributions of far-away actors, and their wishes can be fulfilled only by our contribution. The action chains resulting in value production become longer and longer and embedded in ever more complex networks, including vast numbers of localities and countries. This diagnosis applies to all goods that are highly valued by humans, from the integrity of the natural environment, to food production and distribution, to trade, to finances as well as to security.[26] The production of all these goods is embedded in highly interdependent structures, and will not be achieved if the actions of those involved in that production are not thoroughly coordinated.

The most powerful tool invented in human history for coordinating the actions of large numbers of actors (millions or billions of humans, thousands of large companies, hundreds of states) is law. Law as a system of generalized and generally accepted norms and rules is superior to any other coordination mechanism, notably to power. Power holders wanting to achieve a particular outcome by coordinating the behaviour of other parties need to keep issuing rules and enforcing them by consuming their power resources. Law, once accepted, needs sanctions only in the rare cases of deviant behaviour; it thus consumes far fewer resources. Law, in addition, has a much greater propensity to create, attract and maintain legitimacy. Power used as a crude coordination instrument without the backing of law may create submission but also resentment. If there are opportunities to evade it or to rebel against it, circumvention or revolt will predictably occur. Circumvention of the law and lawless rebellion do occur, but with much less regularity and salience than against power-based coordination.[27]

From this discourse it follows that, the more complex and interdependent an interaction system, the more important and relevant is the role of law in achieving the coordination needed to produce and distribute the values desired by actors. In the current globalized international system, the role of law is more relevant than ever. The system of value production is extremely decentralized. If the system of coordination is, in contrast, centralized – as power coordination systems are – pathologies will ensue in the form of rebellion.

The good news is, of course, that interdependence foments strong interests to create coordination law and the instruments to uphold it against the relatively rare cases of breaches, if and when actors become aware of being spun into networks of interdependence. Without this awareness, coordination ideologies other than law-oriented ones may persist. With this awareness, the inclination to negotiate law will be strong.[28]

Negotiating law is no easy task. An interest in having it as the appropriate system of coordination does not eliminate conflicts of interest over the distribution of values. Actors are torn between these two impulses. Since, however, the failure to achieve consensus on the norms and rules of coordination usually results in suboptimal value production, the expectation is that, after some rounds of (possibly painful) learning processes, actors will finally develop the law needed to achieve the desired results.

Globalization and fragmentation

There is a second aspect of globalization that makes law both more necessary and more difficult to achieve. By focusing on interdependence, I have identified its unifying forces, the creation of common interests in lawful coordination. However, globalization occurs in a world that is still very heterogeneous, socially, politically and culturally. Because globalization has been driven by forces emerging from "Western" culture, other parts of the world see it as an alien intrusion. Even in the Western world, the speed of these developments has disturbed people and made them feel exposed to hostile forces. As a consequence, heterogeneity is reinforced rather than overcome. In reaction to the perceived deleterious intrusion, people re-emphasize the elements of their identity that they believe are at the root of their difference. Socio-cultural and political fragmentation is thus a corollary of globalization and, indeed, the twin of its unifying, amalgamating force.[29]

Fragmentation need not be, but can be, the source of horrendous violence.[30] The opposition of collectivities that see each other as the hostile "other" contains an enormous escalation potential that, as Clausewitz said about war, tends to move towards "the absolute".[31] By increasing diversity, fragmentation may create curiosity, recognition of legitimate otherness and friendship based on a genuine interest in differences. But it may as easily create alienation, resentment, fear and an increased readiness to treat the alien violently. It very much depends on how the existing or emerging order takes care of fragmentation.

Which brings us back to legitimacy. In a heterogeneous world society in which actors are conscious of their "otherness" because of the cycle of fragmentation and emphasis on identity, the legitimacy of an order is measured not only by whether the value obtained by any single actor is seen as satisfactory in itself, but by whether, compared with what "others" have got, one's own share is reasonably fair. Concerns about relative, rather than absolute, gains in distribution systems are always virulent. They define the stability of an order in a world society where fragmentation is accentuated.[32]

Similar reasoning applies on the input side of legitimacy. Because each party in a fragmented world is particularly eager to get its own voice heard in the forums where major decisions are made, decision-making systems that are exclusionary face distrust, resentment and, eventually, violent resistance. Despite all the convergence between cultures that globalization has engendered, even mainstream cultural codes and value systems are still sufficiently different to make it impossible for the members of a particular – Western – cultural system to design patterns of value distribution that would be acceptable to the majority of members of other cultures; this is particularly true when the design is undertaken without the faintest idea of the essence of the other cultures. If inter-cultural dialogue is not integrated into decision-making, cultural cleav-ages are bound to arise. This, in turn, requires assured participation and representation across cultures when high-level decisions with global re-percussions are taken.

International law, once again, can help to solve the problem. Law has two aspects, procedural – how law is made and how it is executed and interpreted – and substantive – which rules and norms the members of a law community are supposed to observe, and by which prescriptions and proscriptions their behaviour has to be guided. These two aspects roughly correspond to the input and output aspects of legitimacy. In terms of procedural law, the attraction of the present international legal fiction of sovereign equality is that each country has the same formal right and opportunity to ensure that its interests are taken into account when international law is made. It is a fiction because, in reality, the states with the most power and resources exert the greatest influence; this is not completely unjust because they usually also invest dispropor-tionately in the production of the collective goods desired by all. How-ever, in comparison with hegemonic rule-setting, the input asymmetry – unequal participation – is greatly mitigated in a law-guided procedure for law production, where the various actors get a fair opportunity to make their views known as rules are made. In a hegemony, rules are im-posed without regard to the interests of anyone but the hegemon. Even the United States, the classic country of immigration, is not capable of thinking with the brain and soul of all world cultures, being dominated still by its "Western" heritage.

The degree to which substantive law reflects the world's diversity is thus, of course, a direct reflection of its procedural twin. If procedural law follows the principle of sovereign equality, international order will be guided by a legal system adapted to a fragmented but globalizing world. I hasten to add that, today, it is appropriate to give civil society the opportunity to contribute to the process of law development, because non-governmental organizations (NGOs) can represent those unrepre-sented by governmental circles. On the other hand, if NGOs are admitted to the law-making table, procedural precautions have to be taken to en-sure that universal representation is achieved. At present, there is not even a rule of sovereign equality among NGOs, and northern ones are much more numerous and resourceful than their "southern" counter-parts.[33] Without some procedural mitigation, the asymmetry of power that exists among states would repeat itself with a vengeance in civil society.

The above reflections point to the enormous importance of the United

Nations. With its universal membership, the UN General Assembly is the appropriate body to initiate and oversee law-making and to host negotiating forums in which everyone has the opportunity to participate. This key role represents the best chance that the diverse parties in a fragmented world will see some legitimacy in the outcomes. The implication of this is that the Security Council – which is much less representative – should be very cautious and reluctant to use its prerogatives under Chapter VII to act as a universal legislator. In Resolutions 1378 and 1540, it did so under the assumption that a clear and present danger existed that had to be addressed forthwith; it could not wait for the inevitably cumbersome proceedings of universal negotiations for a response. It may appear reasonable that loopholes in international law that open the gates to imminent threats should be addressed by the Council, acting as representative of the whole threatened international community. Nevertheless, doubts and considerable distrust remain. It might thus be advisable to attach sunset clauses to such universal rules, combined with a request to the General Assembly – or the appropriate international legal community consisting of a subset of UN member states – to create a negotiating forum to produce a set of rules to close the loophole permanently, while the rules set by the Security Council remain valid in the interim.

Power over resources versus power over outcomes

Thus far, I have compared order based on hegemonic rule-making with order based on international law. My standard was the requirements emerging from globalization. My conclusion is that order based on international law is clearly superior in terms of efficiency because it attracts much greater legitimacy and thus meets much less resistance. Resistance to the implementation of rules meant to help coordinating behaviour, however, inevitably causes a loss in efficiency.

This is not to say that hegemonic order cannot achieve something. Indeed it can, since, behind its rules, raw power waits in the wings to punish deviant behaviour. Beyond this limited objective, however, the hegemonic project adopted by neoconservatism, recognizing the difficulties caused by the fragmentation, diversity and heterogeneity of the world community, has developed the lofty ambition of spreading democracy, if necessary by the use of force, in order to reduce and, in the long run, eliminate heterogeneity as a serious problem for world order. Although, in theory, eliminating the existence of variation in political systems, societal organization and underlying culture is a possible solution to the problem, in practice it is not likely to work well.

As the Iraq experience indicates, power measured by resources is capable of helping to vanquish an inferior enemy. The allies' military victory over the Iraqi forces was crushing, professional and impressive. Power over resources also means power over enemies, at least those who are willing to fight on the field chosen by the superior power. What it does not mean is power over outcomes. Although military victory can be ensured, the desired results cannot. This is typical in a world where such results depend on the collaboration of many actors. As I said above, hierarchical systems of rules help little in this regard, since motivating the many is the secret of success. Motivation, in turn, depends on legitimacy. That legitimacy is lacking if the majority of Iraqis view their "liberators" as occupiers because they themselves are not at all involved in making the rules that are applied in their country.

Imposing democracy is, in many ways, a contradiction in terms. Democracy, after all, is self-determination by the people on their own conditions, not those of a foreign power. There are not many examples of successful externally imposed democracies. Germany and Japan are frequently cited, but one should recognize the special circumstances in these cases: in both cases the *ancien régime* was profoundly discredited not by a short and decisive war, but by the agony of many years of warfare, the loss of a whole generation through death, torture and long-term imprisonment, the destruction of the homeland and an ensuing, deep-seated trauma in the nation. Both countries had experienced a liberal, democratic period in the past, and the politico-societal structures that had supported the political system in those periods were still intact and able to be reinvigorated after the defeat of the dictatorships. These conditions are absent in current targets for democratization, and the cultural gap, notably between the West and the Islamic world, is not conducive to the imposition of anything external, i.e. alien, being greeted with enthusiasm by the Muslim world, which has been on the receiving end of world politics for the better part of 200 years.

This is not to say that world order would not be preferable in a community of democratic states, or that democracy is not compatible with social structures and culture outside the Western world. Democracy has been flourishing in Latin America, India, East Asia and Africa, and it is increasingly successful in Muslim Turkey. However, these were cases not of imposition but of hard-fought change, based on the terms of the people living in these countries. They knew how best to adapt the principles of democracy and respect for human rights to their own value systems and conditions on the ground. Only by creating a consensus among a large proportion of the domestic population could the democracy "outcome" succeed in these transformation processes; societal power made the decisive difference.

Thus, in order to achieve power over outcomes, power holders have to understand power in the sense that the late Hannah Arendt used it – as the synergy of many individual human beings mobilized around a single common project.[34] Because such mobilization is not possible unless people believe in the legitimacy and rightness of the objective they are supposed to be pursuing, only a legitimacy-creating and legitimacy-projecting order will lead to the availability of this particular type of power. And the resources to be used to create it are much closer to the "soft power" spectrum than to the end of the resource continuum where military power is located.[35]

Of course, this does not mean that military power is, in principle, useless and dysfunctional. Clearly it is not. The power to use force effectively is needed as an instrument for upholding the law; thus it is an indispensable part of any law-based order. But such power is connected to the law in a double way: as the ultimate enforcer if and when the law is violated, and, at the same time, as its obedient servant, bound by the law in the way power is used and its use is decided. Only in this capacity, and with this constraint, can military power be assumed not to stand in the way of the other notion of power: power as the mobilization of human will to achieve common purposes on the basis of a belief in their legitimacy and rightness.

Conclusions

The war in Iraq was the attempt by a single state, endowed with historically unprecedented superior power and actively supported by a few allies, to impose its own idea of good governance on a resistant dictatorship, to eliminate a supposed current and future danger to the region and the world at large, to reform the shape of a critically strategic region, and thereby to affect world order in a positive way. This attempt was challenged by the more limited efforts of a majority of the international community to grapple with the possible threat from weapons of mass destruction (WMD). The attempt to establish a model way to deal with non-compliance and the WMD proliferation issue in a well-conceived, multilateral manner failed because of the determination of the superpower to prevail with its own approach. This was not successful because the superpower ignored the most fundamental trends of our time engendered by globalization, namely interdependence and fragmentation, both of which call for an order based on multilaterally established, legitimate international law, and because it confused power over resources with power over outcomes; the latter notion of power is becoming ever more relevant as these trends increasingly shape international interactions.

Bringing order into this interdependent world is a difficult endeavour. At the same time it is also essential because, without orderly coordination, it will be impossible to provide the goods and values needed for 6 billion people in nearly 200 states and some 5,000 ethnic groupings, and as more and more actors – state and non-state – gain access to modern weapons technology with its enormous destruction potential.

In our age, hegemony will not suffice to provide the necessary public goods but will rather stimulate more and more disorder born of the resentment of fragmented identities at the imposition of an alien will. The only route to sustainable order is through international law, negotiated in a broad, participatory fashion, reflecting a fair distribution of values on the basis of such participation, and with effective international organizations supervising the implementation of this law. Power will be extremely useful for law enforcement in the (presumably rare) deviant cases when the law is broken. Law without power is toothless; power without law becomes criminal. Only together can they stand as the pillars of a viable world order. Iraq was a painful reminder of this enduring truth.

Notes

1. Harald Müller, "Das zerrissene Erbe der Aufklärung. Die ideologische Polarisierung zwischen Deutschland und den USA", *Internationale Politik*, Vol. 59, Nos 11/12 (2004), pp. 15–24; Harald Müller, "Germany's Conditional Solidarity", *Internationale Politik. Transatlantic Edition*, Vol. 1, No. 1 (2005), pp. 43–48; Tuomas Forsberg, "German Foreign Policy and the War on Iraq: Anti-Americanism, Pacifism or Emancipation", *Security Dialogue*, Vol. 36 (June 2005), pp. 213–231.
2. Sebastian Harnisch and Hanns W. Maull, eds, *Germany as a Civilian Power? The Foreign Policy of the Berlin Republic* (Manchester: Manchester University Press, 2001).
3. Besides the studies cited in note 1, see Harald Müller, "German National Identity and WMD Nonproliferation", *Nonproliferation Review*, Vol. 10, No. 2 (Summer 2003), pp. 1–20; Volker Rittberger, ed., *German Foreign Policy since Unification* (Manchester: Manchester University Press, 2001); John Duffield, *World Power Forsaken: Political Culture, International Institutions and German Security Policy after Unification* (Stanford, CA: Stanford University Press, 1999); Thomas Berger, *Cultures of Antimilitarism. National Security in Germany and Japan* (Baltimore, MD: Johns Hopkins University Press, 1998); Peter J. Katzenstein, ed., *Tamed Power. Germany in Europe* (Ithaca, NY: Cornell University Press, 1997); Harald Müller, "German Foreign Policy after Unification", in Paul Stares, ed., *The New Germany and the New Europe* (Washington, DC: Brookings Institution, 1992), pp. 126–173.
4. This is not to say that people in other countries do not prefer the same principles for world order.
5. See the debate between Gunther Hellmann, "Sag zum Abschied leidse Servus! Die Zivilmacht Deutschland beginnt, ein neues 'Selbst' zu behaupten", *Politische Vierteljahresschrift*, Vol. 43, No. 3 (2002), pp. 498–507, and Volker Rittberger, "Selbstentfesselung in kleinen Schritten? Deutschlands Außenpolitik zu Beginn des 21. Jahrhunderts", *Politische Vierteljahresschrift*, Vol. 44, No. 1 (2003), pp. 10–18.

6. William Walker, *Weapons of Mass Destruction and International Order*, Adelphi Paper 370 (London: International Institute for Strategic Studies, 2004), Chapter 4.

7. Jeffrey W. Sanders, *Peddlers of Crisis. The Committee on the Present Danger and the Politics of Containment* (Boston: South End Press, 1983).

8. Ernst-Otto Czempiel, *Machtprobe. Die USA und die Sowjetunion in den achtziger Jahren* (Munich: Beck, 1989); Raymond Garthoff, *Détente and Confrontation. American–Soviet Relations from Nixon to Reagan* (Washington, DC: Brookings, 1985).

9. Excerpts from "Pentagon Plan: 'Prevent the Emergence of a New Rival'", *New York Times*, 8 March 1992, p. 14; The White House, *The National Security Strategy of the United States of America* (Washington, DC: The White House, September 2002).

10. Paul Wolfowitz, "Clinton's First Year", *Foreign Affairs*, Vol. 73, No. 1 (January/February 1994), pp. 28–43; Samuel P. Huntington, "Why International Primacy Matters", *International Security*, Vol. 17, No. 4 (Spring 1993), pp. 71–81; Charles Krauthammer, "The Unipolar Moment", *Foreign Affairs*, Vol. 70, No. 1 (1990/1991).

11. Joseph Nye, "U.S. Power and Strategy after Iraq", *Foreign Affairs*, Vol. 82, No. 4 (July/August 2003); Madeleine K. Albright, "Bridges, Bombs, or Bluster?", *Foreign Affairs*, Vol. 82, No. 5 (September/October 2003), pp. 2–19; G. John Ikenberry, "America's Imperial Ambition", *Foreign Affairs*, Vol. 81, No. 5 (September/October 2002), pp. 44–60; Ivo Daalder and James M. Lindsay, *America Unbound. The Bush Revolution in Foreign Policy* (Washington, DC: Brookings, 2003).

12. Robert Kagan, *Power and Weakness*, Stanford University, Policy Review, June 2002, ⟨http://www.policyreview.org/JUN02/kagan_print.html⟩.

13. *The National Security Strategy*.

14. Hans Blix, *Disarming Iraq* (New York: Pantheon Books, 2004).

15. Barbara Tuchman, *The Proud Tower* (New York: Macmillan, 1966). The term stands for the arrogance of the European élites before World War I, their militant social Darwinism, their blindness to the horrors of the imminent war, and their ignorance of the negative dynamics of the forces they had unleashed.

16. Chris Brown, "Reflections on the 'War on Terror'. Two Years on", *International Politics*, Vol. 41, No. 1 (2003), pp. 51–54.

17. The Pew Research Center for the People and the Press, *Views of a Changing World 2003*, ⟨http://people-press.org/reports/display.php3?Report=185⟩.

18. Blix, *Disarming Iraq*, Chapters 11 and 12.

19. Nick J. Rengger, *International Relations, Political Theory and the Problem of Order* (London: Routledge, 2000).

20. Shmuel N. Eisenstadt, "Sociology: The Development of Sociological Thought", in David L. Sills, ed., *International Encyclopedia of the Social Sciences*, Vol. 15 (New York: Macmillan, 1968), pp. 23–36, at pp. 24–25.

21. Morton A. Kaplan, *Systems and Process in International Politics* (New York: Wiley, 1957).

22. Stephen M. Walt, *The Origins of Alliances* (Ithaca, NY: Cornell University Press, 1987); Randall L. Schweller, "Bandwagoning for Profit: Bringing the Revisionist State Back In", *International Security*, Vol. 19, No. 1 (1994), pp. 72–107.

23. Janne Nolan, ed., *Global Engagement. Cooperation and Security in the 21st Century* (Washington, DC: Brookings, 1994); John Steinbruner, *Principles of Global Security* (Washington, DC: Brookings, 2000).

24. David Easton, *A Systems Analysis of Political Life* (New York: Wiley, 1967).

25. Fritz W. Scharpf, "Die Handlungsfähigkeit des Staates am Ende des 20. Jahrhunderts", in Beate Kohler-Koch, ed., *Staat und Demokratie in Europa* (Opladen: Westdeutscher Verlag, 1992), pp. 93–115.

26. Marianne Beisheim, Sabine Dreher, Gregor Walter, Bernhard Zangl and Michael Zürn,

Im Zeitalter der Globalisierung? Thesen und Daten zur gesellschaftlichen und politischen Denationalisierung (Baden-Baden: Nomos, 1999); David Held, Anthony McGrew, David Goldblatt and Jonathan Parraton, *Global Transformations. Politics, Economics and Culture* (Cambridge: Polity Press, 1999).

27. Thomas M. Franck, *The Power of Legitimacy among Nations* (New York: Oxford University Press, 1990); Lori Fisler Damrosch and David J. Scheffer, *Law and Force in the New International Order* (Boulder, CO: Westview, 1991).

28. Robert O. Keohane, *After Hegemony* (Princeton, NJ: Princeton University Press, 1984).

29. Harald Müller, *Das Zusammenleben der Kulturen. Ein Gegenentwurf zu Huntington* (Frankfurt: Fischer TB, 1998), pp. 58–72.

30. This is the concern voiced in Samuel Huntington, *The Clash of Civilizations* (New York: Simon & Schuster, 1996).

31. Carl von Clausewitz, *Vom Kriege*, ed. Werner Hahlweg (Bonn: Suhrkamp, 1990).

32. Joseph M. Grieco, *Cooperation among Nations: Europe, America and Non-tariff Barriers to Trade* (Ithaca, NY: Cornell University Press, 1990).

33. Margaret E. Keck and Kathryn Sikkink, *Activists beyond Borders. Advocacy Networks in International Politics* (Ithaca, NY: Cornell University Press, 1998), pp. 210–217.

34. Hannah Arendt, *Macht und Gewalt* (Munich: Beck, 1970); see also Joseph S. Nye, "The Decline of America's Soft Power", *Foreign Affairs*, Vol. 83, No. 3 (2004), pp. 16–21.

35. Joseph S. Nye, "What Is Power and How Can We Best Use It?", in Benjamin Ederington and Michael Mazarr, eds, *Turning Point: The Gulf War and U.S. Military Strategy* (Boulder, CO: Westview, 1994).

17

Avoiding a strategic failure in the aftermath of the Iraq war: Partnership in peacebuilding

Chiyuki Aoi and Yozo Yokota

Introduction

The Iraq war presented a particularly difficult challenge to Japan, the United States' most important, long-term ally in Asia. Although relations with the United States remain the most important strategic priority for Japan, the unilateral nature of the Iraq war and its implications for the United Nations greatly worried the Japanese leadership, which had placed "UN-centrism" at the centre of its post–World War II foreign policy. In the end, Japan opted to side with the United States diplomatically – while mildly reminding it of the virtues of multilateralism – and to support the coalition-led post-war stabilization operation in Iraq militarily.

Limited as it was, Japan's support for the United States and the coalition made relations between Japan and the coalition even closer. The Japanese support for the post-war stabilization operation, with the Japanese Self Defense Forces (JSDF) providing humanitarian and reconstruction assistance in Iraq, marked a milestone in Japan's post-war security and defence policy. It may also suggest a more independent, proactive Japanese military and security policy in the future, especially in the area of post-conflict stabilization and rehabilitation.

The long-term implications of the Iraq war and of Japan's choices in responding to it are, nonetheless, still largely unclear. Both structural shifts in the international system and a rather unusual situation involving asymmetric threats account for the Iraq war, which leaves many issues unresolved, most notably the roles of multilateral international organizations and formal alliances in an age of strategic coalition-making. Japan needs urgently to clarify the foreign policy goals and principles upon which its future roles in both bilateral and multilateral security affairs will be established. Given Japan's economic power and military capabilities, its actions will have a greater influence than ever in the past on the stability and nature of the international system. Japan's pacifist past may well qualify it for the role of post-conflict peacebuilding, with the JSDF providing non-coercive humanitarian/developmental assistance. Nonetheless, such activities must be placed within an overarching strategic vision that clearly links Japan's long-term national interests and its views about world order.

The significance of the Iraq war: A preventive war, a strategic error?

The lack of a legal framework in which to justify the US attack on Iraq signifies the deeply psychological and strategic nature of the US action. The Iraq war can be perceived as a preventive war, an attempt to forestall a possible future threat.[1] Such a felt need for prevention can be explained as the product of heightened psychological fear in the wake of the terrorist attack of 11 September 2001. The 9/11 attack, the first-ever attack on the US mainland, in which more than 3,000 civilian lives were lost, was a deeply traumatizing experience for the United States. The unconventional nature of the attack, involving seemingly undeterrable opponents forming a loose terrorist network, shocked the Americans. The resulting sense of vulnerability is an important factor that explains the course of war that ensued. Uncertainties and unreliable intelligence regarding the precise nature and level of the threat posed by Saddam Hussein only exacerbated the fear.

In strategic terms, the US action is in line with the behaviour of great powers in previous times that failed correctly to judge the limits of expansion.[2] The United States' "pre-emptive" strategy is more a product of the unipolar structure of the international system, which increases the propensity for hegemonic powers to use force unilaterally, than an idiosyncratic reaction to terrorist attacks by the neoconservatives in Washington. Concurrently, the foreign policy goals of the neoconservatives are defined in such liberal terms that working toward those goals requires a variety of forms of intervention, including forced regime change. This particular combination of liberal purposes and propensity for the unilateral use of force makes the current US foreign policy especially aggressive.[3]

No other single nation can realistically be expected to counter US power at the moment. However, it is unrealistic to assume that the United States' hegemonic position will automatically give it the power to impose order, or "win the peace", in foreign-occupied areas without legitimacy in the eyes of other states and also local people. In a period when terrorism, insurgencies and civil wars are so prevalent, the ability to "win the peace" is ever more critical. More attention will need to be paid to the kinds of operation the US military establishments have long been averse to – for example, peacekeeping and stabilization operations and, indeed, nation-building missions. In both Afghanistan and Iraq, it is precisely these types of operation that will determine the ultimate outcome, and even the legitimacy, of wars fought against the Taliban and Saddam. Having chosen to invade these nations, the United States should remain committed to rebuilding these "failed states", because leaving them would go against the goals it sought to achieve by going to war with them in the first place.

Nonetheless, both situations, especially Iraq, remain challenging. Realists have long warned that the use of force comes with a variety of costs, including those incurred through the "unintended" consequences of military involvement, including the exacerbation of conflict and an increase in underground resistance. There was a warning that military action might not be the right strategy to deal with terrorism, that terrorists and their supporters might gain the strategic upper-hand by exploiting anti-West feelings that were certain to be encouraged by military action and post-war chaos. Unless the United States is able to orchestrate a coherent and broad-based strategy towards peacebuilding in both Afghanistan and Iraq, the coalition forces may risk a strategic failure, which would compromise future US attempts to de-legitimate and counter terrorism.

Japan's responses to the Iraq war

Diplomatic support

Japan's support for the US and coalition forces puts it in the same boat with the coalition forces in their arduous and long-term challenge of re-building Iraq. The Iraq war posed a very difficult foreign policy dilemma for Japan, the dilemma of having to choose between loyalty to its most important ally, the United States, which seemed determined to go to war against Iraq even if a new UN Security Council resolution authorizing such action was not adopted, and the post-war bedrock policy of "UN-centrism", which is still supported by the majority of Japanese citizens. The Iraq war therefore challenged the untroubled, if not entirely realistic, assumption of compatibility between three pillars of post-war

Japanese foreign policy: UN-centrism, alliance with the United States and other Western powers, and friendly relations with Asian countries.

Facing this dilemma, the Koizumi cabinet resorted to a pragmatic policy of assuring the Bush administration of Japanese support on Iraq, while somewhat awkwardly pointing out the importance of unified UN action. In February 2003, Prime Minister Junichiro Koizumi as well as Minister for Foreign Affairs Yoriko Kawaguchi informed the Bush administration that, although obtaining a new Security Council resolution was desirable, should the United States decide to take action without such authorization Japan would still support it.[4] Japan thus clearly departed from the position of France and Germany. As the United States and the European nations debated the possibilities for another Security Council resolution to authorize military action in Iraq, the Japanese government's argument was consistently that, unless the Security Council showed unity, the United Nations would risk losing its credibility. However, rather than trying to mediate between the differing positions of the French/German side and the United States, the Japanese government joined in the US and UK attempts at persuading the French and German governments to accept the draft resolution presented to the Security Council days before the start of the war.[5] Once the United States launched the war on Iraq, the Japanese government immediately expressed "understanding" and supported the US action and its stated goal of disarming Iraq and establishing democracy and prosperity in that country.[6]

Lacking sufficient intelligence of its own, and unable as a result to question the credibility of US intelligence on Iraq's weapons of mass destruction (WMD) programme, the Japanese government justified the Iraq war and Japan's support for it on identical bases to those presented by the US government. Rather than perceiving and presenting the war as a preventive war, the Japanese government justified the war on the basis of the need for pre-emption (given Iraq's defiance of UN Security Council resolutions and the likelihood that WMD programmes existed in Iraq) and liberal foreign policy goals (establishing democracy and bringing prosperity to Iraq), as well as the legal basis of Iraqi non-compliance with past UN resolutions. At a press conference, Prime Minister Koizumi stated that, although the Japanese government had hoped for a peaceful settlement of the crisis, it was likewise the case that Iraq had defied the UN weapons inspection process (violating the terms of Security Council Resolutions 678, 687 and 1441).[7]

The Japanese public were deeply divided on the issue of the Iraq war but, in general, surveys revealed their pragmatism. The public supported the government's policy of siding with the United States while having reservations about the legitimacy of the war itself. Public opinion surveys show a considerable degree of fluctuation depending upon the poll. According to the *Yomiuri Shimbun* newspaper, with a large number of right-wing readers, more than 70 per cent of those surveyed supported (*Hyouka suru*) the fall of the Saddam regime, and more than half were in favour of the Koizumi cabinet's policy of supporting the United States.[8] But other surveys reveal considerably less support. For instance, according to a *Japan Economic Journal* telephone survey, 25 per cent approved of the Iraq war and 68 per cent disapproved of the war, while 40 per cent supported the Koizumi policy of siding with the United States and 49 per cent opposed Koizumi's policy.[9]

Supporting post-conflict stabilization in Iraq

Japan also supports the US and coalition forces militarily. This kind of support is meant to show that Japan is making a substantive contribution, not just a nominal or financial one, through the provision of personnel (*jinteki koken*) to the maintenance of international peace. In July 2003, following the Security Council resolution calling on member states to provide humanitarian and reconstruction assistance to Iraq,[10] the Koizumi cabinet succeeded in obtaining Diet approval of special legislation, the Special Measures Law on Humanitarian and Reconstruction Assistance in Iraq, which enabled Japan to send its Self-Defense Forces to provide humanitarian and reconstruction assistance but not to engage in combat. After the passage of Resolution 1546,[11] which returned sovereignty to the Iraqis in June 2004, the JSDF continued to operate in Iraq, this time "within" the UN-authorized multinational force there, but without coming under the command of the multinational force.

The decision of the Koizumi cabinet to send the JSDF to Iraq was calculated to satisfy the political and economic interests of Japan. The most important of these interests is for Japan to reaffirm and strengthen the existing Japan–US security arrangement, particularly in the face of the growing potential threat posed by North Korea. Despite various diplomatic efforts during the 1990s to forestall North Korea's declared ambition to possess WMD, a series of crises in the region have had the effect of alerting the Japanese leadership and public to the need to strengthen the US–Japanese security arrangement. Japan's dependence on US deterrent capabilities in the region explains the difference in response to the Iraq war between Japan and Germany. Germany, following the thaw of the Cold War in Europe and embedded deeply in political institutions in Europe, no longer relies as heavily on US military protection.

Another source of political pressure is the Japanese policy of seeking a permanent seat at the UN Security Council. Japan is aware that US support is indispensable to gaining a permanent seat. Prime Minister Koizumi declared this goal for the first time as Japanese prime minister at the UN General Assembly in September 2004, in a speech in which he cited Japan's recent contribution in UN peace operations and assistance to Afghanistan and Iraq.[12] Since Japan's bitter experience during the 1991 Gulf war, when its contribution of US$13 billion was received with little appreciation by the coalition, Japan has tried to make its contribution to UN peace activities "visible" – in that human as well as financial resources are provided.

There was also an economic factor behind Japan's decision to support the United States in Iraq. Being aware that Japan's economy depends heavily on the US economy, the Japanese leadership normally avoids a hostile policy towards the United States. Although Japan is likewise averse to hostile relations with the Middle East on which it relies for vital resources, particularly oil, Japan gambled that the United States would win. Pro-American Japanese Foreign Minister Kawaguchi's background as an economic bureaucrat made a difference in advancing that calculation. In the ministry of foreign affairs, too, relations with the United States take precedence over other matters in practically all circumstances. That stance is reflected in the bureaucratic structure, in which regional desks (especially the Northern American desk) exert more influence in decision-making than do functional desks (including the UN and legal affairs desks).

The JSDF operation in Iraq

JSDF deployment in Iraq is a significant development given Japan's pacifist, anti-militarist posture. The JSDF operation in Iraq, following the passage of Security Council Resolutions 1483 and 1511 (2003), gave practical support to what was de facto the military occupation of a sovereign nation by the coalition, albeit under UN resolutions (of somewhat dubious nature), although Japan remained outside and independent of the coalition command. Further, after the passage of Resolution 1546 (2004), the JSDF began operating "within" the UN-authorized multinational force in Iraq, which marked the first such JSDF operation in a multinational force.[13]

However, the JSDF Iraq operation is deliberately limited; the force level is just above 600 and geographically the operation is limited to Al Muthanna Province in south-eastern Iraq, inside areas under the overall responsibility of the UK military. It is significant that, although the Japanese forces are deployed in a strategically unstable situation, their roles are consciously restricted to civil affairs (humanitarian assistance and reconstruction) and no security-related tasks are mandated to the JSDF.

Both the significance of the JSDF deployment and the limitations on that deployment have to be understood in the historical context of Japan's post–World War II security policy. The main factor that has historically limited Japan's military action is the political culture of pacifism, which, as in the case of post-war Germany, laid the foundation for Japan's post-war identity and policy as a civilian power.[14] Throughout the post-war era, Japan's engagement in military actions, independently or jointly with other nations, has been considered legally problematic given the nation's pacifist constitution, especially with reference to Article 9.[15] Certain interpretations of the pacifist constitution have questioned the legality of self-defence and the JSDF itself, interpretations countered by the official interpretation in 1954 that Japan possessed the right to self-defence and that the JSDF, meant primarily for the defence of Japan's territories, was therefore constitutional.[16]

Even more controversial has been JSDF participation in both collective self-defence and collective security. In both areas, domestic political debates developed in such a way as to question the constitutionality of the JSDF's dispatch "overseas". As regards collective self-defence, against the background of the leftist attack on the legality of the JSDF and of the US–Japan Security Treaty, the Japanese government endorsed the view that the JSDF, which was meant strictly for self-defence when Japanese territories were under attack, would not be sent abroad. In June 1954, the upper house unanimously passed a resolution reaffirming that the JSDF could not be sent overseas.[17] The 1956 official interpretation stated that Japan possessed the right to collective self-defence as a sovereign nation but that it was illegal for it to use military force in pursuit of that right.

In the area of collective security, to avoid getting involved in the use of force, Japan has refrained from participating in UN-authorized multinational forces, where "participation" is understood to mean operating under the command of a multinational force. At the time of the first Gulf war (1990–1991) the Japanese conservatives failed to get legislation passed that would have allowed the JSDF to assist the coalition operation in the Gulf. Popular resistance to the idea of "enforcement" has not since been overcome.

As far as UN peacekeeping is concerned, Japan lacked any legal framework within which the JSDF could take part in such missions until 1992, despite heated debates in the Diet through four decades. The central issue remained the legality of the dispatch of the JSDF overseas in whatever capacity – whether to conduct UN "policing" or cease-fire monitoring or to provide logistical support. In 1980, the government stated that it considered it constitutional for Japan to participate in UN peacekeeping, provided its purpose and means were not forcible; the obstacle, in the government's view, was not the constitution but the lack of relevant provisions in the current Self-Defense Forces Law covering JSDF activities in situations other than direct and indirect attacks on Japan.[18] There was, nevertheless, no consensus in the Diet. Given these domestic controversies, Japanese participation in UN collective action was limited before 1992 to civilian assistance to some limited UN peace-keeping operations.

It was not until 1992 that an initiative by three major political parties resulted in the passage of the International Peace Cooperation Law (IPCL), which provided for the participation of the JSDF in UN peace-keeping and humanitarian assistance missions. As a result, Japan partici-pated in the UN Transitional Authority in Cambodia, as well as in sev-eral other UN peacekeeping missions. Japanese forces served in the United Nations Operation in Mozambique in logistical planning and command and control operations; in Zaire in 1994 assisting refugees; from 1996 in the United Nations Disengagement Observer Force in the Golan Heights, providing transportation; and in East Timor since 2002 providing engineering units as well as command and control.

Nevertheless, the law contained some inherent limitations as a result of successful manoeuvres by left-wing political parties in the Diet. The most obvious limitation was the ban on JSDF participation in so-called "core" activities (*Hontai Gyomu*), such as patrols and cease-fire monitoring, until such time as there was international and domestic "understanding" towards Japan's participation in peacekeeping. This ban was lifted in De-cember 2001.

Nonetheless, this ban on "core" activities, and its eventual lifting, probably had little practical significance given that such "core" activities are relatively simple tasks routinely carried out by traditional players in UN peacekeeping. A more significant limitation was the so-called "five conditions" set for Japanese participation in UN peacekeeping: (a) the existence of a cease-fire; (b) consent by the local parties; (c) strict impar-tiality (these three conditions are, needless to say, the conditions for tra-ditional UN peacekeeping); (d) in the absence of these conditions, Japan's right to decide whether to maintain its forces in the operation; and (e) minimum use of force strictly for self-defence. These conditions limited Japanese participation to cases of relatively stable, traditional peacekeeping in spite of the fact that the nature of peacekeeping was changing and might require limited enforcement measures to control local parties' fluctuating levels of consent toward peacekeeping deployments. The five conditions have also prevented Japan from providing much-needed advanced logistical support for UN-authorized coalition missions, such as INTERFET in East Timor.[19] These conditions are increasingly understood within the Japanese leadership to be out of date, for they do not recognize the strategic fluidity in which many of UN missions find themselves in the post–Cold War environment.

Debates about the legitimacy of humanitarian intervention, active as they have been among Japanese academics, the majority of whom grow wary at any hint of the term "enforcement", have had no practical consequences. This is an aspect that is similar to the German situation. Germany shifted its pacifist military posture towards taking an active part in multilateral peace operations by the United Nations and the North Atlantic Treaty Organization (NATO) through an often uneasy involvement in the humanitarian crises in the Balkans and Somalia. Japan did not contemplate joining in UN peace support operations, for instance in the Balkans, not to mention the unilateral Kosovo war, not only because the conflicts there were considered largely a European and a NATO problem, but also, and more importantly, because the use of force there ruled out Japanese participation under the current law.

When the JSDF had participated in missions in the past, it had to operate under extremely restrictive rules, especially concerning the "use of weapons". These restrictions were self-imposed, within limits set by civilians interpreting the pacifist constitution. Unlike in most other nations, the manner in which weapons might be used in various (hypothetical) circumstances is scrutinized in the national Diet prior to the passage of authorizing legislation, which then reflects the general agreement. With regard to self-defence as applying to the "lives and bodies" of JSDF personnel, other personnel serving with the JSDF (in the Peace Corps or humanitarian and reconstruction assistance) and those who, while conducting their missions, have come under the control or protection of the JSDF (including foreign nationals, UN staff and staff of nongovernmental organizations), Japanese regulations do not differ from those of other nations.[20] Nonetheless, the JSDF operates under tight rules of engagement, which cast legitimate doubt on the JSDF's ability to defend itself, or its missions, should the security situation deteriorate in any peacekeeping or humanitarian assistance missions.[21] Further, the JSDF is currently prohibited from responding to requests for assistance from foreign military contingents and is also prohibited from protecting civilians outside its areas of control. It is natural therefore for the Japanese leadership to be extremely cautious in managing the cost-performance aspects of missions in which the JSDF participates.[22] The extremely cautious management by the Japanese leadership of peacekeeping and other deployments has resulted in zero casualties, so far, among the JSDF personnel deployed.

Given the controversy aroused in domestic Japanese politics by any discussion of JSDF deployment "abroad", JSDF deployment in the Indian Ocean during the US war against the Taliban in Afghanistan was quite significant. In this context, it cannot be denied that the 9/11 attacks had a substantial impact on Japan's security policy. Most importantly, the 9/11 attacks had the effect of accelerating and justifying the expansion of Japanese military actions in support of US forces, which were an extension of the bilateral defence arrangement through legal as well as political discretion, a trend that had been under way since the mid-1990s. In the autumn of 2001, after as little as a month's debate in the Diet, the Koizumi cabinet succeeded in getting the Anti-Terrorism Special Measures Law passed by the Diet. Under this law, Japanese naval vessels were dispatched to the Indian Ocean to provide logistical support to the coalition forces during the war against the Taliban. This law was extended in 2003 and again in 2005.

This uncharacteristically swift response by the Koizumi cabinet is in line with Japanese activism in the area of bilateral defence during the 1990s. Triggered in great part by the crises in the Far East in the mid-1990s, Japanese actions in bilateral defence were considerably more proactive than in previous eras. The crises in the Korean Peninsula, most notably the repeated defiance by the North Korean regime of WMD non-proliferation agreements, resulted in a widely held recognition that the existing US–Japanese defence cooperation needed upgrading. The 1996 Hashimoto–Clinton communiqué declared the US–Japanese alliance to be the basis of "world peace and regional stability and prosperity", and agreed on a revision of the 1978 Guidelines for Japan–US Defense Cooperation (Defense Guidelines) in order to clarify the extent of collaboration between the two nations in light of the current security environment.[23] In 1997, revised Defense Guidelines were adopted, which spelled out closer US–Japanese cooperation in a full spectrum of contingencies but especially those related to "situations in areas surrounding Japan". The ensuing passage of Laws Concerning Measures to Enhance the Peace and Security of Japan in Situations in Areas Surrounding Japan clarified and expanded the areas of US–Japanese collaboration in situations in areas surrounding Japan in concrete terms.

The JSDF deployment in the Indian Ocean should be understood as an important extension of this bilateral security arrangement. The Japanese Maritime Self-Defense Force (JMSDF) is deployed in the area on the basis of the Anti-Terrorism Special Measures Law, which inherited much from the Laws Concerning Measures to Enhance the Peace and Security of Japan in Situations in Areas Surrounding Japan, particularly in terms of the definition of the "rear area". Further, the most significant point is that the JSDF began deploying *during* the war in Afghanistan, provoking a domestic debate about whether the JSDF was being sent to a "combat area". The opposition parties worried that, as a result of the

JSDF being deployed in a combat area, it would inevitably take part in (be "integrated" in or "*ittaika*") combat. The government responded to this by arguing that the JSDF would not be "integrated" in combat, but would serve only in areas outside combat zones and would provide only logistical support.[24]

The passage of the Anti-Terrorism Special Measures Law was significant also because it justified JSDF deployment in the Indian Ocean on the basis of international peace and security.[25] It is important to mention that the Koizumi cabinet characterized the JSDF deployment as forming part of Japan's "efforts to cooperate with the rest of the international community in [its] endeavors to prevent and eradicate international terrorism in order to ensure the peace and security of the international community including Japan itself".[26] It was notable that the Japanese government refrained from mentioning the issue of self-defence, which was the main argument given by the US government in justifying its military action against the Taliban. Avoiding self-defence as a justification for the action was supposed to keep controversial issues relating to collective self-defence from being raised in the Diet, which might have precluded swift government action. But it was also the government's position that the US action in response to the 9/11 attacks could not be fully justified as self-defence.[27] The latter interpretation may constitute another point of significance regarding the Japanese deployment in the Indian Ocean. The JSDF may have assisted coalition military activities with an uncertain status under international law, although the Japanese government based its decision to send the JSDF to the Indian Ocean on Security Council Resolution 1368 (2001),[28] which did link international terrorism with international peace, although it failed to endorse collective military action while citing the inherent right to individual or collective self-defence under the Charter.

JSDF deployment in Iraq under the Special Measures Law on Humanitarian and Reconstruction Assistance in Iraq of July 2003 and the Basic Plan, adopted by the cabinet in December 2003, was likewise significant in that it again extended both bilateral and multilateral justifications for Japanese military action. The most important issue for the government was the need to strengthen bilateral relations with the United States. However, the government again used multilateral logic to justify its decision. This legislation cited Resolution 1483 (2003), which recognized the authority (occupying powers under unified command) in an ex post facto manner and established the United Nations' humanitarian role in Iraq.[29] The resolution called for contributions from member states to provide humanitarian and reconstruction assistance, and the Japanese government placed JSDF activities in that context. As in the case of Afghanistan, the Japanese government defined the JSDF activities in Iraq as

Japan's contribution to the international community's effort to bring peace and prosperity to Iraq.

Nonetheless, the uncertain legal status of the Iraq war and subsequent occupation made the legitimacy of the coalition operation much contested. As a result, Japan may be understood to have assisted military activities resembling an occupation of a sovereign nation, which is unprecedented in its post–World War II history. Further, as with the case of Afghanistan, the JSDF was deployed in a strategically fluid situation, with counter-insurgency operations being conducted by the coalition. Although relatively stable, Samawah was a careful and deliberate choice by Japan; the situation there could easily destabilize, as pointed out by the opposition parties as well as by some in the governing coalition.

The latter possibility poses a rather sticky question about the current JSDF approach to force protection and security. The JSDF, which is devoted to civil affairs, does not have any mandate to provide security in Sector South-East, where security-related tasks have been performed by the Dutch, UK and Australian troops. The JSDF is reliant on the coalition for the provision of security-related information. As noted above, current Japanese domestic laws allow for the JSDF to provide for the direct protection of its own force through the exercise of the right of self-defence. Operating under tight rules of engagement, and without the authority to maintain general security in the area of its operation, however, the JSDF provides for indirect force protection, primarily through the management of hostilities in the area of its operation.[30] Hence the JSDF leadership is keenly aware that the success of its civil affairs projects as perceived by the local Iraqis ("hearts and minds" operations) is a matter of primary importance from the force protection standpoint as well as from the humanitarian viewpoint.

The Japanese government's decision on 18 June 2004 to extend JSDF activities beyond the 30 June deadline for the return of sovereignty to the Iraqis (in fact the handover was done two days early) was significant in that it resulted in the first ever JSDF operation "within" a multinational force. It is noteworthy that it is taking place in a post-conflict context, not in a clear-cut case of aggression. Nonetheless, as a result of the government's attempt to keep JSDF activities in Iraq compatible with past legal interpretations, it is again the case that the actual operation of the JSDF is quite limited. The JSDF operates independently of, although it coordinates its activities with, the unified command. While continuing to provide humanitarian and post-conflict development assistance, the JSDF is strictly prohibited from getting involved in the use of force by the multinational force. JSDF activities are also limited to "non-combat" areas. These rules are consistent with the four principles of JSDF participation in the multinational forces in Iraq proposed by Koizumi: (1) no use of force that is banned under the constitution; (2) no activities in combat areas; (3) no "integration" with the use of force by other states; and (4) command under the JSDF.

What was most notable, given the pacifist political culture of post-war Japan, was the constant very high support by the Japanese public for the provision of humanitarian assistance by the JSDF in Iraq. The *Yomiuri* newspaper reported that more than 80 per cent of those surveyed supported the JSDF's providing humanitarian assistance in Iraq.[31] A *Japan Economic Journal* telephone survey showed 52 per cent supporting the Iraq Special Measures Law.[32] Another *Japan Economic Journal* survey suggests that, in April 2004, 42 per cent supported the JSDF assisting the coalition in Iraq while 40 per cent opposed it. Those who opposed it increased in May 2004 to 44 per cent, while 43 per cent still supported it.[33]

It is notable, however, that the Japanese government's decision in June 2004 to participate in the multinational force in Iraq was not as popular as the initial JSDF deployment in Iraq. A *Japan Economic Journal* survey revealed that 49 per cent opposed Japan's taking part in the multinational force, whereas 35 per cent supported it.[34]

The deployment of the JSDF has so far not been affected by the repeated hostage-taking of Japanese nationals in Iraq, although these incidents attracted high public attention and opposition parties questioned the government on its Iraq policy based upon these highly publicized incidents. In April 2004, three Japanese volunteers, including a female worker, were taken hostage by a rebel group, later to be released with the help of Iraqi religious leaders. In the same month, two journalists were taken hostage, again later to be released. In the same year, however, three Japanese nationals were murdered, two of them journalists. These added to the deaths of two Japanese diplomats in 2003 in an ambush near Tikrit. The concern that the Japanese government's policy in Iraq might be endangering Japanese nationals, as in fact claimed by opposition parties, will continue to pose a difficult challenge for the government in maintaining support for the coalition.

Conclusion

In sum, Japan has clearly sided with the United States and the coalition in their post-9/11 actions and in their vision about how to restore international order in the post-9/11 world. In both Afghanistan and Iraq, concern for bilateral relations with the United States has driven Japanese policy. To a significant extent the Japanese response to the Iraq war exposes the nation's strategic reliance on the United States and the readiness of the majority of Japanese to accept that fact. To many observers, there is a significant lack of focus on multilateralism in Japan's response to the Iraq war. Yet Japan's response probably also reflects the fact that there are indeed few security guarantees except that offered by the United States in North-East Asia.

The Japanese government nonetheless opted to support coalition efforts in Afghanistan and humanitarian and reconstruction work in Iraq under the proclaimed umbrella of UN resolutions, despite their lack of clarity, presenting a case that peace, democracy and prosperity in these nations are a matter of international peace. On this basis, a partnership has been forged between the coalition and Japan in long-term peacebuilding in Afghanistan and Iraq. In this process, the Japanese government has defined counter-terrorism and peacebuilding as matters of international concern and linked these with international peace. The Japanese government is now "bound" by its instrumental use of legitimacy. Having supported the Iraq war and the ensuing stabilization operation largely on the basis of their relevance to international peace and security, Japan needs to be committed to and present itself as a credible actor in post-conflict peacebuilding and reconstruction. It will need to prepare a stronger theoretical argument for its use of the Self-Defense Forces for post-conflict peacebuilding purposes, and to present a consistent framework within which the Self-Defense Forces can operate effectively in such contexts.

For this, coming to terms with the past (both pre-war imperialism and post-war pacifism) would seem to be an urgent task for Japan. As JSDF officials privately acknowledge, Asian nations still express relief that the JSDF is operating side-by-side with their militaries (rather than independently) in places such as East Timor. The establishment of mutual confidence, based upon the firm recognition of Japan as a nation committed to multilateralism, is a foreign policy priority yet to be achieved. On the other hand, given the current security environment and the transforming roles of military organizations in supporting peace, Japanese post-war pacifism, which had generally prohibited Japan from utilizing its Self-Defense Forces for the international public good, should likewise be revised. There needs to be a clear, transparent standard, justifiable in light of domestic conditions as well as international standards, upon which the JSDF can conduct UN peacekeeping and humanitarian assistance missions. Such a standard should reflect consensus within Japan about Japan's diplomatic role and the role of Japan's Self-Defense Forces in international peace maintenance as well as a realistic assessment of the capabilities needed to support peace in volatile situations.

What is strikingly lacking in Japan's response to the Iraq war is a clear foreign policy vision. Japan seems to be struggling to strike a balance between multilateral justifications and obvious bilateral needs to strengthen defence, as well as between its militarist and pacifist past and its current political needs. The Japanese government has resorted to special laws to allow for controversial JSDF deployment abroad. The result, which is typical of past Japanese debates on security affairs, is the glossing over of the overall strategic vision in favour of tedious legal arguments with no relevance to the issues of international concern. The issues to be considered and clarified are numerous, and legitimately include both principles and practical considerations: how to strike a new balance between bilateral and multilateral commitments; how to strengthen the UN system to address new security requirements such as dealing with terrorist threats; how to deal with the types of situation now encountered on the ground in Iraq and Afghanistan; and how Japan should prepare to deal with these situations – in terms of the legal framework and doctrinal thinking. More conceptual and strategic thinking seems to be required of the Japanese government and people in order to make wise judgements about its own security and international security, which are becoming increasingly interdependent.

Notes

1. See Robert Jervis, "Understanding the Bush Doctrine", *Political Science Quarterly*, Vol. 118, No. 3 (Autumn 2003); Lawrence Freedman, "Prevention, Not Preemption", *Washington Quarterly*, Vol. 26, No. 2 (Spring 2003).
2. Jervis, "Understanding the Bush Doctrine", p. 366; Paul Kennedy, *The Rise and Fall of the Great Powers: Economic Change and Military Conflict from 1500 to 2000* (New York: Random House, 1987).
3. Jervis, "Understanding the Bush Doctrine".
4. *Mainichi*, 23 February 2003.
5. *Mainichi*, 13 March 2003.
6. *Yomiuri*, 21 March 2003.
7. Ibid.
8. Ibid.
9. Nikkei Denwa Yoron Chosa, March 2003, ⟨http://www.nikkei-r.co.jp/nikkeipoll/qandres/y200303a.htm⟩.
10. UNSCR 1511 (2003).
11. UNSCR 1546 (2004).
12. The speech by Prime Minister Koizumi at the 59th UN General Assembly, 21 September 2004.
13. The government does not use the term "participation". The original Japanese in the decision of 17 June 2004 in the Security Council of Japan reads: *"Takokuseki gun no naka de"*. *Iraq Jindo Hukko Shien Tokoso Ho ni motozuki Jieitai ga Iraku ni oite okonau Jindou Hukko Shien Katudou nado ni Tsuite* [About JSDF humanitarian and reconstruction activities in Iraq based upon the Law Concerning the Special Measures on Humanitarian and Reconstruction Assistance in Iraq] (Security Council of Japan Decision on Heisei 16 (2004) 17 June).

14. Hans Maulle, "Germany and Japan: The New Civilian Powers", *Foreign Affairs*, Vol. 69, No. 5 (Winter 1990/1991); Takashi Inoguchi, Saori Katada and Hans Maulle, eds, *Global Governance: Germany and Japan in the International System* (London: Ashgate, 2004).

15. Yozo Yokota, "PKO and Japan's Domestic Politics: A Legal Analysis", in Soo-Gil Park and Sung-Hack Kang, eds, *UN, PKO and East Asian Security: Currents, Trends and Prospects* (Seoul: Korean Academic Council on the United Nations System, 2002).

16. Akihiko Tanaka, *Anzen Hosho: Sengo Gojunenn no Mosaku* (Tokyo: Yomiuri Shinbun-sha, 1997), pp. 148–149. This interpretation was coupled with the so-called "three principles" of self-defence, adopted in the Diet in 1954.

17. The Nineteenth Session of the Diet, cited in Shigeru Kousai, *Kokuren no Heiwa Iji Katsudo* (Tokyo: Yuhikaku, 1991), pp. 478–479.

18. Kousai, *Kokuren no Heiwa Iji Katsudo*, pp. 500–501.

19. On the basis of the five conditions, the Japanese leadership ruled out a Japanese response to the call to provide medical support to the Australian-led coalition force in East Timor.

20. See Article 24 of the International Peace Cooperation Law, and Article 17 of the Special Measures Law on Humanitarian and Reconstruction Assistance in Iraq.

21. See also the discussion below on force protection.

22. Confirmed in an interview with a JSDF official.

23. "Japan–U.S. Joint Declaration on Security: Alliance for the 21st Century", 17 April 1996, ⟨http://www.mofa.go.jp/region/n-america/us/security/security.html⟩.

24. "Combat" is defined in the Anti-Terrorism Special Measures Law as acts to kill people or destroy objects as part of international armed conflicts (Article 2(3)).

25. For a similar assessment, see Akio Watanabe, "The Higuchi Report and After: Evolution of Japan's Defense and Security Policies during the Past Ten Years", *Kokusai Anzen Hosho*, Vol. 31, No. 3 (December 2003).

26. Statement by Prime Minister Junichiro Koizumi on the Passing of the Anti-Terrorism Special Measures Law by the Diet of Japan, 29 October 2001.

27. Watanabe, "The Higuchi Report and After".

28. UNSCR 1368 (2001).

29. UNSCR 1483 (2003).

30. Interview with JSDF officials.

31. *Yomiuri*, 21 April 2003.

32. Nikkei Denwa Yoron Chosa, March 2003.

33. *Nihon Keizai Shinbun*, 5 July 2004.

34. Ibid.

18

Iraq and world order: A Latin American perspective

Mónica Serrano and Paul Kenny

Introduction: Latin America and US hegemony

A Latin American perspective on world order – isn't there a whiff of the incongruous about this? Even if there is one, why should it count?

Latin America's place in world order *is* peripheral. Whether it be a UN or US world order, Latin America at worst hosts a set of endemically disordered states, and at best is too far removed from the centres of order to register. Yet whether world order means UN or US order also clearly makes a difference in Latin America. As Ramesh Thakur and Waheguru Pal Singh Sidhu write in Chapter 1, the shock over Iraq between "the world's indispensable power" and "the world's indispensable institution" was of seismic proportions. Peripheral though it is, Latin America could hardly fail to register the effects. Latin America's very peripherality in fact lent an added sensitivity to its perspective on the large shifts discussed by Thakur and Sidhu.

For Latin America, the question of the United States' preventive intervention in Iraq became a reflexive question about its own relative global powerlessness; in other words, a question about its continuing subjection to US hegemony. US hegemony over Latin America is a self-evident truth, impossible to elude even in projections of what a *non*-US-centric world order might look like. Contrast, for example, the title of Joseph Nye's globally ranging critique of US unilateralism, *The Paradox of American Power: Why the World's Only Superpower Can't Go It Alone*, with the three entries under "Latin America" in the index:[1]

- adoption of American standards by
- democratization
- foreign-born Americans from

Nye's is a US-centric argument against US unilateralism. There's nothing wrong with that, but his index still confirms Latin America's low ranking in a US-centric view of world order.

Putting it in shorthand, the continent both falls under US hegemony and shares the basic democratic values of the Western hemisphere. "The Hispanic challenge", the last item, deserves mention as a source of US concern, although not for Nye himself. Generally, however, Latin America is not a US priority because it is not a problem.

It might seem that Latin America would be more of a priority in its own right if its disorder were more of a problem for the United States. In fact, the paradox of Latin American powerlessness works differently. As long as it does not pose a problem, Latin America is subsumed by US hegemony; when it does create trouble, US hegemonic intervention faces no obstacles in fixing it on its own terms. Why is Latin America peripheral, then? Because it has no way of escaping the United States.

From the 1980s on, Latin America's political élites gave up looking for the exit. Given the choice between oblivion in outer space or subscribing to the Washington consensus, signing free trade agreements and securing US military aid, élites fell over themselves to hitch their bandwagons to the United States. The more desperate embraced the United States' war on drugs; the more ambitious would enthusiastically adopt far-ranging economic liberalization. In different ways, but with only few exceptions, Latin America consented to US hegemony.

Latin America thus experienced the implications of a US-centric world order before the rest of the late-twentieth-century world. It has not been a salutary experience, with things turning out badly for both the desperate and the ambitious. The deeper lesson of the experience, however, has been that consent to hegemony means losing visibility: only one perspective counts.

Nye's entry under "democratization" provides a benign but also a particularly apposite example of the double-edged logic at work. Latin American democratization can indeed, from a US perspective, be pretty much tantamount to the adoption of an American standard since the demise of both military dictatorships and, with the exception of Colombia, armed insurgencies. From a Latin American perspective, however, the transition to democracy has in many countries precipitated grave crises of governance and rising tides of anti-systemic protest. Human rights records have not necessarily improved; the coup d'état has returned; corruption scandals refuse to go away; and the gap between rich and poor only widens. These are the problems that currently have most of Latin

America in their grip, yet they hardly register for the United States. Whether paradoxically or not, the transition to democracy has reduced the international profile that Latin America had in the troubled epoch of dictatorship and insurgency.

If one re-writes the index for Latin America under US hegemony, it is not hard to see why this should be so:

- Colombia: drugs, war on
- Mexico: border with United States; migration from
- Andes: drugs, balloon effect of
- Paraguay, Brazil, Argentina: terrorist havens on triple frontier of

Such are the US realities of Latin America. They reflect, above all, the securitizing logic of the war on drugs. So long as a country such as Bolivia does not challenge that logic, it may go to the wall without so much as a murmur from the United States. From Argentina to Venezuela, Latin American countries enjoy the sovereign right to descend into disorder without US interference, so long as the chaos presents no security challenge to the United States.

Already blinkered by its own security concerns vis-à-vis Latin America before the terrorist attacks of 11 September 2001, the United States intensified its securitized vision afterwards. With its homeland security under direct threat, the United States was convulsed first by tragedy, then by an apparently consuming urge to divide the world into friends and foes. As al-Qaeda sought to convert anti-Americanism into the cause of a global war, so the natural allies of the United States and major institutions such as the United Nations came under pressure to show their solidarity with the United States as never before. The new pressure on Latin America, however, produced a crack within the hegemonic order. The United States, as ever, wished for an echo to its own reality; not all Latin American countries found they could give it.

The key case was Mexico. The most natural of the United States' Latin American allies, given the depth of regional integration under the North American Free Trade Agreement (NAFTA), Mexico's supply of sympathy was short. President Fox delayed for days after 9/11 before making the gesture of a telephone call to President Bush. The limit to the adoption of American standards was in turn noticed.

For Mexico, 9/11 spelled the end of any hopes of a deal with the United States over the illegal status of millions of Mexican migrants. For Latin America generally, 9/11 also marked the end of any chance of making its realities count against US perceptions. The hemispheric consequence of 9/11 was to sharpen the hegemonic dilemma: to submit and be counted on US terms, or not to react and be discounted.

Many Latin American countries found themselves too dependent upon the United States to refuse the new demand for support. But many were not going to rise to the level of commitment demanded by the United States either. In the test case of Colombia, Brazil and Venezuela declined to categorize the insurgents as terrorists on a par with al-Qaeda, and Ecuador and Peru drew back from the regionalization of the conflict envisaged by Plan Colombia. At the same time, the near presidential victory of Evo Morales in Bolivia on a platform of opposition to US drug eradication policies signalled a new trend of anti-Americanism within Latin America, one synergized by a confluence between opposition to neoliberalism and anti-globalization.

As the war on Iraq loomed, the signs of hemispheric fissure increased. On the one hand, Latin America as a whole shares a diplomatic tradition that is explicitly opposed to military intervention in general, and to US military intervention in particular. On the other, the inescapable reality of hegemony would still dictate the terms of Latin American resistance: it would have to make itself felt without coalescing into an overt challenge to the United States. The Latin American perspective on Iraq would be marked by the peculiar mixture of rifts and constraints within the hegemonic relationship with the United States. Insofar as a matter of diplomatic principle was at stake, leading Latin American countries did oppose the United States. Hegemony reached a limit. The question was how to articulate that a limit had been reached while still bowing to the inevitable.

The Latin American dilemma of divergence within dependence would have remained utterly peripheral had not two of its states, Mexico and Chile, come into the UN Security Council in 2003. The drama that ensued would itself be a test of the implications of a US-centric world order.

The Security Council offered a world stage for the submerged continent to rise up and be seen. That, at least, was how the leading Mexican actors in the drama saw their role in 2003. In the words of Foreign Minister Jorge Castañeda, Mexico came to the Security Council looking to participate "in the design and construction of the new post Cold War world order, simultaneously characterized by the hegemony of the United States and the effort of the rest of the world to limit and control that hegemony".[2]

This chapter is about the fate of that Latin American design. Since the drama was driven by perspectives, we begin with these before moving on to the acts. In the conclusion, we turn our own critical perspective upon the Latin American protagonists. Were Mexico and Chile up to playing a constructive international role on behalf of the world order represented by the United Nations? Or was their divergence from the United States itself limited and controlled by its hegemony?

US order in Latin American perspective; Latin American disorder in US perspective

The virtual veto of the Security Council robbed the US war on Iraq of international legitimacy; but into the gap the Bush administration wedged its doctrine of the preventive use of force in assuring its own national security. If the spiral of terrorism from political Islam is the most alarming short-term consequence of the invasion of Iraq, for many the long-term implications of this new US doctrine for world order are no less troubling. With its willingness to bypass the United Nations now established, what is the post-Westphalian limit to US military intervention?

From the start of the Iraq crisis, this question was uppermost in Latin America. Indeed, the continent was uniquely well – or badly – placed to hear the alarm bells:

The *only* zone of the planet constantly wronged by the United States has been Hispano-America. In 1847 Mexico suffered the mutilation of half of its territory. It was an unjustifiable act of historical piracy which haunted Mexican governments like a nightmare until 1927 ... Along with Mexico, the "banana republics" of Central America and the Caribbean islands of "the US' Mediterranean" were the next victims of *gunboat diplomacy*: the annexation of Puerto Rico, the compulsory protectorate for Cuba ...[3]

The list goes on: Sandino in Nicaragua, Arbenz in Guatemala, Allende in Chile. For most of Latin America, US military intervention is an ever-present threat to world order because it is a memory that refuses to die.

The exceptional significance of this historical consciousness for Latin America's perspective on world order cannot be overestimated. It accounts, in particular, for the high stock set in Latin America upon the United Nations and institutions such as the International Court of Justice. Latin American commitment to them is the genuine commitment of the protection seeker. Equally, behind Latin America's adherence to the general principle of multilateralism often lies the specific interest in non-intervention, along with the bargaining advantages opened for it in a multipolar world.

More than an interest, though, Latin American opposition to US intervention is deep-seated. Even in Colombia, where US involvement in the counter-insurgency has been democratically validated, the number of US military personnel actually in Colombia in 2003 was a mere 358. Colombia is a vivid demonstration of the more general Latin American paradox by which visceral opposition to direct US intervention sits side by side with submission to US hegemony. Latin America does not want to let the United States in; but it does not want it to go away either.

These are the terms of acceptance of US order. Understandably, whether in Latin America or in Iraq, they pose a difficult challenge to the United States – to exercise its hegemony virtuously but not to intervene. Ought there not to be a bigger trade-off? With so many Latin American countries clamouring for economic integration through free trade agreements with the United States, ought they not to be counted as natural allies of the United States? When the United States has genuine security concerns, should it not be allowed to tell its allies how to put their houses in order?

As with the war on drugs, so with the war on terrorism: it is the introduction of a security dimension by the United States, with the call for militarized regional responses, that tests the limits of the acceptability of its indirect hegemonic rule. In a US world order, the responsiveness of its allies to its security concerns is the measure of those allies' standing. To the degree that they do not wake up to US concerns by militarizing, allies lose their right to be treated as partners.

It is not even, after all, the case that the continent is immune from terrorism. Colombia's insurgents may be a controversial case in Latin America, but the presence of Islamic terrorists in Paraguay's Ciudad del Este has been incontrovertible since Iranian-linked Hezbollah terrorists killed 117 Jews in Buenos Aires in the bomb attacks of 1992 and 1994. Likewise, a report by the US–Mexico Binational Commission in 2004 spelled out not just how devastating a terrorist attack in Mexico could be, for both Mexico and the United States, but also what some of the petroleum installation targets could well be.[4] Is it not time that Latin America woke up to the threats it poses to the United States?

Certainly, few Latin American countries can afford not to respond to US alarm calls. Despite its unhappiness with Plan Colombia, Brazil is taking unprecedented measures to tighten its northern border; despite its rebuff over immigration, Mexico is cooperating with US security measures along its border. But, from a US perspective, Latin America more complies with than fulfils US expectations. Less directly imposing than in the past, US hegemony now takes the form of an invitation to share its security perspectives, along with a flat refusal to credit the existence of any others. The failure of the region to intervene in, or even form a plan for, Colombia is one of many upshots: when the United States is involved on its terms, the region backs off. However, once the issue is the security of the United States itself, its expectations are exponential. If it is drugs today, what can Latin America do when it is migration tomorrow?

On different levels, the more prominent Latin American states put up resistance to the United States just when the United States expects them to fall into line. The more the United States securitizes threats, the more wary becomes the Latin American response. The historical precedents become reactivated, fears for the future intensified. *Wherever* the United States intervenes, Latin America sees *its* history being repeated.

No level of response to the US intervention in Iraq was deeper than that of Latin American domestic opinion. Far from finding an echo there, the security concerns of the United States were represented as the thinnest of imperialist disguises; Iraq was just one more case in a litany of US interventions, one more banana-cum-oil republic. Opinion formers found parallels, not between Hussein and Castro, but between the pattern of US intervention in Latin America and in the Middle East, one in which the United States had installed friendly dictators over the heads of suffering peoples.[5] Politicians came in on cue. When at the height of the Iraq crisis President Fox said "there are threats from outside", for his Mexican audience he could mean not al-Qaeda or weapons of mass destruction, but only the United States.[6]

At this crudest level, the significance of Iraq in Latin America was that it exposed the limits of the hegemonic arrangement for both sides. For the United States, if it listened, the message was that Latin America is behind the real time of the new world order in which new threats have to be responded to. For Latin America, the crisis over Iraq brought home the untenability of simultaneously opposing and submitting to the hegemon. Both sides found themselves looking for the exit. For the United States, the exit was unilateralism, with the attendant dilemmas noted by Thakur and Sidhu. For the more chafing Latin American states, the exit was the United Nations, the only forum in which opposition to the United States might be expressed without risking the benefits of interdependence with the United States.

Even without the test of Iraq, some of those states were already voicing their discontent with the structural situation in which they are removed from a world order that in turn neglects them. Take this message, delivered by Luiz Felipe de Macedo Soares, Brazil's under-secretary of foreign relations:

Mexico and Brazil, as Latin America's two great countries, can or ought to jointly express their concern about the situation of Latin America ... so as to attract the attention of the other centres of power.[7]

In its hesitant urgency ("can or ought to"), the message catches the plight of Latin America at the start of the twenty-first century: where can Latin America count? Yet the message was delivered just as the attention of the world was becoming mesmerized by Iraq and the prospect of US invasion. Was this a time for Latin America to count?

For one utopian Latin American protagonist, Mexico, it was. It could not forget 1847, but Latin American history might at last be changed by the creation at the other centre of power, if not of a non-US-centric world order, at least of a US-constraining world order. Driven by its particular historical consciousness, Mexico's utopianism would test the power realities of both the US and the UN world orders.

Mexico: The anatomy of a crisis

Mexico obtained its place as a non-permanent member of the Security Council two days before 11 September 2001; it would assume the presidency on April Fool's Day 2003.

The inauspicious story of Mexico's role in the Security Council began not on 1 January 2002, when it took its seat, but in the country's transition to democracy in 2000. After 71 years of rule by the PRI (Party of Institutional Revolution), President Fox's foreign minister, Jorge Castañeda, was keen to project a new international image of Mexico. The administration would assert itself with the United States over the status of the 3.5 million illegal Mexican migrants there, and would promote human rights, even if this meant breaking with its traditional policy over Cuba. Mexico was going to gain a voice that could now legitimately count in the world.

The story, however, would not be Mexican if it did not have a deeper sub-plot. The last time Mexico had been in the Security Council, in the early 1980s, its ambassador, Porfirio Muñoz Ledo, won notoriety by carrying a gun on the streets of New York. In 2003 he was more diplomatic, if somewhat ungrammatical:

Evidently now, the theme of the new world order, of the reconstruction of the UN's authority and above all of the struggle for a multipolar world in which Latin America, Europe can coordinate themselves, well it's going to help to get a better world.[8]

Mexico was propelled into the Security Council in 2003 by a group of politicians and diplomats with ambitions for the United Nations, the world and Mexico.[9] The Security Council offered them the only arena in which to put a Latin American mark on world order. In it, the latent conflict between Latin America and the United States could, on the one hand, come out into the open, and, on the other, be set to one side of the reality of the ongoing, free-trade-driven bilateral relationships.

When the crisis over Iraq blew up, it must have seemed to observers of Mexico that here once again was a case of one of its projects being overtaken by events out of its control – 9/11 all over again. Yet, although Mexico could not have anticipated that its position on Iraq would be critical, it could well have anticipated that its votes were going to be weighed in the balance with the United States. President Bush had supported Mexico's campaign to join the Council in place of the Dominican Republic (which, along with all the Central American Republics, would later approve the invasion). The US position over Mexico's vote on Iraq was in turn delivered by US Ambassador Tony Garza: "We'll respect the position of any country, but what we most want is that Mexico give its support, and understand our position."[10] By the time President Bush spoke on the telephone to President Fox, the message was simpler: "The security of the United States is on the line. I want your vote."[11]

As Mexico's business community was not slow to point out, Mexico's interests clearly lay in supporting the recipient of 90 per cent of its exports. There was also the vulnerable situation of the still illegal Mexicans in the United States to think of. Yet Mexico had two reasons for deciding not to "do the right thing". Unfortunately, the two reasons did not find a single mouthpiece.

On the surface, Mexico's participation in the Security Council was strictly on the basis of its own historical and constitutional commitment to principles of non-intervention and the peaceful resolution of conflicts.[12] If Mexico's ethically sovereign reasons of state inhibit it from sending soldiers to UN peacekeeping missions, it could hardly be expected to approve a US-led intervention in Iraq.[13]

Below the surface, though, the crisis over Iraq offered an ideal test for the more ambitious Mexican design of checking US unilateralism. Could Mexico dissuade the United States from doing what it wanted over Iraq? No. But could it lead the veto of world consensus against the United States? If yes, the case for an expanded Security Council would be strengthened, along with the authority of the United Nations.

These are the considerations that broke through in the otherwise inopportune exuberance of Jorge Castañeda's assessment in the aftermath of the crisis:

Instead of the Council having decided that it was not going to approve this Resolution and that therefore the Americans, English [sic] and Spanish would not be able to present the second Resolution, they would have had the nine votes. If it wasn't for Mexico and for Chile, they would have had the nine votes and so, of course, it was worth it.[14]

With even greater diplomatic immunity, Castañeda went on to opine: "It was a great piece of luck for Latin America" that the seats on the Council fell to Mexico and Chile. "Just imagine what would have happened if another two countries from Latin America had taken them."[15] Only Mexico and Chile were up to leading what became known in the United Nations as the "revolt of the Latins".

No Mexican figure was more pivotal than Foreign Minister Castañeda. He alone could have played the two cards Mexico had in its hand against the United States.[16] Yet Castañeda resigned at the beginning of 2003, soon to pursue independent presidential ambitions. When he went, he took with him the copy of the script that had the prompts marked for President Fox. From February 2003 on, the president had only the surface reasons in which peace was always the only end Mexico could pursue.[17] President Fox was not the protagonist of the Mexican Security Council drama; the moment he assumed centre-stage was the moment of transition from well-laid plan to grief for Mexico.

Not that President Fox's insistence on a peaceful resolution to Iraq did not meet positive acclamation in Roman Catholic Mexico. To the contrary, he achieved an apotheosis of popularity, gaining a positive rating of 76 per cent compared with one of 17 per cent for Bush in Mexican opinion polls between 18 and 29 March. Opposition to Mexico's lending "moral support" to the United States increased from 49 per cent to 59 per cent.[18] Peace, in other words, was less a policy of neutrality than one of Mexico's other religion, nationalism.

When deputies from President Fox's PAN (Party of National Action) referred to a "despot", they meant George W. Bush;[19] when a leading opposition deputy talked of "war, horror, death, genocide and holocaust", he was referring not to Saddam's Iraq but to "policies" that should not be supported by Mexico.[20] Fox played his part in whipping up this national frenzy; but he was also playing on an uneven terrain with a Goliath whom his diplomatic Davids had attempted to shift. From a Mexican perspective, the point was that Mexican governability depends upon giving in to Mexican anti-Americanism. From a US perspective, this was just one more of those Latin American realities that cut so little ice with it.

Even as Mexican society gave its veto, President Bush both threatened Mexico with "discipline" and turned up the pressure for Mexico's backing, which new Foreign Minister Ernesto Derbez would later call "brutal".[21] Mexican business leaders took to the op-ed pages to warn that Mexican beer was going to go the way of French wine in the United States. President Fox received the dreaded call from President Bush, hedged, and promptly took refuge in hospital to avoid having to return it. The roof appeared to be collapsing on the administration's head.

The point of the Security Council plotters had thus been made: for Mexico to challenge the United States on bilateral terms may produce a fleeting domestic catharsis, but no diplomatic (much less world-historical) sequel. Indeed, one of the few things the Bush and Fox administrations agreed on was that there would be no deal over migration (as perhaps Castañeda had originally hoped) as a reward for Mexico's vote. Instead, for both the United States and Mexico the issue of Iraq came down to basic allegiance – unconditionally expected by the United States, unconditionally refused by Mexico.

President Fox had led Mexico to an unsustainable stalemate with the United States and also foreclosed Mexico's exit options in the Security Council. Mexico's position there, articulated through the traditional "pacifist militarism" of Ambassador Adolfo Aguilar Zínser, allowed no room for bargaining with the United States. But because Mexico was now dancing to a patently nationalist tune in the Council, the option was in turn open to the United States of turning its back on diplomacy there with Mexico and piling on the pressure at source. The new foreign minister began to communicate a policy of "wait and see", of principled – or pressurized – indecision. The United States had opened a breach in Mexican diplomatic discourse. Even when given, "No" was not an answer for the United States.[22] "Did they [the United States] behave badly? Tell them. If they block you, it doesn't matter, tell them," advised Marín Bosch, ex-under-secretary of foreign relations, after the event.[23] Instead, Mexico had only been able to tell them it was going to tell them.

On the one hand, the exercise of US pressure on Mexico, as on Chile, was nakedly hegemonic. Both Mexico and Chile went as far as they could in opposing the United States, paradoxically finding in their very dependence upon the United States an incentive to resist it. The crucial point, on the other hand, is that they were unable to oppose the United States *together*.[24] If opposing the United States was "worth it", what was the value to multilateralism of Mexico and Chile's disjoined opposition?

Chile: Multilateralism in principle and in practice

Three overlapping features made Chile a prominent player over Iraq. First, Chile has a tradition of legalistic respect for international law.[25] Combined with Chile's interest in maintaining economic and trade stability (Chile is the third-largest user of the Panama Canal, for example), this makes for a deep commitment to the United Nations and multilateralism. Secondly, as in Mexico, and Argentina before it, Chile's diplomatic activity reveals a country ambitious to capitalize internationally on its transition to democracy.[26] Finally, and unlike Mexico, Chile had in Ricardo Lagos a president fully in control of the diplomatic script. The first feature had already made Chile loyal to the United Nations. The second and third enabled it to become a protagonist in the Security Council.

Chilean protagonism in early 2003 advanced on the traditional premise, expressed thus by Foreign Minister María Soledad Alvear: "Multilateralism is a permanent interest of Chile."[27] It was a motto that would survive intact for Chile, even in the face of the 2003 defeat for multilateralism. It was also a motto that set Chilean off from Mexican diplomacy. Where Mexico adhered to an orthodox interpretation of its foreign policy principles and fell back on pacifism, Chile established itself as a genuine multilateral player and, as a result, took up a more nuanced position. Notably, Soledad Alvear registered a condemnation of Saddam Hussein's regime that Mexico scarcely attempted. She also endorsed both the urgency and the unambiguity of Resolution 1441, as well as the build-up of US troops on Iraq's borders. A confrontation with Iraq was "indispensable", but so too was "the maintenance of a multilateral control of the crisis".[28] For Chile, the credible authority of the United Nations over Iraq and the "common aim of disarming Iraq by peaceful methods" could be maintained through the "only instrument" available, the weapons inspections.[29] Chilean diplomats remained in close contact with Hans Blix, the UN chief weapons inspector.[30]

Had Iraq been a crisis like any other, Chile's multilateral faith would have been exemplary. As it was, once the permanent members of the Council split, Chile's principled position became untenable. Its powerlessness at the abandoned centre came to symbolize that of the United Nations.

Chile had been in the Council before, most recently in 1996–1997. It came in 2003 as the undisputed economic growth leader of Latin America. A lesson in powerlessness was not what it expected, much less – for this regionally isolated country – one in specifically Latin American powerlessness. Chile was prepared to defend multilateralism; it was less prepared for the confrontation with the United States this would entail. The US–Latin American dimension of Chile's experience came as a shock.[31] Chile could go as far as intimating to the United States that it was with it so long as the United States was with the United Nations; beyond that, Chile had no scenarios.

Yet, in Spring 2003, Chile was also in a situation of unique vulnerability to the United States. A free trade agreement, pursued by Chile for 12 years, was pending US congressional ratification, as was the purchase of F-16 fighter airplanes. Its more nuanced diplomacy notwithstanding, Chile was not that far removed, after all, from Mexico's predicament.

As with Mexico, Chilean society was both opposed to the US invasion of Iraq and apprehensive of the consequences of its opposition. Guido Guirardi, president of the Party for Democracy, the other party in the coalition government, may have declared: "The Free Trade Agreement is not worth a war."[32] But whether Chile could afford an open "No" to the United States remained another, agonizing matter.

From this point on, Chile's unprotected situation mirrored Mexico's. On the one hand, the game with the United States was to intimate "No" without actually saying so for as long as possible. On the other, the rule of the game was that neither government would form a proposal against the United States.[33]

In keeping with its principles, Chile continued to hark on the theme of multilateral consensus; in practice, it now had no position. Not only did Chile now occupy the centre of the Security Council when the centre could not hold; but, as diplomats also later admitted, both the United States and France considered Chile to be on their side.[34] It was in this predicament that, within a matter of days, President Lagos revised his own position and proposed the three-week extension for Blix's weapons inspectors. It was Chile's polite way of saying "No" to the United States.[35] But it was also the moment when Chile broke, in practice if not in principle, with its own multilateral good faith. Critically, the proposal was made with no expectation of Mexican support. As its predicament with the United States had deepened, so had Chile's solidarity with Mexico. Chile was intent on getting itself off the hook, not on putting Mexico on it. In the gratefully acknowledging words of Ambassador Zínser, "these are proposals from the government of Chile".[36] The proposal was withdrawn the same day it was made; already informed in advance about its content, thanks to espionage, the United States was prompt to express the offence it had taken.

The "what might have been" interest of this last-minute episode in the Iraq crisis increases if one credits suggestions that the Chilean proposal had a behind-the-scenes sponsor in UK Prime Minister Tony Blair.[37] But if even such an actor was looking at that late stage for a way out of the rupture between the United States and the United Nations, Chile by now was an actor looking for its own exit.

After the Chilean failure, both the Chilean and Mexican ambassadors were instructed by their governments to "forget about the word 'condemn'. They could 'lament' as much as they liked the drift to war, but condemn, no."[38] Under Mexico's presidency of the Council there was no call for a cease-fire either. So ended the "revolt of the Latins".

The emotive words of Chile's ambassador Gabriel Valdés for the "bitter" experience were "grief" and "horror".[39] But the equally unpalatable fact was that Chile, at the critical moment, had had to privilege a Latin American perspective over a multilateral one. As it came to appreciate Mexico's vulnerability first-hand, so Chile backed off from joining forces with it. Chile may have succeeded in delivering a "No" to the United States, but only as a lone voice. That was as much as the hegemonic rules allowed. The United States was unable to secure legitimation from the Security Council, but it was able to avoid a collective delegitimation.

Conclusion: A Latin lament

At the beginning of 2003 a Latin American dream appeared to come true: through the UN Security Council the peripheral would become central. Two of Latin America's leading states would, in the words of Ambassador Zínser, "facilitate the reinvigoration and transformation of the United Nations".[40] For the diplomatic and political élite who took Mexico into the Security Council, Mexico's mixture of oligarchy with participatory democracy was institutionally unsatisfactory. Transformation was the deep Mexican ambition. Chile's protagonism was more modestly suited to multilateral reinvigoration.

If there was a Latin American script, it was no better expressed than by the lost Latin American leader in the crisis, Jorge Castañeda:

> You cannot on the one hand support multilateralism, the United Nations and international law, and on the other refuse participation in the Council; you cannot denounce US unilateralism and refuse to belong to the only mechanism which can, perhaps only every so often, set limits to it.[41]

The story of Mexico and Chile's participation in the Council is in many ways the story of what went wrong with this script.

Before Iraq, "to be there or not to be there" might well have been the nub of the Latin American soliloquy. The unfolding of the crisis itself would also vindicate Castañeda's premise that only Latin America's leading states could be expected to test the limits of US hegemony and restore visibility to the continent. But, at the end of the crisis, the logic of participation had been reversed: only those leading states that did *not* participate in the Security Council were able openly to oppose the United States.[42]

To the extent that its ambition was more quixotic, Mexico's was the greater failure. Having selected the Security Council as the site of a conflict it could not wage openly with the United States, Mexico found it had landed in the one place where it could not say "No" to the United States. Mexico was also an unlikely protector of a UN system it hoped in any case to transform. Proceeding on the untenable assumption that the United States was a greater threat to peace than Iraq, only reluctantly did Mexico concede to the United Nations' own resolution that Iraq should be made to disarm. And only when it was back in the traditional position of being a victim of the United States was Mexico comfortable. Then, as it saw its history being repeated, it could speak for the world order represented by the United Nations as a whole. Until then, Mexico had no initiative with which to engage either the concerns of the United

States or the role of the United States in the UN world order. The "rogue hegemon" was there only to be constrained. Mexico thus contributed to the opposite of what it intended: a weakened Security Council. Not unjustifiably, Mexico would also lose out to UN peace keeper Brazil as the regional candidate for permanent membership of an expanded Council in an EU-backed reform plan touted towards the end of 2004.

Chile's diplomacy showed a more advanced appreciation of the argument presented by Thakur and Sidhu – that opposing multilateralism against US unilateralism is a limited game. Chile's opening stance conveyed institutional commitment to the United Nations without implying that a UN world order needs to be an anti-US order. But Chile was unprepared either for the conflict between the UN and US world orders or for its subsequent ramifications. Chile's traditional defence of multilateralism could lead it only to a diplomatically empty position over Iraq. Perhaps in recognition of this, the United States did not in the end veto the Free Trade Agreement. While escaping a penalty for its lamentation, Chile also returned to the original Latin American position in relation to the United States.

On the surface, this position allows multilateralism to be defended in principle against the United States. If multilateralism fails to constrain the United States on one occasion, then it is neither the fault of the principle nor for want of trying: better luck may be had next time. Yet, at a deeper level, Chile's experience also revealed some of the complexities and complicities of the hegemonic game with the United States. The United States cannot impose allegiance, but it can ensure that a "No" doesn't translate into a veto. Within the bounds of the game, Mexico was able to confront the United States without opposing it; Chile to oppose without confronting. Both were finally content to escape the consequences of a "No" that really meant what it said.

The crisis over Iraq took this private dialogue of equivocation to the limit without changing the fundamental hegemonic pattern of submissive opposition or resistant acquiescence. A crisis over Cuba might be another matter. Would thinking that "No" had been said to the United States, even though it either had not really been said or had been said but had not been heeded, suffice?

The dilemma of Latin America's role in the world order has been posed as one of participating or shutting up. To judge by the failures of Mexico and Chile over Iraq, Latin America's UN role in a crisis closer to home would be one of participating, denouncing *and* shutting up – inside the United Nations. The uncomfortable question begged as much by the absence of Brazil from the Council in 2003 as by the presence of Mexico and Chile is, ultimately, whether the United Nations *is* an alternative forum to a US world order in the twenty-first century.

Notes

1. Joseph Nye, *The Paradox of American Power. Why the World's Only Superpower Can't Go It Alone* (Oxford: Oxford University Press, 2002).
2. Jorge Castañeda, "América Latina, ante una disyuntiva desgarradora", *El País*, 13 March 2003.
3. Enrique Krauze, "Los Estados Unidos: Un balance histórico", *El País*, 5 March 2003.
4. See Ana María Salazar, "Atentado terrorista en México?", *Reforma*, 30 April 2004.
5. Enrique Krauze, "Ecos de 'pequeñas guerras'", *El País*, 10 April 2003.
6. *Reforma*, 6 March 2003.
7. *El País*, 21 February 2003.
8. *Reforma*, 26 March 2003.
9. The theme of Security Council reform, specifically a widening of the membership with a right to the veto to "some countries important at a regional level", was taken up by Enrique Berruga, Mexico's under-secretary of foreign affairs (*Reforma*, 23 March 2003).
10. *Reforma*, 19 February 2003.
11. Bob Woodward, *Plan of Attack* (New York: Simon & Schuster, 2004), p. 344.
12. Unlike its NAFTA partner Canada, Mexico lacks any legal mechanisms to sanction the use of force abroad. The lack in turn is one pointer to the continuity within Mexico's foreign policy after the transition to democracy. With Iraq, Mexico repeated its non-interventionist stance over Kosovo, where the legitimacy of intervention was more widely seen to outweigh the issues of legality.
13. In May 2004, new Foreign Minister Ernesto Derbrez would call Mexico's refusal to participate in UN peacekeeping operations hypocritical.
14. *Reforma*, 18 March 2003.
15. Ibid.
16. Castañeda was unwilling to share the role of protagonist with Mexico's ambassador to the United Nations, Adolfo Aguilar Zínser. Castañeda opposed Zínser's nomination, and would spend a year without speaking to him. See Jeffrey Davidow, *El Oso y El Puercoespín Testimonio de un embajado de Estados Unidos en México* (Mexico: Editorial Grijalbo, 2003). On the other hand, Castañeda's connections with the Chilean political and diplomatic élites were strong.
17. President Fox had literally read out the wrong script at the United Nations when he was expected to present Mexico's position on UN and Security Council reform. Interview with ex-ambassador Aguilar Zínser, Mexico City, September 2004.
18. *Reforma*, 3 April 2003.
19. *Reforma*, 26 March 2003.
20. *Reforma*, 4 March 2003.
21. In an appearance before the Mexican Congress, 7 May 2004.
22. In late February, it was being reported that both Mexico and Chile were coming over to the US side, that at the very least they had agreed with Bush not to say "No" too early (*El País*, 27 February 2003).
23. *El Universal*, 26 March 2003.
24. From a Canadian perspective, Mexico's behaviour in 2003 could well have evoked recent memories of a Canada–Mexico alliance to pressure the United States to recognize the jurisdiction of the International Criminal Court, an alliance that Mexico at the last minute ditched under US pressure. Interview with ex-ambassador Aguilar Zínser, Mexico City, September 2004.
25. Chile's adherence to the principle of non-intervention was given practical expression in its displeasure at the arrest warrant issued against General Pinochet by Judge Baltasar Garzón in 1998.

26. Or, more accurately, on its still incomplete transition to democracy. The post-transition constitution prohibits elected officials from having a say on the military budget, which is fixed at the level of the last year of the Pinochet government.

27. 7 March 2003, ⟨http://www.un.int/chile/Discursos/disc20030307⟩.

28. 5 February 2003, ⟨http://www.un.int/chile/Discursos/disc20030205⟩.

29. Ambassador Juan Gabriel Valdés, 29 January 2003, ⟨http://www.un.int/chile/Discursos/disc20030129⟩.

30. Interview with Ambassador Pedro Oyarce Yuraszeck, Director of Multilateral Policy, Foreign Ministry, Santiago de Chile, May 2004. Blix co-authored the last-minute Chilean proposal with President Lagos in March 2003.

31. See, for example, the reaction of Gabriel Valdés to the arrival of US special envoy Otto Reich in Chile: "The indignity hurts. Chile can be a partner, not a lackey" (El País, 1 March 2003).

32. El País, 14 March 2003.

33. El País, 11 March 2003: "'It's one thing not to support the resolution of the United States and another to promote an active group,' admitted a [Chilean] source."

34. Interview with the Multilateral Policy team, Foreign Ministry, Santiago de Chile, May 2004. President Chirac directly requested an abstention from President Lagos, and complained at the tone with which he was refused.

35. "Uff, you don't know how hard it was," Lagos is quoted as saying in "Aniversario de la Invasión a Irak", El Mercurio, 21 March 2004.

36. Reforma, 15 March 2003.

37. Interviews carried out in Santiago de Chile, May 2004. Both Blair and Foreign Secretary Jack Straw were prepared to travel to Chile (and to trade Straw's credit over the arrest of General Pinochet) to seek its support. They were also prepared to assist the United States with its spying on Chile in the United Nations.

38. El País, 24 March 2003.

39. 19 March 2003, ⟨http://www.un.int/chile/Discursos/disc20030319⟩.

40. 27 March 2003, ⟨http://www.un.int/mexico/2003/interv_cs_032703.htm⟩.

41. Castañeda, "América Latina, ante una disyuntiva desgarradora".

42. Colombia joined the Central American Republics in supporting the US invasion; Bolivia, Ecuador and Uruguay remained ambiguous; Peru deplored it; Argentina and Brazil opposed it. See FLASCO, Chile, "América Latina se divide frente a Iraq", 28 March 2003, ⟨http://www.flasco.cl/flasco/main.php?page=noticia&code224⟩. Opposition to the United States over Iraq was a factor in the concurrent electoral victory of Nestor Kirschner over pro-US Carlos Menem in Argentina.

19

Iraq and world order:
A Pakistani perspective

Hasan-Askari Rizvi

The Saddam Hussein era came to an end on 9 April 2003, when his statue was toppled in Firdous square, Baghdad, soon after US troops moved into the official sectors of the capital city. This was a moment of triumph for the United States because it demonstrated that it had enough military power and political determination to pursue its global agenda in the face of strong diplomatic opposition.

The US-led war in Iraq (March–April 2003) can be described as an important turning point in international politics. It has such wide-ranging implications for the international system that we may talk in terms of before and after the Iraq war. There are several major implications of the Iraq war for the international system, especially for developing countries.

Major implications of the Iraq war

First, the United States has demonstrated its military primacy and outreach by conducting successful military operations in a distant country. Though a large number of countries criticized the military operation or questioned its legitimacy, hardly any state was willing or capable of making even a symbolic countervailing military move in the region. This reflected the reality of power politics in the post–Cold War era, marked by the military preponderance of the United States. It was not surprising that many in official and non-official circles in the United States talked of restructuring the Middle Eastern political arrangements to protect and promote US interests. The United States kept up pressure on Syria and Iran, two countries viewed as a threat to US interests in the region, during and after the war. Iran had been declared to be one of the three states labelled as the axis of evil in January 2002. During and after the Iraq war, the United States warned Iran against any support for anti-US elements in Iraq. Syria was accused of supplying some military equipment (night vision goggles) and of providing a safe haven to Iraqi officials in the course of the war.[1] Later, Syria was blamed for allowing Islamic militants to enter Iraq from its territory.[2] These warnings were viewed in the Middle East as a US attempt to expand the dividends from the successful military operation in Iraq.

Second, the United States advocated "unilateralism" and "pre-emptive military action" to counter the threats of terrorism and weapons of mass destruction to US territory, citizens and interests. The use of such an expanded notion of security by the US policy makers to justify their military action against Iraq created a dangerous precedent. It amounted to giving a licence to a militarily powerful state to pursue its political agenda against a weaker state on the pretext that it feared a military or terrorist attack from the latter. In a way, it justified the use of military power at will against another state on the pretext of pre-empting a similar action by the other side. This perturbed many states that had serious problems with powerful neighbouring states in different parts of the world.

Third, the US military action in Iraq faced diplomatic opposition from two members of the European Union (France and Germany) and Russia. They were joined by China from time to time in opposing military action in Iraq. These countries were opposed to the unilateral use of military power by the United States and wanted UN channels to be used for obtaining the desired results. They also wanted to give more time to the UN inspectors to locate weapons of mass destruction in Iraq.[3] This was the first major instance in the aftermath of the terrorist attacks of 11 September 2001 when the leading European states and Russia diverged publicly from the United States on its policy on combating terrorism. This did not mean that they supported Saddam Hussein; they objected to what they viewed as a premature use of force against Iraq without authorization from the United Nations. The leaders of France, Germany and Russia who met in St Petersburg on 11–12 April 2003 demanded that the United Nations should be actively involved in the management of post-Saddam Iraq. This proposal has been repeated by these and other countries time and again since then but the United States favoured a restricted role for the United Nations in Iraq so that the primacy of its military presence was not compromised.

Fourth, the Iraq war had two divergent implications for the United Nations. On the one hand, it demonstrated the helplessness of the United

Nations because it was unable to restrain the United States from using force against a member state without specific authorization by the UN Security Council. The United States refused to wait for the UN inspectors to complete their investigation of the presence or otherwise of weapons of mass destruction in Iraq and launched an attack on Iraq, which adversely affected the reputation of the United Nations.

Despite the US disregard for the United Nations, most other states repeatedly emphasized the need to assign a central role to the United Nations in Iraq. It was not merely France, Germany, Russia and China that favoured a UN role during and after the Iraq war. A large number of other states put their confidence in the United Nations and criticized the United States for its unilateral use of massive force in Iraq. The demand for a UN role gained momentum as resistance developed in Iraq.

One could therefore argue that the Iraq war and its aftermath had conflicting implications for the United Nations. The United States manifested an arrogance of power and bypassed the United Nations. Some of its actions can be interpreted as defiance of the international body. However, the United Nations won greater international support and acceptability during and after the Iraq war. Though the US military action in Iraq could not be moderated, the emphasis on a role for the United Nations showed that most states continued to have confidence in the United Nations.

The US emphasis on unilateralism and pre-emption perturbed the smaller and weaker states, especially those that had problems with powerful states. They felt that the US precedent could be used by other powerful states to coerce weaker states into submission. Therefore, the small and weak states viewed the UN system as a possible safeguard for them against other powerful states that might decide to follow in the footsteps of the United States in advancing their individual agendas. Most states advocated that, in an Iraq-like situation, individual states should be discouraged from taking unilateral decisions to use military force against another state.

Why did the United States employ military power against Iraq?

US military action in Iraq was shaped by several factors. These included the policy makers' perception of security threats in the aftermath of 9/11, the power dynamics of the international system that enabled the United States to make unchallenged use of military power, the political profile of the Bush administration, and the divisions and disharmony in the Middle East that enabled the United States to obtain the support of two neighbours of Iraq, while other neighbours stayed aloof from the conduct of the war.

The terrorist attacks on two important symbols of US economic and military power on 9/11 shattered the Americans' sense of security in the post–Cold War era. There was a realization in the United States in the pre-attack period that terrorism was on the rise in the international system and often targeted US interests. However, the US policy makers never visualized that such a massive operation could be carried out on its mainland. The adversary was not a state but a transnational underground group that could not be easily located.

The US administration adopted a host of stringent security measures inside the country, some of which compromised the civil and political rights and freedoms of ordinary people. The United States assigned the highest priority to combating terrorism in its foreign policy and mobilized international support through the United Nations and by direct interaction with other states. The new US strategy of counter-terrorism focused attention on all the states that had adversarial relations with the United States as suspects for terrorism against the United States. Iraq was one such country.

The 1990s brought many achievements to the United States at the international level. In particular, 1990 witnessed the end of the Cold War between the United States and the Soviet Union, which was tottering under domestic political and economic pressures. In December 1991, the Soviet Union breathed its last as a state; its constituent republics became independent. Russia was recognized as the successor to the Soviet Union but its leadership had neither the capability nor the determination to pursue the Soviet agenda at the global level; it sought Western, albeit US, support to put its economic house in order. The United States thus did not face any credible countervailing military threat at the global level and most analysts began to describe the United States as the sole superpower.

Earlier, in January–February 1991, a US-led military coalition had expelled Iraqi troops from Kuwait, which they had occupied in August 1990. This demonstrated the United States' ability successfully to employ its military power to achieve political and military targets in a far away place. It was against the backdrop of these two major events – i.e. the demise of the Soviet Union and a successful military expedition in the Gulf region – that the US President talked of a new world order, emphasizing liberal democracy, civil and political rights, privatization and free trade, non-proliferation of weapons of mass destruction, control of narcotics trafficking, and counter-terrorism.

This strategy was revised after the terrorist incidents of 9/11, when the highest priority was assigned to combating transnational terrorism. Coercion and military force became the cutting-edge of US counter-terrorism policy. President George W. Bush's famous words when seeking the co-operation of a number of world leaders after the terrorist attacks – "Are you with us or against us?" – reflected the changed US disposition. This recalled the peak days of the Cold War when US leaders thought that a country would be supportive either of Western liberal democracy or of the Soviet-led communist system. They did not recognize that a country could maintain a distance from both positions and adopt a non-aligned posture. In the aftermath of the 9/11 terrorist attacks, the US leadership thought that a country friendly to the United States ought to be on board with the United States for combating terrorism. The eradication of ter-rorism and the denial of weapons of mass destruction to other states were adopted as cardinal concerns by US policy makers.

The US President and his advisers represent the right wing of the po-litical spectrum and are backed by religious conservatives and others who think that the United States must assert its military primacy in the world. They developed a security paranoia after the 9/11 terrorism incidents and favoured a hard line towards all sources of terrorist threat. The absence of any competing military power made it possible for the US leaders and their supporters to adopt unilateral measures for the elimination of ter-rorism. They were convinced that the United States had to take effective measures to eliminate every kind of threat to US interests and restruc-ture the world to its political preferences. Terrorism was viewed as the most serious threat to US interests and global peace and economic stabil-ity. Therefore, they argued that the United States should use all possible means at its disposal to check the menace of terrorism. The military action against the Taliban regime in Afghanistan (October–November 2001) had given confidence to US policy makers that they could success-fully use their overwhelming military power and technological superiority in a far-away country without being challenged by any state.

Political cleavages in the Middle East and the dependence of some of the Gulf states on the United States contributed to the US decision to undertake military operations against Saddam Hussein's regime in Iraq. Kuwait had suffered humiliation at the hands of Iraq in August 1990 when Iraq's troops overran it. The US military coalition expelled Iraq's troops from Kuwait and restored its independence. Naturally, Kuwait supported the use of overwhelming force against Iraq and offered the necessary facilities to the United States. Qatar was another state that actively supported the United States against Iraq. The US Central Com-mand operated from Qatar. Saudi Arabia and Jordan adopted a cautious approach towards the Iraq war. Although they wanted to protect their cordial relations with the United States, they did not want to be seen to be helping the US war effort in Iraq. Neither Jordan nor Saudi Arabia trusted Saddam Hussein and they had a host of complaints against him. But they did not want to be a party to the war against Iraq. Given such a regional context, the US policy makers were rightly confident that they would not face strong diplomatic opposition from the region and no neighbouring state would be willing to offer credible military support to Saddam Hussein.

The overwhelming use of military power enabled the United States to dislodge Saddam Hussein from power. However, this success lacked diplomatic support at the global level and the United States faced a lot of criticism for undertaking unilateral military action and for totally disregarding the United Nations. The demand for an increased UN role in Iraq grew as the US military encountered insurgency in parts of Iraq within two months of capturing Baghdad. The insurgency intensified by early 2004, which contributed to the US decision to assign a limited role to the United Nations in Iraq. However, the United States jealously guarded its military primacy in Iraq.

Pakistan and the Iraq war

The US-led war on Iraq created a difficult situation for Pakistan. Its policy makers did not denounce the United States because they attached importance to the reinvigorated Pakistan–US relations against the backdrop of the global efforts to combat terrorism. However, they could not publicly support the US invasion of Iraq, not only because domestic public opinion was extremely critical of US military action but also because the United States had disregarded the United Nations. Pakistan viewed the US emphasis on unilateralism and pre-emptive action as guiding principles for the war as a dangerous precedent. Expressing concern at the outbreak of the war, Pakistan demanded that the war should be brought to an end as soon as possible. However, it avoided public condemnation of the US military action in Iraq.

Pakistan was a non-permanent member of the UN Security Council during 2003–2004, which kept it actively involved with the UN-centred diplomacy on the Iraq war. In the pre-war period, Pakistan emphasized the need for a peaceful resolution of the Iraq problem and favoured giving more time to the UN inspectors to complete their assignment in Iraq. The government of Pakistan maintained that "every effort should be exhausted" for a peaceful resolution of the Iraq crisis,[4] and that, if military action became imperative, it should be "taken within the framework of the United Nations".[5] While outlining Pakistan's policy on Iraq, President General Pervez Musharraf maintained that Pakistan believed in "the supremacy of the UN and [felt] that the Security Council [was] the correct forum to take decisions".[6] Addressing the National Assembly, the lower house of the Pakistani parliament, Prime Minister Zafaullah Khan Jamali said that Pakistan would not become a party to "any decision which leads to bloodshed in Iraq".[7]

The government of Pakistan "regretted" the outbreak of the war without commenting on the US decision to initiate the war. However, the leaders of public opinion, the major political parties (especially the Islamic parties) and the media were very critical of the US decision to undertake unilateral military action against Iraq. The non-official political circles condemned the US-led attack on Iraq and most Islamic parties expressed solidarity with Saddam Hussein.[8] The Islamic parties staged protest rallies and marches in different cities against the United States. However, their protests did not catch on. Other political parties stayed away from the agitation launched by the Islamic parties.

As domestic pressure mounted on the government of Pakistan to adopt a more explicit position, the government adopted a firm position on the war but continued to avoid harsh comments against the United States. Pakistan's foreign minister declared that his government "deplored" the military action – which could be described as a mild criticism. Other issues raised by the foreign minister included that (i) measures must be adopted on a priority basis to avert a humanitarian disaster for the people of Iraq; (ii) civilian casualties and infrastructure damage, especially to civic services and religious/holy places, must be avoided; (iii) military action should not be prolonged; (iv) the territorial integrity and sovereignty of Iraq and its rights over its natural resources must be preserved; (v) the fundamental rights of the people of Iraq should be respected; (vi) the UN Security Council must resume its primary responsibility under the UN Charter for the maintenance of international peace and security.[9]

The government of Pakistan established contacts with the Organization of the Islamic Conference (OIC) in order to adopt a shared approach on the war in Iraq. However, the Arab members of the OIC were divided on the issue and could not agree on a clear-cut and forthright stand. Meanwhile, Pakistan demanded that the military operations should be stopped at the earliest opportunity, and measures should be adopted to reduce the hardships of the Iraqi people caused by the war. It also advocated assigning primacy to the United Nations in Iraqi affairs.

Pakistan was perturbed by three major aspects of the Iraq war. First, the United States launched the attack without any authorization from the UN Security Council. Pakistan felt that Security Council Resolution 1441 did not authorize the United States unilaterally to launch an attack to disarm Iraq. Pakistan maintained from the beginning of the Iraq crisis that the United Nations should be assigned an active role and its inspectors should be given time to complete their task of locating the weapons of mass destruction in Iraq. Even after the end of the war, Pakistan continued to urge that the matter should be handed over to the United Nations,

The United States approached Pakistan to make its troops available for support activities in post-war Iraq. This matter was taken up during President Pervez Musharraf's visit to the United States in June 2003. Pakistan agreed in principle to make its troops available but it insisted on a UN Security Council mandate or "an invitation from the people of Iraq" for any such assignment.[10] President Musharraf declared in September 2003 that Pakistan would not send its troops to Iraq if that made them an extension of the US occupation. He said that Pakistan would send its troops to Iraq "when there [was] a request from the Iraqis, when he [felt that] the troops would be welcomed, when there [were] other Muslim troops participating in a multi-lateral force, and when there [was] a Security Council resolution authorizing such a force".[11]

In July 2004, the appointment of a Pakistani diplomat, Jahangir Ashraf Qazi, as the UN representative in Iraq triggered speculation that the appointment was part of a deal that Pakistan would make its troops available for Iraq. UN Secretary-General Kofi Annan denied any such connection. Meanwhile, Pakistan modified its earlier position on the supply of troops by emphasizing three conditions: (1) Iraq's interim government should make a formal request for troops; (2) other Islamic countries should commit their troops; (3) Pakistan's parliament should approve the dispatch of troops.[12]

Pakistan's refusal to send troops to Iraq was partly caused by strong domestic opposition to military involvement in Iraq. It was not just the Islamic groups that opposed the deployment of Pakistani troops in Iraq; most other political leaders and groups did not want to send troops to Iraq as long as the United States maintained its control over Iraq. They argued that Pakistani troops could not function in Iraq as an appendage to US occupation troops there. The general consensus was that any peacekeeping operation in Iraq should be undertaken under an appropriate UN Security Council resolution.

Second, Pakistan was perturbed by the expansion of US goals in Iraq. Initially, the United States described the main aim of its Iraq policy to be the destruction of weapons of mass destruction. It was willing to achieve this objective through the United Nations. Later, the United States demanded the replacement of Saddam's regime as a prerequisite for destroying the weapons of mass destruction. It also began to talk about deploying its troops in Iraq to achieve this objective. Subsequently, the introduction of democracy was declared to be the goal in Iraq. This implied the removal of Saddam's regime from power and the installation of a government that the United States considered to be democratic and humane. US officials contacted Iraqi dissident elements based in the United States, the United Kingdom and Europe to use their links in Iraq to subvert Saddam's regime. When this did not work, the United States unilaterally resorted to military invasion.

For all practical purposes, the US policy makers manufactured the Iraq war. The administration launched a major propaganda campaign against Saddam's regime by mixing facts with fiction. Unauthenticated data were used by US officials to show that Saddam's regime possessed weapons of mass destruction. This propaganda isolated Iraq at the international level, which made it easy for the United States to take military action against Iraq.

Third, Pakistan's policy makers felt that the US emphasis on unilateralism and pre-emptive strikes for tackling Iraq created a dangerous precedent that other powerful states might emulate to threaten weak states in the neighbourhood. They might resort to military action against a weak neighbouring state on the pretext of pre-empting a military attack from the latter.

Pakistan did not have to wait long to encounter a threat of pre-emptive military action. India's foreign minister, Yashwant Sinha, described Pakistan as a "fit case" for an Iraq-type military action because it had weapons of mass destruction, sheltered terrorists and lacked democracy. He maintained that India had "a much better case to go for pre-emptive action against Pakistan than the U.S. has in Iraq".[13] Speaking in the Rajya Sabha, the upper house of the Indian parliament, Sinha said, "If lack of democracy, possession of weapons of mass destruction and export of terrorism were reasons for a country to make pre-emptive strike in another country, then Pakistan deserved to be tackled more than any other country".[14] Pakistan took exception to these statements and threatened to respond with full force if India undertook military action. US Secretary of State Colin Powell rejected the Indian remarks comparing Pakistan to Iraq and urged India and Pakistan to resolve their differences peacefully.[15] The British High Commissioner to India, Rob Young, also rejected the comparison of Pakistan to Iraq.[16]

The United States and the United Kingdom rejected the Indian comparison of Pakistan to Iraq because Pakistan was an active partner in global efforts to combat terrorism. Furthermore, they wanted to discourage other states from using unilateralism and pre-emptive strikes for advancing their political agendas. This was reassuring for Pakistan but its leadership continued to take issue with unilateralism and pre-emptive strikes as instruments of foreign policy.

Pakistan's prime minister and finance minister met with senior Iraqi officials (members of Iraq's Governing Council, the trade minister and the governor of Iraq's central bank) in Saudi Arabia and Dubai in August and September 2003. In December 2004, Iraq's foreign minister, Hoshyar Zebari, visited Islamabad to discuss bilateral and regional affairs. Pakistan's foreign minister declared in October 2003 that Pakistan was committed to "Iraq's territorial integrity and an early restoration of sovereignty and political independence for the Iraqi people". Pakistan condemned the truck-bomb attack on the UN headquarters in Baghdad on 20 August 2003.[17] It also condemned the reported mistreatment of Iraqi prisoners by the coalition forces. Pakistan expressed "deep concern" over the outbreak of violence in Najaf and Karbala in 2004 and demanded that the sanctity of the holy places in these cities be respected.[18]

Positive signs

Though the United States was able to achieve its immediate objectives in Iraq by using overwhelming military power, it could not muster enough diplomatic support to obtain widespread acceptability of its success. A military success devoid of positive diplomatic backup does not offer enduring political dividends. Astute diplomacy, multifaceted peaceful interaction and a mutuality of interests are no less important than military power for playing a sustainable role at the global level. The US military triumph suffered from a diplomatic deficit.

The United States was not able to get UN Security Council endorsement for its decision to attack Iraq. France (a permanent member of the Security Council) and Germany (a non-permanent member of the Security Council) openly questioned the US impatience for military action. This perspective was supported by Russia and China (permanent members of the Security Council). The absence of the required diplomatic support made it difficult for the United States to cope with the post-war problems in Iraq. One inescapable conclusion is that, despite what happened in Iraq, the role of diplomacy has not become redundant in global affairs.

Another interpretation of the diplomatic opposition to US policies in Iraq is that a new "pole" is gradually emerging in global politics that will transform the US-centric "unipolar" system into a "multipolar" system in which Russia, France, Germany and China coordinate their policies to restrain the United States at the global level. This pole is expected to enjoy the moral support of international public opinion that was reflected in the anti-war protests during the course of the Iraq war in several countries, including the United States and the United Kingdom.

A large number of other states expressed varying degrees of reservation about or criticism of the US action in Iraq without the explicit sanction of the Security Council. This engendered the hope that, despite the

US policy of disregarding the United Nations, this international body will continue to enjoy the confidence of a large number of states. The demand by a large number of states that a more active role should be assigned to the United Nations in Iraq shows that they view the United Nations as relevant to maintaining and promoting peace and stability in the international system.

It can be argued that the Iraq war had both positive and negative implications for the United Nations. On the one hand, the Iraq war showed the limits of the United Nations in performing its main task of preserving peace and security. When a powerful state such as the United States decides to defy the United Nations, it cannot be restrained in the short run. On the other hand, the repeated calls by a large number of states for the United Nations to be given an active role in Iraq show that the United Nations has not become irrelevant. Many countries continue to have faith in it and they would like to strengthen this organization. However, the United Nations has to chart its course in the context of the exigencies of power politics in the international system. These constraints pose a challenge to those who want to assign primacy to the United Nations and the peaceful resolution of international disputes.

Diplomatic opposition and street demonstrations in a number of states against the US attack on Iraq showed that the United States is not going to get a free hand to manipulate the international system. For the first time in the post–Cold War era, a clear divergence emerged between two key European states and the United States. France and Germany continued to build pressure on the US policy in Iraq in the post-war period (2003–2004), leading the United States to seek the cooperation of the United Nations in creating new political arrangements in Iraq. UN Security Council Resolution 1546 (8 June 2004) sanctioned the transfer of full sovereignty to the new Iraqi Interim Government and formally brought an end to Iraq's military occupation. The Interim Government was to work in collaboration with the US-led multinational military force, which would help the Interim Government to maintain law and order.[19] Earlier, the UN Secretary-General's representative, Lakhdar Brahimi, had helped to set up the Interim Government.[20] The United Nations helped the Iraqi government to hold new elections in January 2005. The OIC also endorsed the Interim Government at its meeting of foreign ministers in Istanbul in June 2004.

This may well be the beginning of a new political trend at the global level that may gradually transform the present-day unipolar world into a multipolar international system, in which France, Germany, Russia and China are expected to play a more active role, partly neutralizing the edge the United States currently enjoys in the international system. Much depends on the ability of Russia and China to overcome their internal economic problems, which would enable them to play a more active role at the global level. Two other factors are likely to influence the nature and direction of the international system in the future: first, the way in which France and Germany play their role to assert their autonomy in the international system; second, the dependence of their role on their ability to mobilize support from other states.

The Iraq war has demonstrated US military primacy in the international system. However, this does not necessarily mean that the United States will be able to pursue its global agenda unilaterally all the time. The restraining influence of other states and the problems the United States has faced in Iraq and Afghanistan demonstrate the limits of military power and underline the importance of diplomacy. The United States needs the cooperation of other states for ensuring political stability in Iraq and combating transnational terrorism in an effective manner. Therefore, the United States may find it difficult to pursue its policy of unilateralism and pre-emptive strikes indefinitely in the future. This realization is expected to reintroduce realism into US foreign policy, which would moderate the United States' aggressive posturing as manifested in Iraq. Diplomacy would be assigned priority over the use or the threat of the use of force. This engenders hope for an active UN role in global politics. However, the recurrence of the negative implications of power politics cannot be totally discounted.

Notes

1. *Asia Times*, 31 July 2003.
2. *Gulf News*, 6 November 2003.
3. See Patrick E. Tyler, "A Fissure Deepening for Allies over Use of Force against Iraq", *New York Times*, 6 March 2003; Thom Shanker, "Rumsfeld Rebukes UN and NATO on Approach to Baghdad", *New York Times*, 9 February 2003.
4. See the statement by Pakistan's Permanent Representative to the United Nations: *Dawn* (Karachi), 15 February 2003.
5. See the statement by the prime minister of Pakistan: *News* (Lahore), 31 January 2003. In a statement in Kuwait City, Pakistan's prime minister maintained that he wanted a peaceful resolution of the Iraq problem "without a shot from the gun". He said that Pakistan supported Kuwait when Iraq captured it in 1990. However, Pakistan did not want to see Iraq destroyed and the miseries of its people (*Dawn*, 28 January 2003).
6. *Daily Times* (Lahore), 9 February 2003; see also *Dawn*, 15 February 2003.
7. *Dawn*, 11 March 2003.
8. A traders' group that supported the Islamic parties announced a boycott of US and UK goods in protest against the war on Iraq (*News*, 1 April 2003). This move did not catch on and the appeal for a boycott proved completely ineffective.
9. See Hasan-Askari Rizvi, "Pakistan's Principled Stand on Iraq?", *Daily Times*, 24 March 2003.
10. See the statement by the Spokesperson of Pakistan's Foreign Office: *Daily Times*, 22

July 2003; see also *Dawn*, 9 July 2003; Ijaz Hussain, "Should We Send Troops to Iraq?", *Daily Times*, 9 July 2003.

11. *Dawn*, 27 September 2003.
12. Farhan Bokhari, "Troops for Iraq", *News*, 5 August 2004; see also *Daily Times*, 25 July 2004; and the editorial entitled "Troops for Iraq", *Dawn*, 26 July 2004.
13. *Khaleej Times*, 7 April 2003; see also *Gulf News*, 4 April 2003.
14. *Hindu*, 10 April 2003.
15. *Gulf News*, 11 April 2003.
16. *News*, 7 April 2004.
17. *Dawn*, 21 August 2003.
18. *Dawn*, 14 August 2004.
19. *Nation* (Lahore), 9 June 2004.
20. Warren Hoge, "UN Chief Says Iraq Elections Could Be Held within a Year", *New York Times*, 24 February 2004. See also Warren Hoge and Steven R. Weisman, "Surprising Choice for Premier of Iraq Reflects U.S. Influence", *New York Times*, 29 May 2004. The new Iraqi Interim Government was installed on 28 June 2004.

20

Iraq and world order: A perspective on NATO's relevance

Fred Tanner

Introduction

It is undeniable that the transatlantic dispute over the war in Iraq has altered the horizons of international relations. It has changed the relationship amongst the most powerful countries and between these countries and the United Nations. By challenging some of the most fundamental precepts of international law, the conflict itself has had a serious and far-reaching impact on the "world order", the full implications of which probably still remain to be thought through.[1]

The North Atlantic Treaty Organization (NATO) did not play any essential role in the US-led war on Iraq. Nor did it play a role in the US retaliation against the Taliban-controlled Afghanistan. Thus, the question arises of how relevant NATO will be as an international security institution in the twenty-first century and what its standing will be in the post-Iraq world order. With the disappearance of the Soviet Union and, thereby, of collective defence as NATO's main "raison d'être", the Atlantic Alliance has been looking during the past 15 years for new roles and missions. NATO continues to be relevant through its expansion eastwards. Its membership during the Cold War of 15 grew in 1999 to 19 members to include Central European states and then in 2004 to 26 members to include, among others, the Baltic states, formerly part of the Soviet Union.

Today the United States is the only superpower and Europe is no

longer one of its major strategic concerns. The Atlantic Alliance is a primary "victim" of this development. The 2002 *National Security Strategy
of the United States of America* elevates the defeat of "global terrorism"
to the top US security policy priority. Within this rationale, the United
States would accept an ongoing commitment to NATO only if it is "able
to act wherever our interests are threatened".[2]

Europe, in contrast, is preoccupied with the consolidation of its enlarged Union, which encompasses an additional population of 100 million
stretching from the Baltic sea to Central Europe, the Mediterranean
and soon also to the Eastern Balkans. It tries to deal with its unstable
neighbourhood with partnership-building in the political, economic, development and "soft security" domains. The European Union has also
developed a security policy and is trying to give some depth and military
operations capabilities to its European Security and Defence Policy
(ESDP).

In order to explore various perspectives of where NATO is heading,
and what kinds of role and mission it will be able to play in a US-centric
world order, I shall first discuss the spectre of irrelevance on the one
hand and the transatlantic dispute over Iraq on the other. I shall then examine where NATO could add value to the world community's quest for
peace and security.

The spectre of irrelevance and Iraq

A spectre is haunting NATO, not the spectre of peace but the spectre of
irrelevance. The terrorist attacks on the heartland of America and the
military interventions in Afghanistan and Iraq have demonstrated to the
Atlantic Alliance the considerable problems in finding a consensus on
collective security. The United States is not prepared to fight its wars
through NATO any more. At the same time, the Iraq war has triggered
profound intra-Alliance disagreements on topics such as the role of the
use of force, international law and multilateral engagements.

The spectre of irrelevance

During the Cold War, the Atlantic Alliance was the basic instrument of
the West to "keep the Russians out, the Americans in, and the Germans
down".[3] All of these objectives are obsolete today. Russia is in a process
of profound transformation and has neither an interest nor the power any
more to threaten the "West". Germany has become a "normal" country,
is deeply integrated into European Union structures and will face eco-

nomic problems for many years to come. Finally, the United States is withdrawing most of its forces from Europe because the Euro-Atlantic area has lost its strategic relevance to the United States.

The transatlantic security relationship today is too diverse and too extensive for NATO to handle. Global issues such as the fight against terrorism, the relationship with Russia and China or issue areas related to the Middle East, including Iraq and Israel/Palestine, are not comprehensively dealt with in NATO. Here other mechanisms such as the G-8, US–European summits or bilateral relations with the United States are more in demand than NATO.

This reduced role for NATO in international security affairs contrasts with its role in the 1990s, when it found a key mission in the Balkans to manage and finally overcome the successive wars in the former Yugoslavia. NATO's intervention in Kosovo – the first war NATO had fought in its 50-year history – left two footprints on NATO as a regional and international security institution, footprints that continue to have serious consequences for NATO's future. First, NATO used force against Serbia without UN Security Council authorization. The ensuing legitimacy issue tarnished NATO's reputation, irrespective of the "retroactive" UN Security Council Resolution 1244 (1999).[4] Second, the NATO bombardment of Serbian forces in Kosovo and throughout Serbia demonstrated the ineffectiveness of a war conducted "by committee". The military operation was subject to the consensus of all 19 member states and, according to General Wesley Clark, who was in charge of the operation, "each bomb dropped represented a target that had been approved, at least in theory, by each of the alliance's 19 governments".[5]

After the Yugoslav wars, the United States and Europe began drifting apart for a number of reasons. The strategic convergence of the post–Cold War era had come to an end: Europe was focusing on its wider neighbourhood, whereas the United States was concentrating on global strategic questions. This drifting apart was accelerated by the Bush administration's neoconservative agenda, which emphasized the use of military force abroad. For Europeans, the constants and imperatives in their international conduct are the construction of a liberal and civil European model, multilateralism and international law. For the United States, in contrast, "support for universal rules of behaviour really is a matter of idealism".[6]

With the terrorist attacks on the United States of 11 September 2001 NATO invoked for the first time in its history the collective defence clause – Article 5 of the Washington Treaty – but not much happened as a consequence of this "historic event". Formally, the United States acknowledged that NATO's invocation of Article 5 demonstrated "the commitment of America's partners to collective defence, which bolsters the security of the United States".[7] In practice, however, the United States did not call on NATO for its military campaign against the Taliban.

Broadly speaking, the Europeans continued to look to the Alliance for a "common strategy" and for help in modernizing their collective military capabilities whereas the Bush administration considered NATO more as a "toolbox" or a "coalition generator" than as a security actor in its own right. The military relevance of NATO to US policy makers in the aftermath of 9/11 and the unilateral US war against the Taliban has been reduced to what US Defense Secretary Rumsfeld called the "mission makes the coalition". This means that "mission performance" will determine the extent to which US policy makers call on the Atlantic Alliance.

In view of these developments, NATO as a collective defence organization will have to bank on remote scenarios of "traditional threats" such as the re-emergence of potential aggression on the massive scale of a country or an alliance against NATO countries. The notion of collective defence has, however, gained more currency with the 2004 NATO enlargement, as several of the seven new member states are bordering zones of instability.[8]

Outside the defence realm, NATO will be in much higher demand for international crisis management and peace missions. As this study will show, in these areas NATO may find a new lease of life in the post-Iraq world order. Here, the relevance of a "transformed" NATO will depend more on its ability to act as a coalition generator and with rapid engagement in response to the United Nations' increasing demand for robust peace operations.

Iraq and the transatlantic dispute: Profiling the perspectives

Fundamental differences between the ways in which various NATO members perceive the Alliance have also affected the debate around Iraq. NATO as an institution did not remain immune from the major shifts on the world scene. Transatlantic relations were seriously damaged by the dispute over Iraq, and NATO was one of the main victims. As Ronald Asmus succinctly put it, "somewhere between Kabul and Iraq" the United States and Europe "lost each other".[9]

The United States, supported by the United Kingdom, Italy and initially also Spain, favoured the immediate inception of hostilities against Iraq as a means to forcibly "disarm" the country of its alleged weapons of mass destruction. Meanwhile France, Belgium and Germany, supported by Russia and less vocally by China, opposed immediate military action, instead calling for the continuation of inspections by UN weapons inspectors. Numerous Central and East European countries, notably Bulgaria, Poland and Romania, also supported the US position – these countries have subsequently become NATO members. These dramatic events were played out in the UN Security Council, the international media and national capitals, against a backdrop of massive anti-war demonstrations, running to millions of people, on almost every continent.

Therefore, there was no shared NATO position on Iraq at any stage during the crisis. NATO's paralysis almost turned lethal with the short but intense controversy over Turkey's request for NATO's assistance in strengthening Turkey's defensive capabilities against potential retaliatory attacks by Iraq in the event of a US attack. The failure of NATO to support Turkey with defensive means has led to widespread warnings of "The End of NATO".[10] In fact, Belgium, in the name of three European NATO countries, vetoed the deployment of AWACS reconnaissance planes and Patriot anti-missile batteries to Turkey. Turkey had appealed to its allies for help under NATO Article 4, fearing an Iraqi attack as a response to the impending US-led invasion against Saddam Hussein's regime. France, Germany and Belgium opposed Turkey's request because they felt that their support – before the adoption of an enabling UN resolution – would legitimize unilateral US pre-emption in Iraq.[11]

The positions of the NATO members with regard to Iraq largely remained defined in relation to the United States. Poland and the United Kingdom played a significant role in Iraq.[12] France and Germany, in contrast, insisted on an enhanced role for the United Nations.[13] Moreover, France made the point that NATO was "simply not the right place" for decisions on Iraq once sovereignty was returned by its occupying powers.[14] The German government expressed concern that NATO involvement in Iraq would overstretch troops and resources, given that commitments already exist in Afghanistan, in Kosovo and for fighting "terrorism". The conflicting perspectives of NATO countries were only superficially addressed at the Istanbul NATO Summit in June 2004. NATO's main deficit remains the lack of a shared strategic vision among all partners.

Visions, transformation and capabilities

The new "threats agenda" and Iraq have presented an enormous challenge to NATO because it does not have the capability to cope with a plethora of security problems in transatlantic relations and globally. In this section I shall discuss the difficulties of finding strategic convergence in threat assessments and identify areas where NATO may be able to preserve its relevance in international security.

In search of a shared strategic vision

The debates about the desirability of NATO's involvement in Iraq reveal and underline some of the deep-seated challenges that NATO itself is facing. These concern not just short-term strategic or political choices about particular conflicts, but rather a long-term definitional problem relating to NATO's own identity and purpose in the twenty-first century. NATO's 1999 "Strategic Concept" began the transformation of NATO in response to a new threats agenda that included "complex new risks to Euro-Atlantic peace and stability".[15] The 2002 Prague NATO Summit confirmed and updated the new threats paradigm under the profound influence of the terrorist attacks of 9/11.

As a result of 9/11 and the US strikes against the Taliban, NATO has been solicited to engage in peacebuilding operations in Afghanistan. NATO's involvement in Afghanistan lies outside the "traditional" area of operations. In this sense, it may seem that NATO is searching in a rather haphazard manner for a new identity to replace its previous role. For any new policy direction to be meaningful, the Alliance must agree on a shared strategic vision.

With regard to "roles and missions", NATO is still an organization that can muster forces, command and control, a robust deployment and resources for sustained action. In search of a new strategic vision, the NATO Secretary General highlighted NATO's "ability to conduct robust military operations" as a unique feature of this organization.[16] President Bush's vision of NATO's twenty-first-century responsibilities, in contrast, is about "fighting terrorism and promoting democratic values".[17] These visions are not necessarily incompatible, but they both rest outside the realm of collective defence, which formally still represents the constituent mandate of NATO.

From a geographical or regional perspective, the new security environment obliges NATO to think and act well beyond its traditional Euro-Atlantic area. In fact, the 2004 Istanbul Summit clearly demonstrated that henceforth NATO will embrace a global agenda. With the latest enlargement of NATO in 2004, the Cold War "Eastern border" has all but disappeared. NATO now considers the Caucasus and Central Asia as regions of "special focus". In this spirit, the NATO Secretary General appointed Robert Simmons to the position of the Secretary General's Special Representative for the Caucasus and Central Asia in September 2004.

At the same time, the United States has been pushing for NATO to get involved in the Middle East, both militarily and in terms of partnership-building. The former US ambassador to NATO, Nicholas Burns, argued that NATO's mandate to defend Europe and North America can be achieved only by deploying "our conceptual attention and our military forces east and south. NATO's future, we believe is east and is south. It's in the Greater Middle East."[18] The NATO Secretary General too sees NATO's regional orientation moving towards the Middle East. At the 2005 Munich Security Conference he intimated that NATO could assume a peacekeeping or stabilization role "in supporting a Middle East peace agreement".[19]

Finally, NATO's involvement in Afghanistan has become the litmus test of the organization's post-9/11 credibility. Its involvement did not begin very well because NATO proved unable to muster sufficient forces. When it tried to send more troops to Afghanistan, European countries failed to comply because their deployable forces had already been committed to missions in the Balkans, Côte d'Ivoire and elsewhere. A failure in Afghanistan would lead to another profound crisis for NATO and would also seriously affect global security in the long term.

The fight against terrorism and weapons of mass destruction

NATO has only limited capabilities to serve as a transatlantic forum in the fight against terrorism. NATO forces cannot deter terrorism. Furthermore, counter-terrorist activities such as homeland defence, the protection of critical infrastructures and law enforcement are not in NATO's domain. Here the European Union is of more relevance. But NATO could usefully serve as a conduit for transatlantic security cooperation on the military aspects of the fight against terrorism, which now is called "consequence management". This is why EU–NATO cooperation in counter-terrorism and counter-proliferation will be particularly important.[20] General Wesley Clark went even further and argued that "full cooperation in the fight against terrorism is unlikely without an overall consensus-building mechanism, like NATO, to drive the process".[21]

The "Partnership Action Plan against Terrorism", launched at the NATO Prague Summit in November 2002, represents a normative framework for NATO allies and member states of the Euro-Atlantic Partnership Council (EAPC) to "co-operate across a spectrum of areas ... that have relevance to the fight against terrorism".[22] At the Istanbul Summit, NATO countries followed up with the statement that their "approach to terrorism, and its causes, will include the full implementation of the United Nations Security Council Resolution 1373 on the fight against terrorism, and will continue to be multi-faceted and comprehensive, including political, diplomatic, economic and, where necessary, military means".[23]

NATO can also hedge against asymmetrical attacks under the legal cover of the collective defence clause. For instance, "Operation Active Endeavour", which was launched in the Mediterranean after 9/11, is still considered an operation under Article 5 of the Washington Treaty. The task force includes hundreds of NATO vessels patrolling throughout the Mediterranean Sea, monitoring ships and helping to detect, deter and protect against terrorist activity. Active Endeavour's tasks include intelligence-gathering and the security and safety of non-combatant shipping. In addition, NATO naval forces escort allied non-combatant ships in transit through the Straits of Gibraltar. In a significant move reflecting the broad convergence in the fight against terrorism, Russia and Ukraine announced at the Istanbul Summit that they would contribute maritime assets to Operation Active Endeavour.

In areas related to asymmetrical threats, NATO is called upon to play an increasingly important role, particularly when it comes to rapid intervention against terrorists, the use of weapons of mass destruction (WMD) and consequence management. The key for NATO is to make its NATO Reaction Force fully operational and to work together with other institutions such as the European Union or the United Nations.

With regard to the fight against the spread of WMD, NATO countries agreed at the Istanbul Summit to "consider addressing, in accordance with international law, the risk of terrorist-related trafficking in, or use of, nuclear, chemical and biological weapons, their means of delivery and related materials".[24] Moreover, NATO formally endorsed the US-led Proliferation Security Initiative (PSI), which focuses on the interdiction of proliferation shipments of WMD, delivery systems and related materials at sea, in the air or on land.[25]

However, PSI is yet another typical security initiative that has been launched outside the NATO framework on the assumption that an ad hoc coalition of the willing can implement effective measures against WMD proliferation. For instance, the interception of a shipment of centrifuge parts for uranium enrichment bound for Libya was a joint venture between the United States, the United Kingdom, Italy and Germany. At the same time, NATO and its Operation Active Endeavour were pressured by the US and other NATO governments to subscribe to the PSI principles.

"Soft power" projection and the promotion of democracy

The uniqueness of NATO is its ability to combine robust, military operations with soft power to assist countries in the reform of their security and defence sectors. The notion of soft power includes a large spectrum of cooperative activities that engage partner states in interoperability, security governance, defence reforms, defence education, the fight against small arms and light weapons and other activities in the area of civil–military partnership-building. Institutional frameworks for soft security cooperation include the Partnership for Peace and the Mediterranean Dialogue, which was elevated at the Istanbul Summit to a "Partnership". The launching of a Partnership Action Plan on Defence Institution Building (PAP-DIB), intended primarily for Central Asian partners, belongs to this category.

These areas of activity are becoming ever more important to NATO, particularly with regard to the increasing efforts to promote governance and democratic reform in countries adjacent to the Alliance. In a speech to a Ukrainian audience, the NATO Secretary General defined NATO as "an organisation that protects the values that underlie our societies: Freedom of speech, democratic participation, human rights and the rule of law".[26] However, democracy promotion is an activity that encounters important competition from other international organizations, notably the European Union, the Organization for Security and Co-operation in Europe (OSCE) and the United Nations. NATO's Membership Action Plan (MAP) has also acquired the status of a normative reference for countries outside the enlarged NATO, particularly for Ukraine, countries in the Balkans and possibly also countries in the Caucasus and Central Asia.[27]

NATO, its Partnership for Peace (PfP) and the EAPC remain indispensable forums for the promotion of interoperability, standardization and mission management, not just for NATO operations but also for EU missions and possibly also for future UN missions. NATO has also created institutional arrangements for bilateral consultations with Russia and Ukraine. The 2002 NATO–Russia Council followed on from earlier attempts in the 1990s to institutionalize relations between the former enemies. The Council allows Russia to interact with NATO on a one-to-one basis on security issues ranging from counter-terrorism to conflict management in areas of mutual interest. This institutional interface is increasingly competing with the OSCE, which sees itself as the guardian of comprehensive security in the Euro-Atlantic and Eurasian regions.

At the Istanbul Summit, NATO agreed on three "soft power" initiatives in order to assume a greater presence in the Mediterranean and the Middle East. The first was an effort – which falls far short of a "Greater Middle East Initiative" – to deepen the existing NATO Mediterranean Dialogue with seven countries in North Africa and the Middle East and to transform it into a genuine Partnership. It is not yet clear what the "deepening" should entail, particularly in view of the sombre mood of some Arab states regarding the US occupation of Iraq. Formally, the objectives of the Partnership are dialogue, interoperability, defence reform and the fight against terrorism.

The second was the "Istanbul Cooperation Initiative". With this initiative NATO reached out for the first time to countries of the Middle East and the Gulf states ("the broader Middle East region"). The objective was "to develop the ability of countries' forces to operate with those of the Alliance including by contributing to NATO-led operations, fight against terrorism, stem the flow of WMD materials and illegal trafficking in arms, and improve countries' capabilities to address common challenges and threats with NATO".[28]

NATO's third offer was to train the new Iraqi army. At the 2004 G-8 Summit at Sea Island, France opposed any NATO commitment that would endorse the military presence of US forces in Iraq. It continued to stonewall progress of the NATO Training Implementation Mission in Iraq (NTIM-I) by opposing the creation of a NATO training academy in Iraq. France argued that its costs should be covered only by those NATO allies that are part of the US-led coalition.[29]

Human trafficking is the latest initiative that NATO is trying to assume as part of its new policy orientation towards soft power and human security. The initiative aspires to provide normative guidance to NATO-led personnel, both civilian (including police) and military. The proposed guidelines would include the existing UN Protocol to Prevent, Suppress and Punish Trafficking in Persons, especially Women and Children.[30] The United States and Norway proposed this initiative, which was approved by the North Atlantic Council on 9 June 2004 and by all 46 members of the Euro-Atlantic Partnership Council on 16 June 2004. The comparative advantage of NATO's launching this kind of initiative is to carry it from its conceptual origins within the North Atlantic Council to the legitimacy of the 46-state platform of the EAPC, then to insert it in the curriculums of their defence colleges and peacekeeping centres, and finally to implement it in NATO-led field operations.

Crisis management and peace operations

After more than 40 years of pursuing the single objective of collective defence, at the 1991 Rome Summit NATO turned its attention to crisis management and peacekeeping. A new chapter of NATO's history began with the deployment of NATO forces in Bosnia and Herzegovina in 1995. The rise of complex emergencies, humanitarian disasters and state failure has led today to the involvement of a multitude of organizations that are trying to reassert their mandates and relevance by addressing such challenges. NATO is attempting to find its niche in the global demand for reconstruction and stabilization.

According to Carl Bildt, the former UN Secretary-General's Special Envoy for the Balkans, NATO is "developing into a somewhat more robust equivalent of the UN's peace-keeping operations department".[31] Currently, NATO is subcontracted by the United Nations for peace missions in the Balkans (the Kosovo Force, KFOR) and in Afghanistan (the International Security Assistance Force, ISAF). NATO's operations in both cases are "robust", i.e. the mission spectrum ranges from peace-keeping to the threat and the use of coercive measures against spoilers. KFOR and ISAF have shown that NATO is capable of conflict prevention, robust peace operations and peacebuilding. NATO can project forces for long-term stability operations and it can provide the planning, force generation and mission-intensity continuum of operations in complex emergencies and peace operations. In Afghanistan, NATO has also embraced a new model of civil–military cooperation with the Provincial Reconstruction Teams.

Without a secure environment, serious state-building efforts have no chance of success. For instance, only NATO was able to provide security guarantees to Macedonians and Albanians in the wake of the Ohrid Framework Agreement in Macedonia in 2001. Operations "Essential Harvest" and "Amber Fox" were key to the disarmament and stabilization measures taken in that fragile country. Even though the European Union replaced NATO in Macedonia and also in Bosnia, the Atlantic Alliance is the only organization that could intervene effectively in the region should a deadly conflict break out again. Thus, the need for an indirect NATO presence in the area will remain until the countries of the region have integrated into both NATO and the European Union.

Future demand for peace operations will depend very much on NATO's performance in Afghanistan. The Istanbul Summit confirmed that Afghanistan will remain the priority. However, the inability of NATO to raise sufficient troops and resources to contribute in a meaningful way to the country's stabilization, especially in provincial regions, means that the Afghan situation is likely to receive members' main attention for some time to come.[32] More demand for peace operations will most likely come to the United Nations for robust missions in Africa. NATO Secretary General Jaap de Hoop Scheffer stresses NATO's relevance for the United Nations also in the context of the United Nations' current reform efforts and the recommendations of the UN Secretary-General's Report of the High-level Panel on Threats, Challenges and Change: "As the United Nations looks at how to implement the panel's recommendations, I am convinced that NATO, with its unparalleled experience and expertise, will feature high up on the United Nations' list of preferred suppliers."[33]

NATO's effectiveness in the twenty-first century: Capabilities and "institutional interoperability"

If Europe intends to keep NATO relevant, it has to make credible commitments to spend more on defence and to modernize and transform its forces for missions across the conflict spectrum. NATO's future capabilities will depend on several factors. First, the deployability of forces needs to be increased. Of 1.5 million soldiers theoretically available from European member states for NATO operations, fewer than 100,000 can actually be deployed. At the 2002 Transformation Summit in Prague, NATO leaders unanimously agreed to the creation of a NATO Response Force – a fully interoperable and integrated high-readiness capability, able to act as "the first boots on the ground" in the Alliance's full conflict spectrum. This force should be ready for deployment in the autumn of 2006. In order to increase the general deployability of NATO forces, the member states agreed at the Istanbul Summit to make 40 per cent of their troops deployable on Alliance operations and 8 per cent instantly deployable.[34] Second, Europeans have to spend more on defence. European countries in NATO spend about one-third as much on defence as the United States. Third, NATO members have to rethink the organization of their national armed forces. Countries such as Germany still maintain a conscript system that puts political and practical constraints on sustainable force deployments. Fourth, future NATO capabilities depend on the relationship with the European Union and vice versa. NATO will not be able to achieve its capability objectives if the European Union increases its demand for *autonomously* deployable forces within its European Security and Defence Policy (ESDP) and the "battlegroup" concept. In recent years, the European Union has been using civilian and military ESDP contingents in Bosnia, Macedonia and the Congo.

The effectiveness of NATO in the twenty-first century will also depend on its working relations with other institutions involved in crisis management. The relationship with the United Nations will be a key for NATO's future. NATO could assume the function of a resource organization for the United Nations around the globe. NATO could also be used as a framework at the military level for integrating non-NATO countries in robust peacekeeping missions that would rely on NATO rules of engagement and command and control. The legal basis for this practice was established by UN Security Council Resolution 1244, annex 2 (10 June 1999). The Istanbul Summit confirmed this NATO objective by encouraging the new partner states from the Middle East and the Gulf states to an "additional participation ... in NATO-led peace-support operations on a case-by-case basis".

NATO could also assume a lead role in the context of the G-8 Action Plan for Expanding Global Capacity for Peace Support Operations. The programme calls for providing "interoperability training for peace operations, combating organised crime and border control and to improve the UN ability to provide peace and stabilities through chapter VII operations".[35] In order make better preparations for its cooperation with the United Nations, NATO is participating in bi-annual high-level meetings of regional and intergovernmental organizations organized by the United Nations.

The key institutional partnership remains, however, between NATO and the European Union. The European Union has growing ambitions in the area of crisis management in and around Europe: "With new threats", declares the European Security Strategy of December 2003, "... the first line of defence will often be abroad."[36] The EU–NATO partnership should be based on the principle of complementarity, but it "is too often mired in the political mud of contemporary transatlantic relations from which it can never be divorced".[37] There are, however, permanent arrangements between the European Union and NATO that work well, in particular Berlin Plus, and they provide the framework for the strategic partnership between the organizations in crisis management.[38] The establishment of a small European Union cell at SHAPE (Supreme Headquarters Allied Powers Europe) and of NATO liaison arrangements at the EU military staff will improve the preparation of EU operations that have recourse to NATO assets and capabilities under the Berlin Plus arrangements.

Regarding crisis management, the French tend to privilege the European Union over NATO. Germany and the United Kingdom, in contrast, continue to give NATO "first choice" for crisis operations involving European and US partners. NATO will continue to be the first choice for robust action as long as the United States is interested in empowering NATO, because, as Chris Patten puts it, the European Security and Defence Policy "is still in its infancy".[39]

Conclusions

For NATO, the period of collective defence is over: it has "lost an enemy" but has "not yet found a role".[40] At the same time, NATO, and transatlantic relations more generally, experienced a very serious blow over the war in Iraq and in particular over questions related to the use of force, the legitimacy of intervention and the role of the United Nations in global and regional security issues. The European allies struggle over how to deal with US power, while, for the Americans, Europe has lost much of its strategic relevance. This asymmetry is accentuated by diverging threat perceptions: since 9/11 the United States is "at war", whereas the Europeans have a more diffuse and differentiated perspective on new threats and challenges.

What role can NATO play in the US-centric world order? This chapter suggests that NATO should be able to remain a relevant security institution provided that it is prepared to act globally and muster the necessary capabilities for force projection and sustainable operations. With these provisos, NATO could also act in the future as a "consensus-building engine" between the two sides of the Atlantic.[41] Despite all its weaknesses, NATO continues to be the only mechanism in transatlantic relations in which security issues are politically debated and where instruments for robust responses to challenges are available. Furthermore, NATO is still the only institution that can tie the United States to European security concerns.

NATO can find new functions and utility for regional and global security in the realms of military activities against terrorism and WMD proliferation, as well as in "soft security" areas such as crisis management and peace operations. On the normative side, NATO can use its rich and successful experience with the Partnership for Peace to engage Mediterranean and Middle Eastern countries in dialogue and cooperative programmes dealing with defence reform, interoperability and civil–military relations. Furthermore, the standards and governance requirements that are part of the NATO Membership Action Plan have become recognized norms well beyond the NATO territory.

The problem remains that NATO is made up of 26 countries with different policy agendas and divergent security policy preferences. They include the United States, which, during the George W. Bush administration, repeatedly bypassed the organization. The Europeans resent this and argue that a "NATO which is limited to a 'toolbox' role will not be viable".[42] At the same time, NATO had been instrumentalized politically by several allies both before and after the US intervention in Iraq. The Istanbul Summit was a damage control exercise that tried to mitigate the negative effects of the divisions between Europe and the United States. This is why the successes of the Summit have been primarily in the area of "soft power".

The key to NATO's future is to remain useful to its member states, including the United States, and to become more relevant for international organizations such as the European Union and the United Nations. This requires NATO to continue to reinvent itself and to adapt in both form and substance to the rapidly changing security environment of the post–Cold War era.

Notes

1. See, for example, Richard Falk, "Opposition to War against Iraq", Transnational Foundation for Peace and Future Research, 20 September 2002, ⟨http://www.transnational. org/forum/meet/2002/Falk_AgainstIraqWar.html⟩; Richard Falk and David Krieger, "After the Iraq War: Thinking Ahead", Nuclear Age Peace Foundation, 1 May 2003, ⟨http://www.wagingpeace.org/articles/2003/05/01_falk_after-iraq.htm⟩.

2. *The National Security Strategy of the United States of America* (Washington, DC: The White House, September 2002), ⟨http://www.whitehouse.gov/nsc/nss.pdf⟩.
3. NATO Secretary General Lord Ismay, 1948.
4. Albrecht Schnabel and Ramesh Thakur, *Kosovo and the Challenge of Humanitarian Intervention* (Tokyo: United Nations University Press, 2000).
5. Wesley Clark, "An Army of One", *Washington Monthly*, September 2002.
6. Robert Kagan, "Power and Weakness," *Policy Review*, No. 113 (June/July 2002).
7. *Quadrennial Defense Review Report*, US Department of Defense, 30 September 2001, ⟨http://www.defenselink.mil/pubs/qdr2001.pdf⟩.
8. The new member states are Bulgaria, Estonia, Lithuania, Latvia, Romania, Slovakia and Slovenia.
9. Ronald D. Asmus, "Rebuilding the Atlantic Alliance", *Foreign Affairs*, Vol. 82, No. 5 (September/October 2003), p. 21.
10. See, for instance, "The End of NATO", *Wall Street Journal*, 10 February 2003.
11. In February 2003 France, Germany and Belgium issued a joint declaration that a NATO accord on Turkey's defences would "not in any way prejudge ongoing efforts" within the framework of the existing UN resolution (UNSC Resolution 1441 on Iraq), which abstains from authorizing the use of force.
12. When Poland assumed command of the Multinational Division in the south of Iraq as part of the international stabilization force, NATO supported the mission with tasks such as providing intelligence, logistics expertise, movement coordination, force generation and secure communications support. This support function did not, however, provide NATO with a presence in Iraq.
13. Recent reports suggest that France would require the United Nations to have "responsibility for all operations" ("No NATO Role before UN in Charge – France", Reuters, 6 April 2004).
14. John Chalmers, "Divisions on Iraq Cloud NATO's Enlargement Party", Reuters, 3 April 2004.
15. "The Alliance's Strategic Concept, Approved by the Heads of State and Government participating in the meeting of the North Atlantic Council in Washington D.C. on 23rd and 24th April 1999", NATO Press Release, NAC-S(99)65, 24 April 1999, ⟨http://www.nato.int/docu/pr/1999/p99-065e.htm⟩.
16. Jaap de Hoop Scheffer, NATO Secretary General, "Projecting Stability", speech to the "Defending Global Security" conference, Brussels, 17 May 2004, ⟨http://www.nato.int/docu/speech/2004/s040517a.htm⟩.
17. "NATO Affords Gains for U.S. Foreign, Security Policy", *Washington File*, 30 June 2004.
18. R. Nicholas Burns, "The New NATO and the Greater Middle East, Remarks at Conference on NATO and the Greater Middle East", Prague, 19 October 2003, ⟨http://www.state.gov/p/eur/rls/rm/2003/25602.htm⟩.
19. Jaap de Hoop Scheffer, NATO Secretary General, speech to the Munich Security Conference, 12 February 2005, ⟨http://www.securityconference.de/konferenzen/rede.php?menu_2005=&menu_konferenzen=&sprache=en&id=159&⟩.
20. See Julian Lindley-French, "The Ties That Bind", *NATO Review*, Istanbul Summit Special, May 2004, p. 53, ⟨http://www.nato.int/docu/review/2003/issue3/english/art2.html⟩.
21. Clark, "An Army of One".
22. For the text see *Partnership Action Plan against Terrorism*, NATO Basic Texts, 22 November 2002, ⟨http://www.nato.int/docu/basictxt/b021122e.htm⟩.
23. "Istanbul Summit Communiqué, Issued by the Heads of State and Government participating in the meeting of the North Atlantic Council", NATO Press Release (2004) 096, 28 June 2004, ⟨http://www.nato.int/docu/pr/2004/p04-096e.htm⟩.

24. Ibid.

25. NATO supported the "aims of the Proliferation Security Initiative (PSI) and its Statement of Interdiction Principles to establish a more co-ordinated and effective basis through which to impede and stop shipments of WMD, delivery systems, and related materials flowing to and from states and non-state actors of proliferation concern" (Ibid.).

26. Speech by Jaap de Hoop Scheffer, NATO Secretary General, National University of Kyiv-mohyla Academy Kyiv, Ukraine, 20 October 2005, ⟨http://www.nato.int/docu/speech/2005/s051020a.htm⟩.

27. Heiner Hänggi and Fred Tanner, "Promoting Security Sector Governance in the EU's Neighbourhood", Chaillot Paper No. 80 (Paris: European Union Institute for Security Studies, July 2005).

28. *Istanbul Cooperation Initiative*, NATO Policy Document, Istanbul Summit, 28 June 2004, ⟨http://www.nato.int/docu/comm/2004/06-istanbul/docu-cooperation.htm⟩. The suggested areas of cooperation include NATO-sponsored border security; access to appropriate Partnership for Peace (PfP) programmes and training centres; and promoting cooperation in the areas of civil emergency planning (offering NATO training courses on civil emergency planning, civil–military coordination, and crisis response to maritime, aviation and surface threats; invitations to join or observe relevant NATO/PfP exercises as appropriate; and provision of information on possible disaster assistance).

29. "France and Belgium Block NATO Iraq Training Plan", *Financial Times*, 18–19 September 2004.

30. See *NATO Policy on Combating Trafficking in Human Beings*, NATO Policy document, 29 June 2004, Appendix 1, ⟨http://www.nato.int/docu/comm/2004/06-istanbul/docu-traffic.htm⟩.

31. Carl Bildt, "We Must Build States and Not Nations", *Financial Times*, 16 January 2004.

32. "Afghan Troubles Will Test NATO's Quest for New Role", *Financial Times*, 27 May 2004.

33. NATO Secretary General, Jaap de Hoop Scheffer, "A Transforming Alliance", speech delivered to the Cambridge Union Society, Cambridge, 2 February 2005, ⟨http://www.nato.int/docu/speech/2005/s050202b.htm⟩.

34. "Those Who Can't Fight, Train", *The Economist*, 3 July 2004, p. 38.

35. *G8 Action Plan: Expanding Global Capability for Peace Support Operations*, G8 Summit, Sea Island, GA, 10 June 2004; available at ⟨http://www.g8.utoronto.ca/summit/2004seaisland/peace.html⟩.

36. *A Secure Europe in a Better World*, European Security Strategy, Brussels, adopted by the European Council on 12 December 2003, p. 6, ⟨http://ue.eu.int/uedocs/cmsUpload/78367.pdf⟩.

37. Lindley-French, "The Ties That Bind", p. 51.

38. The Berlin Plus agreement regulates the use of NATO assets and other capabilities in crisis management operations that are led by the European Union.

39. Chris Patten, "A Security Strategy for Europe", *Oxford Journal on Good Governance*, Vol. 1, No. 1 (2004), p. 13.

40. *The Economist*, 26 June 2004, p. 15.

41. Clark, "An Army of One".

42. Peter Struck, "The Future of NATO", speech at the 40th Munich Conference on Security Policy, 7 February 2004, ⟨http://www.securityconference.de/konferenzen/rede.php?menu_2004=&menu_konferenzen=&sprache=en&id=125&⟩.

21

The Iraq crisis and world order: A perspective from the European Union

Luis Martinez

The overthrow of Saddam Hussein provoked a crisis within the European Union over the objectives, principles and resources of its foreign policy, particularly in the Middle East. Since 1995, the European Union has developed its neighbourhood policy within the framework of the Euro-Mediterranean Partnership (Barcelona process), but it has remained marginal in the Middle East and in the Gulf. Therefore, the Iraq crisis has forced the European Union to define its policy towards a region that is largely subject to the influence of the United States. Three major obstacles prevented the Union from defining a common policy towards Iraq: first, the deep mistrust of European public opinion about the real intentions of the Bush administration in Iraq; secondly, objection to war as a means of diplomatic action; thirdly, the preventive war in Iraq appeared to be an aggravating factor in relations with the Muslim world. Besides these three major obstacles, there were internal disagreements between member states of the Union. These member states were divided between a British pro-US model and a Franco-German axis that was hostile to the methods of the Bush administration and its utopian vision of the Middle East.

The side-effects of the trauma caused by the attacks of 11 September 2001 were incomprehensible to European and Arab/Muslim opinion. The "war against terrorism" launched by the Bush administration seemed disproportionate compared with the attacks. Even worse, the invasion of Iraq destroyed the sympathy gained after the drama of the World Trade Center. Being more a reactive war (owing to the trauma of the attacks) than a strategic one, the occupation of Iraq represents a problem. In the first place, how is it possible to keep the US troops in Iraq without provoking violent resistance from Iraqi society? On the other hand, how can the Americans leave Iraq without provoking instability in the region? Finally, how is it possible simultaneously to carry out the "war against terrorism" and the war against the guerrillas in Iraq? The United States is confronted with a deep feeling of incomprehension in Europe and of animosity from the Arab/Muslim world. In May 2003, US President George W. Bush announced that the war in Iraq was over: the regime of Saddam Hussein had been overthrown. A new period would begin for the Iraqis: freedom, democracy and development were the expected results.

In the post-trauma atmosphere, the Bush administration had accused the Iraqi regime of acting in complicity with the al-Qaeda network and producing weapons of mass destruction likely to be used by terrorists.[1] Then, in a more general way, the Iraqi state became the symbol of a new policy towards the Arab/Muslim world: the Bush administration undertook to promote democracy by force.[2] The purpose became "to liberate" societies subjected to dictatorial regimes in order to promote the development of new values. The post-war plan of the Bush administration has been confronted with very serious obstacles (a lack of soldiers in Iraq, increasing rejection of the occupation forces by the Iraqi population, the development of torture, etc.). Symbolically, on 28 June 2004, Iraq regained its sovereignty and the US administrator, Paul Bremer, left Baghdad. With a view to rebuilding a legitimate political system, legislative elections were scheduled for January 2005. Approximately 14 million electors were invited to vote in order to elect the 275 deputies of the Provisional National Assembly, the members of the Baghdad Council and 17 regional councils, and the 111 members of the Kurdistan autonomous parliament. More than 7,000 candidates were registered on 109 lists to participate.

Iraq, Europe and the United States: A persisting incomprehension

Shortly after the attacks of 11 September 2001, the French newspaper *Le Monde* had the headline: "We Are All Americans". Jacques Chirac was the first European head of state to visit the ruins of the World Trade Center in honour of the victims. A wave of compassion tempered European opinion, which considered it legitimate that the United States should respond to this aggression. The overthrow of the Taliban regime in Afghanistan seemed to be a logical consequence. It was only when the Bush administration pointed to the Iraq of Saddam Hussein as a potential target that a kind of incomprehension started to develop. A series of vague and unconvincing explanations, which supposedly justified the war against Iraq, were poorly received by European opinion. Several factors explain this European "resistance" to the media propaganda of the Bush administration.

Iraqi society was already suffering

In the first place, Iraq was not considered to be a dangerous state. Rather it was a destroyed state where the population faced great adversity. Contemplating a new war against Iraq meant accepting that once again its population would suffer new traumas. Whereas US opinion was seemingly indifferent to the humanitarian consequences of the sanctions imposed on Iraq, Europeans were informed about the plight of this country. For five years after the Gulf war of 1991, Iraq was subjected to a total embargo, with devastating socio-economic impacts on the population. As a result of UN Resolution 687 (3 April 1991), the US administration imposed a quasi-total embargo that seemed to be more of a collective punishment rather than real economic sanctions. The embargo was the most severe of the century – not even the Versailles treaty went so far. Certainly, the conquerors of Germany had amputated its territory, obliged it to pay reparations and blocked its military power, but nothing impeded it from re-establishing regular commercial relations and rebuilding its infrastructure. In Iraq, although it was authorized to export a small amount of oil, at a price set by the United Nations, the international community prohibited the import of the necessary materials for restarting refineries and electricity power stations, arguing that these materials could have had "dual" civil and military use. Basic medication and commodities were blocked under the pretext that they could be used for the fabrication of chemical weapons. Owing to a lack of aerosols, asthma became a deadly disease. It is estimated that approximately 500,000 children under the age of five paid with their lives for the severity of the embargo. In 1996, when US Secretary of State Madeleine Albright was questioned in front of the cameras about the human cost of the sanctions and the death of 500,000 children, she answered: "I think this is a very hard choice, but the price – we think the price is worth it."[3] In 1995, the Food and Agriculture Organization of the United Nations and UNICEF announced that 4 million Iraqis were living in a state of "pre-starvation" and that the lives of 1 million, particularly children, were threatened.

To relieve the suffering of civilians, an "Oil-for-Food" programme was set up in 1996. One of the conditions was that 25 per cent of the oil revenues should be directed to Kuwait for war reparations. In order to supervise the programme, a large number of inspectors were mobilized. After 1996 the Iraqi authorities were authorized to sell US$2 billion of oil every six months, and in 1998 the authorized amount was increased to US$5 billion. Iraqi oil was sold mainly through trade companies (83 per cent) and its main client (60 per cent of exports under UN supervision) was the US market. Iraq nevertheless succeeded in appropriating US$2.5 billion each year from the oil revenues without the United Nations' knowledge.

Loulouwa el Rashid describes three stages of economic recovery.[4] The first, 1995–1996, was a period of inflation. The government printed money as a redistribution method but this caused the collapse of the Iraqi dinar. Moreover, the government used up strategic stocks accumulated during the war against Iran and goods appropriated from Kuwait at the time of its invasion. In short, during this period the regime relied on its reserves. It was also during this period that the government encouraged smuggling and deregulated external trade. The second period, 1997–1998, was characterized by an increase in external trade, reflected in massive imports of commodities. The market improved and the shortages of products and goods of the 1993–1995 years started to disappear. The third period started in 1998 and was characterized by a disengagement of the state (privatization of the public sector, enterprise self-financing, financial self-sufficiency, remuneration of civil servants according to results, etc.). The regime was successful in supplying some of the needs of the population.

From this point of view, the Bush administration's determination to overthrow the regime seemed incomprehensible. In the face of the Iranian or North Korean menace, how was it possible to claim that Iraq was a danger? No Iraqis figured among the 9/11 terrorists and yet it was the Iraqi regime that was made out to be a threat. This lack of explanation led European opinion to vacillate between growing scepticism (which would become total mistrust among the French, Germans, Spanish and Italians) and moderate understanding (in the UK and the Scandinavian countries). In general, the Bush administration's interest in launching the war against Iraq would seem to have been the result of psychological factors (finishing Bush senior's work), therapeutic factors (overcoming the trauma of 9/11), economic factors (taking control of oil resources) and military factors (establishing US supremacy in the region). The war against Iraq was not considered to be a "just war", and mistrust turned to hostility when, in the face of the German, French and Russian refusal to support the war in Iraq in the Security Council, Condoleezza Rice was quoted as allegedly saying "we must punish France, ignore Germany and forgive Russia".[5]

A war with irreversible consequences

Apart from a lack of understanding of the reasons for launching a war against Iraq, there was concern that an "illegitimate war" would provoke irreversible consequences in terms of the rise of terrorism. For the Europeans, the best way of disarming "rogue states" is to use UN mechanisms. The United Nations had already given proof of its capacity in this matter in Iraq. To use war for such an objective means to take the risk of provoking a "clash of civilizations". The Arab/Muslim world is already confronted with numerous wars that it considers hostile to its community (Palestine, Kashmir, Chechnya, etc.). Besides, a war against Iraq would create a feeling of "hatred" within the Muslim world that would be difficult to control, and whose long-term effects could undermine international relations. The geographical proximity of Europe to the Muslim world and the depth of its economic, migratory, tourist and cultural exchanges lead it to perceive the war against Iraq in a very different way from the United States. Having a long history formed by crusades, colonization and decolonization wars, Europe views the Arab world with cautious concern. The experience of the British and the French in North Africa and the Middle East prompts Europe to be prudent in its relations with the Arab world. Besides, Iraq could not emulate the German or Japanese post-war model enunciated by Donald Rumsfeld. As Philip H. Gordon emphasized: "Americans imbued with the experience of creating democracy in Japan and Germany after the Second World War cling – perhaps naively – to the belief that if one can just get rid of the current Iraqi dictator, democracy and freedom will flourish in the region ... The European historical pessimism (or realism, depending on one's perspective), contrasts significantly with Americans' historical 'can-do' optimism and helps explain why some Americans believe that invading Iraq would be a first step toward creating a new and better Middle East."[6]

The violence of the occupation: Proof of US failure

The overthrow of Saddam Hussein and the occupation of Iraq marginalized Europe. In spite of opposition from European public opinion and the major European governments, the US administration launched a unilateral war against Iraq. As European public opinion emerged, its objection to war sometimes opposed the decision by their head of state to participate in the war (the United Kingdom, Spain, Ukraine, Poland). Once the illusion of a "lightning victory" and of a constructive occupation had passed, Franco-German pessimism about the impossibility of imposing change by armed force became the point of reference. The French and German analyses proved to be justified and accurate. From this perspective, Europeans have three possibilities: progressively leave the Iraqi territory to the states that got involved and let the United States get bogged down in an endless war; become involved in the economic and political domains in order to alleviate the suffering of the population; participate indirectly in the war by training the security forces.

In fact, the official end of the war was accompanied by the development of a guerrilla war that has undermined and destroyed Iraq's reconstruction project. For example, sabotage of oil pipelines has caused the loss of US$10 billion. Furthermore, out of US$18 billion of aid intended for reconstruction, only 2 per cent was used in 2003. The political and security situation made it impossible for the Iraqi economy to take off, and insecurity and unemployment became a reality. From this perspective, is the reconstruction of Iraq possible? The attitude of the Iraqi population towards the US occupation forces is critical. Because of the US presence in Iraq, Iraqis doubt the sincerity of the United States' proclaimed motives (liberty and democracy), they reject the US war methods (torture, humiliation, the destruction of insurgent cities) and they believe that the United States' real objective is civil war. This Iraqi mistrust of the US occupation forces is based on recent history, current operations and uncertainties about the future. Nationalist sentiment is very strong and constitutes the best antidote to the supposed or real threat that Iraq's diverse communities might cause its collapse.

This insecurity is a real obstacle to the reconstruction of Iraq. During the Madrid Conference on 24 October 2003, the European Union reconfirmed its engagement on behalf of the development of a prosperous and stable Iraq and concluded that it was prepared to participate in the reconstruction of Iraq within the framework of United Nations Security Council Resolution 1483.[7] Since then it has deployed €320 million "with a view to restoring key public services, boosting employment and reducing poverty as well as strengthening governance, civil society and human rights"; and more than one European country is militarily engaged with the coalition.[8] It is clear that very few concrete modes of participation exist for the European Union. However, the EU contribution could be essential for projects that are as important as reconstruction. Also, after the elections of 30 January 2005, the emergence of a new authority in Iraq less subjugated to US tutelage than was the first prime minister, Iyad Allawi, will have the responsibility of facilitating the engagement of the European Union in Iraq.

In June 2004, the Coalition Provisional Authority's Programme Management Office (PMO) confirmed that US$18.4 billion would be invested in infrastructure reconstruction projects. The PMO stated that, as of that date, "we have committed over $9 billion out of a total of $18.4 billion and are employing nearly 20,000 Iraqis".[9] After the overthrow of Saddam Hussein's regime, the fear of a major humanitarian crisis had emerged. Several million Iraqis depended on the distribution of basic products under the "Oil-for-Food" programme. The United Nations quickly restored the rudimentary rationing system that had existed before the war and delivered more than 1.5 million tons of food between May and July 2003. However, supplies of water and electricity and the treatment of waste water have not reached pre-war standards.[10] This has aroused resentment among the population. In fact, by August 2003 more than 585 schools had been rehabilitated and all the universities had reopened,[11] but, for a country ruined by two decades of war, sanctions and a war of "liberation", the lack of progress on reconstruction projects does not give the population confidence in a rapid improvement in the socio-economic situation.[12] Only Iraqis who are able to enlist in the security forces or in the oil sector can expect an improvement in their living conditions.

Even worse, the destruction of cities and districts that support the insurgency has provoked waves of refugees to the interior of the country and an already weakened population is sinking into an ever more precarious situation. The reconstruction of Iraq is undoubtedly the most important challenge for its future. Yet it is clear that, even though Europe could play a major role in this, it is not happening, owing to the lack of convergence between the Iraqi government, the Bush administration and the European Union.

The resistance to the US occupation

Whereas European public opinion expressed doubts about the legitimacy of the war against Iraq, European governments were sceptical about the pertinence of the link between Iraq and al-Qaeda. Whereas the Bush administration associates the fight against world terrorism with the war in Iraq, France and Germany consider that the war against Iraq is only increasing world terrorism and making the world less safe. The exponential development of armed groups in Iraq reinforces this point of view. For the Europeans, the persistence of an armed resistance in Iraq reminds them of their colonial experience and concerns them. From this point of view, the armed forces cannot do anything against a society in revolt.

The resistance to the US occupation is multifaceted. According to Samir Haddad and Mazin Ghazi, it is structured around several tendencies.[13]

1. The main Sunni resistance groups, which primarily target the US occupation:
   - The Iraqi National Islamic Resistance (The 1920 Revolution Brigades). Its declared aim is to liberate Iraqi territory from foreign military and political occupation and to establish a liberated and independent Islamic Iraqi state. A statement issued by the group on 19 August 2004 explained, that between 27 July and 7 August 2004, the group had carried out an average of 10 operations every day.

- The National Front for the Liberation of Iraq, which comprises 10 resistance groups. It consists of nationalists and Islamists, and its activities are concentrated in Arbil and Kirkuk.
- The Iraqi Resistance Islamic Front, which comprises a coalition of a number of small resistance factions (Salah al Din, Sayf Allah al Maslul Brigades, Al Rantisi Brigade). Its political and jihad programme stems from a jurisprudence viewpoint that allows it to fight the occupiers.
- Other Sunni groups are acting against the coalition, and some of these armed groups are considered to derive from Saddam Hussein's regime – Al Awdah, Saddam Fedayeen, and the Iraqi Liberation Army (which warned foreign countries against sending troops to Iraq and pledged to attack those troops if they were sent).[14] Finally, autonomous groups are leading the jihad: Awakening and Holy War, The White Banners, Al Haqq Army.

2. Shiite resistance groups:
   - The Al-Sadr group (Mahdi's army).
   - Imam Ali Bin Abi Talib Jihadi Brigades.
   - A large number of Islamist groups operating against the coalition forces: Assadullah Brigades, Islamic Retaliation Movement, Islamic Anger Brigades, Khalid Bin al Walid Brigades, Iraq's Martyrs Brigades, Secret Islamic Army.

3. International groups operating in the name of al-Qaeda – Abu Musab al Zarqawi, Al Tawhid wa al Jihad, Ansar al Sunah Movement.

In the face of the Iraqi armed resistance, the European Union finds itself confronted with the worst possible dilemma: either remain as a spectator of a dramatic conflict with no certain ending; or participate in a conflict that it opposed. The re-election of George Bush and the determination of the US administration repudiate the hypothesis of a speedy withdrawal of US forces from Iraq. From this point of view, the European Union is participating, in a very modest way, in the Iraqi conflict. The French and German governments are cooperating in the training (outside of Iraq) of Iraqi police. In this conflict, the issue for most European states is to not provoke the US administration. Only the United Kingdom continues actively to support the US troops in Iraq.

The way forward

There are three possible scenarios for the evolution of the situation in Iraq: keeping the coalition forces in Iraq and entrenching the resulting violence; the departure of the coalition forces after 2005 and the preservation of a suspended regime; the construction of a political peace plan.

It is this last proposition that the European Union is more likely to follow.

Maintaining the coalition, entrenching violence

The fact of keeping 150,000 US soldiers in Iraq is perpetuating the state of violence. The United States has failed to establish a climate of trust with Iraqi society. After the overthrow of Saddam Hussein's regime, the political choices by the Provisional Authority and, above all, the behaviour of the coalition soldiers provoked hatred and rejection of the coalition troops, which shifted from "liberator" to "occupying" status. According to the Iraqi political analyst Nabil Mohamed Salim:

The American intervention has touched the moral, symbolic and material components of the national power. The manifestation of the first element was illustrated by the dissolution of the Iraqi army – emblem of the State power – by the occupation forces; the second element lies in the total paralysis of Iraq's economic and industrial sectors after the destruction of its infrastructure. It is like this that Iraq continued and continues to be emptied of all possibilities that will allow it to reconstitute the elements of a sovereign independent State.[15]

Salim emphasizes that nationalist sentiments were completely ignored in the preparations for the post-Saddam period. The inability to formulate a plan that foresaw a rapid transfer of real sovereignty to the Iraqi people explains the present violence. The occupation is experienced as a humiliation. From this point of view, the "liberation" of Iraq is incomprehensible because it was not accompanied by a return of sovereignty. The conviction that the coalition forces are predisposed to transfer power not to the Iraqis but to their chosen representatives has increased participation in the Shiite resistance, the Mahdi army of Moqtada al-Sadr, as well as the Sunnis.

Even worse, ulterior motives are attributed to the coalition forces, which only emphasizes the disillusion and disenchantment of the Iraqis: "when we had realised that the United States invaded us, guided by their economic (oil), political and security interests (remodeling of the region's political and force relations in the international level) in fact we had just apprehended a part of the truth".[16] It is clear that the fear of seeing Iraq completely remodelled, according only to the regional and international imperatives of the United States, has provoked the rise of a conspiracy theory. From the perspective of Iraqi, Shiite and Sunni nationalists, the war in Iraq will be the first step in a search to divide the territory. They fear that behind "the federalist project" lies a programmed division of Iraq into three regions, grouping the Kurds in the north, the Shiites in the south and the Sunnis in the "resistance triangle". The lack of trust between the coalition forces and Iraqi society reinforces the most alarmist visions among opposition members who find in violence the only way to bring an end to violence.

The departure of the coalition forces

For European public opinion, the departure of the coalition forces would endorse the feeling of fairness that sustained their opposition to the war. But for the European Union the viability of Iraq would be threatened if the United States withdrew. The reasoning is simple: the Iraqi guerrilla forces are growing all the time. Those in charge of the US administration increasingly express surprise and astonishment in the face of the continuation of this resistance. Whereas the war against Saddam Hussein's regime was carefully prepared, the war against the guerrillas was not. Far from weakening, the insurgent groups have increased their troops and their capacity to inflict harm. The number of armed coalition victims continues to grow (1,250 deaths and 10,000 injured). From this point of view, the gradual withdrawal of the coalition forces becomes a possible option in the short term. Beyond the costs of war, the absence of a conclusive victory leads to the fear of dealing with a never-ending guerrilla war. However, the hope that a viable Iraqi security organ could take over from the coalition forces is fading away. It is clear that the coalition forces are caught up in a war against a section of Iraqi society that is directly challenging the occupying forces, the Sunni Arabs, and another section, the Shiites, who are manipulating the political process to gain power and to demand the removal of US troops. In the long term, the US presence is not viable because it is deeply rejected.

The paradox is that departure of the US forces troubles the Iraqis. There is a very real fear that a civil war would ensue. From this perspective, there appears to be a similarity with the withdrawal of Soviet troops from Afghanistan after establishing a pro-Soviet regime in Kabul. As in Kabul, the pro-US government in Baghdad would not resist the attacks of the opposition for long.[17] The seizing of Baghdad by the insurgents would considerably weaken the war against terrorism launched by the Bush administration. For the Islamist movements, such a victory would mean that the US forces, just like the Soviets in Afghanistan, are just "paper tigers". For Europe, such an eventuality would seriously destabilize the "conservative" regimes of the Middle East. The premature withdrawal of the US troops would thus represent the worst scenario if it accompanied a civil war in Iraq. This probability would recall the withdrawal of Israeli troops from Beirut, after which Lebanon descended into the chaos of civil war and regional conflicts.

The construction of a political peace plan

For Europe, the issue is to convince the Bush administration that military force alone is useless in the face of resistance by a society. Like many other states (India in Kashmir, Israel in Palestine, Russia in Chechnya), the United States is confronted with the delusion of the military solution. These conflicts remind us of the stalemate of the armed option. The military response to the insurgency (for example, the destruction of the cities of Samara and Fallujah) is an acknowledgement of political power-lessness. The inability of the coalition forces to formulate political options flexible enough to be accepted in Iraq demonstrates a policy based on imposition by force. The construction of a peace plan requires this policy to be questioned. Such a plan should not be proof of the failure of the US project in Iraq, but would acknowledge that developments in Iraq necessarily affect the stability of the region.

From this point of view, the international community must take some share of the responsibility; it should not just accept that the occupier, the United States, is responsible. Moreover, politically and economically, there is very little hope of the situation becoming stable. The international conference at Sharm el Sheikh on 22 and 23 November 2004 highlighted a series of announcements and principles. In the first place, EU Commissioner Ferrero-Waldner recalled that "one of my first tasks is the European Union's support to the preparation of credible and truly competitive elections in Iraq. It is essential that polling ... should take place in all parts of the country".[18] The European Union has become involved (politically, economically and financially) in the Iraqi conflict. But is it possible successfully to construct a peace plan for Iraq?

First, it is necessary to bring to an end the illusory idea that Iraq is the front-line in the war against Islamist terrorism. Secondly, it is necessary to consider the nationalist sentiment in Iraq that makes any kind of foreign occupation unbearable. Finally, one needs to start from the principle that the political system should be applicable to all communities and minorities. Such a plan cannot be created in a political climate where insecurity and a state of occupation prevail. The legitimacy of the new Iraqi political institutions remains weak owing to the presence of US troops. To ensure greater legitimacy it would be wiser to leave the management of this political transfer in the hands of the United Nations. For historical and diplomatic reasons, the United States does not have available a stock of sympathy in Iraq that could allow it successfully to carry out the Iraqi transition. It would therefore be appropriate to call on the United Nations again to reach a consensus on ways of approaching the presence of foreign forces in Iraq. The Bush administration's unilateralism constitutes a serious problem for the construction of peace in Iraq.

Conclusion

Iraq illustrates the deep disagreements between the Bush administration and the European Union. The faith in achieving political change by force is in contrast to the European project of a Euro-Mediterranean Partnership made with the countries of the Mediterranean southern shore in 1995, in which economic reforms, democratization and disarmament are the negotiating objectives.[19] The past colonial experience of the Europeans means that they no longer have the superiority complex that made them colonize the Mediterranean basin during the nineteenth and twentieth centuries. For the Europeans, the Great Middle East project is an illusion. In any event, as the 2002 *Arab Human Development Report* underlines, the Arab population, estimated at 280 million in 2000, is expected to grow to 480 million by 2020, but revenues per capita will take 120 years just to double.[20] It is probable that the development of anti-Americanism and anti-Zionism comes not only from the propaganda of the Arab authoritarian states[21] but also from the situation in Iraq. In fact, there is no guarantee that, once liberated from servitude, the newly democratized Arab societies will no longer have a reason to share "the hatred" for the United States,[22] if it provokes unjustified destruction and violence.

Notes

1. *WMD in Iraq. Evidence and Implications* (Washington DC: Carnegie Endowment for International Peace, January 2004).
2. Daniel Brumberg, *Moyen-Orient: L'enjeu démocratique* (Paris: Michalon, 2003).
3. An interview with Madeleine Albright by Leslie Stahl, "60 Minutes", 12 May 1996.
4. Françoise Rigaud, "Irak: Le temps suspendu de l'embargo", *Critique internationale*, No. 11 (1998).
5. See, for example, Toby Harnden, "Americans Find Ways to Punish the French", *Daily Telegraph*, 25 April 2003.
6. Philip H. Gordon, *Iraq: The Transatlantic Debate*, Occasional Papers No. 39 (Paris: European Union Institute for Security Studies, December 2002), p. 16.
7. Commission of the European Communities, "Communication from the Commission to the Council and the European Parliament: The Madrid Conference on Reconstruction in Iraq, 24 October 2003", COM (2003) 575, Brussels, 1 October 2003, ⟨http://europa.eu.int/comm/external_relations/iraq/intro/com03_575en.pdf⟩ (accessed 2 February 2006).
8. "European Union Factsheet: EU Support for Iraq", June 2005, ⟨http://ue.eu.int/uedocs/cmsUpload/Factsheet-Iraq-June2005.pdf⟩.
9. Coalition Provisional Authority, ⟨http://www.cpa-iraq.org/⟩.
10. Iraqi Interim Government, ⟨http://www.iraqigovernment.org/reconstruction.htm⟩.
11. See "100 Days of Progress in Iraq", ⟨www.whitehouse.gov/infocus/iraq/part5.html⟩.
12. The unemployment rate varies from 25 per cent to 50 per cent of the active population

depending on the estimate ("Reconstructing Iraq", Middle East Report No. 30, International Crisis Group, Brussels, 2 September 2004).

13. Samir Haddad and Mazin Ghazi, "An Inventory of Iraqi Resistance Groups: Who Kills Hostages in Iraq?", *Al Zawra* (Baghdad), 19 September 2004, ⟨http://www.freeArabvoice.org⟩.

14. Scott Ritter, "A Weapons Inspector Saw 'Blueprints' for Monday's Insurgency", *Christian Science Monitor*, 10 November 2003.

15. Nabil Mohamed Salim, lecture at CEI-Sciences-Po, Paris, June 2005.

16. Ibid.

17. "Given their extreme frailty, Iraqi institutions would probably not survive a precipitous disengagement, handing the insurgents a significant victory" ("What Can the U.S. Do in Iraq?", Middle East Report No. 34, International Crisis Group, Brussels, 22 December 2004).

18. Cited in "Sharm el Sheikh: The EU Offers Iraq Support and Partnership", 22 November 2004, at ⟨http://www.delsyr.cec.eu.int/en/whatsnew/detail.asp?id=91⟩ (accessed 3 May 2006).

19. As Javier Solana emphasizes: "In no way does this new Union responsibility move it away from the original European project based on the values of peace, law, justice and democracy. My conviction is entirely the opposite: it is these very values that the Union embodies and seeks to promote in its international action, whether in the Balkans, in the Middle East, in Africa, or with respect to Iraq. Develop a greater degree of international justice and respect for law, build patiently the minimum conditions for good governance and democracy, favour negotiation rather than conflict, but agree to intervene and coerce when coercion becomes necessary: these are the strategic principles on which the construction of the ESPD was founded five years ago" (*EU Security and Defense Policy: The First Five Years (1999–2004)*, Paris: EU Institute for Security Studies, 2004, p. 10).

20. *Arab Human Development Report 2002: Creating Opportunities for Future Generations*, United Nations Development Programme, 2003, ⟨http://hdr.undp.org/reports/detail_reports.cfm?view=600⟩.

21. Anthony H. Cordesman, "The Bush Administration has touched upon all these issues in its call for democracy in the Arab world, but the end result has been slogans rather than substance ... The end result is that the Administration's efforts have generally appeared in the region to be calls for regime change favourable to the US, rather than support for practical reform" ("The Transatlantic Alliance: Is 2004 the Year of the Greater Middle East?", Center for Strategic and International Studies, Washington, DC, 12 January 2004, ⟨http://www.csis.org/index.php?option=com_csis_pubs&task=view&id=1363⟩, accessed 2 May 2006).

22. "In a matter of only a few years, Palestine will be one of two new Arab democratic states. The other neonatal Arab democracy will be Iraq. These unthinkable developments will revolutionize the power dynamic in the Middle East, powerfully adding to the effects of the liberation of Afghanistan to force Arab and Islamic regimes to increasingly allow democratic reforms. A majority of Arabs will come to see America as the essential ally in progressing liberty in their own lands" (Michael Kelly, *Washington Post*, 26 June 2002; see also "Democracy Mirage in the Middle East", Carnegie Endowment for International Peace, Washington DC, October 2002).

22

Quicksand? The United Nations in Iraq, 2001–2005

David M. Malone and James Cockayne

Introduction

In Chapter 2 of this volume, we described five phases of UN peace operations in Iraq in the period 1980–2001. In this chapter, we aim to describe the role of the United Nations in addressing a series of crises affecting Iraq since 2001, and to reflect on their implications for the United Nations. Given limitations of space and not wishing to tax the patience of readers well acquainted with recent news, we compress many of these developments. Instead, our narrative presents a broad overview of the United Nations' role in Iraq in four periods: from 2001 until the coalition invasion on 20 March 2003; from invasion to the bombing of the UN headquarters in Baghdad; the implications of that bombing; and the period since. Finally, we examine the implications of these events for the United Nations' future role in promoting world order.

11 September 2001 to 20 March 2003: The United Nations as one coalition among many?

The terrorist attacks on American soil of 11 September 2001 radically altered the strategic calculus perceived by decision makers in the United States. All too suddenly, the strategy of containment underpinning the inspections-plus-sanctions regime imposed on Iraq after the 1991 Gulf war appeared to many of them as inadequate. The risk of proliferation of weapons of mass destruction (WMD) from Saddam Hussein's Ba'athist regime to terrorists – or even a closer strategic partnership between the two groups – became a point of obsession for a number of policy makers in an atmosphere of national apprehension.[1] Against this backdrop, having first addressed the immediate threat of al-Qaeda and its host Taliban regime in Afghanistan, the United States, ultimately without the authorization of the Security Council, led a new push for the disarmament of Iraq and the overthrow of Saddam Hussein, precipitating a crisis for UN norms and institutions.

In the first half of 2001, the Security Council's inspections-plus-sanctions approach instituted by Resolution 687 was in some disarray. After French support shifted between 1996 and 1998 away from the aggressive US–UK approach to implementing the resolution towards the more conciliatory Russian and Chinese approach, both the inspections and sanctions regimes were gradually rolled back. The procedures of the sanctions regime had slowly been reformed to allow for greater oil export revenues and consequently more humanitarian imports. Sanctions fatigue slowly turned to sanctions defeatism.[2] Inspections had been suspended following Operation Desert Fox in December 1998. By 2001, patience with the inspections-plus-sanctions approach was wearing thin, both in capitals and amongst democratic electors. Deep divisions amongst the permanent five members of the Security Council (the P-5) remained. Whereas, for a combination of economic, political and humanitarian reasons, the Russians, French and Chinese preferred to mitigate sanctions and move away from the intrusive inspections-plus-sanctions regulatory approach back to a more traditional model of inspections as a tool for containment, the United States and the United Kingdom still aimed for permanent Iraqi disarmament.

Slowly, a common ground emerged between these divergent approaches, aiming at relaxing sanctions while bringing further pressure to bear on Saddam to cooperate with weapons inspectors. But Saddam remained defiant, convinced perhaps that the United States and the United Kingdom would never lift sanctions while he was in power, no matter what he revealed or how he limited his military capacity, and sensing, perhaps, the deepening divisions between the members of the P-5.[3] After 11 September 2001, the United States and the United Kingdom seemed intent on removing Hussein from power, once and for all.[4] Within the Bush administration, there was a determination not to allow the terrorist threat represented by al-Qaeda to come together with the WMD threat, which, in US eyes, Saddam Hussein had come to symbolize. The US–UK approach to inspections became more aggressive. By November 2002, they had forged agreement amongst the P-5 to step up inspections, giving the inspections-plus-sanctions approach one final chance.

In Resolution 1441 of 8 November 2002, the Security Council decided that Iraq had been and remained in "material breach" of its disarmament obligations, and gave it one "final opportunity" to comply with those obligations, failing which it would face "serious consequences". Resolution 1441 required Iraq not only to agree to allow the inspections of the UN Monitoring, Verification and Inspection Commission (UNMOVIC) to resume, but also to provide a complete and final disclosure of WMD activities. The Bush administration congratulated itself for what it considered a neat trap: if Hussein admitted possessing WMD, he was acknowledging a violation of UN resolutions; if he did not, he would be deceiving the world, and again violating those resolutions.[5] Either way, the United Nations would have delivered the United States the legitimacy it sought for armed intervention. (That, of course, assumed that Saddam Hussein did have WMD. Ultimately, it was this misreading that hoist the United States by its own non-existent petard.[6])

At first, the apparent consensus embodied in Resolution 1441's creatively ambiguous language of "material breach" and "serious consequences" held. Hussein delivered a document purporting to be a "full disclosure" on time, by 7 December 2002, but Hans Blix, the UNMOVIC head, reported on 27 January 2003 that "Iraq appears not to have come to a genuine acceptance, not even today, of the disarmament that was demanded of it".[7] In response, Iraq increased cooperation – and it was here that the veneer of P-5 unity began to dissolve. France, Russia and China pointed to limited UNMOVIC evidence as indicating the need for further inspections, whereas the United States, and to a lesser extent the United Kingdom, pointed to Iraqi behaviour, rather than specific evidence, as the basis for moving from inspections to enforcement.[8] US Secretary of State Colin Powell presented a detailed dossier of evidence of Iraqi deception to the Security Council on 5 February 2003[9] but when, on 14 February, Blix not only cast doubt on some of Powell's claims but also claimed that Iraq had decided to cooperate with inspectors the United States derided the prospects of successful inspections.

Embarrassingly for the United States and the United Kingdom, the United Nations' agencies in UNMOVIC and the International Atomic Energy Agency (IAEA) began to produce tentative evidence of Western intelligence failures, visiting sites identified by the United States and the United Kingdom without finding anything of substance.[10] The IAEA declared that Iraq was not in the process of reconstituting its nuclear programme.[11] The United States began to disagree openly with some of the tactics adopted by the veteran Swedish lawyer-diplomat Hans Blix, who had deliberately kept a greater distance from Western intelligence agencies than had his predecessor at the UN Special Commission (UNSCOM), Richard Butler.[12] Despite – or perhaps even because of – this increasing gap between what the United Nations was producing (doubt) and what the United States had sought from it (legitimacy), the United

States push to war accelerated. UK Prime Minister Tony Blair pressed hard for a second UN resolution[13] but, when it became clear that a vote would only expose further the already public P-5 rift and that the votes required to carry a second resolution were in doubt, the United States and the United Kingdom acted on Bush's September 2002 threat to the General Assembly. Choosing to act outside the Council, the United States and the United Kingdom unilaterally invaded Iraq on 20 March 2003.

This seemed to signal a new approach by the United States, looking to the United Nations as just one potential source of legitimacy and support, one coalition among many. The unique features of UN legitimacy, including its alignment with international legality, were no doubt understood; but in the end, if the United Nations did not offer the path of least resistance for the achievement of US foreign policy goals, the United States would dispense with it. Even during the drama, WMD appeared to many to represent only a convenient spin for selling a decision to go to war that – as appeared later to be confirmed[14] – had already been made in Washington. The United Nations seemed to be only a partner of convenience to the United States: the United States saw the existing UN resolutions as offering a ready-made *casus belli* linking Iraq with the threat of WMD proliferation, and going to the United Nations helped to keep the United States' key ally, the United Kingdom, on board. It began to appear that, without these considerations, the United States would not have considered the United Nations as the framework for assembling a coalition. Bush's speech to the General Assembly on 12 September 2002,[15] warning the United Nations of an imminent choice between supporting the United States or being deemed irrelevant, had not been idle talk: when the UN Security Council did not, ultimately, offer the United States the legitimacy it had hoped for, it had little to offer the United States, which chose rather to act outside the UN framework.

Lawrence Freedman has characterized the invasion of Iraq as "something of an experiment" by the Western powers, using a pre-emptive strategy rather than a responsive one.[16] But it was equally an experiment in US–UN relations, in which the United States tested whether UN legitimacy would offer the path of least resistance to the achievement of its foreign policy goals. Instead, it offered significant resistance, and so, in the end, was jettisoned from US plans.

20 March 2003 to 19 August 2003: The United Nations sidelined

The US-led invasion of Iraq, which highlighted the willingness on the part of the United States to bypass the United Nations, brought to a head two growing sources of criticism of the United Nations. One critique held that the failure of the United Nations' inspections-plus-sanctions approach to Iraq proved the United Nations' ineffectiveness and growing irrelevance. Another held, almost conversely, that it was the United Nations' failure to contain the United States, rather than Iraq, that proved its ineffectiveness and irrelevance. So serious was this crisis of legitimacy that the Secretary-General decided to establish a High-level Panel on Threats, Challenges and Change, which reported in December 2004, presenting member states with a number of ideas and options for more effective UN action against global threats, including suggestions for institutional reform. As we go to print, the ultimate outcome of these creative recommendations remains in doubt, with the September 2005 World Summit having balked at clearly ruling in – or out – many of the key reforms countenanced, with the notable exception of accepting the creation of a Peace-Building Commission to coordinate post-conflict recovery policy.

For most of 2003, the United Nations was largely sidelined on security issues in Iraq. In early April, Secretary-General Kofi Annan appointed Rafeeuddin Ahmed – a low-key, senior Pakistani UN official with development experience and admired for his wisdom – as his Special Adviser to coordinate thinking on the role the United Nations could play in post-conflict Iraq. This was highly controversial, because any significant UN presence could arguably be seen as retrospectively legitimating the coalition invasion. However, at a senior level the majority UN view was that, regardless of the legality of the coalition action, the United Nations could not shirk its humanitarian and peacebuilding vocations in Iraq. The coalition, however, seemed uninterested in any significant UN role beyond humanitarian assistance. A sensitive issue was the role the United Nations could play in political transitions in Iraq, not least respecting the end of coalition authority and military occupation. On 22 May 2003, the Security Council adopted Resolution 1483, which legitimized the administrative role of the Coalition Provisional Authority (CPA), while requesting the appointment by the Secretary-General of a Special Representative to Iraq (SRSG). The SRSG was mandated to coordinate action in the areas of humanitarian relief, reconstruction, infrastructure rehabilitation, legal and judicial reforms, human rights and the return of refugees, and also to assist with civilian police.[17] Additionally, the resolution authorized the CPA, "working with" the SRSG, to appoint an interim Iraqi administration.[18]

Annan appointed Sergio Vieira de Mello, the charismatic former head of the United Nations' post-conflict mission in East Timor (UNTAET) to the key post of SRSG, taking him away from his responsibilities as UN High Commissioner for Human Rights for a projected four months.

Soon after de Mello's arrival in Baghdad, it became clear that the United States would allow him only a very limited role in the development of a permanent Iraqi constitution, the holding of elections and the establishment of a government (thus rejecting a template for UN involvement developed in East Timor and applied in Afghanistan). The United Nations was therefore to be confined almost exclusively to a technical role, with the United States continuing to call the shots. This was not to be a UN peace operation in any traditional sense.

In this uncertain atmosphere, Annan played a delicate diplomatic game, carefully preparing the ground so that the United Nations would have the support it needed in the capitals that mattered to move into action on a broader footing when the time was right (clearly not yet). He envisaged a broad, multidisciplinary assistance operation, going even further than past peace operations by including the World Bank and the International Monetary Fund from the outset. In a report to the Security Council on 17 July 2003, he set out a range of tasks that the United Nations might undertake in Iraq in relation to the constitutional process, judicial and legal reform, police training, the demobilization and reintegration of former military forces, public administration, economic reconstruction and sustainable development, and technical assistance and advisory services to Iraqi ministries.[19] These activities were to be discharged by a UN Assistance Mission for Iraq (UNAMI), totalling around 300 local and international staff. At the same time, Annan brought pressure to bear on the coalition to lay out a clear timetable for the withdrawal of occupying forces. Given the complex security situation in Iraq, it was widely thought that any such withdrawal would ideally be followed by the deployment of a significant UN security operation (if feasible in terms of Iraqi sensitivities). Whether such a mission may one day be mandated remains an open question today.

19 August 2003: The United Nations' 9/11

On 19 August 2003, the United Nations suffered the largest loss of life of its civilian employees in its history. A massive truck-bomb was detonated at the corner of the UNAMI headquarters in Baghdad, directly under de Mello's office, killing him and 21 others and wounding 150 more. The terrorist attack shocked the UN community and cast doubt over the security of its remaining staff in Iraq. After a second attack within a month left 20 injured, and with the International Red Cross headquarters in Baghdad soon after being destroyed by a bomb attack, Annan radically downsized the UN presence.[20] An independent inquiry condemned what it described as a failure to provide adequate security to UN staff in Iraq.[21]

The bombing made clear that the United Nations' existing security management structures were woefully inadequate and would need radical surgery if the United Nations was to continue to play its key role within some of the world's hottest spots in an age of transnational terrorism.

Three key changes resulted from this report. First, in a much-publicized move, Annan took strong disciplinary measures against senior UN staff.[22] Second, in an important but largely unheralded move away from traditional doctrine, the United Nations countenanced engaging a private firm to provide security for its global operations.[23] Third, in Resolution 1546, adopted in early June 2004, the Security Council for the first time supported the creation of a distinct component within a UN-authorized multinational force devoted specifically to UN security.[24]

The attacks on UN staff made clear two other aspects of the new operational environment. First, the attacks signalled that the United Nations' traditional image of impartiality was once again under attack, this time from Islamic fundamentalists who saw the United Nations as a stooge of Western interests. The United Nations had long been a target of violence in states in which it operated. The United Nations had also learned, in Bosnia and Rwanda, that impartiality cannot be equated with moral equivalence among the parties to a conflict or with unwillingness to intervene to prevent atrocities.[25] Iraq cruelly reminded the United Nations that some interventions would make even its most senior officials the target of violence.[26] Second, the attacks drove home that terrorism posed a fundamental threat not only to the United States but also to the United Nations.[27] The diffuse and asymmetric nature of terrorism calls for a different kind of international policing, with a greater focus on cooperative regulation. As a consequence, some states are increasingly pushing to use the Chapter VII powers of the Security Council not as the basis for UN peacekeeping but as the basis for global legislation and regulation of terrorism. This regulatory style emerged first in the 1990s with the establishment of the ad hoc criminal tribunals and the Oil-for-Food programme in Iraq, but it has moved to centre-stage with the establishment and operation of the Counter-Terrorism Committee under Resolution 1373 and with the criminalization of activities resulting in the proliferation of weapons of mass destruction (WMD) under Resolution 1540.[28] Thus, in the future, UN peacekeeping may have to compete for scarce resources with other forms of UN security regulation.

Terrorism also offers an entirely new set of parameters for UN peace operations, as the Iraq experience makes clear.[29] It offers a new justification for UN intervention, not only as a response to state failure but also as a measure to prevent state failure lest it provide the conditions for the incubation of transnational terrorism. The rise of transnational terrorism may also affect the strategies of state-building adopted by the United Nations, placing a premium on the short-term establishment of a strong state that can combat terrorism, with the transition to democratic statehood remaining a longer-term goal.[30] That inevitably risks undermining long-held goals relating to the promotion of the rule of law in state-building, as we have seen with the West's frequent support for warlords in post-Taliban Afghanistan.[31] In Iraq, US support for the CIA-backed strongman Allawi for a time left questions hanging over the commitment of the central Iraqi authorities to the rule of law country-wide.

One dangerous outgrowth of the 19 August 2003 bombing was arguably an overreaction among UN staff that has risked paralysing the United Nations' capacity to respond meaningfully to those Iraqi needs that the organization might best be placed to address. Grief and rage among UN staff over the carnage ran deep. Internal criticism of Secretary-General Kofi Annan and his senior staff for allowing a UN deployment to Baghdad in dangerous circumstances grew. UN staff sought sympathy and expressed resentment at Annan's attempts to forge a bridge between the coalition occupiers and the rest of the international community in support of Iraqi needs. Increasingly, it seemed to be Annan's political judgement, not the United Nations' security mistakes, that some staff were targeting. Over time, this staff discontent led to perverse results. The United Nations' new representative in Baghdad, Ashraf Jehangir Qazi, insisted in mid-2004 that security is "not only the first consideration, it is the first priority, the second priority and the third priority" for his Baghdad mission.[32] But if UN staff security is the United Nations' only significant priority and if Annan's margin for diplomatic and operational manoeuvre is to be constrained by staff challenges to his judgement, the United Nations will simply not be able to play much of a role in Iraq, or indeed in any of the theatres of war where it is most needed.[33]

After 19 August 2003: The United Nations as escape route?

The attacks on the United Nations in Iraq in August and September 2003 were by no means isolated; they were part of a much wider deterioration in security. The coalition appeared at times to drift from crisis to crisis, unable to meet the most basic security needs of Iraq's citizens and increasingly abandoning its vaunted economic reconstruction objectives.[34] An October 2003 resolution of the Security Council reaffirmed the "vital role" of the United Nations in humanitarian relief, reconstruction, development and the transition to representative government, but did not significantly broaden its mandate beyond calling on the United Nations to support the constitutional drafting processes established by the Iraqi Governing Council.[35] The resolution also authorized the presence of a multinational security force in Iraq under US command, indicating that the United Nations would not take over security obligations in post-conflict Iraq any time soon. By November, however, the situation had become so dire for the US-led coalition that the Bush administration was once again ready to contemplate a significant UN role in Iraq. Annan argued that more time was needed for the security situation to be assessed and for US plans to become clear. He waited until 10 December to name a replacement for de Mello, even then naming only an Acting SRSG.

Coalition forces captured Saddam Hussein on 14 December 2003. Sensing that the moment provided "an opportunity for a new beginning in the vital task of helping Iraqis take control of their destiny", Annan pressed for the Security Council to clarify the United Nations' future role in Iraq.[36] By mid-January 2004, consensus emerged that the United Nations should play an advisory role on the timing and organization of elections. The coalition and Iraqi authorities were pushing for elections before 30 June 2004, when the coalition aimed to "hand over" sovereignty to Iraqis, well before the US presidential elections in November 2004. On 3 February, Annan was invited to the White House, a sign of how far the Bush administration's earlier antipathy to the United Nations had been reversed. Now, it seemed to look to the United Nations as its escape route from the quicksand of Iraq.

By 7 February 2004 a UN team led by the Secretary-General's Special Adviser – Lakhdar Brahimi, a former Algerian diplomat and chief architect of the eponymous 2000 Report on peace operations – had arrived in Iraq to discuss with the Iraqis and the coalition possible ways forward towards representative government, including the possibility of elections before the end of June 2004. The team also included the head of the United Nations' Electoral Assistance Unit, Carina Perelli, and two members of her staff. By the end of February 2004, Brahimi had brokered an understanding over the timing of elections: there was broad agreement that they could not safely and properly be conducted before 30 June 2004. Instead, the United Nations would work with coalition and Iraqi authorities to generate a mechanism for interim government until elections could be held, possibly before the end of 2004 if security conditions permitted (these were later scheduled for January 2005, a highly optimistic target given the deteriorating security situation throughout 2004). On 19 March, the anniversary of the invasion, the Secretary-General decided to dispatch Brahimi to Baghdad again, in response to written requests for assistance by the president of the Iraqi Governing Council and the CPA administrator, to help form an interim government.[37] Brahimi briefly appeared to have been ordained king maker; he had managed to do what the United States could not, engaging with Iraqi society to such an extent that the United States had come to rely on him to "cultivate legitimacy for a step-by-step political process".[38] But selection of the Iraqi government was marked by a degree of controversy, when the US-backed Iraqi Governing Council nominated one from their ranks, a former CIA source, Ayad Allawi, as prime minister. The broader government and cabinet bore the stamp of Brahimi's consultative diplomacy, with posts carefully allotted to the main religious and ethnic groups, but the impression remained that the United States had imposed Allawi and that the United Nations had been traduced.[39]

Just one indication of the extent of coalition policy incoherence was the disconnect between the effort put into promulgating a Transitional Administrative Law, signed into force by CPA Administrator Paul Bremer on 8 March 2004 and containing many minority protections, and the decision only months later to allow this forward-looking text to lapse at the time of the hand-over to Iraqi sovereignty in deference to Ayatollah Sistani's reservations over a text that could qualify Shiite dominance of Iraqi politics in the future.[40]

By mid-2004, the coalition was rocked by scandals over prisoner abuse, which undermined its claims to the moral high ground. In a sign of how far rhetoric and reality had become divorced, given the United Nations' limited role on the ground, on 8 June 2004 the UN Security Council adopted Resolution 1546 establishing a multinational force to provide security in Iraq, at the request of the Interim Government of Iraq, and giving the United Nations a "leading and vital role" – as the US Permanent Representative to the United Nations and future ambassador to Iraq, John Negroponte, described it – in the transition to democracy.[41] On 12 July, Annan named the Pakistani ambassador to Washington, Ashraf Jehangir Qazi, as his Special Representative for Iraq, but it was not clear what significant role, if any, he would play.

Events had come almost full circle. Like his predecessor Waldheim in 1980, Annan now was confined to using his good offices to broker an accommodation among recalcitrant belligerents, without much geo-strategic back-up from a still deeply divided Security Council. It is remarkable, though, to consider how different these two "good offices" processes have been, and how radically different are the visions of the United Nations' role in maintaining world order that they reflect. Where Waldheim and his successor used their good offices to separate two warring states, Annan's good offices addressed a complex array of challenges at the intersection of social, political, economic and security rehabilitation tasks in Iraq. The United Nations' role in underpinning world order has, analogously, shifted from neutral umpire between warring states to something much more complex. Where Waldheim was confronted by a Security Council split by bipolarity, Annan was confronted by a Council rent by unipolarity. In the next section, we reflect on some possible broader implications of the UN role in Iraq.

What Next?

Over almost a quarter of a century, the United Nations has slid deeper and deeper into the quicksand of Iraq, particularly as a result of its joyless embrace with the United States since the end of the Cold War. By 2003 the depth of the crisis had become clear, throwing the role of the United Nations in maintaining world order starkly into question. Although the flexibility and creative potential of the Secretary-General's good offices were once again demonstrated to be considerable, the Security Council revealed itself prone to both ambiguous (Resolution 1441) and unambiguous but unhelpful (Resolution 1546) compromises that did little to paper over deep splits within the body, instead handing unachievable tasks to the Secretariat. Council pronouncements, often initiated by the occupying powers and weakly resisted at the margins by some other Council members, increasingly smacked of a flight from reality as the situation within Iraq continued to deteriorate.

Nevertheless, recent years of often adverse developments on Iraq suggest possible new directions for the United Nations in the security sphere in years ahead. This final section of the chapter looks at the different challenges confronting the United Nations and speculates on possible new directions for the United Nations, centred on its (somewhat tattered) global legitimacy and its (frequently impressive) technical expertise, capitalizing on its network of global regulatory mechanisms and its pivotal, if often unsuccessful, role in state-building. Above all, the reforms must aim to improve the universality of the UN framework and restore it to its central position as a forum for the peaceful resolution of normative differences.

The politics of state-building

Under any scenario, a meaningful UN re-engagement with Iraq will be complex and fraught with normative and operational risk. The impetus to capitalize on the United Nations' experience in areas such as security sector reform and justice sector reform will be enormous; but so, too, will the complexity of the task in Iraq. Although the United Nations has had a limited involvement (with mixed success) in rehabilitating these sectors in failed states, it has never been confronted with the challenges of reforming the massive security apparatus of a police state in a manner consistent with democratization, while, at the same time, seeing off terrorist and ethnic threats to the existence of the state itself against a backdrop of historically entrenched and widespread state corruption.

Perhaps most striking in 2004 was how openly the UN Secretariat became involved with the process of political reconstruction in Iraq. Whereas the Secretariat and subsidiary organs of the Council managed the complex regulatory roles of inspections and sanctions prior to the 2003 crisis, the Secretariat's role after the crisis was one of political brokerage (even the search for Iraqi WMD was taken out of UN hands). Since the end of the Cold War, UN peace operations have increasingly been mandated in support of internal political processes, the organization of elections and the defence of democracy, for example in Haiti, Cambodia, El Salvador, Mozambique, Kosovo, East Timor and Afghanistan.[42] Democracy has become both a reason for intervention and an exit strategy: the holding of free and fair national elections, perhaps after a longer democratic process of constitutional reform, marks one of the few clearly agreed indicators of performance success in complex state-building peace operations.

The evolutionary nature of this change has robbed it of media coverage, although some acute observers in the academic community have advanced helpful analysis, notably Elizabeth Cousens and Karin Wermester, who argue – rightly in our view, though not uncontroversially – that the type of peacebuilding in which the United Nations engages is much more political in nature than are most developmental programmes or narrowly defined peacekeeping efforts.[43] Peacebuilding now overlaps with state-building, an inherently political exercise that requires some groups to be favoured over others and inevitably creates division and perhaps even conflict.[44] Brahimi's role in Iraq in the first half of 2004 makes clear that the United Nations cannot duck the difficult choices involved.

In looking to the future – even the immediate future of the United Nations in Iraq – it is now more widely understood that the process of state-building cannot be narrowly equated with the holding of elections. Electoral assistance – like other specialized programmes run by the UN Secretariat and UN agencies[45] – has emerged as one of the key competencies of the United Nations, as the 200 or so related requests for UN involvement received by the United Nations during the 1990s indicate. At the same time, the reliance on representative democracy carries terrible risks, most clearly illustrated in East Timor in 1999. And the Security Council today understands that one election says little about the sustainability of democracy. The United Nations' expertise in this field has been on display in the rapid and efficient work of Carina Perelli and her staff in Iraq in 2004, although differences in judgement emerged between her ground-up view and the politically influenced top-down view on offer in New York, where the risks of UN involvement in a bungled exercise weighed more heavily. Her technical report of February 2004[46] reflected recognition of the complexity of timing elections in post-conflict peace operations: held too early after an internal conflict, they may be hijacked by extremists; held too late, and they may either never be held at all or serve simply to consolidate the hold on power of those with initial access to government levers. The January 2005 elections in Iraq met with mixed success: although 58 per cent of the electorate voted, the elections were marred by a Sunni boycott, setting the stage for a slow slide into sectarianism that impeded the search for constitutional consensus thereafter.[47] Elections, this experience suggested, were necessary but not sufficient for the emergence of genuine democracy; in addition, a genuine social contract was needed, the result of deliberately political state-building.

A political conception of state-building requires above all strategic planning, especially to marry the sometimes contradictory objectives of peacebuilding and state-building. Peacebuilding may require power-sharing; but power-sharing may prevent democratic state-building. Peacebuilding may mean incentivizing a turn away from violence and an acceptance of the status quo (as in Afghanistan, to a degree); but that status quo may itself perpetuate a democratic deficit. Conversely, an early emphasis on democratic state-building may inflame unresolved social tensions. In Iraq, for example, the creation by the coalition of an Interim Governing Council formed by representatives allotted by ethnic and religious quotas – of Shiites, Sunnis and Kurds – may have served to "entrench and radicalize" existing ethnic and religious identities and tensions.[48] The coalition seems to have underestimated the challenge of calibrating these risks through its policies. The United Nations, with its experience of many post-conflict situations, will be required to do better.

If anything, the difficulties faced by the coalition in post-war Iraq have only highlighted that the United Nations is, to adapt a phrase used by former US Secretary of State Madeleine Albright, the "indispensable organization" for the political management of international crises involving the interests of several powers (internal and external, with the influence of neighbouring countries being a complicating factor in much peacebuilding).[49] But the United Nations' learning curve as "virtual trustee" has been steep.[50] The policy content of virtual trusteeship and state-building would benefit from the creation of a strategic planning capability within the United Nations. Too often, peace operations arise as an ad hoc response by the Security Council to a situation spiralling out of control.[51]

To be successful, state-building must address the connections between conflict prevention and development, between human rights and security.[52] It requires the involvement of actors whose mandate has traditionally been perceived as falling outside that of "peace operations": the World Bank, the UN Development Programme (UNDP), even the World Health Organization. It requires a more deliberate, whole-of-organization approach, with the Secretary-General and the Security Council providing leadership (and coordination). The new Peace-Building Commission – one of the few unambiguously positive products of the September 2005 World Summit – will offer opportunities for realizing just such an approach, although its capacity will be limited as a result of member states' refusal to grant it a centralized strategic planning capacity.

Normative challenges: Rethinking sovereignty

Structural reforms to the United Nations must adapt it to a changed world order and will require reinterpretation of traditional norms such as sovereignty. Although sovereignty is still the lingua franca of UN diplomatic discourse, the degree of intrusiveness the Security Council was prepared to mandate throughout the 1990s – particularly in Iraq – was striking, responding to a sharp redefinition in practice of what constitutes a threat to international peace and security.

The growing gap between de jure and de facto sovereignty fuels perceptions of a North/South divide in world politics. It serves to intensify concern that currently fashionable discourses on human rights and humanitarianism serve as so many Trojan horses for the political interests of the North. The United Nations' increased humanitarian focus is, for the South, a two-edged sword: on the one hand, it offers a basis for arguing that the North should focus its resources as much on dealing with the threats of poverty, deprivation and disease as on terrorism and the proliferation of weapons of mass destruction; on the other, it offers the North a platform to argue for greater intervention in Southern countries where they fail to guarantee their citizens' human security. Accordingly, when the Brahimi Report on peace operations recommended in 2000 the creation of a new information and strategic analysis unit to enhance conflict prevention activities, representatives of the South worried about the potential intrusiveness of improved UN information management. (In contrast, the North worried about financial, personnel and materiel overcommitment in the peacekeeping field.) Similarly, contemporary calls for a revival of the Trusteeship Council to deal with situations where the United Nations is called upon to act as a proxy administration meet with concerns from the South about the resurrection of Northern colonialist tendencies, and with worries in the North about open-ended financial and military commitments. Many saw the Iraq confrontation as a clash of civilizations; but, even more than that, it is about the emerging confrontation between two sets of security needs, between the North – with its justified fear of terrorist assault on its prosperity and political stability – and the South – with its justified fear of poverty, deprivation and disease.

Increasingly, sovereignty is coming to be seen not just as a source of rights but also as a source of duties to provide security to individuals and groups within society – a "responsibility to protect". This idea was born from the Canadian-inspired International Commission on Intervention and State Sovereignty (ICISS) in December 2001.[53] However, taking the responsibility to protect seriously would have consequences not only for states but also for the United Nations, which has recently been sidelined at the operational level by the existence of "coalitions of the willing". The United Nations' partial commitment to this responsibility in the Outcome document of the September 2005 World Summit[54] raised the rhetorical stakes considerably; yet the test will come when troops must be committed. Serious enforcement action now occurs only where there is a militarily capable country or an adequate coalition of countries willing to make available the necessary lift, troops, finance, political capital and military hardware.[55] Countries working together within "Groups of Friends", often spanning the North/South divide, can serve to build support at the United Nations for intervention in specific instances.[56] They can also help avoid the institutionalization of normative differences such as those just discussed. Whether the emerging approach, which leans more heavily on front-line action by regional organizations rather than by the United Nations itself (for example, the Security Council's response to the crisis in Darfur in 2004), represents a flight from responsibility rather than a sensible division of labour remains an open question.

The structural challenge of unipolarity

Perhaps the greatest imponderable in the future of UN action in Iraq, and more generally in security issues, is how US–UN relations will develop. The unipolarity produced by US pre-eminence poses a fundamental challenge to the United Nations, particularly the Security Council. But if Iraq taught the United States and the United Nations anything, it must surely be the extent to which they need each other. Those who, like Michael J. Glennon, pre-emptively declared the demise of the Security Council,[57] have made the same mistake as the Bush administration: they underestimate the long-term costs of acting outside the Council and the framework of law.[58] But the clash of visions for the United Nations' role inherent in speeches by US President George W. Bush and UN Secretary-General Annan before the UN General Assembly on 21 September 2004 suggests continuing trouble in Bush's second term, however much the

United States may need the United Nations instrumentally.[59] The Dayton Accord (on Bosnia) of 1995, brokered by Washington, was a turning-point in UN affairs, consecrating the United States as "the supreme power", according to one Security Council ambassador in early 1996.[60] The challenge for the Security Council in the future will remain to engage the United States on the major security challenges without acquiescing in dangerous initiatives; to "have the courage to disagree with the USA when it is wrong and the maturity to agree with it when it is right".[61] It must "keep intact its integrity, while improving its effectiveness".[62] The Security Council must assert its indispensability rather than becoming just one coalition among many available to the United States.

Iraq suggests the continuing risk for the Council that Washington conceives the United Nations' role, at best, as one of long-term peacebuilding following short and sharp US- or Western-led military interventions (the latter whether mandated by the Council or not). The United Nations would be confined to "picking up the pieces", as we saw in 2004 in Haiti and Afghanistan, which would undermine the legitimacy – and consequently the effectiveness – that the United Nations retains in the security sphere.

Performance challenges

UN effectiveness is more important to its future than is often thought on the East River. Although much attention among UN delegates has focused on Security Council and other structural reforms to improve perceptions of UN legitimacy, the "performance legitimacy" described by Ramesh Thakur as deriving from good results in the field will be at least equally vital to enhancing the United Nations' standing with élite and public opinion around the world.[63] As we have seen, in some areas the United Nations is well positioned to engage in complex administrative and regulatory tasks, from electoral assistance through to the specialized programmes of the World Food Programme, UNICEF and the UNDP. UNSCOM and UNMOVIC also suggest that the United Nations can – given the right political support – make such a regulatory approach work in the security field. But the Oil-for-Food programme and the sanctions experience suggest there are also serious risks involved.

The growing operational role of regional organizations in international security, together with new legislative and regulatory roles of the Security Council, may point to a new phase in UN peace operations that, in the best of circumstances, might take shape in the sands of Iraq. From what is already discernible of this new model, the United Nations might come to play the role of independent arbiter and global security regulator at the apex of a pyramid of regional, local, state and even civil society regulatory mechanisms.[64] This pyramidal structure might be governed by a principle of subsidiarity, with successively higher layers taking up the responsibility to protect as the layer below fails or is ill suited to the task. At the same time, it will see the UN Security Council, at the apex of the pyramid, projecting, monitoring and, where necessary, enforcing global security regulation standards.

Where lower layers of the security apparatus fail or are unavailable (for example in much of Asia), this approach would continue to dictate UN operational leadership in the provision of humanitarian assistance or even virtual trusteeship. (The international community's combination of active and passive approaches to northern Iraq since 1991 merits some reflection from this perspective.) Elsewhere, the United Nations' global enforcement strategy may take on a more administrative and bureaucratic sheen, inspired by the inspections-plus-sanctions regime in Iraq in the 1990s, although the difficulties confronted by that project must sound a warning of the need for adequate resourcing and staffing. In yet other circumstances, the United Nations' role could simply be one of advice, support and advocacy, working in partnership with governments to improve the lives of their citizens. This is a role for which the UN Development Programme, working in partnership with other organizations and sometimes under the political leadership of the Secretary-General, seems well suited.

The United Nations' experience in post-war Iraq makes clear that expectations of what the United Nations can achieve there must be carefully managed and tailored.[65] The operational environment in Iraq stands as a catalogue of all the obstacles that a post-conflict society faces in its transition to stable post-conflict governance: a brutalized and disintegrated population, society and economy, an easy supply of small arms, large numbers of disgruntled soldiers struggling with demobilization and reintegration, ethnic and religious divisions, corruption and terrorism. Additionally, UN state builders face the challenge of grafting norms that grew out of the European Enlightenment onto societies with entirely different historical legacies.[66]

Restoring universality: Avoiding the embedding of normative differences

Behind all of these challenges, the common theme confronting the United Nations is to find ways – through structural and procedural reform and through normative dialogue – to restore its tattered universality. The sense of crisis produced in 2003 by the quarter-century drama of UN–

Iraq engagement reflected concern that normative differences had reached an impasse. The danger is one of embedding these normative differences in social identities, setting a "unilateralist" United States against a "multilateralist" Europe, setting the global North with its focus on security against the global South with its focus on development, setting Western capitals against Western publics, setting Northern states against Southern social movements such as a growing grassroots Islamism. The power of the United Nations for the past six decades has been precisely that it has mediated these normative conflicts, offering groups an international social identity – as members of the United Nations – larger than identities based purely on these points of conflict. To be sure, normative contestations and even ideological conflict might be conducted *through* the United Nations, as they were during the Cold War; but without the United Nations, or something analogous, those contestations would occur on battlefields and not in informal meeting rooms and formal assembly halls.

Universality cannot be restored unless the United Nations reforms itself to give the contesting groups a voice in security decision-making. As we have discussed, that will require reforms to the Security Council and other processes that bring the South back in, and that ensure that the United States appreciates the benefits of multilateralism. But, equally, it may require more creative reforms that allow non-state actors a chance to buy into the process. Brahimi's success in negotiating between local social, religious and ethnic groups and the coalition states shows that the United Nations can play this role, given the necessary combination of political backing and creative thinking. But absent such thinking, social movements, particularly in the global South, will continue to feel marginalized by and excluded from the UN-centred world order and will continue to attack it, as they did with devastating effect on 19 August 2003. That risks a slide into an even deadlier quicksand than that in Iraq – a world order structured on a politics of identity, founded on normative, religious and ethnic differences. For six decades, the United Nations has offered a vision of a world order transcending sectarianism, racism and other forms of discrimination, a vision of a common political space in which differences could be resolved peacefully. Without careful reform, that vision may be at risk.

If one thing is likely, it is that the sands of Iraq will soon shift again, blurring existing lines for Iraqis, the United Nations and other international interveners. That the United Nations and Iraq will remain engaged with each other in a variety of ways is certain. That the shape, depth and outcome of these links will matter critically to the future of the United Nations (and other international actors) can be in no doubt.

Notes

James Cockayne is an Associate at the International Peace Academy; David M. Malone is Assistant Deputy Minister (Africa and Middle East), Department of Foreign Affairs, Canada. The chapter does not necessarily represent the views of either author's organization.

1. See Lawrence Freedman, "War in Iraq: Selling The Threat", *Survival*, Vol. 46, No. 2 (Summer 2004), pp. 7–50.
2. The phrase is taken from an influential Brookings Institution report, Meghan O'Sullivan, *Iraq: Time for a Modified Approach* (Washington, DC: Brookings Institution, 2001).
3. See Kenneth M. Pollack, "Spies, Lies, and Weapons: What Went Wrong", *Atlantic Monthly*, January/February 2004.
4. See Bob Woodward, *Bush at War* (New York: Simon & Schuster, 2002), pp. 83–84, and *Plan of Attack* (New York: Simon & Schuster, 2004), p. 25.
5. Comments of White House spokesperson Ari Fleischer, cited in Woodward, *Plan of Attack*, p. 232.
6. Freedman, "War in Iraq", p. 29.
7. See Hans Blix, *Disarming Iraq: The Search for Weapons of Mass Destruction* (London: Bloomsbury, 2004), pp. 141–142.
8. See Philip H. Gordon and Jeremy Shapiro, *Allies at War: America, Europe and the Crisis over Iraq* (New York: McGraw Hill, 2004); and Michael Clarke, "The Diplomacy That Led to War in Iraq", in Paul Cornish, ed., *The Conflict in Iraq, 2003* (London: Palgrave/Macmillan, 2004).
9. See Statement by Secretary of State Powell to the Security Council, 5 February 2003, ⟨http://www.whitehouse.gov/news/releases/2003/02/20030205-1.html⟩.
10. Blix, *Disarming Iraq*, pp. 157, 167.
11. Mohammed ElBaradei, "The Status of Nuclear Inspections in Iraq: An Update", Statement to the United Nations Security Council, 7 March 2003, available at ⟨http://www.iaea.org/NewsCenter/Statements/2003/ebsp2003n006.shtml⟩.
12. See Susan Wright, "The Hijacking of UNSCOM", *Bulletin of the Atomic Scientists*, Vol. 55, No. 4 (July/August 1999); and see Blix, *Disarming Iraq*.
13. See John Kampfner, *Blair's Wars* (New York: Simon & Schuster, 2003).
14. See Woodward, *Plan of Attack*, p. 220.
15. UN Doc. A/57/PV.3, 12 September 2002.
16. Freedman, "War in Iraq", p. 39.
17. S/RES/1483 (2003), 22 May 2003, para. 8.
18. Ibid., para. 9.
19. See Report of the Secretary-General pursuant to paragraph 24 of Security Council Resolution 1483 (2003), UN Doc. S/2003/715, 17 July 2003.
20. See Dexter Filkins and Raymond Bonner, "Series of Blasts across Baghdad Kill at Least 15", *New York Times*, 27 October 2003, Section 1, p. 1; and see Alex Berenson, "U.N. Chief Orders Further Reduction of Staff in Baghdad", *New York Times*, 26 September 2003, Section A, p. 8.
21. United Nations, *Report of the Independent Panel on the Safety and Security of UN Personnel in Iraq*, 20 October 2003.
22. See UN News Centre, "Annan Takes Strong Disciplinary Measures after Probe Reveals Security Failures in Iraq", 29 March 2004. Annan refused to accept the resignation of Louise Fréchette, who had chaired the Steering Group on Iraq that had recommended the United Nations' return to Iraq before the 19 August 2003 bombings.
23. See Edith M. Lederer, "U.N. Intends to Hire a Security Firm", *Newsday*, 4 March 2004.

The United Nations later backed away from this strategy: author's interview with senior UN security officials, July 2005.

24. See "Text of Letters from the Prime Minister of the Interim Government of Iraq Dr. Ayad Allawi and United States Secretary of State Colin L. Powell to the President of the Council", Annex to S/RES/1546 (2004), at p. 11.

25. See, especially, *Report on the Fall of Srebrenica*, UN Doc. A/54/549, 15 November 1999; *Report of the Independent Inquiry into the Actions of the United Nations during the 1994 Genocide in Rwanda*, UN Doc. S/1999/1257, 15 December 1999; and the Brahimi Report, *Report of the Panel on United Nations Peace Operations*, UN Doc. A/55/305– S/2000/809, 21 August 2000, which argued for the primacy of "impartiality" over "neutrality" in peace operations.

26. Just how high became clear in early May 2004, when al-Qaeda offered 10 kg of gold as a reward to anyone who murdered Annan or his senior Iraq negotiator Lakhdar Brahimi.

27. See, generally, Edward C. Luck, "Tackling Terrorism", in David M. Malone, ed., *The UN Security Council from the Cold War to the 21ˢᵗ Century* (Boulder, CO: Lynne Rienner, 2004), p. 85; and Andrés Franco, "Armed Nonstate Actors" in ibid., p. 117.

28. S/RES/1540 (2004), 28 April 2004.

29. See International Peace Academy (IPA), "The Future of UN State-Building: Strategic and Operational Challenges and the Legacy of Iraq", New York, December 2003.

30. Ibid., p. 6.

31. See Antonio Donini, Norah Niland and Karin Wermester, eds, *Nation-Building Unraveled? Aid, Peace and Justice in Afghanistan* (Bloomfield, CT: Kumarian Press, 2004).

32. See Jim Wurst, "U.N. Iraq Envoy Says Security, Electoral Assistance Are Priority", *U.N. Wire*, 23 July 2004.

33. See David M. Malone, "UN Anger over Iraq: Nobody Said It Would Be Safe", *International Herald Tribune*, 30 September 2004.

34. See Peter W. Galbraith, "How to Get out of Iraq", *New York Review of Books*, Vol. 51, No. 8 (13 May 2004), and "Iraq: The Bungled Transition", *New York Review of Books*, Vol. 51, No. 14 (23 September 2004); Seymour M. Hersh, "Chain of Command", *New Yorker*, 17 May 2004. The abandonment of reconstruction objectives was made obvious to all when the Bush administration sought congressional authorization to shift funding from reconstruction to security; see Richard W. Stevenson, "Seeing Threat to Iraq Elections, U.S. Seeks to Shift Rebuilding Funds to Security", *New York Times*, 14 September 2004, Section A, p. 12.

35. S/RES/1511 (2003), 16 October 2003.

36. UN News Centre, "Annan Asks Security Council for Greater Clarity on UN Role in Iraq", 16 December 2003.

37. See letter dated 18 March 2004 from the Secretary-General addressed to the President of the Security Council, UN Doc. S/2004/225, 19 March 2004. President Bush had earlier met with Brahimi in Washington to ask him to undertake this delicate mission.

38. Edward Joseph, "A Balancing Act for the UN's Brahimi", *International Herald Tribune*, 15 May 2004.

39. Mats Berdal, "The UN after Iraq", *Survival*, Vol. 46, No. 3 (Autumn 2004), p. 88.

40. See Peter W. Galbraith, "Iraq: The Bungled Transition", *New York Review of Books*, 23 September 2004.

41. See S/RES/1546 (2004).

42. For the only clear-cut case in which the Security Council authorized the use of force to restore democracy, see David Malone, "Haiti and the International Community: A Case Study", *Survival*, Vol. 39, No. 2 (Summer 1997), pp. 126–146. See, generally, Gregory H. Fox, "Democratization", in Malone, *The UN Security Council*, p. 69.

43. See Elizabeth M. Cousens, Chetan Kumar and Karin Wermester, *Peacebuilding as Politics: Cultivating Peace in Fragile Societies* (Boulder, CO: Lynne Rienner, 2001). See also Stephen John Stedman, Donald Rothchild and Elizabeth M. Cousens, eds, *Ending Civil Wars: The Success and Failure of Negotiated Settlements in Civil War* (Boulder, CO: Lynne Rienner, 2002); and Chester A. Crocker, Fen Osler Hampson and Pamela R. Aall, eds, *Herding Cats: Multiparty Mediation in a Complex World* (Washington, DC: United States Institute of Peace, 1999).

44. See Stephen Stedman, "Introduction", in Stephen Stedman, Donald Rothchild and Elizabeth Cousens, eds, *Ending Civil Wars: The Implementation of Peace Agreements* (Boulder, CO: Lynne Rienner, 2002).

45. Mats Berdal makes the point that Iraq has highlighted the comparative efficiency of the World Food Programme, UNICEF, UNDP and other UN specialized agencies and programmes: Berdal, "The UN after Iraq", pp. 86–87.

46. See UN Doc. S/2004/140, 23 February 2004.

47. Marina Ottaway, "Iraq: Without Consensus, Democracy Is Not the Answer", *Policy Brief 36*, Carnegie Endowment for International Peace, March 2005. On the grim realities of the election, see also Mark Danner, "Iraq: The Real Election", *New York Review of Books*, Vol. 52, No. 7 (28 April 2005), pp. 41–44.

48. IPA, "The Future of UN State-Building", p. 8.

49. See Simon Chesterman, *You, The People: The United Nations, Transitional Administration, and State-Building* (Oxford: Oxford University Press, 2004); and also Simon Chesterman, "Bush, the United Nations and Nation-building", *Survival*, Vol. 46, No. 1 (Spring 2004), pp. 101–116.

50. See Simon Chesterman, "Virtual Trusteeship", in Malone, *The UN Security Council*, p. 219.

51. See IPA, "The Future of UN State-Building".

52. See, for example, Chandra Lekha Sriram and Karin Wermester, *From Promise to Practice: Strengthening UN Capacities for the Prevention of Violent Conflict*, Final Report (New York: International Peace Academy, May 2003).

53. See ⟨http://www.iciss.gc.ca/menu-e.asp⟩.

54. United Nations General Assembly, *2005 World Summit Outcome*, UN Doc. A/60/L.1, 15 September 2005.

55. Except in Africa, enforcement actions are increasingly advocated, then carried out, by the global North, whereas traditional peacekeeping operations are executed mostly by the global South. The industrialized countries (especially those in NATO) often provide troops that operate under national, NATO or European Union command. The United States in effect operates as a free agent.

56. One of the key means of securing this cooperative approach to security governance may be reform of the working procedures – if not the structure – of the Security Council. See Teresa Whitfield, "Groups of Friends", in Malone, *The UN Security Council*, p. 311.

57. Michael J. Glennon, "Why the Security Council Failed", *Foreign Affairs*, May/June 2003.

58. This and many related points are made in a powerful piece by Thomas Franck, "What Happens Now? The UN after Iraq", *American Journal of International Law*, Vol. 97 (2003), p. 607.

59. See UN Doc. A/59/PV.4, 21 September 2004.

60. Interview with Egypt's then-ambassador to the United Nations, Nabil Elarabi, January 1996.

61. Interview with Mexico's then-ambassador to the United Nations, Adolfo Aguilar Zínser, 26 January 2003.

62. Interview with Michael W. Doyle, New York, 16 May 2003.
63. See, for example, Ramesh Thakur, "How to Build a Better Brains-Trust", *Globe and Mail*, 3 June 2004.
64. Civil society has become increasingly involved in security regulation through mechanisms such as the Global Compact.
65. See IPA, "The Future of UN State-Building", p. 3.
66. Ibid., pp. 3–4.

Part V

International legal and doctrinal issues

23

The war in Iraq as illegal and illegitimate

David Krieger

The Iraqi dictator must not be permitted to threaten America and the world with horrible poisons and diseases and gases and atomic weapons.

(George W. Bush, 7 October 2002)

I think unless the United Nations shows some backbone and courage, it could render the Security Council irrelevant.

(George W. Bush, 17 February 2003)

We now know that there were no weapons of mass destruction in Iraq, despite repeated allegations by President Bush and other members of his administration. And, contrary to President Bush's allegation that the United Nations showed no backbone and courage, the Security Council did, in fact, stand up to the Bush administration's pressure and did resist authorizing war before the UN weapons inspectors had completed their task. It was the Bush administration's impatience with the Security Council process and unwillingness to abide by it that led it to initiate an unauthorized attack on Iraq in violation of international law. Although the war in Iraq is widely regarded throughout the world as illegal under international law, few consequences seem to be flowing from this in terms of holding to account the perpetrators of the war, including leading figures in the Bush administration.

At issue is a view often articulated by detractors of the war, such as former Secretary of State Madeleine Albright, who described the war in Iraq as a "war of choice" rather than a war of necessity.[1] This would suggest that those with sufficient power have choices in matters of war and peace in which they can initiate war without being held accountable, or, at best, being held accountable only by the democratic process of defeat in the next election. The implication is that an illegal war of aggression, although it may be neither wise nor necessary, is a prerogative of power.

The two main justifications offered by the Bush administration for the war against Iraq prior to its inception have by now been completely discredited. First, administration spokespersons repeatedly pointed to an imminent threat that Iraq would use weapons of mass destruction against the United States or its allies, or would transfer these weapons to terrorist organizations. UN weapons inspectors in Iraq prior to the war reported that they were not finding weapons of mass destruction and needed more time to complete their inspections. The Bush administration, however, continued to assert that Iraq had such weapons, despite a lack of credible corroboration, and finally warned the UN inspectors to leave Iraq before the United States initiated what it called a "preemptive" war. Secretary of State Colin Powell, in his presentation to the United Nations Security Council, asserted without question that the United States had knowledge of Iraqi weapons of mass destruction and proceeded to produce intelligence photographs of the sites where they were being manufactured and stored.[2] His assertions turned out to be false.

In the aftermath of the war, despite extensive efforts by UN inspectors and US military personnel, no weapons of mass destruction were located in Iraq. This wholly discredited the numerous pronouncements by members of the Bush administration that they not only knew there were such weapons but even knew where they were located within Iraq.

The second justification for the war made by the Bush administration prior to initiating the war was that there was a link between Iraq and the al-Qaeda terrorist organization. The evidence establishing this link has also proven to be false or, at best, extremely tenuous. This led the United States to come up with new *post hoc* justifications for the war, such as the assertion that Saddam Hussein was a bad man and evil dictator, even though the United States supported him despite his poor human rights record when it believed that it served its interests to do so. Although these *post hoc* justifications may be true, they do not make an effective case for the legality, or even the legitimacy, of an aggressive war initiated without UN authorization.

If allowed to stand unchallenged, the US initiation of war in Iraq and the rationale that permitted it could set an extremely dangerous precedent. Such actions could also undermine the legal and normative system to prevent wars of aggression, centred in the United Nations and enunciated in the Nuremberg Principles, which were the basis for the trials of Axis leaders in the aftermath of World War II. The Nuremberg Principles list "crimes against peace" as first among the crimes punishable under international law and define crimes against peace as: "(i) Planning, preparation, initiation or waging of a war of aggression or a war in violation of international treaties, agreements or assurances; (ii) Participation of a common plan or conspiracy for the accomplishment of any of the acts mentioned under (i)."[3]

The words of the US chief prosecutor at the Nuremberg Trials, Justice Robert Jackson, are relevant. Jackson was adamant that the true test of what was done at Nuremberg would be the extent to which the Allied victors, including the United States, applied these principles to themselves in future years. In his opening statement to the court, Jackson placed the issue of "victor's justice" in context: "We must never forget that the record on which we judge these defendants is the record on which history will judge us tomorrow. To pass these defendants a poisoned chalice is to put it to our lips as well. We must summon such detachment and intellectual integrity to our task that this Trial will commend itself to posterity as fulfilling humanity's aspirations to do justice."[4] For Jackson, such "aspirations to do justice" included applying the law equally and fairly to all. "If certain acts in violation of treaties are crimes," he stated, "they are crimes whether the United States does them or whether Germany does them, and we are not prepared to lay down a rule of criminal conduct against others which we would not be willing to have invoked against us."[5]

The illegality of the Iraq war

The UN Charter is clear that wars of aggression are prohibited. Article 2(4) states: "All Members shall refrain in their international relations from the threat or use of force against the territorial integrity or political independence of any state, or in any other manner inconsistent with the Purposes of the United Nations."[6] This prohibition on the use of force finds an exception in Article 51 of the Charter, which allows for the possibility of self-defence.[7] Article 51 states:

Nothing in the present Charter shall impair the inherent right of individual or collective self-defence if an armed attack occurs against a Member of the United Nations, until the Security Council has taken measures necessary to maintain international peace and security. Measures taken by Members in the exercise of this right of self-defence shall be immediately reported to the Security Council and shall not in any way affect the authority and responsibility of the Security Council under the present Charter to take at any time such action as it deems necessary in order to maintain or restore international peace and security."[8]

It should be emphasized that this exception to the general prohibition against the use of force is valid only in the event of "an armed attack" and only "until the Security Council has taken measures necessary to maintain international peace and security".

In the case of the US war against Iraq, there was no armed attack against the United States by Iraq, nor any substantiated threat of armed attack. There was no credible evidence that Iraq had any relationship to the 11 September 2001 terrorist attacks against the United States. There was, therefore, no appropriate justification for the invocation of the self-defence exception to the UN Charter's prohibition against the use of force. If the United States could proceed to war against Iraq on the basis of a claim of potential future attack, it would open the door to a broad range of assertions of potential future attacks by one country against another that would justify unilateral initiation of warfare, whether or not based on factual foundations, paranoia or simple expediency. It would throw the international order into a state of chaos.

Further, the matter of Iraq's failure to complete the disarmament obligations imposed upon it by the Security Council following the 1991 Gulf war was actually placed before the Security Council by the United States for action, and the Security Council resisted US pressure to provide the United States with authorization to use force. The Bush administration, at the urging of Secretary of State Colin Powell and over the objections of other administration officials, sought a Security Council mandate to initiate what the United States called a "preemptive war" (but was actually a "preventive war" since it involved no imminent threat of attack but sought only to prevent the imagined possibility of a future attack) against Iraq.

The Security Council did agree to one resolution, UNSC Resolution 1441, which called on Iraq to disarm its weapons of mass destruction (WMD) and cooperate with the UN inspectors but did not include an authorization for the use of force against Iraq.[9] In Resolution 1441, the Security Council indicated that it would remain "seized" of the matter, meaning that it continued to assert its authority as the final international arbiter of the use of force in the matter. When the United States went back to the Security Council for a second and follow-up resolution to 1441, this one to provide authorization to proceed to war against Iraq, the Security Council refused to comply with the US demand for such authorization on the grounds that it wanted to give the UN inspectors more time to finish their work.

Rather than awaiting authorization from the Security Council or abiding by the Council's unwillingness to provide such authorization, the United States, under the Bush administration, which had been gradually repositioning its military forces into the Middle East in preparation for war with Iraq, abandoned its quest for UN authorization and proceeded to attack and invade Iraq. The Bush administration sought to justify its illegal actions on the basis of Security Council Resolution 678, a 1990 resolution that authorized "all necessary means" to uphold previous resolutions related to Iraq's invasion and occupation of Kuwait and to restore peace and security in the area.[10] The resolution authorized the use of force unless Iraq fully complied with previous Council resolutions by 15 January 1991. This resolution was used as the legal justification for the attack against Iraq on that date by the US-led coalition and also by the Bush II administration for its attack in March 2003. Although the justification is relevant, at least legally, to the 1991 Gulf war, it is basically used as sophistry in relation to the 2003 attack.

Following the first Gulf war, Iraq accepted a ceasefire contained in Security Council Resolution 687.[11] This resolution imposed certain conditions on Iraq, including WMD disarmament obligations. In justifying the 2003 war in Iraq, Bush administration officials continued to rely upon the Security Council resolutions preceding and immediately following the 1991 Gulf war. US State Department Legal Advisers, for example, argued, "As a legal matter, a material breach of the conditions that had been essential to the establishment of the cease-fire left the responsibility to member states to enforce those conditions, operating consistently with Resolution 678 to use all necessary means to restore international peace and security in the area."[12]

These officials further argued that the provision in Resolution 1441 indicating that Iraq was in "material breach of its obligations" to cooperate with UN inspectors on WMD inspections under previous resolutions, including Resolutions 678 and 687, allowed the United States legally to initiate its attack on Iraq.[13] In fact, however, Resolution 1441 offered Iraq "a final opportunity to comply with disarmament obligations",[14] and Iraq was doing so. Iraq was cooperating with UN inspectors on these issues, and the arguments to the contrary, by Colin Powell and others in the Bush administration, have since been exposed as misrepresentations.[15] Most important, though, Security Council Resolution 1441 stated that the Security Council would remain seized of the matter, thus indicating that, without further Council authorization, there was no legal justification for the United States and its allies to proceed to war against Iraq.[16]

The US-led attack against Iraq constitutes a clear undermining of established Security Council authority in the realm of war and peace. The attack and initiation of the Iraq war would later be described by President Bush in terms of the United States not needing a "permission slip", presumably from the United Nations, when US security interests were threatened.[17] As was subsequently revealed, however, US security interests were not threatened, as had been alleged by the Bush administration, and the war therefore had no legal basis. It was considered by the opposition party in the United States to be at best a "war of choice". More realistically, it was understood by large majorities of the populations of nearly all countries in the world to be an aggressive and illegal war of the type for which Axis leaders were held to account by the Allied powers after World War II. UN Secretary-General Kofi Annan said unequivocally that the war was illegal. Referring to the war, he stated, "I have indicated it was not in conformity with the UN charter. From our point of view and from the charter point of view it was illegal."[18]

The Security Council could have chosen to act under Article 39 of the UN Charter to authorize the use of force against Iraq if it determined that there had been a breach of the peace or an act of aggression. Article 39 states, "The Security Council shall determine the existence of any threat to the peace, breach of the peace, or act of aggression and shall make recommendations, or decide what measures shall be taken in accordance with Articles 41 and 42, to maintain or restore international peace and security."[19] Article 41 refers to actions the Security Council can take that do not involve the use of force. Article 42 refers to acts of force the Security Council can take if it finds the measures under Article 41 to be inadequate. These include "such action by air, sea, or land forces as may be necessary to maintain or restore international peace and security".[20] No such actions were authorized by the Security Council in relation to the Iraq war initiated by President Bush and other US and coalition leaders in March 2003.

The illegitimacy of the Iraq war

Despite the nearly universal understanding of the illegality of the war, it might be asked under what conditions it might nonetheless be considered legitimate, even if not legal. This line of enquiry takes into account the argument that the threat of a possible attack with weapons of mass destruction, particularly nuclear weapons, would allow for some bending of international law to fit the extreme dangers associated with such weapons. In response to this line of enquiry, it seems reasonable to suggest that evidence of the development of weapons of mass destruction, when combined with further evidence of *imminent intent to use such weapons*, could constitute a sufficient threat to justify pre-emptive war in an attempt to prevent the use of weapons of mass destruction. (Would the 2001 US *Nuclear Posture Review*,[21] which calls for the development of contingency plans for the use of nuclear weapons against seven countries, suggest imminent threat and constitute sufficient grounds for a pre-emptive attack by one of these states against the United States?)

Hans Blix, the former chief UN weapons inspector in Iraq, analysed the pre-war situation in Iraq in this way:

Any government learning that a 9/11, perhaps with weapons of mass destruction, is about to happen cannot sit and wait, but will seek to prevent it. However, such preventive action, if undertaken without the authorization of the Security Council, would have to rely critically upon solid intelligence if it were to be internationally accepted. The case of Iraq cannot be said to have strengthened faith in national intelligence as a basis for preemptive military action without Security Council authorization. Saddam Hussein did not have any weapons of mass destruction in March 2003, and the evidence invoked of the existence of such weapons had begun to fall apart even before the invasion started.[22]

Based on this analysis, Blix concluded: "Saddam Hussein was not a valid object for counterproliferation. He was not an imminent or even a remote threat to the United States or to Iraq's neighbors."[23]

It should be understood that, even if there had been weapons of mass destruction in Iraq, this alone would not have been a sufficient justification for pre-emptive war. The mere presence of weapons of mass destruction, *absent evidence of imminent intent to use them*, would be insufficient to justify a pre-emptive war, let alone a preventive war. If the mere presence of weapons of mass destruction were sufficient, it would mean that any country possessing weapons of mass destruction would be a legitimate target of preventive attack by a potential enemy of that country. Such logic would push all states in the direction of preventive warfare and would substantially increase both the likelihood and the danger of such wars. It would allow for attacks against Israel on the basis of its secret but widely recognized nuclear weapons programme, for attacks by either India or Pakistan against the other, and for attacks by any of the nuclear weapons states against one another. This is, in part, why the International Court of Justice, in its 1996 Advisory Opinion on the legality of the threat or use of nuclear weapons, stated: "There exists an obligation to pursue in good faith and bring to a conclusion negotiations leading to nuclear disarmament in all its aspects under strict and effective international control."[24]

Following further this line of enquiry, a distinction needs to be drawn between a state possessing weapons of mass destruction and non-state extremist groups possessing the same weapons. In the former case, a country has a fixed location and is therefore far more likely to be deterred by the threat of retaliation from using such weapons. In contrast, the same weapons in the hands of extremists who are not easily locatable and who may be suicidal as well, and therefore are not subject to being deterred by threats of retaliation, present a far more dangerous threat.

In the case both of states of concern – such as Iraq, Iran and North Korea – and of extremist groups, however, the best remedy is surely policies to prevent nuclear proliferation and achieve nuclear disarmament rather than a pre-emptive war. An aggressive war could stand only as a final barrier and one that is unacceptable and illegal unless under the mandate of the international community through authorization by the United Nations Security Council.

Given the after-the-fact findings in Iraq that there were neither weapons of mass destruction nor links to extremist organizations, there was no reasonable justification, either in legality or in legitimacy, for the US-led war against that country. US leaders continue to make the claim that previous Security Council resolutions provide the necessary justification, but this is a poor argument that is not borne out by scrutiny of the earlier resolutions and, in any event, is overridden by the fact that the Security Council had decided in Resolution 1441 to remain seized of the matter.

The costs of the war

Defenders of the Iraq war claim that the removal of Saddam Hussein by the rapidly diminishing "coalition of the willing" will make it possible for democracy eventually to take root in the country, and that a new Iraq will serve as a model to other countries in the region, transforming a troublesome but oil-rich part of the world into one that is stable, peaceful and democratic. This is an unlikely scenario, given the realities that have ensued as a result of the war.

Although many Iraqi citizens are pleased that Saddam Hussein was dislodged from power, the result of the Iraq war has been the death of some 100,000 innocent civilians, severe injury to tens of thousands more, and enormous destruction of the infrastructure of the country.[25] Iraqi society has been devastated by warfare and its citizens subjected to death, injury, torture and humiliating abuses such as were revealed at Abu Ghraib prison. The price for regime change has been very high in terms of death and destruction. Iraq will now have to struggle with re-establishing itself as a sovereign state, finding its own means of governance in a post-Saddam and post-US occupation country. As part of this struggle, it will have to come to terms with its relationship to the United States, which undoubtedly seeks to ensure special privileges with Iraq with regard to Iraqi oil supplies and the continued presence of US troops in the region, particularly on newly established US military bases in Iraq itself. Of course, the United States has also paid a price for the war in terms of its financial costs, currently estimated at over US$200 billion, the death and injury of its soldiers, the spreading thin of its armed forces to levels considered dangerous by leading US military figures, and the loss of respect for and credibility of the United States in the world community.

A second area of equally severe costs of the war against Iraq is its unfortunate implications for world order in the twenty-first century. If the US precedent of aggressive war under false pretences against Iraq is allowed to stand as a *fait accompli* without some form of international sanction against the United States and its leaders, it bodes ill for the continuation of the world order system established after World War II to prevent "the scourge of war".[26] Clearly, the United States is a key actor in the international system and, with its overwhelming military and economic power, it is not easy for the international community to stand up for principles of international law against US actions that violate the UN Charter. Yet the continued viability of the Charter demands principled action by the members of the United Nations even in the face of US pressure. One extremely important principle of law is that no person or nation stands above the law. Law can be respected and ultimately enforced only when it applies to all, equally and' alike. The US-led invasion of Iraq, under false pretences and without UN Security Council approval, is a direct challenge to the principle of prohibition on the use of force in the UN Charter. Had the Security Council actually authorized the US attack on Iraq, it would have undermined the credibility of the United Nations itself, including its commitment to the basic principles of its own Charter.

The need for accountability

Throughout the world, there have been an ongoing series of inquiries into international crimes committed by US and coalition leaders in initiating and conducting the war against Iraq in the form of international people's tribunals.[27] These tribunals, in the spirit of the Bertrand Russell War Crimes Tribunals during the Viet Nam war, are amassing evidence of international crimes and will be reporting these to the public throughout the world. This is an important initiative of civil society, and it promises to help educate people and governments about the dangers and criminal nature of wars of aggression as well as crimes committed in the conduct of the war. Something more is needed, however, than leaving this matter to be dealt with only by civil society. The United Nations, for the health and integrity of the organization, also needs to initiate its own inquiry into the nature of the US war against Iraq. This could be done either in the General Assembly or by a committee of selected representative members of the United Nations and brought back to the General Assembly and, through it, to the people of the world. If the facts bear out the circumvention of the UN Charter by the United States in direct defiance of the Security Council, at a minimum the United States should be censured for its actions. Further recommendations by the General Assembly could include a call for reparations to the Iraqi people, prohibitions on the United States profiting from its aggression, the disgorgement of profits already obtained, and the trial and punishment of responsible US and coalition leaders for their actions.

An early act of the Bush administration was to "unsign" the treaty establishing an International Criminal Court (ICC).[28] Under the Bush administration, the United States has been hostile to the ICC, arguing that it did not want to subject US military personnel to the dictates of this international court. In light of the US circumvention of international law in its initiation of an aggressive war against Iraq, it becomes clearer that US leaders were seeking to give themselves greater degrees of freedom to commit serious violations of international criminal law without being subjected to the jurisdiction of the court.

No country, even the most powerful, should be immune from international law. The United Nations owes it to itself and to the principles for which the organization stands not to allow the law to be violated without, at a minimum, drawing public attention to the violations. Although a report by the United Nations on illegal actions by a member state might upset the government of that state, it would also help to draw the attention of the people of that country to illegal acts being committed in their name. This would bear some resemblance at the international level to the truth aspect of the Truth and Reconciliation Commission that was successfully used in South Africa after apartheid ended and Nelson Mandela was released from prison to become president of that country.[29] It would be useful for a UN committee examining the violations of international law in the US-led war against Iraq also to look carefully into the more than a decade of sanctions imposed upon Iraq and the results of those sanctions in terms of human life and suffering of innocent parties.

The Iraq war and weapons of mass destruction

At the heart of world conditions that provided the ostensible reason that the United States went into Iraq are the extreme threats posed by weapons of mass destruction. Many countries are now concerned about the incendiary mix that lies at the intersection of weapons of mass destruction and terrorism. The need is greater today than ever before to bring weapons of mass destruction under effective international control, and many countries have voiced their concern that more must be done to keep weapons of mass destruction from proliferating to states of concern and non-state extremist organizations. President Bush has spoken out on the importance of preventing nuclear terrorism. His plans involve attempting to keep what he refers to as the world's most dangerous weapons out of the hands of the world's most dangerous states and extremist organizations. Bush has organized a Proliferation Security Initiative that seeks to prevent the further proliferation of nuclear and other weapons of mass destruction to other states and to terrorist groups.[30] To accomplish this, cooperating countries are tightening export controls, criminalizing transfers of weapons of mass destruction and the materials to create them, and making arrangements to board and inspect ships at sea suspected of transporting contraband materials.

Bush has noted the "loophole" in the Nuclear Non-Proliferation Treaty that allows states to develop peaceful nuclear programmes that could be converted to nuclear weapons programmes.[31] He has called for the closing of this "loophole", although the treaty itself calls the peaceful uses of nuclear energy an "inalienable right".[32] Additionally, he has called for tighter controls on nuclear materials by the International Atomic Energy Agency and particularly international controls on the technologies for reprocessing plutonium and enriching uranium. Bush has not, however, raised the key obligation of the nuclear weapons states in the treaty, the Article VI obligation to engage in good faith negotiations for nuclear disarmament, which, more than any other single act, could limit the possibilities for nuclear weapons or the materials to make them falling into the hands of terrorists.[33]

A major problem in the international system related to preventing the proliferation of weapons of mass destruction is the double standard on nuclear weapons that the permanent members of the UN Security Council attempt to uphold individually and collectively. Although these states continue to maintain nuclear arsenals, all seek also to prevent other states from developing these weapons. In the end, such double standards cannot be maintained. It is not likely, for example, that the United States would have initiated its aggressive war against Iraq if it truly believed that Iraq possessed weapons of mass destruction that it was prepared to use. A consequence of the Iraq war is that it demonstrates to non-nuclear weapons states that there are advantages to possessing these weapons if only to deter a stronger power, such as the United States, from an unprovoked and illegal attack. This message does not seem to be lost on either North Korea, which announced that it has developed nuclear weapons, or Iran, a country that appears to be pursuing a nuclear weapons programme.

The initiation of warfare by a state possessing weapons of mass destruction to prevent the proliferation of weapons of mass destruction reflects the ultimate double standard in the current international system. It is a standard that ultimately cannot hold, and in the end will bring the current international order tumbling down. In a sense, the nuclear weapons states are holding the world hostage to this double standard by failing to fulfil their obligations under the Nuclear Non-Proliferation Treaty. Projecting into the future a continuation of the effort to maintain these double standards, despite long-standing obligations under the Nuclear Non-Proliferation Treaty, suggests the possibility that aggressive "wars of choice" may increase and become a regular occurrence in relations among countries. Such a future will also increase the likelihood of the use of weapons of mass destruction, either pre-emptively by a nuclear weapons state or by extremist organizations intent on inflicting maximum damage on powerful states in the only way they are capable of damaging them, that is, by attacks on innocent civilians.

The need for action by the United Nations

The world continues to stand at a crossroads. In one direction is a continuation of the status quo based on double standards related to weapons of mass destruction; in the other direction is a world in which international law applies to all countries, even the most powerful. The world's countries, acting through the United Nations, must find a way to end double standards relating to weapons of mass destruction and, at the same time, to fulfil the promise of the Nuclear Non-Proliferation Treaty to achieve total nuclear disarmament through the phased elimination of all nuclear arsenals. Prohibitions already exist on chemical and biological weapons, but the international community must find a way to ensure the viability of these prohibitions through robust inspection and verification mechanisms.

In the short run, the war against Iraq has alerted the world to the dangers of a breakdown of accepted international norms and prohibitions against aggressive war. In the longer run, however, the resolution of this problem will require the strengthening of the United Nations itself and the ending of current double standards applied to the possession of weapons of mass destruction. The starting point for addressing this problem is for the United Nations to take responsibility for reviewing and evaluating what happened leading to the war against Iraq and to draw attention to violations of the UN Charter that occurred when the United States and its coalition partners proceeded to invade and occupy Iraq without authorization by the Security Council. In doing so, it is likely that the inescapable conclusion will be that the US-led war was neither legal nor legitimate.

Some final questions

Finally, let us consider some remaining questions that might be raised about the Iraq war.

Was it a defining moment for international law? If it was a defining moment, it was so only in calling for a clear response from the international community that no state, including the most powerful, stands above the law. Otherwise, the Iraq war represents aggressive warfare of a type that has occurred throughout history. Nonetheless, we might enquire about the right of states, individually or collectively, to remove from power a dictator who has a long record of violating international law and committing crimes against his own people. Certainly the international community has some responsibility in such a case, but it is a responsibility that must be exercised with proper authorization of the UN Security Council. Absent such authorization, there is no right under the law for a state to proceed to intervene forcibly in the internal affairs of another sovereign state.

Was the Security Council's refusal to authorize war a triumphant moment for it, as some would argue, or was it an abdication of responsibility, as others, particularly the United States, would argue? If it was a triumphant moment, it was certainly a hollow one. The Security Council, to its credit, did not authorize the use of force in violation of the UN Charter, but it was unable to prevent its most powerful member from acting without its authorization. Thus, although the Security Council may have been right, its authority was weakened by the non-compliance of the United States, acting without UN authority, and thereby illegally, in a spirit of exceptionalism.

Should the legal norm of non-intervention in the internal affairs of sovereign states be abandoned? This norm deserves review by the Security Council in an attempt to better delineate in what circumstances this norm should be set aside by the Security Council. Examples of overriding circumstances could include when genocide or crimes against humanity are occurring or are believed, based on sufficient evidence, to be imminent. A strong case can be made for establishing a UN Emergency Peace Service, a well-trained force composed of international volunteers, which would be available for rapid deployment upon authorization of the Security Council to prevent genocide or crimes against humanity.[34] In relation to genocide and crimes against humanity, it would be appropriate to place limits on the veto power of the permanent members of the UN Security Council.

Does the Iraq war provide a model for future instances of controlling weapons of mass destruction? It is a very poor model for this purpose.

Wars to control weapons of mass destruction are costly in terms of life and treasure, and sometimes, as in the case of Iraq, the wars may be based on faulty information, manipulated intelligence, false premises, misrepresentations and deceptions. The control of weapons of mass destruction can ultimately be achieved only by doing away with double standards and placing all weapons of mass destruction and the materials to make them under verifiable international control while they are being dismantled and destroyed. This will entail the strengthening of the chemical, biological and nuclear non-proliferation regimes; and this, in turn, will require a much higher level of political will by the states currently possessing such weapons of mass destruction.

A step backward for international law

The Iraq war has been a step backward for international law, has harmed the authority of the UN Security Council and has undermined the credibility of the United States in the eyes of the world. The United Nations is faced with the dilemma of reasserting the post–World War II emphasis on ending the "scourge of war" in the face of a disturbing pattern of unilateralism, exceptionalism and disregard for international law displayed by the United States. The international community, acting through the United Nations, needs to establish effective limitations on unilateral action by all states and to censure and apply sanctions to any country, including the most powerful, that defies the dictates of international law. At a minimum, the UN General Assembly should conduct a thorough review of the circumstances leading to the initiation of war against Iraq, and determine authoritatively whether that war was conducted legally with reference to international law.

This matter cannot be left in the hands of the UN Security Council since the United States, as a permanent member, would exercise its veto power to prevent such a review from going forward. If the General Assembly deems it appropriate, it can turn to the International Court of Justice for an advisory opinion on the matter. The UN report or advisory opinion of the Court should be made public and widely disseminated. The General Assembly should make proposals on preventing aggressive wars in the future and on the circumstances in which humanitarian interventions are appropriate. Were the United Nations thoroughly to review the matter and issue a strong report, it is possible that the international community could learn from what has happened and attempt to control such unauthorized and costly interventions more effectively in the future.

Notes

1. See, for example, Madeleine Albright, "Medallion Speaker Address", Commonwealth Club of California, 12 February 2004, ⟨http://www.commonwealthclub.org/archive/04/04-02albright-speech.html⟩. Albright stated, "Because although the war in Iraq was a war of choice, not necessity, winning the peace is a necessity, not a choice."
2. "U.S. Secretary of State Colin Powell Addresses the U.N. Security Council", 5 February 2003, ⟨http://www.whitehouse.gov/news/releases/2003/02/20030205-1.html⟩.
3. General Assembly Resolution 95(1), 11 December 1946.
4. Quoted in Telford Taylor, *The Anatomy of the Nuremberg Trials* (New York: Alfred A. Knopf, 1992), p. 168.
5. Quoted in Ann Tusa and John Tusa, *The Nuremberg Trial* (New York: The Notable Trials Library, 1990), p. 81.
6. United Nations Charter, entered into force 24 October 1945, ⟨http://www.un.org/aboutun/charter⟩.
7. Ibid.
8. Ibid.
9. Security Council Resolution 1441, 8 November 2002, 42 ILM 250 (2003).
10. Security Council Resolution 678, 29 November 1990, 29 ILM 1565 (1990).
11. Security Council Resolution 687, 3 April 1991, 30 ILM 846 (1991).
12. William H. Taft IV and Todd F. Buchwald, "Preemption, Iraq and International Law", *American Journal of International Law*, Vol. 97, No. 3 (July 2003), p. 559. The authors work for the US State Department: Taft is Legal Adviser to the US State Department; Buchwald is Assistant Legal Adviser for Political-Military Affairs.
13. Ibid., pp. 560–561.
14. Security Council Resolution 1441, operative paragraph 2 states: "Decides, while acknowledging paragraph 1 above, to afford Iraq, by this resolution, a final opportunity to comply with its disarmament obligations under relevant resolutions of the Council; and accordingly decides to set up an enhanced inspection regime with the aim of bringing to full and verified completion the disarmament process established by resolution 687 (1991) and subsequent resolutions of the Council."
15. "U.S. Secretary of State Colin Powell Addresses the U.N. Security Council", 5 February 2003. Powell was later reported to have "told The Washington Post that he doesn't know whether he would have recommended the invasion of Iraq if he had been told at the time that there were no stockpiles of banned weapons". See CBS News, "The Man Who Knew", 4 February 2004, ⟨http://www.cbsnews.com/stories/2003/10/14/60II/main577975.shtml⟩.
16. Security Council Resolution 1441, operative paragraph 14 states: "Decides to remain seized of the matter."
17. George W. Bush, "State of the Union Address", 20 January 2004, ⟨http://www.whitehouse.gov/news/releases/2004/01/20040120-7.html⟩.
18. See Ewen MacAskill and Julian Borger, "Iraq War Was Illegal and Breached UN Charter, Says Annan", *Guardian*, 16 September 2004, available at ⟨http://www.commondreams.org/headlines04/0916-01.htm⟩.
19. United Nations Charter.
20. Ibid.
21. Excerpts from the classified *Nuclear Posture Review*, submitted to Congress on 31 December 2001, can be found at ⟨http://www.globalsecurity.org/wmd/library/policy/dod/npr.htm⟩.

22. Hans Blix, "The Importance of Inspections", Carnegie Endowment for International Peace, *Proliferation Brief*, Vol. 7, No. 11 (2004), ⟨http://www.carnegieendowment.org/publications/index.cfm?fa=view&id=1591⟩.
23. Ibid.
24. "Advisory Opinion of the International Court of Justice on the Legality of the Threat or Use of Nuclear Weapons", General Assembly Doc. A/51/218, 15 October 1996, p. 37.
25. Elisabeth Rosenthal, "Study Puts Civilian Toll in Iraq at Over 100,000", *International Herald Tribune*, 30 October 2004.
26. United Nations Charter.
27. See, for example, "World Tribunal on Iraq – Platform Text", Istanbul, 29 October 2003, ⟨http://www.brusselstribunal.org/wti_platform_text.htm⟩.
28. The Treaty Establishing an International Criminal Court entered into force on 1 July 2002. The treaty was signed by President Clinton on 31 December 2000. President Bush took the unprecedented step of "unsigning" the treaty in May 2002.
29. See Desmond Tutu, *No Future without Forgiveness* (New York: Doubleday, 1999).
30. On the Proliferation Security Initiative, see John R. Bolton, "The Proliferation Security Initiative: A Vision Becomes a Reality", US Department of State, 31 May 2004, ⟨http://www.state.gov/t/us/rm/33046.htm⟩. For a more critical perspective, see Colin Robinson, "The Proliferation Security Initiative: Naval Interception Bush-Style", Center for Defense Information, 25 August 2003, ⟨http://www.cdi.org/friendlyversion/printversion.cfm?documentID=1667⟩.
31. See Dana Milbank and Peter Slevin, "Bush Details Plans to Curb Nuclear Arms", *Washington Post*, 12 February 2004.
32. Treaty on the Non-Proliferation of Nuclear Weapons, entered into force 5 March 1970, ⟨http://www.armscontrol.org/documents/npt.asp⟩. Article IV(1) of the Treaty states: "Nothing in this Treaty shall be interpreted as affecting the inalienable right of all the Parties to the Treaty to develop research, production and use of nuclear energy for peaceful purposes without discrimination and in conformity with articles I and II of this Treaty." This clause may be viewed as an obstacle to achieving the non-proliferation and nuclear disarmament goals of the Treaty.
33. Article VI of the Treaty on the Non-Proliferation of Nuclear Weapons states: "Each of the Parties to the Treaty undertakes to pursue negotiations in good faith on effective measures relating to cessation of the nuclear arms race at an early date and to nuclear disarmament, and on a Treaty on general and complete disarmament under strict and effective international control." This critical element of the nuclear non-proliferation/disarmament bargain has been largely ignored by the nuclear weapons states.
34. See Justine Wang, "A Symposium on Genocide and Crimes against Humanity: The Challenge of Prevention and Enforcement", Nuclear Age Peace Foundation, 8 January 2004, ⟨http://www.wagingpeace.org/articles/2004/01/08_wang_symposium.htm⟩.

24

Legitimacy as an assessment of existing legal standards: The case of the 2003 Iraq war

Charlotte Ku

Introduction: Legitimacy and legality

Power, legality and legitimacy are all crucial to a rule-based international order. Politics is the mechanism that maintains an appropriate tension and balance between these elements.[1] International institutions provide the structure for pursuing politics and provide the means to transmit the outcomes and decisions. The 2003 war in Iraq caused widespread concern about the future ability of the international order to regulate the use of force because the war appeared to push legality aside with a decision both to exercise power and to bypass the most widely recognized source of authority for such action, the UN Security Council. But why did the war in Iraq cause such concern when neither the exertion of power nor the sidestepping of the UN Security Council is new? The answer can probably be found in today's international power structure.

With the end of the Cold War, the United States became the world's only superpower. This role created both new responsibilities as well as new opportunities. But the US failure to send a clear multilateralist signal to the world created concern that nothing would or could restrain this superpower. This concern was fuelled by the US rejection of major international agreements such as the Mine Ban Treaty, the Kyoto Protocol to the Climate Change Convention, and the Statute of the International Criminal Court. Yet, despite the harsh rhetoric, there is little to indicate that, in fact, the United States wishes to operate without restraint, even the restraint of the existing UN collective security framework. But has the United States embarked on a course of no return with regard to the UN security system following the 2003 Iraq war? Not so far, and one way to measure how far the United States has strayed from the existing system may be to assess the legitimacy of its actions.

On the eve of the US-led war in Iraq, Anne-Marie Slaughter published a controversial opinion piece in the *New York Times* in which she noted: "By giving up on the Security Council, the Bush administration has started on a course that could be called 'illegal but legitimate,' a course that could end up, paradoxically, winning United Nations approval for a military campaign in Iraq – though only after an invasion." She concluded the piece on a tentative note: "Overall, everyone involved is still playing by the rules. But depending on what we find in Iraq, the rules may have to evolve, so that which is legitimate is also legal."[2] Legitimacy in the case of Iraq depended heavily on what was found.

One year later, she wrote:

A year ago, when the U.S. and Britain decided to send troops to Iraq without a second UN resolution, I argued that their action was illegal under international law but *potentially* legitimate in the eyes of the international community. I set forth three criteria for determining the ultimate legitimacy of the action: 1) whether the coalition forces did in fact find weapons of mass destruction; 2) whether coalition forces were welcomed by the Iraqi people; and 3) whether the U.S. and Britain turned back to the UN as quickly as possible after the fighting was done. A year later, I conclude that the invasion was both illegal and illegitimate. The coalition's decision to use force without a second Security Council resolution cannot stand as a precedent for future action, but rather as a mistake that should lead us back to genuine multilateralism.[3]

Although UN Security Council Resolution 1511 (2003) authorizing UN involvement in post-conflict reconstruction and nation-building in Iraq brought the United Nations back into the picture, Slaughter's conclusion was that, because of the failure to meet what she outlined as the tests of legitimacy, the action taken in Iraq cannot be regarded as a precedent for future such actions. But had the tests been met, what would legitimacy have provided? It would have provided grounds for *post hoc* UN approval and it might have served as a precedent for future action. Slaughter's initial assertion that the war might be legitimate was controversial enough, but what seemed particularly difficult for many to accept was her view that "overall, everyone involved is still playing by the rules". Perhaps the sentence should have read that, "overall, everyone involved is still trying to play by the rules", but that "the rules may have to evolve, so that which is legitimate is also legal". This conclusion accepts that a gap between legitimacy and legality cannot exist indefinitely and that, if a case can be made for the legitimacy of an otherwise illegal action, this may indicate that the rule needs to be changed. Considerations of legitimacy therefore are crucial to the functioning of the law even when legality and legitimacy diverge.

Nevertheless, the war in Iraq triggered much concern that basing an action on legitimacy, even though it was illegal, would lead to self-serving unilateral judgements whenever multilateral authorization was not available. Yet, can a nation realistically be expected to wait for a collective decision if it feels under threat? Slaughter addressed this problem in her March 2003 *New York Times* article: "The United Nations imposes constraints on both the global decision-making process and the outcomes of the process, constraints that all countries recognize to be in their long-term interest and the interest of the world. But it cannot be a straitjacket, preventing nations from defending themselves or pursuing what they perceive to be their vital national security interests."[4] The larger question is whether alternatives existed that might have been more acceptable to the collective body. The failure to explore such alternatives fully (in the opinion of most voices outside the United States) is perhaps the key problem in arguing the legitimacy of the war. A further problem is the ripple effect that the US action might have on the entire UN security system by tempting others to follow the US example and act without specific UN authorization.

UN Secretary-General Kofi Annan addressed this concern in his charge to the High-level Panel on Threats, Challenges and Change in 2003:

The past year has shaken the foundations of collective security and undermined confidence in the possibility of collective responses to our common problems and challenges. It has also brought to the fore deep divergences of opinion on the range and nature of the challenges we face, and are likely to face in the future.

Specifically, he asked the Panel to:

(a) Examine today's global threats and provide an analysis of future challenges to international peace and security. Whilst there may continue to exist a diversity of perception on the relative importance of the various threats facing particular Member States on an individual basis, it is important to find an appropriate balance at a global level. It is also important to understand the connections between different threats.[5]

Whether we individually conclude that the 2003 war in Iraq was legal or illegal, the question is whether the UN Security Council system can respond effectively and retain its "unique standard of international legal legitimacy".[6]

The central role of the United Nations Security Council

In 2000, the Panel on United Nations Peace Operations appointed by the UN Secretary-General concluded that "the United Nations does not wage war. Where enforcement action is required, it has consistently been entrusted to coalitions of willing States, with the authorization of the Security Council, acting under Chapter VII of the Charter."[7] This is how the United Nations was envisaged to work. "Instead of being a substitute for great powers, [the United Nations] was designed to depend on them."[8] The great powers were to provide the means for the United Nations to carry out its decisions. But this created a reliance on strong military powers and an expectation that these powers would act within the confines of the UN community's interpretation of the scope of an authorization. The effort to institute international control or oversight over the use of national military assets is one of the less developed parts of the UN security system. At the same time, relying on one or two large military powers has caused much of the UN membership concern. The views of UN scholar Ramesh Thakur well express this point of view:

there has been a perceptible undercurrent of unease since the end of the Cold War that the will of the UNSC has been bent too easily and too often to the wishes of the sole superpower.... Developing countries fear that in some sections of the west today, the view has gained ground that anyone *but* the legitimate authorities can use force. If this is then used as an alibi to launch UN-authorized humanitarian interventions against the wishes of the legitimate governments of member states, the international organization would quickly be viewed more as a threat to the security of many countries than as a source of protection against major-power predators.[9]

In the post-1945 world, the UN Security Council plays a central role in determining both the legality and the legitimacy of uses of force. This was recognized by US President George W. Bush in his address to the UN General Assembly on 12 September 2002.

The conduct of the Iraqi regime is a threat to the authority of the United Nations, and a threat to peace. Iraq has answered a decade of U.N. demands with a decade of defiance. All the world now faces a test, and the United Nations a difficult and defining moment. Are Security Council resolutions to be honored and enforced, or cast aside without consequence? Will the United Nations serve the purpose of its founding, or will it be irrelevant?[10]

Although the questions are pertinent, the course ultimately chosen by President Bush to force Iraq's compliance is one that has increasingly been regarded as premature and beyond the scope of the authorization of any UN Security Council mandate. This difference in view is at the heart of the disagreement about the legality of the 2003 war in Iraq. The United States acted alone when it became clear that no UN Security Council resolution authorizing additional action would be forthcoming, following France's declaration that it would veto any such resolution. US authorities, however, argued that there was adequate authority in existing UN Security Council Resolutions 678, 687 and 1441.

The United States' close ally, the United Kingdom, concurred, as expressed by the UK Attorney General, Lord Goldsmith, who provided the following legal basis for the use of force against Iraq:

Authority to use force against Iraq exists from the combined effect of resolutions 678, 687 and 1441. All of these resolutions were adopted under Chapter VII of the UN Charter which allows the use of force for the express purpose of restoring international peace and security.[11]

The British government's interpretation was that "Resolution 1441 would in terms have provided that a further decision of the Security Council to sanction force was required if that had been intended. Thus, all that resolution 1441 requires is reporting to and discussion by the Security Council of Iraq's failures, but not an express further decision to authorise force."[12]

Australia's Attorney General and the Department of Foreign Affairs and Trade also agreed that "deployment of Australian forces to Iraq and subsequent action by those forces would be consistent with international law". The opinion was based on the authority of existing UN Security Council resolutions "directed towards disarming Iraq of weapons of mass destruction and restoring international peace and security to the area. This existing authority for the use of force would only be negated in current circumstances if the Security Council were to pass a resolution that required Member States to refrain from the use of force against Iraq."[13]

Iraq in 2002 raised the question of how to deal with threats that have the potential for widespread deadly effects but that have not yet materialized. This led to the debate over whether undertaking "regime change" in Iraq without specific international authorization to do so could be legal. In November 2002, the Legal Adviser of the US Department of State, William H. Taft IV, outlined the changing character of self-defence and the possible need to rethink the rules governing self-defence. He noted that the question of when self-defence could be exercised was not new and he cited President John F. Kennedy's observation during the Cuban Missile Crisis in 1962: "We no longer live in a world where only the actual firing of weapons represents a sufficient challenge to a nation's security to constitute maximum peril."[14] But what constitutes "a sufficient challenge", and who can be the judge of this in the absence of a determination by the UN Security Council? Who is responsible and accountable for determining the appropriateness of action taken? This is the crux of the problem related to the legality of the war in Iraq. And, in a world threatened by terrorists and in which the proliferation of weapons of mass destruction is virtually inevitable, the question will not go away.

The answers to the question of who can decide to act in the specific case of Iraq vary. The differences turn on the amount of reliance placed on UN Security Council Resolutions 678 (1991) and 1441 (2002), which were to regulate Iraq's disarmament programme. William Howard Taft IV argued that these resolutions provided sufficient authority: "Resolution 1441 ... gave Iraq a final opportunity to comply, but stated specifically that violations of the obligations ... would constitute a further material breach.... Iraq has clearly committed such violations, and accordingly, the authority to use force to address Iraq's material breaches is clear."[15]

At the same time, Anne-Marie Slaughter noted that "a large majority of specialists in international law believe explicit Security Council authorization is required to confer legality on such a military campaign".[16] A letter to the *Guardian* signed by 16 professors of international law expressed the problem: "Before military action can lawfully be undertaken against Iraq, the Security Council must have indicated its clearly expressed assent. It has not yet done so."[17] Among official views that the war in Iraq was illegal, the view of the Russian Federation is a good example: "As the legal basis for the military action against Iraq references are made to Security Council Resolutions 678 (1990), 687 (1991), 1441 (2002). In our view the above-mentioned resolutions considered in their entirety and in combination with other resolutions on Iraq, official statements of States on their interpretation and provisions of the UN Charter which were the basis for their adoption, show that the Security Council did not authorize Member States in this case to use force against Iraq."[18]

Among those who did not share the majority academic view was Christopher Greenwood, who wrote that "limited and proportionate action may be taken in self-defense if and when an armed attack is reasonably believed to be imminent".[19] Ruth Wedgwood also dissented from the academic majority, basing her reasoning on existing UN resolutions on Iraq:

The founding legal framework for action against Iraq remains intact and available to those who are willing to use it. Resolution 687 is the mother of all resolutions, setting out the requirements for post-Gulf-war Iraq. This 1991 resolution requires, in perpetuity, that Iraq give up its weapons of mass destruction and permit verification ... Resolution 687 designates Iraq's acceptance of this requirement as a continuing condition of the Gulf war ceasefire. Teeth are also supplied by resolution 678, authorizing the allies to expel Iraq from Kuwait and to use force in support of all "subsequent relevant resolutions" needed to restore regional peace and security.[20]

The key point of contention is whether these resolutions authorized the use of force in the case of an Iraqi failure to comply with their provisions. Those opposing the war argued, first, that the resolutions did not authorize the use of force, and then that the renewed programme of arms inspections had begun to meet the objective of disarming Iraq. The US and UK position was that, short of immediate and complete compliance with the disarmament provisions of Resolution 687, regime change was needed in order to ensure stability and peace in the region and, indeed, in the world. In remarks to the UN General Assembly on 12 September 2002, President George W. Bush said:

With every step the Iraq regime takes toward gaining and deploying the most terrible weapons, our own options to confront that regime will narrow. And if an emboldened regime were to supply these weapons to terrorist allies, then the attacks of September the 11th would be a prelude to far greater horrors.[21]

Although relying on UN Security Council Resolutions 678, 687 and 1441 as the bases for action, President Bush also based his action on the "sovereign authority [of the United States] to use force in assuring its own national security".[22] This latter point, coupled with the present power of the US military, has caused worldwide concern about whether the United States intends to break away from the UN security system that it helped to create after World War II in order to address other "deviant states" that it might regard as a threat to its own or the world's security. Joseph Nye wrote that the reason for thinking about preventive war is "the fear ... that certain deviant states, such as Iraq and North Korea, might become enablers of ... terrorist groups" seeking now to privatize war.[23] But where does all this lead us in the long term? Does it lead to more wars of the type we saw waged in Iraq? Does this spell the end of the UN system seeking to restrain the use of force, which has been in place since 1945?

The consensus remains strong in the United States – despite foreign scepticism – that it needs multilateral frameworks. It needs them to address the broad range of issues and areas that it knows have transnational implications. And it needs them perhaps even more urgently in areas where the international standard is not yet clear. One of the harshest critics of US policy, former French Foreign Minister Dominique de Villepin, put it well when he noted:

Legitimacy ... is the key to the effectiveness of international action. If we want to develop the right answers to the challenges of the modern world and to take appropriate measures – including the use of force – we must do so with the authority of collective decisions.[24]

The present urgent international task is therefore to maintain a multilateral structure within which states can disagree. As with any political contest, winners and losers in a situation must maintain sufficient common purpose and interest to make it possible to work together in the future. Power disparities may present a special problem when the disagreement is with the most powerful member or members of the system. Nevertheless, the United Nations' history during the Cold War demonstrates that this can be done. Sidestepping certain disputes comes at the price of removing some conflicts from the United Nations' field of responsibility. But, as the end of the Cold War showed, having the institution available and capable when political conditions are right for it to play a more active role is also important and should not be overlooked – not by the United States and not by critics of the United States. Although there is a serious disagreement among the most important UN members, all have a stake in maintaining a security role for the United Nations and should be careful not to destroy it.

The war in Iraq and its aftermath pose a serious challenge to the UN system, but the system thus far still remains. Whether that system will be effective in addressing the security concerns of the future will depend on whether UN members are willing to work with each other to make it so.

Establishing legitimacy

In 2001, the International Commission on Intervention and State Sovereignty initiated by the Canadian government noted that, although linked, legality and legitimacy were not synonymous and that legitimacy takes on increased significance when the law is unsettled.[25] But what happens if the chief source of legitimacy happens to be the same body that confers international legality on an action but finds that it can provide neither legality nor legitimacy? This was the case with the 2003 Iraq war, since the UN Security Council declined explicitly to authorize the war in Iraq, making the war illegal in the eyes of many. And are we on the verge of facing more such cases where the United Nations is unwilling to authorize action but some state or group of states nevertheless feels compelled to act? The 2003 Iraq war was not the first time this question arose.

Under very different conditions, but addressing the United Nations' failure to act in Rwanda in the wake of the 1999 Operation Allied Force in Kosovo, UN Secretary-General Kofi Annan asked:

To those for whom the greatest threat to the future of international order is the use of force in the absence of a Security Council mandate, one might say: leave Kosovo aside for a moment, and think about Rwanda. Imagine for one moment that, in those dark days and hours leading up to the genocide, there had been a coalition of states ready and willing to act in defence of the Tutsi population, but the council had refused or delayed giving the green light. Should such a coalition then have stood idly by while the horror unfolded?

To those for whom the Kosovo action heralded a new era when states and groups of states can take military action outside the established mechanisms for enforcing international law, one might equally ask: Is there not a danger of such interventions undermining the imperfect, yet resilient security system created after the second world war, and of setting dangerous precedents for future interventions without a clear criterion to decide who might invoke these precedents and in what circumstances?[26]

The dilemma the Secretary-General posed about the adequacy of the UN security system to respond to security concerns unforeseen by the Charter's founders is a crucial one and existed before the questions raised by the 2003 Iraq war. A rigid requirement of Security Council authorization for military forces to be used legally could preclude, and has precluded, their use when morality and international law would otherwise seem to require it, as in humanitarian emergencies. On the other hand, authorization of the use of military force on an ad hoc basis by bodies or groups of states other than the Security Council or action taken by a single state put at risk the decision-making structure of the present international security system. Since NATO's actions in 1999, for example, new claims to be a legitimate source of authorization have already been made, notably in 2000 by the Economic Community of West African States (ECOWAS), which adopted a protocol explicitly stating that the ECOWAS Council could authorize the use of military force even without a Security Council mandate.[27]

Concern over possible unregulated intervention based on the judgement of a small but powerful number of states caused the International Commission on Intervention and State Sovereignty to insist on objective evidence of a conscience-shocking situation and the conception of a "responsibility to protect" rather than a "right to intervene". The Commission's work was guided by "a clear indication that the tools, devices and thinking of international relations need now to be comprehensively reassessed, in order to meet the foreseeable needs of the 21st century".[28] The Commission's report continued that any new approach needed to meet at least four basic objectives:

- to establish clearer rules, procedures and criteria for determining whether, when and how to intervene;
- to establish the legitimacy of military intervention when necessary and after all other approaches have failed;
- to ensure that military intervention, when it occurs, is carried out only for the purposes proposed, is effective, and is undertaken with proper concern to minimize the human costs and institutional damage that will result; and
- to help eliminate, where possible, the causes of conflict while enhancing the prospects for durable and sustainable peace.[29]

The Commission further noted that: "In the face of legal ambiguity, lists of possible thresholds and criteria assume increasing importance. The establishment of a set of criteria has been offered as one way to mitigate the potential for abuse. While not legally binding, they could nevertheless provide a benchmark against which the legitimacy of an intervention could be measured."[30]

These criteria produce useful general standards by which to judge any claim to legitimate action. They seek to maintain order through rules, procedures and criteria even when such existing standards somehow proved inadequate. They accept the concept of necessity, although only when all alternatives have been exhausted.[31] They apply the just war standard of acting only where there is a likelihood of success in meeting the objectives stated. And, finally, they maintain a focus on supporting durable solutions and institutional structures over pursuing specific national objectives and interests. These criteria well state the tests that can be applied to actions taken outside of the generally accepted frameworks for authorizing action and may provide the conditions necessary to consider legitimate an action that otherwise fails to meet existing legal standards. Given these conditions, it would appear that legitimacy can often be determined only after the action has taken place if the conditions that triggered action are not observable prior to acting. This is, of course, where persuasive and credible intelligence becomes important.

Yet, even though no weapons of mass destruction were found in Iraq, the threat of such weapons finding their way into terrorist networks remains. Are there any standards of legitimacy that might aid in addressing such threats if existing rules and institutions appear unable to respond? One such effort was advanced by Lee Feinstein and Anne-Marie Slaughter in the idea of a "duty to prevent". This would apply under the following conditions:

First, [the duty to prevent] seeks to control not only the proliferation of WMD but also the people who possess them. Second, it emphasizes prevention, calling on the international community to act early in order to be effective and develop a menu of potential measures aimed at particular governments – especially measures that can be taken well short of any use of force. Third, the duty to prevent should be exercised collectively, through a global or regional organization.[32]

Again, if we put the above criteria to the test, we find that they emphasize alternatives to the use of force and address the problem of proliferation in ways that try to bring the action back into a multilateral setting. Should the international community fail to act through the United Nations or some other widely recognized body, capable states, alone or with allies, may be compelled to act to prevent harm from coming to their citizens and others for whom they are responsible. As suggested by the responsibility to protect, the duty to prevent also begins from the premise that individual states are responsible for the security and well-being of their populations. However, in the case of the responsibility to protect, states from the outside may have to act against a state that is abusing its population, whereas, in the duty to prevent, a state may have to act to protect its population from a potential outside threat.

The duty to prevent is also a reaction to possible threats posed by closed societies developing weapons of mass destruction and lacking any internal political checks on the actions of a despotic regime. The duty to prevent seeks to legitimate early action to prevent mass murder through the use of WMD. It attempts to establish criteria in order to determine the existence of a threat so that the difficulty of mounting evidence to support a response prior to an attack is overcome. If a threat is imminent, international law allows pre-emptive action. However, in a world of weapons of mass destruction and technology, the time available for response once a threat materializes may be very short, rendering the classic approach to pre-emptive action insufficient. As described in the *National Security Strategy of the United States of America* in September 2002: "We must adapt the concept of imminent threat to the capabilities and objectives of today's adversaries. Rogue states and terrorists do not seek to attack us using conventional means. They know such attacks would fail. Instead, they rely on acts of terror and, potentially, the use of weapons of mass destruction – weapons that can be easily concealed, delivered covertly, and used without warning."[33]

At the same time, as we have seen from the current war in Iraq, if war is waged on such a pre-emptive basis, then evidence to justify such a war is essential to maintain support for such war efforts on three levels: by citizens in states that wage the war, by the population in the affected state, and by the international community. Whatever the merits of removing Saddam Hussein from power, when the United States waged war in March 2003 on the basis of Iraq's possession of weapons of mass destruction, prior to the completion of the UN weapons inspectors' mission and without further authorization of the UN Security Council, it imposed a burden to find weapons of mass destruction or evidence of their production. The failure to do so has eroded support of the effort in the United States, overseas and within Iraq and has damaged the credibility of both the Iraqi operation specifically and the general effort to address the threat described above by the *National Security Strategy*.

Legitimacy cannot substitute for legality over the long run. Therefore, if change to the existing system is necessary owing to new conditions and circumstances, relevant international and domestic institutions need to reflect seriously on how to address these new circumstances. Failure to do so will result in the kind of unilateral state response that over time will dissipate the advances made in multilateral international cooperation since 1945. As UN Secretary-General Kofi Annan noted: "Whilst there may continue to exist a diversity of perception on the relative importance of the various threats facing particular Member States on an individual basis, it is important to find an appropriate balance at a global level."[34] Implicit in his view is that a balance needs to be found within the UN system itself.

As the International Commission on Intervention and State Sovereignty focused on the responsibility of states and the international community to protect against gross violations of human rights, so is it the responsibility of states and the international community to protect against the potential of mass murder through the use of weapons of mass destruction. The political tensions created among members of the UN Security Council by the war in Iraq demonstrate the complexity of the current security environment. However, both the legitimate and the legal use of force require multilateral cooperation. Yet, militarily capable states can be expected to seek such cooperation only if cooperation will provide effective responses to threats as they emerge.

Conclusion

In an article titled "Unilateral Action and the Transformations of the World Constitutive Process," Michael Reisman wrote:

Actions inconsistent with the procedures prescribed for them may erode the authority of the law and increase the probability of abuse. Hence the law's ceaseless quest for organization and institutionalization and its discomfort with and inherent resistance to legally unauthorized actions, no matter how urgent the circumstances or morally imperative the impulse.[35]

Reisman continued by reflecting on the correlation between "the ineffectiveness of a political system and the resort to and toleration of unilateral action: the less effective the system, the more the impulse for and use of unilateral action and vice versa".[36] These two observations capture well the dilemma faced by the present UN security system.

There is great pressure to avoid changing the existing system lest any effort to improve it result in the destruction of even the modicum of organization and institutionalization that the UN Charter system now provides. At the same time, because the political system does not wholeheartedly embrace this legal framework, the potential for acting outside the framework increases. This explains why any action that challenges the basic tenets of the present system is regarded with such hostility. It triggers a deep worry that each move away from accepted procedure and standards of conduct may prove to be a step towards no organization or order at all. Understanding this, however, leaves open the question of how change can be made in the fragile and fragmented political environment that is the UN community of states.

Arguments of legality should not cloud assessments of the adequacy of multilateral institutions to meet ongoing and emerging needs. Though the tests for legitimacy in Iraq may have proven empty, the questions of security posed throughout the debate about going to war in Iraq may still require attention. These issues included that of closed societies subject to no internal controls developing and brandishing weapons of mass destruction. But if this is the concern, then the need should be clearly spelled out and subjected to legal review. In the case of the 2003 war in Iraq, there was a widespread view that change of the kind sought by the United States and its allies in Iraq was not warranted. For those who will assess these actions in the future, the question will be whether change was not needed or whether the case for change was poorly made.

US actions may have made any change more difficult, but these actions should not overshadow efforts to assess the capacity, effectiveness and accountability of the UN Security Council. This assessment goes beyond Security Council decision-making to its ability to carry out and oversee the decisions it makes. All of this, however, relies on the members of the UN Security Council, and particularly its permanent members, to provide the kind of political system that will decrease the likelihood of behaviour outside the generally accepted framework of conduct.

It would be wise to recognize that, over time, acting on the basis of legitimacy without legality will not contribute to orderly international relations, particularly where the bases for state action may not be easily verifiable. Legitimacy may provide a priori justification where legality is debatable, but it cannot be used on a routine basis and will normally rest on a *post bellum* consensus on the causes of war, as Slaughter argued. For such justification to have any credibility, it must be applied carefully, resting on broadly accepted standards, on clearly articulated needs and on criteria based as much as possible on objective conditions. The action must further be subject to outside review, including assessing whether the stated goals of an operation have been achieved and whether the conduct of the operation was appropriate and acceptable. Providing a framework for ongoing interaction between the states that opted to act and those that did not is particularly important at a time of change when existing standards may be in flux.

Understanding the differences between legality and legitimacy may provide an immediate answer on whether or not permanent change is required where the existing framework appears inadequate. Whatever the answer, states must work to bring legitimacy and legality back together following any significant episode of acting outside the framework. However, this can happen only if institutions are willing and able to recognize new needs and to respond to them. As the debate over humanitarian intervention demonstrated, the credibility of the UN system rests not just on how effectively it can constrain its members but also, and perhaps more significantly, on how well it can enable states to take appropriate preventive and other measures to forestall threats to peace and security. Under the influence of globalization, the speed with which threats can materialize and the scope of the damage that can be done have increased. The ability of states to stave off such attacks will need to adapt at a comparable pace, and this may include the adaptation of the institutions they rely on to provide security both for prevention and for protection.

Notes

1. See Andreas Paulus, "The War against Iraq and the Future of International Law: Hegemony or Pluralism?", *Michigan Journal of International Law*, Vol. 25 (Spring 2004), pp. 732–733.
2. Anne-Marie Slaughter, "Good Reasons for Going around the U.N.", *New York Times*, 18 March 2003.
3. Anne-Marie Slaughter, "Reflecting on the War in Iraq One Year Later", *ASIL Newsletter*, March/April 2004, p. 2.
4. Slaughter, "Good Reasons for Going around the U.N.".
5. "Secretary-General Names High-Level Panel to Study Global Security Threats, and Recommend Necessary Changes", UN Press Release SG/A/857, 11 April 2003.
6. "Jim Carter Becomes ASIL's 41st President", *ASIL Newsletter*, May/July 2004, p. 10.
7. *Report of the Panel on United Nations Peace Operations*, UN Doc. A/55/305–S/2000/809, 21 August 2000, para. 53, p. 10.
8. Anne-Marie Slaughter, "The Will That Makes It Work", *Washington Post*, 2 March 2003, p. B3.

9. Ramesh Thakur and Dipankar Banerjee, "India: Democratic, Poor, Internationalist", in Charlotte Ku and Harold K. Jacobson, eds, *Democratic Accountability and the Use of Force in International Law* (Cambridge: Cambridge University Press, 2003), p. 204.

10. George W. Bush, "Remarks by the President in Address to United Nations General Assembly", 12 September 2002, USUN Press Release 131 (02), ⟨http://www.un.int/usa/02_131.htm⟩.

11. Lord Goldsmith, "Legal Basis for Use of Force against Iraq", 17 March 2003, ⟨http://www.pmo.gov.uk/output/Page3287.asp⟩.

12. Ibid.

13. "Memorandum of Advice on the Use of Force against Iraq, provided by the Attorney General's Department and the Department of Foreign Affairs and Trade, March 18, 2003", available at ⟨http://www.pm.gov.au/iraq⟩ (accessed 5 November 2004).

14. As quoted in William H. Taft IV, "The Legal Basis for Preemption", Memorandum to Members of the ASIL-CFR Roundtable on Old Rules, New Threats, 18 November 2002, ⟨http://www.cfr.org/publication/5250/legal_basis_for_preemption.html⟩.

15. As quoted in Peter Slevin, "U.S. Says War Has Legal Basis", *Washington Post*, 21 March 2003, p. A14.

16. Ibid.

17. "War Would Be Illegal", *Guardian*, 7 March 2003.

18. Legal Department of the Ministry of Foreign Affairs of the Russian Federation, "Legal Assessment of the Use of Force against Iraq", reprinted in "Current Developments: Public International Law", *International and Comparative Law Quarterly*, Vol. 52 (October 2003), p. 1059.

19. As quoted in "Why the Sword Is Mightier Than the Law", *Telegraph*, 19 March 2003.

20. Ruth Wedgwood, "Comment & Analysis: Legal Authority Exists for a Strike on Iraq", *Financial Times*, 14 March 2003, p. 1.

21. Bush, "Remarks by the President in Address to United Nations General Assembly".

22. "President Says Saddam Hussein Must Leave Iraq Within 48 Hours: Remarks by the President in Address to the Nation", 17 March 2003, ⟨http://www.whitehouse.gov/news/releases/2003/03/20030317-7.html⟩.

23. Joseph S. Nye, "Before War", *Washington Post*, 14 March 2003, p. A27.

24. Dominique de Villepin, "Law, Force and Justice", International Institute for Strategic Studies Annual Lecture, 27 March 2003, ⟨http://www.iiss.org/showdocument.php?docID=114⟩.

25. *The Responsibility to Protect: Research, Bibliography, Background. Supplementary Volume to the Report of the International Commission on Intervention and State Sovereignty* (Ottawa: The International Development Research Centre, December 2001), section C.7, ⟨http://www.iciss.ca/00_Intro-en.asp⟩.

26. Kofi Annan, "Two Concepts of Sovereignty", *The Economist*, 18 September 1999, p. 49.

27. As reprinted in *Journal of Conflict & Security Law*, Vol. 5, No. 2 (December 2000), pp. 231–259.

28. *The Responsibility to Protect: Report of the International Commission on Intervention and State Sovereignty* (Ottawa: The International Development Research Centre, December 2001), para. 2.2, ⟨http://www.iciss.ca/report-en.asp⟩.

29. Ibid., para. 2.3.

30. *The Responsibility to Protect: Research, Bibliography, Background*, section C.7.

31. See Andreas Laursen, "The Use of Force and (the State of) Necessity", *Vanderbilt Journal of Transnational Law*, Vol. 37 (March 2004), pp. 485–526.

32. Lee Feinstein and Anne-Marie Slaughter, "A Duty to Prevent", *Foreign Affairs* (January/February 2004), p. 137.

33. *The National Security Strategy of the United States of America* (Washington, DC: The White House, September 2002), p. 15, ⟨http://www.whitehouse.gov/nsc/nss.pdf⟩.

34. "Secretary-General Names High-Level Panel to Study Global Security Threats, and Recommend Necessary Changes", 11 April 2003.

35. W. Michael Reisman, "Unilateral Action and the Transformations of the World Constitutive Process: The Special Problem of Humanitarian Intervention", *European Journal of International Law*, Vol. 11 (March 2000), p. 6.

36. Ibid.

25

The multinational action in Iraq and international law

Ruth Wedgwood

In the rear-view mirror of a difficult war, reassessing legality may seem beside the point to both critics and supporters. The war for the liberation of Iraq has unfolded in unpredictable ways for all sides. In a real sense, the war is not yet over, even as the United Nations and coalition forces support the attempt by Iraqi citizens to establish a working democracy and federal structure. The ongoing terror by Ba'athist insurgents against Iraqi citizens who have worked bravely to adopt a constitution, elect a government and restore an economy, is a reminder of the nature of the former regime. Students of peacekeeping may be reminded of the parallel attempt by old regime militias in East Timor to use a scorched-earth policy to cripple that country's hard-won independence. In Iraq's nascent democracy, there is the additional challenge of an insurgency that is in part directed and financed from across the border, by senior Ba'athist leaders who fled to Syria in anticipation of the capture of Baghdad, a reminder that some problems cannot be fully solved in isolation. Judgements about the intervention in Iraq will inevitably have a broad reach, beyond a spot assessment of the decision in March 2003 to proceed to the use of military force. Alongside the important questions of legality and legitimacy, one would wish to look over time at its effect on international institutions, security doctrine and the transformation of the Middle East. Nonetheless, there are important observations that can clarify a judgement even now.

First, a fast-forward summary. From the viewpoint of a doctrinal international lawyer, the argument in support of the March 2003 intervention

413

is straightforward, even though contested by some. The justification is founded on Iraq's extended and stubborn failure to account for its weapons programmes under the mandatory Security Council resolutions imposed at the end of the 1991 Gulf war. Rather than attacking Baghdad, the coalition in the first Gulf war had hoped to demonstrate that Iraq's threat to the region could be contained by a monitored course of mandatory disarmament. The disarmament and reporting requirements imposed by the UN Security Council in 1991 were not disposable, despite Iraq's remarkable history of defiance. In November 1990, in Resolution 678, the Council voted to authorize member states cooperating with Kuwait to use "all necessary means" in order to expel Iraqi forces from Kuwait and to restore peace and security in the region, as well as to "uphold and implement ... all subsequent relevant resolutions". In April 1991, after the successful ground campaign, the Security Council granted a ceasefire in the war. But the ceasefire was explicitly conditioned on Iraq's compliance with the Council's requirements of Iraqi disarmament and full accounting for prior weapons programmes. Iraq's deliberate breach of Resolution 687 over a 12-year period served to suspend the ceasefire, leaving in place the authorization for the use of force found in Resolution 678, as well as, arguably, an inherent right of collective self-defence stemming from the 1991 war.

The claim that only a second act of authorization would suffice to permit enforcement of Resolution 687 ignores the teeth of the original resolutions. Resolution 678 authorized member states "co-operating with the Government of Kuwait, ... to use all necessary means to uphold and implement resolution 660 (1990) and all subsequent relevant resolutions and to restore international peace and security in the area". Resolution 687 was indeed a subsequent relevant resolution, and was central to the restoration of peace and security in the Gulf. There is nothing in the text of Resolution 687 that limits its duration or suggests expiry. Nor is there any conceivable claim of desuetude or abandonment. To the contrary, the enforcement of Resolution 687 was front and centre in international debate for over a decade, consuming political and military resources that would have had other important uses in meeting human catastrophes. The sanctions regime imposed on Iraq was testament to the seriousness with which the international community regarded Iraq's obligation to disarm. Any claim that Iraq was not given a fair chance to comply with the requirements of Resolution 687 is belied by Iraq's dangerous game of brinksmanship over the course of a decade. This was not a voluntary regime, whose force was contingent on a later ratifying act. And, as a law professor argued in the *Financial Times* on 13 March 2003, "Security Council resolutions are not yet so airy as to expire with the term of a particular secretary-general".[1] One may note the sober voice of Sir Adam Roberts:

How much weight attaches to the past decisions of the Security Council in authorising force? If the Council authorises certain member states to undertake a task, but is then unable to agree on follow-up action, does the original authorisation still stand? ... The simple guiding principle has to be that a resolution, once passed remains in effect. In the absence of a new resolution repudiating earlier positions (which will always be hard to achieve, granted the existence of a veto) a presumption of continuity is plausible.[2]

There is nothing in Resolution 1441, voted by the Security Council in November 2002, that suspended the force of the earlier resolutions.[3] To the contrary, Resolution 1441 recorded the Council's finding that Iraq "has been and remains in material breach of its obligations under relevant resolutions, including resolution 687". Iraq was permitted a "final opportunity" to come into compliance, beginning with an "accurate, full, and complete declaration" of its programmes. But the resolution warned that false statements and omissions would, in themselves, "constitute a further material breach of Iraq's obligations".

Iraq's disregard of the final opportunity provided by Resolution 1441 (and its continuing breach of Resolution 687) was in evidence in its filing in December 2002. Once again (as so many times in the past), Saddam Hussein spurned the obligation to give a complete accounting of Iraqi weapons programmes. This, without needing more, sufficed as *casus belli*, alongside the regime's persistent refusal to permit any interviews of Iraqi weapons scientists outside the country, the inspectors' discovery that Iraq was still deliberately violating the 150 km limit on ballistic missiles, and the discovery that Iraq had retained growth stocks of anthrax and other prohibited biological reagents.[4]

The invasion of Kuwait in August 1990 was the culmination of a long record of aggressive conduct by the Ba'athist Iraqi leadership. The regime had previously invaded Iran and gassed Iraqi Kurds in the Anfal campaign,[5] and, when faced with this dismaying record, the United Nations Security Council reacted with admirable dispatch against Iraq's invasion of Kuwait, not least because of the additional threat to Saudi Arabia. To point out a factor of self-interest in the world's swift reaction to Iraq's attempted domination of an oil-rich Gulf is no insult to the shared principle that other countries should not be swallowed up. The economic facts of life, however, serve as a reminder that collective security mechanisms lack any automatic supply of police power. Even where the Security Council votes to authorize the use of force, the employment of that authority depends upon coalitions of the willing – countries willing to raise and contribute military forces. Council authorization may be stymied as well by the particular ambitions and conflicting agendas of Council members. One may note, for example, the potential effect of Chinese energy relationships on the Security Council's delayed response to Iranian violations of the Treaty on the Non-Proliferation of Nuclear Weapons and to Sudan's genocidal acts in Darfur.

In August 1990, the Security Council demanded Iraq's withdrawal from Kuwait and imposed economic sanctions against the regime. Sanctions and diplomacy were given several months to work. In November 1990, the use of armed force was authorized by Security Council Resolution 678, under Chapter VII, with a 90-day time delay to permit Russian Foreign Minister Primakov and others to undertake one final round of diplomacy. The potential costs of "last chance" diplomacy were later shown in a dramatic discovery made by United Nations weapons inspectors. As it turned out, Saddam had used the 90-day diplomatic interval in 1990–1991 to get ready for battle, producing and loading biological reagents into aerial bombs and warheads.[6] It was also revealed, after the fact, that, following the invasion of Kuwait, Saddam attempted to accelerate the production of a nuclear weapon, hoping for a weapon within a year's time.[7] Iraq did not employ chemical or biological weapons during the March 1991 ground war, but this may have been the result of the deterrence provided by US Secretary of State James Baker's warning that "devastating consequences" would follow if such weapons were employed. (Whether this should be considered a belligerent reprisal is a different legal debate.[8])

In February 1991, after a month-long air campaign, coalition forces swept into Kuwait and Iraq with the famous "Hail Mary" flanking manoeuvre that carried allied forces around Iraqi troops. The coalition's pursuit of Iraqi republican guard divisions stopped short of Baghdad, allowing Saddam to preserve substantial military forces. A ceasefire was offered to the Iraqis and was formalized in Security Council Resolution 687.

This constitutive resolution required that Iraq abide by unique limitations on its military capacity for the indefinite future. Iraq would have to give up any missiles with a range exceeding 150 km, together with any chemical, biological or nuclear weapons, and any components and precursors. In addition, Saddam would have to provide a full and accurate accounting of these weapons programmes, subject to verification by United Nations weapons inspectors, and agree to ongoing monitoring to prevent any reconstitution of these programmes.

The expected compliance by Iraq was not forthcoming. The UN Special Commission (UNSCOM) on Iraq, formed under the leadership of

Swedish diplomat Rolf Ekeus, originally expected to complete verification of Iraq's weapons disposal within 6–12 months. But Iraq refused to grant international inspectors open access to the records, scientists and sites that would have permitted a rapid assay of the state of the regime's weapons programmes. Records were removed from sites scheduled for inspection, travel by the inspectors was delayed and impeded, and air inspections were subjected to landing restrictions and, on at least one occasion, a physical struggle over a helicopter's controls. It was not until four years later, in 1995, that Iraq finally acknowledged it had established a research programme on biological reagents such as anthrax, botulinum and aflatoxin. This admission was not forthcoming until UNSCOM succeeded in piecing together supplier records that showed unaccountably large purchases of biological growth media, ultimately totalling 39 tons (grossly excessive for medical laboratory cultures but useful in biological weapons research and production). Admission that the programme had proceeded to the stage of weaponizing reagents came only after Saddam Hussein's son-in-law defected to Jordan, with knowledge of the programmes. Skilful concealment of weapons production capability within dual-use research and manufacturing facilities also thwarted verification.

Iraq produced a parade of last and final accountings throughout the 1990s, each sworn to be the true and complete version. Iraq's ambassador to the United Nations in New York showed evident chagrin when he was reduced each time to the argument that Iraq's admissions of prior lies now proved its incontestable good faith.

Iraq regularly threatened to withhold future cooperation from the UNSCOM inspectors unless economic sanctions against the regime were lifted. France and Russia also challenged the sanctions regime, and criticized the inspection methods of UNSCOM, suggesting that the burden of persuasion lay upon UNSCOM rather than Iraq. Even after the "Oil-for-Food" programme was introduced in late 1996, the ambivalent stance of these two members of the permanent five (the P-5) continued. Saddam Hussein's political skill was evident, as well, since any fracture in the Council alliance was translated into resistance on the ground. The Iraqi regime refused access to various sites of interest to the inspectors, including so-called presidential palaces, and persistently argued that it was up to UNSCOM to prove that Iraq still had weapons, rather than Baghdad's burden to show the opposite. The doe-faced claim that Iraqi personnel had poured chemical weapons and biological reagents into the desert sand, without keeping records of the disposal or recording the place, was met with understandable incredulity. Attempts to study Iraq's methods of denial and concealment in order to avoid evasion of the inspection methods had limited success. The same closed Iraqi security apparatus was charged with supervision of weapons research and with Saddam's personal security. The situation continued to deteriorate despite the 1997 appointment of a new director of UNSCOM, Australian diplomat Richard Butler, a conciliatory trip to Baghdad by UN Secretary-General Kofi Annan, who obtained a short-lived memorandum of understanding with the regime, a review of UNSCOM inspection results by Brazilian diplomat Cesare Amorim, and the further reorganization of UN inspection efforts (and a nearly wholesale change of inspection personnel) in a new UN group headed by Hans Blix (the United Nations Monitoring, Verification and Inspection Commission, or UNMOVIC). When Iraq refused to admit US inspectors as part of the UNMOVIC teams, on-site inspections were terminated in late 1998. This was followed by a brief air campaign against Iraqi military sites, dubbed Operation Desert Fox.[9] Perhaps one should have expected at the outset that Saddam was unlikely to comply with any international programme of monitored disarmament, even after a defeat. As Rolf Ekeus has observed, when a leader comes to power through stealth and violence, the same pattern of behaviour is likely to manifest itself internationally.

There is no need to summon a controversial theory of preventive war or pre-emptive self-defence as a basis for obtaining Iraq's compliance with a Council-mandated disarmament regime. The legal argument against Iraq can be modest and confined. As a recidivist aggressor against its neighbours, Iraq was assigned and accepted singular duties, under Council Resolution 687, to shed its development of weapons of mass destruction, to abstain from any renewal of those programmes in perpetuity, and to show the international community that it had done so. To be sure, the attacks of 11 September 2001 challenged classic strategic doctrine by exposing the potential failure of deterrence against non-state actors. Any future attacks with weapons of mass destruction may lack a "return address". A state could pass weapons materiel to a non-state actor seeking to target a shared enemy, and yet avoid the matter coming to light. Deterrence of such conduct would not be available, unless one were prepared to announce an unprecedented strategic doctrine that would threaten a response against any possible source of the anonymous attack. Thus, in a brave new world of non-state actors, even where there is no established relationship or integration between a state and a private network, strategic deterrence may not prevent deadly hand-overs. As with 9/11, there may be no warning of an "imminent" attack. It may be a bolt from the blue, or from a container on an ocean barge.

Unlawful production of weapons of mass destruction and deliberate evasion of reporting requirements thus posed an aggravated danger after the occurrence of al-Qaeda's terrorist attacks of 9/11. Earlier in the 1990s, Iraq may (or may not) have exported chemical weapons production to Sudan, where Osama bin Laden maintained important links.[10] Iraqi agents may (or may not) have met in Prague with a leader of the 9/11 attacks. Regardless of the interpretation of intelligence sources on these matters, the deliberate evasion of inspection requirements by an irresponsible regime could not be ignored or indulged, even in 2003.

This helps to explain the willingness of the United States and its allies to flow significant numbers of troops into the Gulf region in mid-2002, in order to persuade Iraq that it needed to readmit the UN weapons inspectors and comply with the verification requirements of Resolution 687. Under Resolution 1441, Iraq was given what the Security Council deemed a "final chance" to give an adequate accounting, and failed to do so. UNMOVIC inspectors directed by Hans Blix did re-enter Iraq and conducted some on-site inspections. Even then, the UN inspectors could not interview weapons scientists in private or gain permission to interview scientists and their families out of the country, where they would enjoy some safeguards against retaliation. Blix was reduced to playing needle-in-a-haystack. He could not follow the records or materiel that might have been removed to Syria, a Ba'athist neighbour. He could not dig up the Iraqi desert, though the intriguing discovery of a Soviet MiG buried in the desert sand suggests that unusual storage methods were not beyond Saddam's imagination. Indeed, Saddam's scientific expert on nuclear centrifuges admitted after the war in 2003 that he had become expert in cleansing inspection sites to thwart UNSCOM inspectors, and had ended up burying crucial design blueprints in his own garden under a tree.[11]

Shortly before the coalition's military intervention, there was a reported meeting in St Petersburg between French President Jacques Chirac, German Chancellor Gerhard Schröder and Russian President Vladimir Putin to discuss their positions. Several public international lawyers from each country were reportedly invited to this affair of state in order to attempt to frame arguments in opposition. But the fat was thrown in the fire by President Chirac's statement to the press on 10 March 2003 that in no circumstances would France vote in favour of renewed authorization of the use of force.[12]

The Security Council was thus blocked from further action. The United States, the United Kingdom and Australia, acting in cooperation with the Emirate of Kuwait, decided to proceed with a military intervention, without extending the UNMOVIC inspections for any further period. Factors that may have argued in favour of an earlier start were the challenges in maintaining battle-readiness in a desert bivouac, and the difficulties of fighting in summer temperatures (especially in chemical protective suits, since Iraq was believed to have chemical arms). In addition, there was an advantage in achieving tactical surprise once the Turkish parliament refused to allow the US Fourth Infantry Division to deploy on Iraq's northern border, and post-war analysts have credited that surprise as a factor in the coalition's success in getting to Baghdad with unexpected speed. Saddam's calculated exploitation of the 1991 diplomatic pause also showed the hazards of granting an adversary extra time to prepare, once an operation was widely seen to be inevitable.

The race to Baghdad went better than anyone expected. The occupation has been difficult and costly to human life, both civilian and military. The war planners saw the possible difficulties of house-to-house fighting in the initial assault on urban areas. But the melting away of Iraqi forces and the organization of a funded, well-supplied and sustained urban insurgency in Sunni areas turned the occupation into a continuation of combat by another name. Even the capture of Saddam Hussein in a "spider hole" near Tikrit has not sufficed to quell the insurgency.

Still, several things have happened since the conclusion of major combat operations that may cast a warmer light on events. First, there is the remarkable and uplifting celebration of Iraqi democracy. Iraqi women and men courageously went to the polls in January 2005, and again in December 2005, defying the danger of car bombs and suicide attacks, in order to cast their ballots. Their forefingers were painted with indelible purple ink, to show that they had voted. This safeguard against double voting provided a view of women and men proudly holding up their purple fingers, in defiance of the repression of the old regime. Iraq's example was reinforced by the events of Ukraine's "orange revolution", sustained by the power of civil disobedience and public demonstration in rebuffing outside interference in national elections.

Since that time, there has been a "domino effect" of democracy – as if other regimes newly understand that their citizens will claim the same voice. The results of a democratic ballot are not always easy in the short run, especially in the wake of a fundamentalist Islamist movement that has radicalized some actors. But the long-term trend toward democracy may be the best chance to bring prosperity and stability to the region. With the death of Yasir Arafat, the Palestinian people voted for Mahmoud Abbas as the new president of the Palestinian Authority, upon his pledge to rid the Authority of its debilitating financial corruption. A year later, in 2006, the parliamentary showing of Hamas has been startling to some observers, but its role as a governing coalition may mitigate its radicalism towards coexistence with Israel. Saudi Arabia held municipal elections in February 2005, and has indicated that women may be permitted to vote in 2009. President Mubarak of Egypt held presidential elections in September 2005, though his first impulse was to arrest the most prominent opposition candidate. The people of Lebanon reacted to the brazen assassination of former prime minister Rafiq Hariri by demanding an end to Syria's 30-year military occupation of Lebanon. The

Security Council followed suit by demanding the immediate withdrawal of Syrian troops in Resolution 1559,[13] and the United Nations authorized an astonishing investigation of Hariri's murder that pointed to the complicity of Syria's leadership. It is too early to speak of a "Basra" or "Baghdad" spring, but the demonstration effect of the Iraqi vote has been extraordinary.

Second, there is the impact of the United Nations High-level Panel on Threats, Challenges and Change, commissioned by the UN Secretary-General to assay future dangers facing the international community. The panel members include a striking array of former international and national leaders, including former UN High Commissioner for Refugees Sadako Ogata, former Egyptian foreign minister Amre Moussa, former head of the French Conseil Constitutionnel Robert Badinter, and former Australian foreign minister Gareth Evans. One of the prime threats identified by the panel is the problem of weapons of mass destruction in the hands of bellicose regimes.

Customary international law has never purported to limit the acquisition of weapons capability by independent states. Limits on the acquisition of biological weapons, chemical weapons and nuclear weapons have developed as a matter of treaty law, and countries can leave those treaties. But the panel faced a new and more dangerous world with the examples of North Korea and Iran, as well as the evident dangers of the attempted acquisition of weapons of mass destruction by private terror networks. The panel observed that there is a new type of collective threat facing the international community, namely, "nightmare scenarios combining terrorists, weapons of mass destruction and irresponsible States". For the first time, the United Nations community – which reacted with great scepticism to the United States' *National Security Strategy* in 2002 – has acknowledged that weapons capacity can itself be dangerous and potentially actionable. The acquisition of weapons of mass destruction by an "irresponsible State" might "conceivably justify the use of force, not just reactively but preventively and before a latent threat becomes imminent".[14]

To be sure, the High-level Panel concludes that threats should be countered collectively rather than unilaterally. But the panel also acknowledges that this preference for multilateral response depends upon the temper and sense of responsibility of Council members. The Security Council must rise to the occasion. In considering the tension between unilateralism and multilateralism, one may remember the Secretary-General's own conundrum about who could authorize humanitarian intervention. In 1999, in a speech to the General Assembly, Kofi Annan posed a more-than-rhetorical question about genocide in Rwanda and ethnic cleansing in Kosovo. He asked what states should do if the Security Council refused to act.[15] Was humanitarian intervention permissible without Council approval? The Secretary-General's suggestion was that the successful maintenance of a collective system for decision-making would depend upon the Council's willingness to respond to threats. Quite apart from the effect of Resolutions 678 and 687, the same point might be drawn in relation to an irresponsible regime such as the Ba'athist dictatorship of Saddam Hussein. As the Secretary-General noted in his visit to Washington in December 2004, "where there is a convincing and persuasive case, the council must face up to its responsibilities and act, rather than create a situation where a member state feels it has to go outside the council to take – to get redress or to take action".[16]

As a third factor, one should note the sobering effect of post-war assessments of Saddam Hussein's weapons programmes. To be sure, the post-war Iraq Survey Group discovered no stockpiles of chemical weapons or biological weapons. But the reticent voice of former UNSCOM director Rolf Ekeus has reminded post-war observers of the central role of Saddam's intention and his interest in break-out capability. In an essay called "Don't Be Fooled, They Found More Than You Think", Ekeus notes that the work of the post-war weapons inspectors "convincingly demonstrates that Iraq's biological weapons experts developed and maintained a clandestine network of laboratories and facilities within the security apparatus". This infrastructure for experimentation was not reported in Iraq's declaration, and this was "an obvious violation of Iraq's reporting obligations under UN Security Council resolution 1441". In addition, recorded Ekeus, "Iraqi scientists have also admitted to investigating how to improve and simplify fermentation and spray-drying capabilities of BW-simulants for application to anthrax". Ekeus also stated that he was "struck ... by information on Iraq's production of liquid rocket fuel and oxidiser. This does seem to support the argument that Iraq had maintained its interest in longer-range missiles (over the 95-mile range allowed)".[17]

The ultimate challenge, notes Ekeus, is how to handle a regime leader who seeks to engineer the lifting of multilateral sanctions in order to go back to his interest in prohibited weapons systems. Ekeus reaches the unvarnished conclusion that "[i]t is difficult to believe that, had there not been a war, it would have been possible to control and monitor Iraq's dual-use capacities for any length of time". The problem was something that no inspector could extirpate – namely, Saddam's commitment to weapons of mass destruction as a central stanchion of his regime's power and prestige. In a challenge that is unusually blunt for UN diplomacy, Ekeus states: "I put it to those who criticised the decision to go to war against Iraq to outline an alternative route and explain what should have been done with Saddam's weapons programmes."[18]

So, too, the results of the Iraq Survey Group corroborate that Saddam had not abandoned his ambitions. Iraq Survey Group director Charles Duelfer, who had also served as Deputy Executive Chairman of UN-SCOM under both Ekeus and Butler, concluded that the Iraqi Intelligence Service "maintained throughout 1991 to 2003 a set of undeclared covert laboratories to research and test various chemicals and poisons, primarily for intelligence operations".[19] In addition, the Survey Group "uncovered Iraqi plans or designs for three long-range ballistic missiles with ranges from 400 to 1,000 km and for a 1,000 km-range cruise missile". Although these were still in the design phase, this was a forbidden enterprise and was accompanied by the importation of engines from Poland, and possibly Russia or Belarus, which would have supported longer-range missiles, and by the importation of missile guidance and control systems. The Duelfer report concluded that Saddam Hussein "wanted to end sanctions while preserving the capability to reconstitute his weapons of mass destruction (WMD) when sanctions were lifted". Yet, of course, the regime created by Resolution 687 would not be satisfied by a momentarily empty larder. Rather, it required the dismantling of WMD programmes in perpetuity. It is hard, then, to know how inspections would quell this commitment. Inspectors, supported by 225,000 troops in the desert, would have had to continue their work until Saddam and his heirs had finished their natural span of years.

The final post-war development that has put the assessments of Resolutions 678, 687 and 1441 into a different light is the so-called "Oil-for-Food" scandal. Starting in 1997, the UN sanctions programme permitted Iraq to sell significant amounts of oil for the purpose of raising money for humanitarian supplies, as well as to pay reparations demanded by the Iraqi Claims Commission, a body sitting under UN auspices in Geneva. The investigative report by former Federal Reserve chairman Paul Volcker, appointed by the Secretary-General, concluded that a UN director of the Oil-for-Food programme obtained a cash pay-off for steering valuable oil purchase vouchers to a favoured company.[20] Oil allotments were allegedly given by Saddam to prominent politicians of Security Council member states, to outspoken opponents of the Iraqi sanctions, and to two family members of a former UN Secretary-General, acting for an Egyptian oil company. The steady flow of illicit cash to Iraq as kickbacks on oil purchases and surcharges on contracts for the supply of humanitarian goods meant that the regime had a steady supply of hard currency to use as it might wish, including for the purchase of weapons components. Thus, the Oil-for-Food scandal means that economic sanctions had, in a sense, already been lifted against Iraq, at least as regards high-priority regime purchases. There could be no guarantee that forbidden fruit was really out of reach, even while UN weapons inspectors might be travelling around the countryside in pursuit of a site inspection. This re-supply chain – sustained by cash and shaped by intention – could overcome any inspector's ability to separate Saddam from WMD. The breach of Resolutions 687 and 1441, as shown in the false declaration of December 2002, was thus more than a technical failure. It was yet another sign of Saddam's totemic attachment to weapons of mass destruction as symbols of power and as a club with which to overawe his neighbours and his own population. That is what Resolution 687 was designed to prevent.

Notes

1. Ruth Wedgwood, "Legal Authority Exists for a Strike on Iraq", *Financial Times*, 13 March 2003.
2. Adam Roberts, "Law and the Use of Force", *Survival*, Vol. 45, No. 2 (2003), p. 31. See also Adam Roberts, "International Law and the Iraq War 2003", Memorandum for the Select Committee on Foreign Affairs, *Written Evidence for the Tenth Report: Foreign Policy Aspects of the War against Terrorism* (London: HMSO, 31 July 2003), available at ⟨http://www.publications.parliament.uk/pa/cm/cmfaff.htm⟩.
3. See Ruth Wedgwood, "The Fall of Saddam Hussein, Security Council Mandates and Preemptive Self-Defense", *American Journal of International Law*, Vol. 97 (2003), pp. 25, 29.
4. The suggestion has been made that a "material breach" of a Council resolution is different from the material breach of a treaty, and may lack the same suspensive effect. But the Council itself has used the idea of material breach in just this way throughout the 12-year history of Resolution 687. See Ruth Wedgwood, "The Enforcement of Security Council Resolution 687: The Threat of Force against Iraq's Weapons of Mass Destruction", *American Journal of International Law*, Vol. 92 (1998), pp. 724, 727 and accompanying notes.
5. See, e.g., Human Rights Watch, *Iraq's Crime of Genocide: The Anfal Campaign against the Kurds* (New Haven, CT: Yale University Press, 1995).
6. *Report of the Secretary-General on the Status of the Implementation of the Special Commission's Plan for the Ongoing Monitoring and Verification of Iraq's Compliance with Relevant Parts of Section C of Security Council Resolution 687 (1991)*, UN Doc. S/1995/864, p. 29, para. 75(w).
7. See Mahdi Obeidi and Kurt Pitzer, *The Bomb in My Garden: The Secret of Saddam's Nuclear Mastermind* (Hoboken, NJ: John Wiley, 2004). See also "Statement by David Kay on the Interim Progress Report on the Activities of the Iraq Survey Group (ISG) before the House Permanent Select Committee on Intelligence, the House Committee on Appropriations, Subcommittee on Defense, and the Senate Select Committee on Intelligence", 2 October 2003, ⟨http://www.odci.gov/cia/public_affairs/speeches/2003/david_kay_10022003.html⟩.
8. See, generally, Frits Kalshoven, *Belligerent Reprisals* (Leiden: Martinus Nijhoff, 2005).
9. There was no additional Security Council resolution preceding Operation Desert Fox. So, too, in 1993, US, UK and French aircraft took part in limited air attacks against Iraqi radar sites as a means of coercing Iraqi compliance with inspection requirements. See Wedgwood, "The Enforcement of Security Council Resolution 687", pp. 724, 727–728.

10. See Ruth Wedgwood, "Responding to Terrorism: The Strikes against Bin Laden", *Yale Journal of International Law*, Vol. 24 (1999), p. 559.

11. Obeidi and Pitzer, *The Bomb in My Garden*.

12. See "Interview Télévisée sur l'Iraq du Président de la République, M. Jacques Chirac (10 mars 2003), par Patrick Poivre d'Arvor (TF1) et David Pujadas (France 2)", Palais de l'Elysée, ⟨http://www.elysee.fr/elysee/francais/les_dossiers/iraq/de_janvier_a_mars_2003/de_janvier_a_mars_2003.21454.html⟩.

13. Security Council Resolution 1559, 28 February 2004.

14. *A More Secure World: Our Shared Responsibility. Report of the Secretary-General's High-level Panel on Threats, Challenges and Change* (New York: United Nations, 2004), p. 64, para. 194.

15. Kofi Annan, *On Sovereignty and Intervention*, reprinted in "Secretary-General Presents His Annual Report to General Assembly", UN Press Release SG/SM/7136, GA/9596 (20 September 1999). See also Kofi Annan, "Two Concepts of Sovereignty", *The Economist*, 18 September 1999.

16. Remarks of Secretary-General Kofi Annan, *A More Secure World: Who Needs to Do What?* (Washington, DC: Council on Foreign Relations, 16 December 2004).

17. Rolf Ekeus, "Don't Be Fooled, They Found More Than You Think", *Sunday Times* (London), 9 October 2003, News Review, p. 7. See also Rolf Ekeus, "Iraq's Real Weapons Threat", *Washington Post*, 29 June 2003.

18. Ekeus, "Don't Be Fooled, They Found More Than You Think", p. 7.

19. "Key Findings", in *Comprehensive Report of the Special Advisor to the DCI on Iraq's WMD* [Duelfer Report], Vol. I, 30 September 2004, at ⟨http://www.cia.gov/cia/reports/iraq_wmd_2004/⟩.

20. Independent Inquiry Committee into the United Nations Oil-for-Food Programme, *Third Interim Report*, 8 August 2005, available at ⟨http://www.iic-offp.org/documents.htm⟩.

26

Iraq and the social logic of international security

Jean-Marc Coicaud

I don't care what the international lawyers say; we are going to kick some ass.
(George W. Bush, 11 September 2001)[1]

The most conservative views of the Bush administration have shaped US foreign policy since the beginning of 2001. Four assumptions are at the basis of these views: national security prevails absolutely over solidarity considerations (including the importance given to humanitarian and human rights issues); the United States has the right to define on its own what is legitimate US foreign policy; the United States has the power to influence international legitimacy and, subsequently, international legality; US foreign policy is, by and large, accountable to no one but the United States itself. These assumptions amount not only to a self-centred and asocial conception of US foreign policy, but also to a self-centred and asocial conception of international order. As such, the search for international security equates with the search for US security; and the principles and institutions of collective security are only as good as they serve US national interest.

In the past four years or so, the Bush administration has taken action on the basis of these assumptions. The difficulties it has encountered indicate, however, that these beliefs and this world view are misled. This is what is considered in this chapter. The argument proceeds in three steps. First, the question of how these assumptions unfold in the theory and practice of Bush's foreign policy is examined. Second, the argument reveals that, although there is some truth in Bush's foreign policy postulations, they have been largely proven wrong in the aftermath of the war against Iraq. Third, the chapter explores how the international order could be improved. Here it calls for a social conception of international security – one reconciling power and principles and making the search for international legitimacy a key element of international order.

National security versus principles of multilateralism and solidarity

Since 2001 the Bush administration has not hesitated to state in the clearest manner the main beliefs that shape its foreign policy and to have these words followed by actions. A rapid analysis of Bush's foreign policy in theory and practice suffices to show this.

Bush's foreign policy and the theory of US power

The radicalism of the *National Security Strategy of the United States of America* report published by the White House in September 2002 caught the eyes of many, in the United States and abroad.[2] The vision, and the ends and means it put forward for US power, outlined a grand strategy leading to the doctrinal sidelining of multilateralism and the philosophy of international solidarity that it partly encompasses.

The vision and ends of Bush's foreign policy

Overall, Bush's grand strategy is based on and expresses a rather dark vision of the world. The world is seen as a fundamentally dangerous place. Bush's world vision has four main characteristics. First, it entails the largely confrontational conception of international relations, and the sense of mistrust associated with it. Second, it is shaped by the exceptional situation in which the world and the United States found themselves after the terrorist attacks of 11 September 2001. A third characteristic is the friend/enemy divide. This divide is used to distinguish those countries collaborating fully in the war against terror from those reticent to give their unrestricted backing. Fourth, there is the moral clarity with which the Republican administration entrusts itself. Moral clarity is meant to provide an analytically sound appraisal of the current international situation but also to ground the ends and means of US grand strategy in values.

The primary end of Bush's grand strategy is homeland security. In the September 2002 document, the fixation on homeland security is at work on four levels. First, US national security appears as the only thing that truly matters on the international chequerboard. Second, the report elevates terrorism to a phenomenon of gigantic historical significance, as part of a struggle between good (the United States and its values) and evil. Third, there is the stated goal of defending national security by not allowing any other nation to challenge US military dominance. Fourth, the impression is given that the United States, to counter its vulnerability and insecurity, has to get as close as possible to absolute security through the neutralization of opponents, potential or real, present or future.[3]

The means of Bush's foreign policy and the doctrinal sidelining of multilateralism and international solidarity

Within the means, the doctrinal sidelining of multilateralism and international solidarity entailed in the vision and ends of Bush's grand strategy appears most clearly. The 2002 report evokes four defining tools for the defence of US interests in the world: an ad hoc approach to international issues; unilateralism as a rather standard procedure; the pre-emptive use of force; and regime change. These means are a significant depreciation of international rules, treaties and security partnerships as they had previously been conceived.[4]

The *National Security Strategy* document may express, along with its support to alliances, an endorsement of the United Nations and multilateralism.[5] But the minimal attention and place accorded to them, and the introduction of reservations about their overall usefulness and validity, reveal how low Bush's grand strategy ranks them in its list of tools. The rejection of the International Criminal Court (ICC), which the 2002 report makes a point of insisting on in its closing paragraphs, provides a further indication of the circumstantial value attributed to the United Nations and multilateralism.[6]

In addition, the 2002 report hardly gives any attention to the issues of international solidarity associated with peace operations and humanitarian interventions. Peace operations by and large do not enter into the security mindset of President Bush. The term "peace operation" is mentioned no more than once, in the context of Africa and *en passant*. The same disregard applies to humanitarian crises. To be sure, the report refers to the importance of providing humanitarian assistance in the specific case of Afghanistan.[7] It also evokes a number of ways of helping regions and populations that have suffered from humanitarian crises, including economic, legal and political aid.[8] But it moves away from the position put forward in the Clinton years, which envisioned the use of force to end humanitarian crises perhaps not as a priority but at least as a possibility. In the 2002 document, nothing indicates that humanitarian crises could constitute a good reason for the use of force. Typically, when humanitarian crises in Africa are mentioned, they are referred to not primarily as humanitarian crises but in the context of how they constitute national security and terrorism threats.[9] It is the danger represented by rogue states, and not their human rights violations track record, that causes them to forfeit their national sovereign rights and be exposed to military intervention.

The geopolitics of US national interest in practice

The Bush administration did not wait for the hijacked jetliners to hit the Twin Towers in New York and the Pentagon outside Washington DC in September 2001 to act upon its radical conservative assumptions about US power and its relations with the world. The presidential campaign of 2000 made it clear that the Republicans intended to be as little constrained as possible by the United Nations and multilateralism and to give close to no attention to non-security issues. From 2001 onwards, Bush's foreign policy, including its response to 9/11 and the war against Iraq, illustrated this state of affairs.

The road to unilateralism prior to 9/11

In the first eight months of his presidency, President Bush showed no inclination to have the United States involved in peace operations or humanitarian interventions. When fighting broke out in Macedonia in March 2001, despite the potential for a widespread confrontation between Macedonian Slavs and the country's sizeable ethnic Albanian minority, the Bush administration essentially vetoed direct US involvement. Later on, in August 2001, when NATO sent troops into Macedonia to disarm the Albanian rebels in the wake of a peace accord, the United States took a minimal role. Only US troops already stationed in the region to support peace operations in Kosovo joined in, and their mission was restricted to providing logistical support and intelligence to European troops. The Bush administration showed equal reluctance vis-à-vis humanitarian and human rights crises. It stayed away from the emergencies generated by war in the Democratic Republic of the Congo. Nor did it manifest serious concerns for human rights violations in Afghanistan prior to 9/11.

During the same period, the Bush administration paid lip-service to the United Nations and multilateralism. Its actions showed that it refused to be bound and constrained by them. It opposed several compacts that the international community, and especially US allies, had pushed forward in recent years. It abandoned the Kyoto Protocol to the United Nations Framework Convention on Climate Change. It rejected protocols enforcing a ban on germ warfare. It demanded amendments to an accord on illegal sales of small arms. And it vowed to withdraw from a landmark pact limiting ballistic missile defences.

"What you are going to get from this administration is '*à la carte* multi-lateralism'", said Richard Haass, at the time the US State Department's director of policy planning, coining a term for the administration's approach in its pre-9/11 months.[10] Ultimately, the value of the United Nations and multilateralism – not seen as ends in themselves – was to be assessed in a purely instrumental way, based on their utility for US national interest.

The war against terror and Bush's multilateralism "de circonstance" in the aftermath of 9/11

In its fight against terrorism, the White House opted for an attitude of active engagement in the international arena, eager to get as wide support as possible from other nations. Did this mean that Bush's foreign policy moved away from à la carte multilateralism and endorsed the binding modalities of multilateral cooperation? Did this mean that it renounced unilateralism? The answer is "no".

For the Bush administration, enrolling the United Nations in its war against terror in the immediate aftermath of the terrorist attacks was simply a matter of convenience. It welcomed Security Council Resolution 1373 (adopted on 28 September 2001), which called upon all states to take a variety of measures to curb terrorism. After the quick victory of the US-led Operation Enduring Freedom over al-Qaeda and Taliban forces in Afghanistan in October–November 2001, the Bush administration also supported the establishment in December of the International Security Assistance Force to help the Afghan Interim Authority create a secure environment in Kabul and its surrounding areas. In March 2002, it buttressed the creation of the United Nations Assistance Mission in Afghanistan. But, once the United Nations and multilateralism proved to be an obstacle to the pursuit of US objectives, the Bush administration did not take long to move away from them.

From bullying the United Nations to the war against Iraq

The argument put forward to justify going after Iraq was its assumed possession of weapons of mass destruction (WMD) and its links with al-Qaeda.[11] The hawks holding positions of responsibility at the White House and in the Department of Defense were determined to do whatever it took, with whoever would want to join the coalition, to bring down Saddam Hussein.[12] To them, going through the United Nations was ill advised. This view was not universally shared in the Republican administration. Secretary of State Colin Powell epitomized those who favoured building support for the US policy towards Iraq via the United Nations.[13] He managed to convince the President. In the powerful speech that he delivered to the UN General Assembly on 12 September 2002, George W. Bush stressed that his administration would work with the Security Council to adopt new resolutions as the instrument for forcing Saddam Hussein to disarm or, if he refused, as the basis for military action.[14] He also warned the United Nations that it risked becoming irrelevant if it allowed Iraq not to comply with the Security Council resolutions. Bush's tactic worked. After a few weeks of intense negotiations, the Security Council unanimously passed a resolution with teeth. Approved on 8 November 2002, Resolution 1441 stressed the imperative that Iraq disarm totally or face "serious consequences".[15]

Eventually, the multilateral route led to a blind alley. The divisions within the Bush administration on the need for a UN endorsement hampered the effectiveness of the US efforts to bring other countries on board. While Colin Powell was "sweet-talking" member states to obtain their support, at times it seemed as if the main goal of the hawkish elements of the Bush administration was to undermine his diplomatic efforts. In the process, not only were they attempting to keep the United States free of UN and multilateral entanglements. They were also making the point that the United Nations and multilateralism were in no position to contribute to giving legitimacy to US foreign policy. In addition, the difficulty of convincing other member states of the existence of WMD in Iraq, illustrated by the mixed reports of the United Nations weapons inspectors, and the even greater challenge of demonstrating the link between Iraq and al-Qaeda proved to be significant obstacles for the United States in the Security Council.[16] The more the United States and the United Kingdom insisted that they had a case (without supporting it with incontestable evidence), and the more they expressed the need to use force, the less the other permanent members (especially France) and the non-permanent members (in particular Germany) of the Security Council were willing to go along.

This multilateral deadlock was not enough to stop the Bush administration. The war was launched on 20 March 2003 without Security Council backing.[17] With this, the White House showed that it was ready to bypass the multilateral rules of the game to pursue its objectives. True to its credo of limiting the role of the United Nations to US needs, in the immediate aftermath of the war the Bush administration also rejected the idea of the United Nations taking the lead in the post-war reconstruction of the country and having a say in the modalities of the transition towards the restoration of full Iraqi sovereignty. The appointment, in May 2003, of a Special Representative of the UN Secretary-General for Iraq, who did not have much power, was the greatest involvement from the United Nations allowed by the Bush administration.[18]

Iraq as a testing ground for Bush's foreign policy assumptions

The difficulties encountered by the United States because of the war in Iraq, on the ground and at the international level, have put in question the claimed validity of the key assumptions of Bush's foreign policy. The war against Iraq has shown that these assumptions contained some elements of truth. But it has proved them wrong as well. Moreover, the effects of Bush's foreign policy, although marginally positive, have been mainly negative for the reputation and influence of the United States and for the stability of international order. It is proving to be a challenge for the relatively successful election of 30 January 2005 in Iraq and the constitutional referendum of 15 October 2005 to undo this state of affairs.

The war against Iraq and Bush's foreign policy assumptions: From right to wrong

To a certain extent, the aspects of Bush's foreign policy assumptions that state the awesome scope of US power and its capacity to act alone have been confirmed by the facts. On the other hand, other facts have proven wrong the assumptions betting on the US ability to achieve legitimacy, including international legitimacy, through a self-centred foreign policy and the unilateral use of power.

Bush's foreign policy assumptions vindicated by the war against Iraq

The predominant position of the United States in the international distribution of power has given Washington ample possibilities to define the international agenda and act unilaterally. Following the ways in which the United States has more or less conceived and conducted on its own the war against terrorism in the aftermath of 9/11, the war against Iraq certainly makes this point. The scepticism and opposition expressed by most nations towards the Bush administration's eagerness to act against Saddam Hussein were not enough to stop the war. The fact that the United States had the power to go to war on its own terms won the day.

In that sense, the foreign policy assumption stating that the United States has the power to act internationally as it sees fit is correct.

Bush's foreign policy ideology at odds with reality

This does not mean, however, that the United States enjoys a free hand and has the possibility to ensure international security and redesign international order at will. This does not mean either that, because of the assumed global primacy of its national interest, it is more or less accountable to no one but itself. The obstacles faced by Bush's foreign policy in

Iraq show that the US national interest is not the sole yardstick for assessing the legitimacy of US foreign policy and international legitimacy as a whole, let alone of the political order favoured by the United States in the countries in which it intervenes.

To begin with, the fact that the strategic reasons put forward by the Bush administration for going to war were fallacious has not helped. Weapons of mass destruction are nowhere to be seen in Iraq. And in June 2004, the National Commission on Terrorist Attacks Upon the United States (also known as the 9-11 Commission), put in place to inquire into 9/11, stated that there was no proven link between al-Qaeda and Saddam Hussein's regime.[19]

The ways in which force has been used by US troops on the ground have also been a major problem. Rules of engagement (with an inclination to shoot first and ask questions later) and torture (if not officially decided, at least encouraged and informally approved at the highest level[20]) did not boost the United States' reputation and ability to translate its power into influence and legitimacy.[21]

Moreover, the Bush administration has experienced first hand how difficult it is to ensure security and reconstruct Iraq more or less on its own. It has learned the hard way that the United States needs the political, military, financial and logistical support of as many countries as possible. In this regard, the Bush administration has painfully learned that it is difficult to ignore the United Nations, in spite of all its shortcomings. This is particularly the case because the European allies that it needed the most – France and Germany – were eager to have the United Nations involved. Subsequently, in occupying Iraq by and large alone, the United States contributed less to the redesigning of international legality and legitimacy than to the undermining of its own credibility and legitimacy.

As a whole, the failures of Bush's foreign policy in Iraq illustrate the social dimension of legitimacy. Legitimacy is not a self-declared phenomenon. It requires at minimum the recognition and consent of others. This is true at the national level; it is equally true, if not more so, at the international level. Because competition, tension and confrontation tend to shape international life, any sense of legitimacy at the international level has to be a shared view.[22] This social dimension is a requirement of international legitimacy in general; but it is also a requirement for the legitimacy of any given foreign policy. This requirement is of particular importance for the United States, considering its global reach and democratic claims. Unlike the rather inconsequential international impact of a country of secondary importance, the overwhelming international power of the United States is certain to have a tremendous effect on other nations. If these nations are not consulted, a rift is destined to emerge and deepen, as has happened in recent years.

Bush's Iraq policy and its impacts on international order:
From positive to negative

Against this background, it does not come as a surprise that the mix of right and wrong that characterizes Bush's foreign policy assumptions had more negative than positive impacts on international order and on the norms and institutions underwriting it.

Looking for the positive impacts of Bush's foreign policy

Among the positive effects of Bush's foreign policy in Iraq, it helps to distinguish between intentional and unintentional effects.

The main intentional positive effect of Bush's foreign policy in Iraq is, of course, the elimination of Saddam Hussein and his regime. No matter how uncomfortable people may be with the invasion of Iraq, nobody argues that ousting Saddam Hussein from power was a bad thing. By and large, nobody regrets Saddam Hussein's removal from power.

Arguably, the decisiveness with which the Bush administration has acted against Iraq can also be seen as a positive aspect. Over the years, the willingness of the United Nations to leave the arms inspection issue unresolved and the forced departure of the inspectors in 1998 unchallenged de facto paved the way for thinking that no solution could come from the multilateral body. Furthermore, the sanctions and the no-fly-zone regimes imposed upon Iraq for more than a decade could not possibly go on forever. Something had to be done. Yet, on inspections and sanctions, the United Nations seemed to be paralysed. The White House's will to act showed that there was an alternative to the status quo and to inaction on Iraq.

What are the unintentional positive effects of Bush's foreign policy in Iraq? Three come to mind. They concern intellectual, political and institutional benefits.

The intellectual benefit of Bush's foreign policy vis-à-vis Iraq amounts to the fact that its radicalism and "outside the box" character serve as a wake-up call.[23] Bush's departure from a routine approach to international relations forces us to reassess the nature and role of the norms and institutions of international law and multilateralism and the ability to change them. Are international law and the United Nations (the values, rights and duties that they promote) simply organized hypocrisies, or should they be taken seriously and therefore defended seriously? How can international law and the United Nations contribute better to the socialization of international life? How do international law, its institutions and its norms evolve? How does the adaptation of international law and multilateralism to reality take place? Conversely, how does the adaptation of reality to international law and multilateralism take place? And where (and how) should decision makers draw the line in this dual process of adaptation?

The second benefit of Bush's foreign policy vis-à-vis Iraq is political. Its radicalism brings about political clarification. Other actors now tend to go beyond the usual diplomatic ambiguities. With the war against Iraq, European countries have for instance been forced to take a position. They have had to state the extent to which they value their alliance with the United States and multilateralism. Overall, political clarification is helping to define the extent and limits of the flexibility of international legality and legitimacy, of what is acceptable and what is not from the point of view of member states.

The third unintentional benefit of Bush's foreign policy vis-à-vis Iraq is institutional. It concerns the United Nations. To be sure, the United Nations is politically a rather weak organization at the moment. At the same time, Bush's foreign policy has contributed to fuel the debates on the role of the United Nations in international political life. It has also contributed to making the UN stakeholders more aware of the challenges that the United Nations and multilateralism are likely to face down the road if they do not address their limitations.[24]

Bush's Iraq policy and its negative effects on international order

The positive effects mentioned above are only a small part of Bush's foreign policy impact on international order.

To begin with, even the intentional positive effects of Bush's policy in Iraq are questionable. The ousting of Saddam Hussein will not necessarily lead to a better situation in Iraq. It is still far from sure that Iraq will become a more democratic regime. Iraq could remain unstable and a source of tension in the region and in the world at large.

As for the unintentional positive effects, they were not pursued per se by the Bush administration. In fact, Bush's foreign policy tends to oppose changes that could capitalize on these unintentional positive effects. Because the Bush administration tends to favour a self-serving, self-centred version of international law, the United Nations and multilateralism, any development that might go against this is unwelcome.

More to the point, the main negative effects on international order of Bush's Iraq policy are closely associated with the three following facts: the war against Iraq was launched with no regard for international legality and legitimacy (there was no formal green light from the UN Security Council); the war was launched for dubious reasons (the existence of weapons of mass destruction in Iraq and links between al-Qaeda and Saddam Hussein's regime are unproven); and significant aspects of the conduct of the war have ignored the Geneva Conventions (torture, lack of due process). The cumulative impact of this state of affairs has weakened international order at three levels at least.

The self-serving conception and discretionary use of the multilateral mechanisms and obligations put forward by Bush's foreign policy have undermined the system of international legitimacy that multilateralism seeks to provide. By promoting a double standard attitude – with a maximum of entitlements and a minimum of duties for the United States, and a maximum of duties and a minimum of rights for other states – the Bush administration has made it even less attractive for other states to accept the constraints associated with international reciprocity and with the dynamics of rights and duties.[25] Its unilateral approach to international affairs and its self-serving multilateralism have been an invitation to more one-sided attitudes. Ultimately, the idea and possibility of a credible regime of international cooperation and of international legality and legitimacy are endangered.

The credibility of the United States and of its message concerning democratic values has been weakened as well. As a result, the ability of the US leadership in particular to rally other nations in the service of international law and multilateralism has been altered. This is a problem for the last resort role that the United States plays in international order and for international order itself. It means that the United States' foreign policy is not seen as being the expression and tool of international legitimacy. Considering the pivotal role that the United States plays in the international distribution of power, this tends to cripple the international order with a sense of international illegitimacy.[26]

Finally, there is the negative effect of Bush's policy on the Middle East. Three elements come to the fore here. First, far from contributing to a reduction in terrorism, Bush's foreign policy has allowed it to spread in the region, and has contributed to its internalization in Iraq. The policy has also contributed to the establishment of a link between terrorism in Iraq and regional terrorism, if not international terrorism. Secondly, rather than bringing stability to the Middle East, Bush's foreign policy has increased its instability. Various actors, inside and outside Iraq, see the possibility of the descent of Iraq into a civil war as an opportunity to further their interests. Thirdly, the difficulties encountered by the United States in Iraq give hope to non-democratic Arab regimes. The failure to make Iraq stable helps their case. Authoritarian rule, once more, could emerge as the surest way to preserve stability in the Middle East.

The impact of the January 2005 Iraqi election

The relatively successful election of 30 January 2005 has certainly been a cause for optimism. The election day did not turn into the Armageddon that the insurgency had promised – no major violence was unleashed on that day. Although most of the Sunni Arabs decided not to vote, Shiites and Kurds went to the polls in their millions. Capitalizing on this positive development, President Bush travelled to Europe in late February 2005 for a fence-mending tour and to call for a "new start" in European–US relations.

Yet the terrorist attacks did not stop after the election. And in the autumn of 2005, after the constitutional referendum of 15 October, it was still not clear how and to what extent it would be possible to bring Sunnis into the Iraqi political process. Finding a way for the Shiite alliance, now the majority in parliament, to coexist in the long run with the Kurds and, more importantly, with the once-privileged Sunni minority was not a settled issue. It therefore remained very much an open question whether or not 2005 would mark the turning point for a better future for Iraq and the rehabilitation of Bush's foreign policy.

What is next for the international order?

The war against Iraq and its aftermath have shown that the United States and the United Nations (or multilateralism) are largely mutually dependent. It is difficult for one to do without the other. It is true that the United States is able to act unilaterally. Doing so, however, raises the question of the legitimacy of its foreign policy, if not the legitimacy of the international system that it underwrites. Conversely, without the United States playing by multilateral rules, the United Nations runs the risk of being reduced to a second-class international citizen. In the process, its overall relevance and legitimacy are in jeopardy.

Furthermore, a divorce between the United States and the United Nations would be likely to increase global instability. Since most countries favour a multilateral approach, resentment towards the United States would grow. Moreover, the rest of the world (including the Europeans) is neither willing nor able to take up the task of collective security on its own, without the United States. The mission of preserving international security could end up facing two opposite but equally challenging predicaments: too much concentration or too much diffusion of power. In the first case, the United States alone would be more or less in charge of global security, with the various associated dangers. These dangers could include making US power a global scapegoat for whatever went wrong. In the second case, left to the goodwill of local actors, the international order might largely remain unattended to.

Completely getting rid of the tensions between the United States and the United Nations and achieving a fully stable (and just) international order are not on the cards at present. The tendency to a national bias in international life and the inter-state structure that it gives to international order lead to unavoidable tensions, if not conflicts, and limitations on international justice. Nevertheless, there are a number of ways to reduce these tensions and limitations. Two types of change could help: reconciling power and principles; and adjusting US foreign policy.

Reconciling power and principles

The principles and institutions (including the United Nations) of multilateralism are the product of power and of a history of power. They originated in the world influence (economic, political and normative) of the West in modern times. They also go back to the Western willingness and ability in the twentieth century, especially under the stewardship of the United States after World War II, to make multilateral principles and institutions part of the international rules of the game. At the same time, in the past 50 years, the principles and institutions of multilateralism, although underwritten by key member states, have time and time again been undermined by them. Major democratic powers have themselves played a leading role in both strengthening and weakening multilateral culture. As a result, multilateralism has all too often been either the captive of or disconnected from power.

In the aftermath of the Cold War, this divorce between power and principles is more and more problematic, and less and less acceptable. The removal of strategic competition between East and West and the rise of democratic governance make international legitimacy increasingly necessary. Unless ways are found to reconcile power and principles, a sense of legitimacy at the international level will be out of reach.

At a minimum, the reconciliation of power and principles has three requirements. First, it entails intertwining international rights and duties (more than is now the case), which presupposes an awareness of the entitlements but also of the concomitant mutual limitations and restraints. Another key requirement is consistency, rather than expediency, in interpreting and acting upon international rights and duties. Third, both these conditions have to be met to make possible the legitimate use of power at the international level and to favour norms and mechanisms of international legitimacy.

This being said, reconciling power and principles also calls for certain adjustments on the part of the one power most in a position to set the international tone and agenda – the United States.

The need to adjust US foreign policy

Fine-tuning power and principles at the international level requires at least three changes in US foreign policy. The first is a better balance between the US national interest and the international interest. The goal here is not a U-turn in US foreign policy, in which the international interest would become the paramount factor. This is neither possible nor desirable. Nevertheless, changes have to be introduced to mitigate the self-centred character of the United States' power projection.

The second change is to take seriously the constraints of democratic values on US foreign policy. The United States has to become less self-centred and more aware of the need for a legitimate international system. In order to achieve this, the United States has to come to terms with the political and policy implications and with the responsibilities brought about by being not only the sole superpower but also the sole democratic superpower. This presupposes in particular that the demand for democratic and human rights values in the global setting is not a cloak for universalizing an undemocratic hegemony.

The third change concerns the United States and international democratic leadership. A better balance between national and international interests and welcoming the foreign policy implications of being a democratic superpower do not imply that the United States should give up its position of leadership and become a regular actor – if only because the international system needs leadership. Without leadership, the many points of view are likely to cancel each other out and become a paralysing factor. The need for democratic leadership by the United States signifies that the United States has to use its leverage while keeping in mind three elements: international cooperation is not a one-way street; leadership in the context of multilateralism builds upon the consent of other countries, especially since contemporary international life increasingly relies upon a negotiated course of action; taking multilateralism seriously does not mean using exclusively its conciliatory and conflict resolution powers as bargaining chips and opportunities to advance US interests.

Ultimately, an unequal distribution of power at the international level, with the United States at the top of the hierarchy, is not in itself a problem, as long as the dominating position of the United States is accompanied by a commensurate sense of international responsibility. For, in an (international) political culture where factoring in the rights of the other is increasingly important, being perceived as a legitimate power and one that supports a legitimate international system depends largely upon living up to the following standard: the more power one has, the more duties one has.[27] In this perspective, the United States may very well be the first power to be accountable globally.

Is there any hope for the future?

What is the likelihood of a reconciliation of power and principles and an adjustment of US foreign policy? It is rather slim for two reasons: one concerns US foreign policy; the other has to do with the reluctance of other countries to show leadership.

Although in his second term President Bush is adopting a friendlier US foreign policy (at least in style, with the new Secretary of State Condoleezza Rice), it is not a more accommodating one. There are no reasons to believe that he has abandoned the fundamental premises of his world view. Moreover, if Bush's foreign policy were simply an aberration in the history of US foreign policy, overcoming its negative impacts on international order would be a relatively simple proposition. His departure from the White House, at the end of his second term, would bring part of the solution. The problem is that Bush's foreign policy is to a large extent a radical version of characteristics that are now deeply embedded in the United States' foreign policy and its relations with the rest of the world.[28]

As a result, the chances are that the defining features of US foreign policy will continue to be the unequal relationship between the United States and the United Nations, the primacy of national interest and national security issues in US foreign policy, the temptation to reduce the international interest to a US national interest, and the United States' self-centred conception of multilateralism. The tensions between the United States and multilateralism will therefore continue to shape international life. And the imbalance between power and principles will persist.

The reluctance of other member states to adopt a proactive attitude is another reason for doubting that power will be put at the service of the multilateral principles of inclusiveness and reciprocity of rights and duties. In particular, the tendency of the permanent members of the Security Council (other than the United States) and of UN member states in general to take a back seat or to endorse the status quo is not encouraging, and nor is the fact that they appear unwilling to invest much energy or capital in addressing the current shortcomings of multilateralism and the United Nations. In the end, the fact that there is much discussion and little action is probably a sign that, for most member states (including the critics of the current international situation), getting by is the best worst option, and one that seems satisfactory. The limited, and disappointing, results of the UN World Summit of September 2005 serve as a case in point.

The quandary of today's world rests on an age-old problem: the tense relationship between the West (of which the United States is the latest leading model) and the rest of the world. The West has oscillated between domination (with a drive to expand its power and a tendency to predation) and humanism (promoting the universality of human rights and the extension of international solidarity).[29] Before the United States moved into the driver's seat, Europe was for a few centuries the engine and incarnation of this hybrid outlook on international life, which was simultaneously discriminatory and embracing.

Time and time again, the West has had the opportunity to choose between the two paths – domination or humanism – without ever opting decisively for one over the other. The current quasi-unipolar moment offers once again a historic opportunity to choose the rewards of principled international rule over the intoxicating temptation of power and the subsequent trappings of paranoia. Choosing the former would be truly heroic. So far, nobody is volunteering to play that part.

Notes

1. Richard A. Clarke, *Against All Enemies: Inside America's War on Terror* (New York: Free Press, 2004), p. 24.
2. *The National Security Strategy of the United States of America* (Washington, DC: The White House, September 2002).
3. On this point, see, for example, David C. Hendrickson, "America's Dangerous Quest for Absolute Security", *World Policy Journal*, Vol. 19, No. 3 (Autumn 2002).
4. G. John Ikenberry, "America's Imperial Ambition", *Foreign Affairs*, Vol. 81, No. 5 (September/October 2002); and David E. Sanger, "Bush to Outline Doctrine of Striking Foes First", *New York Times*, 20 September 2002.
5. *The National Security Strategy of the United States of America*, Preface.
6. Ibid., p. 30. On this issue, see also Eric P. Schwartz, "The United States and the International Criminal Court: The Case for 'Dexterous Multilateralism'", *Chicago Journal of International Law*, Vol. 4, No. 1 (Spring 2003).
7. *The National Security Strategy of the United States of America*, p. 7.
8. Ibid., pp. 21–22 and p. 31.
9. Ibid., p. 10.
10. Quoted in Thom Shanker, "White House Says the US Is Not a Loner, Just Choosy", *New York Times*, 31 July 2001. A few months earlier, Richard Haass went as far as to call upon Americans to "re-conceive their global role from one of a traditional nation-state to an imperial power" (Richard Haass, "Imperial America", paper presented at the Atlanta Conference, 11 November 2000, ⟨http://www.brook.edu/views/articles/haass/2000imperial.htm⟩).
11. George W. Bush, *The President's State of the Union Address*, 29 January 2002, ⟨http://www.whitehouse.gov/news/releases/2002/01/20020129-11.html⟩. See also David Frum, *The Right Man. The Surprise Presidency of George W. Bush (An Inside Account)* (New York: Random House, 2003), Chapters 10 and 12.
12. On the neoconservatives and their influence on Bush's foreign policy, see, for example, "The Shadow Men", *The Economist*, 26 April–2 May 2003, pp. 27–29.

13. On Colin Powell and his views on multilateralism, see, for example, Bill Keller, "The World According to Powell", *New York Times Magazine*, 25 November 2001.

14. *Remarks by the President in Address to the United Nations General Assembly*, New York, 12 September 2002, ⟨http://www.whitehouse.gov/news/releases/2002/09/20020912-1. html⟩.

15. Resolution 1441 (2002), adopted by the Security Council 8 November 2002, UN Doc. S/RES/1441 (2002), para. 13.

16. In their various briefings of the Security Council – on 9 January 2003, reporting on Iraq's arms declaration; on 27 January, in their 60-day update, since its return to Iraq, of the activities of the UN Monitoring, Verification and Inspection Commission (UNMOVIC); and on 14 February and 7 March – Hans Blix, Executive Chairman of UNMOVIC, and Mohamed ElBaradei, Director-General of the International Atomic Energy Agency, indicated that, based on the information collected, the existence of weapons of mass destruction in Iraq was not proved. See also Glen Rangwala, Nathaniel Hurd and Alistair Millar, "A Case for Concern, Not a Case for War", in Micah L. Sifry and Christopher Cerf, eds, *The Iraq War Reader. History, Documents, Opinions* (New York: Touchstone, 2003), pp. 457–463.

17. On this issue, see Michael Byers, "Agreeing to Disagree: Security Council Resolution 1441 and Intentional Ambiguity", *Global Governance*, Vol. 10, No. 2 (April–June 2004).

18. UN Security Council Resolution 1483, adopted 22 May 2003, UN Doc. S/RES/1483 (2003), requested the Secretary-General to appoint a Special Representative for Iraq, with responsibilities for coordinating humanitarian and reconstruction assistance by UN agencies and between UN agencies and non-governmental organizations.

19. Twelfth public hearing of the National Commission on Terrorist Attacks Upon the United States, Staff Statement No. 15, ⟨http://www.9-11commission.gov/staff_ statements/staff_statement_15.pdf⟩.

20. See the Alberto Gonzales Memorandum to President Bush, 25 January 2002, on the application of the Geneva Convention on prisoners of war to the conflict with al-Qaeda and the Taliban. In the memorandum, the White House Counsel argues that the war against terrorism "renders obsolete Geneva's strict limitations on questioning of enemy prisoners". Memo quoted on the website of the Center for American Progress, ⟨http://www.americanprogress.org/site/pp.asp?c=biJRJ80VF&b=246536⟩. Refer also to "Shameful Revelations Will Haunt Bush", *The Economist*, 18 June 2004; *Beyond Torture: U.S. Violations of Occupation Law in Iraq*, A Report by the Center for Economic and Social Rights, June 2004, ⟨http://www.cesr.org/beyondtorture.pdf⟩; and Seymour M. Hersh, *Chain of Command. The Road from 9/11 to Abu Ghraib* (New York: HarperCollins, 2004), Chapter 1. See also Karen J. Greenberg and Joshua L. Drate, eds, *The Torture Papers. The Road to Abu Ghraib* (Cambridge: Cambridge University Press, 2005).

21. Refer to *Beyond Torture*.

22. Christian Reus-Smit, *American Power and World Order* (Cambridge: Polity Press, 2004), pp. 55–67.

23. This is one of the reasons behind the research project of which this book is the result.

24. *A More Secure World: Our Shared Responsibility. Report of the Secretary-General's High-level Panel on Threats, Challenges and Change* (New York: United Nations, 2004) is part of the efforts of the United Nations to factor in the changes that have taken place in the international landscape in the past few years and to adapt to them in order to preserve, if not enhance, its relevance. The UN World Summit of September 2005, which was meant to implement its recommendations, did not amount to much.

25. See Thomas M. Franck, "The Role of International Law and the United Nations after Iraq", American Society of International Law, Washington DC, 2 April 2004.

26. Francis Fukuyama, "The Neoconservative Moment", *The National Interest*, Issue 76 (Summer 2004).

27. Jean-Marc Coicaud, *Legitimacy and Politics. A Contribution to the Study of Political Right and Political Responsibility* (Cambridge: Cambridge University Press, 2002).

28. For more on this issue, see Jean-Marc Coicaud, *Beyond the National Interest* (Washington, DC: United States Institute of Peace Press, forthcoming 2006).

29. Gerrit W. Gong, *The Standard of "Civilization" in International Society* (Oxford: Clarendon Press, 1984), pp. 81–93.

27

Justifying the Iraq war as a humanitarian intervention: The cure is worse than the disease

Nicholas J. Wheeler and Justin Morris

Introduction

What impact has the US-led intervention in Iraq had on the developing norm of humanitarian intervention in international society? Typically, there are two opposing responses to this question. On the one hand, critics of the invocation by President George W. Bush and Prime Ministers Tony Blair and John Howard of humanitarian claims to justify the war against Iraq argue that this was a classic and dangerous case of state leaders abusing humanitarian rationales for ulterior political ends. Moreover, those who voice such concerns but are themselves supportive of international action to end gross human rights abuses – whom we term "liberal internationalists" – argue that the likely effect of these appeals will be to undercut political support for future interventions that could legitimately be defended on humanitarian grounds. Set against this, supporters of the Iraq intervention – whom we call the "new liberal interventionists" – argue that it is defensible on moral grounds, and that international law should be changed to permit armed intervention to remove tyrannical regimes such as that of Saddam Hussein. Consequently, far from discrediting the emerging norm of humanitarian intervention, this group views the Iraq intervention as setting an important precedent for future actions of this kind.

The premise guiding this chapter is that neither of the above positions should be accepted on grounds of either theory or policy. The first part of the chapter briefly maps out the arguments supporting a new norm of humanitarian intervention in the 1990s. We then turn to an examination of the contention that Iraq is a clear-cut case of states misusing moral arguments for political ends. Although we refute the claim of the new liberal interventionists that the intervention in Iraq has produced – or is producing – a positive humanitarian outcome, equally we reject the argument that, in acting as they did, Bush and Blair were abusing the norm of humanitarian intervention. We reject the argument on two grounds. First, it fails to capture the belief of Bush and Blair – and their closest advisers – that regime change in Iraq was genuinely justifiable on moral grounds. The problem is not that Bush and Blair were manipulating humanitarian claims for selfish purposes, but rather that their conception of humanitarianism, most especially in the case of Bush, is coterminous with the spread of liberal values. Secondly, the argument that the United Kingdom and the United States abused humanitarian claims fails to acknowledge that the dominant justification – and certainly the only formal legal argument pressed into service to justify the war – related to Iraq's non-compliance with existing UN Security Council resolutions regarding possession of weapons of mass destruction.

The final part of the chapter investigates the argument, championed by Blair, that the UN Security Council should intervene militarily in cases where governments abuse human rights on a widespread and regular basis. Whereas currently the emerging normative consensus at the United Nations supports military intervention for humanitarian protection only in cases of genocide and/or mass killing, the proposition advanced by the new liberal interventionists is that the threshold justifying armed action should be lowered to encompass regimes that massively abuse human rights. However, such a move is not going to find political support at the United Nations. The majority of states remain stubbornly committed to the norm of non-intervention except in the most egregious of cases. Moreover, what many governments perceive as the misuse of humanitarian arguments over Iraq has served only to reinforce their concerns about the dangers of legitimizing a new rule of humanitarian intervention in international society. This criticism misconstrues the motives behind the Iraq intervention; nevertheless, the very perception of abuse serves to undermine the further consolidation of a norm of humanitarian intervention. This, however, is not the primary reason that the new liberal interventionist agenda should be opposed. Rather, in seeking to legitimize action outside the UN framework that significantly limits sovereign rights, it risks eroding what progress has been made in moving international society towards a limited doctrine of UN-authorized humanitarian intervention.

A developing norm of military intervention for humanitarian protection?

To understand how attitudes to the idea of military intervention for humanitarian protection changed in the 1990s, it is necessary to look back to the Cold War era when the society of states operated a rigid interpretation of the non-intervention principle. It is true that after the end of World War II, and in the shadow of the Nazi death camps, it was agreed in a series of UN human rights instruments that states should uphold basic humanitarian values. The 1948 non-binding Universal Declaration of Human Rights was followed in 1950 by the adoption of the Convention on the Prevention and Punishment of the Crime of Genocide, which required signatories to punish those who committed the crime of genocide on their territory. But what is crucial to note about the development of global humanitarian norms is that it was clearly understood that they did not provide a basis for states to use force to uphold these standards in the event that particular governments failed to live up to them. The longstanding idea of humanitarian intervention found no support in such legal instruments, and Charter provisions such as Article 2(4), limiting states' rights to use force, and Article 2(7), banning UN organs from interfering in matters that belonged to the "domestic jurisdiction of sovereign states", served significantly to constrain the means by which humanitarian objectives could legitimately be pursued.

If humanitarian ends were to be achieved through military means then, within the United Nations' highly centralized system, it would require the Security Council to utilize the powers at its disposal. But during the years of the Cold War the Council interpreted these powers very narrowly and invariably in a way that was inimical to the protection of basic human rights. A graphic illustration of this proclivity was the Council's response to Pakistan's slaughter of tens of thousands of Bengalis in East Pakistan in the period between March and December 1971. The Council expressed regret at the humanitarian emergency caused by the mass killing, but there was an unusual consensus among its 15 members that Article 2(7) of the Charter prevented the Council from acting to stop the carnage. Cold War rivalries militated against any such intervention, with Pakistan and India allied respectively to the US and Soviet blocs. Even without this geopolitical dynamic, Council members strongly held the belief that mass killing inside Pakistan fell firmly within its sovereign jurisdiction.[1]

Today, it is virtually inconceivable that the Security Council would oppose armed intervention to end genocide, mass killing and large-scale ethnic cleansing on the grounds that this violated a state's sovereign rights. This profound change in attitudes was registered at the 2005 UN

World Summit when the General Assembly accepted a declaration that stated that "collective action" could be taken using "Chapter VII, on a case-by-case basis and in cooperation with relevant regional organisations ... should peaceful means be inadequate and national authorities are manifestly failing to protect populations from genocide, war crimes, ethnic cleansing and crimes against humanity".[2] The fundamental change in normative practice that occurred during the 1990s concerned the Council's willingness to define humanitarian emergencies inside a state's borders as a threat to "international peace and security", thereby legitimating UN enforcement action under Chapter VII of the Charter.[3] But there are three caveats that have to be borne in mind when claiming, as UN Secretary-General Kofi Annan did, that there is a "developing international norm"[4] forcibly to protect endangered populations.

The first is that governments remain extremely sensitive about trespassing on the sovereignty of others. Member states are cognizant that the United Nations was created to prevent wars, not to become an instrument for their propagation. Consequently, in the absence of target state consent, the Council is going to authorize armed action to protect fellow humans only in exceptional circumstances and where it is believed that the costs of military action are massively outweighed by the moral consequences of inaction. The bar, then, for UN-authorized humanitarian intervention is very high, and most states will support such action only in cases of genocide and mass killing and where it does not impinge upon important interests.

The second point to realize about the developing norm is that the consensus over armed intervention does not extend to unilateral action (defined as an intervention not authorized by the Security Council). It is evident from the position taken by the vast majority of states in debates in the General Assembly that there is no support for a legal right of unilateral humanitarian intervention, with many Southern states worried that such a right would become a weapon that the strong would use against the weak. Notably, however, where the Council has been called upon to judge cases of intervention in which it did not give prior authorization (such as the intervention by the Economic Community of West African States in Liberia in 1992 and, much more controversially, NATO's intervention in Kosovo in 1999), it has shown a new-found capacity to interpret flexibly the Charter's firm legal prohibition on the use of force. In so doing it has avoided a situation in which a consistent application of the law offends against moral values that are integral to the Charter itself.[5]

Thirdly, the much-vaunted claim that there is a "developing international norm" to protect civilians appears very hollow when viewed from the perspective of the millions who have perished in the past 10 years from genocide and war in Rwanda, Sudan and the Democratic Republic of the Congo (DRC). In the case of NATO's intervention in Kosovo, the major Western states were prepared to employ force for a complex mix of humanitarian and security reasons. But the emergent norm of civilian protection was insufficient to motivate these same governments to put their troops in harm's way to save Rwandans from genocide in 1994. The problem is that the norm enables new possibilities of intervention, but it does not determine that such actions will take place. The moral limitations of the project of humanitarian intervention in the 1990s can be seen in the fact that in no case have states intervened when there were no vital interests at stake and/or where there were perceived to be high risks to the lives of intervening forces. This produces a pattern of intervention that is highly selective, frequently driven by considerations of national self-interest rather than humanitarian need.[6] It also ensures that, when intervention does take place, it is widely viewed as morally hypocritical, a rhetorical instrument that rationalizes the projection of force by the powerful. Iraq is only the latest intervention where this long-standing critique can be strongly heard.

The use and abuse of humanitarian claims over Iraq

Defending the removal of Saddam Hussein on humanitarian grounds undoubtedly became more pronounced following the failure to find weapons of mass destruction (WMD). But it would be wrong to think that such claims were not invoked by the United States, the United Kingdom and Australia (the three states that contributed combat forces to Operation Iraqi Freedom) in the months preceding the military action. Speaking on 28 January 2003 in his State of the Union Address, Bush addressed the Iraqi people in the following terms: "Your enemy is not surrounding your country – your enemy is ruling your country ... And the day he and his regime are removed from power will be the day of your liberation."[7] And, three days before initiating military hostilities, the President made the following promise to Iraqis: "we will tear down the apparatus of terror and we will help you to build a new Iraq that is prosperous and free. In a free Iraq, there will be no more wars of aggression against your neighbours, no more poison factories, no more executions of dissidents, no more torture chambers and rape rooms."[8]

An appeal to humanitarian rationales was also evident in the justifications proffered by the Australian and British governments. Prime Minister John Howard vigorously defended the morality of Australian participation in military action, arguing that the humanitarian costs of war had to be weighed against the "very powerful case to the effect that the removal of Saddam Hussein's regime would produce a better life and less suffering for the people of Iraq".[9] This sentiment was also strongly held by Blair and his Foreign Secretary, Jack Straw. The Foreign and Commonwealth Office released a report in November 2002 documenting the gross and systematic abuses of human rights that had taken place in Iraq since Saddam came to power. Moreover, speaking at the Labour Party's local government, women's and youth conferences in Glasgow on 15 February 2003, the same day that 1 million people were marching against war on the streets of London, Blair championed the moral argument for war. He challenged delegates to remember that, "if the result of peace is Saddam staying in power ... then I tell you there are consequences paid in blood for that decision too. But these victims will never be seen. They will never feature on our TV screens or inspire millions to take to the streets. But they will exist nonetheless. Ridding the world of Saddam would be an act of humanity. It is leaving him there that is in truth inhumane."[10]

Critics of the war argue that these moral justifications are hypocritical and self-serving. They cite UK and US inaction in the face of Saddam Hussein's terrible oppression of the Kurds in the late 1980s, the establishment of a sanctions regime that inflicted terrible suffering on the civilian population, and revelations regarding the brutal treatment of Iraqi detainees in support of this case. Each of these criticisms is, of course, open to a counter-argument: the West's support for the Iraqi leader and consequent failure to protect the Kurds appear more reasonable when viewed in the context of the Cold War and the perceived threat from Iranian fundamentalism; the US and UK view of sanctions was driven by the expectation that they would produce regime change in Baghdad by triggering an internal uprising and by concerns that lifting the sanctions would enable Saddam to procure components for his nascent WMD programmes; and the US and UK culpability for the mistreatment of detainees depends upon the extent to which political leaders were complicit in the actions of subordinates. Whatever the balance of these arguments, what is important is the perception of many governments and national publics that, to the extent that humanitarian arguments were employed, the United Kingdom and the United States were deliberately using them to cloak the pursuit of baser national interests.

Viewed in this light, the real motivations that led Washington and London to deploy troops to Iraq are seen to be geopolitical and strategic. This is not the place to delve into these factors in great detail, but it is clear that for the United States a mix of the following considerations supported a policy of forcible regime change in Baghdad: long-term anxiety about how to manage a nuclear-armed Saddam; the associated fear that Iraqi WMD might find their way – deliberately or inadvertently – into the hands of terrorist groups such as al-Qaeda; the conviction that there was a war-winning strategy in Iraq that would serve as a demonstration effect to other states about the consequences of challenging Washington; the hope that Iraq could serve as a new beacon of democracy in the Middle East; the desire to remove a long-term foe of Israel; and the desire to secure long-term access to Iraq's major oil supplies. Not all of these rationales played in the UK context but, critically, an additional one did, namely Blair's belief that public and unstinting loyalty to the United States would be reciprocated by greater UK influence over the course of US policy. This article of faith in the so-called "special relationship" has been a hardy perennial in British foreign policy since 1945, and it was never more visible than over Iraq.

Clearly, without at least some of the above motivations, it is inconceivable that Bush and Blair would have acted to overthrow Saddam Hussein, but the fact that the primary – though not exclusive – motivations were non-humanitarian does not necessarily negate a positive humanitarian outcome. Motives matter only if they contradict the stated humanitarian justification for an action.[11] The question is whether, from a human rights perspective, it is reasonable to support a military intervention that has as one of its declared ends the termination of human rights abuses, when this is not one of the motives behind the action or at best is a secondary consideration. Those new liberal interventionists who support the Iraq war but consider that humanitarian motives were not paramount point to the beneficial consequences of the action. Thus, Michael Ignatieff argues that, "if the consequence of intervention is a rights-respecting Iraq in a decade or so, who cares whether the intentions that led to it were mixed at best?"[12] Similarly, William Shawcross, in entering the political minefield over Blair's WMD justification for war, argues that "what really matters ... is to build upon the first opportunity Iraqis have ever had to create a decent society".[13]

Because intervention will rarely be motivated primarily – let alone singularly – by humanitarian purposes, the privileging of humanitarian outcomes over motivations is a good reply to those critics who oppose establishing a doctrine of humanitarian intervention. However, such an argument rests on two key premises, both of which are deeply problematic in the case of Iraq. The first is the accuracy of the claim, frequently reiterated by Bush and Blair, that Iraq is a much better place as a result of the intervention. If Iraq evolves in the next few years into a tolerant rights-respecting society, then this will provide support to those who seek to represent the Iraq war as a justifiable humanitarian intervention. However, any such assessment would have to weigh on the debit side of the equation the thousands of Iraqi civilians killed during the war, the civilians who have been killed, injured or abused by both the resistance and coalition forces during the subsequent military occupation,[14] and the damage done to the civilian infrastructure, which is seriously affecting the health and well-being of many Iraqis. The final conclusions that one should draw from this complex balancing act are yet to be determined. The acceptance of a new Iraqi constitution in late October 2005 bodes well, although in both its build-up and final outcome the referendum says as much about the dangerous cleavages in Iraqi society as it does about national solidarity. And, against this positive outcome, insurgent activity continues and casualties rise. Despite increasing political opposition and an electorate that grows ever more critical, it is probable that the Bush administration has too much political capital invested in Iraq for it to withdraw from the melee. A post-Bush United States may, however, prove far less resolute. In the lap of such political vacillations lie the fortunes of post-conflict Iraq.

The argument's second premise concerns the sustainability of the assumption that there is no link between motivations and outcomes. The contention that outcomes should be privileged over motives is rejected by those who maintain that there is a direct link between the strength of the altruistic impulse to rescue and the effectiveness of the subsequent military operation in meeting this need. "A dominant humanitarian motive is important", according to Kenneth Roth, executive director of Human Rights Watch, "because it affects numerous decisions made in the course of an intervention and its aftermath that can determine its success in saving people from harm."[15] He argues that, if the humanitarian impulse had been a primary consideration in the case of Iraq, the Bush administration would have made better plans, especially in terms of increased troop numbers. Senior US generals requested a much larger force to cope with what they expected to be a chaotic and violent postwar security situation, but this request was turned down by Secretary of Defense Donald H. Rumsfeld. The civilian leaders in the Pentagon were strongly – if ill-advisedly – influenced by those Iraqi exiles who maintained that US forces would be greeted as liberators, and they were openly dismissive of dissenting views such as those expressed by the State Department and some in the military.[16]

Many Iraqi civilians have been killed since the end of the war as a consequence of intense fighting between US forces and local militias. Roth considers that the regular troops deployed in Iraq were – and are – unsuited to the task of local policing, and that the Pentagon's failure to train large numbers of police for such operations is symptomatic of its general lack of commitment to humanitarian protection as a principle guiding US force planning and strategy. He also castigates the UK and US forces for employing cluster munitions in urban areas, arguing that this led to the death or injury of over 1,000 civilians. "Such disregard for civilian life", he laments, "is incompatible with a genuinely humanitarian intervention."[17] This reliance on cluster bombs by UK and US forces reduces the risks facing soldiers compared with the alternative military strategy of moving in closer to engage enemy forces with close air support. However, although it is entirely reasonable that the armed forces should seek to minimize risks, the problem arises, as in Iraq, when this has the direct effect of increasing the exposure of civilians to harm. The difficulty here, and it is one that is overlooked by Roth, is how intervening states should balance the responsibilities they have to their armed forces against the duties they owe foreigners.[18] If the requirement for a legitimate humanitarian intervention is that soldiers should incur high levels of risk to protect non-nationals, this will have the effect of further inhibiting states from acting in humanitarian emergencies.

Critics would argue that the discrepancy between US and UK humanitarian justifications and the military conduct of the intervention supports the argument that Iraq was a case of abuse. Examining how far humanitarian justifications were in conformity with subsequent military actions is an important way of testing for the presence of humanitarian motivations, but it is not definitive, and Iraq demonstrates the limits of this approach. It does not automatically follow from the obvious shortcomings of Operation Iraqi Freedom in protecting civilians that the critics are right to name Iraq as a clear-cut case of abuse. Those like Roth are right to highlight the failure of the US-led coalition to calibrate military means to declared humanitarian ends, and those responsible should be held morally accountable for their failure to factor civilian protection seriously into post-war military planning; to believe that a force of fewer than 100,000 troops could provide for law and order in a post-Saddam Iraq was wishful thinking of the most irresponsible kind and it has produced tragic results. It does not, however, necessarily follow from such culpability that US and especially UK state leaders were disingenuous in advancing human rights as a rationale for their recourse to force.

Iraq would constitute a case of abuse only if the United States and the United Kingdom deliberately manipulated humanitarian claims for ulterior purposes. But those who make such a claim ignore the fact that both Bush and, especially, Blair strongly believed in the moral case for removing Saddam, although the philosophy guiding their respective world views is significantly different. Bush had made clear on many occasions that he believed in the "non-negotiable" values of freedom, human dignity and justice. His neoconservative philosophy is predicated on the belief that US values are universally valid, and that the United States' political and economic system is "a model for the world" – as two of the high priests of the neoconservative movement put it.[19] Moreover, Bush and his neoconservative allies believe that the mission of US power is actively to defend and export these principles. Given this guiding moral impulse, regime change in Iraq was seen by the Bush administration as being justifiable because Saddam was a fundamental obstacle to the realization of those universal moral values shared by both the United States and the Iraqi people.

There are, of course, countless examples in history (the Crusades, the Spanish/Portuguese conquest of the Americas, etc.) where interveners have appealed to universal values when these were merely a reflection of particular values and interests. It is recognition of these dangers that leads opponents of humanitarian intervention to worry that the doctrine merely serves to legitimate the exercise of US preponderance. Moreover, while acknowledging the Bush administration's belief that the notions of human dignity and freedom are synonymous with the extension of US liberal capitalism, it remains important to recognize how selective it has been in its approach to meeting human need. The neoconservatives support using US military power only where there are clear strategic threats to US interests and important political and economic benefits to be gained from intervention. It is this reasoning that explains why Iraq, and not the humanitarian emergencies in Liberia or the DRC, became the object of US military intervention.

In contrast to Bush and the neoconservatives, Blair stands as a leading advocate of the new liberal interventionist agenda. Speaking in October 2001 at the Labour Party Conference, the Prime Minister asserted that "the starving, the wretched, the dispossessed, the ignorant, those living in want and squalor from the deserts of Northern Africa to the slums of Gaza, to the mountain ranges of Afghanistan: they too are our cause". In the same speech, he stated his firm conviction that, were another Rwanda to happen, the world would have a compelling "moral duty" to intervene to stop it.[20] In helping to topple Saddam there is ample evidence that Blair saw himself as acting pursuant to this world view. Although he certainly believed that Iraq posed a long-term threat to regional and global security that could be effectively addressed only by Saddam's removal from power, these considerations served to reinforce his powerful humanitarian instincts.[21] What is certainly the case is that Blair would have been uncomfortable with any ending of the Iraq crisis that left Saddam in power.[22] Peter Stothard, who spent 30 days with the Prime Minister in March 2003, quotes Blair as saying: "What amazes me is how many people are happy for Saddam to stay. They ask why we don't get rid of Mugabe, why not the Burmese lot. Yes, let's get rid of them all. I don't because I can't, but when you can, you should."[23]

Ironically, whereas some critics of the war have sought to cast doubt on

Blair's humanitarian credentials, others have lambasted him for failing to emphasize humanitarian concerns more strongly and for not resting his case for war on such grounds alone. They maintain that he would have secured greater public support had he employed this rationale rather than relying on Iraq's possession of weapons of mass destruction, which lacked credibility among many voters.[24] Aside from smacking of the kind of cynical manipulation of public opinion for which Blair is so often castigated, this argument is open to more substantive objections. First, it fails to appreciate that for Blair there was no incompatibility between the WMD and the humanitarian arguments; he viewed regime change as the only means of effectively addressing both concerns. Secondly, even if humanitarian motives were the primary driver, he recognized there was no prospect of building an international coalition at the United Nations to support regime change on humanitarian grounds alone. Finally, the advice being tendered to the Prime Minister by his legal advisers was that there was no legal basis for removing a regime on account of its brutal character. Reliance on this justification might have triggered more embarrassing resignations among the government's legal advisers,[25] including perhaps the Attorney General himself, Lord Goldsmith, whose private legal opinion to Blair provided no support for the view that Iraq's regime could be overthrown on humanitarian grounds.[26] Whatever Blair's own convictions about the humanitarian case for war, he stated publicly that this is "not the reason we act. That must be according to the United Nations mandate on Weapons of Mass Destruction."[27] The fact that the United Kingdom's legal case for going to war against Iraq rested firmly on the contention that this action was in conformity with existing Security Council resolutions (the 678–687–1441 argument) further undermines the contention that the United Kingdom was abusing humanitarian justifications. The abuse argument relies on the assumption that a humanitarian rationale is the principal reason adduced in defence of an intervention, and this is clearly not the case with Iraq. If anything, it may well be that such arguments were, at least initially, deliberately down-played.

The claim that Blair was strongly motivated by humanitarian reasons over Iraq but felt constrained by international political exigencies and the existing legal framework from pressing this argument too strongly is strongly supported by the attempts he has made since the war both to justify Iraq as a humanitarian intervention and to change international law so that armed intervention would be permissible against tyrants such as Saddam. It is to these efforts, their reception in the wider international community and the implications for the developing norm of humanitarian intervention that we now turn.

Justifying Iraq as a legitimate humanitarian intervention

In a landmark speech on 5 March 2004 in his home constituency of Sedgefield, Tony Blair declared that "we surely have a responsibility to act when a nation's people are subjected to a regime such as Saddam's".[28] He admitted that there was no existing legal basis for intervention of this kind, but maintained that there should be. As we argued at the beginning of the chapter, the emerging normative consensus supports Security Council authorized intervention in cases of genocide and mass killings, but there is no enthusiasm for military action to defend human rights below this level. Blair's contention that the war against Iraq met the threshold for a justifiable humanitarian intervention was partly post hoc rationalization, but it also reflected the worry that establishing a high threshold for intervention allows regimes to abuse human rights secure in the knowledge that this would not trigger outside intervention. A chilling illustration of this reasoning was the Serb general who reportedly said, in relation to ethnic cleansing in Kosovo, "a village a day keeps NATO away". The problem is that addressing this concern by lowering the threshold brings in its wake a whole new set of problems that are likely to make the cure worse than the disease.

There are two compelling reasons to maintain a high threshold for justifying the use of force in humanitarian emergencies. The first is that resort to armed action as a means of halting slaughter must always be a last resort and should be undertaken only in the full knowledge that using force inevitably imposes harm on the civilian population the intervention is aimed at rescuing. Such interventions should be launched only when policy makers are confident that the moral costs of inaction far outweigh the moral consequences of using force, and this inevitably means restricting military intervention to extreme cases of humanitarian emergency. This position was one of the key planks in Human Rights Watch's rejection of the argument that the war in Iraq was justifiable on humanitarian grounds. In his 2004 article, executive director Roth argued that humanitarian intervention without the consent of the target state could be justified only "in the face of on-going or imminent genocide, or comparable mass slaughter or loss of life .... Other forms of tyranny are deplorable ... but they do not in our view rise to the level that would justify the extraordinary response of military force."[29]

The second objection to lowering the threshold is that this opens the door to a range of interventions that could claim, with varying degrees of plausibility, to be humanitarian. Gareth Evans, co-chair of the International Commission on Intervention and State Sovereignty (ICISS), encapsulated the reasoning that led ICISS to establish deliberately narrow threshold principles in its report *The Responsibility to Protect*. "The argument", Evans recalled, "was that unless the bar is set very high and tight, excluding less than catastrophic forms of human rights abuse, *prima facie* cases for the use of military force could be made across half the world." Awful though the chronic human rights abuses inside Iraq were, they could not justify recourse to force because Saddam's "behaviour was not much worse than a score or two of others".[30]

Both Roth's consequentialist argument and Evans' concerns regarding the opening of the proverbial flood-gates require the plotting of a difficult course between navigational points about which there is little international consensus. Although each stands as a major opponent of intervention in March 2003, both have argued that military action would have been legitimate following the 1988 "genocide" against the Kurds and also in the immediate aftermath of the 1991 Gulf war when Saddam's forces brutally suppressed uprisings by Kurds in the north and by Shiites in the south of the country.[31] However unpalatable the implication, the question of when to intervene must always be one of degree. Hence Roth, a tireless campaigner against the barbarous Saddam regime, while recognizing that Saddam killed perhaps as many as a quarter of a million Iraqis over his 25-year rule, concluded that there was no evidence of mass killing – actual or imminent – that justified military intervention in March 2003.[32] Such difficulties go far in explaining the tentative manner in which the international community came to endorse the concept of a "responsibility to protect" at the 2005 World Summit.[33] General Assembly acceptance came at a price, namely the abandonment of criteria that could be employed to address the issue of degree, which for many is at the heart of the question about when the use of force is legitimate.[34]

A further factor in the garnering of support for the "responsibility to protect" was the omission of references to how action could be legitimized in the absence of Security Council authorization. In the eyes of many, the dangers of issuing a licence for intervention to end gross human rights abuses would be significantly lessened if Security Council authorization were accepted as a *sine qua non* of a legitimate intervention. This was Blair's aspiration in raising the issue in his Sedgefield speech, and it is clear that the United Kingdom has a strong interest in ensuring that interventions secure Council approval, given its veto power. But there is no likelihood of the Council agreeing to sanction force to end human rights violations that fall below the level of genocide, mass murder and large-scale ethnic cleansing. China and Russia could be relied upon to lead opposition to such a step, and they would draw considerable support from the non-aligned grouping at the United Nations. These states have long worried that the major Western powers, and especially the United States, might employ human rights justifications as a pretext to legitimate military intervention. These suspicions are seen to have been confirmed by the action in Iraq and, although the General Assembly signed up to a declaration on the "Responsibility to Protect" in September 2005, it remains to be seen to what extent Council members will be prepared to give teeth to this in future cases of egregious human suffering. In this regard, any future expansion of the Council designed to ensure greater Southern representation is likely to prove deleterious from a new liberal interventionist standpoint. Exactly how this will factor into the further development of the norm of humanitarian intervention remains a matter of conjecture, but it is unlikely that increasing representation from Africa, Asia and Latin America will result in a Council more inclined to support humanitarian intervention.

The new liberal interventionists want to use Iraq to advance the case for military intervention to remove tyrannical regimes. However, liberal internationalists who are committed to establishing a new global consensus supporting UN-authorized humanitarian intervention fear that the Iraq war undermines the limited progress made to date. For example, Evans argues that, because Iraq is interpreted in wider international society as a case of abuse, this would make it much more difficult to persuade other governments to support future interventions justified in humanitarian terms. In May 2004 he argued that, as a consequence of the Iraq war, an "emerging international norm of real potential utility was once again struggling for acceptance".[35] Reflecting the same anxiety, Roth cautioned that "the effort to justify it [the Iraq war] even in part in humanitarian terms risk[s] [breeding] cynicism about the use of military force for humanitarian purposes [which] could be devastating for people in need of future rescue".[36]

The dismal failure of the international community to respond effectively to the humanitarian catastrophe in Darfur in western Sudan in 2004 appeared to confirm Roth's worst fears: it is estimated that at least 100,000 Sudanese civilians have been killed by government-sponsored militias in the past two years, and, as of December 2005, 2 million people were internally displaced in Darfur and at risk from malnutrition and disease.[37] US Secretary of State Colin Powell took the momentous step on 9 September 2004 of declaring the catastrophe in Darfur to be a case of genocide,[38] but, if he expected this act of naming to galvanize the international community to respond decisively to the crisis, his hopes were to be dashed. The international community remained stubbornly passive in the face of what was at the time the world's worst humanitarian crisis, and it seemed that the war in Iraq had done little to help those who wished to see a robust response to the unfolding humanitarian emergency. Alex Bellamy points out that some members of the Security Council, anxious that Sudan should not become the next target for US intervention, reaffirmed in Council deliberations the paramount importance of the non-intervention principle.[39] Such language is worryingly reminiscent of the Council debates of the past, but its import should be neither read out of context nor exaggerated.

That in the face of such atrocities no proposal for large-scale military intervention in Darfur was tabled in the Council may be taken as evidence that post-Iraq states are highly reluctant to sanction intervention, particularly where the target state is Islamic. Iraq is also significant in that the ongoing commitment there of the United States and the United Kingdom diminishes their capacity – and perhaps willingness – to become embroiled in additional military ventures. Moreover, in the eyes of many states, their actions over Iraq make them less than palatable agents of the United Nations or norm carriers for humanitarianism.

However, set against these arguments, there exist equally plausible alternative interpretations of the inertia. Principally it should be recognized that the norm that emerged during the 1990s – codified in the *2005 World Summit Outcome* document – is permissive rather than obligatory and, even without the repercussions of Iraq, it is doubtful that there would have been much appetite for military intervention in Darfur given the geographical, logistical and military challenges that such an operation would entail. Such practical questions are an integral part of the ethical reasoning that must inform any decision to intervene and, as noted already, such issues have served in many cases to prevent action being taken. It should also be recognized that, whereas those within the Council inclined to oppose intervention may be emboldened by the post-Iraq discrediting of the United States and the United Kingdom in invoking sovereignty as a shield against intervention, states such as China are doing no more than voicing concerns that pre-date the conflict but that fell silent during a brief period of acquiescence in the 1990s.

In the aftermath of the Iraq conflict, cases such as Darfur serve only to test the continuing validity of the embryonic norm of Council-authorized intervention in which a "coalition of the willing" seeks Security Council authorization to use force to halt a humanitarian crisis. If, pushed to a vote, such a request fails to secure majority support in the Council on the grounds that such action violates the principle of state sovereignty, then this would represent a retreat from the promise made in September 2005 to set definite limits to the non-intervention rule – turning back the clock to the dark days of the Cold War when sovereign rights always trumped human rights.

Conclusion

The war against Iraq has produced a major fissure in the liberal international consensus forged in the 1990s concerning the justifiability of military intervention for humanitarian protection. This was predicated on the assumption that sovereign rights should be limited in cases of genocide and/or mass killings when a government was unable or unwilling to provide protection to its citizens.[40] It is paradoxical that the General Assembly signed up to this principle in September 2005 because the international consensus underpinning this position has been put under great strain as a consequence of attempts by the new liberal interventionists to justify the Iraq war as a humanitarian intervention. This move is condemned across the political spectrum as a convenient rationalization, and those within the liberal camp committed to working through the United Nations worry that defending the Iraq war as a humanitarian intervention sets back the cause of entrenching the norm of the responsibility to protect.

This chapter has argued that the charge of abuse oversimplifies the complex set of motivations that led Bush and Blair to overthrow Saddam Hussein, but endorses the liberal internationalist position that the Iraq war fails as a justifiable humanitarian intervention. However, in arguing that Iraq was not a simple case of abuse, it is necessary to recognize that humanitarian motives were not the primary driver behind the US and UK intervention. The Iraq war is a significant factor in the wider debate about the legitimacy of humanitarian intervention, not because it was primarily justified as such an act but because of the nature and magnitude of the human suffering that resulted from the war. Yet it does not follow that, because the Bush administration accorded a low priority to civilian protection in post-war military planning, the Iraq war is a clear-cut case of abuse. The administration should be held to account for its over-reliance on Iraqi exiles who had their own agenda; for thinking that the Iraqis would greet US forces with open arms; and for ignoring the advice of senior military officers and area experts in the State Department. The US failure to discharge its responsibilities for providing security as the occupying power justifies charges of incompetence and even negligence, but this does not mean that the moral impulse to spread US conceptions of freedom and human dignity was mere subterfuge. That said, what the Iraq war highlights is that those who employ human rights rationales will be believed only if they demonstrate by their actions that military means are supporting humanitarian values.

The fundamental concern that animates many governments, human rights international non-governmental organizations and public intellectuals is the deleterious impact of the Iraq war on the developing norm of humanitarian intervention. The Security Council's reluctance to act over Darfur is cited in support of this position, and it is evident that the Iraq war has made many states, especially in the Arab world, conscious of the need to reassert the primacy of the non-intervention principle. However, before succumbing to the gloomy view that the Iraq war has strangled the emerging norm of humanitarian intervention at birth, two key points should be borne in mind. First, this pessimistic position exaggerates the pre-Iraq propensity of states to act for humanitarian purposes pursuant to the norm. The norm that developed in the 1990s enabled rather than determined intervention, a point graphically illustrated by the failure to prevent and halt the Rwandan genocide. In other words, even without the Iraq war, it is far from clear that the major Western states would have taken the lead in militarily intervening in the Sudan.

The second reason for some limited optimism is that the *2005 World Summit Outcome* document makes it harder for states to evade their declaratory commitment to protect strangers in peril. On the other hand, it does nothing to address the fundamental problem of what should happen if the Council is unable to agree in cases where particular states are seeking a mandate to prevent or stop a humanitarian emergency. In the case of Darfur, for example, the implication of the current position is that, if a majority of the Council support a request for authorization from a coalition of Western and African states seeking to end the atrocities, and this is opposed by one or more of the permanent members, then this would be the end of the matter. Hitherto the willingness of the permanent members to veto such a resolution has not been tested since there has been no enthusiasm from Western states, especially the United States and the United Kingdom, for such an action. With regard to the United Kingdom and the United States, the Iraq war has surely played an important part in sapping their enthusiasm for military intervention. Certainly, it has done little to strengthen their political credentials as entrepreneurs for the emergent norm of humanitarian intervention. Consequently, those with the greatest military capacity to act would face high political costs were they to do so and, in the absence of compelling strategic rationales, these have been deemed unacceptable.[41] This is not, however, to say that, were the United Kingdom and the United States to come to the conclusion that the humanitarian catastrophe in Darfur necessitated military action, members of the Security Council – including those non-Western permanent members most critical of the action in Iraq – would not feel compelled to grant a UN mandate in the face of claims that such action was the only means to end the humanitarian catastrophe. To this extent, the norm of UN-authorized humanitarian intervention might yet prove more robust than the critics fear.

Acknowledgements

We would like to thank Alex Bellamy, Ken Berry, Ian Clark, Cian O'Driscoll, Tim Dunne, Anne Harris, Andrew Linklater, Gerry Simpson and Paul Williams for their comments on earlier versions of this chapter. It was originally presented at a conference on "Iraq and World Order: Structural and Normative Challenges", jointly hosted by the King Prajadhipok Institute, the United Nations University and the International Peace Academy on 17–18 August 2004 in Bangkok, Thailand. We are grateful to all the participants at the conference for their contribution to the ideas in the chapter.

Notes

1. For a fuller discussion of this case, see Nicholas J. Wheeler, *Saving Strangers: Humanitarian Intervention in International Society* (Oxford: Oxford University Press, 2000), pp. 55–77.
2. *2005 World Summit Outcome*, UN Doc. A/60/L.1, 20 September 2005, ⟨http://daccessdds. un.org/doc/UNDOC/LTD/N05/511/30/PDF/N0551130.pdf?OpenElement⟩ (accessed 26 September 2005), p. 31.
3. It would be wrong to give the impression that this pushing out of the boundaries of legitimate intervention was uncontested. Rather, as the deliberations over intervention in northern Iraq in 1991 and in Somalia in 1992 demonstrated, there was resistance from those states that worried about setting precedents that might erode the principle of non-intervention.
4. Kofi A. Annan, "Two Concepts of Sovereignty", Address to the 54th Session of the General Assembly, 20 September 1999, reprinted in Kofi A. Annan, *The Question of Intervention: Statements by the Secretary General* (New York: United Nations, 1999), p. 44.
5. This argument is developed in Thomas Franck, *Recourse to Force: State Action Against Threats and Armed Attacks* (Cambridge: Cambridge University Press, 2002), p. 185.
6. Even where states are not acting according to narrow self-interests, there is no escape from selectivity in the application of moral principles. In some cases military intervention is rightly ruled out on the grounds that armed action would do more harm than good (Chechnya and Tibet are obvious examples here). As Michael Ignatieff notes, "perfect consistency is a test of legitimacy that political action can never meet, and hence the prerequisite of consistency serves (even if it does not intend to do so) either as a justification for doing nothing or as a condemnation of any intervention actually undertaken" (Michael Ignatieff, "Human Rights, Power and the State", in Simon Chesterman, Michael Ignatieff and Ramesh Thakur, eds, *Making States Work*, Tokyo: United Nations University Press, 2005, p. 60; Chris Brown, "Selective Humanitarianism: In Defence of Inconsistency", in Deen K. Chatterjee and Don E. Scheid, eds, *Ethics and Foreign Intervention*, Cambridge, Cambridge University Press, 2003, pp. 31–53).
7. President George W. Bush, "State of the Union" Address, 28 January 2003, ⟨http:// www.whitehouse.gov/news/releases/2003/01/20030128-19.html⟩ (accessed 10 June 2004).
8. Remarks by the President in Address to the Nation, 17 March 2003, ⟨http://www. whitehouse.gov/news/releases/2003/03/20030317-7.html⟩ (accessed 10 June 2004).

9. Transcript, the Prime Minister to the National Press Club, The Great Hall, Parliament House, Canberra, 14 March 2003.

10. Speech by Prime Minister at Labour's local government, women's and youth conferences, SECC, Glasgow, 15 February 2003, ⟨http://www.scottishlabour.org.uk/tbiraq/⟩.

11. This argument is developed at length in Wheeler, *Saving Strangers*.

12. Michael Ignatieff, "Why Are We in Iraq? (And Liberia? And Afghanistan?)", *New York Times*, 7 September 2003.

13. William Shawcross, "Blair Was Right on Iraq", *Guardian*, 21 July 2004.

14. A research team at Bloomberg School of Public Health at Johns Hopkins University in Baltimore estimated in 2004 that as many as 100,000 civilians had died in Iraq as a direct or indirect consequence of the US-led invasion. The methodology underpinning the report has been challenged, and others put the figure much lower. For example, the Baghdad-based Iraqi human rights organizations estimate the figure at 30,000, and Iraq Body Count puts the number at 28,000–32,000 (see Elisabeth Rosenthal, "Study Puts Iraqi Deaths of Civilians at 100,000", *New York Times*, 29 October 2004; Rob Stein, "100,000 Civilian Deaths Estimated in Iraq", *Washington Post*, 29 October 2004; Patrick Wintour and Richard Norton-Taylor, "No 10 Challenges Civilian Death Toll", *Guardian*, 30 October 2004; and Iraq Body Count, ⟨http://www.iraqbodycount.net/⟩, accessed 2 March 2006).

15. Kenneth Roth, "War in Iraq: Not a Humanitarian Intervention", Human Rights Watch Report 2004, ⟨http://hrw.org/wr2k4/3.htm⟩ (accessed 15 June 2004), p. 6. It is noteworthy in this respect that, writing a year after his *New York Times* article cited above, Ignatieff recognized that "insincere intentions may prevent good consequences from occurring. If the United States and the United Kingdom actually do not much care about human rights in Iraq, then they are unlikely to do very much to improve them once they occupy the country" (Ignatieff, "Human Rights, Power and the State", p. 68).

16. See Warren P. Strobel and John Walcott, "Post-war Planning Non-Existent", *Knight Ridder Newspapers*, 13 July 2003, ⟨http://www.realcities.com/mld/krwashington/9927782.htm⟩ (accessed 2 March 2006); Bob Woodward, *Plan of Attack* (London: Simon & Schuster, 2004), pp. 114–115, 117–119, 207–208.

17. Roth, "War in Iraq", p. 7.

18. For a fuller discussion of this problem focusing on the case of US intervention in Afghanistan, see Nicholas J. Wheeler, "Dying for Enduring Freedom: Accepting Responsibility for Civilian Casualties in the War on Terrorism", *International Relations*, Vol. 16, No. 2 (2002), pp. 205–225.

19. Lawrence F. Kaplan and William Kristol, *The War over Iraq: Saddam's Tyranny and America's Mission* (San Francisco: Encounter Books, 2003), p. 64.

20. Tony Blair, speech to the Labour Party Conference, 2 October 2001, ⟨http://politics.guardian.co.uk/labourconference2001/story/0,1220,561988,00.html⟩ (accessed 9 February 2006).

21. For a thoughtful assessment of the mixture of motivations driving Blair over Iraq, see Christoph Bluth, "The British Road to War: Blair, Bush and the Decision to Invade Iraq", *International Affairs*, Vol. 80, No. 5 (2004), pp. 871–893.

22. Ignatieff, "Human Rights, Power, and the State", p. 59.

23. Peter Stothard, *Thirty Days: A Month at the Heart of Blair's War* (London: HarperCollins, 2003), p. 42.

24. Andrew Rawnsley, "The Damaging Questions Keep Coming", *Observer*, 14 September 2003; Nick Cohen, "No Sexing up, Please", *Observer*, 14 September 2003.

25. The Foreign Office's Deputy Legal Adviser Elizabeth Wilmshurst left the Foreign Office in March 2003 because she was unhappy with the legal basis of the government's case.

See Ewen MacAskill, "Adviser Quits Foreign Office over Legality of War", *Guardian*, 22 March 2003; John Kampfner, *Blair's Wars* (London: Simon & Schuster, 2003), p. 304.

26. Lord Goldsmith tendered this advice to Blair on 7 March 2003 and it was finally made public after intense scrutiny of the legal case for war by Parliament, lawyers and the media on 28 April 2005. Attorney General's legal opinion tendered to the Prime Minister on 7 March 2003, at ⟨http://news.bbc.co.uk/1/shared/bsp/hi/pdfs/28_04_05_attorney_general.pdf⟩ (accessed 12 November 2005).

27. Speech by Prime Minister at Labour's local government, women's and youth conference, SECC, Glasgow, 15 February 2003.

28. Tony Blair, speech on Iraq and the threat of international terrorism, Sedgefield, 5 March 2004, ⟨http://politics.guardian.co.uk/speeches/story/0,11126,1162992,00.html⟩ (accessed 7 July 2004).

29. Roth, "War in Iraq", pp. 3–4.

30. Gareth Evans, "When Is It Right to Fight? Legality, Legitimacy and the Use of Military Force", 2004 Cyril Foster Lecture, Oxford University, 10 May 2004.

31. Ibid.

32. Roth, "War in Iraq", pp. 3–4.

33. *2005 World Summit Outcome*, UN Doc. A/60/L.1, p. 31.

34. Nicholas J. Wheeler, "A Victory for Common Humanity", *Journal of International Law and International Relations*, Vol. 2, No. 1 (Winter 2005).

35. Roth, "War in Iraq"; Evans, "When Is It Right to Fight?".

36. Roth, "War in Iraq", p. 1.

37. Rob Crilly, "Darfur 'Sliding into Anarchy'", *The Scotsman*, 5 November 2005; Robert I. Rotberg, "Why Wait on Darfur", *Boston Globe*, 24 October 2005.

38. Glenn Kessler and Colum Lynch, "U.S. Calls Killings in Sudan Genocide", *Washington Post*, 10 September 2004.

39. See Alex J. Bellamy, "Responsibility to Protect or Trojan Horse? The Crisis in Darfur and Humanitarian Intervention after Iraq", *Ethics and International Affairs*, Vol. 19, No. 2 (Summer 2005), pp. 31–54.

40. This idea of "sovereignty as responsibility" received its most eloquent expression in the 2001 report *The Responsibility to Protect* by the International Commission on Intervention and State Sovereignty, ⟨http://www.iciss.ca/report-en.asp⟩ (accessed 9 February 2006).

41. Bellamy, "Responsibility to Protect or Trojan Horse?"

28

The responsibility to protect and the war on Saddam Hussein

Ramesh Thakur

The worst act of domestic criminal behaviour by a government is large-scale killings of its own people; the worst act of international criminal behaviour is the attack and invasion of another country. The international history of the twentieth century was in part the story of a twin-track approach to tame, through a series of normative, legislative and institutional fetters, both internal and external impulses to armed criminality by states. This approach attempted to translate an increasingly internationalized human conscience and a growing sense of international community into a new normative architecture of world order. Saddam Hussein's record of brutality was a taunting reminder of the distance yet to be traversed before we reach the first goal of eradicating domestic state criminality; his ouster and capture by unilateral force of arms were a daunting setback to the effort to outlaw and criminalize wars of choice as an instrument of state policy in international affairs.

But what if the second failure is a response to the first – if one country is attacked and invaded in order to halt or prevent atrocities inside its sovereign territory by the "legitimate" government (which already indicates a troubling appropriation and corruption of the word "legitimate")? For answers to this painful dilemma, read *The Responsibility to Protect* (R2P), a Report by the International Commission on Intervention and State Sovereignty (ICISS).[1] The UN Secretary-General's High-level Panel on Threats, Challenges and Change, borrowing from R2P, proposed five criteria of legitimacy: seriousness of threat; proper purpose; last resort; proportional means; and balance of consequences.[2] With respect to internal conflicts, the panel explicitly endorsed the ICISS argument that "the issue is not the 'right to intervene' of any State, but the 'responsibility to protect' of *every* State".[3] The legitimacy criteria will simultaneously make the Security Council more responsive to outbreaks of humanitarian atrocities than hitherto, and make it more difficult for individual states or ad hoc "coalitions of the willing" to appropriate the language of humanitarianism for geopolitical and unilateral interventions. In March 2005, Kofi Annan made an explicit reference to ICISS and "the responsibility to protect" as well as to the High-level Panel, endorsed the legitimacy criteria, and urged the Security Council to adopt a resolution "setting out these principles and expressing its intention to be guided by them" when authorizing the use of force. This would "add transparency to its deliberations and make its decisions more likely to be respected, by both Governments and world public opinion".[4]

In the event, the "responsibility to protect" was one of the few substantive items to survive the brutal negotiations toward the very end of the negotiations prior to the UN World Summit in New York in September 2005. The *2005 World Summit Outcome* document contained clear, unambiguous acceptance by all UN members of individual state responsibility and collective international responsibility to protect populations from genocide, war crimes, ethnic cleansing and crimes against humanity, and a willingness to take timely and decisive collective action for this purpose, through the Security Council, when peaceful means prove inadequate and national authorities are manifestly failing to do it. The concept was given its own subsection title ("Responsibility to protect populations from genocide, war crimes, ethnic cleansing and crimes against humanity").[5]

The triple dilemma of complicity, paralysis or illegality

The Responsibility to Protect is not an interveners' charter, any more than the UN Charter is a tyrants' charter behind which they can shield their acts of atrocity with impunity. Embedded within the larger framework of human security, R2P concluded that, where a population is suffering serious harm as a result of internal war, insurgency, repression or state failure, and the government in question is unwilling or unable to halt or avert it, the norm of non-intervention yields to the international responsibility to protect. But, in order to ground international intervention in a more widely shared international morality, R2P reformulates "humanitarian intervention" as "the responsibility to protect", and identifies the conditions under which the principle of state sovereignty yields to the international responsibility to protect.

The 1990s were a challenging decade for the international community with regard to conscience-shocking atrocities in many parts of the world. We generally failed to rise to the challenge and the price of our failure was paid by large numbers of innocent men, women and children. The debate on intervention, reinvigorated by the Iraq war in 2003, was ignited in the closing years of the twentieth century by the critical gap between the needs and distress felt in the real world in Somalia, Rwanda, Srebrenica and East Timor, the growing acceptance of human security as an alternative framework for security policy in today's circumstances, and the codified instruments and modalities for managing world order.

The triple policy dilemma – complicity, paralysis or illegality – can be summarized thus:

- to respect sovereignty all the time is to risk being complicit in humanitarian tragedies sometimes;
- to argue that the UN Security Council must give its consent to international intervention for humanitarian purposes is to risk policy paralysis by handing over the agenda either to the passivity and apathy of the Council as a whole or to the most obstructionist member of the Council, including any one of the five permanent members determined to use the veto clause;
- to use force without UN authorization is to violate international law and undermine world order based on the centrality of the United Nations as the custodian of world conscience and the Security Council as the guardian of world peace.

Under the impact of contrasting experiences in Rwanda and Kosovo, UN Secretary-General Annan urged member states to come up with a new consensus on the competing visions of national and popular sovereignty – reflecting national and human security – and the resulting "challenge of humanitarian intervention". Responding to the challenge, Canadian Foreign Minister Lloyd Axworthy set up ICISS as an independent international commission to wrestle with the whole gamut of difficult and complex issues involved in the debate. The ICISS report R2P seeks to do three principal things: change the conceptual language from "humanitarian intervention" to "responsibility to protect"; pin the responsibility on state authorities at the national level and on the UN Security Council at the international level; and ensure that interventions, when they do take place, are done properly.

Because R2P is not an interveners' charter, it does not provide a checklist against which decisions can be made with precision. Political contingencies cannot be fully anticipated in all their glorious complexity and, in the real world, policy choices will always be made on a case-by-case basis. With that in mind, R2P seeks to identify those conscience-shocking situations in which the case for international intervention is compelling and to enhance the prospects of such interventions. In turn, this means that the circumstances have to be narrow, the bar for intervention high and the procedural and operational safeguards tight, because the probability of international consensus is higher under conditions of due process, due authority and due diligence.

From "humanitarian intervention" to "responsibility to protect"

"Humanitarian intervention" is what humanitarian agencies such as the International Committee of the Red Cross and the UN High Commissioner for Refugees do; they object to the phrase being appropriated and debased by states engaged in military intervention. "Humanitarian bombing" as a conceptual oxymoron is immediately obvious to everyone. Yet the discourse over NATO's intervention in Kosovo in 1999 was framed largely in the language of humanitarian intervention – when in fact that intervention consisted of three months of bombing. So, if that was humanitarian intervention, then surely it must necessarily also have been humanitarian bombing? Only those who feel no sense of unease at "humanitarian bombing" should use "humanitarian intervention"; the rest should abandon this phraseology.

It is easy to dub a war a "humanitarian intervention" and so label critics as "anti-humanitarian". "Humanitarian intervention" conveys to most Western minds the idea that the principle underlying the intervention is not self-interested power politics but the disinterested one of protecting human life. It conjures up in many non-Western minds historical memories of the strong imposing their will on the weak in the name of the prevailing universal principles of the day, from the civilizing mission of spreading Christianity to the cultivation and promotion of human rights. The phrase "humanitarian intervention" is used to trump sovereignty with intervention at the outset of the debate: it loads the dice in favour of intervention before the argument has even begun, by labelling and de-legitimizing dissent as anti-humanitarian. This is why the *ex post facto* shift in justification for the war in Iraq, from weapons of mass destruction and links to al-Qaeda before the war to humanitarian liberation afterwards, had the net effect of de-legitimizing "humanitarian intervention" instead of legitimizing the Iraq intervention.

Military intervention for human protection purposes is a polite euphemism for war: the use of deadly force on a massive scale. Politics is at the core of the contested aspects of such interventions, including the threshold of abuse, legal authority for the intervention, and replacement of the repressive regime with a more progressive one. For example, if law and order are to be restored, whose law and whose order will they be? The answer to this central question provides the best clue to the genuineness and extent of the transfer of sovereignty from the US occupying power to an Iraqi government in June 2004.

In any event, answers to all the above questions are profoundly political in content, and they are made by political actors on the basis of political judgements and calculations. Moreover, the privileging of some crises that are securitized over those that are not reflects the interests and perspectives of the powerful and the rich at the expense of the weak and the poor. How else do we explain the attention surfeit syndrome with respect to Iraq alongside the attention deficit syndrome with regard to the Democratic Republic of Congo or the crisis in the Darfur region of Sudan? It also explains why the risk to the soldiers of the intervening, warring-by-choice countries is minimized by transferring the burden of danger to the civilians and soldiers of the other side. And it explains the refusal of the United States, which wields enormously destructive power well beyond its borders, to permit such a global exercise of power to be accountable to international institutions such as the new International Criminal Court, let alone to those who suffer its consequences. Thus it is all right for 600 Iraqis, mainly civilians, to die in revenge attacks on Fallujah for the four Americans killed and mutilated. If done by Saddam Hussein this would have been called mass murder.

From this to abuse of Iraqi prisoners is not such a big step. It results from the attitude that "we" are superior beings above the law and "they" are an inferior species not deserving of the protection of the law. Thus Rob Corddry of the satirical *Daily Show*: "Remember, it's not important that we did torture these people. What's important is that we are not the kind of people who would torture these people."[6] That is, repressive regimes can be held accountable for their use of force internally by foreign governments that insist on exempting their own use of force internationally from any independent international accountability. In the case of Saddam Hussein, in order to oust a regime based solely on might with few redeeming features to make it right, established institutions and conventions for ensuring that force is legitimately exercised were set aside by a power supremely confident of its might.

'Twas ever thus, and perhaps ever will be. William Dalrymple, in his fascinating book on mores governing social intercourse between Europeans and Indians in the eighteenth century, quotes a French writer explaining why Napoleon Bonaparte planned to invade India and how he would be received by the natives:

General Bonaparte, following the footsteps of Alexander would have entered India not as a devastating conqueror ... but as a liberator. He would have expelled the English forever from India so that not one of them would have remained and ... would have restored independence, peace, and happiness to Asia, Europe, and to the whole world ... All the Princes in India were longing for French intervention.[7]

The above was penned by Louis Bourquien in 1923 – *plus ça change, plus c'est la même chose* (the more things change, the more they stay the same).

The cynical deployment of moral arguments to justify imperialist actions in Iraq in 2003 has a direct structural counterpart in the British annexation of the kingdom of Awadh (Oudh in its Anglicized version) in the first half of the nineteenth century. The structure of justification makes use of a specific set of techniques for the mobilization of democratic consent and international support – through political representatives, the press and the interested and attentive public – for decisions taken in pursuit of national interest by an élite group of policy makers. Tracing its origins to John Locke and John Stuart Mill, Chatterjee locates it in the paternalistic belief that people – and hence nations – who are morally handicapped or in a state of moral infancy deserve a benevolent despot who will protect and look after them.[8]

What is remarkable is how many of the same arguments, including the evangelical fervour, the axiomatic assumption of the mantle of civilisation, the fig-leaf of legalism, the intelligence reports, the forgeries and subterfuges and the hard-headed calculations of national interest, remain exactly the same at the beginning of the 21st century.[9]

The collective memory of the people and governments of most developing countries is that, in the name of moral enlightenment, the European powers expanded their empires by defiling the lands and plundering the resources of their subject peoples. This is why the fine talk of humanitarian intervention by Westerners translates in non-Westerners' historical consciousness into efforts to resurrect and perpetuate neo-colonial rule by foreigners. It also explains why so many of them look for the ugly reality of geostrategic and commercial calculations camouflaged under the lofty rhetoric of spreading Christian humanitarianism. They cannot reasonably be expected to be mute accomplices when Westerners substitute their mythology of humanitarian intervention for histories of colonial oppression. To deny the formerly colonized their own history is to negate their independent identity.

Where "humanitarian intervention" raises fears of domination based on the international power hierarchy, R2P encapsulates the element of international solidarity. It implies an evaluation of the issues from the point of view of those seeking or needing support, rather than of the rights and duty of those who may be considering intervention. It refocuses the international searchlight on the duty to protect the villager from murder, the woman from rape and the child from starvation and being orphaned.

Sovereignty as responsibility

Intervention for human protection purposes occurs so that those condemned to die in fear may live in hope instead. It is based in the double belief that the sovereignty of a state has an accompanying responsibility on the part of that state; and that, if the state defaults on the responsibility to protect its citizens, then the fallback responsibility to do so must be assumed and honoured by the international community. Based on changes in the real world and evolving best-practice international behaviour, the ICISS concluded that it is necessary and useful to reconceptualize sovereignty, viewing it not as an absolute term of authority but as a kind of responsibility. Crucially, R2P acknowledges that responsibility rests primarily with the state concerned. Only if the state is unable or unwilling to discharge its responsibility, or is itself the perpetrator, does it become the responsibility of others to act in its place. Thus R2P is more of a linking concept that bridges the divide between the international community and the sovereign state, whereas the language of humanitarian intervention is inherently more confrontational.

The doctrine of sovereign equality and the correlative norm of nonintervention are European in origin and construct and they received the most emphatic affirmation from the newly independent developing countries (although the United States is second to none in the jealous defence of national sovereignty against international encroachments). At one level, the developing countries' attachment to sovereignty is deeply emotional. In the age of colonialism, most Afro-Asians and Latin Americans were the victims of Western superiority in the organization and weaponry of warfare. Most developing countries are former colonies that achieved independence on the back of extensive and protracted nationalist struggles against the major European powers. The anti-colonial impulse in their world view survives as a powerful sentiment in the collective consciousness of the nation. The continuing scars in the collective memory of the former colonized countries are difficult for many Westerners to comprehend and come to terms with.

At another level, the commitment to sovereignty is functional. The state is the cornerstone of the international system. State sovereignty provides order, stability and predictability in international relations. It mediates relations between the strong and the weak, the rich and the poor, and former colonizers and the colonized. With independence, and following the globalization of the norm of self-determination, the principle of state sovereignty was the constitutional device used by newly decolonized countries to try to reconstitute disrupted societies and polities and to restart arrested economic development.

Yet even during the Cold War state practice registered the unwillingness of many countries – not just the major powers but also former colonies such as India and Tanzania – to give up intervention as an instrument of policy. The many examples of intervention in actual state practice throughout the twentieth century did not lead to an abandonment of the norm of non-intervention. Often the breaches provoked such fierce controversy and aroused so much nationalistic passion that their net effect was to reinforce, not negate, the norm of non-intervention.

R2P's core principle is that, although the state has the primary responsibility to protect its citizens, the responsibility of the broader community of states is activated when a particular state is either unwilling or unable to fulfil its responsibility to protect or is itself the perpetrator of crimes or atrocities. The foundations of the international responsibility to protect lie in obligations inherent in the concept of sovereignty; the responsibility of the Security Council, under Article 24 of the UN Charter, for the maintenance of international peace and security; specific legal obligations under human rights and human protection declarations, covenants and treaties, international humanitarian law and national law; and the developing practice of states, regional organizations and the Security Council itself. As a result of agreements they have signed voluntarily, states now accept many external obligations and international scrutiny.

The UN Charter is itself an example of an international obligation voluntarily accepted by member states. On the one hand, in granting membership of the United Nations, the international community welcomes the signatory state as a responsible member of the community of nations. On the other hand, the state itself, in signing the Charter, accepts the responsibilities of membership flowing from that signature. There is no transfer or dilution of state sovereignty. Rather, the United Nations is the chief agent of the system of states for exercising international authority in their name.

Doing it right, doing it well

The substance of the responsibility to protect is the provision of life-supporting protection and assistance to populations at risk. The goal of intervention for human protection purposes is not to wage war on a state in order to destroy it and eliminate its statehood but to protect the victims of atrocities inside the state, to embed the protection in reconstituted institutions after the intervention, and then to withdraw all foreign troops. Thus military intervention for human protection purposes takes away the rights flowing from the status of sovereignty, but it does not in itself challenge the status as such. It is always limited in time to a temporary period, until the capacity of the state itself to resume its protective functions can be restored and institutionalized. Intervention may also be confined to the particular portion of the target state's territory where the abuses are actually occurring (for example, Kosovo and not all of Yugoslavia), and limited to the particular group that is the target of abuse.

The traditional terms of the "humanitarian intervention" debate do not adequately take into account the prevention and follow-up assistance components of external action. Action in support of the responsibility to protect necessarily involves and calls for a broad range and wide variety of measures and responses in fulfilment of the accompanying duty to assist. These may include: development assistance to help prevent conflict from occurring, intensifying, spreading or persisting; support for rebuilding to help prevent conflict from recurring; and, in extraordinary cases, military intervention to protect at-risk civilians from harm.

The responsibility to prevent conflict necessitates addressing both the root causes and the direct causes of internal conflict and other human-made crises putting populations at risk. The responsibility to react requires us to respond to situations of compelling human need with appropriate measures, which may include coercive measures such as sanctions and international prosecution and, in extreme cases, military intervention. The responsibility to rebuild requires us to provide, particularly after a military intervention, full assistance with recovery, reconstruction and reconciliation, addressing the causes of the harm the intervention was designed to halt or avert.

Far from meeting the test of engaging in conflict prevention in Iraq prior to initiating hostilities, the United Kingdom and the United States were the most insistent on keeping in place the comprehensive UN sanctions that caused large-scale deaths, inflicted considerable human misery on Iraqi civilians and negated any efforts at development. The basic cause of this was Saddam Hussein's refusal to comply fully with UN demands, but the price of his intransigence was exacted from his people. Any failure to "stay the course" in Iraq until the security situation has been stabilized and a self-sustaining and economically viable democratic and representative system of government has been instituted will cause still further retroactive erosion of legitimacy of the war.

Threshold criteria and precautionary principles

Military intervention for human protection purposes is an exceptional and extraordinary measure. To be warranted, there must be serious and irreparable harm occurring to human beings, or imminently likely to occur, of the following kind:

- large-scale loss of life due to deliberate state action, neglect or inability to act, or a failed state situation; or
- large-scale ethnic cleansing, actual or apprehended, whether carried out by killing, forced expulsion, acts of terror or rape.

On these criteria, protective intervention would have been an acceptable option in Iraq in the late 1980s. The major difficulty, of course, was that Saddam was the West's "useful idiot" at that time, supported politically and assisted materially as a bulwark against the revolutionary regime in Iran. R2P does not envision retroactive validation more than a decade after the atrocities were committed.

Looking ahead rather than to the past, it would be futile to try to anticipate every contingency and provide a uniform checklist for intervention. Rather, the decision on intervention has to be a matter of careful judgement on a case-by-case basis. Even when the just cause threshold of conscience-shocking loss of life or ethnic cleansing is crossed, intervention must be guided by the precautionary principles of right intention, last resort, proportional means and reasonable prospects.

The primary purpose of the intervention, whatever other motives intervening states may have, must be to halt or avert human suffering, if necessary by defeating a non-compliant state or regime. Right intention is better assured with multilateral operations, clearly supported by regional opinion and the victims concerned. There was and remains confusion about the mix of George W. Bush's motives for war: personal (revenge for Saddam's failed attempt to assassinate George Bush Sr, the unfinished agenda from the 1991 Gulf war for the many policy makers from that era who were part of the US administration in 2003); oil; geopolitical (destroying an existing or imminent WMD capability, eliminating a major node in the international terrorist network with part culpability for 9/11, securing an alternative to a suddenly less reliable Saudi Arabia for a large-scale US military presence in the region, securing Israel's eastern flank, securing Iran's western flank in order to intensify pressure on it, consolidating the entire energy-rich region from Central Asia to the Middle East); and military-technological (using Iraq as the testing ground for the revolutionary new doctrine of strategic pre-emption). But there is consensus that the humanitarian motive was adduced after the fact with the failure to find any WMD in Iraq or to establish credible links between Saddam and Osama bin Laden or 9/11.

If the first principle is not satisfied because there is no clear answer to "Why Iraq?", the second remains problematic because of the failure to answer "Why now?". Military intervention can be justified only when every non-military option for the prevention or peaceful resolution of the crisis has been explored, with reasonable grounds for believing that lesser measures would not have succeeded. The verdict on Iraq is clear by now: all alternative options had not been exhausted, and the UN weapons inspectors under Hans Blix could and should have been given more time to complete their task.

Third, the scale, duration and intensity of the planned military intervention should be the minimum necessary to secure the defined human protection objective. This is difficult to assess in the case of Iraq, since human protection was not the primary objective. It does seem that the main war was conducted with military efficiency, civilians were never the chief target, and indeed the coalition forces tried to minimize civilian casualties as best they could in an insecure and highly volatile environment. But although this was true of the major combat phase at the start, civilians have increasingly borne the brunt of the cross-fire between the belligerents in the post-war insurgency phase. With best-case estimates of 98,000 deaths excluding Fallujah,[10] and then with the all-out assault on Fallujah in November 2004 (which drew a warning from the UN Secretary-General on the risk of civilian casualties), the equation clearly has changed.

And, fourth, there must be a reasonable chance of success in halting or averting the suffering that has justified the intervention, with the consequences of action not likely to be worse than the consequences of inaction. The Iraq war cannot be judged to have met this criterion. On the contrary, the continuing instability and the rise of Iraq as the hotbed of terrorist activity as a *result* of the war were predicted by many analysts.

Right authority and due process

As demonstrated yet again in Iraq, war is a major humanitarian tragedy that can be justified only in the most compelling circumstances regarding the provocation, the likelihood of success – bearing in mind that goals are metamorphosed in the crucible of war once started – and the consequences that may reasonably be predicted. And the burden of proof rests on the proponents of force, not on dissenters. In particular, we cannot accept the alternative doctrine that any one state or coalition can decide when to intervene with force in the internal affairs of other countries, for down that path lies total chaos. The sense of moral outrage provoked by humanitarian atrocities must always be tempered by an appreciation of the limits of power, a concern for international institution-building and a sensitivity to the law of unintended and perverse consequences – of which Iraq offers but the latest example.

Given the enormous normative presumption against the use of deadly force to settle international quarrels, who has the right to authorize such force, on what basis, for what purpose, and subject to what safeguards and limitations? In other words, even if we agree that military intervention may sometimes be necessary and unavoidable in order to protect innocent people from life-threatening danger by interposing an outside force between actual and apprehended victims and perpetrators, key questions remain about agency, lawfulness and legitimacy.

R2P came down firmly on the side of the central role of the United Nations as the indispensable font of international authority and the irreplaceable forum for authorizing international military action. Attempts to enforce authority can be made only by the legitimate agents of that authority. What distinguishes coercive compliance by armed criminal thugs from rule enforcement by police officers is precisely the principle of legitimacy. The chief contemporary institution for building, consolidating and using the authority of the international community is the United Nations. It was set up to provide the framework within which members of the international system can negotiate agreements on the rules of behaviour and the legal norms of proper conduct in order to preserve the society of states. The Iraq experience proves that it is easier to wage war without UN blessing than it is to win the peace – but victory in war is pointless without a resulting secure peace.

The task therefore is not to find alternatives to the United Nations as a source of authority, but to make it work better than it has. Thus, if the veto is the source of the Security Council's ineffectiveness, it should be eliminated or its use curtailed. The Council's authorization must be sought prior to any military intervention. Those calling for an intervention should formally request such authorization, or have the Council raise the matter on its own initiative, or have the Secretary-General raise it under Article 99 of the UN Charter. The United Nations' work can be supplemented by regional organizations acting within their own jurisdictions, for example the Arab League.

The burden of responsibility, from having the power to make the most difference, often falls on the United States and other leading powers. The conceptual connecting rod that links power to authority is legitimacy. In this sense the United Nations is the symbol of what even major powers must *not* do. In the field of state–citizen relations within territorial borders, the totality of Charter clauses and instruments such as the Universal Declaration of Human Rights restricts the authority of states to cause harm to their own people. In the sphere of military action across borders, UN membership imposes the obligation on all powers to abjure unilateral intervention in favour of collectively authorized international intervention.

If the Security Council rejects a proposal or fails to deal with it in a reasonable time, alternative options are: consideration of the matter by the General Assembly in Emergency Special Session under the "Uniting for Peace" procedure; and action within their area of jurisdiction by regional organizations, subject to subsequent authorization by the Security Council. In the case of Iraq, the United Kingdom and the United States tried but failed to obtain a second Security Council resolution explicitly authorizing military enforcement, failed to seek and clearly would not have obtained majority support in the General Assembly, and would have been met with derision had they tried to get Arab League endorsement for war. Even the so-called coalition of the willing was extremely narrow.

The Security Council should take into account in all its deliberations that, if it fails to discharge its responsibility to protect in conscience-shocking situations crying out for action, concerned states may not rule out other means to meet the gravity and urgency of that situation. This carries a double risk. Their actions may not be guided by the just cause and precautionary principles identified in R2P, and so their interventions may not be done well, with due authority, diligence and process. Alternatively, they may do it very well and the people of the world may conclude that their actions were necessary, just and proper, in which case the stature and credibility of the United Nations may suffer still further erosion. Apropos of this comment from R2P, the opposite conclusion may now be proffered: that the United Nations' refusal to authorize war on Iraq in 2003 has been fully vindicated and has restored the organization's authority and credibility. Had UN authorization been given, it would have conferred the veneer of legality on the war but made the organization complicit in an illegitimate war against a sovereign member state. This suggests that, while UN authorization may be a necessary condition for legality, it is not a sufficient condition.

Changing demands, expectations and tools

In sum, Iraq fails the test of an R2P-type intervention. Yet, paradoxically, it highlights the urgency of international endorsement for R2P. The United Nations is dedicated to peace but is not a pacifist organization. Its entire Chapter VII focuses on the coercive instruments of statecraft against wilful transgressors of world order. Sometimes war will be necessary to meet and defeat the challenge from international outlaws. R2P rests on the premise that one such context for the legitimate and necessary use of armed force is large-scale humanitarian atrocities inside sovereign territory by interposing international military contingents between victims and perpetrators. But the will to wage war will weaken if force is used recklessly, unwisely and prematurely. Ill-considered rhetoric about pre-emptive strikes and about Iraq as an example of "humanitarian intervention" risks draining support from R2P rather than adding to the legitimacy of such enterprises.

The world is changing, and changing fast, all around us. Calls for "humanitarian intervention" could arise from any one or more of potential flashpoints; humanitarian carnage could be triggered by any combination of contingencies. The continuing tragedies of Liberia, Burundi, Sudan and the Congo, and the potential tragedy in Myanmar, come readily to mind. Human nature is fallible, leaders can be weak and corruptible, and states can be frail and vulnerable to outbreaks of multiple and complex humanitarian crises. Our ability and tools to act beyond our borders, even in some of the most distant spots in the world, have increased tremendously. This has produced a corresponding increase in demands and expectations to do something.

An analogy with medicine is appropriate. Rapid advances in medical technology have greatly expanded the range, accuracy and number of medical interventions. With enhanced capacity and increased tools have come more choices that have to be made, often with accompanying philosophical, ethical, political and legal dilemmas. The idea of simply standing by and letting nature take its course has become less and less acceptable, to the point where in many countries today parents who refuse all available treatment for their children can be held criminally culpable for failure to exercise due diligence.

Similarly, calls for military intervention happen. Living in a fantasy world is a luxury we cannot afford. In the real world today, the brutal truth is that our choice is not between intervention and non-intervention. Rather, our choice is between ad hoc or rules-based, unilateral or multilateral, and consensual or deeply divisive intervention. If we are going to get any sort of consensus in advance of crises requiring urgent responses, including military intervention, the R2P principles point the way forward. The president of the Security Council at the time of the Rwanda genocide in the fateful month of April 1994, Ambassador Colin Keating of New Zealand, has added his voice thus: "If the international community is ever to be able to act effectively for human protection purposes, then it must pay attention to the recommendations" of R2P.[11]

Establishing agreed principles to guide the use of force to protect civilians under threat will make it more difficult, not less, to appropriate the humanitarian label to self-serving interventions while simultaneously making the Security Council more responsive to the security needs of civilians. To interveners, R2P offers the prospect of more effective results. For any international enforcement action to be efficient, it must be legitimate; for it to be legitimate, it must be in conformity with international law; for it to conform to international law, it must not be inconsistent with the Charter of the United Nations. To potential targets of intervention, R2P offers the option and comfort of a rules-based system, instead of one based solely on might. The challenge is neither to deny the reality of intervention nor to denounce it, but to manage it for the better, so that human security is consolidated, the international system is strengthened and all of us come out of it better, with our common humanity not diminished but enhanced.

Notes

1. *The Responsibility to Protect: Report of the International Commission on Intervention and State Sovereignty* (Ottawa: International Development Research Centre for ICISS, 2001). The Report is also available at ⟨http://www.iciss.ca/report-en.asp⟩ (accessed 9 February 2006).
2. *A More Secure World: Our Shared Responsibility. Report of the Secretary-General's High-level Panel on Threats, Challenges and Change*, UN Doc. A/59/565 (New York: United Nations, December 2004), para. 207.
3. Ibid., para. 201, emphasis in original.
4. Kofi A. Annan, *In Larger Freedom: Towards Development, Security and Human Rights for All. Report of the Secretary-General*, UN Doc. A/59/2005 (New York: United Nations, 21 March 2005), paras 122–135.
5. *2005 World Summit Outcome*, UN Doc. A/RES/60/1 (New York: United Nations, 24 October 2005), paras 138–140, ⟨http://daccessdds.un.org/doc/UNDOC/GEN/N05/487/60/PDF/N0548760.pdf?OpenElement⟩.
6. Quoted by Eric Alterman, "Hawks Eating Crow", *The Nation*, 7 June 2004, p. 10.
7. Quoted in William Dalrymple, *The White Mughals: Love and Betrayal in Eighteenth Century India* (New Delhi: Viking, 2002), pp. 147–148. In the event, Napoleon never got beyond Egypt.
8. Partha Chatterjee, "Empire after Globalisation", *Economic and Political Weekly*, Vol. 39, No. 37 (11 September 2004), pp. 4155–4164, at p. 4158.
9. Ibid., p. 4163.
10. Les Roberts, Riyadh Lafta, Richard Garfield, Jamal Khudhairi and Gilbert Burhnam, "Mortality before and after the 2003 Invasion of Iraq: Cluster Sample Survey", *Lancet*, Vol. 364, 30 October 2004. The survey team was from Johns Hopkins University's Bloomberg School of Public Health and was assisted by doctors from al-Mustansiriya University Medical School in Baghdad. Coalition governments disputed the findings, but failed to provide numbers of civilian casualties themselves whose accuracy can be assessed against the *Lancet* article's.
11. Colin Keating, "Rwanda: An Insider's Account", in David M. Malone, ed., *The UN Security Council: From the Cold War to the 21st Century* (Boulder, CO: Lynne Rienner, 2004), pp. 500–511, at p. 510.

29

Post-war relations between occupying powers and the United Nations

Simon Chesterman

An important aspect of the 2003 invasion of Iraq that is frequently overlooked is its resurrection and transformation of the law of military occupation. Legal analysis of the conflict has tended to focus on the alleged right of "pre-emption" (bluntly asserted in the 2002 *National Security Strategy of the United States of America* but not invoked by the United States on this occasion[1]) and the limits of ambiguous Security Council resolutions that intimate that force might be used but do not authorize it. Council resolutions on the aftermath of the conflict were scrutinized for their potential to legitimize the war retrospectively and for their delineation of the responsibilities of the Coalition Provisional Authority (CPA) and the United Nations for the political and economic reconstruction of Iraq.

The fact that either the CPA or the United Nations should have any such responsibilities was regarded as unremarkable. The first mention of the United States and the United Kingdom as "occupying powers" was briefly noted in the popular press, but Iraq quickly fell into the mould of other post-conflict operations, from Kosovo to Afghanistan. A major criticism of the United States was that it should have sought greater political legitimacy through the United Nations in order to ensure greater support on the ground. Only when the political transformation began to unravel did there appear to be a significant difference between such an operation being conducted under UN as opposed to US auspices.

Military occupation has a long pedigree, but its relation to the United Nations has never been fully clarified. At a time when war itself was not illegal and occupation was accepted as an element of war, complicated rules outlining the rights and responsibilities of an occupying power were developed over the nineteenth century. By the middle of the twentieth century, however, the prohibition of the use of force enshrined in the UN Charter – designed "to save succeeding generations from the scourge of war"[2] – made occupation law something of an embarrassment. Though the latter part of that century was not noted for the absence of conflict, occupation law itself was rarely invoked. The abolition of colonialism and the condemnation of occupation in the 1970 Declaration on Friendly Relations led some to question whether occupation law had fallen into desuetude.

In the 1990s, this reticence in principle coincided with a confusion of practice, as the collapse of government institutions in a series of states saw the United Nations assert some or all government powers in virtually every continent. These responsibilities included staging elections in Namibia in 1990 and Cambodia in 1993, restoring a democratic government in Haiti in 1994, administering the eastern Danube region of Croatia (Eastern Slavonia) from 1996 to 1998, assuming control of the Serbian province of Kosovo for an indefinite period from 1999, and ultimately running the entire territory of East Timor from 1999 until its independence in 2002. A similar role was assumed by an ad hoc international consortium established in 1995 by the Dayton Peace Agreement to oversee Bosnia and Herzegovina. Though the language of military occupation was not used, the presence of large numbers of foreign troops, an international war crimes process and summary dismissal of its politicians by an international administrator in Bosnia bore more than a passing resemblance to occupied Germany of 1945–1949.

Such comparisons were largely academic until the United States, together with the United Kingdom, entered and occupied Iraq in 2003. After some initial resistance, both states ultimately embraced their role as occupying powers, and Security Council resolutions that endorsed this position noted specifically the international humanitarian law instruments concerning military occupation. Occupation law was invoked in part owing to the controversy surrounding the decision to go to war, but also reflected a new-found sensibility that special post-conflict obligations fall to belligerents that choose to enter a conflict voluntarily for reasons asserted to be in the common good. Drawing upon the humanitarian intervention discourse through the 1990s, the International Commission on Intervention and State Sovereignty referred to this in its *Responsibility to Protect* report as the "responsibility to rebuild".[3]

Even the most liberal reading of the instruments governing occupation law, however, finds it hard to reconcile with military intervention and

post-conflict occupation premised on regime change. The essence of occupation law is that occupation should be temporary and balance the
right of an occupying power to protect its forces against the humanitarian
needs of the civilian population. Transformation of the political and legal
structures of an occupied territory runs against the most basic principles
of occupation. Because this was precisely the purpose of the US-led military effort in Iraq, further authority is required – though it is unclear that
this authority is to be found in the Security Council resolutions that gave
ambiguous support to US post-conflict aims in Iraq.

In this chapter, I first survey the law of military occupation before
briefly examining the role of the UN Security Council in post-conflict administration. I then turn to the ambiguous responsibilities accorded to
the United States and the United Kingdom as occupying powers in Iraq
from 2003. Though the series of operations through the 1990s referred to
earlier suggests that the Council has the power to modify the traditional
obligations of occupying powers – most spectacularly displayed in Kosovo and East Timor – the provisions adopted in relation to Iraq in 2003
evince some uncertainty as to whether these operations have changed occupation law itself. The underlying problem is that international law continues to presume the inappropriateness in all circumstances of the coercive use of force to effect political change in another state. Though it is
undesirable to modify this general principle, there is some evidence that,
where use of force takes place in contravention of the norm, there may
nevertheless be an emerging obligation to contribute to reconstruction
that goes beyond providing for the humanitarian needs of the civilian
population.

The law of military occupation

The laws of war – a troubled body of norms suspended between irrelevance to and complicity with its subject matter – provide detailed rules
for the administration of occupied territory. These rules long presumed
that the conclusion of hostilities is marked with a peace treaty or, less
commonly, the destruction of the defeated power and the subsuming of
its territory into that of the victor.

From the end of World War II, however, the acquisition of territory
through military force has been prohibited under international law. This
was merely one aspect of the norm outlawing the use of force more generally. Article 2(4) of the UN Charter provides that states "shall refrain
in their international relations from the threat or use of force against the
territorial integrity or political independence of any state, or in any other

manner inconsistent with the Purposes of the United Nations". The only exceptions to this broad prohibition are the "inherent right of individual or collective self-defence if an armed attack occurs"[4] and Security Council authorized actions under Chapter VII of the Charter.[5]

A consequence of this new-found suspicion of war as a legitimate pursuit in human history is that states are now very reluctant to acknowledge their position as occupying powers. Military occupation, however, is a question of fact rather than intent. The 1907 Hague Regulations, for example, provide that "[t]erritory is considered occupied when it is actually placed under the authority of the hostile army".[6] The Fourth Geneva Convention of 1949 confirms that the provisions on occupation apply "even if the ... occupation meets with no armed resistance".[7] Whether a state formally accepts the role of occupying power is therefore irrelevant in determining whether the relevant occupation law obligations apply. This has been the subject of longstanding disagreement, for example with respect to Israel's obligations in the West Bank and Gaza Strip. In May 2003, Israeli Prime Minister Ariel Sharon stirred controversy when he explicitly referred to Israel's "occupation" of the Palestinian territories. Israel has long argued that the territories are, at best, "disputed" and Sharon later said, confusingly, that he used the word in relation to the Palestinian people but not the territory.[8] The International Court of Justice and the Israeli High Court subsequently held that Israel was indeed an occupying power.[9]

The formal obligations on an occupying power are outlined in complex provisions – at times reaching quite extraordinary detail – in the Hague Regulations and the Fourth Geneva Convention. These obligations comprise responsibilities and constraints. The occupying power is entitled to ensure the security of its forces, but is also required to "take all the measures in his power to restore, and ensure, as far as possible, public order and [civil life], while respecting, unless absolutely prevented, the laws in force in the country".[10] In addition to other positive obligations, such as ensuring public health and sanitation, as well as the provision of food and medical supplies, the occupying power is prohibited from changing local laws except as necessary for its own security and is limited in its capacity to change state institutions.[11]

The underlying premise of occupation, then, is that it should be temporary. The elaborate provisions in occupation law recognize the need for regulation of territory during the period of occupation to minimize the adverse effects on the civilian population, but are inconsistent with occupation for extended periods or for the purpose of transformation of that territory.[12] Occupation law thus provides little support for regime change. As the commentary on the Geneva Conventions observes, attempts to justify such change in the course of occupation are not new:

During the Second World War Occupying Powers intervened in the occupied countries on numerous occasions and in a great variety of ways, depending on the political aim pursued ... Of course the Occupying Power usually tried to give some colour of legality and independence to the new organizations, which were formed in the majority of cases with the co-operation of certain elements among the population of the occupied country, but it was obvious that they were in fact always subservient to the will of the Occupying Power.[13]

This may be contrasted with the doctrine of *debellatio* or subjugation that was asserted by the Allies in their occupation of Germany and Japan after World War II. *Debellatio* refers to "a situation in which a party to a conflict has been totally defeated in war, its national institutions have disintegrated, and none of its allies continue militarily to challenge the enemy on its behalf".[14] Though the Allies' title to Germany was not seriously questioned, the implication that the law of occupation did not apply was convincingly challenged on the basis that international law should not be presumed to abandon its concern for a population simply because their national institutions have disappeared. In any case, the 1949 Conventions and subsequent state practice suggest that the doctrine is unlikely to be applied in the future.[15]

The 1970 Declaration on Friendly Relations – passed as a unanimous resolution of the UN General Assembly and therefore evidence of a widely held view of the law, though not of binding force – appeared to undermine occupation law further. It provided that "[t]he territory of a State shall not be the object of military occupation resulting from the use of force in contravention of the provisions of the Charter".[16] This should be seen, however, in the context of the general prohibition of the use of force it sought to affirm and in the political context of the ongoing dispute at the time over the status of the West Bank and Gaza Strip.

The general position, then, appears to be that occupation is generally frowned upon – not least because it is hard to conceive of situations in which it might lawfully come about. International humanitarian law, of course, has long separated the questions of the *jus ad bellum* (concerning the decision to resort to war) and the *jus in bello* (concerning conduct during hostilities). In the context of the present discussion of *jus post bellum* (concerning post-conflict obligations), what can be said of occupation law is that occupation, where it does occur as a matter of fact, should be limited both in time and in its impact on the relevant territory.

In addition to the prohibition on the use of force, the limitations on an occupying power provide a second layer of legal norms inconsistent with coercive transformation of a political system. Nevertheless, the Declaration on Friendly Relations, quoted earlier, stressed that the provisions condemning occupation should not be construed as affecting the powers of the UN Security Council. The next section considers the potential role of the Council as an occupying power, and the following section considers the ambiguous case of Iraq.

The Security Council's power to administer territory

The power of the Security Council to administer territory is not mentioned in the UN Charter. Nor, however, is peacekeeping, the formula that came to define UN military activities. Here, as in many other areas of the Council's activities, practice has led theory and the Charter has been shown to be a flexible – some would say malleable – instrument.

That the Security Council might be required to administer a state or territory was, in fact, contemplated in the drafting of the UN Charter. At the San Francisco Conference that led to the adoption of the Charter in 1945, Norway proposed to amend the Chapter VII enforcement powers of the Council to provide that it should, in special cases, temporarily assume the administration of a territory if administration by the occupant state itself represented a threat to the peace.[17] This was withdrawn out of a concern that including such specific powers might be interpreted as suggesting that other powers not listed were implicitly excluded.[18]

In 1947, the possibility of Council administration swiftly assumed practical significance in two cases: the Free Territory of Trieste and Jerusalem. Early objections were voiced when the Council initially undertook its obligations in Trieste – notably by the representative of Australia, who abstained from voting on Resolution 16 (1947) on the grounds that the Council lacked the authority to exercise such governmental functions.[19] Secretary-General Trygve Lie argued that the Council enjoyed a broad power to maintain peace and security under Article 24 of the Charter, a position that was accepted at the time by the other Council members and subsequently endorsed by the International Court of Justice.[20]

In the event, however, neither proposal was implemented. As with most of the Council's powers, transitional administration remained largely an intriguing prospect until after the conclusion of the Cold War. And, as with the Council's activities in other areas, the manner in which this power has subsequently been exercised departed substantially from what was envisaged when the Charter was drafted.

In early 1995, UN Secretary-General Boutros Boutros-Ghali issued a conservative supplement to his more optimistic 1992 *Agenda for Peace*.[21] Where the 1992 *Agenda* had been written in the buoyant period of an apparent new concord in international affairs, the *Supplement* followed the failed operation in Somalia, inaction in the face of genocide in Rwanda, and ongoing difficulties in Bosnia and Herzegovina. It noted that these new intra-state conflicts presented the United Nations with challenges that it had not faced since the Congo operation of the early 1960s. Though the language of occupation was not used, the *Supplement* observed that a feature of these conflicts was the collapse of state institutions, meaning that international intervention had to extend beyond military and humanitarian tasks to include "the re-establishment of effective government". Nevertheless, Boutros-Ghali cautioned against the United Nations assuming responsibility for law and order, or attempting to impose state institutions on unwilling combatants.[22]

Such caution notwithstanding, the end of that year saw the United Nations assume responsibility for policing in Bosnia. Twelve months after the *Supplement* was published, a mission was established to administer temporarily the last Serb-held region of Croatia in Eastern Slavonia. In June 1999, the Security Council authorized another "temporary" mission to administer the Serbian province of Kosovo. Four months later another mission was created with effective sovereignty over East Timor until independence. As indicated in the introduction, these expanding mandates continued a trend that began with the operations in Namibia in 1989 and Cambodia in 1993, where the United Nations exercised varying degrees of civilian authority in addition to supervising elections.

The expansion was part of a larger growth in activism by the Security Council through the 1990s, which showed itself willing to interpret internal armed conflicts, humanitarian crises and even disruption to democracy as "threats to international peace and security" within the meaning of the UN Charter – and therefore warranting a military response under its auspices. The "new interventionism" was, however, constrained by the inability of the United Nations to develop an independent military capacity; as a result, Council action was generally limited to circumstances that coincided with the national interests of a state or group of states that were prepared to lead.[23]

There is, today, little doubt that the Security Council possesses the power to administer territory on a temporary basis and that it may delegate that power to the Secretary-General (or his or her representative).[24] Recent practice in Eastern Slavonia, Kosovo and East Timor in particular suggests that this power is now an accepted arrow in the very limited quiver with which the Council may respond to threats to international peace and security.

Acceptance in practice, however, has not meant acceptance in theory. The lack of an institutional capacity to respond to the demands of transitional administration has left the United Nations relying on a variety of structures built around a core of peacekeeping personnel. The different operations have thus adopted idiosyncratic mission structures that reflected the varying capacities of the regional organizations and UN agencies involved in each situation. It is occasionally argued that some form of structural change in the UN system would enable it to respond more effectively to such challenges in the future. Reviving the Trustee-ship Council, which suspended operations in 1994, is sometimes men-tioned in this regard – most prominently by the International Commis-sion on Intervention and State Sovereignty (ICISS). Its report *The Responsibility to Protect* suggests that a "constructive adaptation" of Chapter XII of the Charter might provide useful guidelines for the be-haviour of administering authorities.[25] For the Trusteeship Council to provide more than guidance, however, would require a Charter amend-ment, because Article 78 of the Charter explicitly prevents the Trustee-ship System from applying to territories that are members of the United Nations. In any case, the direct associations with colonialism would be politically prohibitive.

More general political barriers to any such institutional changes were implicit in the Brahimi Report on UN Peace Operations. Despite the "evident ambivalence" among member states and within the UN Secre-tariat, the Report noted that the circumstances that demand such opera-tions were likely to recur:

Thus, the Secretariat faces an unpleasant dilemma: to assume that transitional ad-ministration is a transitory responsibility, not prepare for additional missions and do badly if it is once again flung into the breach, or to prepare well and be asked to undertake them more often because it is well prepared. Certainly, if the Secretariat anticipates future transitional administrations as the rule rather than the exception, then a dedicated and distinct responsibility centre for those tasks must be created somewhere within the United Nations system. In the interim, DPKO [the Depart-ment of Peacekeeping Operations] has to continue to support this function.[26]

This was not the subject of any recommendation and was not addressed in the Secretary-General's response to the Report.[27]

It seems probable, then, that any institutional reforms within the United Nations will be incremental, driven by the exigencies of circum-stance rather than institutional or doctrinal development. Though po-litical resistance may prevent development of a policy or institutional framework for future transitional administrations in theory, it is unlikely to prevent the demand for such operations in practice.

The occupation of Iraq

Occupation is an ugly word, not one Americans feel comfortable with, but it is a fact.

(L. Paul Bremer III, May 2003)[28]

By the time Operation Iraqi Freedom commenced on 20 March 2003, two discrete post-conflict scenarios for Iraq were in the public domain. The first was broadly consistent with the plans leaked by the Pentagon in October 2002 for a US-led military government in Iraq modelled on the US occupation of Japan, with the United Nations providing humanitarian assistance.[29] The second scenario, advanced by the United Kingdom and, to a lesser extent, by the US State Department, included a larger – if essentially undefined – role for the United Nations. The latter position was implicit in the Azores Declaration issued by the leaders of the United Kingdom, Spain and the United States days before the outbreak of hostilities,[30] but was subsequently downplayed by the Bush administration.

Testifying before the US Senate Foreign Relations Committee in February 2003, the Departments of State and Defense affirmed that the United States – rather than the United Nations or some provisional government of Iraqi exiles – would take charge in Baghdad. Civilian tasks would be carried out under the authority of the Pentagon's new Office for Reconstruction and Humanitarian Assistance (ORHA), established by Bush on 20 January 2003. ORHA's director, retired Army Lieutenant General Jay M. Garner, would report to the President through General Tommy Franks of Central Command and Secretary of Defense Donald Rumsfeld. Garner's tenure in Iraq was a debacle, plagued by inexperience, bureaucratic infighting and inertia. In less than a month he was replaced by L. Paul Bremer III.[31]

Discussion within the United States tended to focus on a political function for the United Nations only when considering the question of how the occupation might be paid for. As the war began, US, UK and UN officials were exploring the possibility of transforming Iraq's Oil-for-Food programme, established by the Security Council in April 1995, into a more flexible arrangement to allow the United Nations to control goods purchased under its auspices throughout the country. (Suggestions that oil revenues might actually cover the military expenses incurred by the United States in defeating and administering Iraq were confined to the most radical US think tanks.[32] In fact, the Hague Regulations support this interpretation, allowing an occupying power to administer public assets as a trustee and levy funds for the administration of the territory.[33]) Bringing the post-conflict phase of operations under UN auspices had other financial attractions. Most prominently, Chris Patten, the EU Commissioner for External Relations, stated before the war that, if the United States attacked Iraq without Security Council approval, the European Union might withhold money for reconstruction. This received vocal support from French President Jacques Chirac after military operations commenced, who argued that France would not support any Security Council resolution that gave retrospective legitimacy to the conflict. Companies invited to tender for reconstruction projects also expressed concern about the legal implications of ongoing Council economic sanctions.[34]

Though the outcome of the conflict was never in serious doubt, the manner in which the war was fought served as a proxy for debates within the United States on the size and posture of its armed forces. The swift victory demonstrated a paradox of the "revolution in military affairs": a smaller, faster, more lethal US military might be able to achieve quick victories over anyone who might stand against it, but, as Rumsfeld understated it, the aftermath of such wars can be most "untidy".[35] It soon became apparent that little serious planning had been done on stabilizing the post-conflict situation, perhaps because of reliance upon best-case scenarios in which a minimal US presence could draw heavily upon the pre-existing Iraqi bureaucracy and security sector. Work had commenced in April 2002 within the State Department's Future of Iraq Project, including the development of extensive plans for post-conflict justice mechanisms, but was shelved when responsibility was transferred to the Department of Defense in January 2003.[36]

For its part, the United Nations engaged only in halting planning for post-conflict scenarios. An early planning cell was shut down in December 2002 owing to concerns that its very existence might be interpreted as undermining the position of UN weapons inspectors then in Iraq. A confidential internal "pre-planning" report was requested in February 2003, which was promptly leaked to the press. The report stressed that the United Nations lacked the capacity to take on the responsibility of administering Iraq, preferring a political process similar to that followed in Afghanistan. The favoured option – in the context of what was, as the Secretary-General later emphasized, only preliminary thinking – called for an assistance mission that would provide political facilitation, consensus-building, national reconciliation and the promotion of democratic governance and the rule of law. The people of Iraq, rather than the international community, should determine national government structures, a legal framework and governance arrangements.[37]

There is, of course, a certain irony to this controversy about planning. The United Nations is criticized when, as in East Timor in 1999, it fails to plan for a scenario that many regarded as likely. In Iraq, it was criticized for engaging in preliminary thinking on an eventuality that most regarded as inevitable. But the tension within the planning process also reflected concerns about a role that might be thrust upon the United Nations in order to provide political cover for what was essentially a US military occupation. This suggested an additional incentive for the United States and the United Kingdom to bring the operation under some form of UN umbrella. The Fourth Geneva Convention limits the capacity of an occupying power to change the status of public officials and to impose new laws.[38] As the stated war aims in Iraq included regime change and the transformation of Iraq into a "liberal democracy", Security Council authorization provided a sounder basis for such activities.

Resolution 1483 (2003), adopted by the Council on 22 May 2003, was an uncomfortable compromise that straddled this divide. The resolution explicitly recognized that the United States and the United Kingdom – the Coalition Provisional Authority – were occupying powers in Iraq and called on them to comply with their obligations under the Geneva Conventions and the Hague Regulations.[39] Nevertheless, the resolution also called upon the CPA "to promote the welfare of the Iraqi people through the effective administration of the territory, including in particular working towards the restoration of conditions of security and stability and the creation of conditions in which the Iraqi people can freely determine their own political future".[40] David Scheffer has described this blend of Council powers and occupation law as "both unique and exceptionally risky".[41]

The preamble of the resolution recognized "the specific authorities, responsibilities, and obligations under applicable international law of these states as occupying powers under unified command (the 'Authority')" and noted that "other States that are not occupying powers are working now or in the future may work under the Authority".[42] This unusual provision implied that the United States and the United Kingdom were occupying powers, but that other states could participate in reconstruction efforts without taking on the responsibilities of occupiers themselves. As indicated earlier, occupation is a question of fact rather than intent and it is unclear whether this preambular reference was intended to supplant the existing law. Acting under Chapter VII, the Council went on to call upon "all concerned" to "comply fully with their obligations under international law including in particular the Geneva Conventions of 1949 and the Hague Regulations of 1907".[43]

The contours of Iraq's "political future" were adumbrated in the Council's support for "the formation, by the people of Iraq with the help of the Authority and working with the [UN Secretary-General's] Special Representative, of an Iraqi interim administration as a transitional administration run by Iraqis, until an internationally recognized, representative government is established by the people of Iraq and assumes the responsibilities of the Authority".[44] Other obligations concerned the establishment of a Development Fund for Iraq[45] and the transfer of responsibilities under the Oil-for-Food relief programme to the CPA.[46]

The responsibilities of the United Nations in Iraq were ambiguous. Although its role was repeatedly said to be "vital", the powers given to the Special Representative were intentionally vague: these included "coordinating", "reporting", "assisting", "promoting", "facilitating" and "encouraging" various aspects of humanitarian relief and reconstruction.[47] On the fundamental question of political structures, the Special Representative was empowered to work "intensively with the Authority, the people of Iraq, and others concerned to advance efforts to restore and establish national and local institutions for representative governance, including by working together to facilitate a process leading to an internationally recognized, representative government of Iraq".[48] Senior US Defense Department officials described their relationship with the United Nations as "input but no veto". Sergio Vieira de Mello, previously Special Representative in both Kosovo and East Timor, was appointed Special Representative for Iraq and head of the UN Assistance Mission for Iraq (UNAMI).[49] Vieira de Mello and 21 UN colleagues were killed by a truck-bomb in Baghdad on 19 August 2003 in the worst attack on civilian staff in the organization's history.[50]

Iraq was unique as a transitional administration. Previous operations where international administrative structures were required can be grouped into two broad classes: those where state institutions were divided and those where they had failed. The first class encompasses situations in which governance structures were the subject of dispute, with different groups claiming power (as in Cambodia or Bosnia), or ethnic tensions existed within the structures themselves (such as Kosovo). The second class comprises circumstances in which such structures simply did not exist (as in Namibia, East Timor and Afghanistan). Neither situation applied to Iraq. In particular, Iraq had far greater resources – human, institutional and economic – than any comparable situation in which the United Nations or other actor had exercised civilian administration functions since World War II. Nevertheless, comparisons with occupied Japan and Germany were stretched.

No plan, of course, survives contact with the enemy. As Iraq soon proved, this aphorism of von Moltke applies also to plans coming into contact with those one presumes will welcome you as friends.

Conclusion

The Iraq wars of 1991 and 2003 bookend a period of unprecedented international cooperation in the management of war and peace. Coming soon after the conclusion of the Cold War, Operation Desert Storm, which drove Iraq from Kuwait, was heralded by US President George H. W. Bush as ushering in an era in which the rule of law would replace the rule of the jungle. A newly activist Security Council outlined an expanding agenda for itself and the United Nations. In its first 44 years the

Council passed 24 resolutions citing Chapter VII or using its terms; by 1993 it was adopting that many Chapter VII resolutions every year.

The rhetoric was euphoric, utopian and short lived. Council activism, it was soon revealed, depended entirely upon a coincidence of Council agreement with the willingness of a state or group of states to take action. When agreement was not forthcoming, as in the case of Kosovo in 1999, action took place anyway. The Iraq war in 2003 was seen as more troubling because it was not simply the United Nations that was divided but the European Union and NATO. It was not merely the Council's authority in peace and security that was being challenged but the idea of international law as such.

Although the role of the United Nations in providing relief to the Iraqi civilian population was never questioned – during the second week of the conflict, a unanimous Council resolution extended the application of the Oil-for-Food programme[51] – reluctance to involve it in post-conflict reconstruction led to a reliance on occupation law unprecedented since World War II. The return to older legal forms, however, was at odds with modern sensibilities about the nature of post-conflict responsibilities. As indicated earlier, traditional occupation law would have required the United States to interfere as little as possible in the local political system. The purpose of the US invasion was regime change but, even if it had not been, there would doubtless have been pressure to leave Iraq in a better political and economic situation than it was found.

This changed sensibility can in part be traced to the role played by the United Nations in various post-conflict situations during the 1990s, and in turn to the recognition that contemporary conflict is increasingly connected to the collapse of state institutions. The forms prescribed by occupation law assume both the capacity and the desirability of maintaining existing institutions. In Cambodia, Bosnia and Kosovo, divisions within those institutions had made them unviable; in territories such as Namibia, East Timor and Afghanistan, such institutions simply did not exist. Ironically, Iraq was the one country on this list in which existing institutions might well have been drawn upon – and there is some evidence that key figures within the Bush administration contemplated quickly positioning a pliant leader at the top of those structures. When this proved impossible, deeper obligations quickly had to be assumed.

Former US Secretary of State Colin Powell referred to this as the "Pottery Barn" principle: if you break it, you own it.[52] But the principle has a broader foundation and application. As the International Commission on Intervention and State Sovereignty observed in the context of humanitarian intervention, where military intervention is taken "there should be a genuine commitment to helping to build a durable peace, and promoting good governance and sustainable development".[53] This obligation is

at once ethical and practical. The ethical component is that by intervening in a territory one assumes a special responsibility for the consequences of one's actions that may approach the level of a fiduciary obligation. The pragmatic component is that failure to resolve underlying
political and economic tensions may leave the problem that gave rise to
intervention in the first place unresolved.

Where the United Nations has assumed such obligations, or provided a
framework for such obligations to be undertaken by specific actors, there
has been minimal suggestion that this represents a colonial or imperial
endeavour. The case of Iraq suggests an ongoing suspicion of the motives
of individual states assuming control of a polity even on a temporary
basis. Diffusing responsibility through multilateralism thus removes accusations of self-interest, but may also remove pressures on a national actor
to conclude its obligations quickly in order to satisfy domestic political
imperatives.

The only element of the transition plan adopted by the CPA in November 2003 that remained intact was the 30 June 2004 deadline for the
United States to begin withdrawing its influence – a date clearly chosen
with an eye less to the Iraqi political timetable than to the US presidential election four months later. Appearing on NBC's "Meet the Press" in
mid-April, L. Paul Bremer III, the US proconsul in Iraq, was asked to
whom, exactly, the United States was planning on handing power on 30
June. "That's a good question", was the chilling opening to his reply.
"It's an important part of the ongoing crisis we have here now." President Bush was asked essentially the same thing two days later during a
rare televised news conference. Not known for his love of the United Nations, Bush referred to Lakhdar Brahimi by name as the man "figuring
out the nature of the entity we'll be handing sovereignty over" to.

US President George W. Bush didn't need the United Nations going
into Iraq, but he needed the United Nations' help to get out. This put
the United Nations in an extremely difficult situation: the only thing
worse than the world's most powerful country shoving you aside as irrelevant is when that country hugs you close and calls you the solution to all
of its problems. Such new-found enthusiasm for multilateralism remains
uncomfortable for the United Nations, which is still recovering from the
death of Vieira de Mello and his colleagues. There is no queue of volunteers wanting to return to Baghdad to aid a US withdrawal.

But there are signs that the relationship is quickly becoming strained
for the United States as well. Bush administration officials soon began to
backpedal on exactly how much "sovereignty" was to be transferred in
June and how much independence the Interim Government would have.
This was and remains a disastrous move. Better to delay the handover
entirely than to taint a caretaker government with the appearance of

being mere puppets of the United States. This had been the albatross around the necks of the Iraqi Governing Council. At the same time, the Oil-for-Food corruption scandal stiffened the spines of conservatives in Washington who would rather see the United States fail in Iraq than turn to the organization with the black helicopters for help.

There are no easy options now in Iraq. But there are dangerous signs that expectations have been lowered to the point where the primary objective is to get US casualties out of the news as quickly as possible. Handing power to a dysfunctional Iraqi government – ideally one whose dysfunction can be blamed on the United Nations – has become the most attractive option for Washington. It is unlikely to be received well in Baghdad.

The United Nations itself faces more existential questions. The Iraq war was a direct challenge to the organization's role in maintaining international peace and security by the world's most powerful state, prompting the Secretary-General to appoint a High-level Panel on Threats, Challenges and Change to rethink the very idea of collective security in a world where that state also feels itself to be the most vulnerable.[54] At the same time, the attack on the United Nations' Baghdad compound on 19 August 2003 killed respected staff, prompting a scathing review of internal security procedures and a near-mutiny on the part of staff, who pushed for a complete withdrawal from Iraq.[55] Though it is too soon to draw confident conclusions on this point, there will be more sustained debates in the future concerning whether the United Nations should refuse on principle to become involved in conflicts seen to be wars of choice by the great powers of the day; these debates will turn in significant part on whether the United Nations' presence can be meaningful and independent.

Underlying this is a larger question of what role the United Nations can and should play in the structure of world order, a theme running through much of this book. Does the United Nations exist in order to play a leading role in maintaining peace and security, or to provide legitimacy for those who do? In this context, the history of military occupation provides a cautionary tale: institutions that are designed to legitimize that which is otherwise illegal tend themselves to become discredited and fall into disuse.

Where the United Nations is at its strongest is articulating the normative context within which collective action takes place and establishing the conditions for necessary multilateral cooperation. An example of such norm entrepreneurship may be the Secretary-General's comments on US abuses at the Abu Ghraib prison outside Baghdad at the time the United States was seeking an extension of the immunity of its peacekeeping troops from the International Criminal Court. His observation that such circumstances made it "unwise" to press for an exemption stiffened the spine of Council members, and the United States quietly withdrew the item from the Council's agenda.[56] Such victories – if it was a victory – may be small; they may restrain rather than exercise power. But the test of the "relevance" of the United Nations and international law is not their capacity to force the great power(s) into action or inaction. Rather, it is to provide the grammar for how power is exercised: providing the forum for elaborating shared perceptions of threats, the vehicle for responding collectively where possible, and the normative framework against which unilateralism may be judged.

Acknowledgements

This chapter draws upon some material previously published in *You, The People: The United Nations, Transitional Administration, and State-Building* (Oxford: Oxford University Press, 2004) and "Occupation as Liberation: International Humanitarian Law and Regime Change", *Ethics & International Affairs*, Vol. 18, No. 3 (2004), pp. 51–64.

Notes

1. It nevertheless had profound implications for the use of force. See the chapters by Ruth Wedgwood, Charlotte Ku and David Krieger in the present volume.
2. UN Charter, preamble.
3. International Commission on Intervention and State Sovereignty, *The Responsibility to Protect* (Ottawa: International Development Research Centre, December 2001), available at ⟨http://www.iciss.gc.ca⟩.
4. UN Charter, Art. 51.
5. See, generally, Ian Brownlie, *International Law and the Use of Force by States* (Oxford: Clarendon Press, 1963).
6. Convention (IV) Respecting the Laws and Customs of War on Land and Its Annex: Regulations Concerning the Laws and Customs of War on Land (1907 Hague Regulations), done at The Hague, 18 October 1907, 36 Stat 2277, 1 Bevans 631, available at ⟨http://www.icrc.org/ihl⟩, Article 42.
7. Convention Relative to the Protection of Civilian Persons in Time of War (Fourth Geneva Convention), done at Geneva, 12 August 1949, available at ⟨http://www.icrc.org/ihl⟩, Article 2. The right to resistance is a contested area of the law of military occupation. See Adam Roberts, "Prolonged Military Occupation: The Israeli-Occupied Territories Since 1967", *American Journal of International Law*, Vol. 84 (1990). One important victory in the representation of the conflict in Iraq was the depiction by even mainstream news media of armed resistance to the occupation as "terrorism".
8. Glenn Frankel, "Hopes for 'Road Map' Tempered by History; U.S. Role in Plan Seen as Crucial", *Washington Post*, 3 June 2003.
9. *Legal Consequences of the Construction of a Wall in the Occupied Palestinian Territory*

(Advisory Opinion) (International Court of Justice, 9 July 2004), available at ⟨http://www.icj-cij.org⟩; *Beit Sourik v. Israel* (Israeli High Court, 30 June 2004) HCJ 2056/04.

10. 1907 Hague Regulations, Article 43. On the replacement of "public order and safety" with "public order and [civil life]", see Eyal Benvenisti, *The International Law of Occupation* (Princeton, NJ: Princeton University Press, 1993), p. 7.

11. Fourth Geneva Convention, Articles 54–56, 64.

12. David J. Scheffer, "Beyond Occupation Law", *American Journal of International Law*, Vol. 97 (2003), p. 848.

13. Jean Pictet, ed., *Convention Relative to the Protection of Civilian Persons in Time of War (Fourth Geneva Convention): Commentary* (Geneva: International Committee of the Red Cross, 1958), Art. 47.

14. Benvenisti, *The International Law of Occupation*, p. 92.

15. Ibid., pp. 91–96.

16. "Declaration on Principles of International Law Concerning Friendly Relations and Co-operation among States in Accordance with the Charter of the United Nations", UN Doc. A/5217, 25 GAOR, Supp. (No. 28), 1970.

17. (1945) 3 UNCIO 365, 371–372, UN Doc. 2G/7 (n)(1).

18. (1945) 12 UNCIO 353–355, UN Doc. 539 III/3/24.

19. Security Council Resolution 16 (1947). See further Hans Kelsen, *The Law of the United Nations* (London: Stevens & Sons, 1950), pp. 825–826.

20. (1947) 2 SCOR, No. 3, p. 44; *Legal Consequences for States of the Continued Presence of South Africa in Namibia (South West Africa) Notwithstanding Security Council Resolution 276 (1970) (Advisory Opinion)* [1971] ICJ Rep 16.

21. *An Agenda for Peace: Preventive Diplomacy, Peacemaking and Peace-keeping*, Report of the Secretary-General pursuant to the statement adopted by the Summit Meeting of the Security Council on 31 January 1992, UN Doc. A/47/277–S/24111, 17 June 1992.

22. *Supplement to An Agenda for Peace: Position Paper of the Secretary-General on the Occasion of the Fiftieth Anniversary of the United Nations*, UN Doc. A/50/60–S/1995/1, 3 January 1995, paras 13–14.

23. See Simon Chesterman, *Just War or Just Peace? Humanitarian Intervention and International Law*, Oxford Monographs in International Law (Oxford: Oxford University Press, 2001), pp. 112–218.

24. Danesh Sarooshi, *The United Nations and the Development of Collective Security: The Delegation by the UN Security Council of Its Chapter VII Powers* (Oxford: Clarendon Press, 1999), pp. 59–63.

25. ICISS, *The Responsibility to Protect*, paras 5.22–5.24. The Commission was established by the Government of Canada in 2000 to seek consensus on the question of humanitarian intervention. Its co-chairs were Gareth Evans and Mohamed Sahnoun.

26. *Report of the Panel on United Nations Peace Operations* (Brahimi Report), UN Doc. A/55/305–S/2000/809, 21 August 2000, ⟨http://www.un.org/peace/reports/peace_operations⟩, para. 78.

27. *Report of the Secretary-General on the Implementation of the Report of the Panel on United Nations Peace Operations*, UN Doc. A/55/502, 20 October 2000.

28. Scott Wilson, "Bremer Adopts Firmer Tone for U.S. Occupation of Iraq", *Washington Post*, 26 May 2003.

29. See, for example, David E. Sanger and Eric Schmitt, "U.S. Has a Plan to Occupy Iraq, Officials Report", *New York Times*, 11 October 2002.

30. "Statement of the Azores Summit", *Washington Post*, 17 March 2003.

31. See, for example, Joshua Hammer and Colin Soloway, "Who's in Charge Here?", *Newsweek*, 26 May 2003.

32. See, for example, Nile Gardiner and David B. Rivkin, *Blueprint for Freedom: Limiting*

the Role of the United Nations in Post-War Iraq (Heritage Foundation, Backgrounder No. 1646, Washington, DC, 2003).

33. 1907 Hague Regulations, Articles 48, 49, 55.
34. Jackie Spinner, "Firms Cite Concerns with Iraqi Sanctions", *Washington Post*, 3 May 2003.
35. Peter J. Boyer, "The New War Machine", *New Yorker*, 30 June 2003, pp. 55, 70–71.
36. Peter Slevin and Dana Priest, "Wolfowitz Concedes Iraq Errors", *Washington Post*, 24 July 2003.
37. James Bone, "UN Leaders Draw up Secret Blueprint for Postwar Iraq", *The Times* (London), 5 March 2003. Humanitarian contingency planning – some of which was leaked in December 2002 – was less controversial and more advanced.
38. See above notes 11–12.
39. Resolution 1483, UN Doc. S/Res/1483 (2003), preamble and para. 5.
40. Ibid., para. 4. This was later confirmed in Resolution 1500 (2003), which also welcomed the establishment of the Governing Council of Iraq.
41. Scheffer, "Beyond Occupation Law", p. 846.
42. Resolution 1483 (2003), preamble.
43. Ibid., para. 5.
44. Ibid., para. 9.
45. Ibid., paras 12–14, 17.
46. Ibid., para. 16.
47. Ibid., para. 8.
48. Ibid., para. 8.
49. *Report of the Secretary-General Pursuant to Paragraph 24 of Security Council Resolution 1483 (2003)*, UN Doc. S/2003/715, 17 July 2003, paras 2 and 100.
50. See, for example, Robert F. Worth, "Last Respects Are Paid to Head of UN Mission in Iraq", *New York Times*, 22 August 2003.
51. Resolution 1472, UN Doc. S/Res/1472 (2003). The preamble noted the obligation imposed on an occupying power by the Fourth Geneva Convention to ensure "to the fullest extent of the means available to it ... the food and medical supplies of the population".
52. See Bob Woodward, *Plan of Attack* (New York: Simon & Schuster, 2004).
53. ICISS, *The Responsibility to Protect*, para. 5.1.
54. See Chapter 28 in this volume.
55. See David M. Malone, "Nobody Said It Would Be Safe", *International Herald Tribune*, 1 October 2004.
56. Warren Hoge, "Annan Rebukes U.S. for Move to Give Its Troops Immunity", *New York Times*, 17 June 2004.

30

"Common enemies": The United States, Israel and the world crisis

Tarak Barkawi

From the late 1940s, the Arab–Israeli conflict was woven into the fabric of world politics, with consequences far beyond the Middle East itself. The conflict's wider effects are due not only to the significance of oil but to the ways in which it is implicated in US domestic politics and foreign policy as well as in conceptions of US identity. During the Cold War, and in the wake of the Holocaust, moral and humanitarian concern coupled with domestic political interests led to US support of Israel. But this support had to be balanced against good relations with Arab states, where oil was to be found and where the threat of Soviet influence loomed. From 1967, however, the United States and Israel, despite rocky moments, were drawn ever more closely into one another's orbit. With the advent of the "war on terror", the US–Israeli relationship has taken on a new significance and is now a critical pivot determining events in the Middle East and beyond.

To speak of a conflict as being part of the structure of world politics, as a dynamic form of interconnection between and among Israel, Palestinians, Arab states, US domestic politics, European economies and third world debts fuelled by petro-dollars (to list only a few possibilities), is not the normal way in which many analysts and commentators think about conflict and world order. Typically, conflicts are viewed first and foremost as "problems", as aberrations in the normal flow of relations and as breakdowns of communication and interchange.

Perhaps because of its length and global reach, the Cold War occasioned another kind of analysis. The US–Soviet confrontation was seen as structuring world politics in far-reaching ways. A crucial element that made the Cold War "fungible", allowing its categories to be effortlessly applied to diverse situations around the world by Western analysts and policy makers, was the construction of a common enemy: the communists. Parties to conflicts in the third world, be they Vietnamese or Arab nationalists, Congolese anti-colonialists or peasants struggling against landlords in any of a number of countries, found themselves defined – and acted upon – in terms of competing Western ideologies of modernization, communism or liberal democracy.

During the Cold War, no amount of explaining that third world conflicts had their own local sources or that they had systemic sources other than US–Soviet confrontation (such as decolonization or the world economy) would serve to convince hawks in the United States that US prestige and credibility were not at stake in Angola, or Indonesia, or Timbuktu. "Communism" connected all these conflicts together. In a nutshell, the significance of the Israel–Palestine conflict for contemporary world politics is that, for the United States, the common enemy in the war on terror – in Iraq, in Afghanistan, in the Philippines and elsewhere – has come to be defined in no small measure through certain Israeli categories. The Bush administration and its neoconservative ideologues have powerfully linked this enemy with core aspects of US identity and purpose, in ways strongly reminiscent of the Cold War. As a result, through the close relationship between US identity and US foreign policy, especially in wartime, ideological categories derived from the Israel–Palestine conflict are playing a central role in the present world crisis and the coming long decades of struggle it portends.

Identities, enemies and strategies

Identity relations are a crucial component of conflicts. Identity is as important to conflict as conflict is to identity. Conceptions of the "Self" require imaginings of an "Other". Moments of perceived threat and danger serve as incitements to define the Self against the enemy Other. Studies of this relationship between threat and identity have tended to focus on only one side of a conflict, as in David Campbell's classic *Writing Security*, which concerns US Cold War identity.[1] As valuable as such studies are, they can easily overlook some of the *interactive* identity dynamics in conflict situations. Particular identities facilitate particular strategies and approaches to a conflict, while making other possible strategies appear irrational.[2] This link between strategy and identity means that untoward outcomes on the battlefield can reverberate at home, causing an identity crisis. For if a nation (or voices within it) defines itself in terms of an opposition to the enemy Other, then that national identity becomes in some way dependent on the enemy. Enemy actions and pronouncements can confirm or destabilize that identity.

An example is found in the Tet offensive of 1968. The United States conceived its role in Viet Nam within terms that reflected its construction of the Cold War. The world was seen as divided between two blocs – one slave, one free. It went without question that the denizens of the free world *wanted* to be free, so any "subversion" or resistance was interpreted as emanating from the Soviet bloc countries, infecting the free world. Insurgencies were read as evidence of external attack. "What Chairman Khrushchev describes as wars of liberation and popular uprisings", Secretary of Defense Robert McNamara remarked, "I prefer to describe as subversion and covert aggression."[3] This basic framing of the Cold War – that the United States was assisting "free peoples" in defending themselves against external attack – was already present in the Truman Doctrine speech: "It must be the policy of the United States to support free peoples who are resisting attempted subjugation by armed minorities or by outside pressures."[4] As many have commented, this vision of the Cold War and of the United States' role in it licensed overly militarized responses to multifaceted conflicts in the third world, as in Viet Nam.

As conventionally interpreted, the significance of the Tet offensive is that it exposed as hollow the claims of steady US progress beforehand, fatally undermining domestic support for continued involvement even though the offensive itself failed at heavy cost to the Vietnamese communists. This is not, however, the whole story. Whatever its reality, Tet appeared on television screens and in other media representations as a general popular uprising against the Saigon regime and its US backers. It was no longer possible for Americans to evade the fact that the Vietnamese people were against the "freedom" the United States was offering. After Tet, the United States sought withdrawal rather than victory. The initial framing of the conflict in Viet Nam, as one primarily about "communist subversion" from outside, not only led the United States to adopt a heavily militarized and counterproductive strategy – one pregnant with the possibility of defeat – but also left core US identity constructions vulnerable in the eventuality of such a defeat. Precisely because of the heavy implication of US identity in its Viet Nam venture, the defeat became a more general crisis of the US body politic. It challenged the identity relations and ideological constructs that had inspired intervention in Indo-China in the first place. Was the United States on the side of freedom or of oppression, its citizens asked?

In the years since 1975, the Americans have subsequently discovered that really, despite all appearances and all those dead Vietnamese, they always were on the side of "the people" in Viet Nam. There has been a sustained retelling and reinventing of the meaning of the Viet Nam war in US political ideology and popular culture, turning it into something Americans can take pride in.[5] The neoconservative movement that exerted such profound influence over the Bush administration in the wake of the attacks of 11 September 2001 has its origins in this retelling of the Viet Nam war. Several neoconservatives who became prominent fled the Democratic Party during and after Viet Nam. They felt the Democrats had lost the will to use force in the service of US values abroad. After Viet Nam, two neoconservatives argue, "[t]he suspicion of American power inherent in contemporary liberalism now became a reflexive opposition to the exercise of American power around the world".[6] Because US values are synonymous with liberty and freedom the world over, this was a grave crime indeed. The solution was to narrate US involvement in Viet Nam as a story in which the United States had tried to do the right thing but had been thwarted by nefarious forces in the form of the anti-war movement, the news media, liberals, Washington bureaucrats and faint-hearted politicians. In this way, the verdict of Tet – that the United States was not on the side of "the people" – was erased and the United States reinstated as the defender of the oppressed everywhere, willing to use its military power to liberate them.

This kind of imaginary work was crucial to re-empowering the militarized US internationalism so evident in the "liberation" of Iraq. A strategy to invade and liberate Iraq could appear appropriate and rational only in a United States that had successfully rewritten the history of the Viet Nam war. But this framing of Iraq – as a potentially "free people" oppressed by a tyrant – left both US strategists and ordinary Americans unprepared to meet a popular resistance. As such, resistance to the Americans was once again represented as the work of "armed minorities", this time "Saddam loyalists" and "foreign terrorists". President Bush remarked in October 2003 that "[w]e're working hard with freedom-loving Iraqis to help ferret these people out before they attack".[7] By definition, anyone opposing the United States cannot be a "freedom-loving Iraqi" because the United States stands for freedom. Indeed, the Iraqi insurgents are now referred to as "anti-Iraqi forces" by the US military. Elsewhere, President Bush described the resistance in Iraq as comprising "killers" whose main goal – like that of the opponents of the Viet Nam war – was to "cause America and our allies to flee our responsibilities" for spreading freedom.[8]

This framing of the situation in Iraq, despite its resonances with US élite and popular self-perception, is dysfunctional in strategic terms. The implication is that the sources of resistance are to be found *not* in a complex political, cultural and social context fuelled by totalitarianism, conquest and occupation, but rather in an identifiable group of "cold-blooded killers" who must be "ferreted out" and destroyed. As in the Cold War, subversion is seen as coming from the "outside", not from the people the United States seeks to free, when in fact it is the United States that has invaded Iraq. When the "ferreting out" comes in the form of heavy-handed use of military force, it contains the potential to generate further popular Iraqi resistance, which will only use up more US blood and treasure and try US resolve further, until there is no longer a political coalition in Washington willing to sustain the costs of continued involvement in Iraq.

Crucial to this identity dynamic between the United States and Iraq is a construction of the enemy Other. This construction has much more to do with US identity than with any rational analysis of the security situation. That enemy is of course "terror". "The return of tyranny to Iraq would be an unprecedented terrorist victory, and a cause for killers to rejoice," President Bush remarked.[9] It is here that we turn to Israel–Palestine. This particular idea of terror as the enemy was in part made available to the United States through its implication in the Israeli–Palestinian conflict and through the close identification of the neoconservative movement with the Israeli right. In identifying their enemy as "terror" and in insisting on the cessation of "terror" prior to meaningful negotiations, hard-line Israelis, as well as Palestinian responses to their policies, have shaped the Israel–Palestine conflict in distinctive ways. Of special significance are the ways in which the notion of "terror" serves to obfuscate the sources and nature of violent resistance and makes any other strategy than "no appeasing of terror" appear irrational, for to give in to "terror" is to encourage more "terrorism". A spiral of terrorist attack and harsh reprisal is set in train, one that encourages the digging in of heels on both sides, de-legitimizes negotiation and compromise, and inspires further and ever more violence.

Using "terror" to frame the enemy Other results in particular strategic and identity dynamics. These dynamics are now evident in the developing war on terror, in the fighting in Iraq, and in US constructions of these conflicts. Some of the core ideas and interpretations of events that have driven US leadership, and that have been popularized through various media, are derived directly from and modelled on those of the Israeli right. Tracing out the genealogy of these ideas and some of their consequences illuminates important aspects of the contemporary world crisis and of the United States' role in it.

Incubating the war on terror

In 1995, Benjamin Netanyahu published a slim volume entitled *Fighting Terrorism: How Democracies Can Defeat Domestic and International Ter-*

rorists.[10] Netanyahu's concise treatment encapsulates the state of the then-developing field of terrorism studies and demonstrates the unusual ideological utility of "terror", "terrorism" and "terrorists" as representations of enemies and their violence. This utility rests in part on the facility with which "terror" can be linked to diverse conflicts, particularly those involving the violence of the "weak" against the "strong", creating an imaginary alliance among all those who use "terror". Netanyahu also makes a very important move, although he is by no means the first to do so. He links Israel with the West and identifies "terror" as the common enemy of both. If Israel is at war against "terror", rather than with occupied Palestinians or Arab states, security relations with the United States are that much warmer, because "terror" can be the United States' enemy too.

The linkages between identity, strategy and foreign policy, and this utility of "terror", are evident in Netanyahu's framing passages. "Terrorism is back", the book begins. Rather than defining the term, Netanyahu lists examples: the 1993 attack on the World Trade Center, the Oklahoma City bombing, "terrorist attacks from Beirut to Buenos Aires", a Paris subway bombing and the Aum Shinrikyo attack in Tokyo.[11] What is left entirely unclear, and is never addressed in the book, is why such diverse events, actors and uses of violence should be grouped under one category, even one he goes on to subdivide between domestic and international. What, exactly, "is back"? Even if one granted for the sake of argument that these uses of violence fell under a common classification, it would be ridiculous to suggest – as Netanyahu implies – that these instances were the work of some common enemy. This implied assumption that the use of a "tactic" is indicative of an "alliance" of some kind among all who use it lies at the origins of any notion of a war on terror.

On its own, this move is so transparently absurd as to be unsustainable. It amounts, as some wag remarked, to declaring war on all airplanes rather than on Japan after the attack on Pearl Harbor. What it requires is a vision of a unitary enemy behind acts of terror, and this enemy is of course radical Islam, yet slippage is left to insist that one is at war not with Islam, or Palestinians, per se, only with terror. In laying out the rise of militant Islam and its terror threat, Netanyahu's book serves as a "roadmap" to the war on terror, which was to follow six years after its publication. All of the major terms of debate are present, beginning with references to Charles Martel's defeat of raiding "Saracens" at Poitiers in 732, invoked to establish the supposed long-running, primordial hostility between Islam and the West.[12] Terrorism and dictatorship, an expansive category into which Netanyahu places the Soviet Union, authoritarian Arab states, Iran and so on, are associated in ways that make non-democratic regimes a threat by their very existence: terrorism "is not an incidental characteristic of dictatorships; it is their quintessential, defining attribute".[13] Through this mechanism, he links terrorism to Arab state sponsors and counsels hostility towards these states. This is the same logic that appeared in Bush's pronouncements immediately after 9/11, in which he insisted that the United States would make no distinction between terrorists and the states that harboured them. Netanyahu identifies Gaza as the archetypal terrorist enclave, arguing that Israel's participation in the Oslo process created this enclave – drawing the lesson that negotiation and compromise with terrorists are counterproductive and that terrorist enclaves should be directly controlled by security forces. Finally, his penultimate chapter speculates on the possibilities of terrorist use of weapons of mass destruction (WMD), in particular an Iranian nuclear weapon, sketching out the relations between "rogue states" and WMD that marked justifications for the invasion of Iraq.

Throughout the text, in his discussions of past, present and future, Netanyahu links Israeli security concerns to Western security concerns. This sounds somewhat forced in his account of the "Soviet–Arab terrorist network" and the "Soviet–PLO axis", or in his ham-fisted efforts to liken Ba'athist pan-Arabism to Hitler's pan-German nationalism.[14] However, as he moves into the 1990s, this association of Israel with the West via common enemies becomes progressively more plausible. This plausibility is achieved through the logic of a simple syllogism: terrorism/militant Islam is hostile to Western democracy; Israel is a Western democracy; therefore Israel and the West share a common enemy. Netanyahu argues that Islam was hostile to the West long before Israel came into existence, so no one should assume that, if Israel did not exist or was forced to make peace with the Arabs and Palestinians, hostility between Islam and the West would evaporate. He emphasizes: "*The soldiers of militant Islam and Pan-Arabism do not hate the West because of Israel; they hate Israel because of the West.*"[15] Overall, we are left with a link between terror, Islam and dictatorship, on the one hand, and the West, democracy and Israel on the other. Netanyahu manages deftly to work the 1990s themes of a "democratic peace" into his imagined geography of a war on terror, in which Israel is the West's front-line against the "rest".

The suggestion here is not that Netanyahu's book represents a plan that was later followed by the United States or that, in and of itself, it was directly influential. Rather, the book represents an effective blending of the ideas that would later provide the ideological framing of the "war on terror" after the shock of 9/11. This will become even clearer in consideration of some neoconservative texts below. The linkages between the Israeli right, elements of the US national security complex – especially certain influential think tanks, publications and lobbying outfits – and the neoconservatives themselves are well established and frequently commented upon.[16] It is not a mystery how ideas such as Netanyahu's came to circulate in Washington.

Netanyahu adds another crucial piece to the picture, the idea that "terrorism" is an evil beyond redemption or understanding: "*nothing* justifies terrorism ... it is evil *per se*".[17] His reasoning is simple. The definition of civilized warfare is that it tries to proscribe deliberate attacks on "defenseless civilians"; the notion of a war crime takes on meaning only in this context. In completely ignoring the line between combatants and civilians, in its "uninhibited" and "brazen" resort to violence, "terrorism attacks the very foundations of civilization and threatens to erase it altogether by killing man's sense of sin, as Pope John Paul II put it".[18] Any attempt to excuse terrorism, to justify it or to take seriously the reasons for it proffered by terrorists themselves is to participate in this erasure of civilization: "For if anything is allowable, then even the gassing of a million babies in Auschwitz and Dachau is also permissible", intones Netanyahu, turning ham-fisted again.[19]

A few implications of the equation of terror with evil must be drawn out, for it is a key trope of the war on terror. Like the notion of "peace", which everyone is in favour of, it is easy to condemn "terror", which people find distasteful as well as dangerous. Yet as E. H. Carr pointed out some time ago, those who benefit from the status quo – and want to continue to do so without having to fight for it – are likely to trumpet the virtues of peace while condemning war as evil.[20] What Netanyahu calls "terror" can be an effective weapon in the hands of those who lack other weapons; it is often a form of resistance by the weak against the strong. It is hardly surprising that the strong would seek to discredit such a weapon in moral terms. Doing so has the additional advantage, one that Netanyahu eagerly seizes on, of silencing any justification for using such a weapon in the first place, since, by assertion, nothing can justify it. What Netanyahu has outlined is a kind of principled deafness by which the powerful righteously refuse any dialogue with their opposition until the latter disarm, even though it is the very taking up of arms in the first place that made the strong pay attention. The utility of such a position for sections of the Israeli right, who wish to remain in possession of Palestinian lands regardless of the consequences, is obvious; its value for the West in the war on terror is much less evident.

One more point needs to be made here. Netanyahu defines as civilized those who make war with a distinction between combatant and civilian, whereas those who do not make such a distinction are uncivilized. This idea fits with long-established Western constructions of lawful and just war. Israeli commentators regularly distinguish between suicide bombers who directly target civilians and their own forces, who occasionally harm civilians in their efforts to strike militants and terrorists. That more civilians are killed "accidentally" by Israeli forces than purposely by Palestinian terrorists does not matter in this construction of what is at stake ethically. As Victor Davis Hanson explains: "[W]e in the West call the few casualties we suffer from terrorism and surprise 'cowardly', the frightful losses we inflict through open and direct assault 'fair'."[21] The effect of this kind of attitude in the face of asymmetric war is to dismiss as "collateral damage" the losses inflicted on civilian populations in Iraq and Afghanistan, while feeling Western losses – for example, the far fewer killed on 9/11 itself – particularly deeply. When coupled with the stance of principled deafness, this is a recipe for continued escalation, because those "frightful" losses tend to inspire more "terrorism" and "surprise" on the part of the weak.

From theory to policy

Netanyahu's ideas reflect a particular milieu of security thought and practice in the 1990s. As Stefan Halper and Jonathan Clarke have argued, many of the ideas developed in the 1990s by neoconservatives and others became policy after 9/11.[22] George W. Bush had never intended to be a foreign policy president, and had explicitly rejected the idea of "nation-building". After the strikes on New York and the Pentagon, President Bush required not only a plan but an overall paradigm, and the neoconservatives and their allies in his administration were ready with one. They seized the moment almost immediately. Richard Clarke, National Coordinator for Counter-terrorism in the Bush administration until March 2003, relates how, when he returned to the White House on 12 September 2001, "I walked into a series of discussions about Iraq ... I realized ... that Rumsfeld and Wolfowitz were going to take advantage of this national tragedy to promote their agenda about Iraq."[23] Although the CIA was already certain that al-Qaeda had conducted the strikes, Wolfowitz was insisting – in line with long-held views such as Netanyahu's about state sponsorship of terror – that al-Qaeda must have had assistance from Iraq.

"Having been attacked by al Qaeda, for us now to go bombing Iraq in response would be like our invading Mexico after the Japanese attacked us at Pearl Harbor", Clarke remarked.[24] What seemed so bizarre to him made perfect sense in the context of the neoconservative agenda worked out in the 1990s. That agenda had long included regime change in Iraq.[25] There was simply no place, at least initially, in the state-centric neoconservative outlook that could take on board something like the global network enterprise that is the ever-shifting al-Qaeda. But related and more important was the turn to what Lawrence F. Kaplan and William Kristol

termed a "distinctly American internationalism".[26] This involved the use
of US power aggressively to further "freedom" abroad, exactly the policy
that the neoconservatives argue was an unnecessary casualty of the debacle in Viet Nam.[27] A liberated Iraq was to be the bridgehead of "freedom" in the Middle East, regardless of whether or not this was an appropriate response to the threat posed by al-Qaeda and its affiliates. As Vice
President Cheney put it before the invasion, when Saddam is removed
"the freedom-loving peoples of the region will have a chance to promote
the values that can bring lasting peace".[28] And so an attack by a non-
state actor on the United States, an actor the United States had been instrumental in creating, is turned into a neo-colonial occasion to bring democracy to Middle Eastern states by force.[29]

It is in this context ("democracy" vs. "dictatorship") that the US war
on terror is most easily linked with Netanyahu's vision of an embattled
"Western" Israel fighting the same fight. In early April 2003, with the invasion of Iraq under way, the Project for the New American Century (a
neoconservative "educational" organization) sent a letter to President
Bush on Israel and the war on terror.[30] It was signed by many prominent
neoconservatives as well as other US security analysts. The letter opens
by identifying Israel as a liberal democracy under attack by "murderers
who target civilians", insisting that "we Americans ought to be especially
eager to show our solidarity in word and deed with a fellow victim of
terrorist violence". The differences between the armed resistance of an
occupied people and al-Qaeda's strikes on the United States are here
erased through the magic of "terror". The letter urges the President to
accelerate his efforts to remove Saddam Hussein from power, citing the
fact that "Saddam, along with Iran, is a funder and supporter of terrorism
against Israel". Pressuring Israel to negotiate with Yasser Arafat is
likened to pressuring the United States to negotiate with Osama bin
Laden or Mullah Omar, and the Palestinian Authority is described as a
"cog in the machine of Middle East terrorism". In these constructions,
it becomes increasingly difficult to separate out US from Israeli interests;
they appear as one and the same. "No one should doubt that the United
States and Israel share a common enemy ... You have declared war on
international terrorism, Mr. President. Israel is fighting the same war."

In fact, the United States had come to be fighting Israel's war, at least,
as Netanyahu and his allies might envision it, taking out one of Israel's
most implacable enemies in Iraq and threatening Iran and Syria, the two
next-largest worries for Israeli security planners. The United States was
attacked by al-Qaeda, not by Iraq. Yet notions of state sponsorship of
terror, of the link between "dictatorship", Islam and terror, and of regime change as the solution came to overshadow the actual group that
had attacked the United States. All of these terms were packaged to-

gether by Netanyahu and others long before 9/11. Just before the first an-
niversary of that day, President Bush told some members of the US
House of Representatives: "The war on terrorism is going okay; we are
hunting down al Qaeda one-by-one ... The biggest threat, however, is
Saddam Hussein and his weapons of mass destruction. He can blow up
Israel and that would trigger an international conflict."[31]

"The Israelization of America"

It is not as surprising as it should be that the President of the United
States would downplay to the US Congress an enemy that had directly
attacked the United States in favour of one that might harm Israel. As
Senator J. William Fulbright remarked in 1973, "[o]n every test on anything the Israelis are interested in the Senate ... the Israelis have 75 to 80
votes".[32] If anything, this tally increased after 9/11. In November 2001,
89 senators wrote to President Bush urging him not to restrain Israel
from "using all [its] might and strength" against Palestinian terrorism.[33]
This occurred at a time when many sensible commentators were urging
Israeli restraint because of the utility of the Israel–Palestine conflict for
al-Qaeda propaganda, that is, for the enemy that had only recently inflicted a heavy blow on the US homeland. Many mistakenly attribute US
support for Israel to Jewish influence and the pro-Israeli lobby. To be
sure, this lobby is effective and powerful, but it would not be nearly so
effective if it were not advocating policies that a broad range of Americans see as in US interests and as reflecting US purposes in the world.[34]

The question becomes why do so many Americans find it both congenial and necessary to make common cause with Israel? The reason is that
they define the meaning and identity of the United States in ways that
make Israel a "friend", and supporting this friend is a test of US character and strength. This occurs in several ways – some religious, as when
Israel is seen as a vital prerequisite to the second coming of Christ; some
strategic, as when Israel is seen as a loyal ally against the Soviets or radical Islam; and some Kantian, in that they invoke a fraternity of democratic republics.

None of these different strands is exclusive of the others and each pre-
dates 9/11. They also frequently have purchase across the political spectrum. In a famous article critical of Israeli policies, George Ball (an
Under Secretary of State in the administrations of John F. Kennedy and
Lyndon B. Johnson) wrote in 1977: "Not only must Americans admire Israel, there can be no doubt that we have an interest in, and special responsibility for, that valiant nation."[35] As early as 1969, Gerald Ford (a
Republican and the then House Minority Leader) had stated that "the

fate of Israel is linked to the national security interests of the United States". Eugene Rostow (Under Secretary of State for Political Affairs under President Lyndon B. Johnson) warned in apocalyptic terms:

It is unthinkable that the international community could stand idly by ... if Israel were in danger of destruction. The moral and political convulsion that such an event would engender is beyond calculation. It could spell the end not only of the Atlantic alliance, but of liberal civilization as we know it.[36]

During the Reagan era, Israel was designated a major non-NATO ally of the United States, and relations between the United States and Israel were characterized by frequent dialogue and consultation, including the establishment of a US–Israeli free trade area in 1985. An agreement to intensify political, security and economic cooperation between the United States and Israel in 1988 began by reaffirming "the close relationship between the United States of America and Israel, based on common goals, interests, and values".[37] In April 1996, President Clinton and Prime Minister Peres reaffirmed US–Israeli strategic cooperation, and signed a US–Israel Counter-Terrorism Cooperation Accord, setting up a joint task force to oversee the implementation of the agreement.[38] The US and Israeli militaries developed close relations, ranging from arms procurement to trips for US service academy cadets to Israel.[39]

For present purposes, the hard facts about US–Israeli relations are less important than the sentiments of affinity and emotional attachment of which they are indicative. The effective evocation of sentiments of affinity creates a bond, a sense of shared identity and purpose. Representations of war and sacrifice can intensify these bonds, and in doing so they create an imagined geography of conflict that informs policy in fundamental ways. For example, consider the notion of the "Western allies" in World War II and the associated tropes of liberation through war and conquest. President Bush invoked these tropes to the graduating class of the US Air Force Academy by quoting General Eisenhower's message to the troops who would invade Normandy: "The hopes and prayers of liberty-loving people everywhere march with you."[40] Bush was attempting to link his war on terror with both World War II and the Cold War, likening something called "the ideology of terror" to "the murderous ideologies of the 20th century".[41] The notion of an "ideology of terror" serves to conflate the different reasons for which various groups take up arms against Western values and interests. Much else is at work in these tropes of the West and World War II. There is, for example, the curious disassociation of Nazi Germany from "the West". As Martin Lewis and Kären Wigen observe, imagined geographies are vehicles "for displacing the sins of Western civilization onto an intrusive non-European Other in our midst".[42] Germany returns to the West only after being schooled in democracy by the United States and its allies.

The sometimes expanding, sometimes contracting "West" was very much in evidence in the invasion of Iraq. In US policy pronouncements and in much US news commentary, the West was reduced to an Anglo-American rump, with some assistance from Spain, for a time, and Eastern Europe. Most of Western Europe was considered undeserving of fully fledged membership in the West precisely because of its unwillingness to engage in military action for purposes of liberating a "free people". Robert Kagan's very widely read and influential *Paradise and Power* exemplifies this move.[43] Israel, however, does much better in these terms. "You've worked tirelessly to strengthen the ties that bind our nations – our shared values, our strong commitment to freedom," President Bush told the American Israel Public Affairs Committee (AIPAC) in May 2004, something very difficult to imagine him saying sincerely in regard to France, for example.[44]

After 9/11, rather than seeing the Israeli occupation of the West Bank and Gaza as an underlying cause of terrorism, Israel was viewed as an allied republic under assault from the same enemy. In the immediate aftermath of the strikes on New York and Washington, the number of Americans who said their sympathies lay with the Israelis rather than the Palestinians increased to 55 per cent from 41 per cent the previous month.[45] That the United States had been grievously wounded by this same enemy was represented as creating a new bond between the United States and Israel, one in which the United States had greater empathy with Israel's plight. In April 2002, as Israel was on the offensive in the West Bank, Deputy Defense Secretary Paul Wolfowitz told a rally of US supporters of Israel and Prime Minister Sharon that, "[s]ince September 11, we Americans have one thing more in common with Israelis. On that day, America was attacked by suicide bombers. At that moment, every American understood what it is like to live in Jerusalem or Netanya or Haifa."[46] Later that same month, the House Majority Whip Tom DeLay told AIPAC that Israel should not give up "Judea" and "Samaria" and described Israel as "the lone fountain of liberty" in the Middle East, while referring to the Palestinian Authority as a "holding company for terrorist subsidiaries".[47] This "Israelization of America" was evident in Bush's speech to AIPAC in 2004 too.[48] Invoking the purported common experience of the United States and Israel, President Bush remarked "[w]e experienced the horror of being attacked in our homeland, on our streets, and in places of work. And from that experience came an even stronger determination, a fierce determination to defeat terrorism and to eliminate the threat it poses to free people everywhere."[49] This warmth of feeling is reciprocated in Israel. Israelis, unlike people in nearly every other country around the world, backed the re-election of Bush over his Democratic challenger in November 2004 by over two to one.[50]

That Israel and the United States face a "common enemy" begs the question of who this enemy is. In Bush's AIPAC speech he makes the obligatory concession to reality that "not all terrorist networks answer to the ... same leaders" but then insists that "all terrorists burn with the same hatred" of people who love freedom and that all terrorists kill without shame or mercy, counting their victories in the number of dead innocents.[51] As with Netanyahu, the "terrorism is evil" line is not sufficient on its own and so Bush goes on to list a number of instances of terrorist attack, spread widely over time and space, that have only one thing in common: the nominally Muslim identity of the perpetrators – nominal because at least one case was the work of secular Palestinian nationalists. Bush's list includes Nicholas Berg, beheaded in Iraq; Daniel Pearl, killed in Pakistan; Leon Klinghoffer, killed in the Mediterranean; and "blood on the streets" of Jakarta, Jerusalem, Casablanca, Riyadh, Mombasa, Istanbul, Bali, Baghdad and Madrid. "Every terrorist is at war with civilization, and every group or nation that aids them is equally responsible for the murders that the terrorists commit," Bush concludes.[52] Vice President Dick Cheney produced a similar list in October 2003, referring to a "global campaign" waged by a "terrorist network" ranging from Casablanca to Bali.[53]

The degree to which al-Qaeda represents a tightly controlled hierarchy or a looser network of more or less affiliated organizations, or both in different times and places, is open to dispute.[54] Equally, the notion that various resistance organizations might draw from a similar pool of personnel as well as financial and ideological resources can also be debated. But Bush and Cheney offer expansive views of a common enemy, in ways strongly reminiscent of Cold War representations of a unitary communist threat. On their account, "civilization", of which the Anglo-American–Israeli rump is the main defender, is at war with what they see as a widespread pathology of Islam. To arrive at this vision, they must erase the differences between, for example, the despair of long-term occupation and desire for revenge that inspire many Palestinian suicide bombers; Jemaah Islamiya's strike in Bali in October 2002; and Moro resistance in the Philippines, which has been under way in one form or another since the Spanish arrived in the sixteenth century. Strategically speaking, it would seem to be in US interests to disarticulate these various conflicts by addressing their direct sources, including past and present US policies. However, in terms of US identity, it is precisely the expansive vision of civilization's enemy that resonates.

There is some slippage and mobility in the notion of what "civilization" is being defended. Is it "the West"? It is notable that, in Rostow's formulation, the fate of the Atlantic alliance and of "liberal civilization" hangs on the willingness of the "international community" to aid Israel. A feature of the diplomacy surrounding both the Israel–Palestine conflict since 9/11 and the war in Iraq is increasing tension between the US and West European powers (including the United Kingdom) over Palestine. The warm language of common cause consecrated by blood sacrifice that US leaders reserve for Israel, and the intensity of pro-Israeli feeling among many Americans, are difficult to find in relation to Europe, with the exception of the United Kingdom. "The American people join me in expressing condolences to Prime Minister Sharon and all the people of Israel, and in reiterating our common dedication to the cause of fighting terrorism," President Bush stated after a suicide bombing in Haifa in October 2003.[55] When the Israelis killed the commander of Hamas' military wing in July 2002 by F-16 strike, the CIA station chief in Israel telephoned the Chief of Staff of the Israeli Defense Forces and the Director of the Shin Bet to say "great job".[56] The imagined geography at work here is not the familiar one of "the West", but something new, perhaps "post-Western" in John Gray's term, of which two intensely religious societies are the core: the United States and Israel.[57]

More recently, there has been close cooperation between Israel and US forces over Iraq. Israeli military and intelligence officials have trained US counterparts preparing to go to Iraq, in part to develop a programme of targeted killings designed to dismantle the Iraqi insurgency modelled on Israeli operations in the occupied territories.[58] UK advice to adopt a "hearts and minds" approach has been much less warmly received by the Americans.[59] The British have a much more successful record in counter-insurgency than either the Israelis or the Americans. Israeli tactics in the occupied territories have created isolated cells led by young, often inexperienced and aggressive individuals not subject to central control. More generally, the Israelis have little prospect of winning hearts and minds in the occupied territories and so a coercive, militarized strategy is the only one available. Iraq is a much different conflict and, despite the presence of foreign elements interested in spoiling a positive outcome, a "hearts and minds" strategy was a rational way forward, one fully concordant with announced US purposes to liberate and rebuild Iraq.

The problem is that, in the US/Israel vision of "terror", the enemy is not conceived as someone whose heart and mind are potentially winnable. Rather, the enemy is composed of dedicated, fanatical terrorists. One of the planners involved in the US–Israeli counter-terror initiative in Iraq is Lieutenant-General William Boykin, an evangelical Christian who has likened the Muslim world to Satan, claiming it wants to "destroy us as a Christian army" and that it hates the United States "because we are a nation of believers".[60] To be sure, many US officers have a less eschatological account of the war on terror and the nature of the insurgency in Iraq than Boykin. But Boykin's vision is far more compatible with US identity as the defender of "free peoples" under attack from "armed minorities" who must be found, fixed and destroyed. The tendency at all levels, from the US military to the US public, will be to see policies and strategies that fit with this identity as more rational and appropriate. As a senior British army officer remarked of US soldiers in Iraq, "[they] view things in very simplistic terms. It seems hard for them to reconcile the subtleties between who supports what and who doesn't in Iraq. It's easier for their soldiers to group all Iraqis as the bad guys. As far as they are concerned Iraq is bandit country and everybody is out to kill them."[61]

The US/Israeli vision of the enemy is a recipe for continued escalation of the war on terror, in ways that increasingly take on the form of a clash of civilizations. Neoconservative ideologues eagerly seize on this possibility. Daniel Pipes, whom President Bush has appointed to the board of the US Institute of Peace, speaks of a long-term conflict between the West and militant Islam. Like Bush, he sees Islamism as a "totalitarian movement that has much in common with fascism and Marxism-Leninism".[62] Such claims are now commonplace in US political discourse. But Pipes' "West" is not what it seems at first take: "The Europeans, with their low birth rates, have brought in immigrants from Islamic countries. Indicators suggest that Europe is gradually becoming part of the Muslim world." He sees Christianity and Islam on a collision course, competing for converts and territory: "The main centers of Christian vigor are now in Africa, Latin America and Asia."[63]

This language of religiosity and conversion is at odds with standard accounts of a secular and rational Western modernity. Gray argues that, unlike the United States, Western Europe is "post-Enlightenment" in that it has largely given up on the idea of a "universal civilization", as well as the armed imposition of this civilization on "natives". The United States, in the view of Gray and others, is diverging from Europe across a range of indicators. Not only do more Americans go to church, but their Protestantism is the most fundamentalist in Christendom. "Just under 70 per cent of Americans believe in the devil, compared with a third of the British, a fifth of the French and an eighth of the Swedes ... America's secular traditions are weaker than Turkey's."[64]

One of the key confusions in Samuel Huntington's thesis of a clash of civilizations is the notion that conflicts of belief among different civilizations can lead to war. War and conflict are in fact opportunities for voices within communities to redefine and refashion dominant identities. Such is the case in the war on terror, for the United States, for Islam and for the West. Whereas much commentary has focused on the diplomatic tensions between Europe and the United States over Iraq, less attention has been paid to the kind of increasingly fundamental divergence – across a range of social, cultural and political dimensions – that Gray identifies. The war on terror is both an example and an agent of this divergence. For many Europeans, terror is a problem to be managed, something they have lived with, something that is not eradicable, and something to which the primary response should be increased policing and intelligence. For Americans, terror is an evil against which a crusade must be waged. In this they have in part taken their cue, their language with which to conceive the enemy, from a certain strand of Israeli thinking. The tragedy in the making is that the battlegrounds of the war on terror will come increasingly to resemble those in Israel–Palestine. "Close your eyes for a moment, and you can imagine that the [US] Marines in Karbala are Golani infantry in Tul Karm."[65] Iraqi imaginations need little prompting: they already refer to US soldiers in Iraq as "Jews".[66]

Acknowledgements

Thanks to Brian Job and the participants in the United Nations University and International Peace Academy workshop on "Iraq and World Order: Structural and Normative Challenges" for comments on earlier versions of this chapter. It draws in part on previously published work. See Tarak Barkawi, "Globalization, Culture and War: On the Popular Mediation of 'Small Wars'", *Cultural Critique*, No. 58 (Autumn 2004); "On the Pedagogy of 'Small Wars'", *International Affairs*, Vol. 80, No. 1 (January 2004); and *Globalization and War* (Lanham: Rowman & Littlefield, 2005).

Notes

1. David Campbell, *Writing Security: United States Foreign Policy and the Politics of Identity* (Minneapolis: University of Minnesota Press, 1992).
2. See Tarak Barkawi, "Strategy as a Vocation: Weber, Morgenthau and Modern Strategic Studies", *Review of International Studies*, Vol. 24, No. 2 (April 1998).
3. Quoted in Michael McClintock, *Instruments of Statecraft: US Guerrilla Warfare, Counter-Insurgency, Counter-Terrorism, 1940–1990* (New York: Pantheon, 1992), p. 174.
4. Quoted in John Lewis Gaddis, *Strategies of Containment: A Critical Appraisal of Postwar American National Security Policy* (Oxford: Oxford University Press, 1982), pp. 64–65.
5. See, for example, Susan Jeffords, *The Remasculinization of America: Gender and the Vietnam War* (Bloomington: Indiana University Press, 1989).
6. Lawrence F. Kaplan and William Kristol, *The War over Iraq: Saddam's Tyranny and America's Mission* (San Francisco: Encounter Books, 2003), p. 57.

7. Quoted in Brian Knowlton, "US to 'Stay the Course' in Iraq", *International Herald Tribune*, 28 October 2003, p. 1.
8. "President's Radio Address", 1 November 2003, ⟨http://www.whitehouse.gov/news/releases/2003/11/print/20031101.html⟩ (accessed 3 November 2003).
9. Ibid.
10. Benjamin Netanyahu, *Fighting Terrorism: How Democracies Can Defeat Domestic and International Terrorists* (New York: Farrar, Straus, Giroux, 1995).
11. Ibid., p. 3.
12. Ibid., pp. 82–83.
13. Ibid., p. 75.
14. See, for example, ibid., pp. 60, 62, 85.
15. Ibid., p. 87; emphases in the original.
16. See, for example, Stefan Halper and Jonathan Clarke, *America Alone: The Neoconservatives and the Global Order* (Cambridge: Cambridge University Press, 2004).
17. Netanyahu, *Fighting Terrorism*, p. 21.
18. Ibid., pp. 21–22. The irony of condemning Muslim violence via the Papacy – which licensed the Crusades – does not seem to have occurred to Netanyahu.
19. Ibid., p. 21.
20. E. H. Carr, *The Twenty Years' Crisis 1919–1939: An Introduction to the Study of International Relations* (London: Macmillan, 1946), pp. 51–53.
21. Victor Davis Hanson, *Carnage and Culture* (New York: Anchor Books, 2002), p. 97.
22. Halper and Clarke, *America Alone*.
23. Richard A. Clarke, *Against All Enemies: Inside America's War on Terror* (New York: Free Press, 2004), p. 30.
24. Ibid., pp. 30–31.
25. See, for example, Richard Perle, "Iraq: Saddam Unbound", in Robert Kagan and William Kristol, eds, *Present Dangers: Crisis and Opportunity in American Foreign and Defense Policy* (San Francisco: Encounter Books, 2000).
26. Kaplan and Kristol, *The War over Iraq*.
27. Ibid., pp. 65–67, 115–118.
28. Quoted in ibid., p. 100.
29. On the role of US policy in creating al-Qaeda, see Gabriel Kolko, *Another Century of War?* (New York: The New Press, 2002); and Mahmood Mamdani, *Good Muslim, Bad Muslim: America, the Cold War and the Roots of Terror* (New York: Pantheon Books, 2004).
30. Project for the New American Century, "Letter to President Bush on Israel, Arafat and the War on Terrorism", 3 April 2002, ⟨http://www.newamericancentury.org/Bushletter-040302.htm⟩ (accessed 17 May 2004).
31. Quoted in Bob Woodward, *Plan of Attack* (New York: Simon & Schuster, 2004), p. 186.
32. Quoted in Bernard Reich, *The United States and Israel: Influence in the Special Relationship* (New York: Praeger, 1984), p. 190.
33. Quoted in Dana H. Allin and Steven Simon, "The Moral Psychology of US Support for Israel", *Survival*, Vol. 45, No. 3 (Autumn 2003), p. 130.
34. Ibid., p. 131.
35. Quoted in Reich, *The United States and Israel*, pp. 178–179.
36. Both quoted in ibid., p. 179.
37. "Memorandum of Agreement between the United States and the State of Israel Regarding Joint Political, Security, and Economic Cooperation", *JINSA Online*, 21 April 1988, ⟨http://www.jinsa.org/articles/view.html?documentid=182⟩ (accessed 17 May 2004).

38. "U.S.-Israel Joint Statement on Strategic Cooperation", *JINSA Online*, 30 April 1996, ⟨http://www.jinsa.org/articles/view.html?documentid=184⟩ (accessed 17 May 2004).
39. Jason Vest, "The Men from JINSA and CSP", *The Nation*, 2 September 2002, ⟨http://www.thenation.com/doc/20020902/vest⟩ (accessed 18 May 2004).
40. Quoted in "Remarks by the President at the United States Air Force Academy Graduation Ceremony", 2 June 2004, ⟨http://www.whitehouse.gov/news/releases/2004/06/20040602.html⟩ (accessed 3 June 2004).
41. Ibid.
42. Martin Lewis and Kären Wigen, *The Myth of Continents: A Critique of Metageography* (Berkeley: University of California Press, 1997), p. 68.
43. Robert Kagan, *Paradise and Power: America and Europe in the New World Order* (London: Atlantic Books, 2003).
44. "Remarks by the President to American Israel Public Affairs Committee", 18 May 2004, ⟨http://www.whitehouse.gov/news/releases/2004/05/20040518-1.html⟩ (accessed 18 May 2004).
45. The Gallup Organization, "Americans Show Increased Support for Israel Following Terrorist Attacks", 19 September 2001, ⟨http://poll.gallup.com/content/default.aspx?ci=4915&pg=1⟩ (accessed 10 February 2006).
46. Quoted in NewsMax.com Wires (UPI), "Hard-line Israeli Supporters Boo Wolfowitz", 16 April 2002, ⟨http://www.newsmax.com/archives/articles/2002/4/15/204626.shtml⟩ (accessed 17 May 2004).
47. Quoted in Barbara Slavin, "Don't Give up 1967 Lands, DeLay Tells Israel Lobby", *USA Today*, 23 April 2002, ⟨http://www.usatoday.com/news/world/2002/04/24/aipac.htm⟩ (accessed 18 May 2004).
48. Gideon Samet titled one of his columns in *Haaretz* "The Israelization of America", 4 April 2003, ⟨http://www.haaretzdaily.com/hasen/objects/pages/PrintArticleEn.jhtml?itemNo=280488⟩ (accessed 18 May 2004).
49. "Remarks by the President to American Israel Public Affairs Committee".
50. Alan Travis, "We Like Americans, We Don't Like Bush", *Guardian*, 15 October 2004, p. 4.
51. "Remarks by the President to American Israel Public Affairs Committee".
52. Ibid.
53. "Remarks by the Vice President to the Heritage Foundation", 10 October 2003, ⟨http://new.heritage.org/Research/MiddleEast/DickCheneySpeech.cfm⟩ (accessed 10 February 2006).
54. See, for example, Jason Burke, *Al-Qaeda: Casting a Shadow of Terror* (London: I. B. Tauris, 2003); Mark Duffield, "War as a Network Enterprise: The New Security Terrain and Its Implications", *Cultural Values*, Vol. 6, Nos 1 & 2 (2002), pp. 153–165.
55. "President Condemns Terrorist Act", Statement by the President, 4 October 2003, ⟨http://www.whitehouse.gov/news/releases/2003/10/20031004-1.html⟩ (accessed 17 May 2004).
56. Quoted in Amir Oren, "Facing the Common Enemy", *Haaretz*, 30 July 2002, ⟨http://www.haaretzdaily.com/hasen/pages/ShArt.jhtml?itemNo=192149&contrassID=2&subContrassID=4&sbSubContrassID=0&listSrc=Y⟩ (accessed 17 May 2004).
57. John Gray, *False Dawn: The Delusions of Global Capitalism* (London: Granta Books, 2002), pp. 128–130.
58. Seymour Hersh, "Moving Targets", *The New Yorker*, 8 December 2003.
59. Sean Rayment, "US Tactics Condemned by British Officers", *Daily Telegraph*, 11 April 2004.
60. Quoted in Hersh, "Moving Targets", p. 4.
61. Quoted in Rayment, "US Tactics Condemned by British Officers".

62. Quoted in Manfred Gerstenfeld, "The End of American Jewry's Golden Era: An Interview with Daniel Pipes", *Campus Watch in the Media*, 2 May 2004, ⟨http://www.campus-watch.org/article/id/1138⟩ (accessed 15 May 2004).

63. Ibid.

64. Gray, *False Dawn*, p. 126.

65. Samet, "The Israelization of America". The Golani Infantry Brigade is an élite Israeli unit and Tul Karm is a city and refugee camp on the West Bank.

66. Thomas Friedman, "Jews, Israel and America", *International Herald Tribune*, 25 October 2004, p. 8.

Part VI

Conclusion

31

Structural and normative challenges

James Cockayne and Cyrus Samii

Things fall apart; the centre cannot hold;
Mere anarchy is loosed upon the world,
The blood-dimmed tide is loosed, and everywhere
The ceremony of innocence is drowned;
The best lack all conviction, while the worst
Are full of passionate intensity.

(W. B. Yeats, *The Second Coming*, 1921)

Introduction

The Iraq crisis, which climaxed in the US-led invasion of 20 March 2003, was by many reckonings evidence of a disintegration of the existing UN-centred world order. This world order is the product of the formal institutions centred on the United Nations and the norms and perceptions undergirding those institutions. Seen another way, it is the product of the distribution of power enshrined in UN institutions and the actual distribution of capabilities supposedly justifying those institutional arrangements. Basic elements of this order have been challenged by the crisis over Iraq. The prohibition of aggression has been tested by the doctrine of preventive military action. The international norm of state sovereignty has been brought into question by efforts directed against the proliferation of weapons of mass destruction (WMD), non-state actors' militancy and human rights violations. The apparent incapacity of the United Nations either to prevent or to manage the Iraq crisis raised questions about the organization's continued utility, at least as it is currently constituted. Institutional privileges such as permanent member status in the Security Council are, by some reckonings, out of step with empirical realities. The chapters in this volume helpfully bring together varying perspectives on the causes and implications of the Iraq crisis in this tension-ridden context. A question remains for the UN-centred international community: *quo vadis?*

This concluding chapter addresses that question, focusing on implications for continued UN reform for dealing with international threats and challenges in the twenty-first century. It is too soon to say definitively whether the Iraq crisis was indicative of tectonic shifts in power and beliefs or if the crisis has itself triggered a lasting reconfiguration of world political forces. Nonetheless, the manner in which the crisis unfolded and the behaviours that it elicited have highlighted a number of important trends in contemporary international relations. Grasping these trends is a necessary precondition for effectively designing and reforming institutions in the service of global collective action to promote peace and security.

In the first section we discuss the nature of the disconnect between world order and current realities as revealed by the Iraq crisis and as illuminated by the contributions to this volume. We then focus on structural challenges, in particular on the challenges posed by both the United States' preponderance of power and the lack of inclusiveness in UN decision-making. The third section focuses on normative challenges posed by the disconnect between the norms enshrined by the United Nations and perceptions in the world of legitimate responses to contemporary threats. In the final section we draw out implications for UN reform.

Revealing the disconnect

"World order", in this volume, refers to conventional and institutionalized patterns of behaviour in world politics.[1] The structural aspects of world order include the distribution of empirical and institutional power within the world political system, and the political, social and economic organization of the system. The normative aspects of world order are the ideas and beliefs that undergird institutions and inspire the agents within the system. Challenges within the context of world order arise when the institutions of world politics become disconnected from empirical realities, compelling agents to take action outside existing institutions or to alter those institutions. Structural challenges arise, for example, when the formal distribution of power within these institutions no longer matches the empirical distribution of power in the world. Normative challenges arise when the principles undergirding formal institutions are disconnected from the beliefs and values that prevail in the world. The Iraq crisis exposed a number of structural and normative challenges to the notion of UN-centred world order. Some of these challenges, it seems, can be resolved only with institutional reform. Other challenges may be resolved through the reinforcement or re-articulation of existing norms, or by the creation of new ones by "norm entrepreneurs".[2]

These "disconnects" are produced by both continuous trends and occasional radical transformations, as the Iraq crisis has amply demonstrated. Those emphasizing continuity point to ongoing UN intervention and previous Western unilateralism in Iraq since 1980, for example in the establishment of the no-fly zones.[3] Other continuous factors were also relevant, such as inflammation of militant Islamist sentiment owing to the US troop presence in Saudi Arabia following the 1991 Gulf war.[4] The Iraq crisis and the resulting diplomatic and political fall-out were reminiscent of past episodes, most notably the 1999 Kosovo crisis. Finally, the US–UK approach to the crisis could also be cast as a return to traditional patterns of great power politics after a brief flirtation with institutionalization immediately following the end of the Cold War.[5]

In contrast, one may read the Iraq crisis as either the cause or the effect of radical transformation. This view emphasizes the split between the United States and "Old Europe", a precipitous rise of Islamic militancy, and the consolidation of a global peace movement in the 15 February 2003 demonstrations.[6] Finally, for some, the crisis was not "about" Iraq, but simply and unfortunately played out in Iraq.[7] Both readings are plausible and both reveal the disconnect between the formal institutions of world order and structural and normative realities.

Structural challenges

Current structural challenges arise from a number of sources.[8] One source is the disconnect between, on the one hand, US preponderance and the emergence of new powers and, on the other hand, the anachronistic distribution of institutional power within the UN Security Council. Another source is the "Westphalian myth" underpinning the formal sovereign equality of states upheld in institutions such as the UN General Assembly, and the extreme empirical variation in capabilities of states. These longstanding and increasing structural disconnects have set the stage for more immediate challenges to the centrality of the United Nations. The structural disconnects amplified the sense of disequilibrium triggered by the US decision to take military action against Iraq in 2003 without renewed Security Council authorization.

The contributions to this volume describe a number of structural challenges arising from these disconnects, all of which have implications for restoring the United Nations' special place in the international system. One challenge is immediately relevant to the UN reform process: challenges to the role of the UN Security Council as the central body in multilateral decision-making in security affairs. The Iraq crisis shook beliefs in many corners of the world that the Security Council has truly been entrenched as the primary decision-making body for global security concerns in the post–Cold War era. Another challenge came to those leaders facing the uncomfortable choice between supporting the agenda either of the United Nations, with all of its apparent contradictions, or of the United States, with risks of eroding already institutionalized global commitments to democracy and human rights. As is discussed below, these uncomfortable choices produced many ironic results. The way in which leaders and policy entrepreneurs work to overcome these challenges has important implications for North–South relations – another dimension of the global politics surrounding the Iraq crisis that contributions to this volume have highlighted.

The Security Council: Just another coalition?

Contributors to this volume seem to agree that the United States cannot and does not pursue its security objectives alone, and that it must call on the assistance of coalitions of other actors. Since there is a small group of Northern states on which it calls most regularly, the resulting system could be characterized as one of "uni-multipolarity"[9] or a "unipolar concert".[10] This view is presented as a corrective to the simplistic, although often expressed, notion of the United States as an omnipotent hegemon. The concert may best be understood as congruent with the G-8 or, after its possible expansion, the G-10 (since the G-10 would include all of the permanent five (P-5) members of the UN Security Council plus Japan, Germany, Italy, Canada and India). The unipolar concert is not quite identical with the Security Council, and serves as an alternative centre of international security decision-making.

As a unipolar power, the United States has the ability to vary the membership of the supporting cast on an issue-by-issue basis – the idea of "coalitions of the willing". The Iraq crisis revealed that the UN Security Council might be just one potential coalition among many for Washington. The United States is likely to use the Security Council only when its legitimizing currency for some specific task far outweighs the consequential procedural and political constraints, making it more appealing than other coalitions. In such circumstances, the primacy of the Security Council and the image of a UN-centred world order are illusory. On top of legitimacy and procedural constraints, functional effectiveness serves as another consideration for the United States. This combination of considerations affecting US resort to the Security Council is consistent with the concept of "effective multilateralism" that official US delegations have invoked at major international conferences in recent years. All of these considerations factor into the United States' "coalition shopping" behaviour, even beyond the Security Council. NATO would seem to represent another substitute coalition in the area of post-conflict peace operations, at least in places where NATO members can agree on involvement.[11] This of course was not the case vis-à-vis Iraq, notwithstanding NATO's token role in training Iraqi security forces. This is an important reason for UN reform efforts to think harder about the sources of Security Council legitimacy and to focus on ways to protect and perhaps increase that legitimacy. Security Council expansion may serve this function, contributing to holding the United States' attention to the degree that it increases the Council's legitimizing currency without introducing major procedural and political constraints.

The Iraq crisis made crystal clear the central danger of unipolarity for a UN-centred multilateral system: the destabilization of an institutionalized political system by the knowledge that, at any time, the unipolar power may choose to look elsewhere for its supporting cast. The specific challenge that the United Nations confronts is to find a path between perceptions of irrelevance and complicity. The Security Council's begrudging acceptance of the US-led occupation of Iraq in Resolution 1483, for example, exposed it to charges of complicity.[12] The emergence of alternative centres for decision-making on global security issues – whether in the G-8/10 or in ad hoc groupings such as the Six-Party Talks on North Korea or the Proliferation Security Initiative – exposes the United Nations to charges of irrelevance in dealing with critical security challenges.

Uncomfortable choices and ironic results

The Iraq crisis forced many leaders to face an uncomfortable question in managing their relations with both the United States and the broader international community: does a pro-UN position imply an anti-US position, and does a pro-US position imply an anti-UN position? For Japan, as Chiyuki Aoi and Yozo Yokota put it in their contribution to this volume, "the Iraq war therefore challenged the untroubled, if not entirely realistic, assumption of compatibility between three pillars of postwar Japanese foreign policy: UN-centrism, alliance with the United States and other Western powers, and friendly relations with Asian countries".[13] Other country perspectives presented in this volume invariably describe the choices that leaders faced as "uncomfortable" or "difficult". Mónica Serrano and Paul Kenny make an interesting comparative point by noting that the rest of the world was just getting a taste of what states in the Western hemisphere have been forced to deal with all along. They write, "Latin America ... experienced the implications of a US-centric world order before the rest of the late-twentieth-century world".[14]

The outcomes that these dilemmas produced were often ironic. Given the intensity with which states typically pursue Security Council seats, for example, it is noteworthy to read in the contributions to this volume that Security Council members seemed to have been relieved that an ultimate Security Council vote never came about. Serrano and Kenny point out that, "within the bounds of the game, Mexico [which was on the Security Council] was able to confront the United States without opposing it; Chile [which was also on the Security Council] to oppose without confronting. Both were finally happy to escape the consequences of a 'No' that really meant what it said."[15] In the absence of a vote, Russia could more easily play a "wait and see" strategy. According to Ekaterina Stepanova in Chapter 15 in this volume, this strategy rested on the optimistic belief that the United States would eventually recognize the limits of its power and then seek once again to play by the rules – albeit by slightly modified rules.

Another irony is that the United Nations may have received increased support in some corners as a result of the "with us or against us" choice that the United States forced upon the international community. Jean-Marc Coicaud in his chapter proposes that "radicalism brings about political clarification" by forcing attention to concentrate on what is really at stake and thus pushing actors to clarify their commitments.[16] In the crucible of the crisis, attention concentrated on the costs of a diminution of UN relevance, impelling some states to speak more clearly about their commitments to multilateralism. Kenny and Serrano provide some support for this view, pointing out that the Mexican leadership ended up throwing its weight behind the United Nations, even though prior to the Iraq crisis President Vicente Fox's administration spoke of significant reforms needed for the United Nations to be credible. It is not abundantly clear, however, that such reactionary support for the United Nations indicates a real strengthening of its capacity to discharge its peace and security role, or whether in fact it amounts to a more desultory rearguard action.

There were also complexities in the relationships between states' international behaviour and the quality of their domestic democratic institutions. In the United Kingdom, Prime Minister Blair had to face a largely offended public in choosing to act outside the United Nations.[17] Such was also the case in Spain, Italy and, arguably, Poland, all states in which democratic credentials are not in question. These results demonstrate that democratic constraints on foreign policy decision-making are only one side of the "two-level game" that leaders play in making foreign policy decisions; indeed, opportunities and pressures in the international system may be compelling even for those subject to domestic democratic discipline. On the other hand, Hasan-Askari Rizvi (Chapter 19) proposes that public opinion figured very prominently in President Pervez Musharraf's decision not to join the US-led coalition, even during the post-invasion reconstruction phase. Amin Saikal (Chapter 11) finds similar results for many of the Arab states. In Germany, Chancellor Schröder seized the chance to salvage his sliding re-election campaign through a populist rejection of the US position.[18]

Another notable outcome was that the consensus that has been built in regional organizations and identity-based international institutions hardly featured in the crisis. As Fred Tanner argues in Chapter 20, NATO "did not play any essential role" and the European Union was left divided and inert. The German–US split was drawn into a broader European–US split, and the unified Franco-German opposition to the US–UK axis could be seen as the first real evidence of a genuinely "European" foreign policy. But, clearly, Europeans across the continent were not united on this. Leaders from "new Europe" used the US-led war effort as an opportunity to redefine the post-expansion distribution of authority within the European Union. Karawan, Saikal and Rizvi point out in Chapters 10, 11 and 19 that the Organization of the Islamic Conference was also unable to present a common position. Thus, the crisis showed the limited achievements of such consensus-building processes, at least in relation to the United States and international security concerns.

Unipolarity and the North–South divide

As Ayoob and Zierler discuss in Chapter 3, a unipolar system can be distinguished from an imperial one. A unipolar power contends with sovereignty when trying to exert influence over other states, whereas an imperial power overrides sovereignty. But an automatic tension exists between a unipolar power's sense of privilege, derived from its preponderant power and responsibility, and the other states' sense of privileged autonomy, derived from being part of a system based on the international norm of state sovereignty. Just as unipolarity undermines UN-centred world order, it may contribute to the hardening of the North–South divide. This tension helps to explain the puzzling vitality of the Non-Aligned Movement (NAM), despite the passing of a decade and a half since the end of the Cold War.

The tensions across the North–South divide come not only from clashing senses of privilege but also from divergence in security priorities.[19] Lowering the bar to intervention – whether military or simply reform-minded intervention – is a central concern. Thakur argues in Chapter 28 that "[i]n the real world today, the brutal truth is that our choice is not between intervention and non-intervention. Rather, our choice is between ad hoc or rules-based, unilateral or multilateral, and consensual or deeply divisive intervention."[20] Nonetheless, in multilateral forums such as the UN General Assembly, the global South has tended to see any effort to make the United Nations more responsive to interventionist impulses as a powerful threat to their interests.[21] For the US leadership, following the promulgation of its 2002 *National Security Strategy*, precisely the opposite is true. Such intervention is taken as a necessary action to remove terrorist or WMD threats.

North–South tensions emanate from a sense that each group's priorities imply mutually exclusive policy choices drawing on finite institutional resources in a zero-sum game. The commitment of exorbitant resources and institutional attention to "hard security" crises such as Iraq means lost opportunities for development efforts elsewhere. If the United Nations complies with such prioritization, it may be seen as downgrading part of its mission. At the same time, inclusion of the South's developmental concerns on the global agenda is sometimes characterized as distracting from the security concerns of the North. If the priority gap widens between the United Nations and, for example, the United States and the United Kingdom, then the United Nations is impaired in its ability to organize development assistance. Some have argued that development should be understood as a path to security, in order to break this zero-sum logic between Northern versus Southern priorities. The perception found favour in both the December 2004 report from the United Nations' High-level Panel on Threats, Challenges and Change, *A More Secure World*, and the UN Millennium Project's January 2005 report, *Investing in Development*.[22] The UN Secretary-General released a March 2005 follow-on report, *In Larger Freedom*, which aimed to combine the findings from the two earlier reports into a common agenda for reform and revitalization of the United Nations.[23] However, the March 2005 report hardly attempted to synthesize the findings of the two earlier reports, instead offering a "package" of disparate institutional reform projects. This outcome reflects the difficulty in finding a way to move from conciliatory rhetoric to convincing reforms marrying security and development objectives.[24]

The capacities of the Security Council also require attention in relation to North–South tensions. The 1990s have seen the Security Council take on an increasingly legislative role – especially in Resolutions 687 (the Iraq ceasefire), 1373 (the Counter-Terrorism Committee), 1422 (the first of the ICC-exemption resolutions) and 1540 (criminalizing certain WMD proliferation activities). Resentment of the "unelected 5", as some have termed the permanent five members of the Security Council, will only grow if such rule by legislative fiat is to continue. To prevent this, legislative resolutions would have to be subjected to stringent standards of debate, transparency and accountability.[25]

Normative challenges

In relation to security concerns, normative challenges to UN-centred world order arise from the disconnect between the norms enshrined by the United Nations, particularly state sovereignty and non-aggression, and the nature of contemporary threats.[26] As is made clear in both Chapters 27 and 28, the United States is not alone in sensing this disconnect, which has been noted in relation not only to terrorism and WMD proliferation but also to humanitarian crises. This disconnect may translate into a gap between the legality and the legitimacy of some acts contributing to peace and security. This weakening of the link between legality and legitimacy opens space for "norm entrepreneurs" to promote alternative visions of world order.[27] As is discussed below, some of these alternative visions present formidable challenges to the United Nations in the organization's claims to represent universal interests.

Legality vs. legitimacy

The Iraq crisis is only the most recent crisis provoking consideration of the disconnect between responses to contemporary threats and the norms enshrined by UN institutions.[28] The Kosovo Commission, for example, reflected much contemporaneous commentary in its assessment of NATO's 1999 Kosovo intervention as "illegal but legitimate".[29] In this volume, three interpretations of the US-led intervention in Iraq have been presented. Ruth Wedgwood (Chapter 25) proposes that the invasion was legal, through authorization by Security Council Resolutions 678, 687 and 1441, and legitimate, on the basis of security and humanitarian imperatives. David Krieger (Chapter 23) disagrees, arguing that the invasion was unlawful for not having garnered explicit Security Council authorization, and illegitimate on the basis of norms of non-aggression and the unsupportability of the claims of a threat. Charlotte Ku (Chapter 24) explores the implications of a hybrid view: that the intervention was unlawful but perhaps legitimate.

Although the debate related to legality is likely to continue, a number of possible dangers are associated with a legality/legitimacy gap.[30] According to basic institutional and legal theory, by enshrining norms in law, the costs and benefits of transgression are made more discernible. By leaving legitimacy untethered to law, that discernibility is lost, raising transaction costs, undermining cooperation and encouraging reliance on self-help strategies. As the legitimacy of international law as a general approach is eroded, so too are the legitimacy and effectiveness of all those institutions it permits and sustains, from the United Nations to the International Committee of the Red Cross. Saddam Hussein's ability to undermine the United Nations' efforts to lay down the law certainly weakened the binding force of those laws. But the same might be said of the US-led coalition's reliance on extra-legal claims of legitimacy. This raises questions about whether this reliance on extra-legal legitimacy is an exceptional case or whether it is indicative of a new pattern of international affairs. The suggestion emanating from the United States' approach during the Iraq crisis and after, as many contributors propose in their chapters, is an abandonment of a world order powered by rules for a world order ruled by power.

The importance of the legality/legitimacy distinction in the Iraq case is precisely that it comes as part of a growing perception among many that the two *are not* identical at the international level. In the Middle East, particularly with respect to the Arab–Israeli conflict, the loss of law's legitimacy is frequently linked to the perceived uneven enforcement of UN Security Council resolutions. In the capitals of members of the US-led coalition, a problem is seen in how an outmoded international law protects threatening tyrants but places a straitjacket on political reform by an intervening/occupying power.[31] This comes in addition to what Mark A. Heller notes in Chapter 9 as "the absurdity of granting terrorists and their state sponsors and apologists a seemingly legitimate role in the elaboration, interpretation and enforcement of the law; in properly functioning legal systems, they would be recused on grounds of clear conflict of interest".[32] Such concerns seem to have been reflected in the proposal by Secretary-General Annan in his *In Larger Freedom* to do away with the Human Rights Commission in favour of a more selective Human Rights Council – a proposal that member states accepted at the September 2005 UN World Summit, but without agreeing any of the institutional detail, wherein, no doubt, lurked many devils. In the eyes of civil society activists, UN legitimacy suffers from the inconsistency between, on the one hand, aspirations for enhancing democracy in global institutions and, on the other hand, the United Nations' dependence on international law, which empowers states, not people directly. In the global South, legitimacy is eroded as international law comes to be seen as the rule of the few, for the few and by the few.

The Iraq crisis and norms of humanitarian protection

Three extra-legal claims were made by members of the US-led coalition about the legitimacy of the invasion of Iraq: that it was a legitimate response to (1) the imminent threat of WMD falling into the hands of terrorists; (2) an imminent threat constituted by Iraq's own possession of WMD; and (3) the need for "humanitarian" protective intervention. Domestic reviews in the United States and the United Kingdom showed that the intelligence offered to coalition decision makers in the run-up to the invasions provided only questionable support for the first two justifications.[33] The WMD-based justifications were further undermined by the US Iraq Survey Group's discovery that Iraq was indeed not in possession of deployable nuclear, chemical and biological weapons.

The "protective intervention" justification is not so easily dismissed on evidentiary grounds, but suffers from the lack of consensus on the criteria for such intervention. Nonetheless, in Chapter 28 on the relationship between the invasion and the doctrine of the "responsibility to protect", Thakur neatly sums up a case against humanitarian justifications.[34] For Thakur, the Iraq war, as a humanitarian effort, fails to offer convincing answers to the questions of "why Iraq?" and "why now?". In addition, the scale of force used was incongruous to the scale of the humanitarian crisis, and there was little to ensure that the suffering that justified the invasion would end upon the invasion.

If humanitarianism cannot reasonably be argued to be amongst the coalition's primary motives, then the (perhaps intentional) conflation of humanitarianism and the Iraq war endangers the ongoing "responsibility to protect" project. As Stepanova argues in Chapter 15, "such blatant violations of state sovereignty as this [the US intervention in Iraq] seriously compromised the idea of intervening in a state's internal affairs, even for allegedly benign purposes".[35] Wheeler and Morris (Chapter 27) provide some of the reasons. First, they point to the possibility of increased cynicism when humanitarian concerns are expressed in future crises, pointing to Darfur as evidence of the realization of this effect. Second, that the Iraq war pushed UN procedures to the sidelines may have raised fears among states in the global South, particularly in the Arab world, that extra effort may be required to defend sovereignty, both within and outside the United Nations. Third, the existence of the debate over the validity of humanitarian protection as a justification for the Iraq war has split the pre-Iraq humanitarian consensus, leaving factions arguing among themselves over this issue rather than acting collectively to push the normative agenda forward. Finally, if the United States and the United Kingdom have been discredited in invoking the norm of humanitarian protection, then the norm has been decoupled from the two powers that are most capable of enforcing it.

Alternative visions

As Brian Job discusses in Chapter 4, the shift away from universalistic legal procedures and the invocation of non-legal sources of legitimacy open a space for "norm entrepreneurs" to propose alternative visions of world order, ranging from the global peace movement to "neoconservative" hawks, and from "new liberal interventionists"[36] to Islamist militants. The future of multilateral institutions will be affected not only by the structural challenges discussed above, but also by the efforts and ideas of such norm entrepreneurs. A crucial challenge to the United Nations is for it to serve as an adequate forum to contain such contests of ideas. If it fails to do so, the legitimacy of UN resolutions and guidelines can only erode. The Iraq crisis has brought to the fore competition between visions across two key cleavages, the first of which divides "the West" and Islamist militants, and the second of which divides the transatlantic community.

The competition of ideas between (non-state) Islamist militants and "the West" threatens to engulf the United Nations in a conflict that the organization is ill designed to mediate. Karawan (Chapter 10) and Saikal (Chapter 11) argue that Iraq became a focal point for Islamic *jihad*, similar to the Soviet occupation of Afghanistan. These authors also emphasize that much Islamist militancy is a product of widely held feelings of disempowerment, disenfranchisement and alienation generated by "Western" political and cultural penetration into Muslim countries. The lack of broad and visible agitation in the Middle East following the Iraq crisis may only mean that the "Arab Street" has transformed into the "Arab Basement".[37] As an institution serving the interests of the states that are the expressed enemies of such militants, the United Nations is poorly suited to serve as a venue for mediation in the confrontation between such militants and "the West". In addition, UN-based efforts such as Security Council Resolution 1373 contribute to the sense of some that the United Nations is an instrument of P-5 repression through the "war on terror".[38] What the United Nations could do is to steer likely recruits away from militancy by linking their prospects to the objectives promoted by the UN system. As the chapters by Saikal and Karawan suggest, priority areas would include the Israeli–Palestinian conflict and enhancement of economic and political opportunities.

The contributions by Müller (Chapter 16), Martinez (Chapter 21) and Coicaud et al. (Chapter 14) suggest that, beyond this divide between Islamist militants and counter-terror minded states, another divide may have opened within the United Nations over Iraq – a transatlantic divide resulting from deep normative differences. To the extent that European leaders were trying to manage the interests of their publics, as discussed above, these leaders were constrained by a *principled opposition* to the Iraq war that predominated throughout much of the continent. Martinez proposes that, perhaps as a result of differences in media coverage on either side of the Atlantic, Europeans on the whole exhibited more sensitivity than Americans to the humanitarian tragedy that had been unfolding in Iraq since the initiation of UN sanctions in the 1990s. Martinez argues further that this sensitivity to the humanitarian toll and the devastation of the country made it hard to imagine that the Iraqi regime could be a threat, but made it easy to imagine that the regime was being selected as an easy target. Martinez also argues that Europeans have learned from the colonial experience that dominance is fleeting. Whatever its causes, a divide in the transatlantic community has implications for UN-centred world order that are significant, given that the members of the transatlantic community (perhaps extended to include Japan) provide the bulk of the United Nations' resources.

Implications for the United Nations: Revise or reverse?

Observers debate whether the Iraq crisis is indicative of a functioning or dysfunctional United Nations. One could argue that the denial of explicit Security Council authorization for the US-led invasion was a triumphant moment for the United Nations, in which countries acted through the organization to deny legitimation to the acts of an aggressor (i.e. the United States). Would the United Nations not be in a much worse position had explicit authorization been granted on the basis of the supposed WMD threat? For many, however, such arguments miss the point. As Krieger argues in Chapter 23, "[i]f it was a triumphant moment, it was certainly a hollow one".[39]

The United Nations' own leadership clearly took the latter message. An immediate consequence of the Iraq crisis was that UN Secretary-General Kofi Annan decided in late 2003 to initiate a process of reform by commissioning a High-level Panel on Threats, Challenges and Change. The process was initiated in his speech to the UN General Assembly on 23 September 2003, in which he stated:

[I]t is not enough to denounce unilateralism, unless we also face up squarely to the concerns that make some States feel uniquely vulnerable, since it is those concerns that drive them to take unilateral action. We must show that those concerns can, and will, be addressed effectively through collective action.[40]

The ensuing process attempted to find a number of institutional solutions to many of the structural and normative challenges to the United Nations' central role in world order. But the immediate results, from the 2005 World Summit, fell far short of hopes, perhaps compounding the sense of deep institutional crisis triggered by Iraq. Thus much work remains to be done. As the discussion above suggests, the changes demanded relate to the need not only to make the United Nations more inclusive or to realign the structures to more closely match the global distribution of power, but also to improve the United Nations' performance relative to its stated principles and objectives. The list of complaints is long and in some places possibly even contradictory. In assessing reform options, a key underlying question is this: to revise or to reverse?

The "revise" approach would be to increase UN capacity so that it can better perform the broad range of tasks that have slowly accrued in its domain of responsibility. Proposals for improving UN performance have ranged from the addition of new permanent or long-term Security Council seats, to the creation of new bodies to handle tasks such as peacebuilding and transitional administration, to even greater emphasis on "soft security" issues such as poverty and disease. This may involve cutting away some of the non-performing bodies – and not only the Commission on Human Rights. But the basic sense is to accept the broadened domain of responsibility and to build up institutions accordingly.

The "reverse" approach treats such broadened responsibilities with scepticism, especially as aroused by the United Nations' efforts vis-à-vis Iraq. In a study on the performance of international organizations, Michael Barnett and Martha Finnemore have made a remarkable discovery: following failures, international organizations tend, more often than not, to *expand* rather than cut back on their personnel and on the range of tasks that they take on.[41] It is clear that the United Nations' reform agenda following the Iraq crisis has stayed true to that tendency. Nonetheless, problems such as those associated with the Oil-for-Food programme raise the issue of whether the Secretariat and the Security Council are well suited to such complex operations. Despite the veneer of bureaucratization, do the politics inherent in all UN operations allow for a proper execution of all of the tasks it is asked to perform? A "reversal" approach to UN reform would advocate that the Security Council should, instead, stick to what it has traditionally been good at: brokering peace accords and facilitating the consolidation of peace where there is peace to be consolidated. Any reform need not be uniform: the United Nations might reverse in some areas and on some issues, and revise in others. According to this view, however, the United Nations should not be assumed to hold the cure for all the world's ills, and attempts at reform must be realistic about what the United Nations can and cannot achieve.

Notes

1. Throughout this chapter, by "institutions" we refer to rules *purposively* assigned to produce particular patterns of behaviour. Institutionalization is one such purposive assignment of rules.
2. See Chapter 4 in this volume. Ramesh Thakur and Waheguru Pal Singh Sidhu provide arguments for the desirability of a UN-centred world order in their introduction to this volume.
3. See David Malone and James Cockayne's introductory historical chapter in this volume (Chapter 2).
4. Ibid.
5. These facts lead Charlotte Ku to pose a poignant question at the start of Chapter 24 in this volume: "[W]hy did the war in Iraq cause such concern when neither the exertion of power nor the sidestepping of the UN Security Council is new?" (p. 397).
6. See Chapters 5, 11, 14 and 21.
7. See Chapters 9, 11 and 16.
8. These structural challenges are discussed in more detail in Ramesh Thakur's introduction to the second volume of this series. See Waheguru Pal Singh Sidhu and Ramesh Thakur, eds, *Arms Control after Iraq* (Tokyo: United Nations University Press, forthcoming).
9. See Chapter 9.
10. See Chapter 3.
11. See Chapter 20.
12. It should also be noted that Resolution 1483 highlighted the instrumental approach toward the Security Council of other permanent members – particularly France and Russia, which appeared to support the resolution in hopes of re-entering the Iraqi oil market.
13. Chapter 17, pp. 284–285 in the present volume.
14. Chapter 18, p. 299 in the present volume.
15. Ibid., p. 312.
16. Chapter 26, p. 435 in the present volume.
17. See Chapter 13.
18. For a discussion of the principles behind the German public's rejection of the US-led war effort, see Chapter 16.
19. Hasmy Agam, "Iraq and the Issue of Global Governance: A Perspective from the Non-Aligned Movement", paper presented at the workshop on "The Iraq Crisis and World Order: Structural and Normative Challenges", organized by the International Peace Academy and United Nations University, and hosted by King Prajadhipok's Institute, Bangkok, 16–18 August 2004.
20. Chapter 28, p. 477 in the present volume.
21. Such has been the basis of NAM's apprehensive response toward UN policy agendas associated with "conflict prevention" and "the responsibility to protect" (see note 34 below). Some ground was conceded in the adoption of "responsibility to protect" language in the September 2005 UN *World Summit Outcome* document (UN Doc. A/60/L.1, New York: United Nations General Assembly, 2005). However, no specific mechanisms were outlined for intervention if the Security Council fails to act. The final say on international intervention was thus entrusted to two P-5 members traditionally protective of sovereignty – China and Russia.
22. *A More Secure World: Our Shared Responsibility. Report of the Secretary-General's High-level Panel on Threats, Challenges and Change*, UN Doc. A/59/565 (New York: United Nations, 2004); and United Nations Millennium Project, *Investing in Develop-*

ment: A Practical Plan to Achieve the Millennium Development Goals (London: Earth-scan, 2005).

23. *In Larger Freedom: Towards Security, Development and Human Rights for All. Report of the Secretary-General*, UN Doc. A/59/2005 (New York: United Nations, 2005).

24. The one exception might be with respect to peacebuilding.

25. One option might be for such legislative resolutions to first be debated in or even approved by the General Assembly.

26. See Chapter 1 in Sidhu and Thakur, eds, *Arms Control after Iraq*.

27. See Chapter 4.

28. See Chapter 24 for further discussion of this point.

29. Independent International Commission on Kosovo, *The Kosovo Report: Conflict, International Response, Lessons Learned* (Oxford: Oxford University Press, 2001).

30. The 2005 UN *World Summit Outcome* document affirmed that "the relevant provisions of the Charter are sufficient to address the full range of threats to international peace and security" (para. 79). In other words, no new international consensus was reached on the legal interpretation of the United States' invasion of Iraq.

31. See Chapter 29.

32. Chapter 9, p. 170 in the present volume.

33. See the conclusions in the Commission on the Intelligence Capabilities of the United States Regarding Weapons of Mass Destruction, *Report to the President of the United States, March 31, 2005* (Washington, DC: United States Government Printing Office, 2005).

34. Refer to Chapter 28 for background on the international project initiated by the International Commission on Intervention and State Sovereignty to garner commitment to a normative doctrine of "the responsibility to protect".

35. Chapter 15, pp. 252–253 in the present volume.

36. Wheeler and Morris in Chapter 27.

37. Thomas Friedman, "Under the Arab Street", *New York Times*, 23 October 2002, p. A23.

38. Such was the nature of the indictment of the United Nations made by Osama bin Laden in his address broadcast on Al Jazeera on 3 November 2001 in the wake of the invasion of Afghanistan.

39. Chapter 23, p. 393 in the present volume.

40. UN Secretary-General Kofi Annan's Address to the 57th Session of the UN General Assembly, New York, 23 September 2003. United Nations Press Release SG/SM/8891, GA/10157, 24 September 2003.

41. Michael Barnett and Martha Finnemore, *Rules for the World: International Organizations and World Politics* (Ithaca, NY: Cornell University Press, 2004).

Index

Advertising
  anti-war movement 86
Afghanistan
  elections 128
  NATO peacebuilding in 333
  Turkish involvement in reconstruction
    128
  United Kingdom and 226
al-Qaeda
  financial sanctions and travel restrictions
    on 209
Arab League
  reactions to Iraq war 189–192

Beslan school attacks 209–210

Chile, *see* Latin America
Concert of the North Atlantic 51
  cavalier use of power by 52
Counter-Terrorism Committee
  establishment of 209
  role 209
Crisis management
  NATO and 337–338

Darfur
  international community failure in 158
Debellatio, doctrine of 183

Democracy
  consociational democracy in Lebanon,
    see Lebanon
  "domino effect" 420
  NATO promotion of 335–337
  transition to in Iraq, *see* Iraq

E-mail networks
  and global movement against Iraq war
    79
Egypt
  challenges to UN role 178–182
    Afghanistan conflict and 180
    Egyptian analysts on 178–179
    future of world governance and
      179–180
    viability and effectiveness of United
      Nations 179
  demise of Arab order 182–183
    lack of alternatives to US military
      action 182
  Egyptian state strategies 183–185
    arrest of political activists 184
    call for Arab summit 184
    protests against US action in Iraq
      183–184
  and Iraq war 175–186
    balancing act of Egyptian regime 181

Egypt (cont.)
  Egyptian policy options during
      175–176
  Iraq as haven for terrorists 180–181
  as manifestation of restructuring of
      international system 175
  spillover effects 181–182
  US-dominated world order and 176–178
    positions of states in conflict areas
        177–178
    reversal of strategic realities 176–177
    role of regional actors 177
Elections
  in Iraq 129
  impact of 436–437
Epstein, Barbara
  on global movement against war in Iraq
      75
European Union
  9/11, effect on 344–345
  "We Are All Americans" 345
  and Iraq war 344–356
    definition of Middle East policy 344
    European resistance to, reasons for
        346
      "illegitimate war" 347–348
      suffering of Iraqi people 346–347
    future prospects 351–354
      construction of political peace plan
          354
      departure of coalition forces 353
      maintaining coalition 352–353
    guerrilla war following 349
    humanitarian concerns 349–350
    proof of US failure 348–350
    reconstruction of Iraq 349
    refugees 350
    resistance to US occupation 350–351
      international resistance groups 351
      Shiite resistance groups 351
      Sunni resistance groups 350–351
    sabotage of oil pipelines 349
    US justification for 345

France
  essentials of French foreign policy
      235–236
    commitment to multilateralism 236
    international projection of influence
        235
    primacy of national interest 235

regions where influence sought 235
French foreign policy decision-making
    process 236–237
  demilitarized foreign policy 237
  French constitution 236
  implementation of 237
  president, powers of 236–237
  range of actors 237
opposition to Iraq war, reasons for
    234–248
  assessment of threat 242–243
  lack of evidence of WMD 239
  France's support to Iraq 240–241
  French reticence about change 244
  future prospects 243–245
  interpretation of Resolution 1441 239
  lack of credible alternative 243–244
  no automatic recourse to force 238
  refusal to deploy troops post-war 245
  two-stage UN process proposal 238
  and use of force in Middle East 242
  vision of multipolar world 241

Germany
  and Iraq war 267–270
    9/11 and 268
    imposing democracy 277
    international law and organizations
        268
    as "Proud Tower" illusion 269
    and world order 267–268
  perspective on Iraq war 266–267
    Germany as a civilian power 266
    German peacekeeping 267
  and world order 270–276
    globalization and fragmentation
        274–276
    globalization and interdependence
        272–273
    hegemonic order 276
    imposition of democracy 277
    meaning of world order 271–272
    military power, use of 278
    Monitoring, Verification and
        Inspection Commission 270–271
    power measured by resources 277
    requirements for global order 272–276
    Security Council 270–271
    United Nations 270–271
Global movement against war in Iraq
    75–91

15 February 2003 protests 75
actors 76
Barbara Epstein on 75
impacts 86
    on Bush administration 88
    emphasis of threat from Iraqi WMD
        88–89
    Security Council rebuff to United
        States 87
international coordination 75
international dimension 79–84
    15 February 2003 protests 80
    censure of Australian Prime Minister
        83
    German national elections 82
    international anti-war opinion (table)
        81
    opinion polls 80
    Pakistani elections 83
    political impact of demonstrations
        80–81
    religious opposition 81
    significance of anti-war sentiment for
        US policy 83–84
    South Korean elections 83
    Turkish rejection of US request for
        transit corridor 82–83
and Internet 76
interplay with United Nations 87
media communications 84–86
    advertising 86
    media coverage of 15 February
        demonstrations 85
    message framing 85
    power and influence of media 84
    Win Without War 85
MoveOn, role of 78–79
    "action in a box" 79
    e-mail networks 79
    impact of Internet on 78
    Internet organizing 78–79
    online membership 78
as "superpower" 76
in United States
    on Human Rights Day 77
    two major coalitions 77
    virtual organizing 77–78
    Win Without War coalition 77

Hariri, Rafiq
    assassination of 109

Humanitarian intervention
    Iraq war as, see Iraq war
    meaning 467

"India Shining"
    rejection by Indian electorate 53
Interim Constitution for Iraq 105
International institutions and institutional
        change 59–62
    "big bang" theory of great events 60–61
    and changes in US leadership 61
    formation of institutions: two perspectives
        59–60
    Ikenberry on 59
    institutional change in the aftermath of
        "great events" 60–61
    "institutional compact" 60
    interests of dominant states 60
    norm entrepreneurs 61–62
        "bucking the system" 61
    "social constructions" 59–60
International law
    Iraq war as defining moment for 393
    Iraq war as step backward for 394
    multinational action in Iraq and 413–425
        1990 invasion of Kuwait 415
        1991 Resolutions 414
        blocking of Security Council action
            419
        casus belli 415
        "domino effect" of democracy 420
        economic sanctions against Iraq 416
        French and Russian criticisms of
            sanctions 417
        Iraq Survey Group results 423
        Iraqi democracy 420
        Iraqi weapons disposal 417
        justifications for war 414
        limitations on Iraq's military capacity
            416
        non-state actors' use of WMD 418
        Oil-for-Food scandal 423
        ongoing insurgency 413
        post-war assessments of weapons
            programmes 422
        preference for multilateral response
            421–422
        UN High-level Panel on Threats,
            Challenges and Change, impact of
            421
        unlawful production of WMD 418–419

International law (cont.)
    urban insurgency 420
    weapons inspections 419
  reform of 170
  US immunity from 390
International order
  future prospects after Iraq war 437–441
    need to adjust US foreign policy
        439–440
    reconciling power and principles 438
  impact of US Iraq policy on 434–437
    impact of Iraqi elections 436–437
    negative impacts 435–436
    positive impacts 434–435
International peace and security and state
        sovereignty 57–74
  contesting norms 57–74
  global public goods dilemma 71–72
  "institutional bargain" 58
  instrumental materialism 71
  norm entrepreneurs 57–74
  United Nations, role of 58
  uncertain future 70–72
  and United Nations, see United Nations
  United States: leading state and norm
        entrepreneur 66–70
    attack on US homeland 2001 67–68
    Bush, George W., election of 67
    Cold War, end of 67
    and Iraq war 67
    multilateralism, principles of 68–69
    and NATO 68
    structural logic of US systemic
        dominance 66–68
    United States as norm entrepreneur
        68–70
  United States: prospects for change and
        continuity 70–72
  United States, role of 58
International security
  social logic of, see Social logic of
        international security
Internet
  and Iraq war protests 76; see also Global
        movement against war in Iraq
Iran
  9/11 and 139–142
    Ayatollah Mohammad Emami-Kashani
        on 139–140
    Iranian response to Iraq war 141–142
    national press on 140
    support for United States 139
    sympathy from civil society 140
    Tehran and Washington, relationship
        between 141
  1979 Islamic revolution 134
  assessment of Iraq crisis 134–160
  drive towards regional supremacy 135
  geography of 135
    role in foreign policy 135
  as important regional player 134
  Iraq crisis 142–151
    Afghanistan and 149
    arms-length position 150–151
    consequences for Iran 143
    effect of on factional rivalries in Iran
        145
    geo-economic consequences 151
    inter-Shia politics 146–147
    Iranian domestic politics and 147–148
    Iranian influence in Iraq 144
    Iranian issues with 149
    Iranian security thinking 151
    as mixed blessing for Tehran 143
    political voice of Iraq's Shiite
        community 147
    Qum–Tehran–Najaf relationship 146
    regime change in Iraq 142–143
    relations with Gulf Cooperation
        Council and 146
    security as prime driver 148–151
    Supreme Council for Islamic
        Revolution in Iraq 149–150
    war and its aftermath 143–146
    Washington's intentions towards Iran
        144
  "negative balance" doctrine 135
  nuclear programme 152–156
    and balance of power between Iranian
        factions 156–157
    changes in West Asia and 157–158
    "dual containment", doctrine of 152
    EU "constructive engagement"
        dialogue 153
    flexible acquisition strategy 154
    geopolitical insecurity paradigm
        155–156
    IAEA and 154
    Iranian admission of weapons
        programmes 153–154
    national resources 156
    national security and 152–156

prestige of being nuclear state 155
rights of signatories to NPT 155
Russia on 153
territorial nationalist debates 156
United States' ability to act 152
US position on 157
post-9/11 international order and
    151–158
    national security and nuclear
        programme 152–156
post–Cold War regional politics 137–139
    "both North and South" 138–139
    "three Gs" in foreign relations 137
    views of new international system
        137–138
as rational actor 134
religious dimension to projection of
    power 136
Soviet relations during Cold War 136
support for Islamic groups 136
Turkish rapprochement with 121–122
Iraq
challenge to world order 3–15
Coalition Provisional Authority 129, 349,
    361, 479, 489, 492
elections 129
formation of independent government
    129–130
interim constitution 129
    problems in drafting 129
Iraqi Interim Government, establishment
    of 128–129
occupation of, see Occupation of Iraq
as a political earthquake 11–13
    aims of Bush administration 12–13
political system post-war 102
reasons for US use of military power
    against 317–320
    9/11 attacks 318
    invasion of Kuwait 319
    US security measures 318
sectarian fighting 128
as testing ground for US foreign policy
    assumptions 432–437
transition to democracy in 102–106
    armed resistance to occupation 104
    challenges to 104–105
    federalism 105
    form of democracy 102–103
    Interim Constitution 105
    leadership 106

multi-party system 103
pluralist state, Iraq as 103
political culture 106
political divisions 103
power-sharing arrangement 105
restructuring of social and political
    structure 106
and social reform in greater Middle
    East 104
Iraq Survey Group
results of 423
Iraq war
accountability, need for 389–390
    immunity from international law 390
    international people's tribunals 389
    US "unsigning" of ICC treaty 390
case for 96, 397–412
    adequacy of multilateral institutions
        409
    adequacy of UN security system 405
    Anne-Marie Slaughter on 398
    Attorney Generals' opinions 401
    closed societies developing WMD 407
    "duty to prevent" 406
    establishing legitimacy 404–408
    evidence for pre-emptive wars
        407–408
    Kofi Annan on 398
    need for Security Council authorization
        402
    power, legality and legitimacy,
        importance of 397
    precedent for future actions, Iraq as
        398
    "regime change", legality 401
    resolutions authorize use of force,
        whether 403
    Security Council, role of 400–404
    standards for legitimate action 406
    and UN failure to act in Rwanda 405
    unregulated intervention 405
    US rejection of international
        agreements 397–398
    "who can decide to act" 402
costs of 388–389
    deaths of Iraqi citizens 388
    implications for world order 389
as defining moment for international law
    393
failure to find WMD 97–98
    other justifications for war after 102

Iraq war (cont.)
  global movement against, *see* Global
      movement against war in Iraq
  as humanitarian intervention 444–463
    abuse of humanitarian claims over Iraq
        448–454
    Australian government 448–449
    declaratory commitment to protect
        strangers in peril 460
    developing norm of military
        intervention for humanitarian
        protection 446–448
    and failure to find WMD 448
    failure to respond in Darfur 457–458
    impact of Iraq war on developing norm
        of humanitarian intervention
        459–460
    Iraq better place as result of
        intervention, whether 450–451
    justifying 455–458
    as last resort 455
    legal basis for 455
    legality of humanitarian intervention
        454
    legitimizing action in absence of
        Security Council authorization
        456
    liberal internationalists 444
    link between motivations and outcomes
        451
    military conduct of intervention 452
    moral case for removing Saddam
        Hussein 452
    motivations to deploy troops 449–450
    narrow threshold principles, reasons
        for 455–456
    new liberal interventionists 444
    non-intervention principle of Cold War
        446
    policing 451–452
    positive humanitarian outcome,
        whether 450
    protection of civilians 447–448
    removal of other tyrannical regimes
        457
    Security Council powers 446
    Tony Blair on 453
    trespassing on sovereignty of others
        447
    UK government 449
    unilateral action 447
  use of "collective action" 447
  when to intervene 456
  illegality of 383–386
    authorization for use of force 384
    "final opportunity to comply with
        disarmament regulations" 385
    Iraq's failure to disarm 384
    no attack on United States 384
    terms of 1991 ceasefire 385
    UN Charter 383
  illegitimacy of 386–388
    and dangers of WMD 386
    Hans Blix on 387
    presence of WMD as justification 387
    state and non-state actors, distinction
        387–388
  implications of 211–212, 315–317
    America, role of 211
    "pre-emptive military action" 316
  inevitable, whether 9–11
    United Nations, role of 10–11
  international law and, *see* International
      law
  international system after 161–162
    constraints on US power 163–166
    need for partners 163–166
    United States in 162–163
  invasion of Iraq 97
  legitimacy of 381–396
    al-Qaeda links with Iraq 382
    discredited justifications 382
    "victor's justice" 383
    "war of choice" 381
    WMD 381
  manner of fighting 488
  as model for controlling WMD 393–394
  need for UN action 392
  reactions in Muslim world to 187–200
    almost universal opposition 187
    Arab League 189–192
    élite attitudes 188–189
    élites' private positions 192–193
    moderate Islamists 195–196
    neo-fundamentalists 198
    Organization of the Islamic Conference
        189–192
    popular sentiment 193–199
      destruction of Iraqi state 193–194
      opposition to Saddam Hussein 193
      US application of disproportionate
          force 194

US attempts to influence democratic
processes 194
US support for Saddam Hussein
pre-1991 193
radical Islamists 196–198
radical secular nationalists 198–199
US post-war management of Iraq
194–195
variety of views 187–188
reasons for, *see* Iraq war, case for
responsibility to protect and 464–478
abuse of Iraqi prisoners 468
British annexation of Awadh 469
changing demands, expectations and
tools 476–478
complicity 465–467
doctrine of sovereign equality 470
due process 474–476
follow-up assistance 472
functional commitment to sovereignty
470–471
government criminal behaviour 464
humanitarian intervention, meaning
467
illegality 465–467
international criminal behaviour 464
military intervention for human
protection purposes 467–468
neo-colonial rule, humanitarian
intervention as 469
paralysis 465–467
political considerations 468
precautionary principles 473–474
provision of life-supporting protection
471–472
responsibility to prevent conflict 472
"responsibility to protect" of every
state 465
right authority 474–476
sovereignty as responsibility 470–471
threshold criteria 473–474
triple policy dilemma, summary 466
and social logic of international security,
see Social logic of international
security
as step backward for international law
394
weapons inspections 96
and weapons of mass destruction
390–392; *see also* Weapons of
mass destruction

and world order 519–520
Islamism
reactions to Iraq war
moderate Islamists 195–196
neo-fundamentalists 198
radical Islamists 196–198
rise of in Turkey 120–121
Israel
Israeli perspective on Iraq crisis 161–174
communism and 171–172
international system after Iraq war
161–162
Iraqi WMD 173
Israel's margin of manoeuvre 173
Israel's need for partners 171
need for close relationship with United
States 172
previous conflicts with Iraq 172
United States and, *see* United States and
Israel

Japan
and Iraq war 282–297
"coming to terms with the past" 295
concern for bilateral relations with
United States 294
Japanese Self Defense Forces, use of
282
long-term implications 282–283
support for United States 282
Japanese Self Defense Forces (JSDF)
operation in Iraq 287–294
9/11, effect of 291
activism in bilateral defence 291
Anti-Terrorism Special Measures Law
292
ban on "core" activities 289
collective self-defence 288
deployment in Indian Ocean 291
five conditions for Japanese
participation 289–290
hostage-taking of Japanese nationals
294
International Peace Cooperation Law
289
involvement in Afghanistan 291
and legal status of Iraq war 293
legislation for 292
legitimacy of humanitarian intervention
290
limits of 287

Japan (cont.)
  mandate 293
  public opinion 294
  resistance to "enforcement" 288
  rules concerning "use of weapons" 290
  significance of 287
  UN peacekeeping 288–289
  "within" multinational force,
      significance 293
  responses to Iraq war 284–294
  diplomatic support 284–286
  foreign policy dilemma 284–285
  justification for support 285
  public opinion 285–286
  supporting post-conflict stabilization in
      Iraq 286–287

Khan, A.Q.
  and dissemination of nuclear material 53
Krasner, Stephen
  on North–South relationship 38
Kurds
  future in northern Iraq 118–120

Latin America
  Chile 308–310
    free trade agreement with United
        States 309
    and Iraq 309
    multilateralism 308–309
    powerlessness of 309
    prominence of 308
    proposal for extended weapons
        inspections 310
    public opinion 309
    tradition of respect for international
        law 308
  Mexico 305–308
    foreign minister, role of 307
    non-intervention, principle of 306
    as non-permanent member of Security
        Council 305
    opinion polls 307
    peaceful resolution of conflicts,
        principle of 306
    "revolt of the Latins" 306
    transition to democracy 305
    US threats 307
    "wait and see" policy 308
  US hegemony and 298–301

consent to 299
democratization 299–300
effect of 9/11 300
  Mexico 300
implications of US-centric world 299
and Iraq war 301
Mexico and Chile membership of
    Security Council 2003 301
Plan Colombia 301
powerlessness of Latin America 298
US order in Latin American perspective
    302–305
  domestic opinion 304
  Latin American opposition to US
      intervention 302–303
  Latin American security measures
      303
  Latin American terrorism 303
  preventive use of force 302
  resistance to United States 303–304
  responsiveness of allies to security
      concerns 303
  significance of Iraq 304
  US military interventions 302
League of Nations
  rejection by United States 6–7
Lebanon
  Cedar Revolution 109
  consociational democracy in 106–107
    composition of society 106–107
    power-sharing practices 107
    social structure 107
    stability of political system 107
  impact of Iraq crisis on 108–111
  Lebanese perspective on Iraq war
      95–113
    distrust of US motives 97
    public opinion 97
  Syria's legacy in 108–111
    assassination of Rafiq Hariri 109
    Cedar Revolution 109
    consequences of Hariri assassination
        109–110
    developments following withdrawal of
        Syrian troops 110
    Fitzgerald fact-finding mission
        recommendations 110
    relations between Syria and Lebanon
        108
    revitalized political system 110–111

Syrian intervention in Lebanese
communal conflict 108
Syrian withdrawal from Lebanon
108–109

Media communications
anti-war movement's use of, *see* Global
movement against war in Iraq
Mexico, *see* Latin America
Middle East
building coalition on 166–169
assistance made contingent on
compliance with donor-defined
criteria 168–169
difficulties securing international
cooperation 166
difficulties for United States in
promoting 167
European perspective 167
need for 166
purpose of 167
sanctions 168
building democracy and stability in
125–130
broader Middle East initiative,
legitimacy of 125–127
European regional order as model for
124–125
Military occupation, law of 481–484
acquisition of territory through military
force 481–482
administration of occupied territory 481
debellatio, doctrine of 483
formal obligations 482
jus ad bellum 483
separation from *jus in bello* 483
limitations on occupying power 483–484
prohibitions on use of force 483
reluctance to acknowledge position as
occupier 482
underlying premise of occupation 482
MoveOn
role in global movement against Iraq war
78–79
Multilateralism and unipolarity: artificial
contradiction 45–47
capital mobility 47–48
Concert of industrialized states 47
Concert of the North Atlantic 46
"end of the West" 45–46

National security
versus multilateralism and solidarity
427–431
North Atlantic Treaty Organization
(NATO)
and 9/11 attacks 330–331
during Cold War 329–330
"common strategy" 331
crisis management 331, 337–338
democracy, promotion of 335–337
effectiveness in 21st century 338–340
capabilities 338–340
institutional interoperability 338–340
and European priorities 329
fight against terrorism and WMD
334–335
asymmetrical threats 335
limited capabilities for 334
"Partnership Action Plan against
Terrorism" 334
spread of WMD 335
and Iraq 329–332
"spectre of irrelevance" 329–332
transatlantic dispute 331–332
Turkey's request for assistance 332
key institutional partnership 340
Kosovo intervention 330
new functions 341
new "threats agenda" 332
peace operations 337–338
reduced role of 330
role in Iraq war 328
role in US-centric world order 340–341
shared strategic vision, search for
333–334
peacebuilding in Afghanistan 333
regions of special focus 333
"roles and missions" 333
"soft power" projection 335–337
and US priorities 329
United States–Europe split 330
North versus South: economics 47–48
FDI flows 48
skewed nature of globalization 48
North versus South: politics and security
48–51
Military Technological Revolution 49–50
Revolution in Military Affairs 49–50
and self-interest 49–50
and sovereignty 49

Nuclear Non-Proliferation Treaty
  "loophole" in 391
Nye, Joseph
  on structure and process in the
      international system 40–41

Occupation of Iraq 486–490
  manner in which war fought 488
  obligations of occupiers 489
  political function for United Nations 487
  "political future" 489
  post-conflict scenarios 487
  UN planning for 488–489
  UN recognition of Coalition Provisional
      Authority 489
  UN responsibilities 489–490
  US leadership of 487
Oil-for-Food scandal 423
Operation Desert Storm 7
Organization of the Islamic Conference
      (OIC)
  reactions to Iraq war 189–192

Pakistan
  and Iraq war 320–326
    absence of diplomatic support 324
    comparison of Pakistan to Iraq 323
    difficulties for Pakistan 320
    divisions within the OIC 321
    expansion of US goals 322
    main issues for Pakistan 321
    membership of Security Council 320
    "multipolar" system 324–325
    pre-emptive strikes 323
    public opinion 321
    refusal to send troops 322
    UN authorization, lack of 321–322
    unilateralism 323
Peace operations
  and NATO 337–338
Precautionary principle 473–474
Pre-emptive war, doctrine of 99
  as tool for combating terrorism 99

Regime change
  legality of principle 401
Responsibility to protect
  and Iraq war, see Iraq war
Revolution in Military Affairs (RMA)
      49–50

Russia
  framework for policy on Iraq 251–254
    "axis of peace" 252
    "axis of war" 252
    geo-economics, role of 254
    normalization of foreign policy 251
    "oil and gas factor" 254
    preference for multilateral approach
        253
    two levels 253–254
    UN reform 252
    US refusal to work within international
        framework 252–253
  international security agenda 249
    post–Cold War "damage limitation"
        249
  and Iraq war
    as landmark development 250
  and Iraq and "war on terrorism"
      258–262
    actors capable of "winning the peace"
        261
    anti-terrorism priorities 259
    central role of United States 262
    long-term anti-terrorism strategy
        260–261
    "post-post–Cold War" world order
        261
    range of threats 260
    Russian place in world order 262
    terrorism generated by Iraq conflict
        259
  policy scenarios on post-war Iraq
      254–258
    accommodating steps towards coalition
        powers 257
    accommodation scenario 254
    compromise scenario 257–258
    deteriorating security situation 256
    geo-economics and 256
    "global order" concerns 257
    modification of accommodation
        scenario 255
    non-association scenario 254
    opinion polls 258
    post-war interim political governance
        arrangements 256–257
    post-war reconstruction 255
      pace of 255–256
  war on terrorism, effect of 250

Rwanda
  UN failure to act in 405

Self-defence
  meaning 206
September 11th
  Iranian perspective, 139–142; *see also*
    Iran
  and United Nations, *see* United Nations
  US multilateralism "de circonstance"
    after 430
Social logic of international security
    426–443
  Bush's foreign policy 427–429
    doctrinal sidelining of multilateralism
      428–429
    and theory of US power 427–429
  future prospects for international order
    437–441
  geopolitics of US national interest
    429–431
  impact of US foreign policy on
    international order, *see*
    International order
  Iraq as testing ground for US foreign
    policy assumptions 432–437
    assumptions vindicated by war 432
    foreign policy at odds with reality
      432–433
  Iraq war and 426–443
  national security vs. multilateralism and
    solidarity 427–431
Soft power
  NATO projection of 335–337
Sovereign equality
  doctrine of 470
Structural and normative challenges
    519–534
  alternative visions 530–531
  competition of ideas 530–531
  Kosovo Commission 527
  legality vs. legitimacy. 527–528
  normative challenges 527–531
  norms of humanitarian protection
    529–530
    protective intervention justification 529
    "responsibility to protect" 529
  North–South divide 525–527
    capacities of Security Council 526–527
    sources 526

perceived uneven enforcement of UN
      Security Council resolutions 528
  relations with United States 523–524
  revealing the disconnect 520–521
  structural challenges 521–523
  unipolarity 525–527
  "Westphalian myth" 521
Structure and process in international
    system 40–41
  Joseph Nye on 40
Syria
  legacy in Lebanon, *see* Lebanon
  Turkish rapprochement with 121–122

Terrorism
  definition 204
  pre-emptive war as tool for combating 99
  problems defining 207
  rise in Turkey 120–121
  root causes of 164
Turkey
  building democracy and stability in
      Middle East 125–130
    and Afghanistan elections 128
    Arab-Israeli peace process 126
    imposition of nation-building 128
    Islam and secular nationalism,
      relationship between 127
    military, role in politics 127
    political culture of region 126–127
    protection of secularism 127
    relationship between Islam and
      nation-state-building 127
    Turkey's position 126
    Turkish experience in nation-building
      127–130
    Turkish involvement in reconstruction
      of Afghanistan 128
  divergence of interests from Washington
      118–122
    adjustment of foreign policy goals 119
    attacks on PKK camps in Iraq 119
    future of Kurds in northern Iraq
      118–120
    rise of Islamism and terrorism 120–121
    Turkish rapprochement with Syria and
      Iran 121–122
  place in international system 117
  trans-regional cooperation between
      Europe and Middle East 122–125

Turkey (cont.)
  common interests of Iraq's neighbours
    123
  cross-border issues 122–123
  "danger zone", Turkey as 123
  European regional order as model for
    Middle East 124–125
  "soft power" initiatives 125
  unconventional security challenges
    122–124
Turkish perspective on Iraq war 114–133
  importance of Turkey in Iraq conflict
    114–115
  Istanbul terrorist attacks 117
  Turkey's place in international system
    117
  Turkish membership of NATO 116
  Turkish parliament's rejection of
    Turkey's involvement 116–118
  US pressure to send troops 117

Unipolarity, globalization and the Concert
    of Powers 41–45
  chasm between global North and global
    South 43
  critique of market-driven globalization
    45
  global North 41–42
  globalization, meaning 44
  and multilateral regimes 45
  neoliberal rhetoric 42–43
  New International Economic Order
    (NIEO) 42
  presumed threat of Iranian nuclear
    proliferation 44
  Samuel Huntington on 44
  "unipolarity" 43–44
Unipolarity and multilateralism in the age
    of globalization 37–56
  continuities between Cold War and
    post–Cold War epochs 39
United Kingdom
  development of foreign policy on Iraq
    223–225
  9/11 and 223
  Iraq ("dodgy") dossier 224
  Security Council negotiations 224
  strategy towards Saddam Hussein's
    regime 223
  and Iraq 1990–2001 219–222
  air patrols 221

Chapter VII demands on Iraq 220
  enforcement of withdrawal from
    Kuwait 221–222
  Iraqi invasion of Kuwait 219–220
    international response to 220
    use of force against 220
  no-fly zones 220–221
  violation of UN Charter by Iraq 222
and Iraq 2001–2005 222–229
  Afghanistan and 226
  alliance with US neoconservatives 230
  Commons vote on 225
  criticisms of Prime Minister's policy
    229
  economic costs 231
  legal issues 226–227
  military policy 228–229
  opinion polls 229
  Palestine and 226
  political investigations 227–228
  resignation of ministers 225
  two-level policy 230
and Iraq until 1990 217–219
  Iraqi invasion of Iran 219
  Iraqi membership of League of Nations
    218
  Kuwaiti independence 218
  nationalization of oil interests in Iran
    218
  Ottoman Empire 217
  during World War I 217
United Nations 62–66
  action on terrorism 204–205
  in 1970s 204
  Beslan school attacks 209–210
  and end of Cold War 204
  financial sanctions on al-Qaeda 209
  international rules and norms 205
  and Libya 205
  need for coordination 214
  root causes 211
  terrorism, definition 204
  use of force 211
challenge to from US power 212
challenges to 4, 100–102
  distrust and hostility of Cold War era
    international relations 100
  domestically based international
    conflicts, problems resolving 101
  and ethno-national conflicts 100
  rebuilding of Iraq 101

Charter as "institutional bargain" 62
Counter-Terrorism Committee
  establishment 209
  role 209
creation of 62
damage caused by Iraq war 9
dialectic between civil society and 87–88
double crisis of legitimacy 4–5
evolution of response to terrorism 208
  CTC, establishment of 209
  sanctions, impact of 208–209
  Security Council, role of 208
evolving norms 62–66
forces of change 62–63
fundamental tensions 62–66
High-level Panel on Threats, Challenges
    and Change
  impact of 421
impact of Iraq war on
  American role and 211–212
  condemnation of terrorism 208
  High-level Panel on Threats,
    Challenges and Change 207,·
    531
  negative short-term impact 203
  re-election of George W. Bush and
    203–204
  terrorism, defining 207
  United Nations' future prospects
    211–212
importance of United States to 213–214
  need to re-engage United States 214
increased support 524
institutional compact 62–66
interplay with anti-war movement 87
multilateralism, embodiment of 5
need for action by in Iraq 392
political function in occupation of Iraq
    487
position on terrorism, three linked
    concepts 210
post-Iraq war relations with occupying
    powers 479–496
  Coalition Provisional Authority and
    UN responsibilities 479
  instruments governing occupation law
    480–481
  invoking of occupation law in Iraq
    480
  law of military occupation, see Military
    occupation, law of

military occupation in relation to
    United Nations 479–480
  Pottery Barn principle 491–492
  role of United Nations 491
  role of United Nations in world order
    493
  Security Council's power to administer
    territory 484–486
  UN assertion of government powers
    480
  US need for UN assistance 492
primary responsibility of 6
redefining of security, responsibility and
    use of force 63–66
  change within United Nations itself
    65–66
  David Malone on 66
  "human security" perspective 63–64
  initial norm entrepreneurial leadership
    65
  non-governmental organizations and
    66
  traditional concepts of security and
    sovereignty 64
relations with United States 4–9
  five policy dilemmas 7–8
responsibilities in Iraq post-war 489–490
"reverse" approach 532
"revise" approach 532
role during and after Iraq war 102
role of 3
Security Council 5, 63
  coalition, whether 522–523
  role in Iraq war 400–404
Security Council's power to administer
    territory 484–486
  Bosnia 485
  drafting of UN Charter 484
  growth in activism by Security Council
    485
  lack of institutional capacity 485–486
  political barriers 486
  Trieste 484
and September 11th 205–206
  change in approach to terrorism 206
  change in Security Council 210–211
  Kofi Annan, role of after 206–207
  Resolution 1368 205
  Resolution 1373 205–206
  self-defence, meaning 206
shared interests with America 213

United Nations (cont.)
  states choosing to act outside 525
  US "bullying" of 430–431
United Nations in Iraq 1980–2001 16–33
  five phases 17
  inspections plus sanctions 25–29
  insurgencies and humanitarian crisis
      23–25
  Iran–Iraq: Cold War peacekeeping
      18–20
    and Gorbachev 20
    United Nations Iran–Iraq Military
        Observer Group 20
  Iraq–Kuwait: towards peace enforcement
      20–22
  Iraqi exports 28
  new Iraqi disorder 23–25
  Operation "Provide Comfort" 24
  Resolution 687 26–27
  United Nations Guards Contingent in
      Iraq 24–25
  United Nations Iraq–Kuwait Observer
      Mission 22–23
  United Nations as global regulator and
      proxy administrator 25–29
United Nations in Iraq 2001–2005 357–378
  11 September 2001–20 March 2003
      357–360
    9/11 attacks 357–358
    inspections-plus-sanctions approach
        358
    Resolution 1441 359
    Saddam Hussein's defiance 358
    United Nations as one source of
        legitimacy 360
    Western intelligence failures 359
  19 August 2003 362–364
    overreaction amongst UN staff 364
    terrorist threat to United Nations 363
    truck-bomb attack on HQ of UN
        Assistance Mission for Iraq in
        Baghdad 362–363
    United Nations as stooge of Western
        interests 363
  20 March 2003–19 August 2003 360–362
    development of Iraqi constitution
        361–362
    diplomacy 362
    ineffectiveness of UN approach 361
    sidelining of United Nations 361

  future prospects 367–374
    normative challenges 370–371
    performance challenges 372–373
    politics of state-building 367–370
    restoring universality 373–374
    structural challenge of unipolarity
        371–372
  post–19 August 2003 364–367
    capture of Saddam Hussein 365
    coalition policy incoherence 366
    deterioration in security 364–365
    elections 365–366
    prisoner abuse 366
United Nations Guards Contingent in Iraq
    (UNGCI) 24–25
United Nations Iran–Iraq Military
    Observer Group (UNIIMOG) 20
United Nations Iraq–Kuwait Observer
    Mission (UNIKOM) 22–23
  and muscular peacekeeping 22–23
United States
  Bush's foreign policy 427–429
    doctrinal sidelining of multilateralism
        428–429
    ends of 427–428
    impact of Iraqi elections 436–437
    means of 428–429
    negative impacts on international order
        435–436
    positive impacts on international order
        434–435
    and theory of US power 427–429
    vision of 427–428
  constraints on power of 163–166
    international cooperation, need for
        164
    modernization of developing countries
        165
    need for partners 163–166
    physical space of non-state actors 164
    root causes of terrorism 164
    types of security threats 163–164
    willingness of other actors 163
  exceptionalism 9
  geopolitics of US national interest in
      practice 429–431
    "bullying" of United Nations 430–431
    Iraq war 430–431
    multilateralism "de circonstance"
        post-9/11 430

road to unilateralism 429–430
impact of 9/11 attacks 95–96
isolationism 8–9
Israel and, *see* United States and Israel
multilateralism 8
need to adjust foreign policy of 439–440
post–Cold War order and 98–102
  challenges to United Nations 100–102
  changing profile of world order
    99–100
  disengagement from international
    commitments 98
  doctrine of pre-emptive war 99
  impact of 9/11 98
quest for centrality in world affairs 98
rejection of international agreements
  397–398
relations with United Nations 4–9
unilateralism 5
uni-multipolarity in international system
  169–171
  building of ad hoc coalitions 171
  conflict resolution 169–170
  reform of international law 170
US hegemony and world order 115–118
United States and Israel 497–516
  Arab–Israeli conflict, consequences of
    497
  and Cold War 497–498
  enemies 498–501
  identities 498–501
  incubating war on terror 501–505
    civilized, definition of 504–505
    linking Israeli and Western security
      concerns 503
    roadmap to war on terror 502–503
    "terrorism evil beyond redemption"
      504
    terrorism studies 501–502
    use of "terror" 504
    utility of terror 502

Israelization of America 507–513
  defending "civilization" 510–511
  hearts and minds strategies 511–512
  Israeli influence in Senate 507
  language of religiosity 512
  major ally, Israel as 508
  military cooperation over Iraq 511
  religious background 507
  sentiments of affinity 508
  shared enemy 509–510
  shared vision of enemy 512
  "West", membership of 509
  strategies 498–501
  from theory to policy 505–507
    democracy vs. dictatorship 506
    "distinctly American internationalism"
      506
    neoconservatives' ideas becoming US
      policy 505

Weapons of mass destruction (WMD)
  acquisition of 53
  closed societies developing 407
  double standard on nuclear weapons 391
  existence of in Iraq 96
  and Iraq war 390–392
    "loophole" in Nuclear
      . Non-Proliferation Treaty 391
  Iraq war as model for controlling
    393–394
  non-state actors' use of 418
  and terrorism 390–391
  unlawful production of 418
  and "wars of choice" 392
Wilson, Joseph C.
  on Iraq–Kuwait 19
Win Without War coalition 77
  media communications 85
  virtual organizing 77–78
World order
  meaning 520